# A DOCTOR IN THE HOUSE

# A DOCTOR IN THE HOUSE

The Memoirs of Tun Dr Mahathir Mohamad

**MPH**
PUBLISHING

Published by

MPH Group Publishing Sdn Bhd

Lot 1, 1st Floor, Bangunan TH, No. 5 Jalan Bersatu 13/4

46200 Petaling Jaya, Selangor, Malaysia

email: *mphpublishing@mph.com.my*

Distributed by

MPH Distributors Sdn Bhd

Ground Floor, Bangunan TH, No. 5 Jalan Bersatu 13/4

46200 Petaling Jaya, Selangor, Malaysia

email: *distributors@mph.com.my*

MPH Distributors (S) Pte Ltd

No. 12 Tagore Drive, Habitat Warehouse, Singapore 787621

email: *sales@mph.com.sg*

Photographs courtesy of Perdana Leadership Foundation

Produced by Salt Media Consultancy Sdn Bhd

Perpustakaan Negara Malaysia    Cataloguing-in-Publication Data

Mahathir bin Mohamad, Tun, 1925-
        A doctor in the house: the memoirs of
        Tun Dr Mahathir Mohamad / Tun Mahathir Mohamad.
        ISBN 978-967-5997-22-8
        1. Mahathir bin Mohamad, Tun, 1925-. 2. Autobiography.
        3. Ex-prime ministers—Malaysia—Biography. I. Title.
        923.2595

Printed by

MPH Group Printing (M) Sdn Bhd

No. 31 Jalan 2/148A

Taman Sungei Besi Industrial Park

57100 Kuala Lumpur, Malaysia

For Hasmah and my children,

for their love, support,

tolerance and courage.

# Contents

# Preface

This is the story of Malaysia as I see it. This is also my story.

I have written about the wisdom of our founding fathers who crafted a political system that has enabled the country to democratically and peacefully resolve the problems and challenges inherent in a complex society.

Malaysia may not be styled after the liberal democracies of the West, but it is led by governments elected by the people at the central and state levels. Not many former colonies have been able to make democracy work. We have. In Malaysia, Opposition candidates can win, and be successful enough to gain control of state governments, if not the central government. Although the Alliance Party and its successor, the Barisan Nasional, have won all the national elections since Independence, there have been exhilarating highs and worrying lows. As I write this, the coalition remains vulnerable, having lost five states to the Opposition at the 2008 General Election. To regain its robustness, Barisan Nasional must make an honest assessment of its virtues and its failings, and must be prepared to take radical measures if it is to be a relevant and effective leader of Malaysia in the new millennium.

Because of pragmatic policies, Malaysia made a smooth transition from an agricultural economy to an industrial one. The sons and daughters of subsistence farmers and fishermen now work in air-conditioned factories, handling delicate instruments and producing sophisticated products for the world market.

Today, Malaysia is among the most developed in the developing world. It plays a significant role in international affairs, focusing mainly on the injustices perpetrated by the wealthier nations against poorer ones. It has been one of the most outspoken of Islamic countries.

We have flourished economically. Kuala Lumpur, an unknown capital of 300,000 inhabitants at Independence, has been transformed into a cosmopolitan city of more than two million. Its skyline is characterised by impressive buildings led by the luminous PETRONAS Twin Towers, once the tallest in the world. Our development plans have always taken into account the needs of the day and those of the distant future.

I played some part in all this but it would be remiss of me not to credit my predecessors for Malaysia's phenomenal progress. They set the foundation – and I only built on it. Without their sound judgment and foresight, my task would have been significantly harder.

These memoirs must naturally contain a focus on my role, but essentially it is about my beloved Malaysia, a country which has given me – indeed, all Malaysians – a good life. There will be other books about Malaysia, even about me, from other perspectives. But I hope that here, I have done justice to my country.

In writing this book I have been assisted by many people. My wife Hasmah encouraged me when I despaired over ever finishing it. She made it possible for me to work with peace of mind, organising my daily schedule to accommodate my writing time. My daughter Marina found a team of journalists and researchers to assist me. They went through my manuscript and re-arranged it, giving me valuable tips.

Matthias Chang, my former political secretary helped with suggestions and encouragement. My other children and many friends urged me on.

Fauziah Ismail and Laila Jaafar who have been part of my staff since my years in office, never tired of typing and retyping my drafts, corrections and new drafts. Every chapter was redone at least five times. There was never a word of complaint from them, even when, after typing the draft for the fifth time, I decided to rewrite the whole chapter.

There are several others whose contributions are too many for me to list. I thank them all.

I still wonder if this book is readable. I am assured that it is. But my doubts remain.


**Dr Mahathir Mohamad**
**2011**

# Chapter 1:
## Becoming Prime Minister

I became the fourth Prime Minister of Malaysia on 16 July 1981. Like other UMNO leaders before me, I had dreamt about becoming a member of the Cabinet, even Prime Minister. But I did not believe it would really happen. Until the moment I stood before the King waiting to be sworn in, I remained a highly unlikely candidate to attain the highest office in the country.

The odds had always been stacked heavily against me. I did not come from the Malay ruling elite. Tunku Abdul Rahman Putra Al-Haj ibni Almarhum Sultan Abdul Hamid Halim Shah, the nation's first Prime Minister, was a prince, the son of the Sultan of the state of Kedah.[1] He was also a former Deputy Public Prosecutor and State Superintendent of Education. The Tunku, as he was warmly referred to by all strata of society, was in the Kedah Civil Service and was used to heading government departments. His elevation to Prime Ministership did not go against the social conventions of that time.

Tun Abdul Razak Hussein, the second Prime Minister, came from a distinguished family of administrators. His father was a senior civil servant in the Pahang[2] state government and Tun Razak himself was Pahang State Secretary before he became involved in politics. After the Federation of Malaya was established in 1948, he became the *Menteri Besar*, or Chief Minister, of his state. Holding the number two position in UMNO, he became Deputy Prime Minister and was the natural successor to the Tunku.

As with Tun Razak in Pahang, my predecessor Tun Hussein Onn belonged to the elite of Johor[3] society and, like all his family, was close to the Johor palace. His father and grandfather had both served as *Menteri Besar* of Johor. With them, heading government administration was a family tradition.

---

[1] A state in the northwestern region of Peninsular Malaysia.

[2] A state in the East Coast region of Peninsular Malaysia.

[3] A state in the southern region of Peninsular Malaysia.

I, on the other hand, was a commoner, the son of a former schoolteacher who was drawing a monthly pension of RM90 at the time I became involved in politics. Malays were then still feudalistic and not at all used to commoners rising above their station. But I broke the mould and paved the way for them to head the Government of Malaysia. Today, an ordinary person who becomes Prime Minister is given the same respect as anyone from the ruling classes.

The first three Prime Ministers were also all lawyers trained in London. I was a medical doctor from the University of Malaya in Singapore. That alone put me at a disadvantage. Medicine was not considered the best qualification for a Prime Minister. Lawyers were deemed fit for the office because of the legislative functions involved in governance. Doctors, it was held, had no training in the intricacies of law and administration.

I was also a rebel and a troublemaker. I had no protector. I was expelled from UMNO in 1969 for daring to criticise the Tunku. This alone should have ended my political career. There was a precedent for this. Aziz Ishak, the former Agriculture Minister in the Tunku's first Cabinet, had promoted setting up a fertiliser factory to help local farmers who relied on a foreign producer for their supply. The move displeased the Tunku, who did not want to upset the foreign company, and he dropped Aziz from the Cabinet. He was eventually expelled from UMNO and was never allowed to rejoin.[4]

I was more fortunate. I was eventually reinstated but my troublesome record should have precluded me from holding senior posts in the party or Government. I had no family ties with the top brass and under normal circumstances would not have gone far. My political salvation came from Tun Razak, who overlooked my behaviour with the Tunku and smoothed my way up by making me a full Minister after I won a seat in the 1974 General Election.

Until recently, political convention here dictated that one was first made Parliamentary Secretary and then Deputy Minister before being elevated to full Ministerial rank. I bypassed these two apprenticeship stages.

---

[4]  He was also held in detention under the Internal Security Act for several years; see his autobiographical memoir, *Special Guest*, Oxford University Press, Kuala Lumpur.

Understandably, quite a few in UMNO who were far more senior than I did not take kindly to my leapfrogging. But for Tun Razak, I would have had very little chance of reaching the top. When he died in 1976, my only protector was gone.

Even when he was still alive I had to step carefully. One friend, Datuk Harun Idris, the *Menteri Besar* of Selangor[5] who had helped bring me back into UMNO after my expulsion, believed that I had undermined his chances of a vice-presidency in the 1975 UMNO elections. I ran in that same race and narrowly defeated him. Harun and his children never quite forgave me, but I never forgot what he did for me. He was later charged in court and found guilty of corruption, but he was released from prison during my time as Prime Minister.[6] In 1986, Harun and his son aided Tengku Razaleigh Hamzah, then an UMNO Vice-President, when the latter challenged my presidency of the party in that year's UMNO elections.

Even an endorsement from the top man did not secure the support of senior party members. When Tun Hussein made me Deputy Prime Minister in 1976, I faced continuing opposition from powerful party members such as the ageing UMNO Youth leader Tan Sri Syed Jaafar Hassan Albar, who died of a heart attack while campaigning in Johor. And soon after my appointment as Deputy Prime Minister, two of my close friends were arrested for allegedly being pro-communist.

Tan Sri Abdullah Ahmad and Abdullah Majid were Deputy Ministers in Tun Hussein's administration. Abdullah Ahmad had been Tun Razak's political secretary and was a family friend. He was also one of my strongest supporters. As if that was not enough, three days before I was to be sworn in as Prime Minister, my political secretary, Siddiq Ghouse, was arrested for alleged espionage activities. The then Home Minister Tun Ghazali Shafie said that Siddiq was a spy for the Soviet Union's KGB.

So there I was, the non-pedigreed Deputy Prime Minister whose political secretary was a "spy" and whose friends were "communist sympathisers". Any further rise in the party seemed most unlikely.

---

5   A state in the central region of Peninsular Malaysia.

6   Harun, the Chief Minister of Selangor from 1964 -1976, was convicted in 1976 on corruption charges relating to the 1975 Muhammad Ali-Joe Bugner boxing match in Kuala Lumpur.

Perhaps I was not alone in not having it easy. Tun Hussein also came under attack when Tun Razak appointed him Deputy Prime Minister. Some leaders of the party regarded him as an outsider because he had rejoined UMNO only in 1964, 17 years after he and his father, UMNO founder Dato' Onn Jaafar, had quit the party to set up the Independence of Malaya Party. It was Tun Razak who brought Tun Hussein back into the party – the two men had married sisters and so were related. Tun Hussein became Minister of Education and his elevation was also considered rapid. Later, his choice of me as Deputy Prime Minister would be seen as ill-advised, partly because of my connections with so-called communists. But Tun Hussein was a straight arrow who had served with British forces. No one could believe he, and by extension I, could have anything to do with communism. Besides, Tun Hussein readily detained those suspected of having leftist leanings despite their standing in UMNO and closeness to Tun Razak.

I have often wondered why he chose me to be his deputy. He knew very little about me personally. Perhaps it was because he knew even less about Tun Ghafar Baba, who also ran in the same UMNO race and won the highest number of votes of the three vice-presidential posts. About Tun Hussein's attitude towards the second Vice-President, Tengku Razaleigh Hamzah, I can only speculate. Perhaps an incident that took place when Tun Hussein was Minister of Finance and Deputy Prime Minister left its mark. Tengku Razaleigh, who was then head of PETRONAS, the national oil company, and Pernas, the national trading corporation (now Tradewinds Corporation), had demanded an allocation of RM100 million for each of the two companies and that he report directly only to Tun Razak, bypassing Tun Hussein as head of the Treasury. Perhaps Tun Hussein had not forgotten about this. I believe he did not have much of a choice when picking his deputy, and perhaps Tun Razak's views still exerted some influence. As he once told me, Tun Razak advised him to call me if he ever needed help.

Fate certainly played an important part in my political ascension. When Tun Dr Ismail Abdul Rahman, whom Tun Razak named his Deputy Prime Minister, died, Tun Hussein became Deputy Prime Minister. Not long after, Tun Razak died and Tun Hussein became Prime Minister. Ill health prevented Tun Hussein from being Prime Minister for long, and he stepped down in July 1981.

My rise was considered rapid but I still took 18 years to become a Member of Parliament, and 28 years to become a Minister. Money politics was unknown in those early days and I did not use cash to get to where I was. Even when money was allegedly used in campaigns against me, I still managed to win without any bribery, albeit with a narrow margin. I am thankful for the democracy practised in UMNO, which goes against the feudal nature of the Malays. I had dared to challenge the Tunku in 1969 because I felt I had grassroots support. Even though I was expelled I was able to rejoin UMNO because of this support.

Yet, as Deputy Prime Minister, I was a man chosen by a leader who did not have strong support in the party. I was obviously not going to have an easy time and Tun Hussein could not provide much protection for me. Tun Hussein had depended on Tun Razak for support when he was chosen as Deputy Prime Minister. When Tun Razak died, Tun Hussein had no great grassroots base to speak of. The arrest and detention of the so-called communist sympathisers high in the party seemed to suggest that his office was influenced by communists. His acceding to pressures to effect those arrests is probably a good measure of his own weak political situation. His administration was haunted by the communist bogey that his detractors unleashed in the hope that he would be ousted or would step down early, prompting a leadership struggle in UMNO.

Unable to curb efforts to undermine him in UMNO, Tun Hussein also faced challenges from the Chinese. Under the New Economic Policy (NEP),[7] the Industrial Coordination Act of 1975 required that companies allocate 30 per cent of their shares to the Bumiputera.[8] As most Chinese companies at that time were family-owned, they were naturally averse to having the Bumiputera, who were total strangers, involved at any level, even as directors. But the ICA was inflexible and Chinese businessmen agitated against the Government. There were also demands for a Chinese university.

---

[7] The NEP was designed to narrow the socioeconomic gap between the Malays and other indigenous peoples, and the Chinese and Indian minority groups.

[8] Roughly translated as "son of the soil", this term refers to Malays and other indigenous groups of Malaysia.

To fulfill the NEP requirement, the quota for places for the Bumiputera in government universities was increased. This kept many qualified Chinese and Indian students from enrolling in these institutions. For the rich, this posed no problem as they could afford to study at foreign universities. But opportunities for a good education for the poor non-Malays were much reduced by the quota system.

In those days there were no private universities or non-university tertiary institutions. Many Chinese completed secondary schooling in their mother tongue, so the demand for a Chinese university grew increasingly strident. Led by the Chinese educationist group Dong Jiao Zong,[9] the community united in agitation. Both Tun Hussein and I were in a dilemma. I was then Minister of Education and the issue landed on my desk. If we acceded to the demands of the Chinese, we would incur the displeasure of our Malay supporters. But if we refused them, we would weaken the MCA and Gerakan, UMNO's Chinese partner parties in the ruling Barisan Nasional coalition.[10]

Unlike the Malays, most Chinese voted on the basis of issues rather than political affiliations. On the Chinese university issue, I knew from experience that many MCA and Gerakan supporters would vote for the Opposition party DAP. Loyalty to their race was more powerful than party loyalties. In the 1969 General Election, for example, Chinese voters in my constituency voted for the Malay Islamist party PAS simply to ensure that as a so-called Malay "ultra", an alleged ethnic extremist, I would not win. This choice illustrates the sometimes decisive role of ethnic minority voters in Malaysia, which one ignores only at one's peril.

In these volatile circumstances, some Malay Muslim extremists also presented problems. On 26 May 1979 a small group of them had desecrated Hindu temples, prompting one temple in Selangor to post armed guards. When some Malay troublemakers came, they were attacked and four were killed. This provoked a powerful reaction among the Malays, and anti-Indian feelings remained strong even after the Government arrested and

---

[9]  The United Chinese School Teachers Association of Malaya.

[10]  The Barisan Nasional, or National Front, is the coalition of political parties that has headed the Government since Independence.

tried those responsible. Worryingly, and a sign of future developments, the young Malays who provoked the Indian response were not poor villagers resentful at being shut out from all opportunities but young students who had been educated overseas.

On 16 October 1980, in Batu Pahat in Johor, another group of deviant Malay Muslims attacked a police station. They were repulsed and eight of them were killed, yet this incident too marked the start of the growing problem of deviant teachings among Muslims in Malaysia. A similar but more serious challenge would come in late 1985, when a man who called himself Ibrahim Libya and his heretical followers staged an uprising in Memali, Kedah.

By far the most difficult problem Tun Hussein faced on taking over as Prime Minister was the corruption case involving Harun Idris. The Selangor *Menteri Besar* was also head of UMNO's youth wing and was very popular with the more outspoken Malays. Lacking strong party support and having powerful enemies among UMNO's old guard, Tun Hussein should have been careful in dealing with Harun. But he went ahead with the case. UMNO Youth strongly condemned him. I had no choice but to support him, even though I knew that if he went down, I might well go down with him.

Yet, Tun Hussein was a man of strong convictions. He ignored UMNO Youth and was even prepared to use the police when Harun refused to surrender. Agitation against Tun Hussein continued but the Barisan Nasional victory in the 1978 General Election — greatly aided by the split in PAS, which had left the coalition — helped to secure his position. Flush with this victory, Hussein decided to hold UMNO elections to confirm his presidency of the party. He was challenged by an UMNO member, Haji Sulaiman Palestine, a colourful character who, having lived in Palestine for some time in his younger years (hence his nickname), could surprisingly speak Hebrew. The populist Sulaiman was a very powerful orator, but Tun Hussein won comfortably. I was not challenged and was confirmed as Deputy President. The threat against Tun Hussein and me receded.

My own relationship with Tun Hussein, however, was sometimes strained. He rejected a number of my suggestions and was not pleased that I had ventured to offer them. Increasingly frustrated, I eventually stopped putting forward ideas. I did not want to annoy him and jeopardise my chances of becoming Prime Minister. Then, in 1981, Tun Hussein suddenly informed the Cabinet that he was going to the United Kingdom for treatment for his heart condition. We knew he was not very well but we did not think it was so serious as to require heart surgery — in those days regarded as a far more risky operation than today. The operation itself was successful, but Tun Hussein remained unwell when he returned home. He had to slow down and I offered to take on his extra work. One day in mid-1981, after a meeting at his residence, he asked me to stay behind. He told me that he could not carry on and wanted to step down. I again offered to do his work for him while he rested. But he was adamant and said that his mind was made up. I was to take over from him.

I kept this information to myself and waited for Tun Hussein to make the announcement himself, which he did to his own Johor Baru UMNO division on 15 May 1981. The thousand members attending the annual meeting were shocked when he told them he would not be seeking re-election as party President and would step down as Prime Minister. Shortly after that, he informed the Cabinet and made a public announcement that he intended to resign as Prime Minister. The party was to hold its elections at the Annual General Assembly on 28 June that year. I accepted the nomination for presidency of the party only after it was clear that Tun Hussein would not be contesting.

As no other candidate emerged, I would become President uncontested on 28 June, the day Tun Hussein would officially step down. The focus of interest was upon the contest for the Deputy President's post. There were two candidates, Tengku Razaleigh and Tun Musa Hitam,[11] both of whom were Vice-Presidents.

The Annual General Assembly was held at the then Hilton Hotel's Nirwana Ballroom as the UMNO building[12] was not yet ready. The hall was packed with delegates, observers and guests. After the usual preliminaries, Tun

---

[11]  Tun Musa Hitam served as Deputy Prime Minister from 1981-1986.
[12]  The Putra World Trade Centre (PWTC), which houses UMNO's headquarters, was officially opened on 2 September 1985.

Hussein stepped up to the rostrum and made a brief speech which, according to UMNO practice, was also the opening speech of the assembly. To the hushed crowd he announced that after consulting with me, he had decided to step down as Prime Minister on 16 July. This meant that for 17 days, the Prime Minister would not be the President of UMNO or vice-versa. Though this broke with tradition, it was not a matter of any consequence and no one remarked on it. All eyes were on Tun Hussein as he stepped down from the rostrum at the end of his speech. There was loud applause, and he shook hands with the members of the Supreme Council before returning to his seat.

The meeting was adjourned and the Supreme Council members all retired to the Rajah Room for a break and coffee. Tun Hussein did not stay long. UMNO members gathered around him as he made his way to the hotel's lower entrance, from where the Supreme Council saw him off. After that, party members crowded around me to congratulate me on my uncontested election as President of UMNO. It was good for the ego even though I was not sure how many of them were sincere.

When the meeting resumed, voting for the Deputy President, Vice Presidents and other posts began. In UMNO, whoever became Deputy President also became the Deputy Prime Minister. So naturally, the contest between Tengku Razaleigh and Tun Musa drew the most attention. I resolved to work with whoever won. I could not afford to back either because if my candidate lost, I would be left with an antagonistic deputy. Staying impartial was very important to me as I wanted to be close to my deputy. I did not enjoy this rapport with Tun Hussein and I felt that this was why some of my ideas were rejected. Yet my careful neutrality ultimately did not secure my deputy's lasting support. Within five years, Tengku Razaleigh and Tun Musa would unite against me to contest the UMNO leadership.

Although Harun was still in jail when Tun Hussein ended his premiership, he had been nominated for Vice-President at that assembly. Tun Hussein did not make an issue of it. Besides, there was nothing in the party constitution to stop the nomination. According to the regulations, however, Harun would not be able to take an active post in politics for five years after his release from jail. The UMNO Youth made it clear that they wanted Harun to get a full pardon from the King. I was not sure if even a full pardon would allow his immediate return to active politics, so this UMNO election was critical. It would both determine who my deputy would be and it would indicate the feelings of UMNO members regarding the jailing of Harun. I knew Tun Hussein's feelings about the issue. He had literally thrown the files on Harun's case at me when I had earlier tried to discuss the political implications of continuing legal proceedings against Harun, and I now assumed that he would be offended if I did anything for Harun. On the other hand, I could not risk ignoring the feelings of members and becoming unpopular so soon after becoming President of the party.

There was a great deal of excitement as the votes were being counted. At the usual Supreme Council meeting the night before the General Assembly, all candidates had pledged that, win or lose, they would continue to serve UMNO and the Government. I felt reasonably assured that the party would not be split between the supporters of Tengku Razaleigh and Tun Musa. Tun Musa won with a clear majority with 722 votes against Tengku Razaleigh's 517. There was loud but brief cheering when the results were announced. The delegates had thankfully heeded my appeal not to display their feelings too much over the result.

The next results to be announced were those of the Vice-Presidents. I waited with bated breath over the number of votes Harun would get. There were seven candidates, of whom only Tun Ghafar was an incumbent. The other two, Tengku Razaleigh and Musa Hitam, were not contesting. They had gone for broke, contesting only the Deputy President's post and nothing else. Other than Tun Ghafar and Harun, those standing included Tengku Tan Sri Ahmad Rithaudeen Tengku Ismail, Tun Ghazali Shafie, Tan Sri Senu Abdul Rahman, and Datuk Seri Dr Rais Yatim.[13] As expected, Tun Ghafar came in first with 869 votes. Then Harun garnered 757 votes to come in second. Tengku Ahmad Rithaudeen came in third with 711 votes.

---

[13] Tun Ghafar Baba was the Deputy Prime Minister of Malaysia from 1986 -1993; Tengku Ahmad Rithauddeen Tengku Ismail's last Cabinet position was as Defence Minister until 1990; Tun Ghazali Shafie's last Cabinet position was as Foreign Affairs Minister until 1984; Tan Sri Senu Abdul Rahman was Information and Broadcasting Minister in the Tunku's Cabinet; and Datuk Seri Dr Rais Yatim is the current Information, Communication and Culture Minister.

My worst fears were confirmed. The outcome posed two major problems for me as I began my stint as President of UMNO and Prime Minister. First, there was the possible split in the party between Tun Musa and Razaleigh's supporters and, second, we now had a Vice-President in jail.

On 15 July Tun Hussein chaired his last Cabinet meeting. The following day he submitted his official resignation letter to the Yang di-Pertuan Agong,[14] then Sultan Ahmad Shah of Pahang. At 11am the same morning, a short ceremony was held in the palace's *Dewan Istiadat* or Ceremonial Hall. All the Ministers were present, together with the Inspector-General of Police, the Chief of the Armed Forces and the Attorney-General. Toh Puan Suhaila Mohd Noah, Tun Hussein's wife, and my wife, Siti Hasmah Mohd Ali, were also there. At another table sat the Acting Lord President of the Supreme Court, Tan Sri Raja Azlan Shah, (who later became the Sultan of Perak[15]) and the Chief Secretary to the Government, Tan Sri Hashim Aman.

Tun Hussein walked in with me behind him. We were dressed in dark lounge suits and *songkok* as the ruling requiring Malay Ministers to wear black *baju Melayu* was not yet in force. Then His Majesty the Yang di-Pertuan Agong walked in and sat on the throne flanked by four aides-de-camp drawn from the Police and the Armed Forces. Upon the invitation of the Court Chamberlain I walked up to the Agong, who handed me the official document for oath-taking. After reciting the oaths, one being the oath of office and the other to guard official secrets, I signed them and they were countersigned by the Acting Lord President.

Inscribing those signatures represented a sharp demarcation between my old life and my new one. During my tenure, I would often wonder how an ordinary person like me had risen to this office. Looking back, it was a most unlikely path for a medical doctor, let alone a commoner. Yet I became the fourth Prime Minister of Malaysia.

11

---

[14]   The King and elected head of Malaysia's constitutional monarchy.
[15]   A state in the northwestern region of Peninsular Malaysia.

# Chapter 2
# Family Values

My father, Mohamad bin Iskandar, was a man of unusual character when it came to education. He ran to school and not away from it, and he hid his attendance from his parents. It was this peculiarity that ultimately taught me to revere learning and knowledge.

In the days of his youth, Malay parents were against sending their children to English schools because most of them were run by Christian brothers, or missionaries. They taught Christian scriptures in convents and other missionary schools, and many Malay students had to study it as one of the subjects for examination. Malays, who were Muslim, feared their children would be converted to Christianity if they went to these schools, though there is no record of anyone converting. Naturally, my father did not tell his parents when he decided to attend classes at a Christian school in the British colony of Penang.[1] He was bent on getting an education because he believed it would improve his employment prospects, and that his faith in Islam was strong enough to resist proselytising.

After passing Standard Four, he was accepted by the Penang government as a trainee teacher. He underwent "normal class" training, a kind of on-the-job training for teachers. In 1908 the Kedah government invited him to start an English school in the capital town of Alor Star for the children of the royal household and the elite in Government service. Among his students was Tunku Abdul Rahman, who would later become the first Prime Minister of independent Malaya and Malaysia. My father was a strict disciplinarian and was not much liked by his students, including the future first Prime Minister. This was probably because the Sultan had given my father permission to punish students for not studying, even if they were from royal families. He had no hesitation about doing this, sometimes even resorting to the use of a thin rattan cane.

He was equally strict at home. Because he demanded that we study hard, our relatives sent their children to stay with us so they too would be infused with the same values. Among them was the late Tun Syed Ahmad Shahabuddin

---

[1]    A state in the north of Peninsular Malaysia.

who, among other things, served as Governor of Malacca from 1984 to 2004. We children lived in awe of my father, even though he never laid a hand on us. He didn't have to — the sound of his cough when he came home was enough to send us scurrying back to our books and homework. We all studied together at the big table in the front room, stopping only for dinner.

My father was later transferred from Kedah to Pahang and then Johor to teach in the English schools there. The journeys were often strenuous and took many days. He had to go by steamship, taking my mother and his children with him. One of my sisters, Habsah, was born in Pahang, and my brother Mahadi was born in Johor where my father taught in a school which later became the famed Johor English College. Eventually he got tired of being transferred and of living so far away from home. He resigned from the teaching service after nearly eight years. Being good at mathematics, he then joined the Kedah Audit Department as Senior Auditor. He used to tutor my brother Mashahor, who was two years ahead of me in school, about HCF or highest common factors and LCM or lowest common multiples. These lessons took place at the big table where I was studying and I listened in keenly, becoming quite good at mental arithmetic as a result. My father retired when I was in Primary Two of the Government English School in Alor Star.

It was in the poorer quarters of this town that I was born, in an area called Seberang Perak. My real birthday is 10 July 1925, but my father registered all his male children as born in December. Since the Malayan school year began in January, this avoided any hassles to do with age when registering for entry. That is why my registered birth date is 20 December, making me slightly younger than my real age.

With its stinking earth drains and black scum floating on the water, our neighbourhood verged on being a slum. The area would get very muddy after it rained. During high tide the river water would flow into the drains and spill into the surrounding land, dumping mounds of waste when the tide receded. There was a positive side to this. During this season, my brothers and I would fish for *ikan temekong*, a kind of small catfish. It was inedible, but we liked the fun.

13

A number of local characters frequently passed our house – the transvestite Che Din Ponen; a soya bean cake and bean sprout seller; Encik Sutan Adam, a well-to-do neighbour; and a woman cakeseller who regularly carried four baskets of varied Malay *cucur* or cakes on her arms. On some nights, Pa' Awang Ladeh, known as such because he sold *ladeh*, or curdled milk, would pass by. His son Abdul Rahman Awang later studied dentistry and was in the 1947 batch of medical students with me. After graduating, he joined government service and rose to become Director of the Department of Dentistry in Malaysia. His story proves that anyone can do well in this country if he tries hard enough.

There was also the Indian watercarrier, who was a little eccentric. He had a habit of suddenly putting down his four-gallon tins and dancing noisily. For some reason, he had all kinds of coins attached to his shirt and they would make a jangly "kerching-kerching" sound as he danced and shouted, "Aiyem yuyeh, uhuk-uhuk!" which was quite meaningless. To this day, whenever I wear my state uniform and medals I am tickled by the memory of this man with his many coins. I think I look like him.

14

My father was a Penang Malay. Almost all Malays of the island of Penang have some Indian blood. Migration from India was highest when Penang became a British colony, and since only the men came, they usually married Malay women. Their children were called Jawi Peranakan, literally "Javanese-born", probably because people in those days were unable to distinguish the Malays from the Javanese. To this day, the Arabs call Malays the Jawi people. That the Arabic script used in Malaysia is also called Jawi is a coincidence. Culturally and linguistically, the Penang Malays are Malays. My father could not speak any of the languages of India and knew none of his forebears or relatives there. The connection was completely broken.

My mother, Wan Tempawan, was a Kedah Malay. The pre-fix "Wan" indicates that she was from the ranks of Kedah Malays who usually served the royal households or were in government service. Since my father's own relatives were all in Penang and so did not know the Malay families of Kedah, my parents' marriage was an arranged one, with a few senior Malay civil servants acting as go-betweens. My mother was very well-bred and understood the *adat*, or traditions and codes, of Malay etiquette. Accordingly, she brought us up to behave and carry ourselves as good, well-bred Malays.

My father gave all his children the education they needed to make their way in life. But I have always felt that, of my brothers, I was the luckiest because my father gave me the highest level of education. That is why I was better off than all my siblings.

While my father stressed general education, my mother insisted that her children learn the teachings of Islam early in life. She was good at reading the Quran and she taught us herself. My eldest sister, Rafeah, whose nickname was Putih,[2] was known for her good voice when reciting the Quran. At the Malay school we were taught basic elements of the religion, and we memorised selected verses of the Quran without being given any explanation of their meaning. Later we had a tutor from an Arabic school, Encik Zakaria Mohamad Noor, who taught us to memorise more verses and gave us the translations in Malay. Even now, I can recite these verses from memory. Between my father's emphasis on education and my mother's insistence on knowing my religion, I became enthusiastic about acquiring knowledge and reading all kinds of books.

15

I was closer to my mother than to my father and as a result, she shaped my personality more. She taught me the values that I have upheld throughout my life, especially to be modest and not boastful about what I have done. When I did speak about myself — perhaps in a bragging tone — she downplayed my achievements. She believed that I should always give way in any dispute or quarrel. I used to find this very hard to do because I usually believed I was right. But as far as my memory stretches, she never took my side in a dispute.

She also taught me very clearly that if I wanted something, I had to work for it. When I wanted to buy a pen, she told me to carry buckets of water for her jasmine plants for one sen a day to earn the money. From her, I learnt that this was the honourable way. So when my pocket money was reduced from four sen to two sen after my father retired, I did not

---

2    In Malay, *putih* means "white".

complain. Instead, I tried to earn extra money by selling balloons to my friends. I would buy three balloons for two sen from a shop near my house, usually on Fridays when I had time, and then sell them for one sen each. You could buy a lot with a one-sen profit at that time, like a full plate of rice with curry. But I did not always get to spend it on myself. Sometimes the class bully, who lived near where I did, would take me to the tuckshop and force me to spend the money on him. If I refused, he would punch me and I certainly did not want to get into a scuffle with him. He was one of the tough guys and his father was an ex-police officer. I also made some money by doing more chores at home. My mother kept chickens and ducks under the house, and I helped her to feed them and get them into the coop in the evenings. I also chopped *bakau* logs, a mangrove wood, for the cooking fire. For doing these chores I would get one sen as *upah* or wages.

My mother had a small plot of land on which she grew mostly jasmine and roses. We collected the jasmine flowers and strung them on finely-split, dried long grass stems called *menerong*. An Indian flowerseller would then come to collect the strings of flowers and sell them to women who wore them around their hair buns. In our neighbourhood, my mother was also well-known for the *celak*, or kohl which she made. It was tedious work — she used a porcelain mortar and pestle to crush the kohl to a very fine powder. In addition, she made *bedak sejuk* by dropping liquid rice flour through a banana leaf cone onto a piece of white muslin. When dried it would be stored in bottles in pellet form. In those days women dissolved the solidified paste in water and applied it to their faces to help cool the skin. My mother also made *minyak angin*, a kind of coconut-oil-based liniment that helped to relieve muscle aches and sprained ankles.

I suppose we would have been considered lower-middle class, but my parents were in no way stingy. If my school pocket money was reduced from four sen to two sen it was because my father's pension was now a third of his last-drawn salary of RM270. I knew they loved me, though my father was distant and was not good at showing his affection. I knew that, more than anything, my mother wanted me to be a good and upright man. As a career, there were only two things she didn't want me to become: a police inspector or, ironically, a doctor. Either, she said, would mean that

I would never get any sleep. But when I did go on to study medicine, she didn't object.

We had only two iron four-poster beds at home, one for my parents and the other for any newly-married member of the family. The rest of us slept on thin mattresses laid out on the floor, under mosquito nets hung from nails driven into the wooden pillars. In the morning the nets were taken down and the mattresses rolled up and stacked against the wall with the pillows. When I was Prime Minister and visited Japan frequently, I was amused when the Japanese carefully explained to me their custom of sleeping on the floor because it was no different from my own experience growing up.

Manners were given great emphasis in our home. Malays eat with their fingers but they do not grab food and soil the palm. Food is to be handled with the right hand only. Serving spoons are managed with the left hand so that the handle remains clean. It may sound difficult but I became very skilled, even at getting the meat out of prawns and crabs with my right hand only. Today I wince when I see Malay children using both hands to eat. In my family, which I would call orthodox Malay Muslim, all the women, except for my mother, used to eat after the men had eaten. We had our meals sitting on the floor and did not talk while eating. After the men, including even young boys like myself, had eaten, the food was taken to the kitchen area which was at a lower level, where my sisters ate.

It was my father who taught me to sit at the table and use a fork and spoon to eat. Since we usually sat on the floor for meals, he bought a small wooden table to teach me. But I was not inclined to use forks and spoons until I injured my right hand when I was about eight. I was trying to stop a bench from falling over, but it landed on the middle finger of my right hand, splitting the tip. After that I had to use a fork and spoon most of the time. Now I hardly ever eat with my hands. Indeed, I am now more adept at getting the meat out of prawns and crabs using the fork and spoon than most people are with their fingers. I often shell crabs for Hasmah, and I taught my children the best way to get the meat out. I regard table manners, whether Malay or English, as a measure of one's upbringing, so I am horrified when I see Malaysians — even diplomats — holding forks in their fists as if wanting to stab someone.

My sisters and brothers also played a role in my upbringing. I was the youngest of six children in my mother's[3] family and naturally I was pampered. My three sisters, Rafeah, Habsah and Johara corrected my manners — they would smack my hand if I handled food wrongly — and instructed me about proper deference to the elderly and to family friends who were senior members of the Kedah government service. Apart from these siblings, I had two half-brothers and one half-sister. Aishah, my half-sister, was also close to me, though she married when I was still a small boy and lived with her husband in a house further down the Seberang Perak road. The eldest of my sisters Rafeah was with me the longest. She moved from Alor Star to live with me in Kuala Lumpur and I was always happy and deeply nostalgic when she was around. She passed away on 1 September 2009.

Through teaching me to be modest, my mother also handed down the values of tolerance and respect. When I became Deputy Prime Minister and Prime Minister I never transferred any member of my staff for bad work, as was usually the practice. Instead, I tried to get them to do what I expected of them by gaining their loyalty. They were usually able to improve and raise their performance to a satisfactory level. Many members of my staff are still with me, after decades of service. I strongly believe that it is the boss' responsibility to get on with the staff and get the best out of them. Faults will always be there. Changing staff does not guarantee that the new employees will be any better. I am keenly aware that perfect people simply do not exist. As much as I might have been annoyed with staff members, they must have also been irritated with me quite often. All this early guidance from my family served me well during my tenure as Deputy Prime Minister and Prime Minister. Though I did not agree with some of Tun Hussein's policies and ideas, for example, he was the boss and I respected him.

Observing my parents as I was growing up also taught me to value the concept of the family. My parents were very close. At night my father would sit on the floor, stretch his legs and lean against the main pillar of the house to talk to my mother. The pillar was his favourite spot and

18

---

[3]   My father married my mother after the death of his first wife.

it was worn smooth over the years because he leaned against it so often. He would smoke cheroot cigars and she would chew betel leaves. I do not know what they discussed but they were good companions and seemed to have something to talk about all the time. They did not demonstrate their affection for each other as it was unbecoming to do so, but I know they loved each other very much.

As he grew old and his heart began to fail him, my father refused to go anywhere. I think he feared dying away from home. I was already a medical officer by then and was staying in government quarters, but I visited my parents every day. Eventually the time came when he refused to take the medicine prescribed for him, and he began to fade away. He passed away quietly in 1962. After my father died, my mother no longer had the desire to live. She withdrew from all of us. She did not eat well or talk much. After some time, she just lay down listlessly on a mattress on the floor. She pulled up her legs and did not seem to want to get up. Eventually, her legs froze in that position. When she died, we could not straighten them. I already had a private medical practice at the time and every day, after treating my last patient, I would go home to see her. I would try to cheer her up but it was difficult and frustrating. Three years after my father's death, she too passed away.

19

I cannot imagine what growing up in a polygamous family would have been like. Surely in such a situation, bitterness would eat at the heart of the household. Life could not be peaceful for the husband. Among my brothers, only the eldest, Murad, from my father's first marriage, had two wives. Being brought up in a family that was largely monogamous has helped me keep to the straight and narrow. My father-in-law Haji Mohd Ali also had only one wife. Hasmah and I feel blessed that we come from such a family background.

People often fall back on the argument that Islam allows a man to have four wives at one time, but there is a clause that is always ignored. The Quran says that you *may* marry two, three or even four women, but if you cannot be just to them all, then marry just one. And later in the same chapter, it says that you will never be able to achieve this level of fairness to women. The implication is clear: the Quran advocates one wife, not four.

Undoubtedly, there are sometimes unusual circumstances — such as war — in which the number of women exceeds the number of men. To ensure that someone takes care of war widows, Muslim men are allowed to marry more than one wife. Islam is not merely a system of beliefs and rituals. It guides the community in all the daily activities of life, even in areas such as punctuality, personal cleanliness and protecting the environment.

By shaping our way of life, Islam maintains balance and a well-ordered society. Yet, ironically, it is those who claim to be religiously educated who tend to marry more than one woman. Generally communities are made up of roughly equal numbers of men and women. I have often argued that if a man takes more than one wife, then it would presumably deprive others of spouses. It hits at the heart of society's equilibrium.

By no means am I saying that monogamous marriages are perfect. In practice, disagreements cannot be avoided but they should not cause any break-up in husband-wife relations. For example, I am a stickler for time. In the stories I read as a boy, punctuality seemed a good quality to have, so I developed it. Hasmah, however, is always late, inevitably having something to sort out just before we have to leave. At first this difference caused a lot of friction. But over the years I learnt to accommodate this habit, as she has had to do with many of mine. Now I make jokes about her tardiness and make exaggerated efforts at helping to find what she is looking for. I irritate her by following her around the room. I lie and say we have to leave at 8pm when we actually have to leave later. Still, she is incorrigible. Now I stay in the dressing room until she is finished. I have learnt the hard way that if I were to go downstairs first, she will never emerge. Mutual regard and good humour, as this small example shows, can preserve a marriage. I would never dream of taking another wife and causing Hasmah and my children anguish and pain. To be happy, one must learn to make compromises with grace.

From my mother I also learnt the importance of the extended family. We were very attached to ours, even our relatives by marriage. My maternal grandmother lived with us until she died. Her name was Hawa, and by the time I was born she was already grey-haired. What I remember most about her is that she kept her money in a round cigarette tin, and at night she would sleep using the tin as a pillow. Recently, I watched a television show in which a Malay couple decided to send their aged father, who had had a stroke, to an old folks home. It is an idea that is alien to me. In Malay culture, you cherish and revere your elderly relatives. You do not send them to die alone among strangers. I am horrified at the change in the Malay value system and I mourn the passage of good values of the sort handed down by my parents.

Yet family ties and high office are not always a comfortable combination. When I was Prime Minister, many members of my extended family did not understand that I could not use my authority to get whatever I (or they) wanted. Some expected me to favour them with contracts, licences and the like. They came to my home armed with their brown envelopes containing all kinds of proposals, but the most I could do was play postman and pass the envelopes to the officers concerned. Sometimes I would write, "Please See" on the envelopes. Some say this was enough to influence the officers to give what was asked for, but I also know that most of my relatives and friends got nothing. If they received a positive response, it was because in the opinion of the respective officers, their proposals were sound.

Some of my relatives who failed to get anything are still not on speaking terms with me. In one case, my nephew Ahmad Mustapha, a journalist, attempted to go into business. He tried to persuade me to buy what he said was the Sukhoi 35 aircraft, and I told him any decision to purchase would depend on how good the aircraft was. When I made enquiries from a Russian, he said there was no Sukhoi 35, only the 30 which India had. The mark 35 version has yet to be produced to this day. I even asked Russian President Vladimir Putin about it since I wanted the best for our air force. But he confirmed they did not have the 35, so our Government decided to buy the Sukhoi 30. Mustapha thought I had personally frustrated him and until today, he doesn't talk to me. These are the hazards of public office, and my relatives' displeasure must be endured.

My own children knew my views and they did not bother me. I did not even allow them to bid for positions in UMNO or to become candidates for elections. I firmly believed that my family had no role to play in government. I was the Prime Minister of the people, not of my family. There were occasions when my sons received company shares and Approved Permits, or APs, to import cars. Mirzan, my eldest son, received shares because as a director of the company, that was his entitlement. Mokhzani, my second son, received APs because he was running a legitimate business importing cars and selling them. However, there were many others who received APs to sell them, and not to bring in cars through a genuine business.

After my retirement I felt it was no longer fair for me to deprive my children of playing a role in politics if that was what they wanted. They did not directly benefit from my years as Prime Minister, and although it could not be helped if people connected them to my name, my children built their lives and careers on their own.

Just as I drew moral instruction from my father and mother, my children have also drawn moral guidance from me. Or so I hope. Of all the lessons I hope they have learnt, the most important is not to abuse their position. In the case of my own family most of the public focus is on Mirzan because he sold his company to MISC, which belongs to PETRONAS, which in turn is under the Government's control. But my children did not rely on me to solve their problems. Mirzan handled his himself, as I will relate in a later chapter.

My vision for Malaysia and the policies my administration created were for everybody, not just for a politically-connected elite or a small circle of my own family and friends. I never even gave my children one cent of capital — all I gave them was a good education, a chance to develop and make something of themselves in life. They never asked me for anything and didn't even tell me about the business that they did. We did not discuss business or politics with each other. Politics and public policy was not for them to know. It was always clearly understood among us all: that I was busy with the country and their troubles were their own.

The truth was that, from the moment I became Prime Minister, I ceased to belong to my family. They accepted that as Prime Minister I could not spend time with them or be overly occupied with their problems. It was the same for their mother too. Hasmah never complained if I didn't come home, or was late, or was not paying sufficient attention to the family or the house, both of which she managed. She and the children understood that if they had problems, they might go to her for help, but not to me.

I would not abuse the power that I had, nor did I want them to abuse their connection to me. I often said just that and they knew what I meant. They grew up and matured during the time I was Prime Minister. Even when they went to university, I never asked the Government for scholarships. Earlier Mirzan received a scholarship when I was not in the Government, when I was expelled from UMNO and well before I became a Minister. He got a MARA[4] scholarship on his own merit. He was one of a handful of Malay students who were selected to study in private schools in the UK to expose them to a different culture.

As for other values like consistency, punctuality and reliability, I would tell them they should not behave like children of wealthy parents. When I talked about my school days, about walking to school and the like, they would get bored. Perhaps they will read these pages, especially my recollection of my parents and my own childhood, and find something of interest to them. Perhaps they will learn something that will help explain their father, or some aspects of his character, a little more clearly to them, or perhaps an insight that they in turn may pass on to their own children. There are always lessons to be learnt, if only we have the wisdom to see them.

23

---

[4] Majlis Amanah Rakyat, a government agency that aids Bumiputera participation in the economy.

# Chapter 3:
# I Am A Malay

I am well aware that my ethnic origin has been the subject of much animated debate. Some claim that my father was Malayalee and was fluent in both Tamil and Malayalam. Some have even written that he was a Hindu who converted to Islam to marry my mother. Others say they have seen documents clearly stating my ethnicity. I admit that some Indian, or more accurately South Asian blood flows in my veins, but from which part of the Indian subcontinent my ancestors came I do not know. Malays in the past did not keep track of their lineage, although most of those with Arab blood can trace their roots to Yemen and know which family they belong to.

Some people will see this chapter as racist at worst, and narcissistic at best — it is intended to be neither. I am a Malay and am proud of it. There are many reasons why I state this so strongly and boldly. Those who say that a leader's ethnicity or gender does not matter to the people are fooling themselves. It was only during the 2008 US Presidential elections that a woman and an African-American became serious contenders for the post. To date, the US has only had one Roman Catholic leader, John F. Kennedy. Britain has a similar record. The indomitable Baroness Margaret Thatcher characteristically came from a very English family, and except for Benjamin Disraeli, who renounced Judaism, Britain has had no head of government or Prime Minister who was not white or Christian.

Multiracial democracies have nuances that homogenous countries cannot imagine. Racial tags often have a derogatory taint. In Malaysia, Chinese are popularly seen as money-grabbing and Indians as violent drunks. Malays, the majority race, are said to be lazy and lacking in intellectual capacity. Stereotypes will always persist, even in the most progressive and educated societies. But a good leader does not let them go unchallenged. Every time when, as Prime Minister, I made a mistake or an unpopular decision, people were ready with their "dim-witted Malay" slurs. But when I made good decisions, those that brought progress and prosperity to the nation, it was always because I had Indian blood. I wanted to prove otherwise: that Malays were more than capable of thinking, progressing and leading.

Nearly every Malay in Malaysia has some non-Malay blood. But that fact doesn't make them any less Malay. We seem to categorise ourselves in such puzzling ways that managing our multiracial country is extremely difficult. Racial categorisations make a great deal of difference to the acceptance or rejection of one's leadership and decisions.

The Peninsular Malays have long lived at the crossroads between the East and the West, so they intermarried with others and became mixed earlier than most people. The most common intermarriages were with Indians and Arabs. At one time the offspring of such marriages were classed, often derogatorily, as either DKK (*Darah Keturunan Keling*, Malays of Indian blood) or DKA (*Darah Keturunan Arab*, Malays of Arab blood). Today, such labels are no longer used. Each classification generated its own distinctive stereotypes, some of them negative.

In Malaysia today, being Malay is not a question of descent, of one's family history of intermarriage, and hence the popular idiom of "blood". "Malayness" is a legal construct. One is a Malay if one satisfies certain legal conditions. Constitutionally, a Malay is defined as a person who habitually speaks Malay, practises Malay customs and is a Muslim. An individual who meets these requirements is a Malay and all such individuals are automatically citizens enjoying rights in the nation. Citizens of Malay origin are entitled to certain rights that go with this legal personality. Others, too, become citizens of Malaysia by the operation of the Constitution and the law, but the formal or technical basis of their citizenship is different, at least at this time. Ultimately, all who are born in Malaysia and owe sole allegiance to it will, we hope and also plan, become members of the one people and nation, termed *Bangsa Malaysia*.[1]

Until we reach that point, race relations in Malaysia will remain a topic of perennial interest and controversy. We are often accused of being chauvinistic and the constitutional provision defining "Malay" is sometimes regarded as divisive and exclusionary, and also a trap to lure the unwitting into joining our racial ranks. Yet it was, in fact, meant to deflect racism by

---

[1]    I introduced the Bangsa Malaysia (or Malaysian nation) policy to create an inclusive national identity for all Malaysians. It meant that we could identify ourselves with the country, speak the Malay language and accept the Malaysian Constitution.

placing all Malays — no matter what their ethnic heritage — on an equal footing. To my mind, that approach has worked, although Johor oddly enough does not extend the right to own Malay reserve land[2] to those of Arab origin.

That legal definition became necessary when people without any Malay characteristics or connections began claiming to be Malay in order to enjoy certain Malay rights such as ownership of reserve land. That was when the Malay states were British protectorates. But when the Malayan Union was proposed in 1946, the British wanted to grant the descendants of immigrant Indians and Chinese the same citizenship status as that of the native Malays. In consequence, the question of definition became all the more crucial.

My family and I have always fulfilled those formal criteria. But I am a Malay not just on paper. I am also a Malay in sentiment and in spirit. I identify completely with the Malays and their problems, their past and their present, their achievements and failures. I do not do so sentimentally and uncritically, but thoroughly and thoughtfully. On many occasions I have criticised the Malays for taking the easy way out, for their general lack of desire for self-improvement and for their tendency to be dependent on others. I have confronted the comforting illusions they retreat into when they become afraid of challenges that they face as individuals and as a people. I have even written books on the subject. I have always had my reasons for these frequent expressions of disappointment. They were often outbursts due to my frustration, but they were also strategic. They were intended to provoke the average Malay to improve himself, to stand poised, confident and able, instead of leaning on crutches like affirmative action. I still believe, as I did when I put forth that challenge, that a change in the Malay value system is necessary. No one can deny that the Malays have been instrumental in making Malaysia what it is today because of their good and generous character. Whatever their lack of expertise and skill, to my mind their great strength has been their willingness and ability to work with others.

---

2   As stipulated in Article 89(6) of the Federal Constitution, Malay reserve land can only be owned or transferred to a Malay. There are currently some 4.5 million hectares of Malay reserve land.

So great was their capacity for acceptance that at one time, in the late 1920s and early 1930s, they had become, or were on the verge of becoming, a minority in their own country. If not for an accident of history — namely the Great Recession of the 1930s, which not only discouraged immigration into the country but also led many long-resident foreigners to return to India and China — the Malays could have lost Malaya completely. But by the late 1940s, as a result of events recounted elsewhere in this book, the situation had changed entirely. The war discredited the British and their assumed right to rule. It had lit a new spark of Malay determination. When the British returned after World War II, they tried to impose the Malayan Union, whose citizenship provisions would no longer recognise the Malays as the historic people within the Malay lands. This triggered the appearance on the political stage of a new force that could not be denied — a sleeping giant, Malay nationalism, stood up as UMNO.

For a long time, the Malays of the Peninsula had hospitably acceded to the arrival and the claims of immigrant non-Malays. Now, after some 450 years of colonisation, the Malays stood their ground, but not selfishly. Rather, once they had been assured recognition of their own historic position, they proved themselves able to work with others to build a prosperous and thriving nation in less than 50 years. Others may have had a special talent for commerce and business enterprise. We Malays demonstrated our own distinctive aptitude for social harmony and public administration. That has been the basis of the country's success.

Many other lands that the ethnic Europeans colonised experienced a protracted and violent struggle for liberation. But the Malays appear to have accepted colonisation and foreign domination with equanimity. There was some resistance and a few uprisings, notably in Perak where the British Resident J.W.W. Birch was assassinated at Pasir Salak on the Perak River. In Malacca,[3] the territorial chief Datuk Naning[4] fought against the British for imposing a tax on his district. In Pahang and Terengganu,[5] there were small rebellions led by territorial chiefs, and in the state of

---

[3] A state in the central region of the Peninsula.

[4] Datuk Naning, whose real name was Datuk Abdul Said, was the ninth ruler of Naning, a district in Malacca.

[5] A state in the East Coast region of the Peninsula.

Kelantan[6] the revered Tok Janggut,[7] a village leader from Pasir Puteh, led an insurrection against the British in 1915, not long after they had taken control of the state and its finances. In all these cases, the British hunted down the leaders and some were killed. In Sarawak,[8] Brooke loyalists among the Malays assassinated the British Resident.[9]

For all its heroism, this resistance was always sporadic and local. The Malays mounted no concerted and sustained struggle to regain their independence from the imperialists by violent force. Instead, they always appeared ready to cooperate amiably with their colonial masters — until the British tried to expropriate their *Tanah Melayu*, their Malay homeland, through the Malayan Union proposal. Until that time the Malays had pledged their loyalty to the Rulers of their respective states. Though aware at some level that they were all of the same stock or race, the Peninsular Malays never acted as one group. Their allegiance stopped at state borders and, as a result, one by one the Malay states fell into British hands. Today we talk of nations as if they have naturally existed from time immemorial. Yet many great nations started off as small principalities, not unlike the Malay *negeri*, or state. Japan, China, Italy and Germany were all divided into small states ruled by princes and warlords. In each case, a powerful leader emerged and, by force, fused the states into one country. Giuseppe Garibaldi, who created the cohesive Italian nation, is regarded by many as an outstanding example.

Their resilience and adaptability have allowed the Malays to thrive in a world which has unfortunately borne witness to the disappearance of numerous other indigenous peoples. The native peoples of the Americas and the Caribbean, the aborigines of Australia and the Maoris of New Zealand have all but disappeared due to the onslaught of the ethnic Europeans. Their lands have been expropriated and these lands have now

28

---

6   A state in the northeast region of the Peninsula.

7   Born Mat Hassan Panglima Munas, Tok Janggut led a rebellion against the British over the taxes they had imposed on agricultural goods in Kelantan. He was killed by the British on 24 May 1915. His body was paraded around Kota Baru and then hung upside down in front of the palace.

8   A state in East Malaysia.

9   James Brooke, Charles Brooke, and Vyner Brooke – the three White Rajahs of Sarawak – ruled the state from 1841 until it became a British colony in 1946. During their reign, they protected the rights of the indigenous people, earning their trust and loyalty.

become ethnic European countries. But the Malays — whom so many of their critics see as weak, indolent and inept — have survived European colonisation, raids and threats of conquest by strong neighbours and long submissions as vassals to powerful Asian nations. Because we survived that long history of dealing with powers greater than ourselves, we Malays were able in time to emerge as a people able to take its fate into its own hands. For this we are genuinely admired by many other newly independent nations. The Bosnians in Europe and the Arabs today also look up to the Malays, and often seek our guidance on the management of change and development in their countries.

Of all the ethnic Malays in the region, the Malays in this country are today widely recognised as the most successful. They have been able to administer and develop a multiracial country with an array of inherent problems and challenges. The many races in Malaysia are divided by religion, culture, language and — most important of all — by the disparities in their development and wealth. Yet the Malays have made progress and achieved significant success. While 50 years after Independence the Malays still form the bulk of the poorest stratum in society, there have been great advances.

There are fewer abject poor than there used to be and those who live in poverty are provided with the means and opportunity to better themselves. Some Malays have become prominent national entrepreneurs and corporate leaders. This has been accomplished by good policies, not by indulging the urge to acquire the wealth of others in order to enrich oneself. Malay economic progress has been accomplished ethically and legally, not ruthlessly.

This could only have been achieved under conditions of civil peace and social stability. It has largely been Malay political and administrative skill that has kept the country peaceful and stable and has fast-tracked its development. People rarely wonder about the origins of this talent for public service that the Malays so conspicuously display. Some of those who do not simply take it for granted like to suggest that it is a British legacy — the result of the example and lessons in public administration that the colonial authority taught us. There is, I believe, a deeper reason: a political tradition that dates back to the pre-colonial Malay sultanates.

Today there is a Malay presence everywhere in the world, and most recently in space as well. They have expanded their skills so greatly that now Malays drill for and produce oil, build roads and power plants, and manage multinational corporations and industries, including those involved with sophisticated engineering and high technological content all over the world. They have gone abroad and are accepted as capable contractors, builders and traders. Foreign companies now hire Malay executives for top posts.

Malays have scaled Mount Everest, sailed solo around the world, swum the English Channel, walked alone across Antarctica and travelled in space. Considering that our land is hot and humid, these achievements are doubly remarkable. Given the opportunity and the right attitude, Malays have proved themselves again and again. The basis for these achievements, and of the new Malay sense of confidence, has been our national affirmative action policies, implemented since 1971. These policies are regularly condemned by many ethnic Europeans, both statesmen and journalists. Even years after my retirement, I continue to be vilified for promoting these programmes. So be it. Their achievements are undeniable to those

who can think clearly and are fair-minded.

History, it seems, is easily forgotten. Apart from leaving the Malays with a big immigrant Chinese and Indian population to manage, the British also left the country very poor. The country's per capita income in 1957, the year of Independence, was less than USD350. Under British colonial rule more than 70 per cent of the population lived below the poverty line. The literacy rate was very low and there were only about 100 university graduates in the whole country. Roads that were built served only the British-owned rubber estates and tin mines. Malayan ports were deliberately left undeveloped in order to protect the British colonial port of Singapore. Malacca was destroyed and Penang's growth slowed down to enhance the economic development of Singapore. True, Singapore was strategically located at the tip of the Peninsula in the centre of 13,000 rich spice islands, but as the post-Independence development of Peninsular ports shows, that concentration on the development of Singapore port did not need to be total. Malayan ports could have catered to some of the trade during colonial days. Instead, Malaya was made totally dependent on exports of rubber and tin via Singapore. The bulk of the foreign exchange that these industries earned went to Britain. These cold hard facts are never mentioned in the so-called free Press of the ethnic Europeans.

By sharp contrast, Malaysia's per capita income today is more than USD7,000 (or in Purchasing Power Parity terms, USD14,000). Less than five per cent of the population is below the poverty line (and only one per cent are in absolute poverty). The literacy rate is more than 90 per cent and there are hundreds of thousands of university graduates. A network of modern expressways and tarred roads, reaching the most remote villages, joins all parts of the country together.

The seeds of our recent success were admittedly already there. A combination of the locals' business savvy and the capacity for tolerance made the Malay Peninsula a successful and popular trading locale many hundreds of years ago. The Peninsula is situated at the crossroads between China and Japan in the East, and India, Arabia and Europe in the West. For centuries, traders from all these countries and regions sailed past the Peninsula to do business with each other. Many stopped and some settled down in Malacca, marrying the locals. In those days, women did not travel with the traders. Not surprisingly, most Malays have some mixture of Chinese, Indian, Arab or even European blood in their veins. But the cultural values, the traditions and the religion adopted by all these people were distinctly Malay.

It is not the Malays who developed an obsession with the supposed purity of bloodlines but the Europeans. They displayed that characteristic obsession both in the racial segregation that they imposed upon the colonial societies that they ruled and also among themselves, at home in Europe. But one can build a race or people on a basis other than blood. It may be built, as Malay identity was, on culture and history. To do so on the basis of ethnic origins, using bloodlines as the criterion, was possible in former times because people could isolate themselves. But today, people are very mobile. It is difficult to make ethnicity the sole criterion of race. Even the insular English now have Jewish and Continental European blood, as is evidenced by their names. And the mix is going to increase so that a person's stated ethnicity, or official public identity, will no longer be an accurate indication of his or her race.

For example, an ethnically Indian citizen of the United Kingdom today is British, not English. But how long can this continue as Englishmen keep having children by Indian and African women and vice-versa? One day a legal definition may be needed to identify the English. By then, the English may not look English at all, just as today's Malays often do not have the anthropological physiognomy of Malays. Mixed blood or descent does not make a person any less English — or Malay.

The Malays belong to the brown-skinned people who inhabit almost all of Southeast Asia, including the vast archipelago once known as the Malay Archipelago. Today it is divided among three major branches of the one ethnically Malay people: the Indonesians, the Filipinos, and the Malays of the Peninsula and of the North Borneo states of Sabah and Sarawak, as well as Brunei. The division is purely political, deriving from the history of European colonisation of the region, and is not at all based on any inherent ethnic differences. The Philippines, for example, openly declare that its national hero, Jose Rizal, is a Malay.

The Malays of Malaysia are typically brown, of medium height and are well-proportioned in terms of their body structure. They tend to have flat, almost flaring nostrils, wide-open black eyes, straight or wavy black hair and are generally not hirsute. Their women are usually fairer in skin colour and the girls can be so stunningly beautiful that one — certainly a Malay like me — experiences a sense of deep pride at the sight of them. More than just being comely in appearance, the Malays are a cultured people, always very courteous and formal, with a fine aptitude for the arts. They adhere closely to their traditions, even though these are largely unwritten. They live, above all, according to proverbs and sayings that every Malay child used to learn and which together provide an informal guide to social etiquette and a sound basis for political common sense and wisdom. Adherence to the traditions or *adat* that is preserved within these sayings and proverbs is a mark of good upbringing.

There are thousands of these proverbs and sayings in Malay, perhaps more than in any other language. These really seem to influence attitudes and to shape Malay behaviour, even today. Unfortunately, these sayings often contradict one another. In any situation the Malay can usually find a saying to guide his action or to justify what he intends to do, but he may also draw wisdom from another saying which would allow him to do the exact opposite. Thus the Malay is enjoined to be loyal to his Raja or Ruler, according to the saying *Melayu tak akan derhaka kepada raja* (The Malay shall not betray his Raja). But another saying permits him to fight his Ruler if the latter is unjust. Thus: *Raja adil raja disembah, raja zalim raja di sanggah* (The just Ruler is obeyed, the unjust is opposed).

Malays tend to tolerate the injustices and the foibles of their Rulers to a far greater extent than other races. Rebellions and revolutions do not feature much in Malay history. While many ruling houses were done away with upon independence, often violently, in India and Indonesia, especially Sumatra, in the Peninsula all nine of them survived. It is said that they make up half the remaining royal houses in the world.

The value system of the Malays in the Peninsula often differs markedly from that of the other ethnic Malays of the archipelago. Peninsular Malays tend to be more relaxed and easygoing. They are not violent, dislike physical work and are not naturally given to competition. The other ethnic Malays of the archipelago are, by contrast, naturally hardworking and can sometimes be quite violent and intensely competitive.

33

Malay etiquette is complex and is made up of a subtle set of rules. I was brought up to be polite, to keep my own counsel and to defer to my elders and superiors. Respect for elders and titles[10] is very strong and is shown, among other ways, in the use of honorifics. In Malay speech there are numerous honorifics, all of which come easily to me. Indeed, try as I might I simply cannot address people, especially Malay royalty, without them. I find myself frequently resorting to English to escape the burden of the deference, even obsequiousness, of the Malay language. The Malay language also provides a vast and diverse vocabulary for addressing different people. The closeness between you and a friend is expressed very differently from the closeness you have with a parent or aunt.

More exquisite and tacit than spoken language is body language. This is a very significant manifestation of the code of Malay politeness. When walking past old or senior people we bend slightly forward and lower the

---

[10]    Malays have a complicated system of honorifics that convey esteem or respect.

right arm, as if to prevent the foot from accidentally touching the person in front of whom we walk. Kicking or touching an individual with the foot is considered very impolite. Pointing with the foot at anything to anyone is taboo.

Foreigners are usually unable to grasp these fine gradations of behaviour. In 1985 the *Far Eastern Economic Review* reported that Tunku Abdul Rahman had rejected my attempt to kiss his hand. The incident was interpreted as the Tunku dismissing me curtly. In Malay etiquette a person of low rank kisses the hand of a superior, particularly if he is an aristocrat, as the Tunku was. However, if the aristocrat feels that the person is of some consequence, he pulls his hand away before it can be kissed. This is indicative of good upbringing and is recognition of the other person's status. When the Tunku pulled his hand away before I could kiss it, it was an acknowledgement that I was not a lesser person. He was not being rude nor was he dismissing me. In fact, he was being extremely courteous according to Malay etiquette. Subtlety is opaque to those who are incapable of it themselves or who are ignorant of its ways.

Steeped though I was in such manners, I soon learnt that foreigners, non-Malays and especially Europeans, could not be treated in the same way as Malays as they may not understand the nuances of Malay etiquette. The author Joseph Conrad thought that when Malays address a European as *tuan* (literally, "master"), it was a rightful acknowledgement by the Malays that the European was superior. Conrad in fact translated the word *tuan* to "Lord", hence "Lord Jim" in his book of the same name. Lord Jim was not an English Lord as I had assumed before reading the book. He was simply Tuan Jim or Master Jim, which was the way he was addressed by the Malays he met.

For a long time, Malays expected people to understand that these titles were spoken out of politeness, and were not to be taken as an indication of real status. Thus all Chinese were *towkay*, all Indians *aya* and all Arabs and Europeans *tuan*, irrespective of their individual or personal standing in society. Very early on I decided to reserve my self-effacing Malay manners only for the people who were well-taught in the etiquette, and to adopt the more candid manners of the foreigners, particularly the Europeans, when I dealt with them. Europeans are frank and direct. Being critical is natural to their style of discourse and with it comes the tendency to run people down. In the Malay world, this transgresses the boundaries of good behaviour. Unfortunately, many ethnic Europeans behave as if they are superior and generally know better than Asians.

The thousands of comments made about Malaysia in foreign journals and newspapers seem to reveal a certain smug assurance that they could govern Malaysia far better than any Malay. They are forever offering unsolicited advice, apparently unashamed that when they left Malaya to the Malays in 1957, it was a poor and undeveloped country. I myself, in particular, seem to have been singled out for regular vilification. I usually lose no time in reminding them of their own imperfections and poor behaviour, past and present. Still, they seem blind and deaf to why I will not accept their advice. Many of them think we should uphold liberal democracy modelled on their own national practices, forgetting that our social, cultural, religious, ethnic and economic composition is completely different from theirs.

According to them, we stubbornly prefer to adhere to our own cultural traditions and moral codes and to practise democracy not as a reckless free-for-all, but in a form that we consider suitable for a potentially unstable multiethnic country. Despite their repeated assertions that we should be more open to criticism, they do not take kindly to reminders about the genocide they committed in order to set up new European nations outside Europe. When I bring this up, they redouble their condemnation of me.

They make, for example, disparaging remarks about Malaysia's affirmative action programme and express their disgust over positive discrimination in favour of the Malays and other indigenous people over the Chinese and the Indians. They do not seem to realise the shallowness of this analysis, nor how ill-qualified they themselves are to offer such criticisms. When the British ruled Malaya, they reserved for themselves exclusive rights to jobs in the administration and allocated vast tracts of forest land to be cleared for their rubber estates and tin mines. They have apparently forgotten how they set aside select enclaves for their residences. They have forgotten how even Sultans, the Rulers of the Malay states in whose names they governed, were not allowed to enter their exclusive clubs. There was only one basis for all this unrelenting discrimination: an assumed and false notion of inherent racial superiority. Since then, they have not changed much. They may have retreated from Malaysia but they continue to give unwanted counsel and to forcibly spread their ideas, thoughts and systems.

History is but a cluster of memories and memory is selective. The same people who hasten to chastise us today forget that Malaysia's racial problems were caused by their greed in wanting to extract the wealth of the country without taking any serious responsibility for its economic development or for the welfare of its people. They allowed unlimited numbers of Chinese and Indians into the Malay states until there were more immigrants in the population of the Peninsula than Malays. If Britain had allowed Chinese and Indian immigrants in until they made up 40 per cent of its own population, what would have happened to British workers and their unions? Britain would no longer be the land of the English, Scots and Welsh. Without discrimination, the diligent and skilful Chinese and Indians would have filled up the senior posts in government, run all the businesses and shops, and the original natives would work as drivers and gardeners of the immigrants. The British would certainly not allow into Britain the massive immigration that they permitted into Malaya under their rule. Even now, with only a small part of their population made up of Indians, Chinese and other non-Europeans, they feel uncomfortable. They have many more ugly race riots on their record than we do.

Their Government makes a pretence of being liberal and non-racist. Here and there, one finds the odd Asian customs officer, Member of Parliament and town mayor. But obviously they are restricting the immigration of Asians. Jews and Europeans are welcome but Asians and Africans are subjected to unwritten quotas. The ethnic Europeans will be entitled to criticise Malaysia, the Malays and our affirmative action policies only after they have allowed the free immigration of a few hundred million Chinese, Indians and Africans into their countries. When they themselves only barely outnumber all these immigrants, we should see what tune they will sing: whether they will go on criticising us for what we have done or whether they will do as we did.

The British encouraged the Chinese to immigrate and move to Singapore to provide the economic base and manpower for British trade and commercial activities. By 1963, three-quarters of Singapore's 3.5 million inhabitants were Chinese. Historically and geographically, however, Singapore was a part of *Tanah Melayu*. In other parts of the world, when the lands of indigenous people were taken over by latecomers and immigrants, the locals would fight bloody, prolonged wars to reclaim their birthright. We see the evidence of this in Northern Ireland, Palestine and several African colonies. But in the case of Singapore, it did not happen. The Chinese immigrants swamped the indigenous Malays who became an insignificant minority in a majority Chinese state. Singapore's admission into Malaysia raised the possibility that a very aggressive non-Malay Singapore might attempt to dominate Malaysia. During the short period that Singapore was in Malaysia (1963-1965), this is precisely what its leader Lee Kuan Yew, now Minister Mentor of Singapore, tried to do. Eventually, Singapore had to be excluded. This is the Malay way. Rather than live in acrimony, the Malays simply asked the Singaporeans to leave peacefully.

Ethnic Europeans have ignored the relatively gentle way in which the Malays deal with racial differences. Yet the Europeans surely cannot have forgotten how they themselves dealt with native Americans, the Carib people in the Caribbean, Australian aborigines, and Indians. They should also remember that in order to achieve their preferred notions of equality in the past, thousands were killed in the French and Russian revolutions. The killing and brutality did not stop when the revolutions were over. The Malaysian way may seem unfair to some but it is important to note that, in our growth and development, lives were not sacrificed nor vast properties expropriated. Instead we enlarged the economic cake so that all might get a bigger slice than they had before, and so that the biggest slice could be given to the less fortunate, provided they were ready to work for it. The result, plain for all to see, is a stable country with robust economic growth. Even during the Asian financial crisis Malaysia experienced no racial violence, as there was in neighbouring countries. For this Malaysia gets little credit from its European critics. When they preach their doctrines of equality and fairness to me, I remind imperialists that they never treated their colonial subjects as equals and were rarely fair. So their dislike for me is intense. I am branded a dictator. If my name is mentioned at all, it is followed with insinuations of cronyism and references to the jailing of one of my deputies.

It is the negatives that they see and imagine, not our positive achievements. The great change, the vast and progressive social transformation that turned a poverty-stricken former colony into the Malaysia of today simply does not rate a polite mention. Ethnic European writers, journalists and officials utter hardly a word about the obvious capacity of the Malays as politicians and administrators capable of developing an entire country. Any rare mention of this achievement is prefaced by disparaging remarks about control of the Press, authoritarian rule, and political interference with the judiciary.

Most Malays are reluctant to offend others. They hide their frustration and anger over their humiliation by foreigners. I do not. In this respect I may not be completely Malay. I have learnt the frankness of foreigners and employ it in my dealings with them. I am no longer, like so many Malays, too shy to defend myself and my interests, or too polite to uphold my dignity against crassness and vulgarity. I have learnt their ways and they must pay the price for my having learnt the lessons they taught me so well.

British notions of racial superiority seem to have left their mark in all territories they once held. Once when I flew alone from Australia to Fiji, I was seated at the back of the B747 among South Sea islanders and Indian Australians. There was not a single white passenger at the back of the plane. It could not have been accidental that they were all seated in front. But on my return flight, the seating was very different. I was with members of the Committee of the Commonwealth Association, some of whom were white. It is hard to believe that it was mere coincidence that our seats were in front, where there were no South Sea islanders. The White Australia policy has officially been discarded but remnants of it still remain as demonstrated by the Cronulla incident of December 2005, when beachgoers with Arab features were attacked by white hooligans at the seaside in Sydney.

At the opposite end of the spectrum of criticism, I was once castigated by an Australian writer for censuring my own race and angering them. A Malay, he asserted, would not do this. He is, by and large, right. But I have learnt that in order to be heard on the global stage, different rules apply and you have to play by them. The rules of that game have required me to have the courage to speak up and not care too much about pleasing people, even those of my own race, when I speak my mind and say what I think I must. At times one must speak frankly, and without niceties, even to one's fellow Malays. To reach them one must sometimes deliver a small shock, just to seize their attention. I have never wanted to lull the Malays into self-satisfaction and complacency. If one heaps accolades on people and say they are adept and able, when in fact they are not, they will make no effort to improve themselves and to rise to challenges. They will have no motivation or incentive to do so. A stern but caring rebuke can provide that motivation.

One simply cannot say all is well when it is not, when things are far from perfect. The NEP has largely been a success, and an impressive one. Today, many Malays have become successful in business and in the professions, and the Malay middle class has grown considerably. That said, when one considers the many opportunities made available to them, there ought to be a bigger percentage of successful Malays in our society by now. And there would have been, had they been prepared to work harder. I am personally ashamed when I hear of incidents in which Malays do not pay their debts, when they abuse the trust people place in them, when they sell the permits, licences and contracts made available to them by the Government through the NEP. Sadly, while the NEP has done much good to those who were ready to make an effort to realise the possibilities it offered, it has also created a disabling culture of entitlement among many other Malays with less wholesome values and motivations. So, while the NEP has produced a number of Malays with good ethical values, many more have been weakened by the privileges that come with positive discrimination. I fear for our coming generations. I worry that the children of those who have made it good will take the policy for granted and never learn to be intellectually and economically self-reliant. At the risk of being more unpopular, I will continue to press, goad and cajole them with the idea of making them stand tall.

I believe firmly in leadership by example. In my own code of behaviour, I make a point of refusing typical Malay stereotypes by practising the values which I want the Malays to adopt. For instance, I have often been asked where I get my energy. The general perception is that Malays are incapable of working hard. To correct this notion, throughout my 22 years as Prime Minister, I never took the full leave I was entitled to. Returning from visits abroad, I would go back to the office the same day. My working hours were longer than those of most government employees and Ministers. I did not play golf, I seldom watched such games as football or badminton and I rode horses only once a week. What drove me was the simple fact that I enjoyed working. When I was Minister, Deputy Prime Minister and Prime Minister, what I looked forward to most was seeing the results of my ideas, policies and directives taking shape: to see what I had glimpsed in my imagination become reality.

When I saw how the trainees, who went through programmes facilitated by the Look East policy[11] were sought after, I was gratified. I saw that this new generation of Malaysians did not display the usual diffidence. I saw how highly regarded they became outside Malaysia. I had to work hard myself in order to impress on everyone, the Malays in particular, the virtue of hard work. They had to be made to understand that this was the only way to succeed in life and develop the country. I am always in a hurry to see results. This is uncommon for a Malay. If only our whole community would do this, success would be the natural outcome. And the harder you work, the earlier you get to see results. There are many reasons, of course, for my intense drive. After closely studying the history of Malaya I recognise how greatly the industriousness of the Chinese and Indians has contributed to Malaysia's remarkable success.

In commerce Malay acumen and work ethics leave much to be desired. They do not seem to realise that prompt repayment of loans and creditworthiness are prerequisites for commercial growth. Many borrow money for business purposes but use only half the loan for genuine business activities, effectively doubling their interest rate. With half the capital, it is difficult to make enough to repay the whole loan. When this happens, they have no choice but to cut corners and deliver inferior work. They then lose the trust of their customers, banks and subcontractors. They get blacklisted and all other Malays get tarred with the same brush. A petrol service operator I once met invested his cash earnings in another business.

40

---

[11]　This policy sought to model Malaysia's growth on the development of East Asian countries such as Japan and South Korea.

That business failed and he was unable to pay for the stock of oil he had obtained on credit. After he failed to pay several times, the supplier started demanding cash payments. The operator had no more cash and could not raise another loan from his bank. He finally lost his service station business. I got to know about this because he appealed to me directly to instruct the oil company to let him continue operating the station. When I made enquiries about his case, I found that he had not been paying for his petrol supply. It appears he was not the only one who did this. Because of a few bad eggs, Malay service station operators must now pay upfront in cash for their supply of oil. These are market forces, pure and simple.

The reputation of small Malay contractors has been blighted in the same way by incidents involving the construction of school computer laboratories. These were meant to be simple buildings wired for computers. Instead of building the laboratories themselves, the contractors sold their contracts to other contractors, who then sold the same contracts for upfront money to yet another set of contractors. This process devolved until the profit margin became negative and the contract was no longer viable. The final contractor then tried to construct the laboratories using inferior materials and, in some instances, by not paying suppliers and subcontractors. The result was either failure to complete the projects or the collapse of the building before it was even used. This problem was repeatedly highlighted in the Press and Malay contractors got a blanket reputation for being unethical and irresponsible. The reason why these things happen can be explained in one word: greed. It is the desire to get rich quickly without doing anything to deserve the wealth.

History has in this instance proven to be a true teacher but its students have been inattentive. In the early twentieth century, the Malay Rulers did not get the revenue due to them because their Malay tax collectors pocketed much of what they collected. Along came a Chinese *towkay* who offered to guarantee a lot more tax for the Ruler if he was given the right to collect taxes for the royal house. That was common practice in those days. Gradually, opium monopolies, clove monopolies, tax collection and so on were farmed out to Chinese *towkays* because they guaranteed higher returns to the Rulers. Over time, the need for Malay administrators diminished and they became less skilled in administration, less powerful and poorer

41

while the Chinese became richer and more influential. These lessons still need to be heeded, even today. Unless the Malays work hard, they may wake up one day to find that this country is no longer theirs, that they are dispossessed in their own land. This scenario is not farfetched. If Malays become corrupt they may be financially persuaded to elect governments that may be prepared to sell their birthright to the highest bidders, who are unlikely to be Malays.

In making disparaging remarks and offering critical analyses about the Malays, I wanted not to insult them but to encourage a habit of self-scrutiny, which I hoped might lead to self-improvement. The Malay people have notable weaknesses and defects. But they also display many attributes in which they can take pride. Among them is the fact that Malaysia is what it is today because of how well and generously the Malays have accommodated those who have made this country their home. Many non-Malay Malaysian citizens have emigrated but there is no rancour. Those who remain are still regarded as loyal fellow citizens.

When I became Prime Minister in 1981, Malaysia had a population of 13 million, of whom seven million were Malays. Today the population is 25 million, nearly twice the number in 1981. The proportion of Malays has increased somewhat but their contribution is not commensurate with their number. They have responded to my appeal to play a bigger role in the development of this country but they need to do more. People in developing countries all over the world speak highly of the rate of Malaysia's progress. I am proud, but it is a pride tinged with sadness. We can do better. The Malays can do better. I know they can. In retirement, apart from appealing to them, I can do very little. I pray, but I know that Allah will not change the fate of any people unless they seriously attempt to change it themselves.

I worry about the Malays and fear for their future, but that does not change the fact that I am proud to be a Malay. I would not want to be anything else. In earlier times a Roman, wherever he went in the world, was always proud to declare himself a Roman citizen. For my part I wanted to be able to go anywhere in the world and say with equal pride, "I am a Malay".

# Chapter 4:
## The Story Of The Malays

To understand the Malays we need first to examine their origins and the journey they have taken to reach where they are today. I began my study early, knowing that if I was to champion their cause, I would need to know them more intimately.

What I had been taught in school was very sketchy. Apart from text books, I read books on Malayan history by British administrators such as Sir Richard Winstedt, Sir Frank Swettenham and many academics. I also read the *Sejarah Melayu* or *Malay Annals*, the *Hikayat Hang Tuah* and *Hikayat Merong Mahawangsa*. In world history, the Malays are mentioned in documents going as far back as the time of Alexander the Great. Ptolemy, the Greek astronomer and mathematician of the first century of the Common Era, referred to the Peninsula as the "Golden Chersonese". To the Indians it was *Suvarnadvipa*, "the Golden Peninsula". The Portuguese apothecary Tomé Pires wrote that Malacca was of such importance and profit that it had no equal in the world. The Peninsula had a reputation for being rich in gold.

From these readings I discovered that the Malay people who inhabited the Peninsula from ancient times were believed to have made their way there from southern China. To this day there are people of the same physiognomy in the Yunnan Province of China. They apparently emigrated down to the Peninsula, which formed the southernmost part of the Asian land mass. Some even crossed the seas to the islands of the huge archipelago, which has today become the Republic of Indonesia and the Philippines. Others apparently traversed vast oceans to settle in the Easter Islands, Hawaii and Madagascar.

Eventually, the Malay peoples developed a complex and distinctive civilisation based upon the institution of hereditary rulers who set up principalities. Apart from indigenous animism, the inhabitants were also influenced by the Hindu and Buddhist religions and cultures of India. Indian merchants had voyaged to the Peninsula from as early as 1,700 years ago, and they brought with them the ideas of Hindu-Buddhist teachings. These elevated the princely rulers to the status of god-like kings who commanded the complete obedience of their subjects. Life centred upon the courts of the Raja, the hereditary ruler. His god-like status was enhanced by elaborate rituals and ceremonies. His subjects — even the most senior members of court — literally had to crawl on all fours to make obeisance to him.

This remained the situation until the arrival of Islam in the region. Islam did not so much replace the Hindu-Buddhist cultural world as graft itself upon that older social order. But it also introduced changes. Far from subscribing to the caste system which had become common practice, Islam preached equality before God. It must have been difficult for the Malay Rajas in the Peninsula and the archipelago to accept this egalitarian principle, but the Muslim traders from the Arabian Peninsula and India who introduced Islam into the region were rich, successful and intelligent, and therefore very influential. The Rajas could not help but be impressed by them, especially since the goods they brought were highly sought after by the Malays. With certain exceptions, they were willing to accept Islam's moral egalitarianism, even while maintaining much of their old ways.

The Rajas traded jungle produce gathered by their subjects for the silk, lacquer ware, brassware, gold and so on that the traders brought. Personal relationships must have developed (as they do even today) between the rich traders and the Malay Rajas. Eventually most of the Rajas converted to Islam, interpreted in a way that maintained their high positions and most of the old court practices. But they ceased to claim that they were gods and accepted that like everyone else, they were "*hamba Allah*", the "slaves of Allah". While it was a big step down for them, they remained the anointed group.

The Malay states of the archipelago and the Peninsula flourished through trade. Situated on the sea routes between east and west, they benefited from the passage of trading vessels calling at their ports to replenish supplies and water. The region produced spices, scented wood and various gums from forest trees, which were much in demand by the foreigners. Trade with the merchants of China, India and Arabia developed, bringing prosperity to the numerous principalities on the sea coast.

The first of these entrepôt ports was Fu-Nan in the Gulf of Siam. It was already a thriving commercial centre in the second century CE. Strategically located, it was accessible by land to ports on the west coast of the Isthmus of Kra, where goods from India, Arabia and even the Mediterranean countries landed. The overland route to Fu-Nan was preferred because the voyage down the coast of the Malay Peninsula was very long and the sea there was infested with pirates. Because of this, the exchange and sale of goods from China, India, the Arabian Peninsula, and the Southeast Asian islands took place in Fu-Nan. From there, Chinese ships would carry goods back to China, while the Malay ships took theirs to the budding entrepôt ports in Southeast Asia. Later the ethnic Malay traders from the archipelago bypassed Fu-Nan and sailed straight on to China. According to European records their ships weighed more than 200 tonnes, clearly the creation of master shipbuilders. Chinese traders did the same and sailed to ports in Southeast Asia. Fu-Nan went into decline and in its place, the great entrepôt ports of Java, Sumatra and the Malay Peninsula developed.

All these trading ships, and later those that came to Southeast Asia from Europe, sailed with the help of the monsoonal or "trade" winds.[1] They were dependent upon these biannual wind patterns because naval architecture of the time did not allow the traders to build ships capable of "tacking into", or sailing against, the prevailing wind. So the ships from China, India, Arabia and the outlying Southeast Asian islands had to remain in port at their destination for almost half a year, waiting for the winds to change and blow them back to their homelands.

The enforced stay of traders of many nationalities gave these ports an international or cosmopolitan flavour. Their human diversity enriched the culture of the region's states and cities. In its heyday, Malacca had a population of 100,000 — at a time when the population of London was about 200,000. Sometimes the rulers of these port cities also involved themselves in trading activities, naturally giving themselves various privileges above those of their own subjects. This was not unusual in those days, when European royalty in the same era also used to invest in the trading expeditions of their merchants. A taste or inclination for trade has

---

[1]   The winds upon which those engaged in the growing international trade relied.

remained characteristic of a number of the ruling families of the region. In modern Malaysia, for example, the royal family of Negeri Sembilan has become one of the nation's major corporate and entrepreneurial forces.

The commercial life and success of these maritime trading ports required great administrative and negotiating skills among their local ruling classes. Competition was keen as new ports emerged, always seeking to attract canny traders through better security, efficiency and the fairness of the Rulers of the states. In the administration of entrepôt ports, some foreigners played functional roles in governing foreign merchant communities and overseeing port activities. But the life of the maritime port city remained under the overall supervision of the local Ruler, together with his close family and associates. They had to maintain the success of the city as a trading centre, or else other Rulers would seize the opportunity to build their own ports. Taxes and dues were levied by the Ruler's administration, but care was taken that they did not become excessive and drive the traders away. The same approach is evident in Malaysia today; far from new, the business-friendly attitude of the Malaysian Government has deep cultural origins and historical precedent. The competing entrepôt ports of Southeast Asia set out to be attractive to foreigners long before modern Malaysia was ever imagined.

In the early fifteenth century CE, the new entrepôt port of Malacca was founded on the west coast of the Malay Peninsula. There were already ports in Kedah and Perak, and in Terengganu on the east coast. But these were small and not as successful or as well administered as Malacca. The Hindu prince Parameswara, who founded Malacca, and his successors were far more astute. Parameswara built an entrepôt port at the mouth of the Malacca River. Coming from Palembang, part of the powerful Sri Vijaya empire, he saw how wealth had been created through providing port facilities and the exchange of goods at entrepôt ports. The Malays of Malacca adapted easily as they were an urban people. The city was surrounded by forest and there was little cultivated land. Evidently, the Malays in those days thrived in a trade-based urban economy. It was only later that they were driven into the countryside as peasants.

Beginning with Parameswara, who founded Malacca in 1400, the Rulers of Malacca built up a sound administration, providing laws for both land and sea. The Ruler managed the city's affairs through his high officers headed by a *bendahara* (Prime Minister or Chief Minister), a *shahbandar* (harbour master), and various *panglima* (generals or commanders) and *laksamana* (admirals). In Malacca, as in Sri Vijaya, success was due to Malay nautical skills and organising abilities. Location also played a role, as it did later with Singapore. But without the right human talent and abilities — or social infrastructure as we would now say — location by itself was no guarantee of commercial success.

Of the foreign traders, the most numerous were the Chinese. They were everywhere, from Manila in the Philippines to Aceh in North Sumatra. Like all other traders, they did not bring their women along, and as a result many married locals. When their numbers were small they assimilated, adopting the language, culture and religion of the locals. This locally integrated Chinese community was favoured by Chinese mainland traders when making commercial transactions in the region. Some of these mixed and locally assimilated Chinese became involved in the cultivation of cash crops. In the Philippines, Java and elsewhere, as their numbers increased, they tended to keep more of their Chinese character. They gradually became a separate component of society, distinct from the local people.

When the Europeans came to Southeast Asia in the sixteenth century CE they introduced a monopolistic trade culture. Under these arrangements the Chinese traders and settlers took on a greater role since it was they who collected various kinds of produce from the local people and supplied them to the European traders. Close and strong connections were also formed from the high level of intermarriage between Spanish traders and Chinese women. A Spanish/Chinese Mestizo community soon emerged and the Spanish and the Chinese naturally gravitated towards them. Gradually, as the Chinese and Mestizo communities in Southeast Asia began to take away the business of the locals, tensions grew between the two groups. In the Philippines and Java, clashes took place and many Chinese were killed. Conflict arose now and then, but the business potential of the Southeast Asian entrepôt ports and their hinterlands was so great that, as soon as things settled down again, the Chinese would come back.

Chinese businesses in Southeast Asia expanded. Very soon they were building ships for inter-island trade and trade with China. As a result, more Southeast Asian locals lost their role in trade as Chinese junks replaced the ships of the Malays. Chinese influence also grew when they were able to offer their services to the local Rulers. At their suggestion, the Rulers farmed out the task of tax collection to them to take advantage of their efficiency and the larger sums that they were able to collect. Next, they were licensed to operate the opium, nutmeg, pepper and other monopolies. As the Chinese expanded their businesses their participation in administrative activities also increased, and the locals retreated further. Meanwhile, the superior skills of the Chinese in various crafts put the local craftsmen out of business. When the Chinese in the Philippines were expelled, the Spanish colonialists, the Mestizos and the local elites found themselves without shoes and other basic goods. Now indispensable, the Chinese had to be brought back.

It was the same in the Dutch East Indies, Siam, Burma, Malaya and Indochina. Everywhere the Europeans established their colonies, the

Chinese moved in as middlemen in business and provided good craftsmen who were able to meet the needs of the European and local communities. In time the number of Chinese had so increased that their assimilation was no longer possible. When they brought their women with them, intermarriage with the locals stopped. Chinatowns started to become a feature of almost every urban area in Southeast Asia. The Chinese community's usefulness ensured its protection by the European colonial powers as well as by the local Rulers.

The Indians and the Arabs, however, behaved differently. Their communities were never big nor did they encroach into the trading activities of the locals. They tended to blend with the locals and to intermarry when they wished to settle. They would eventually forget their own languages completely and would identify fully with the locals, whether they were Malays, Sumatrans, Javanese or the numerous tribes found in the eastern islands of the Malay Archipelago. When the Arabs and the Indian Muslims introduced Islam, no animosity was provoked as there was no forcible conversion of the indigenous people. Much of the missionary work was carried out by local converts.

The Europeans also behaved differently, arriving not in trading ships but in armed merchantmen. Nor did they believe in free trade. One of the Rulers of Macassar – now Ujung Pandang in Indonesia – had to point out to the Dutch that "God made the land and the sea; the land be divided among men and the sea he gave in common. It has never been heard that anyone be forbidden to sail the seas."[2] European nations wanted monopolies and so began by setting up fortified trading stations. Eventually, as a final solution, they conquered their trading partners to ensure supply and exclusivity.

Among the Europeans, the Spanish, and to a lesser degree the Portuguese, believed it was their God-given task to Christianise the locals. In Spain, after the re-conquest by the Catholics, Muslims and Jews who had been forcibly converted had to prove the genuineness of their conversion by eating pork. The same occurred in Southeast Asia. In this way, the Christian converts in the Philippines were also separated from the Muslims. It is only lately that the Filipinos have learnt to respect the Muslim aversion to pork. But the schism between Christians and Muslims remains very deep and has become a cause for conflict and war among the Filipinos. Since it was the Chinese who converted to Christianity more readily, they would get on better with the Europeans in the colonies. Changed religious belief caused no division within the Chinese community, nor were the Chinese active in spreading their own religions. The locals, whether Muslim or Christian, were much more tolerant of the Chinese than they were of each other.

49

To varying degrees, this was also the situation in the states of the Malay Peninsula and the British colonies of Singapore, Malacca and Penang. With the exception of Singapore, the Malay Peninsula had the largest number of Chinese immigrants anywhere in Southeast Asia. Their inflow was encouraged by the British, and the ethno-demographic consequences of that fact persist until the present day.

When the British colonised Malaya, the demography of the Malay Peninsula changed rapidly. In the Straits Settlements, the Chinese community dominated and, by the first quarter of the twentieth century, Singapore had become a de facto Chinese state. Only about 15 per cent of the population

---

2 *Cambridge History of Southeast Asia: Volume One, Part Two, From c. 1500 to 1800*, edited by Nicholas Tarling, Cambridge University Press, 1992.

was Malay. Had the Malays been in the majority, Singapore would have been included as part of Malaya and Malaysia.

Before the Chinese came it was the Malays who had been the region's traders. The peoples of Southeast Asia, including Malays, had formerly collected spices and forest products for shipment to the entrepôt port of Sri Vijaya, where they were exchanged with products from China, India, Arabia and Europe. But eventually all this business also came under the total control of the Chinese traders, who in time started their own spice gardens which displaced the Malay farmers. When the Europeans came, therefore, the Chinese were well positioned to act as the middlemen. Over time, more Chinese immigrants came to Southeast Asia to provide all the services that the European traders and colonialists needed, and in the end, even the Malays began to depend on the Chinese for their supplies and services.

That was the status quo ante upon the arrival of the European powers. The Malays were not just the indigenous people of the region but also the demographically preponderant part of the population. They still set the shape and form of the social and political order in which trading activities were carried out. But all that was to change. Under European domination of the region, the Malays lost their central position within the new framework of sociopolitical and commercial life.

The Malays might have prevented their land from being inundated by foreigners had they shown some inclination to take up the new jobs required to service the rubber and tin industries established by colonialists. But, now concentrated in the countryside and not the port cities or commercial and administrative centres, they preferred to remain padi planters and fishermen. As a result, the British brought in Indians and encouraged the Chinese to seize the many opportunities created by the new industries. In response, the Malays retreated further and further from all the urban activities in which they had once been involved. As the indigenous people became ever less involved in business, the commercial skills that they possessed deteriorated. Had they persisted, they would not have been as marginalised as they were after the Europeans gained total control over their land.

50

By the time the Pacific War began, the various Southeast Asian natives (or ethnic Malays) had been sidelined and had become the poorest people in their own countries. In most parts of Southeast Asia that had been colonised by the Europeans, the social and economic order was roughly the same: the Europeans were at the top, followed by the Eurasians, the Chinese, and others, with the indigenous people trailing at the bottom. In the Malay Peninsula, the most extreme examples of economic and social stratification were found in the British colonies of Singapore, Penang and Malacca. The Malays did not relish the prospect of becoming a poverty-stricken minority in the Peninsula as they had become in Singapore.

An awareness of history and the knowledge of what had happened in Singapore caused the Malays to be anxious about their position in a world where others exerted economic — and ultimately political control — over them. Some argued they were too pessimistic about their future in a British-ruled Malayan Union, but anyone who looks at Singapore today must see that they were not being overly cautious. Although the Malays make up 15 per cent of the population of Singapore, they are hardly visible and form the poorest segment of the population, working mainly in blue-collar jobs there.

By contrast, Malaysia is far more open. The Chinese do hold senior posts in both the Federal and state governments. Despite affirmative action in favour of the Malays, it is the Chinese community that takes the lead in business. They make up 90 per cent of Malaysia's millionaires, and more than a handful are billionaires. Even though the Malays are supposedly privileged, the Chinese in Malaysia are nowhere near as deprived as the Malays of Singapore.

It was not simply a Malay demand but an imperative of national social cohesion and survival that a serious plan of government action had to be devised and implemented to remedy the disadvantaged position of the nation's Malay population. This was necessary to undo the close identification of race or ethnicity with economic function and status, a legacy of the racially organised division of labour created by British colonial rule. It was important to do so in the overall context of the reduction and ultimate elimination of poverty in Malaysian society as a whole. Hence the

New Economic Policy or NEP, an affirmative action programme to redress the disadvantaged position of the Malays and secure their socioeconomic future.

The case for positive discrimination is reasonable. It is now universally accepted that in taxation, the rich must be taxed at a higher rate than the poor. Yet if the revenue of a country is spent only on people who pay high taxes, lower income groups in villages and slums would become forgotten people. There would be no sanitation, fewer schools — if any — and no medical facilities for them. Because of their high financial contribution to the administration, the rich would enjoy safe, clean environments, whereas the poor would be consigned to disorder and squalor. To prevent the rich from exploiting the poor, trade unions and labour laws have been established. Without discriminatory laws and taxes on wealth to protect workers, the wealth generated by industry and business would accrue only to the rich capitalists and entrepreneurs. Malaysia would not be the stable and prosperous country that it is today but for this discriminatory policy.

Malays must take the next phase of history and their future into their own hands. They must master the knowledge, wisdom and understanding that can enable them to do so effectively. They must acquire important skills that will empower them. But these alone will not be enough. The Malays must revisit their past and learn from history's tough lessons in order to secure their place in the world.

# Chapter 5:
# From Infatuation To Disillusionment

In 1933 I was among the lucky few in Kedah to gain admission into the Government English School. Unfortunately, thousands of others did not get that opportunity. Had they all been armed with a good education, they might have improved their own lives and society's well-being.

Unlike most Malay boys, I was not admitted into the English medium school through the Special Malay Class. Before World War II Malay students who finished Standard Four in the Malay schools were placed in Special Malay Classes in the English schools for two years, where they studied the English language and other subjects in English. Instead, when I was eight, my father took me out of the Malay School in Seberang Perak, where I was in Standard Two, and had me admitted into Primary One in the Government English School. Having been a teacher himself in an English school, he believed his children would get a better education there. All my siblings followed the same route, except one of my brothers who went to an Arabic school first before going to the Government English School.

My classmates in school were mostly non-Malays. I made friends with several of them, including Munusamy, Ooi Eng Ban, his brother Ooi Eng Hooi, and Tan Kiat Seng. Kiat Seng's father was a rice dealer and was quite well off. Eng Ban's family rented out rickshaws. I had a friendly rivalry with him because it was always either he or I who would come first in class. Most of my classmates could speak only colloquial Malay and this forced me to speak English with them. It was not easy but I managed fairly well, and I mastered the language faster than the boys in the Special Malay classes. Since I had started reading in English much earlier, I had a bigger vocabulary than most of the other boys. By the time I reached Standard Seven I realised I could express myself in English as well as I could in Malay. I came in first in our Standard Four class and four of us — including Eng Ban — got a double promotion to Standard Six. All the teachers and students — Malays, Indians and Chinese — mixed well. I do not think we noticed ethnic differences at the time. We took it for granted that this was the way things were.

As a teenager, I used to wonder why education was not available to more people. This thought grew more powerful when I went to university. There were only seven Malays among the 70-odd medical and dental students in my batch. That made me determined to see an increase in the number of Malays reaching higher education. All they needed was the creation of more opportunities. Throughout my career I made education a top priority and worked to make it as accessible as possible, especially to Malays.

My own education was supplemented with the books and magazines I read while growing up. Before the war I was class librarian for Standard Four. It was my job every Thursday to buy magazines like *Rover*, *Champion*, and *Film Fun* for the library. The Kedah weekend was from Thursday to Saturday so I had two-and-a-half days to read all the stories — even captions and advertisements — before putting the new issues in the class library. I loved stories about fictitious British heroes like Rockfist Rogan and Mad Carew, ace fighter pilots who shot down German planes with ease. Then there was Jack Keen 'Tec, the detective who never failed to get his man.

I saw those characters as typical of the White Man, or *Orang Putih*, and I wanted to emulate them, particularly their bravery, the way they planned their moves and their coolness in the face of danger. They were disciplined men who kept their word. They never gave up, despite the terrible dangers they faced. Becoming like them, I believed, might help me become a person who stands up to challenges. I too wanted to coolly assess my situation, weigh my weaknesses and strengths against those of my opponents, calmly plan my strategies and put them into action.

I grew up not minding being ruled by the British. When I was learning the history of the British Empire in school, I was naïve enough to feel proud to be a part of it. I even contributed my pocket money to the Malaya Patriotic Fund, which the British Colonial Administration set up to help pay for World War II. Every 11 November — Armistice Day, marking the day the First World War ended in 1918 — I would buy an artificial poppy flower and pin it to my shirt to help support the war veterans. On that day the normally aloof wives of British expatriates would come to the school with their trays of paper flowers and slotted tin cans to collect donations. To my adolescent eyes, the "mems" were gorgeous. I was truly a young Anglophile, but I believe most people in Malaya were pro-British in those days. I accepted British news reports as the truth because there was no other source of information to rely on. Malaya, our teachers told us from our early years, was so peaceful, and its different races lived together without jealousy, animosity, or history of racial conflict. In fact, they said ours was a country with no history at all. With that one, short, ill-informed sentence, the whole history of my country was dismissed. It was as if there had been no Malaccan Empire, no Portuguese conquest, and no European colonisation. Our history began and ended when the country mysteriously became British Malaya.

Since we had no past of our own, we learnt only the history of the British Empire. We were familiar with the Wars of the Roses, the Seven Years' War, the Kings and Queens of England, Oliver Cromwell, the Norman invasion and the Hundred Years' War in Europe. We learnt about the Roman Empire and the Napoleonic Wars. There was no mention of the 800 years when Spain was under Muslim rule, except for a vague reference to the Moors. Nor was there any mention of Eastern Europe being under Turkish rule. We read of the scalp-hunting Red Indian savages, the Spanish Main, the setting up of Australia as a penal colony, and about the rest of the Empire on which the sun never set. Every classroom had a map of the world with British Imperial territories marked in bright red, encircling the globe.

Strangely, when Malays spoke of the *Orang Putih*, they seemed to refer only to the British. They would speak about the *Orang Puteh* fighting the Germans, as if the Germans themselves were not white. We were always on the side of the British. I remember reading about the dervishes fighting against General "Chinese" Gordon in Khartoum, Sudan. I was glad when I read that they were mowed down by Gatling machine guns as they charged the British forces. That Sudan belonged to the Sudanese and that they were fighting to rid their country of British imperialists did not make them right or the British wrong. It came naturally to me to identify with the British heroes when they were fighting and killing the natives. I forgot that I was one of the natives. Sir Francis Drake, the Duke of Wellington, Lord Horatio Nelson and other British warriors were my heroes too. In those days I knew and took pride in their great battles — Waterloo and

Trafalgar — won against Britain's European foes. Looking back, it now seems odd that I considered it patriotic to uphold British imperialism and the colonisation of my country. Yet somehow they made us believe that we belonged to the Empire.

There were not many *Orang Putih* in Alor Star. Those who lived there were all British and they secluded themselves in a special enclave along Jalan Maxwell, in the northern part of Alor Star. The land belonged to the Government and was easily the best residential area in the state. No locals lived there. The houses stood on large grounds with shady angsana trees, well-kept lawns and flower beds. It was a different world entirely. It was quiet and clean, a far cry from where I lived. Our house was surrounded by squatter huts and wooden barracks with thatched roofs. My modest surroundings did not depress me as I thought them normal, and that everyone lived this way. Until I was in Standard Six I was not allowed to cycle on the main roads as my father feared I would get run over by a car. My world widened when he finally gave me permission to cycle to school. Together with my schoolmates, I would cycle in the evenings to where the expatriates lived. The European residents would be playing golf, trailed by their caddies carrying their golf clubs in leather bags. This was the only golf course in Kedah. Occasionally some Europeans and a few members of the Kedah Royal Family would be seen riding horses. There was a racecourse belonging to the Kedah Gymkhana Club where races were held once a year. I never thought I would live in that area, but years later I did when I became a Government Medical Officer.

The Kedah Club was where the Europeans would congregate in the evenings, drink and hold their dance parties. It was exclusive, but not as exclusive as the Royal Lake Club in Kuala Lumpur where even the Sultan of Selangor was not allowed to enter.[1] A few senior Malay officers were members of the Kedah Club. When Tunku Badlishah ibni Sultan Abdul Hamid[2] was Regent of Kedah, he played tennis there. The Malay officers of the Kedah Civil Service had their own club in the southern part of Alor Star, while

---

[1]  The Royal Lake Club of Kuala Lumpur was founded on 16 August 1890. The decision to bar the Sultan of Selangor from joining the club was later rescinded, and the British officer responsible was banished from Selangor.

[2]  Tunku Badlishah ibni Sultan Abdul Hamid became the 29th Sultan of Kedah in 1943.

subordinate officers had their club in front of my school. Clubs provided a kind of recreation for the elites in those days. Badminton was popular but tennis was regarded as elitist. Some of the very senior civil servants smoked opium. Emulating the Europeans, quite a few drank alcohol.

It was only when we began the struggle against the British proposal to create the Malayan Union that I realised the full extent of our colonisers' shrewdness and skill. They did not have to fight to colonise the Malay states. They merely offered the Rulers and their families regular political pensions, more than they had ever received from the taxes they used to collect. All these were paid from the taxes which the British collected locally with great efficiency. The treaties that they imposed upon the Malay states and the concessions extracted from the Malay Rulers were beginning to offend intelligent Malays, not just because they were permanent but also because of their doublespeak. These agreements referred to the Malay Sultans as "Rulers", while the most senior British officer was designated "Adviser". But the treaty provided that when the British Adviser gave advice, it had to be followed. Obviously, he was not advising but directing the government of the state. The Ruler might reign but he clearly would not be able to rule. He was merely a figurehead.

This duplicity is integral to the English language and etiquette. During the Commonwealth Heads of Government meeting in Harare, Zimbabwe in 1991, I, as the previous host of the Commonwealth Heads of Government meeting, was required to make a speech at the formal dinner for the Queen. By then I had already gained a reputation for being caustic and outspoken and British officials were very worried that I would say something that might offend the Queen.

To play safe, palace officials as well as several Commonwealth Secretariat officers took pains to inform me that Queen Elizabeth II would only be making a very short speech and that I should therefore keep mine short as well. This of course was not the tradition. In previous Commonwealth meetings, speeches were long and full of praise for the Queen and the great British Commonwealth of Nations. Apparently, no one had told the other Heads of Government to keep their speeches short. The Queen had also made much longer speeches in previous Commonwealth functions.

But I was not irked by this attempt to muzzle me. I had grown used to it so I had prepared a fairly short appropriate dinner speech. Still, I cut it, leaving what I really wanted to say intact, which was to illustrate that what is said in English is usually not what is meant. I said that while the person presiding over the Parliament is called Mr Speaker, he cannot speak. The British Adviser did not merely advise and the Malay Rulers did not rule. They both did just the opposite. And in the Commonwealth, the wealth is not common. The Queen was evidently amused and the BBC recorded her laughing uproariously. Later, when the British celebrated the Queen's Golden Jubilee, the video clip of my speech and the Queen's laughter was aired by the BBC several times.

The British Colonial Administration was not altogether bad. Apart from their high-and-mighty attitude and the decidedly superior status they accorded themselves in society, they did a fairly good job. The boundaries between the states were defined, land holdings were properly surveyed and documents or grants were issued. Still, it was not until Malaysia became independent that proper surveys were carried out together with Malaysia's neighbours to determine and mark out the international boundaries between Thailand and Malaysia, and Indonesia and Malaysia. There are still disputes over river and sea boundaries with these countries, and with Singapore.

The British introduced modern administrative methods and allocated specific duties and responsibilities to the various departments of the administration. Malay officers who worked under British officers could understudy them and were thus able to take over without too much difficulty when Independence was achieved. Proper state treasuries were set up to collect and manage revenue. It no longer went to the Rulers. The practice of farming out tax collection and opium monopolies to the Chinese *towkay* was stopped.

There was also much about the years of British rule that should have angered us. However, we were brainwashed into accepting the superiority of the *Orang Putih*. So in the Federated Malay States (FMS)[3] all senior posts

---

[3]  The Federated Malay States lasted until 1946, when it formed the Malayan Union with Singapore, Malacca, Penang and Province Wellesley, Perlis, Kedah, Kelantan, Terengganu and Johor.

in government service were filled by British officers who drew expatriate pay, at a far higher rate than the locals. Every three years they would go on home leave paid by the Government. Their designations were also different. In the Public Works Department, the Europeans were Engineers while Asians were Technical Assistants. In the medical service, British doctors were designated Medical Officers, but Asian doctors were only Assistant Medical Officers. In the Malay regiment, British officers did not salute Malay officers because the latter were commissioned by the High Commissioner of Malaya, while the British were commissioned by the King. In business the British companies controlled all the agencies and were given all government contracts. All supplies for all the governments — Straits Settlements, Federated and Unfederated States — had to be procured through the Crown Agents. Huge areas of land for plantations and tin mining were granted only to British companies at nominal prices.

Perak,[4] Selangor, Negeri Sembilan[5] and Pahang had each entered into agreements to become British protectorates, but in 1895 they were persuaded to federate. The administration of the FMS was in the hands of British officers of the Malayan Civil Service. British rule in the FMS was therefore direct and complete. A Federal Legislative Council was set up, consisting largely of British ex-officio members, British business representatives and a representative each from the Malay, Chinese and Indian communities. But the High Commissioner could overrule their decisions. He was answerable only to the Colonial Secretary in Whitehall in London. The idea of a protectorate was to protect the state from foreign aggression, but the British interpreted "protection" to mean their control of all aspects of the administration, except those concerning Malay custom and the Muslim religion. The Malay states and their peoples were essentially to be protected from themselves, from (as the British saw the matter) their own poor character and vices, and from the consequences of managing their own affairs. The administration and the status of the FMS were not that different from those of the Straits Settlements which, without the doublespeak of the Malay treaties, were directly ruled colonies.

---

[4]    A state in the northwestern region of Peninsular Malaysia.
[5]    A state on the west coast of Peninsular Malaysia.

My home state of Kedah was one of the Unfederated Malay States, those that came under British control after the creation of the FMS and stayed outside of its centralised administration. The other Unfederated States were Johor, Terengganu, Kelantan, and Perlis.[6] When the Malay Rulers of the FMS lost control over their own states, the Rulers of Kedah and Johor turned down the invitation to join the Federation. They even refused to have a customs union and a postal union. Kedah went further and insisted on its own police force, which at one point was headed by a Malay Chief Police Officer, Tunku Yahya Sultan Abdul Hamid. All District Officers in Kedah were also Malays from the Kedah Civil Service.

The Kedah state government wanted more local personnel appointed to head the administration. Accordingly, Malay students who did well were sent to England to study engineering, law and veterinary science. Students were also sent to Singapore and Hong Kong to study medicine. Police officers were trained in Kedah's own Police Depot. That is why when Malaya became independent, most of the professional departments were headed by Kedah Malays. After my father stepped down as the founding headmaster of the Government English School in Alor Star, two other Malays who were also from Penang — Abdul Manaf and Ismail Merican — succeeded him. But after them all the headmasters of the Government English School in Alor Star were European. The Government's technical and professional departments were also headed by British officers. My father never said anything to me about what he thought of colonial rule, but like everyone else I think he accepted that it was the way things were.

Malay, written in the Jawi script, was the official language in the Unfederated Malay States' administration. In Malay schools, we learnt both the Jawi and the Rumi (or Romanised) script. Gradually, the British pushed for the latter, and in Malay schools, students learnt Jawi only to be able to read the Quran. In English schools, the study of the Quran was not among the subjects, although in the Government English School where I studied, there were afternoon religious classes. I continued my study of the Quran at home, initially under my mother and then under a senior student from the Mahmood Arabic School.

---

[6]     Perlis is a state in the northwest region of the Peninsula.

Although the Rulers of the Federated States were paid higher political pensions and had a more affluent lifestyle, all the Rulers were aware of and mildly resented the fact that British control was more direct and extensive in the Federated States. The language of administration in those states was largely English. Since there were few Malays with an English education, English-educated Indian and Ceylon Tamils were brought in to man senior posts. Where they controlled recruitment, these officers would fill new posts with their relatives from India and Ceylon. By the early twentieth century an ethnic social stratification had emerged in the Straits Settlements and the Federated States, with the white officers at the top, followed in turn by the Eurasians, the Ceylon Tamils, the Indians and the Chinese. At the bottom of this ladder were the Malays. That was the price of not getting a good education, and it is something I have never forgotten.

When the British entered into treaties with the Malay Rulers, it was not clear over which areas these Rulers would exercise their authority. So the British were able to move boundaries at will. Province Wellesley[7] was enlarged when its southern boundary was moved to include Perak territory. Down south, when Singapore was ceded to the British, they set its boundaries to include islands in the Johor Straits. In the north, much of Kedah territory was ceded and became Siamese territory under the Anglo-Siamese Bangkok Treaty of 1909. Colonial administrative convenience and economic advantage seemed to supercede all other considerations, everywhere. Meanwhile, Japan and Siam were adopting European systems of government. Kedah and Johor also attempted to do likewise before accepting British protection. Penang was the model for Kedah, and Singapore for Johor. But the re-organisation was not conducted well, as too many people with vested interests interfered.

Under British colonial rule large areas of forest land were given out to British companies for rubber plantations and tin mining. They paid just a few Straits dollars per acre. Where Malay reserve land was involved, the Government obligingly made available forest land to replace the Malay reserve land which was excised. These companies made huge profits from both the plantations and the big tin mines where dredges were used. They

---

[7] The part of Penang state that is located on the mainland, opposite Penang island.

were listed on the London Stock Exchange and their shareholders were almost exclusively British. Chinese miners operated the open-cast mines and sand pumps. There were also American-owned plantations, but needless to say, the bulk of the money accrued to Britain. Malaya collected no tax on the profits, as income tax was introduced only after World War II. Improving public amenities and infrastructure for local society was not an objective of colonial "protection". Revenue was to be collected for other purposes and more distant beneficiaries.

Initially, Malay states had their own money in the form of brass, silver and gold coins. When trade with the Europeans flourished, the Spanish silver dollar was accepted for payment. When Penang was ceded to the British, the agreement provided for a yearly payment of 6,000 Spanish silver dollars. Then a slice of the mainland opposite Penang was ceded for 4,000 Spanish silver dollars. Since politics in those days was the prerogative of the Sultan, no one questioned the deal. British plans benefited from the deep feudal loyalty of the Malay *rakyat* to their Rulers. And 10,000 Spanish silver dollars was a lot of money then.

After silver dollars were replaced by currency notes issued by the Government of the Straits Settlements, the payment to Kedah was made in Straits dollars. The note guaranteed the value in gold of the Straits dollar, but in practice no redemption in gold ever took place. The Straits dollar was never the same in value to the Spanish silver dollar and, over time, it depreciated. But in the absence of any paper money issued by the Malay states, the currency notes issued by the Government of the Straits Settlements (and later by the Currency Board of the Straits Settlements and the Federated States) became legal tender in all the states of Malaya. Prior to this, the major British banks had made huge sums of money issuing banknotes. And when the governments of the Straits Settlements took over, they too made money printing currency notes. No one knew in those days whether there were any gold reserves to back the Straits dollar, but so long as nobody wondered or, more to the point, sought to redeem notes for gold, it did not matter.

When Malaya became independent in 1957 the value of the Straits dollar was fixed at 8.30 to one pound sterling and three to one US dollar. Malaya belonged to the Sterling bloc and all its reserves were kept in pounds. The

British Government assumed that the Straits dollar, which became the Malayan dollar after Independence, would depreciate in value. And so in the Independence agreement, the British insisted that their pensioners be paid in pounds. However, it was the pound which devalued and the payment of pensions to British retirees cost the Malayan Government less in terms of the Malayan dollar than at the time of Independence. But in 1967, Malaysia lost quite a lot of money following the sudden devaluation of the sterling because its reserves were held in British pounds.

The systematisation of the administration and the introduction of proper currency and financial systems improved the administration of the Malay states and Malaya as a whole. Even the foreign-owned rubber plantations and tin mines helped enrich Malaya so that at the time of Independence, Malaya's administration and finances were on a much better footing than many other colonies which gained independence after World War II. But the annual per capita income of the five million people living in the Peninsula was below USD350. Unemployment was high and poverty rampant.

The British lauded the concept of constitutional monarchy of the kind that they practised as the ideal form of government. But they never mentioned that democracy or elections were not practised or held in British Malaya. British colonial rule was autocratic and discriminatory against the locals, especially the Malays. Today the British, like other ethnic European imperialists, demand that their former colonies be democratic. They really do not have any right to do so but they show not the slightest embarrassment over their own past.

Yet many Malays must have admired British parliamentary democracy and constitutional monarchy. When UMNO finally got around to seeking self-government and independence, there was no talk about republicanism. Instead, the discussion focused on how to merge nine Malay states with their Sultans into a single nation to be called the Federation of Malaya, which would replace the Malayan Union. On what basis might the Rulers agree to this merging, even submerging, of their separate identities and state sovereignty into a new central structure? It was a stroke of genius on the part of the Malay leaders to suggest a rotation of Kings, who would be elected for five-year terms from among the Malay Rulers. The Rulers were happy to accept this new constitutional status. It was far better than the MacMichael Treaties, which provided the basis for the much disliked and quickly repudiated Malayan Union of 1946. Those proposed arrangements would have reduced them to mere heads of the Islamic religion and custodians of Malay customs and traditions, and ultimately perhaps to the status of princely anachronisms like those who were so easily cast aside in India.

To some extent the British can claim credit for solving the problem of retaining the system of Malay states and Sultans while uniting them into one entity and nation. The system has worked well even after the admission of Sabah and Sarawak into Malaysia. Malayan constitutional monarchy and parliamentary democracy reflect the good sense of our people as a whole, the Malays in particular. The Malays had learnt a lot from the British and the Colonial Government. There was no initial hostility towards the British. We Malays were used to being vassals of more powerful nations from before. The suzerainty of the British was not unusual. When the Chinese communists resorted to armed struggle against the British Colonial Government of the Federation of Malaya, few Malays joined them, whereas they readily joined the security forces to fight alongside the British.

It was the Chinese who created problems for the British administrators. Their secret societies actively extorted money from the rich and they operated brothels, opium dens and illegal gambling operations. They formed *kongsi* or clandestine organisations seeking to control monopolies and to dominate selected economic niches, and they warred among themselves.[8] Influenced by events in China, they started to spread communism. They organised a *hartal*, or a general strike like those engineered by Gandhi, and boycotted Japanese goods. Despite these problems, the British Colonial Government seemed to think the contribution of the Chinese towards the colonial economy was worth the trouble. A Protector of the Chinese was appointed. During the Malayan Union dispute, Victor Purcell, who was the most prominent holder of that position, strongly defended Chinese rights.

---

[8]  *Kongsis* were Chinese immigrant associations which were founded by various clans to provide economic and social contacts for their members who came in large numbers to work in tin mines and plantations.

The British kept the three races apart. While the Malays were immersed in peasant life in rural areas, the Chinese were concentrated in urban centres and the Indians in rubber estates. Malay peasants were reluctant to leave their *kampung* homes to take up wage labour under the unrewarding and difficult conditions that destitute imported Indian labour had to accept. Not unreasonably, they preferred to remain in the countryside, earning cash from rubber cultivation when they could, otherwise growing and subsisting on rice cultivation or fishing. This choice made immediate short-term sense for every individual Malay farmer and Malay family. But in the long run, it meant that Peninsular Malay society became ever more sidelined from development. Socially and culturally, not just economically, the Malay peasant world became a backwater. In time, Malays became outsiders not only to advancing modernity but to the desire to acquire its benefits and to master its new skills and knowledge.

Their British "protectors" were happy to let this happen. They liked the idea of a simple, changeless Malay world. Yet, damaging as it would prove, their divide-and-rule strategy must have been successful, for during the colonial days there were hardly any racial clashes. British Malaya may well have remained a trouble-free part of the great British Empire had the Japanese not decided to invade it.

Some people believe that my being critical of the British and other Europeans stems from the fact that I was not educated in the UK, as the three Prime Ministers before me were. In fact, my dislike for the British and British colonialism was retrospective, something that developed upon hindsight. Had it not been for the Malayan Union proposal, which would have deprived the Peninsular Malays of their land, I would likely have continued to be unquestioningly pro-British. But the struggle against the Malayan Union caused me to look back on the period of colonial rule and see much that I did not like. It resulted in a feeling of humiliation that led to my mental and emotional revolt against the British. It was then that the decolonisation of my own mind and soul began.

# Chapter 6:
## A Wartime Entrepreneur

Just days after I sat for the Junior Cambridge Examination for Standard Eight in 1941, Japan attacked Pearl Harbour on 7 December and the British and Dutch-ruled territories in Southeast Asia on 8 December. By then the Germans also appeared to be gaining ground in Europe, with Hitler invading Russia that June after France had surrendered in July of the previous year. An Empire patriot, I never doubted that the British and their allies would eventually prevail. My history lessons had taught me that when Napoleon attempted to conquer Russia, he had been defeated by the Russian winter. I had no idea what winter was like, but I was convinced that it would again beat back the Germans.

Encouraged by Germany's successes in Europe, the Japanese decided to enter the war and attacked the United States by bombing Pearl Harbour. I remember thinking that it was foolhardy of the Japanese to attack America. I could not imagine a small nation like Japan invading and conquering a huge country like the US. In the end, all they succeeded in doing was to force the US to enter the war on the side of the Allies. From the imprudent Japanese attack I learnt a crucial lesson that served me well in later years when I entered politics: never add to the ranks of your enemies. If you must take on another foe, do so only after tackling the first successfully.

I had never imagined that the Japanese would invade Malaya, but the collapse of France had enabled them to station their troops in French Indochina. The US had imposed sanctions against oil exports to Japan which, even then, was completely dependent on fuel imports. By then, the British were worried enough to station Blenheim bombers[1] and the East Surrey Regiment[2] in Alor Star. Gurkha troops, whom I initially mistook for Malays because they wore the pill-box caps then worn by Malay policemen, also appeared.

The Government initiated civil defence preparations and the Air Raid Precautions (ARP) included tacking black cloth over windows, switching

---

[1]　A British high-speed light bomber plane used extensively in the early days of World War II.

[2]　A regiment of the British Army founded in 1881.

off street lamps, and sirens to warn of air raids. I joined the Auxiliary Fire Service and was proud to wear the khaki uniform, with an axe hanging from my belt. We were trained to handle hoses and to evacuate casualties by rope through windows — which was no great feat since the houses in Alor Star were only two storeys high. Incendiary bombs were used to show us how to handle the fires. Once, one was thrown from a temporary observation platform built on the roof of the main government building, but it failed to explode. When someone instructed me to pick it up and take it back to the platform, I did just that, completely unaware that the bomb could have exploded in my hand. Later, when I realised the danger I had placed myself in, I literally broke out in a sweat.

Around this time British troops began appearing in droves in Alor Star. There had never been so many white men in town. They frequented the local coffee shops, drinking beer and making loud, disparaging remarks about the Japanese. British propaganda in Malaya was very strong and the *Straits Times*,[3] the Penang *Straits Echo*[4] and Radio Malaya all declared Britain's ability to eventually defeat the Germans. The hasty retreat from Dunkirk was made out to be a tactical withdrawal and a great victory. The Battle of Britain, in which the Royal Air Force shot down dozens of German Messerschmitt[5] fighter planes and Junker bombers,[6] was reported at great length.

Before Japan entered the war, its ties with Malaya were both minor and friendly. In Alor Star, a number of Japanese shops sold toys. One of them was K. Shiba on Jalan Raja. As the leader of the tiny local Japanese community, the owner Mr Shiba was always invited to the Sultan's birthday ceremony. But when war broke out, all Japanese residents were arrested. It was said that a Japanese photographer in Alor Star, Mr Miyamoto, had taken pictures of the Alor Star airport where the Blenheim bombers were parked. When the Japanese landed in Songkhla, in Thailand, and in Kota Baru, Kelantan on 8 December 1941, not a single British warplane was in the air. Those bombers, it seems, had been withdrawn to fight in other

---

3    A national English-language broadsheet newspaper.

4    Another English-language newspaper.

5    The first jet fighters designed by a German aeronautical engineer Willy Messerschmitt.

6    Used in both World Wars, the German military aircraft were designed by Hugo Junkers.

theatres. A flying club plane, which was used to observe the Japanese troop movements, was shot down over north Kedah.

The Japanese troops advanced rapidly and quickly overcame the so-called Jitra line, made up of a series of "pill-boxes" or defensive entrenchments near the roads north of Alor Star.[7] From the town, people could hear the sounds of guns shortly after Japanese troops crossed the Siam-Kedah border. But when I went to the town centre after the Japanese had occupied Alor Star, only a few shop houses had been destroyed by shellfire – the British troops' quick retreat had saved Alor Star from extensive destruction. My father's family was still staying in the Seberang Perak house when the sounds of guns signalled the Japanese advance. We decided to evacuate to my sister's home in Jalan Kota Tanah, about a kilometre away. Looking back, the measures we took to protect ourselves were quite amusing. We felt that moving one kilometre would make all the difference and keep us safe. Meanwhile, those who lived there moved another kilometre away. These were hopeful gestures more than strategies. On hearing a loud explosion, we guessed it was the Wan Mohamad Saman Bridge, a beautiful, old-fashioned structure over the Kedah River, that had been blown up. We had earlier seen the British soldiers wiring it in preparation for its detonation. It was only two kilometres away and we later found that pieces of concrete from the bridge had fallen through the roof of our neighbour's house in Seberang Perak. Luckily, they too had evacuated.

Rain fell and the earth road next to my sister's house was thick with mud. We watched, anxious and fearful as weary British troops trudged through the sludge and rain to escape the advancing Japanese. It was a shock for me to see the *Orang Putih* being defeated, and by Asians at that. We heard of stragglers who somehow got left behind. One British soldier hid in the Royal Theatre in Alor Star, while another was found near the Lower Court, close to where the Wan Mohamad Saman Bridge had been. The Japanese did not bother to take the two soldiers prisoners and bayoneted them on the spot.

68

---

[7]   Jitra was a strategic town in Kedah. The Jitra line extended for about nine kilometres from the beach on the left to the mountains on the right.

I often thought of them, especially the one who had been found near the old bridge. Here was this young Tommy, thousands of kilometres away from home. What were his last thoughts as he was pushed to the ground, a Japanese bayonet pointed at him? To this day, I can feel his fear and the pain as the bayonet was thrust into his body. People said later that they had heard him screaming before there was an abrupt silence. His body was kicked into the river and when I went to the spot later, I could still see his blood. I found it hard to imagine being killed so far away from home and family. I thought of myself dying at that age, and how horrifying it must have been for him moments before his excruciating death. The cruel wasteful wars I have seen since then always take me back to that day, to that frightened lone soldier, and it has only increased my abhorrence of war.

Several days after the Japanese had driven the British out, the people of Alor Star began to emerge from their homes and hiding places. The town centre was deserted. Terrified of being targeted by the invaders, the Chinese shopkeepers had fled and looting soon began. People used axes to break down shop fronts and for some time after, looted goods were referred to as *chap kapak* or "axe brand". A week after the British left town, we returned to our Seberang Perak house. We had evacuated in a great hurry yet found the place just as we had left it, but with the food rotting on the plates.

We had heard of the atrocities that Japanese soldiers had committed against local populations elsewhere. Many Malayans, especially the Chinese, had been put to death and we were afraid that they would rape our women and kill our men. Many young girls hurriedly cut their hair very short and hid above the flimsy ceilings of their houses. But the Japanese were apparently too busy fighting and for the most part the horrors we feared did not take place. But throughout the Occupation we lived in fear of the *kempeitai*, the Japanese military police. They detained people suspected of supporting the enemy, of being spies or being involved with the anti-Japanese guerrilla movement. Before the Occupation some of those arrested had been involved in helping China against the Japanese. The *kempeitai*'s favourite method of torture was to force water through a prisoner's mouth with a high-pressure hose. The stomach would expand and then the water would be forced out by stomping on the abdomen. After a few times, if the prisoner was not dead, he would certainly confess.

Yet, the number of people killed during the Japanese Occupation of Malaya was relatively small. The Japanese even recruited Malays for their *heiho*, a paramilitary force. Proud young Malay officers strutted about in their uniforms, which included curved swords just like the Japanese officers'. I became firm friends with one of these *heiho*, Azahari Taib, who later became a member of the Kedah State Council and then Member of Parliament after Independence. Later I learnt that Tan Sri Azahari (he has recently passed away) did not become a member of the *heiho* to fight for the Japanese. He was a Malay patriot and nationalist and was among the first to join the struggle for Independence. Jobs were scarce and joining the paramilitary force meant he could get food.

Others joined the *heiho* because they were anti-British. I was very surprised that there were Malays who felt that way. There was, for example, the Kesatuan Melayu Muda (KMM), or Young Malays Association, started by teachers who were trained at the Malay Teachers Training College in Tanjung Malim, Perak. I heard that they actually aided the Japanese invasion by arranging goalposts in the form of arrows pointing towards British military installations. There was also close collaboration between the Malayan and the Indonesian *heiho*, which formed the core of the Indonesian Army of liberation. With their friends in Java and Sumatra, the KMM radicals planned to form Indonesia Raya, which would have included the Malay Peninsula. Sukarno,[8] the leading activist for the independence of Indonesia, visited Malaya during the Japanese Occupation to meet with leaders of the KMM. But the majority of Malays were wary of this nascent independence movement. They wanted the Allies to win the war against the German, Italian and Japanese Axis.

They also welcomed the involvement of the US, seeing them as liberators. Most Malays were very pro-American. I myself was in awe of Americans, whom I had seen only on cinema screens before the war. They were big people who always fought and won against the Indians in cowboy films. As the yelling Indians were shot off their horses, falling like nine pins and dying, I cheered. Today such films are no longer acceptable. Roles have changed, as have the attitudes of filmmakers and audiences, and it is no longer unusual for Westerns to portray Native Americans and African

[8]    Sukarno went on to become the first President of Indonesia from 1945 -1967.

Americans as heroes. We are also less likely these days to cheer the Americans as they seek out and take on their enemies worldwide.

With the Japanese invasion, the Government of Kedah ceased to function and all my brothers and brothers-in-law who were working with the state government suddenly found themselves unemployed. The Straits dollar was still valid but very soon we had gone through all the money we had. Something had to be done urgently, so my brothers decided to sell bananas on the street. We had no shop so we just spread mats on the road in Jalan Pekan Melayu and laid the bananas out for display. Food grew scarce despite our best efforts and we began having to skip meals. Very quickly, we sank into poverty.

Our daily diet consisted of rice and shrimp curry with long beans. We lived near the coast so shrimp was plentiful and cheap. Even so, I would first eat the rice mixed with curry and beans, saving the shrimp for the last mouthfuls. For years after that, I kept to the habit of saving the choicest morsels for last. Meat and chicken were scarce; there was no coffee or tea and above all, there was no sugar. Fortunately, rice was plentiful in Kedah. In fact, during the early part of the Japanese Occupation, there was an excess of rice as it could not be transported to other parts of Malaya.

71

Yet we were poorly nourished and many suffered from beriberi,[9] which caused their bodies to bloat. Others developed suppurating sores, while a number contracted fever and died. My parents were concerned about us catching a fever because there was no medicine available. The only treatment was to be sponged down with a cold compress, or to take a bath in hot water in which herbal leaves had been boiled.

Meanwhile, the Japanese began forcing the staff of the Malayan Railways and other civilians to join a workforce that was building what became notoriously known as the Death Railway[10] in Burma to transport troops, weapons and other war materials to the Indian front. Those conscripted had to live and work in mosquito-infested jungles with little food, clean water, or a proper place to sleep. Many Malayans died working on that

---

[9] A disorder of the nervous system, caused by a lack of Vitamin B1.

[10] An estimated 180,000 Asian workers and 100,000 Allied prisoners of war were forced to work on the railway, which stretched over 415km between Burma (now Myanmar) and Thailand.

railway. When the war was over, the survivors walked all the way back from Burma. A few of my relatives and their friends who worked on the railway stayed with us for a few days before continuing their walk home. They were emaciated and sick, with festering sores all over their bodies. Thankfully, after a few days of nourishing food and rest, they began to recover.

Since there was no school during the early days of the Occupation, I stayed at home. I ransacked the house and found the books from the Reader's Library belonging to my father which I had already read. I read them again, having nothing else to do. Later I found some American business magazines that someone had thrown away, probably out of fear that the Japanese would object to them. Deciding that the soldiers would be busy with more serious things, I took all the magazines home and read every page thoroughly. I read through everything I could get my hands on, except for one thick volume I had found called *The Wandering Jew*. It was about the misfortunes which befell any community that the title character visited, but it was so dull — and so very long — that despite my determination, I could not make it to the end. It remains the only book in my life that I have not been able to finish.

Kedah was then administered by what I believed to be a senior Japanese military officer, who went by the title of *Cho Kang Kakka*. At the beginning of every month, the people of Alor Star had to gather on the Padang Court, the field in front of the old courthouse, so that the *Cho Kang Kakka* could harangue the crowd with a long speech in Japanese. Even when I could understand a little Japanese, I could not make out what he was saying except for his reference to *Ei Bei Koku*, that is, America and Britain. I knew that the Japanese wanted us to hate the British and the Americans, but I don't think they made any impression on the people.

Despite our earlier fears and the scarcity of food, life under the Japanese was not as tough for us as it was for some. It was mainly the feeling of being cut off from the rest of the world that depressed me. It was not that I was used to travelling widely — it was just that I could not get news about what was happening anywhere else, news that I used to read regularly in the local papers. And I really missed the magazines which I had so enjoyed reading in the school library.

I tried to follow the progress of the war through the English-language tabloid, the *Syonan Shimbun*[11] published in Singapore. Initially, as the Japanese were advancing everywhere, there seemed to be no stopping them. They had already occupied Papua New Guinea and were apparently poised for the invasion of Australia. They moved through Burma and eventually reached Imphal, the capital of Manipur. The way had been cleared and India was now within reach. Many Indians in Malaya were excited at the possibility of fighting alongside the Japanese to liberate their homeland. Fearing disloyalty, the British did not attempt to recruit Indians into the anti-Japanese guerrilla force. Many Malayan Indians ended up joining the Indian National Army, set up by Subhas Chandra Bose[12] and Ras Behari Bose[13] to achieve Indian independence through force of arms in concert with the Japanese.

Most of the Pacific Islands were also already conquered by then. Siam had allowed the Japanese Army in after its government decided to throw in its lot with Japan. As a result, there was practically no war damage in Siam. Around this time Siam decided to rename itself Thailand, meaning Land of the Free. As a reward for their support, the Japanese decided to transfer to them the four northern Malay states — Kedah, Perlis, Kelantan and Terengganu. The Kedah Sultan, Tunku Badlishah, was not too unhappy about this. He had been educated in Bangkok as a ward of the Siamese King. When the transfer was effected, he rang up the Siamese Prime Minister. No one knows exactly what was said during this conversation but there was no open opposition against the Thais when they came to take over from the Japanese. The Malays still took it for granted that they would always live under foreign rule.

73

Soon I began seeing Thai military and civil service uniforms in Alor Star for the first time. They were made of silk as this was the only textile available during the war. The military wore green uniforms while the civil servants had black trousers and white tunics. Upon Independence, Tunku Abdul

---

11  *Syonan* was the Japanese word for Singapore.

12  Subhas Chandra Bose was one of the most prominent leaders of the Indian independence movement against the British Raj. He was elected President of the Indian National Congress for two consecutive terms.

13  Ras Behari Bose was the President of the Indian Independence League and head of the first Indian National Army founded by General Mohan Singh.

Rahman adopted the same uniform. The Ministers and Governors of Penang had an addition to their outfits — a cork hat with ostrich feathers similar to what the British Governors used to wear. It made them look so ridiculous that the headgear was soon discarded in favour of the *songkok*.

I resented the way the Japanese had so cavalierly transferred control of Kedah to the Thais. It seemed to me that Kedah and the other northern states were just pieces of real estate which could be moved around like personal property. We Malays had no say over what happened to our own country. We did not count for anything at all. By this time I had become conscious of my identity as a Malay, and was also developing a distinct distaste for foreign rule. I wanted Malays to be respected.

During the Siamese occupation of Kedah, the Malays lived in fear of their girls being abducted by the Siamese soldiers. The Malays even now remain a very superstitious people. In olden days they really believed the Siamese possessed great magical powers and could supposedly make potent love potions that bewitched Malay girls to run to them. Stories were told of two or three Malay girls leaving their families and apparently converting to Buddhism. While nobody could confirm these tales, they created much anxiety and fear. But aside from this, Thai rule did not make much difference to our lives during the war. They actually allowed the Kedah State Council to be revived and to administer the state.

There was one incident, however, that angered me greatly. The Thais insisted that every evening, when their flag was lowered and their anthem was played, everyone had to stand still as a mark of respect to these symbols of the Thai nation. One evening while walking near the Alor Star police station, I heard the Thai anthem being played so I stood still where I was. There were several Thai soldiers on the street and they stood to attention, turning to watch the Thai flag being lowered slowly atop the police station. An old man on a bicycle appeared and pedalled past. He did not seem to hear the anthem or notice that everyone on the street was standing still, and he continued cycling past us slowly. As soon as the anthem came to an end, a Thai soldier ran after the old man and gave him a hard flying kick to the side of his head. He fell with his bicycle and lay quite still on the street.

I must admit that I was a coward. Like the others on the street, I just stood there, shocked by what had just happened and unable to move. The Thai soldier looked as if he was going to kick the man again, but instead he shouted something in Thai, turned, and stalked off. I cannot really remember what happened after that. Some people eventually went to help the old man up. I stood there, transfixed, all kinds of thoughts pounding in my brain. Strangely, I was not angry at the soldier. I just detested the fact that foreigners could kick our people and we could do nothing about it. We were a people with no rights, who could literally be kicked about. That incident remains etched indelibly in my mind and to this day, I cannot tell this story without feeling emotional. Yet I had not begun to think of Independence. It was too foreign, too strange an idea. I simply wanted the Japanese to lose and the Thais to get out of Kedah, or Saibury as they called it. I wanted the British to come back and resume protecting us. At that time I forgot that, far from protecting us, the British had in fact abandoned us.

After some time with nothing to do, I was persuaded to go to the Japanese school, the Nippon Gakko, when I was 17. The school was run by an old Japanese lady who was married to a European. Her husband had been interned and she had a pretty daughter named Nora with whom all the older boys fell in love. A senior student from the Ma'ahad Mahmood Religious School, Syed Abbas Al Habshee, was appointed *kumicho*, or head prefect of my class, and I became the *fukucho*, the number two. I tried to study Japanese but my heart was not in it. I believed that the British would eventually return and the Japanese language would then be of no use to me. How wrong I was. After the war, whenever I visited Japan, I always regretted not being able to speak the language. It would have been an asset, especially when I was in the Government and had to deal with Japanese businessmen and government officials.

What I liked about the Japanese school was Radio Taisho, or drills during which we all exercised to music and instructions from the radio. In class the teacher would also stop teaching at certain times for us to do breathing exercises, which helped to keep us awake and attentive. The drills also included running long distances in formation. You get less tired as many feet beat a rhythm on the ground. I would start bravely at the head of the group but usually I could not keep up. I have never been physically strong. I did not have, and have never had, the muscular physique I admired in other boys.

But I do have stamina. If you do something you really want to do, you will not tire. With the passing years, and especially after Independence and when I became a Minister, my belief in the positive contribution of discipline, initially taught by my father and enhanced by Japanese school training, strengthened. I believe anybody can do anything if he is disciplined in carrying out his work properly. Discipline means controlling or overcoming one's base desires — like cheating, for example, or being lazy — so that the proper results or objectives may be achieved. Discipline has played a big role in my life, contributing to whatever successes I may have attained.

I left the Japanese school in order to earn a living by selling rice and curry with my friends at a canteen in the government office where the *kempeitai* had installed themselves. One day they ordered us to leave, tossing our tables and chairs into a nearby concrete drain before we even had time to move our things. We then set up a stall in Pekan Rabu, the weekly market in Alor Star, to sell ginger water and Malay cakes. Of my three partners then, one became an engineer and another became, for a time, the secretary of UMNO. The third one joined the government service in Kedah and now lives in retirement. We later sold off the stall and I started selling bananas and other fruits in Pekan Rabu. I also fried and sold banana fritters, as well as firewood, bamboo baskets and rattan products. I cycled to Gurun, about 33km south of the town, to buy the bamboo products from a Chinese man who made them himself. When my brother Mahadi got hold of some dried tamarind from Thailand, I helped sell it to an Indian Muslim provision shop. I think I did quite well in my little business. Certainly I was better off than my brothers, who kept trying to work with the Government.

I also struck up a friendship with a Northern Indian Muslim who sold cloth and precious stones, including loose diamonds. He had named a price for one of his diamonds and I took it to have a good look. I knew nothing about gems but I noticed that this particular stone was not reflecting light very well. I hazarded a guess and said there was something wrong with the diamond, and that's when he sheepishly admitted that it did indeed have a flaw. I felt very proud, although I did not really see this flaw. He showed me more respect after that. He also taught me how to cheat a little when measuring cloth with the yard measuring stick. The trick was to slip the cloth between your fingers so that you began the measurement slightly after the starting point. But you had to do it very quickly. I also learnt how to use the Chinese weighing device, the *kati*, and how to depress the marked horizontal bar with the little finger in order to increase the weight.

The businesses I was involved in may seem small and insignificant now but I learnt the essentials. Later, when I was writing *The Malay Dilemma* and *Panduan Peniaga Kecil* (*Guide to Petty Trading*), I suggested the use of better weighing machines with two trays to balance the goods against certified weights. You cannot cheat with this type of weighing device. The counterweights are marked and can be checked by weighing against each other. The Government Inspector of Weights cannot overlook any meddling with such weighing machines. There were lots of other things that I learnt from my foray into small business during the Japanese Occupation which stood me in good stead as I took on more and more responsibilities in life, including running the Government and its numerous companies.

During the Japanese Occupation there was no subsidy or support of any kind from the Government. If we did not work hard to earn a living we would literally starve. I worked very hard and so did my friends, and I made sure I owed nothing to anybody. I hated being in debt and still do. It gives me sleepless nights. By the time the war ended I had saved enough Japanese "banana currency" to surreptitiously buy Straits dollars.

By 1943, the war was clearly not going well for the Japanese. The momentum of their advance had slowed and finally stopped. They were stuck in Papua New Guinea, in the remote Pacific Islands, and in Burma, close to the Indian border. The Allied forces had begun to counterattack, but the fighting was terrible as the Japanese held their ground despite the heavy shelling and huge casualties. They appeared to be willing to die rather than retreat, so their positions could only be taken after their forces were almost totally annihilated. Luckily, Malaya was very far from the fighting fronts so it was relatively peaceful. I continued selling bananas in Pekan Rabu. But I noticed the soldiers who patronised our stalls were getting younger and younger, and they tended to behave more like playful teenagers than soldiers. They could not wait to eat the cheap *pisang mas air*, the poor cousin to the good *pisang mas*, or golden bananas. They ate the bananas there and then, finishing bunches in no time.

We followed the progress of the war through reports in the *Syonan Shimbun*. Not surprisingly, the reports were biased in favour of the Japanese, but they could not hide the fact that they were not advancing any more. We also obtained news through some people listening to Allied broadcasts. It was dangerous but the listeners took the risk and spread whatever news they heard. We learnt about the retreat of the Germans from Russia and Eastern Europe. I managed to get a map of this part of the world from an old school atlas and I could follow the German retreat. I knew that the German-Italian Axis was breaking up and was going to lose. The Italians had lost in North Africa. Field Marshall Erwin Rommel and the German Afrika Korps, which took over from the Italians, could not withstand the Allied onslaught.

As the Allies advanced in the Pacific theatre, B-24 bombers flew over Alor Star and other parts of Malaya, dropping leaflets which carried news of the Japanese retreat and of the defeat of the Japanese navy in the Battle of Midway. Clearly, Japanese rule in Malaya was not going to last. I felt justified in not learning Japanese. Then, one day as I was bathing, my brother Mashahor ran home and shouted to me that a huge bomb had been dropped on Hiroshima. He had heard the news from someone who kept an illegal radio. I had read about the atom bomb in various magazines and immediately concluded that this must have been the bomb that was dropped on Hiroshima, and later, Nagasaki.

All I could think of was how Japan would now have to surrender. There would be no opportunity for them to carry out any scorched earth tactics during their retreat through Malaya, as they had threatened to do. We would be spared and that was all I cared about. I knew nothing about the effects of nuclear fallout then. No one did. Even the US assumed it was safe as long as you were a long distance away and were not blown up by the explosion. The long-term effects of nuclear fallout were only discovered much later, when those exposed in Hiroshima and Nagasaki suffered from radiation sickness and developed various forms of cancer. Had the US known how destructive they were, would it have refrained from using nuclear weapons? Were nuclear bombs used because the enemy was Japanese and not European? The Allied carpet bombings of German cities such as Dresden were undoubtedly devastating, but I don't think the Europeans would have visited such a horrible fate on their own kind.

Still, the two atomic bombs forced the Japanese to surrender. The Japanese field commanders, not knowing the extent of the devastation, could not believe their country was surrendering. They wanted to keep fighting, so the Emperor of Japan had to send Count Terauchi, one of the imperial court officials, to convey the decision to surrender to the Japanese commanders in Southeast Asia. In several places, the Japanese soldiers committed mass suicide rather than face the humiliation of defeat.

I was elated when the Japanese Occupation ended. It meant I could go back to school. Unable to wait, I broke into the school building and vandalised it by signing my name with charcoal all over the walls of the assembly hall. I felt like Zorro, slashing my initials everywhere. It was childish and later, when the school finally did reopen, one of my teachers Mr Lim Chien Chye roundly scolded me and made sure I cleaned up the mess. But that did not dampen my excitement, especially when I found out soon after that my Junior Cambridge Examination papers, which I had sat for just before the war broke out, had reached England. With the war now over, the examination results were announced and I discovered that I had passed.

I had gone through a war, a World War, and seen two foreign armies occupying my country. It was a strange and unique experience, and it had a profound effect on me. It shattered many of my perceptions of things and many of my beliefs. The White Man was not as invincible as I had thought. He was not as smart as I had believed. He could be outsmarted and defeated. Deep down inside me a new feeling stirred. I became more conscious of my origins, my Malayness. I began to resent the dishonour and the humiliation of my people and my country. I saw how historically it was always the vassal of powerful countries, occupied, colonised and transferred from one country to another at will. I also saw how Malays were regarded as people of no consequence, their land as mere property to be literally traded or given as gifts for services rendered by foreigners to other foreigners, and even kicked and abused mercilessly for not deferring to others.

These various feelings did not crystallise at one single moment or with immediate clarity. They came slowly, with no order or sequence. But they formed the basis of my reaction to the Malayan Union, and helped to propel me into politics with deep commitment.

# Chapter 7:
## Awakenings

I read about the Japanese surrender in the newspapers more than a week after it happened. As a symbol of Japanese surrender, General Tomoyuki Yamashita, the Tiger of Malaya, handed over a samurai sword to Admiral Lord Louis Mountbatten on the steps of the Court House in Singapore on 12 September 1945. Humiliated by the surrender of their commander-in-chief Lieutenant-General Arthur Percival in Bukit Timah, Singapore, in 1942, the British were determined to make an elaborate, well-publicised show of the Japanese defeat.

A large number of the local Chinese gathered to watch the ceremony on a field facing the Court House. Their feelings were clear: the hated Japanese had lost and it served them right. That meant that not only Malaya, but China too would be liberated from the Japanese.

The Malays, on the other hand, seemed unmoved by the surrender. I was told that they simply looked on at the solemn and momentous spectacle. I do not remember celebrating nor did my friends and other people in Alor Star appear jubilant. True, *Tanah Melayu,* our homeland, was now free from the Japanese, but for the Malays it was just another change of colonial masters. We were happy the war was over, but that was all. We were back to being under British rule.

All I could think about was going back to school. I was 19 years old by then and missed the company of my friends and schoolmates, many of whom had returned to their *kampung* during the war. A few had died. My close friend Aziz Zain, who had lived near my house, had contracted a high fever when he was 16 and passed away. Medical treatment was not available during the Japanese Occupation.

As soon as school re-opened, I was re-admitted to Standard Nine. I remember all of us crowding into the classroom on our first day back. Most of us were not wearing the school uniform of black shorts and white shirts. Later, when we had time to obtain our uniforms, my family could not afford to buy cotton shirts for me, so I wore a white T-shirt instead. I would continue to do this throughout my remaining time in school.

Our class master was Mr Zain Rashid, whom I remember well. He was a remarkable man who spoke English meticulously. All of our old teachers returned as well, except the geography teacher Mr M. Veeramuthu, who had died during the war.

Mr J.F. Augustine, the most senior teacher, was appointed our temporary headmaster. He was a Eurasian from the Philippines and he had a family big enough to fill all the positions in a football team. Mr Augustine also taught English, and he always gave me good marks for my work. It was he who made me Chairman of the Literary and Debating Society and Editor of the school magazine, *The Darulaman.* My first editorial for the magazine was a commentary about the war and the Japanese. I set out to write a grand piece, beginning with "Much water has passed under the bridge" to show how good my English was. But Mr Augustine thought it was bombastic, perhaps because I had insisted on using big words, so I had to revise it.

He was headmaster for only a few months when he was succeeded by a young Englishman, Mr G.E. Marrison. Although Mr Marrison was only in his late twenties, he was considered more senior than all the other Malayan teachers. He was a linguist and picked up Tamil very quickly by talking to the hawkers in the canteen. He became a priest a few years later and I attended his ordination at St Andrew's Cathedral in Singapore when I was at medical college.

I did not play games much in school because I was not very good at them. Even in football you have to know how to pass the ball to another player. But I did play rugby. Rugby does not require skill, just the willingness to get hurt. I don't think I was a good player, but I could pick up the ball with my hands and run. I enjoyed the push and shove of the scrum. I was a member of the team in medical college as well, and was a reserve player for the Singapore All Blues — though I never got a chance to play.

Textbooks were not available so soon after the war. We had to share notes and whatever old books there were. The Japanese had destroyed the science laboratory too, so the school did not begin teaching science subjects again. Whatever I knew of science, I had learned before the Japanese Occupation. This would later prove a handicap for me when I studied medicine. But at the time not being able to study science did not worry me. I did not know I would be going on to study medicine. In fact, I did not even think I would make it to any form of higher education.

Mathematics was my favourite subject. It bothers me greatly that my own children and grandchildren are reliant on calculators and not adept at mental arithmetic. My father was very particular about mathematics and used to tutor me and my brother at home. Mathematical skills are absolutely essential in life, especially in business. I had reasoned that because the Chinese boy grows up behind the shop counter where he has to calculate the change, he is more skilful in mathematics. The Malay boy in front of the counter does not need to do any calculations after his purchase. My argument may be simplistic but this regular exposure to the exchange of money must necessarily make the average Chinese boy better at mathematics than the Malay boy. I myself often did not count the change after purchasing items from local shops.

When I was still very young I could hear the Chinese shopkeeper behind my house shaking his abacus for good luck when he opened for business in the morning. Someone told me that if you went to a Chinese shop first thing in the morning, you could name any price for what you wanted to buy because the Chinese believed it was bad luck to turn down the first sale of the day. I tried it one day, and named a ridiculous price for something, I don't remember what. Of course, the shopkeeper said no. Today no abacus is used and I am sure that Chinese shopkeepers do not shake their calculators. But I remain committed to the empirical method, to trying things out and testing what I am told.

In school, we went back to studying the history of the British Empire. They had not yet changed the curriculum for the Senior Cambridge Examination. But we did not discuss the Japanese defeat of the British during the war. History was supposed to be about the past, not current events — that was the teacher's attitude anyway. I still find history fascinating. It has so many lessons to teach us that can be applied to our own times.

I did not, and still do not, remember historical dates very well. I did not want to clutter my brain with too many things and dates were among what I chose to forget. Unfortunately, I also tend to forget people's names, an unforgivable shortcoming in a politician. But I was good at history in school and obtained an "A" in the Senior Cambridge Examination. I also did well in geography and mathematics, the former because during the war I had pored over maps of European towns and cities where great battles were fought.

But, though I was regarded as a good student, my teachers did not quite like me. I was perhaps "too-clever-by-half", as they say. I wasn't the obedient type, and obedience was what they looked for when choosing a student to be head boy or prefect. I was not made a school prefect until just before I left. My teacher Mr Lim, who had admonished me for vandalising the classroom, recommended me and told me to accept the position because it would help my prospects for employment or a scholarship.

As I settled back into the routine of classes and studies, memories of the war remained. We had all expected the British to win and I had waited eagerly for them to return to Malaya. But creeping into these memories was an increasing disillusionment about the *Orang Putih*. They were not the invincible people I had thought they were and I was also unhappy that they had taken no action against Thailand for allowing Japanese troops to land on its coast and march down the Isthmus of Kra[1] to invade Malaya.

There was also the matter of the Malay States being British protectorates before the war. In 1909, Kedah had been among the last of the Malay states to accept British protection. It too entered into one of those ridiculous treaties which handed administration of the state over to the British for as long as, according to the words of the treaty, there was "the sun, the moon and the stars". The Malays did not seem to mind the permanency of these agreements – they could not imagine that the future might be different. They embraced British rule for eternity with no way out.

The British had clearly failed to protect the Malay States and their Rulers from Japanese occupation. This failure should have made the treaties null and void, or at least prompted some re-negotiation ending the permanency clause. Yet when the British returned, the Malays acted as if the treaties were still valid. The Malay Rulers, especially those who had ascended the

---

[1] The narrow landbridge that connects the peninsula to mainland Asia.

throne during the Japanese Occupation, were afraid that the British might not recognise their legitimacy. Far from questioning continuing British claims in Malaya, they were only too willing to submit to British rule so long as their own positions were assured.

Well aware of this, the British made recognition conditional upon the Rulers accepting the new treaties hatched up in London during the war. These were the infamous MacMichael Treaties, which would merge the Malay States, together with the Crown Colonies of Penang and Malacca, into a single colony called the Malayan Union. From this point onwards, the Malay States, instead of being British protectorates, would become British crown colonies. The Malay Rulers would only oversee matters concerned with Malay *adat* (custom and tradition) and Islam, and the states over which the Rulers reigned (rather than ruled) would lose their historical identity and political reality. Under the new treaties, the position of the Rulers themselves would be greatly diminished. Yet – albeit under British duress – they were ready to consent to this humiliation of all Malays, but especially themselves. The British apparently regarded their victory in the war as an opportunity and a right to consolidate their Empire. Churchill, after all, famously said he was not elected to preside over the dismantling of the Empire.[2]

Perhaps most significantly, the Malayan Union would create not just a unitary Malayan state but a unitary or homogeneous citizenship within it, for Malays and non-Malays alike. Granting equal citizenship to the immigrant Chinese and Indians would imperil Malay rights to land and opportunities. Wealth disparities in Malaya would also widen, leaving the Malays the most deprived group in their own country.

The schoolmates I mixed with were interested in politics and the struggle against this latest British proposal. How could I not be distracted from my studies by these developments? In a series of discussions at my house a small group that I formed became convinced that the British had no right to impose the Malayan Union without consulting us. Although some

---

[2]  "Let us therefore brace ourselves to our duties, and so bear ourselves that if the British Empire and its Commonwealth last for a thousand years, men will say, 'This was the finest hour.'" – Sir Winston Churchill's speech to the House of Commons on 18 June 1940.

members eventually dropped out to focus on their studies, most wanted to do something to protest. Among them were Aziz Ahmad, who later graduated as a mechanical engineer in the United Kingdom; Zulkifli Hashim, who later became the Secretary-General of UMNO, and Osman Abu Bakar, who we all called Man Kuda (or "horse") because he had buck-teeth.

By early 1946 the British were already pushing for the Malayan Union to come into effect. Time, I believed, was of the essence. Something had to be done. The rest of the group accepted me as a leader, I suppose because I naturally took on a more prominent role and pushed us to take action. I had always scorned people who would rather talk about things when they were in a position to do something. I used to poke fun at my elder brother Mashahor, who always talked about wanting to rear goats or chickens but never did. Now I asked myself, "What about me?" Here was a cause that I felt passionate about. What was I doing about it?

Our parents' generation had a strong sense of loyalty towards the Rulers, and though we never discussed this matter with older people generally, we could sense that they felt beholden to the royalty. Malays believed politics was not for the *rakyat*, the subjects of the Rulers. It was the prerogative of the high-born in their palaces, not the ordinary folk in their villages. My generation was the first to break away from that acceptance of the ban on politics. We recognised the role of the Rulers, but we also felt very disillusioned by the treaties that they had entered into with the British.

Our little group read the newspapers avidly for any scrap of information about the Malayan Union, while news also reached Malaya through Malay students who were studying in the United Kingdom. One of them who opposed the proposal was a law student named Ismail Mohd Ali, who had been stranded in England by the war. I wrote to him supporting the Malay students' opposition to the Malayan Union. I did not know him, but I had read about the Malays in London protesting and the newspaper article had mentioned him. He did not reply to my letter, but I would meet and get to know him years later, when he became my brother-in-law and eventually, the first Malaysian Governor of Bank Negara.

The student group I organised in the Sultan Abdul Hamid College later teamed up with the religious school students of the Ma'ahad Mahmood, the premier Government Arabic and religious school. We had heard that the teachers and students there were as concerned about the Malayan Union as we were. The headmaster Sheikh Abdul Halim from the Al-Azhar University in Cairo was particularly against the British. I wrote letters to other Malay groups, including one in Tangkak, Johor, which was very active in opposing the Malayan Union. I also wrote to the Press, mainly to the *Straits Times,* which had resumed publishing after the war. In one letter I criticised the use of English on certain occasions and argued that we should use Malay instead. It got a very harsh response from one reader, who accused me of trying to impose Malay on everyone.

The non-Malay students seemed indifferent to what was going on. The Chinese and Indians in general did not react either positively or negatively to the Malayan Union. Ultimately, it would be good for them because its intention was to give citizenship to them all, but some of them were not all that keen to become Malayan citizens. The Chinese had always put up Chinese national flags during China's festivals and identified themselves either with the Kuomintang or the Chinese Communist Party. Meanwhile, the Straits Chinese were so British that they regarded themselves as the King's Chinese. At one stage they wanted Penang, where many of them had settled, to stay out of the Federation of Malaya and continue to be a British colony.

For their part the Indians focused mainly on events then unfolding in India. During the Japanese Occupation they had set up the Indian National Army for men and the Rani of Jhansi Regiment for women. They wanted to fight alongside the Japanese at the border between Burma and India. India's struggle for independence became more determined immediately after the war was over. The Malayan Union was therefore not at the forefront of their political concerns.

As my respect and liking for the British withered, I grew more politically active. From the history of the American colonies that I had studied in school, I remembered the Boston Tea Party and the slogan "No taxation without representation". I strongly believed that we Malays, the definitive people of the Malay Peninsula with whom the British had entered into treaties, should be consulted about plans for the Malay states. I did not yet have Independence in mind; in fact, when the Tunku first talked about it, I thought we were not yet ready. I thought the British were still qualified to rule us. I just wanted them to respect Malay status and rights.

If the Malayan Union materialised, it would mean the land of the Malays would become an international settlement under British colonial rule. Anyone could become a citizen. Since there was no provision for renouncing former nationalities, the Chinese, Indians and others could effectively have dual citizenship. We Malays could have only one: that of the Malayan Union. There were already rumblings at this time that a part of Palestine should be given to the Zionists for the State of Israel and I was concerned that Malays would suffer a similar fate as the Palestinians — marginalised, then squeezed and perhaps even expelled from their own land.

At that time the Malays were by far the poorest people in the Peninsula. There were only a handful of university graduates among them and the literacy rate was very low. Most were padi farmers, fishermen or labourers. There was hardly a Malay shop in any of the towns and most rural areas were served by Chinese or Indian sundry goods shops. There were quite a few Malays in the civil service in the Unfederated Malay States and some in the Federated Malay States, but there were practically none in the Straits Settlements of Penang, Malacca and Singapore. Indians and Ceylon Tamils dominated the clerical services and the Malayan Railways.

I knew about the structure of British rule in Malaya because it was taught in school. But I also saw for myself what had happened to the Malays. Those in Penang looked down on those in Kedah because we were a rural people. We were wide-eyed when we went to towns like Penang and saw buildings that were four storeys high. But Penang Malays were actually of a lower economic status than the Kedah Malays. In Kedah, the government officers were all Malays. In Penang there was only one Malay doctor. When I visited my relatives in Penang I saw that my uncles lived in what would be considered slums back home. Some of them worked with the Government, but only in low-paying jobs.

In the Federated Malay States the Malay Rulers were able to get some Malays into the Malayan Civil Service and the Malayan Administrative Service. Some of the traditional district chiefs were able to lease their tin-bearing land to the British or the Chinese. But while they were relatively well-off, most other Malays lived in poverty, if not as rice farmers and fisherman then as wage earners — clerks and drivers of the Europeans and the Chinese *towkays*. A few had some rubber smallholdings.

There was much less British control in the Unfederated Malay States. Malay was the administrative language and almost all the civil servants were Malays. Becoming a government servant with a regular salary and pension was every Malay's greatest ambition. Getting involved in business was, by and large, regarded with disdain.

The Unfederated Malay States were less well-endowed with tin than the FMS and except for Johor, these states were poor. More numerous than in the FMS, the Malays of the Unfederated States were generally also poor. Overall, the Rulers themselves were badly off and, probably as a result, were quite ready to lease or cede parts of their state for income.

By recognising another claimant to the Johor throne, the British gained for themselves a piece of strategic and valuable real estate, Singapore. In those days only the British had survey teams and they also claimed the islands in the Johor Straits, or Selat Tebrau. Quite a number of islands belonging to the Malay states were lost to the neighbouring countries because Malay Rulers did not know the full extent of their states and borders. In the late twentieth and early twenty-first centuries this problem returned to haunt Malaysia in the dispute over Pulau Batu Puteh, or Pedra Branca, which the International Court of Justice awarded to Singapore in May 2008.

Singapore was so valuable to the British that they excluded it from their proposed Malayan Union. As Singapore developed, the Malays there became a small minority, and were even poorer than the Malays of the Peninsula. The number of Malays with tertiary education in Singapore at Independence could be counted on the fingers of one hand. When I was at medical college there were a few Malay *kampung* in Singapore. One was Kampung Gelam where the dispossessed former Sultan of Johor had his so-called *istana*, or palace. The Singapore Government has since repossessed the *istana* and all the Malay *kampung* have now disappeared.

Whether in the Straits Settlements, the Federated Malay States or the Unfederated Malay States, the Malays were the poorest and most backward community. They also lagged behind in education. Except in Kedah and Johor, the number of Malay children attending Government English schools was not high. Their abject situation was not entirely due to neglect by the British or the Malay Rulers. The Malays themselves had made little attempt to adapt to the changing situations in their country. Because they refused to work in the modern economy, the British brought in Indian indentured labourers and Chinese coolies. As the modern economic sector grew, there were more Chinese and Indian small businessmen and those capable of becoming clerks and low-grade technicians. After them came the doctors and better-trained technicians. Malays came to regard these types of work as the preserve of Indian and Chinese immigrants.

Their Rulers were in no position to help them because their own powers had been reduced. As before, the Rulers would not rule but only reign — now not over their states but over the *kathi*[3] and *adat* officials[4] who would serve them personally under *istana* and *balai* (royal audience hall) supervision. The Rulers would be no more than decorative symbols of the customs and traditions of the Malays and heads of Islam among their subjects.

In the Municipal Councils of the colonies of Singapore, Penang and Malacca there was only one Malay Councillor each. That, the Malays believed, would be as much representation as they would get in the State and Federal Legislative Councils after the Malayan Union was formed. As for the Malay language, it would become the language only of the Malay community. The official language would be English and thus a major symbol of the Malay origin and character of the Peninsula would be removed. Most Malays were sure that in the Malayan Union, the more dynamic and better-equipped Chinese would dominate the country. They would not only control the business sector but soon the political arena as

---

3    A *kathi* was appointed for each district to administer Muslim affairs, try cases within his jurisdiction, and supervise the operation of mosques in his district.

4    Experts on Malay customs and protocol.

well. Government service, they envisioned, would be largely filled from the ranks of those who were qualified and competent, namely Chinese and Indians. Malays would be left to take up low-ranking posts.

Perhaps this was too pessimistic or suspicious a view. Many Malays did not want to admit this possibility. But even if the future were to be brighter, the Malays would still be in a vastly inferior position vis-à-vis the non-Malays who would now get full and equal citizenship rights and privileges under the Malayan Union.

We did not have the full text of the Malayan Union proposal and we had to get most of our information from newspapers. Yet what I read left me deeply troubled. I had grown quite proud of being Malay and believed I had inherited a land and culture that I could call my own. Even today, there are many peoples in the world who have no land of their own. But the Malays had always had their *Tanah Melayu*, just as England is the land of the English and Scotland, the land of the Scots. I did not relish the idea of becoming dispossessed in my ancestral land, a land that was mine to begin with, or seeing my own people's land becoming everybody else's. I dreaded the possibility of my fellow Malays becoming the servants of others because equal citizenship would mean just that — behind formal equality was a substantively unequal and inferior citizenship for all Malays.

91

As I would later elaborate in my book *The Malay Dilemma,*[5] I already feared that my fellow Malays were incapable of competing with the country's other races. They lacked all the necessary skills and education and had already succumbed to a culture of dependence in colonial times. They avoided hard work and always looked for the easy way out. In a competitive situation against others who were more motivated and capable, that would now work against them. But it was not Malay peasants alone who deserved to be blamed, for the problems began at the top.

Their Rulers had so easily handed over their land to the British because they were promised easy money and easy lives. Why work when the British would pay you for not working? The political pension, or allowance, was really a bribe offered by the British to the Sultan, his family and his

---

[5]    See Chapter 18: The Malay Dilemma.

grandchildren for them to surrender the governance of their states. Not a single British soldier died so that the Malay states might be quickly and effectively colonised. They were taken over from within, and when the ruling families were won over their autonomy and that of Malay society as a whole were compromised. Before, Nature had been gentle to the Malays, assuring them of abundance without great effort; now it was British protection and their Rulers' participation that disabled them by depriving most Malays of the incentive to pursue success energetically.

As a people the Malays had gone through the colonial period without having to face tough challenges. Weakened by their self-induced diffidence, they were now expected, with the setting up of the Malayan Union, to compete with people who had many advantages over them: people who were hardworking, educated and skilled, people who also already possessed more wealth than they had. If allowed to proceed, the results of the Malayan Union would be disastrous for the Malays.

At that time no organisation represented the Malays of the Peninsula as a whole. The Malays regarded themselves as subjects of the various Malay states and their respective Rulers. They had no paramount ruler then and they did not think of themselves as belonging to a single nation.

Not understanding the vast dimensions of the task, I started organising my fellow students to be active in an anti-Malayan Union campaign. Though many people, including our teachers, were aware of our political discussions and meetings, they did not expect us to actively oppose the creation of the Malayan Union. But they did not try to stop us either.

What could a small group of schoolboys do against the mighty British Military Administration? A few of us decided on an anti-Malayan Union poster campaign in Alor Star and nearby towns. We scraped together what little money we had and bought large sheets of paper from the printing shops. About 10 of us were involved in making the posters. That took several days, at my house and Aziz Ahmad's. At first we tried drawing the outline of the letters in pencil and filling the space with Chinese ink, but it was slow going. Then Aziz tried carving bold capital letters from potatoes. We used makeshift stamp pads and Chinese ink to print the posters with our chosen slogans "Equal Citizenship Not Wanted" and "No Malayan Union".

On the day that we were ready to put our posters up, we divided ourselves into groups and headed to different areas. Worried about getting caught and taken in by the police for questioning, we waited until it was dark before we set out. The blackout[6] was still on as the electricity supply was poor.

I was glad to be finally doing something about the situation. It was our first time going against the establishment and it was thrilling. The night activities went well, and only two or three of the boys who were supposed to put posters up in Jitra lost their nerve. Some of us put up posters on the Public Works Department storehouse in front of my home. We did not realise at the time that there was a man sleeping on the cement pavement skirting the building. We must have woken him up because when the police came around the next day to ask questions, he said he had seen some people near where he slept. Thankfully, because of the blackout, he was not able to recognise any of us.

My father was one of the very few people who knew what we were doing, but he did not try to stop me. My mother was not involved — if she did know anything, she did not show it. When I asked her how to make glue for our posters, she showed me how to create a homemade version using tapioca flour and hot water. No questions were asked.

Our time-consuming political activities encroached on our studies but strangely, my father did not object. In fact, it was quite the opposite. He appeared supportive and for the first time in our relationship, we discussed politics man to man. I remember exactly when he broached the subject with me. He was sitting on the steps of our veranda one day and I was leaning against the railings. He asked me what I thought about the Malayan Union. I was hesitant at first, but grew more comfortable the more we talked. To my surprise, he was just as much against the Malayan Union as I was. He had followed every development through the *Straits Echo* and the *Straits Times*. What I found even more surprising was that he wanted to discuss these serious topics with me, a mere boy. I realised at that moment our relationship had changed. I was no longer just a child in his eyes. Having

93

---

[6] During the war all windows were switched with black cloth, or lights were switched off, to prevent bombers from locating towns.

my father's recognition added to the confidence I felt in my first serious dip into politics.

My father depended entirely on his meagre pension to support us. During the Japanese Occupation he had to sell two pieces of land, one of them a fruit orchard. I was very upset about this as I thought that it was important to keep landed property. He sold it with a plan in mind, to gain the capital to invest in a trishaw. He then rented it out to the younger brother of a *satay* seller who lived in a wooden squatter hut behind our house. But this boy always came up with some excuse not to pay the rent and my father ended up not making a single cent from his enterprise. I really do not know how he made ends meet. We had enough to eat and I had five cents for pocket money when I went back to school. This was the money I used to buy the paper for our posters.

Though funded from these modest resources, our campaign was so convincing that the police thought the posters had been produced by a subversive organisation with a printing press. They tore the posters down the very next day and questioned all the printing presses in Alor Star. The printers honestly denied all involvement, but they were fortunately not asked whether they had sold white sheets of paper to anyone. My brother-in-law was working as a clerk in the police department, so we knew that the police were both mystified and worried by the posters.

Everyone in our group was startled by the reaction to our little campaign. The police believed that behind the big white sheets was a major movement to defy the British. They never suspected that mere schoolboys were behind it — nobody did, though it became a hot topic in the coffee shops. The people's general knowledge about politics then was minimal, but they knew that the Malayan Union was not good for the Malays and they were relieved that someone was doing something to oppose it. We had wide popular support.

News of the posters spread throughout Malaya and there were other attempts to put up anti-Malayan Union posters. Sir Harold MacMichael was charged by the Crown with securing the agreement of each of the Rulers of Malaya to the Malayan Union. When he came to Alor Star to get the consent of the Sultan of Kedah to the Malayan Union proposal, we put up more posters in front of the British Adviser's Residence, where he was staying. He was very annoyed. The British were not used to opposition in Malaya.

Legally, in the eyes of many people including the Malays, the Malayan Union was a done deal once the MacMichael treaties were signed. The Malay civil servants and most of the prominent Malays were ready to accept the full colony status of their *Tanah Melayu*. But on the ground, feelings were strongly against the surrender of the Malay States to the British. Even the Malays of the colonies of Penang, Malacca and Singapore were set against it.

Malay resentment became more apparent and *rapat raksaksa*, or giant gatherings, were held everywhere to protest against the Malayan Union. Street marches were also held. In Alor Star, the march might have turned ugly as many of the padi farmers brought their *parang,* or machetes. I knew some of the leaders who took part in the marches, but while I went to watch them parade in protest, I did not join them.

The Malay papers reported these protest demonstrations, as did the *Straits Times* and the *Straits Echo*. Posters condemning equal citizenship and the Malayan Union were seen everywhere.

This was an important period for me. As with so many other Malays, the attempt to impose the Malayan Union focused my growing dissatisfaction with the British and forced my own political consciousness into the open. But I was still just a schoolboy. I needed credibility so that people would listen to my opinions. I believed that a sure way to gain this was to get a university education. I was not too particular about what field I would enter — I studied hard to qualify and when I passed, I decided to apply for a scholarship to study law. Instead, I got a scholarship to study medicine.

# Chapter 8:
## A Political Triumph

By refusing point blank to accept the Malayan Union proposed by the British, the apolitical, easygoing Malays broke with tradition and banded together for the first time in history to fight for their rights. Previously, they had always been loyal to their respective Sultans, never questioning their actions or rebelling against them. But this was different. The British proposal amounted to dispossessing them of their *Tanah Melayu*, their Malay land. If this happened, the Malay states would become *de jure*[1] as well as de facto colonies of the British like Singapore.

Knowing how badly the Malays of Singapore had fared under British colonial rule, the local Malays were not about to remain passive. Instead, they reacted with great vigour, which surprised both their Rulers and the British. The Malayan Union proposal can be said to have changed the culture and character of the Malays completely.

Through the ages the Malay states of the Peninsula had remained separate, as no powerful warlord or prince emerged to forcibly fuse these states or principalities into one nation. Perlis only became a state after a Kedah Sultan decided to give away a part of his fiefdom. Kubang Pasu, a district in Kedah and my former constituency, very nearly became a state after another Sultan of Kedah presented it to a relative of the ruling family. Fortunately, this was aborted. To survive, these small Malay states sought protection from powerful neighbours and agreed to become their vassals as long as they were allowed to administer their internal affairs. When their overlord or suzerain weakened, they would append themselves to other powerful nations. They could even be vassals of more than one country.

The main symbol of their vassalage was the yearly tributes they gave their overlords, the most important gifts being gold and silver flowers. Delegations would be sent with these tributes and, once in a while, the Ruler himself would accompany the offerings. When he did this, he would receive gifts in return from the rulers of the countries he submitted to. Frequently, these would include concubines, sometimes even a wife. The powerful Asian

---

[1] Ordained by law.

countries did not regard the Malay states as their colonies and so appointed no governors or proconsuls. But Siamese soldiers would sometimes raid the northern Malay states, killing the inhabitants, destroying their crops and burning their wooden houses. After they withdrew, however, they would leave no occupying forces. The status quo would be restored and the Malay states would continue to be self-ruled vassals of Siam.

Fearing these raids however, the Malay states tried to find new protectors. The Rulers thought they had found them when the Europeans arrived with their well-trained fighting force and superior weapons. In 1786, Kedah offered to cede the island of Penang to the British in return for their help against Siamese raids. The Rulers thought that they could become vassals of the European powers and still retain their autonomy. Unfortunately, the Europeans had very different ideas. In their scheme of things, international relations did not merely mean yearly tributes of gold and silver. The British readily accepted Penang but ended up not protecting Kedah against the Siamese. The Sultan of Kedah tried to regain Penang but failed. Instead, the British acquired a strip of the mainland opposite Penang to strengthen the defences of the island.

The Malays never expected that their status would change so drastically under European protection. The British used what seemed like mere poetic language in their agreements — that they would honour their word for as long as there were "the sun, moon and the stars". All agreements between the Malay states and the British contained this phrase. If all these agreements to become British protectorates were indeed permanent, then independence for the Malay states or Malaya would be impossible. With hindsight, it may seem naïve, but it is unlikely that the Malay Rulers, used to a lyrical oral tradition, considered the literal meaning. To them, it was just a figure of speech; unfortunately, to the other parties, it was legally binding.

The Rulers' subjects were apolitical and considered it an absolute right of the Rulers to dispose of their territories as they thought fit. There may have been intrigues in the courts, but there were no rebellions by the people. Even if a Ruler was incapable, cruel or irresponsible — with the notable exception of Sultan Mahmud Shah II of Johor-Riau who was assassinated[2] — his subjects would not rise against him. Malay feudalism was deep and abiding. The ancient story of Hang Tuah and Hang Jebat[3] merits elaboration within this context. The legendary Malay warrior, Hang Tuah, reputedly declared that "the Malay will not betray his Raja." His loyalty was total and never wavered, not even when he was wrongly accused of an illicit relationship with one of the Sultan's concubines and ordered to be put to death. However, the *bendahara* did not carry out the sentence. Tuah's close companion and fellow warrior Hang Jebat, believing that his friend had already been put to death, ran amok and killed a number of palace officials. Despite the injustice done to him, Tuah never hesitated to obey the Sultan when ordered to kill Jebat.

To this day Malays glorify the loyalty of Hang Tuah. When there was a suggestion that a Malaysian warship be named *Hang Jebat,* the Tunku vetoed the idea. Jebat was a *penderhaka,* a traitor — and a betrayer of the sacrosanct principle of absolute loyalty to the Ruler. The decision was based on the belief that he did not deserve to have his name perpetuated. Nevertheless, we now have a naval vessel named *Jebat.*

Despite the fact that the Sultans had no real authority during the colonial days, the Malay *rakyat* dutifully abstained from politics, considering it the prerogative of their Rulers. The British benefited greatly from these feudal ways. Apart from minor opposition to British rule, there was no violent uprising as seen in other colonial territories. Initially, the British East India Company did not care to extend its rule beyond Penang and Province Wellesley, but everything changed when tin was discovered in Perak. The Chinese in Penang began to move into Perak to mine tin and the industry helped in the growth of Penang. However, the wars between the Chinese tin-mining *kongsi* or gangs proved disastrous for the tin smelting and trading business of Penang. Seeing that the Sultan of Perak was unable to maintain law and order, the British persuaded him to accept their assistance to end the *kongsi* wars.

---

[2]    Sultan Mahmud Shah II (1675-1699) was known for his cruelty and was said to have had any of his wives who became pregnant killed so that no heir could be born to challenge him. He was assassinated by Laksamana Megat Sri Rama, whose wife and child he had killed in a palace intrigue.

[3]    Hang Tuah and Hang Jebat are the two most celebrated members of the court of Sultan Mansur Shah of Malacca who ruled from 1456 to 1477.

Most likely, the Sultan thought that Perak was about to become a British vassal state, and would continue to be self-administered. The British stipulation that there should be a British Resident seemed harmless enough. He was, after all, just a Resident, a figure who would reside in Perak to advise the Sultan on the administration of the state. It was assumed that this provision would not affect the authority of the Sultan or the autonomy of his state. Even the condition that the Resident's advice had to be followed did not arouse the Sultan's concern.

Soon after the Pangkor Treaty[4] was signed, the British revealed their hand. They took over the administration of Perak and pushed aside the Sultan and his administrators. The upshot was the murder of J.W.W. Birch,[5] the first Resident of Perak, after which the British were more careful. H.W. Low, the next Resident, was more diplomatic, although the execution of Birch's alleged killer and banishment of the Sultan impressed upon the other members of the Perak ruling houses – and no doubt the other Rulers — that the British were not to be trifled with.

Despite what happened to Perak, three other Malay states — Selangor, Negeri Sembilan and Pahang — signed treaties with the British to accept protection. Through their Residents and their attendant powers to "advise", the four states were forced into a federation, losing their rights to act individually. British Officers completely took over the administration of this new federation through the setting up of the Malayan Civil Service, which excluded the Malays, none of whom were regarded as having the required qualifications.

By 1914 the other five Malay states had agreed to become British protectorates. But seeing the loss of autonomy of the members of the Federated Malay States, Kedah, Perlis, Kelantan, Terengganu and Johor refused to join the Federation. They were therefore negatively branded "the Unfederated Malay States", or "Non-Federated Malay States". So

---

4    The Pangkor Treaty of 1874 between Raja Muda Abdullah of Perak and Sir Andrew Clarke, the Governor of the Straits Settlements, recognised Raja Abdullah as the legitimate Sultan of Perak. In return, Abdullah had to accept, among other things, the advice of a British Resident in all matters except the religion and customs of the Malays.

5    J.W.W. Birch (1826-1875) was assassinated on 2 November 1875 after he angered local Malay chiefs by outlawing slavery and reportedly showing disrespect to the Malays.

wary were these five states of losing their authority that they refused to even join the Customs and Postal Unions proposed by the British. They were determined to retain whatever autonomy they had, even if they were now regarded as British possessions in the eyes of the world.

By the time the Pacific War broke out in 1941, the Malay Peninsula had seven different governments. The Straits Settlements of Penang, Malacca and Singapore were administered as British Colonies with a Governor residing in Singapore. The Federated Malay States of Perak, Selangor, Negeri Sembilan and Pahang had a federal government with Kuala Lumpur as its capital. Each state had a British Resident answerable to a British High Commissioner, who was under the Governor of the Straits Settlements. The federal administration was headed by the High Commissioner assisted by a Legislative Council made up of officials and nominated members. In all the states the Sultans remained responsible for the religion of Islam and Malay *adat*. Political pensions were paid to all the Sultans and members of their families for *not* taking part in administration. The five Unfederated States each had its own government and civil service. Except for those in technical departments, the administration was headed by Malay officers. The Rulers of these states also received political pensions but they chaired the state councils.

All the Sultans acknowledged only Malays as their subjects. Muslim immigrants from the Dutch East Indies (now Indonesia) who were permanent residents in these states were also accepted as subjects of the Rulers. Non-Malays (Chinese and Indians largely), whether born in the Malay States or permanently resident, were all regarded as foreigners. The notion of citizenship did not arise during this period, and at no point did it occur to the Sultans that these "foreigners" would one day seek citizenship rights. When the Malay states became British Protectorates and the number of Chinese and Indians increased, the British administration created departments to look after these two groups. There was an officer designated the Protector of Chinese heading the Chinese Affairs Department in the federated states. As most of the Indians were workers in rubber estates and ports, a South Indian Labour Board was set up to look after them. The labourers would return to India every few years, sometimes with their passage paid by the Board.

For Malays, their status as subjects of the Sultans was important as the Malay states were feudal and the Rulers the legal heads. All treaties and agreements were entered into by the Rulers or, at the very least, in their names. This recognition was of great significance, especially when the Malayan Union agreements were signed and later revoked to be replaced by a new Federation agreement.

When the Japanese conquered Malaya, their policies concerning the governments of the Malay States and the Straits Settlements were not consistent. They did not depose the Malay Rulers, but the state councils were not allowed to function. Instead, each state came under a military administration headed by the *Cho Kang Kakka*. In October 1943 the Japanese transferred the four northern states of Kedah, Perlis, Kelantan and Terengganu to Siam as reward for facilitating the Japanese invasion of Malaya. These four states had been vassals of Siam earlier, until a treaty was signed in 1909 between the British and Siamese Government in Bangkok. The agreement stipulated that the four states would be under the British sphere of influence. The other four Malay states north of Kedah, Perlis and Kelantan, that is, Setol, Patani, Narathiwat and Yala, were put under Siamese jurisdiction.

As with the Bangkok Treaty, the Malay Rulers were not consulted when the Japanese transferred their states to Siamese rule. Still, they were content as the Siamese allowed the state councils to be revived and the state governments to function. In the meantime the British, believing in their eventual return, decided to plan the structure and administration of post-war Malaya. They envisioned a return by invasion and military conquest. By extension, they would therefore be dealing with a conquered territory and would no longer be bound by past treaties with the Sultans. They never saw their failure to protect the Malay states as a breach of the treaties they had signed. Their first priority was to unify the administration of the Malay states, purportedly in order to help them prepare for self-government.

In 1943 work began in the Colonial Office in London on the Malayan Union plan. Not surprisingly, no Malay was consulted. Even the well-known British officers who had served in Malaya were ignored. The plan was for the Sultanates to be joined with the colonies of Penang and

Malacca to make up the Malayan Union, administered by one Governor. Singapore was to remain under British colonial rule. The Malay Rulers would transfer jurisdiction to His Majesty's Government, but they would continue to preside over the affairs and administration of Malay customs and Islam. While they would have no role to play in the administration or the Union government, they would continue to receive political pensions. In the Malayan Union, anyone who wished to make Malaya their permanent home, irrespective of race or religion, would be entitled to citizenship. This meant that immigrants and their descendants would enjoy equal status with the indigenous Malays and other subjects of the Sultans. There was also no condition that citizenship of other countries had to be renounced, providing immigrants with the opportunity for dual citizenship.

The invasion forces of the Allies were at sea when the Japanese surrendered. This somewhat altered the Malayan Union project, but the British were unfazed by this turn of events. They complacently thought that the Rulers could still be made to sign new treaties, which would completely transfer jurisdiction to the British Crown. At that early stage there was no thought given to the reaction of the *rakyat*, as the British fully expected that the consent of the Rulers was all they needed in order to create the Malayan Union. The Malay Rulers must have been aware of the fate of the Indian Maharajas and the rulers of the numerous states of neighbouring Indonesia. The Maharajas merely lost their status when India achieved independence, but most of the Indonesian Sultans were killed by their people during their struggle for independence. Still, they thought it was unlikely that the gentle Malays would emulate the Indians or the Indonesians.

In September 1945, before the arrival of Sir Harold MacMichael, who was to be responsible for obtaining the consent of the Rulers, the British Military Administration decided to test the Malayan Union proposal. Brigadier H. C. Willan, the Deputy Chief Civil Affairs Officer, was assigned to see the reigning Sultans who had been recognised by the British before the Japanese invasion. He was also to meet with new Rulers who had been installed during the Occupation. The British decided that they would use the official recognition of each throne to strong-arm the Sultans into surrendering jurisdiction to the British Crown.

Willan met the Sultan of Johor first, believing that if he could get him to sign, the others would willingly follow suit. On 8 September 1945, he travelled to Johor Baru to see the Sultan in his Pasir Pelangi Palace. Willan commented that the Sultan was "genuinely pleased to see us and not once throughout the interview even hinted that the British had let him down by losing Johore".[6] He noticed a change of attitude and a subtle shift of allegiance in favour of the British. During the meeting, the Sultan said that the 20,000-dollar allowance the Japanese paid him was the same amount the British Government paid him. To Willan, this was significant. Before the Occupation, the Sultan's monthly allowance had come out of Johor state funds. Willan explained why it was necessary to have a Military Administration and why the Sultan and his state council could not begin functioning. The Sultan fully agreed and said his only desire was to see the parade in Singapore marking the Japanese surrender, after which he wanted to proceed to England as soon as possible.

Next, Willan visited Selangor, which had had a change of Sultan during the Japanese Occupation.[7] The new Sultan was considered an unsuitable heir apparent by the British even before the war and they made it clear that he would not be recognised. As such, Willan chose to speak only with the candidate approved by the British. But there was no talk of installing him as Sultan. Instead they dangled a carrot, saying that they would recognise him if he signed the treaty. It came as no surprise when he readily agreed to the Military Administration, the suspension of his council and restrictions on his movement.

The next stop on Willan's carefully plotted path was an appointment with the Sultan of Kedah, who had also been installed during the Occupation. Willan pointedly referred to Tunku Badlishah as the Regent and not the Sultan. He recited his usual spiel, but when he said that neither the Regent nor his state council were allowed to function, the "Regent seemed a bit

---

[6]  *Malaya, Part 1: The Malayan Union Experiment 1942-1948*, Editor A.J Stockwell, British Documents on the end of Empire, Series B, Vol. 3.

[7]  Sultan Hishamuddin Alam Shah (1898-1960) was deposed by the Japanese for having made pro-British speeches prior to the Occupation. He was replaced by his older brother Tengku Musaeddin (b. 1893), who became Sultan Musa Ghiatuddin Riayat Shah. Sultan Hishamuddin was restored in 1945 on the return of the British, and Sultan Musa was exiled to the Cocos Keeling Islands, but was returned to Malaya just before he died in 1955.

shaken".[8] He also told the Sultan that "His Majesty's Government could not recognise him as Sultan because the present policy is not to recognise any Sultan who had been appointed during the Japanese period, and that was also why he could not perform any functions of a lawful Sultan".[9] The encounter with the Sultan of Kedah, however, rattled Willan and it was a sign that the Ruler was likely to make negotiations with MacMichael difficult.

Willan made reports on all his interviews and suggested how the British should deal with recalcitrant rulers. He also suggested the sequence of royal signatures to be obtained. First on the list was the Sultan of Johor, who had readily agreed to the terms. Next was Selangor, then Negeri Sembilan and Pahang. After these four had signed, Willan was certain that the Sultan of Perak would not refuse to join them.

After getting the signatures of the Ruler of Johor and the Federated States, MacMichael was to approach Kedah and the other northern states. Kedah would offer some resistance as the Sultan was bound to consult his state council. Haji Sheriff Awang Osman, the State Secretary who was close to the Sultan and who was likely to be a stumbling block, had to be convinced first. This, the British believed, was a sure-fire way of getting the Sultan's endorsement. No problems were expected in Perlis, Terengganu and Kelantan as all three Rulers had ascended to the throne during the Japanese Occupation and would rely on British recognition of their positions.

Following Willan's reports, MacMichael was dispatched to Malaya the next month. By this time the *rakyat* of Malaya had heard about the Malayan Union proposal and were agitated, even though they did not know the full content. Because they lacked reliable information, they assumed that the British wanted to make a colony of Malaya and confer citizenship on everyone living in the country. The Malays were very conscious of their poverty, poor education and lack of involvement in the country's enriching economic activities. They feared they would become the lowest, most deprived stratum in Malayan society.

---

[8]   *Malaya, Part 1: The Malayan Union Experiment 1942-1948.*
[9]   Ibid.

However, unlike their brothers in the Dutch East Indies, the Peninsular Malays were not thinking of independence. All they wanted was a return to the comfortable *status quo ante* they had enjoyed before the war. They wanted to stay as British Protectorates where, as the indigenous people and subjects of the Sultans, they would remain the legitimate definitive people of the Malay states. Everyone else would remain foreigners.

As reports and stories grew of the British determination to implement their Malayan Union plan, the *rakyat's* confidence in their Rulers began to erode. They were no longer content to be excluded from politics. As treasonable as it may have been, they felt that their Rulers were not up to resisting British pressure. The incipient idea of Malay unity slowly spread through the states of Malaya, but they were not confident they could frustrate British plans. The call became louder and more insistent for the Malays to think of themselves as people of *Tanah Melayu* and not as subjects of the Rulers of the different states. Newspapers began to promote Malay unity and proposed the setting up of a single body to represent all Malays. The *rakyat* envied Indonesia for having a charismatic leader in Sukarno, and some even considered a union between the two countries. Still, the majority believed that if they succeeded in setting up a grouping open to all Malays from all the states, a leader would emerge.

The British noted this increasing level of Malay political activity and their opposition to the Malayan Union, but they were not deterred. They still believed that if the Sultans acquiesced, their plan to unify the Malay states and rule them directly as a Malayan Union would succeed. MacMichael arrived in Malaya in October 1945. On Willan's advice, he went to see the Sultan of Johor first. Although I was at that time still a student in the Sultan Abdul Hamid College, I watched MacMichael's progress closely. I wanted to find out what I could do to show Malay displeasure at what he was doing.

The meeting was held in Pasir Pelangi Palace. MacMichael explained that His Majesty's Government was concerned only with the welfare of the country and that his own work was limited to the congenial task of obtaining the cooperation of the Rulers. For His Majesty's Government to properly and efficiently carry out the policy, it needed powers of jurisdiction which it did not have at the time. The treaty to be signed by the Sultan would grant this jurisdiction. MacMichael said he had an explanatory note giving more details, strictly for the Sultan's personal and confidential information. In his notes on the encounter with the Sultan, MacMichael remarked, "that these documents had been printed at very short notice and with really remarkable efficiency, together with the text of the Treaty all ready for signature."[10]

The Sultan insisted that a British official head every department to ensure that it was properly administered. He stated he had lost faith in Malays — this was duly recorded in the files kept in the archives. The Sultan also expressed concern over such matters as the fate of postage stamps and police badges after the Union, perhaps because he was concerned that these items would not carry Johor's crest. He said he wanted time to study the papers and to prepare a memorandum, so it was agreed that another meeting would be held two days later. On 20 September, H.T. Bourdillon,[11] Assistant Secretary in the Colonial Office, produced the documents for signature. Both MacMichael and the Sultan signed without formality or

discussion.

MacMichael, having served in Palestine, marked the occasion by saying "Praise God" in Arabic. The Sultan did likewise. The Sultan's memorandum (containing his views on British-Johor relations) was produced and he said MacMichael could take it for what it was worth, and, if he saw fit, could throw it in the wastepaper basket. MacMichael then expressed a hope to meet the Sultan in England, mentioning that General R. Hone, the Chief Civil Affairs Officer, had wired an urgent request for passage to England for His Highness.

Jubilant over this coup, MacMichael knew that he would thereafter encounter fewer difficulties with the other Rulers. As he anticipated, they all signed without demur, except for Tunku Badlishah, the Sultan of Kedah.

MacMichael then noted when he went to the palace in Anak Bukit, Alor Star, where Tunku Badlishah was waiting for him, that "he was a small

---

[10]   These notes are kept in the Istana at Pasir Pelangi.

[11]   H.T. Bourdillon served in Malaya and later worked in the Colonial Office in London.

stocky man whose figure hardly permits him any great natural dignity".[12] Nevertheless he impressed the British envoy "as a man of sense and honesty, courteous and friendly and possessed of considerable self-assurance". Tunku Badlishah must have been aware even at that time that if he failed to sign, someone else more pliable would be anointed by the British. MacMichael explained his mission along the same lines and made a point of telling the Sultan that "he had been granted discretion by His Majesty's Government in the matter of recognising him as Sultan of Kedah".

Tunku Badlishah read the copy of the new Treaty and the Explanatory Note handed to him carefully and without comment. When the British officer remarked that he hoped there was nothing unpalatable in the agreement, Tunku Badlishah replied that it was "very devastating".[13] The point which disquieted him most, and which he constantly returned to in the discussions, was the surrender of power by the Rulers. He noted that Rulers would advise the Resident Commissioner and the Governor (a reversal of roles) but neither would have to heed the advice. This was a reference to the role of the British Adviser, whose advice could not be refused whereas the Sultan's instructions could be ignored without fear of reprisal. To this, MacMichael said that it was no more than a formal recognition of the existing state of affairs. He said that pre-war, the Governor had always exercised the real power and it was foolish to deny this fact. Under British rule, he said, Sultans had been bound to accept the advice of the Residents or Advisers, and it was only right that this power and overt responsibility should remain in the same hands.

His Highness demurred to the suggestion that the Rulers had always been bound to accept the advice of the Residents and referred to the right of appeal to the High Commissioner or the Secretary of State under the old treaty. This made MacMichael unpleasant. He issued a veiled threat, saying it was fortunate that His Majesty's Government had not concluded — as would have been consistent with modern conceptions of democratic Government — that Sultanates were altogether out of date. What Tunku Badlishah thought of this we do not know, but MacMichael went on to

107

---

[12] These notes are kept in the British Archives.
[13] Also from the British Archives.

say that even if the policy were to be modified, the change would not favour the Rulers. Despite these menacing undertones, and MacMichael's insistence on referring to him as the Regent, the Sultan would not readily accommodate himself to the surrender of nominal power. He continued to argue about the independent status of the Unfederated Malay States, Kedah in particular. He went on to say that Malaya would be reduced once again to the status of a colony.

Brigadier Sir Alex Newboult, who later became Chief Secretary of the Federation and who was also present, snidely suggested that perhaps His Highness was thinking of returning to Siamese control as an alternative. This ill-mannered comment was followed by MacMichael remarking that if His Highness' qualms had been well founded, they would surely have been voiced by the Sultan of Johor. To this the Sultan of Kedah retorted that he was not bound to follow Johor's example. Finally, he said that he would consult members of the state council. Before MacMichael left, Tunku Badlishah reverted to his courteous Malay self by showing his guest the wedding regalia of the Kedah ruling house. But the strength of his sentiments had registered with MacMichael.

The Sultan again expressed his sense of shock to Colonel E.V.G. Day, the Kedah Senior Civil Affairs Officer, who had accompanied MacMichael and had stayed back after the meeting. Tunku Badlishah added that although the British were far more polite, their bullying tactics were similar to those of the Japanese. For four days MacMichael was kept waiting as Tunku Badlishah consulted the state council. Offers by Colonel Day and Brigadier Newboult to help explain the issue were not taken up.

Finally, there were no more excuses. On 3 December, MacMichael prepared to see the Sultan again to get his signature. But Tunku Badlishah said the signing should take place the next day. When MacMichael refused on account of having other engagements, the Sultan agreed to the signing only after he had had his lunch. At 4pm, before the signing, the meeting of the state council was questioned by the state council members themselves as the British Adviser had not been present. Perhaps this was their way of delaying the signing. MacMichael then took pains to explain that Colonel

Day — later to be appointed British Adviser of Kedah — had all the powers and functions of the British Adviser. This authority was only revealed after the fact.

Minutes of the state council meeting, without which the treaty could not be signed, were then prepared. But before signing took place, it was cleverly pointed out by a council member that the Sultan was the President of the state council. This meant that Tunku Badlishah could not sign the minutes before he was made Sultan and therefore the legitimate Council President. Having obtained the assurance of all members that the treaty would be signed, MacMichael was then forced to formally declare that His Majesty's Government recognised His Highness as the Sultan of Kedah. The minutes of the state council were then signed by all. Tunku Yaacob, the State Agricultural Officer and brother of the Sultan, stated in no uncertain terms that he gave his consent only because he had no choice. Bourdillon then produced the treaty itself for signature. At this stage, the Sultan stood up and announced that he would like to say a few words. Speaking firmly, he said that this was the most distressing and painful moment of his whole life. MacMichael did not let that pass. He stood up and expressed regret at the Sultan's pessimism, insisting that the treaty would be good for Kedah, and Malaya as a whole. He indicated that he had to report the Sultan's declaration to the Secretary of State. Finally, the treaty was signed at 5.10pm.

While the Sultan was negotiating with MacMichael, the people of Alor Star were starting to get restless. This was also when my friends and I produced the anti-Malayan Union posters, tacking several of them onto a tree opposite the residence of Colonel Day, where MacMichael was staying. We had heard about the Sultan of Johor readily signing the treaty, then we learnt that four other Sultans had done the same. To us, the treaty was grievously wrong, for it was no less then the surrender of the Malay States to the British. Many of us felt betrayed by our Rulers.

Disappointed though the people were with their Sultans, they still felt that only the Rulers could right the wrongs caused by the treaties. If the Rulers did not repudiate them, these treaties would remain legal. This was the dilemma faced by the nascent political leadership of the Malays. They needed to get the Rulers on their side if they wished to overturn the proposed Malayan Union. Fortunately, the Rulers sensed the change in the attitude of their subjects and a few of them tried to undo the damage. But the British were adamant. This was the catalyst needed to make the Sultans more amenable to the suggestions by the newborn United Malays National Organisation to boycott the installation of the first Governor of the Malayan Union. However, all these issues would soon be overtaken by an outbreak of civil strife that threatened to throw Malaya into conflict.

110

# Chapter 9:
## The Emergency

From the end of the Japanese Occupation until Independence, the British kept a watchful eye on the activities of the Chinese, especially the communists. When the Kuomintang (KMT) and the Communist Party split in China in 1927, their Malayan counterparts were also divided. Viewed with suspicion by the British, the Chinese communists set up an underground party and initially confined themselves to organising demonstrations against Japan for invading China. They also initiated boycotts of Japanese goods and threw Japanese products into the sea at the Esplanade[1] in Penang. They even banded together with other Chinese groups in Singapore to raise funds for China.

During the Japanese Occupation, a number of Chinese activists, both communist and KMT, were arrested and executed. Relentless Japanese hunt-downs had forced both groups to retreat into the jungles where they set up guerrilla resistance. The two guerrilla groups were distinguished by the stars they wore on their caps — the KMT supporters had one star, while the communists had three, to symbolise that the Malays and Indians were also with them. They wanted to show they were Malayans and not just Chinese communists. Among the Malays in their ranks was Rashid Maidin who, together with Chin Peng, the Secretary-General of the Malayan Communist Party (MCP),[2] was selected to attend the Victory Parade in London after the war. They had been leaders of the Malayan People's Anti-Japanese Army or MPAJA, which collaborated with the British during the Japanese Occupation. When World War II was being fought, the British had been quite willing to supply both the one-star and three-star guerrillas with weapons and rations. They also set up a third stealth force, Force 136, which was almost purely Malay. Besides local recruits, Malay students studying in England and other Malays living abroad were also brought in to help with the resistance.

---

[1]   The Esplanade is today a popular tourist destination, but was originally the heart of Penang's colonial administration.

[2]   Initially a supporter of Sun Yat-Sen, Chin Peng (né Ong Boon Hua) was the longtime leader of the Malayan Communist Party (MCP). After WWII, the MCP fought against the British colonial government, which led to the Malayan Emergency. The Emergency lasted for 12 years until 1960.

British officers parachuted into the jungle as designated liaison representatives for the guerrilla groups. Malay members of Force 136 from abroad were either parachuted into the jungle or brought in via submarines. Among those who landed on the shores of Peninsular Malaya was Tun Ibrahim Ismail, an officer of the Johor Military Force who had been sent to Dehradun, the British military college in India and who later rose to become Malaysia's third Chief of Armed Forces. Two Kedah Malay students who qualified as engineers in England were also parachuted into the jungles. They were Mohamad Yusof, who later became the first Malay director of the Federation's Public Works Department, and Abdul Hamid who returned to Kedah to join the Department there. Tun Hussein Onn, too, served in the British Indian Army. All these locally-based guerrilla forces were readying themselves to support an Allied landing and to recapture Malaya from the Japanese.

The Allies had planned Operation Zipper involving some 100,000 troops to be landed in the Peninsula. While the invasion force was still on the high seas, Hiroshima and Nagasaki were bombed, forcing the Japanese to surrender on 16 August 1945. As soon as news of the surrender broke, the Chinese guerrillas started to behave differently. They emerged from the forests and occupied several police stations in remote areas, arrogantly claiming that Malaya was now under their rule. This resulted in clashes with Malay villagers whom they accused of collaborating with the Japanese. We were told that over 2,400 Chinese, Indians and Malays were killed by the guerrillas. Among those who were taken away by the guerrillas was a close friend of mine, Sithampalam. He was working in the police force and was suspected of collaborating with the Japanese Military Police, the *kempeitai*. After he was taken, we never saw him again.

Where government should have stood, there was only a power vacuum. An all-out bloody war between the Chinese guerrillas and the Malays was avoided only because British forces, after landing in Selangor and Penang, were quickly deployed to areas where tension had arisen between the Malays and the Chinese.

British liaison officers who had been working with the Chinese guerrillas were able to convince them to leave the jungle and to disarm. In Alor Star, guerrillas in full uniform, after much persuasion, laid down arms in the field near the old palace of the Sultan, adjacent to the Japanese school where I had once studied. But the British knew that a substantial number of arms previously supplied by them had not been surrendered. This was a mistake that would be repeated around the world in years to come: supplying heavy-duty arms and training friendly forces that would later turn hostile. Meanwhile, the guerrillas were hedging their bets. They did not quite trust the British, who were aware of the MCP's openly-declared intention to rule Malaya.

After disarming and shedding their uniforms, the MCP went about organising trade unions. Soon every town had English and Chinese signboards with yellow characters on a red background proclaiming workers' unions of every kind. Suspecting the intentions of the MCP, the Police Special Branch watched the activities of these unions closely. Among the most dedicated Special Branch officers were the anti-communist Chinese. These officers were naturally better able to penetrate the communist organisations and their guerrilla units, and they provided valuable background information on the activities and plans of the armed insurgency which soon followed.

All this took place against the backdrop of the British Malayan Union proposal, about which the communists appeared singularly unconcerned. When the Malayan Union was inaugurated, they continued organising their trade unions. But when the Malays forced a review of the Malayan Union Constitution, the communists joined the All-Malaya Council of Joint Action, a group of political organisations and NGOs created to take part in developing a constitution in preparation for Independence. The Malayan Union would have given the communists citizenship and the right to participate in the country's politics. After the British abandoned the Malayan Union, the Federation of Malaya that took its place denied non-Malays the right to automatic and unrestricted citizenship. Only certain specific categories of non-Malays would qualify. No longer eligible to become citizens, most Chinese would be barred from participating in politics, so they opposed the Federation.

Meanwhile, the communist-led unions organised strikes and used physical intimidation on a large scale. Unemployment then was very high and small businesses were struggling in the immediate post-war years. Lacking confidence in the Government's ability to deal with the communists, many Chinese allowed themselves to be intimidated into joining them, thinking that at least they would have food and safety. Except for a rare few, the Malays resolutely refused to join the communists, even though they had become increasingly disenchanted with the British.

Had there been elections, most Chinese would not have been able to stand as candidates or to vote. As non-citizens they could not organise or lead trade unions. Many activists were deported to China where the communists, after defeating Chiang Kai-shek and the KMT, had set up their government. Their scope for open and legitimate political action severely limited, the Malayan communists felt increasingly pressured to resort to different options. Whatever the immediate trigger, the Chinese communists in Malaya decided to abandon civil action and take on the British Colonial Government in open armed confrontation. They were prepared to fight tooth and nail to make Malaya a communist state. Doubtless, they were in no small way encouraged by the success of the communists in China.

In 1948, I followed these developments in the newspapers as I was studying my medical texts. The former guerrillas, I read, had slipped back into the jungle to begin their armed struggle against the British Colonial Government of the new Federation of Malaya. Bent on proving that they meant business, and to signal the beginning of the armed insurrection, they killed three British planters in Perak. From then on, British estate managers would become their principal targets. The British authorities reacted by arresting and detaining suspected communists.

A few Chinese medical and arts students in my batch at my college were also interrogated and detained. Upon their release two of them, presumably with strong communist sympathies, decided to leave the country for China. More left-leaning than politically committed, the others who decided to continue with their studies at the Medical College and Raffles College were harassed by the police in Singapore. Every now and then the police would come to visit them in their dormitory or call them in for questioning. I saw for myself how this affected their studies, but at the time we all accepted the fact that if you were a communist, the Government would take action against you.

Yet most people in Malaya were very anti-communist. They remembered that after the Japanese surrender, the communists had tried to rule the country. This was also a time of political awakening in Singapore. With the island's large Chinese majority, the communists seemed set to dominate Singapore politics for good. They quickly gained control of the trade unions and the Chinese schools. Indian trade unionists in Singapore also teamed up with the MCP-controlled unions, in particular the Harbour Workers Union. Had Singapore become communist, the insurrection in Malaya would have been stepped up.

Meanwhile, the guerrillas were getting more active and their well-planned ambushes resulted in many security personnel being killed. British and other Commonwealth troops, together with Malay soldiers, were among the casualties. The guerrillas were well organised — a sure sign that they were receiving support from sympathisers among the Chinese population. Called the Min Yuen, or People's Movement, this support arm of the party was made up of Malayan Chinese who worked silently to provide food, medical supplies and money to the guerrillas.

The British authorities responded to the communist challenge by declaring a state of Emergency. Under this rule, ordinary operations of the law were largely suspended. Communist suspects, for example, could be detained without trial for as long as it pleased the Government, a move that would be the precursor to the Internal Security Act (ISA).[3] The situation served the British well for, as far as they were concerned, the longer the Emergency went on, the longer ordinary laws could be ignored. The power of the Government would be unlimited and would also be free from scrutiny by the courts. There was no right to challenge arrests and detentions in court during colonial days and even after Independence. It was only after

---

[3] The Internal Security Act 1960 provides for preventive detention without trial. Under the Act, police are allowed to detain a person without a warrant for 60 days, after which they may recommend to the Home Minister further detention for up to two years. This second period is renewable.

I became Prime Minister that, in a case brought by lawyer and Opposition politician Karpal Singh, the age-old legal mechanism of *habeas corpus*[4] was invoked to obtain the release of ISA detainees.

The British, however, made their classic error of underestimating the strength of an opposing Asian force. The determination of the MCP should have been amply clear: there was an escalation in trade union activities and in the intimidation of the workers. In response, the British brought in trade unionists from the UK to advise the workers and their leaders, which was clearly an exercise in futility. When a dispute arose between the workers and the General Transport Company (GTC) — a British company which operated buses in Kuala Lumpur — the communist trade union activists simply sabotaged the vehicles, puncturing the tires and damaging the engines. But the strike was only in town where the GTC operated the bus services. Other locally-owned companies were permitted to bring passengers from the outlying areas into town. The GTC, incidentally, would in later years be sold and renamed Sri Jaya, making it the first major Malay bus company.

116

In Malaya, Indian unionists also backed the MCP. Prominent among them was the communist R.G. Balan, the Tamil publicist of the MCP in the Kampar and Tapah areas during the Japanese Occupation. He was later to control 90 per cent of the estate workers in Kedah and the Kinta Rubber Factory Workers Union in Perak. The MCP also made attempts to get Malay support, but made no headway as most Malays rejected communism as atheistic and anti-Islam. Gruesome memories of how MPAJA guerrillas had taken over rural police stations in the immediate post-war period, abducting and executing Malays they randomly accused of being Japanese collaborators, were still fresh. The MCP also formed a peasant party, the Kaum Tani, and managed to gain control of the youth wing of the Malay Nationalist Party, the Angkatan Pemuda Insaf (API). When it was banned by the Government, a new youth party, Ikatan Pemuda Tanah Ayer (PETA), was set up. Members of the API, PETA and a party called

---

[4]  The full Latin formula *habeas corpus ad subjiciendum et recipiendum* refers to a mediaeval writ requiring that authorities "have the body (person detained) brought to the court to undergo and receive" the court's judgment.

the New Democratic Youth League[5] were given military training by the communists.

The communists also gained control of the Pan-Malayan Federation of Trade Unions (PMFTU), which began to talk about taking the offensive. At a PMFTU Congress in Singapore, the Secretary of the Penang Federation of Trade Unions said that workers should be prepared to sacrifice their lives for the cause. Balan, on a visit to a European estate, claimed that his union had a membership of 13,700, covering 133 estates, and had the strength to take on anyone. Tough talk and bold, inflammatory propaganda were rife in 1948. A mass meeting of 100,000 was organised for May Day and further incitement to violence was planned throughout the Peninsula.

Only when the three European planters were murdered did the British realise the seriousness of the situation. The Government now had to admit it was not prepared and that its police force was far too small to tackle the growing number of armed and trained insurgents. Having the army and the air force at its disposal helped but the task was too big, so they decided to increase the strength of the police by setting up a special constabulary (SC). Almost all the Special Constables were Malays, men and women equipped only with shotguns and outdated rifles. They made up for this inadequacy in firepower with grim determination.

Their tenacity and courage won them an honoured place in our history books, as they fought valiantly during an MCP guerrilla attack on their doomed Bukit Kepong police station in Johor on 23 February 1950. More than 100 MCP guerrillas had laid siege on the poorly-manned station. Though they were heavily outnumbered the policemen, together with four Home Guardsmen, would not give up. When they did not respond to calls from the besieging force to surrender, the guerrillas set fire to the wooden building. The trapped policemen and their families, together with the Special Constables, died fighting desperately or were burnt alive. The

---

5    The New Democratic Youth League (NDYL) was formed in Singapore in 1945. "Although the NDYL's sponsors tried to project it as non-partisan, it lay at the apex of communist youth bodies, promoting 'free democratic education' and civil liberties through such events as International Youth Week 1946… It was specifically a Malayan organisation, although it mirrored similar groupings in China." See T. N. Harper, *The End of Empire and the Making of Malaya*, Cambridge University Press, 2001, p69.

Home Guardsmen under Penghulu Ali,[6] who had set off from a village just a mile away to help the policemen, became unsuspecting victims of a cruel ambush. One of the Guardsmen was shot and killed. The bloody battle only stopped at dawn when the murderous guerrillas retreated. By that time, the police station had been completely razed. All that remained of that act of heroism were the charred remains of the policemen, their families and the four Home Guardsmen. In his book General Tun Ibrahim, who had been in charge of training the Home Guard, documented a horrific sight that met him when he arrived at the scene: the burnt body of a woman, who lay with her baby still clutched closely in her arms.

The situation was demonstrably beyond the Government's capability, and the appointment of Sir Henry Gurney as Governor (he had been Chief Secretary to the Government of Palestine) did not improve matters. The Malays were wary of Gurney. They appreciated the complexity of the Malayan communist problem and Malay-Chinese antagonism, and did not want Gurney to conveniently equate it with the Arab-Jewish problem. This was at a time when Jewish terrorist groups, such as the Haganah and the Irgun Zvai Leumi, were violently attacking the British, blowing up the King David Hotel, the biggest international hotel in Jerusalem, where the British administration was based. The British Government delayed Gurney's appointment slightly but set to work to get the Chinese community to back the Government in Malaya against the mainly Chinese insurgents.

Meanwhile, the communists continued their campaign of terror and intimidation, especially against those Chinese who were not their sympathisers. People who admitted to contributing money and food to the guerrillas did so, they said, not because they believed in the cause but because they had little trust in the Government's ability to protect them. Events in China continued to influence the local Chinese. The communists had gained ground there and were also doing well in Burma and Indochina.

To the British, the Chinese in Malaya fell into four categories. The first were local-born Chinese who had been in Malaya for at least two generations. These included the Babas or Straits Chinese who identified closely with the

---

6    See Gen Tun Ibrahim Ismail, *Ibrahim Pahlawan Melayu*, Pelanduk, 2005

country. They tended to speak English or Malay and were regarded as being naturally loyal to Malaya. The second consisted of local-born Chinese with immigrant parents. Although they spoke English, Chinese family traditions remained strong among them and they looked to the KMT to protect them from both the communists and possible threats from the Government. Politically, they were ambivalent, and their allegiance was uncertain. The third category consisted of local-born, non-English speaking Chinese of the first generation, whose fathers were immigrants. They had done well, valuing Malaya as a safe place for making money. A sub-group was made up of the labourer-children of labourer-immigrants who had little in common with other Malayan communities. The British described them as Chinese colonists in Malaya, saying that nothing could be done to convert them into Malayan citizens. Their outlook was entirely Chinese, and they occupied squatter areas at the fringe of the jungle where they built Chinese schools. Some of these areas housed Chinese secret societies. In the fourth classification, the British identified newcomers born in China who had the same qualities, only more intensely so.[7]

In facing the challenge of armed insurrection, the British had to devise a plan to counter the communist influence upon the Chinese community. A political grouping or party of loyal Malayan Chinese seemed to be the appropriate answer to this. It would be based largely in the first of the four sub-categories, but it had to be capable of drawing support from the others, especially the second. One of the tasks of this party would be to neutralise Malay resentment against the Chinese. To do this, it had to be centred on a nucleus of Chinese who were already Federal citizens. One year after Gurney sent a letter on "Disorders and Ways of Enlisting Chinese Support" to the Colonial Office in London, the Malayan Chinese Association (MCA) made its appearance, led by Tun Tan Cheng Lock, a Straits-born Malay- and English-speaking Chinese from Malacca.

To win local allegiance, the British administration needed to draw into its structure a few local political leaders. Sir Malcolm MacDonald, Governor-General for the Federation of Malaya and Singapore, created the Communities Liaison Committee and appointed Chinese, Indian and

---

[7]    These notes are in the British Archives.

Malay leaders to it. Prominent among its members were Tan Cheng Lock, Datuk E.E.C. Thuraisingham of the Indo-Ceylonese community and Dato' Onn Jaafar of UMNO. Yet the British reading of the situation lacked finesse — one may even suggest that it lacked sincerity. In fact, there was no need to persuade the Malays to cooperate as they had not objected to the formation of the MCA. The issue at hand seemed to be the opening of UMNO to all races, which the British wanted before talks on self-government could begin.

For this, they turned to Dato' Onn, who was not easy to convince. He noted that every time a new proposal was made, the British, preoccupied with their tactical objective of enlisting and consolidating Chinese support, would ask only what the Chinese thought. An increasingly bitter and irritable Dato' Onn complained that it was the Malays who should have been asked what they thought.

It became clear to him that if he did not take steps to protect Malay interests, no one would, certainly not the British. He went to London to meet the Colonial Secretary, mainly over his concern about the appointment of the Deputy High Commissioner. Dato' Onn was the obvious Malay choice for Deputy High Commissioner and he was backed by UMNO. But the British and the Malay Rulers were against it as the High Commissioner took precedence over the Rulers. If the Deputy High Commissioner ever served as Acting High Commissioner, he would have precedence protocol-wise over the Rulers and that was not acceptable to them. When it came to subtleties, gradations and entitlements of status, British colonial proconsuls and Malay Rulers shared similar sensitivities. Furthermore, Dato' Onn alienated the Colonial Office by asking for 10 million pounds to help the Malays go into business. This was born out of his worry that as more and more Chinese became federal citizens, the Malays would be further sidelined. He also blamed the British for the communist insurgency, saying that they had been the ones to bring in the Chinese. This frankness did not endear him to the British.

Usually cool-headed, Dato' Onn lost his temper on many occasions during his discussions with the British. He did not understand why the Colonial Government could not see the fairness of his requests. As far as the British were concerned, he only wanted Malaya for the Malays when in fact, he was trying to keep watch over the Malay community and its endangered interests in the flurry of fast-unfolding developments. Despite all this, MacDonald believed that Dato' Onn was a genuine and skilled statesman and the true leader of the Malays. He also observed that Dato' Onn had pushed for the entry of non-Malays into the Johor State Civil Service.

In the end, MacDonald, a consummate diplomat, was able to persuade Dato' Onn that allowing non-Malays into UMNO was the right thing to do. The British were especially fearful that if the Malays came to power after Independence, they might suppress other races, which would gravely affect British investments. Their concern over the development of a stable multiracial polity in Malaya was not about human rights — it was driven by business.

Misreading the feelings of Malays towards the Chinese, Dato' Onn brought the proposal to open UMNO's membership to non-Malays to the party's Supreme Council, which emphatically rejected it. As a gentleman, he now found his position untenable. He left the party, accompanied by his son, Tun Hussein, the Datuk Panglima Bukit Gantang (Abdul Wahab Toh Muda Abdul Aziz), Datuk Zainal Abidin, Datuk Nik Kamil and several other senior leaders of UMNO. This was unfortunate as he should have been the one to gain independence for Malaya. As it was, he went on to set up the Independence of Malaya Party, which disbanded in 1953.

Bereft of leaders of calibre, UMNO was forced to look around. Tun Razak Hussein, the most senior of the remaining leaders, proposed Tunku Abdul Rahman as head of the party even though he was not involved in UMNO at that time. Two others indicated their willingness to replace Dato' Onn: Haji Ahmad Fuad and Haji Mohamad Yusof. In the contest which followed, the Tunku won hands down. A disappointed Ahmad Fuad left to found the Pan-Malayan Islamic Party, or PMIP, later known by its Malay acronym PAS.

Meanwhile on the security front, the Emergency was still on and guerrilla attacks were frequent. Despite this the Tunku set about rehabilitating and strengthening UMNO. He was not as eloquent a speaker as Dato' Onn but his royal background and his friendly and approachable ways made him popular.

In this whirlwind of events in Malaya, it is worth noting that the British believed the African countries were making better progress than Malaya towards self-government. One key issue of concern to the British was the economic position of the Malays. They feared that, should the Malays gain full political control without holding any substantial economic stake in the country, they would expropriate non-Malay interests. They expected greater stability in West Africa at that time, where the groundnut and cocoa crops were the products of thriving peasant enterprise. On the road to national freedom, it was evident that ordinary Africans enjoyed a greater role in the economy of their countries than the Malays did in theirs.

Our own pace towards Independence was slowed because the insurgency showed no sign of abating. The number of communist bandits had increased to an estimated 5,000. Malayan civilians were frequently murdered by the communists and wherever they could, the guerrillas isolated and intimidated entire communities by cutting power lines and blocking water supplies. Since the British were responsible for the security of Malaya and its defence, funds for operations against the terrorists had to be provided by the treasury of His Majesty's Government. The communists were proving to be a tough and tenacious force. Despite realising that the cost of keeping them at bay was rising, the British Government failed to allocate the necessary funds. This was despite the fact that Sir Shenton Thomas, Governor and High Commissioner before the Japanese invasion, acknowledged that Malaya had contributed a great deal to the British war effort. It seemed the British were now beating a hasty retreat, not from violence but from rising prices.

When Lieutenant-General Sir Harold Briggs was appointed Director of Operations for the army in 1950, he drew up the Briggs Plan to clear the Peninsula of the "bandits", beginning in the south in Johor and moving north right up to the Thai border. The thick jungles were the guerrillas' secret weapon: once an area had been officially cleared, they emerged from hiding and resumed their earlier positions. But Briggs was not to be outfoxed. Part of his plan was to starve the guerrillas out by rigidly controlling the movement of foodstuff. This eventually led to the resettlement of squatters from the fringes of the jungle to New Villages near urban areas, where they could be prevented from supplying food and money to the guerrillas.

When Sir Gerald Templer became High Commissioner in 1952, he was determined to make an impression. When the people of Tanjung Malim, a town in south Perak, refused to give the authorities information on a communist attack there, Templer imposed a curfew on the whole town and regulated the supply of food to it. By this one decidedly unyielding move, he showed that he meant business. Thereafter he received much more cooperation and terrorist attacks dwindled. The areas in which their activities had stopped completely were declared "white", meaning completely free from communist terror. Night curfews were lifted in these parts and people were once again able to move around freely. Still, a large portion of the Peninsula remained black. With the appointment of Templer, the character of the anti-terrorist campaign changed and the Government began to recover its nerve and seize the initiative.

Fijian soldiers, the East African Rifles and Gurkhas were given a bigger role alongside the British. The combined force was known as the Malaya Command, not the Malayan army, though its forces were augmented locally. Templer insisted that the officer corps in the Malay forces be multiracial and include Chinese, Indians and Eurasians. His forces soon had the communists on the run. Once the Chinese squatters were relocated to the New Villages, it was communist supply lines that were now cut off. The importance of the New Villages in the anti-guerrilla war cannot be overstated.

Many Western writers equate new villages with concentration camps. When I was in Amherst, Massachusetts, I was asked by a young American couple how many new villages there were in Malaysia. I did not know but I hazarded a reply, saying there were about one hundred.

The Americans expressed horror. "How can you have so many concentration camps?"

But the new villages were not concentration camps even if there were barbed wire fences all around. The jungle-fringe Chinese squatters, under threat of violence by the communists, had been supplying food and money to them. Their resettlement in the new villages would protect them and enable the authorities to control food supplies.

Today the new villages have prospered and many settlers have been given land titles. The critics can come and verify what I say.

By the time Templer left and Sir Donald MacGillivray, his deputy, took over, most of the Peninsula had been declared white. Three years after Independence, in 1960, the Emergency was ended. But the guerrillas who had retreated to southern Thailand continued to mount sporadic attacks against the security force. In 1974, when I became Minister of Education, Tun Razak also made me a member of the National Security Council (NSC), which directed the war against the remnants of the guerrillas. Every week until the end of 1989 — when the communists finally laid down arms — the police and the military chiefs gave a briefing on the progress of the anti-terrorist war. I was impressed with the information gathered by the intelligence agencies. They could identify all the communist units, their locations, leadership and strength. With this intelligence, the security forces were able to position their people and to mount attacks. They were often able to locate food dumps and money, thus forcing the terrorists to depend on their own vegetable gardens in the jungle and supplies from the Orang Asli. Far from any government presence, the Orang Asli often saw the need to stay on the side of the armed and feared guerrillas, who at times made a point of marrying Orang Asli women to gain their support. On its side, the Government had set up an Orang Asli unit in the police force, the Senoi Praak.[8] A number of Malay officers learnt to speak the languages of the Orang Asli and led the unit very effectively. Their knowledge of the jungle and trekking came in very useful. Gradually, they stopped helping the terrorists as they gained confidence in the Government's ability to protect them.

The briefings I attended when I was first appointed to the NSC convinced me that the insurrection could not last. For one thing our police personnel

124

---

[8]   Also spelt Senoi Praaq, the unit was formed by Templer in 1956 at the instigation of colonial officer R. O. D. Noone (who eventually commanded it). Original members were trained by the elite British Special Air Service, and their highly successful operations gave communist insurgents pause. Today the unit (now with two batallions) is part of the Royal Malaysian Police General Operations Force, and plays a leading role in search and rescue missions.

had managed to infiltrate the guerrilla bands and the information they collected was accurate. Another crucial contribution to the Government's success was the setting up of a War Room or Operations Room, which was an idea adopted from the military and is still used today by the Government to monitor development projects. Now this method has become technologically sophisticated with computers linked to projectors that can display enlarged images, maps, data and the like. This is a great advance from the mid-1970s, when briefings on the security situation at the Operations Room employed more basic technologies such as sliding boards and flip charts, with maps showing the positions of the enemy throughout the country. Layers of transparent sheets over a map enabled us to follow changes that were taking place. Terrain models were also constructed to enable us to appreciate the nature of the operations and the difficulties involved.

By the late 1980s, there were no more casualties from booby traps and the cross-border raids stopped completely. Intelligence reports indicated that the guerrilla fighters had either surrendered or had settled down in south Thailand. But the insurrection was not over until the MCP agreed to officially lay down arms in December 1989. Police intelligence said that the communists no longer saw any prospect of military victory as Malaysia was strong and independent. After communication through go-betweens, discussions took place between our Inspector-General of Police Tan Sri Rahim Noor and the MCP's Chin Peng. Even though the guerrillas laid down arms, they insisted they had not surrendered. They claimed that they had only decided not to fight anymore. To us, that was a distinction that made no difference.

In his recently published memoirs, Chin Peng claims that he was the one who truly struggled for the independence of Malaya. Yet he cannot deny that the number of Malaysians murdered and the MCP's attacks on the Malayan police and the armed forces, even after Independence, prove that his fight was not about achieving national liberation. It was about trying to seize power by force of arms from a sovereign country that was ruled and defended by its own people. As late as 2008, Chin Peng was still fighting in the Malaysian courts to prove that he had never renounced his Malayan citizenship, and so was entitled to return "home" to Malaysia.

The British had been involved in the campaign to get rid of the communist threat when Malaya was their colony, but after Independence we were completely on our own. The Five Power Defence Agreement (FPDA) with Australia, New Zealand, Britain and Singapore could not be invoked. In fact, Australia made it clear that the FPDA was entirely concerned with attacks against Malaysia by foreign invaders — the communist insurgency was considered a domestic affair. In the end, it was our own security forces, both police and military, the Home Guard, the Special Constables, the Senoi Praak and the people of Malaysia who defeated the MCP guerrillas.

Among the world leaders who have expressed their admiration for how we defeated the guerrillas is former president of South Africa Nelson Mandela. I first met him in Zambia when he was released from detention. I expected to see a broken man, someone embittered by captivity. But he was very calm, rational and free of rancour. He had been trained in guerrilla warfare in Libya and Yugoslavia. According to his trainers, he told me, guerrillas could not be defeated. But we, Malaysians, proved them wrong. We fought our own fight, trusted only in our own military and political strength, and

prevailed.

# Chapter 10:
## Going To Medical College

I wanted to be a leader so that I could get things done. At school, my schoolmates had readily accepted me in this role, but older people did not take me as seriously as I wanted them to. I decided that the only way I could get them to listen to my ideas and opinions was to improve my credentials. The key was a university degree as graduates were a rarity then, so I turned my mind to my textbooks, determined that I should qualify for entry.

I had my heart set on studying law because I enjoyed debating. Besides, it also meant an opportunity to go to England, a strange but exciting foreign country. My family could not afford the expenses of a higher education, so I needed a scholarship. A small number of my classmates had already gone overseas on scholarships and I waited eagerly for news of my own application. It would be ages before I heard anything and in the meantime I grew very dejected. A tertiary education was the only way to achieve my dream of being heard and heeded. But when I finally received a scholarship, it was to study medicine in Singapore. I had never seriously considered medicine and it was clearly not my first choice, but Fate had played its hand. I was to appreciate its intervention greatly in later years, as medicine would prove to be a strangely appropriate education for a political career.

My medical training, for example, came in useful when tackling the problems of administration. Running a country is not just about debating in Parliament or making laws, but also about curing social, economic and political diseases. At least in principle, the treatment resembles medical procedures. The British colonialists were better disposed towards colonial subjects who were doctors because they believed doctors were less likely to give them political trouble. Lawyers, on the other hand, were a pain in the neck and could be critical, and tended to talk back. They were likely to lead movements against the colonialists, who therefore preferred producing doctors rather than lawyers.

It was in 1947 that I was accepted as a medical student at the King Edward VII College of Medicine in Singapore. It was then one of the two higher education facilities in all of Malaya, which at that time included Singapore.

I was 22 years old, a little above the average age for admission, but allowance was made for three years because of the Japanese Occupation.

I had applied for a scholarship when I heard that a selection team was going around the country to interview potential candidates for medicine, dentistry and pharmacy. They would also be recommending suitable students for government scholarships. On the team was a Professor A. Sandosham, who later taught me biology in my first year. I remember him particularly because he once joked that he chose medicine because when he went to see his girlfriend, her mother said she was in bed with her doctor. Three whole months passed before I would hear anything about my application. Finally, I received a letter saying that I had been successful. I would receive government financial aid, which entitled me to get all my fees paid by the Government and an allowance of 25 Malayan dollars per month. In today's money it would be about RM200, maybe less. That was adequate for me to buy soap, toothpaste and other personal items, and I would have enough left over to go to the cinema.

Though my mother had warned me many times that a doctor's life meant having to forgo sleep and work odd hours, she and my father seemed silently pleased that I was going to go to college. I was working as a clerk in the office of the Custodian of Enemy Property at that time, with no prospects of promotion or acquiring new skills. Moreover, when I was on contract with the office, I had been paid $80 a month. Now that I had become full-time and pensionable, I was only being paid $60 monthly.

A classmate who was also admitted into the medical college was R.P. Pillay, the son of a Hospital Assistant at the Alor Star General Hospital. His elder brother, R.G. Pillay, was already in his third year at the college. It was agreed that R.P. and I would go by train to Singapore, where his brother would be waiting for us. One of my distant relatives, Sutan, who was studying dentistry, would also be waiting for us at the Tanjong Pagar railway station. My parents were relieved that there would be no chance of me getting lost on arrival in Singapore.

Singapore was the biggest city I had ever been to and everything seemed large and impressive. Being there felt like being in a foreign country. When I went to register myself as a student I passed through the General Hospital, which sprawled over acres and acres of undulating land. The Grecian columns which formed the college's façade towered over me and I could not think of anything else except that I was going to be a doctor. I was going to be like the man who would come to my house with a Gladstone bag to see to my asthmatic sister. One jab and her suffering would stop — I would now learn to do the same.

I discovered what ragging was on my very first night at the college. I was sharing a room with two other boys, a second-year student named Chong Chun Hian, who came from Sarawak, and a big, jovial fellow named Carleel Merican, who was also a second-year student. The previous year the punishment for a freshie had been to carry and dump him in an earthenware tub they used for bathing. Chong and Carleel lost no time in warning me that if I made any noise at all, they would tub me. I was very fearful of my head being pushed underwater. I thought I would definitely lose my breath and drown. Even now, an element of that fear lingers and I automatically open my mouth to breathe every time I am in water. This is probably why I still cannot swim.

Our room was furnished with creaky iron folding beds and I was so conscious of the noise that I did not move at all that night. I woke up the next morning in the exact same position as when I went to sleep. The three of us shared a room for several nights until another room was allocated to me. This time, thankfully, I was sharing with another freshie.

I still got tubbed a few times though. The seniors ragged me and the 3As I had earned in the Senior Cambridge exam were mercilessly ridiculed. With those grades, they said, I really did not deserve to be there. I was told to pack my bags and go home. Our seniors also made us do ear squats. Far worse were push-ups, because my arms were never strong. Even the girls got ragged and were made to suck pacifiers. The seniors appeared to be having great fun with all this but there were a few bullies among them who went too far. When I became a senior I too enjoyed ragging, but I did not ever cross the line and become sadistic.

I took most of the ragging on the chin but some of the remarks were offensive. All the Malay boys were called *tanam padi* (literally, "plant rice" since the seniors did not know the Malay for "padi planter") or *pancing ikan* ("catch fish", though what they meant was "fisherman"). These were crude references to the lowly position Malays held in the Malayan social order back then. They were hurtful names, but they only made me even more determined to do well.

When the term began, I was interviewed once more by a Mr Austin Hill, the college bursar. He wanted to know whether my family would be sending me any money. When I told him I would be getting $10 a month from my father, my monthly government allowance of $25 was immediately reduced to $15. But I did not complain — I learnt to be frugal. I went out only once a week and did not buy extra items like new clothes. If I had any money left over after buying what I needed, I would treat myself to a film at the imposing, 12-storeyed Cathay Cinema, the tallest building in Singapore at the time. Otherwise, I would go to Marine Parade by the sea where I could get a plate of *tauhu bakar* (grilled tofu) at a reasonable price. The Singapore Traction Company operated a good and affordable bus service. Things were priced in multiples of ten cents or less in those days, and $25 turned out to be quite adequate.

In between swotting, I also earned a side income from writing for the *Straits Times* and *Sunday Times*. With one or two articles a month, I could supplement my income by as much as $50. The most I ever earned for one piece was $40. Most of my articles were about the problems of the Malays, and had titles like "Malay padi planters need help", "Plight of the fisher folk" and "New thoughts on nationality". I urged for Malay to be made the national language, pointing out that it was not just the language of a few Malays in Malaya, but also the language of 120 million Indonesians.

Allington Kennard, then the editor of the *Straits Times*, eventually offered me a job as a full-time journalist. At that time in the late 1940s, the *Straits Times* had very few Malay journalists on its staff but I politely declined. Getting a degree and thereby developing my political career was much too important to me. Perhaps it was a happy coincidence but my articles appeared quite regularly in the *Sunday Times* after that meeting. I used the *nom de plume* of "C.H.E. Det". "Det" was my family nickname and I masked my identity by separating the letters C, H and E of the Malay "Che", an abbreviation of 'Inche' which loosely meant "Mr". This byline also veiled the gender of the writer. Some years after I became Prime Minister my "C.H.E. Det" articles were compiled in a book published by Berita Publishing, at one time one of the biggest publishing houses in the country. Datuk A. Kadir Jasin, who was head of Berita Publishing and chief editor of the New Straits Times group at that time, wrote the foreword. I had not bothered to keep the articles, so Kadir had to find them himself in the newspaper archives.

At college, I found myself among mostly Chinese and Indian students as Malays made up only 10 per cent of the 70-odd students. The non-Malay students were brilliant, each having entered with a minimum of 6As. I believe that, with my 3As, I gained entry partly due to the fact that the Government of the Malayan Union wanted some Malay students to take up medicine. Once, in Physics class, I tried to help a Chinese student by explaining how to carry out a particular experiment. He ignored what I said and turned to another student, probably because he did not trust my grasp of the subject. That semester was my first, and I topped the class in Physics. The snooty student failed the first-year examinations and had to leave.

I made friends with many of the seniors as well as those in my class, irrespective of race or religion. I was not very involved in student politics and did not contest any posts in the Students' Union as I could not afford to spend time away from my studies. I was, however, appointed editor of the Medical College magazine, *The Medico*, when I was in my third year. The publication was supported by advertisements from pharmaceutical companies. An editor's life, I was to learn, had unimaginable pitfalls. I was horrified when, in one issue, "propanol cream" came out as "propaganda cream". The company concerned was naturally very annoyed, and I was asked to produce new copies with the correct word. Fortunately, I was not charged extra for the copies.

The Class of '47 was an unusually close-knit group. We had all been through a war and the Japanese Occupation and we were unusually mature for our age. We had suffered ragging together. We had also been thrown together on the journeys by military truck between the Medical College and Raffles College, where the Chemistry lessons were taught. The military truck was the only form of transport we had then, and we would all get in the back and hang on, standing up throughout the 20-minute journey. The Medical College was only about four kilometres away from Raffles and there were not that many vehicles on the road in those days.

My first roommate had served in the British Royal Air Force and had been a prisoner of war in Japan. We often had dinner together in Harrower Hall, debating the issues of the day with one another. After a year in the Tan Tock Seng hostel I moved to the Federal Hostel, which was closer to campus. My accommodation was a temporary annex, a shed that had been converted into 12 single rooms, known as The Stables.

For a few years as a student, I managed to refrain from getting involved in campus politics. I wanted to focus on my books, but I couldn't help but be distracted by the political events in Malaya. Unable to be directly involved in mainland politics, I joined the Muslim Society of the Medical and Raffles Colleges. The majority of the Muslim students were Malays and the society afforded us an opportunity to discuss politics and the fate of the Malays. Forming a Malay society would have been regarded with suspicion, and I was very conscious that the financial aid I was receiving could be withdrawn if I displeased the authorities.

Inevitably, the small number of Malays admitted into the Medical and Raffles Colleges in the universities attracted our attention. We decided something had to be done to increase the Malay student body. In the group with me was Aminuddin Baki, a student from Perak who was studying Arts. He was a great nationalist and was very passionate about education. He later joined the Government service in Malaysia and quickly rose to become the Director of Education. Unfortunately, his intensity and dedication to his job affected his health and brought him an early death in 1964, at the age of about 40. It was a great loss to the Malays.

Aminuddin suggested that the Muslim Society conduct a survey of Malay students in the senior classes in schools with a view to helping them achieve good results for university entry. I was given a stack of forms to conduct the survey in Kedah during my first semester holidays. Back home, I went about meeting Malay students in the senior classes in the English schools. But the Police Special Branch thought I was up to something subversive and called me in for questioning. Despite my explanations, I was told to stop the survey. Not wanting to get into any trouble that might affect my studies, I did as I was told.

In Malaya, the political terrain was changing rapidly. The Malayan Union had been replaced by the Federation of Malaya on 1 February 1948. Dato' Onn Jaafar was the first Malay who was confident enough to publicly envision and articulate the case for a free Malaya. But it was the Tunku who eventually led us to Independence. In 1951, after he took over the presidency of UMNO, a group of Malay students from the colleges in Singapore decided to see him. Although he was already talking about self-government, Malays in general doubted their ability to take charge.

This fear stemmed from various factors. Most Malays were extremely poor and very few had tertiary education or professional qualifications. They were also totally uninvolved in the economic activities of the country. There was widespread apprehension that the Chinese, despite their smaller numbers, would dominate an independent Malaya. The situation in Singapore, where most Malays lived in slums and worked as drivers and manual labourers, was an eye-opener for Malay students at the two colleges.

Without a sufficient number of Malays qualified to take over from the British, we students felt that Independence would not enhance the position of the Malays. We might well end up exchanging British rule for Chinese and Indian rule. In 1947 one British officer, H.T. Bourdillon, stated that "to give Malays full self-government within the next five years would probably mean the rule of the Malays by the Chinese." We did not know the official British view then, but our assumption was apparently shared by some British observers.

It was with trepidation that we journeyed to Johor Baru to see the Tunku at the dilapidated shop house that served as the UMNO headquarters then. There were six of us, and Aminuddin Baki naturally assumed leadership. I had met the Tunku in Kedah when I was in the Pemuda Melayu Kedah[1] (PMK) and he was the Superintendent of Education, but

---

[1] I was a founding member of the PMK.

I did not know him well. Of all my siblings, he knew my brother Mahadi best. They had been very naughty together as boys and would harass rickshaw pullers by throwing stones at them or stealing their rickshaws. From a young age, the Tunku loved playing practical jokes. He would tell people that someone they knew had died. They would rush to the house for the funeral or to comfort the grieving, only to discover the person alive and well, drinking tea.

At the time I did not think that the Tunku was of Dato' Onn's calibre. I could not imagine his leadership of UMNO bringing about significant changes, and I certainly could not see him leading Malaya to Independence. I was so wrong.

At that meeting, we argued with the Tunku about Malay readiness for Independence. He was not very patient and was not inclined to explain his views in depth. Needless to say, the meeting did not last long. Although the UMNO-MCA Alliance had not yet been formed at the time,[2] he was convinced that he could get the Chinese to support him and to cooperate. I remember him hinting that we Malays had the guns to do the job, possibly in reference to the overwhelming number of Malays in the police force at that time. We did not force the issue. *Adat* dictated that we had to show him respect.

But we were not convinced by his political strategy. I know that I was not. I did not relish the idea of using violence to maintain Malay rule in independent Malaya. Besides, I doubted the British would allow a situation in which the Malays used force against the non-Malays.

By 1948, the communists had already launched their armed struggle and the British were less than successful in the anti-guerrilla war. How, I wondered, could a Malay government do better? This was just one of my doubts about Independence.

We returned to Singapore far from happy. Though I badly wanted to, there was nothing I could do to influence the developments in Malaya. I was just a medical student and a nobody in UMNO and I had not updated

---

[2]  UMNO and MCA formed an electoral pact in the 1952 Kuala Lumpur Municipal Council elections, paving the way for political cooperation between the parties.

my membership in the party. The only option left was to concentrate on passing my examinations and getting through all of them in the shortest time possible.

I worked very hard, reading my textbooks over and over again. Soon I found that by doing this, I could literally see the pages of text and illustrations in my mind. In examinations I could reproduce the information accurately. When I was leading the Government many years later I remembered this technique and urged all Malaysians to read their materials several times, to be able to retain the information and use it with ease. It is the same with manipulative skills, oratory, or any kind of work, including administration and management. It is always difficult in the beginning but with repetition, everything can be mastered. Experience, and most certainly repeated experience, is the best teacher.

When I first entered college, six years seemed like a long time to my young mind. Very quickly though, the course came to an end. The last two years were devoted to the subjects to be taken for the final qualifying examinations: medicine, surgery, obstetrics and gynaecology. When the examinations came round, I was well prepared. I knew I did well in medicine and surgery because my professors did not ask too many questions during the viva voce.

135

I got through all my examinations in the Medical College except for obstetrics and gynaecology in my final year. It was very disappointing, especially as I had no intention of being an obstetrician or gynaecologist — all I wanted to do was pass my examination. Professor Benjamin Shears, who later became the second President of Singapore, was the professor of obstetrics and gynaecology.[3] He had gone to the United States and returned an exponent of American obstetric and gynaecological procedures. We were therefore taught the American way of doing things, but this apparently differed from the methods favoured by the British school.

Unfortunately, the external examiner for that year was a Miss Gladys Dodds from England, who apparently did not care much for American

---

[3]    An obstetrician at the Kandang Kerbau Hospital, Dr Shears was also the first Chancellor of the National University of Malaya and the first Chancellor of the National University of Singapore.

procedures. I cannot remember the exact question she asked me during the viva, but she clearly disapproved of my answer and failed me. It shook me — I had never failed an examination before. I sent a telegram to my father, telling him that this meant I would be in college for at least another six months. I did not want him to hear it from anyone else.

College was not only about examinations and student issues. Until I got into medicine, I had only gone to boys' schools. There was no co-education in those days. At college, though, there were girl students. Of the seven Malay students in our batch, one was a girl named Hasmah, who wore her hair in two pigtails. The boys fell over each other to carry her books. Aside from female relatives, I had never really met girls before and had no idea how to behave around them. Some boys seemed very comfortable interacting with girls. I envied them, because I was very awkward and never knew what to say. But I did not want to be left out, so I finally plucked up the courage to offer her my book-carrying services. She readily accepted my offer, but then she did this with many others. I persisted and gradually we grew closer to each other.

Eventually, she asked whether I could help her with some of her lessons. This would prove near-fatal to our friendship. I was a very impatient young man, and I simply did not understand why she was unable to follow my explanations. At first, it was easy to conceal my irritation, but in due course it became very taxing. I suppose what helped us avoid too many quarrels was our natural tolerance of other people. There were times when she and I would lose our tempers, but it was nice when we made up.

We grew very close, Hasmah and I. One day, after the usual quarrel-and-make-up episode, we took an STC bus to Marine Parade, which was a favourite spot for students. The food was cheap and it was soothing to be by the sea. We had our favourite *tauhu bakar* with *kangkong* (water spinach) and squid. We had such a grand feast that I finished all my money and had to ask Hasmah for a loan of $5 for the fare back.

Sometime during the course of the day, I plucked up the courage to tell her exactly how I felt about her. To my great relief, she said she felt the same way about me. That was 23 April 1949 — it was such a happy day that we still celebrate it every year.

Because she came from Kuala Lumpur and was a city girl, I had assumed that her family was "modern." They took me in as Hasmah's boyfriend and even allowed me to take her to Alor Star. Looking back, I am astonished at this broad-mindedness, because they were actually a very conservative family. I'm even more shocked at how audacious I was. Hasmah and I were not even engaged. We were, to all intents and purposes, just friends. Moreover, she was a girl, a Muslim Malay girl, and in those days visiting and staying in a boyfriend's house was unusual to say the least. It was uncharacteristically forward on my part to assume that I would be accepted without the formality of being engaged. But maybe her parents sensed that we were serious about each other, and that I would marry her. In those days married couples did not attend university, so they knew we had to wait until we graduated.

With my earnings from the articles I wrote for the *Sunday Times*, I bought a second-hand BSA 250cc motorcycle. That eased my journeys to Holne Chase, the girls' hostel, to see Hasmah. It also meant we had a set of wheels to go out together, sometimes even for weekends to Johor Baru.

Later I bought a second-hand 500cc Fiat Marvelette, which broke down all the time. My next purchase was not much better. I bought a dilapidated, second-hand Standard Coupe, in which Hasmah and I decided to drive to Kuala Lumpur for the holidays. The roof would collapse every now and then and Hasmah had to hold it up with both hands whenever the road was rough and bumpy — and the road was rough and bumpy most of the way. Perhaps this was why I wanted to develop high-speed expressways when I became Prime Minister.

In Kuala Lumpur, I persuaded Hasmah to get her parents' permission to allow her to go with me to Alor Star. I had no doubt I would marry her eventually and I wanted my parents to meet her. I drove the Standard Coupe all the way to Alor Star. The previous owner was astounded when I told him that the car and I had both survived the journey.

The price of second-hand cars in those days was not high. You could get one for just a few hundred dollars, depending on its condition. Since the Standard Coupe was breaking down all the time, I wanted to borrow money from my brother-in-law Ghani Pak Chik to buy a better car. Instead of giving me money, he gave me a Triumph Mayflower, which was still in good condition. He had always looked out for me. When I eventually went into private practice he financed me and in return I gave him 10 per cent of my takings. When he gave me the Mayflower, in 1950 I think, I was not a houseman (a medical intern) yet, but I kept it when I was working as a houseman in Penang. I returned it to him when I got a government loan to buy a Morris Oxford. I was very close to Ghani Pak Chik. He had helped me attend the fateful Congress of Malay Organisations gatherings in Kuala Lumpur in 1946.[4] He subsequently died of liver cancer, an illness that I had diagnosed. I felt his loss terribly.

Throughout my university days I tried to be with Hasmah as often as possible. We would sit in the garden at her hostel, studying together or just talking. I was sore about failing the O&G exam, but it also meant that I could be with Hasmah for another six months. She was still in her fifth year then.

We were only able to get married nine years after we met. I had to wait for her to graduate and finish her housemanship first, so we married only in 1956. The ceremony was held at Jalan Imbi in Kuala Lumpur. I stayed with an uncle in Kampung Baru, the old Malay settlement in the heart of the city.[5] It was a fairly large wedding for that time and we had a few hundred guests. It was a lengthy ceremony, since tradition dictated that the bridal couple had to appear in several outfits during the course of the celebrations. One of the dresses that Hasmah wore was a traditional Chinese dress fashioned after those worn by the Chinese concubines of the Sultan of Malacca. I teased Hasmah ceaselessly after that about being my own concubine. Nowadays Malay brides no longer wear this dress or the accompanying *sanggul lintang*, a special hair bun.

During the six months I had to stay back, I made sure I studied hard, determined to pass the examination. I prayed and hoped Miss Gladys Dodds would not be the external examiner again. In the event, she was not and I got through my O&G examination with marks to spare.

138

---

[4] These meetings led to the formation of UMNO on 11 May 1946.

[5] Kampung Baru (New Village) is the oldest Malay residential area in Kuala Lumpur and was founded in 1899 as a Malay agricultural and handicraft settlement. Today it is completely surrounded by modern Kuala Lumpur, but still retains a village-like air.

When the results were put on the board in the main hall of the college building, it was with a stab of sadness that I realised my college days were over. Suddenly the whole place seemed empty. Those of us who had had to repeat examinations left very early. The only ones around were my juniors, and Hasmah was among them.

I spent two or three days there after the results were released, partly to be with Hasmah and partly to visit the familiar places I had frequented during my six years in medical school. One of the stops we made was at Ah Leng's Canteen where we had Hasmah's favourite *meehoon* (rice noodle) soup.

When it was time to leave, Hasmah saw me off at the Tanjong Pagar railway station. It was a sweet and sad train journey home. My college days were truly over, and so were six memorable years of my life.

# Chapter 11:
## An Alliance Is Born

I was in my second year at medical college when the Federation of Malaya was inaugurated on 1 February 1948. It was almost two years after the Malayan Union had been established and several years before I completed my degree.

I followed the events keenly in the newspapers, for these were exciting times that would change the lives of Malayans forever. The *rakyat*, as represented by UMNO, wanted the Malay states to come together as one nation, the Malay nation. They had opposed the complete surrender of the Malay states to form the Malayan Union that had been promoted by the British. General fatigue had set in, and Malayans had lost faith in the Colonial Government. No longer would the Malays do exactly what the British wanted. But there was still one obstacle to get around: the MacMichael Treaties.

A union implied a totally unitary state with only one government, whereas a federation would recognise the existence of component states. The degree of autonomy of the components could be determined by mutual agreement and so could the degree of federal authority over the states.

The Sultans, finally realising the depth of feeling among the *rakyat*, tried to repudiate their agreements with the British. They were unsuccessful, but by this time they understood that their only choice was to back their people's demand for a Federation and to do it on Malayan terms which were acceptable to the country's now politically awakened Malays.

Sir Edward Gent was the Governor at the time and Sir Malcolm MacDonald was the Governor-General. The Colonial Office sent out MacDonald to make sure that the Malayan Union would continue. But MacDonald appeared to be of a different mind — he wanted to listen to the views of the Malays. He came to agree with Gent that the Union was not workable and that a Federation of Malaya as proposed by the Malays was needed instead. When MacDonald eventually saw that the Malayan Union plan was dead, he recommended that the Colonial Office accept the Federation proposal. This was a complete and quite unexpected reversal of British policy for post-war Malaya.

A cohesive federal government was therefore formed and the states regained nearly all the powers they had when they were protectorates. But now, after what had happened in 1946, their desire to be independent of the British as well as the new federal government was more pronounced. Their state councils were headed by Chief Ministers or *Menteri Besar,* nominated by the respective Rulers. Conscious of their autonomy and power, and the duty that went with them, they insisted on having a say in the decisions taken by the federal authorities.

The Federation initially recognised mainly Malays as citizens. As a result, the number of Chinese and Indians who were eligible to vote made up only 11 per cent of the total number of voters in the 1955 Federation-wide elections for self-government. This was a startling contrast to the ratio of voters in the Malayan Union, where the proportion would have been roughly 50 per cent Malays and 50 per cent non-Malays. For me this was half a victory, half a solution. While the plight of the Malays had been addressed to some extent, the Federation had obviously disenfranchised most of the non-Malays. The Chinese formed the All-Malaya Council of Joint Action (AMCJA)[1] with Tun Tan Cheng Lock as leader to protest that the Federation had been formed after consultation almost exclusively with the Malays. The Indians on the other hand, were generally still focused mainly on India, which had become independent.

The Head of the Federal Government was still Gent, the British High Commissioner. He was to be assisted by a nominated Federal Executive Council and a Federal Legislative Council, but the High Commissioner could overrule both councils.

Soon after the Federation of Malaya was inaugurated, the Malayan Communist Party (MCP) decided to mount an armed struggle to wrest the country from the British. The majority of Chinese had always been much more interested in the political goings-on in China than the events in

141

---

[1] The AMCJA was a union of mainly Chinese and Indian non-governmental organisations that pursued independence for Malaya and citizenship for the Chinese and Indians.

British Malaya. They did not regard the country as their home and pledged no allegiance to it.

On every Chinese festival day, the local Chinese would fly the Chinese flag from their shop windows. They had actively supported the setting up of the Chinese Republic by Dr Sun Yat-sen. Aware of this backing, the revolutionary leader even visited and stayed in Penang and funds were collected to finance his struggle. Only a few Baba, or Straits Chinese,[2] thought of Malaya as their home.

But by this time, communist rumblings had begun in China and filtered to Malaya. Once again, the British underestimated the enemy. It seemed to me that the only history they remembered was their grand old Empire, and not their recent defeat at the hands of a newly developed Asian nation. They genuinely did not believe that the communist insurgents would succeed. But soon the guerrillas were mounting hundreds of attacks against civilians and military targets.

Gent was forced to declare a state of emergency. Despite this, the guerrillas were able to mount attacks throughout the country. Malay animosity towards the Chinese impeded the political progress of the Federation towards self-government. It was unclear how the three main communities could work together. People were thinking of a single party which everyone, from all communities, might join, but that was not feasible. So the Federation arrangements which preserved Malay identity and centrality, and excluded the Chinese and Indians, prevailed.

Gent was regarded as weak and incapable of tackling the insurgency. He also bore the stigma of responsibility for the demise of the Malayan Union. When the communists surfaced with ferocious violence, the British planters and miners campaigned through the British-owned *Straits Times* for Gent's removal and the appointment of a "Supremo" — a supreme commander responsible for both the civil administration and the conduct of the war against the terrorists. The way to meeting their demands was opened by

142

---

[2]   The British Colonial Authorities in India established the Straits Settlements (made up of Penang, Malacca and Singapore) as a single administrative unit in 1826. The descendents of Chinese traders who married local Malay women and settled in the settlements were known as Baba (men) and Nyonya (women), or Straits Chinese.

fate: Gent was killed in an air crash and in 1949, was replaced by Sir Henry Gurney. Gurney had served in Palestine — where the Jews had adopted terror tactics against the British — and so had some experience with guerrilla warfare. He brought in 500 British police sergeants who were serving in Palestine to combat the problem, but this raised the matter of status. In the Malayan Police the British sergeants would have had to serve under Malay officers. This was not acceptable to the British Government and so to close the gap, the sergeants were given the rank of Police Lieutenants, a rank that had not previously existed. Naturally, they were not able to integrate smoothly into the force. Later, many of them were promoted to the rank of Deputy Superintendent of Police, which enabled them to outrank Malayan Police Inspectors and Assistant Superintendents. Nor were the police and the army able to work together either — Colonel W. N. Gray, the Commissioner of Police who was also from Palestine, was particular about his authority over the police force and did not cooperate with the officers of the military forces.

Things were not going well at all for the Government. The MCP had announced the setting up of the Malayan Peoples' Liberation Army (MPLA) and actively tried to recruit Malays and Indians. But they had little success and, in the end, the MPLA remained an almost exclusively Chinese force. One of the very few Malays who joined was Shamsiah Fakeh. She ended up living for many years in China but during the 1990s, our Government allowed her to return to Malaysia in her old age. She passed away in 2008.

Despite measures to eradicate the communist threat, including the establishment of New Villages to cut off their food supply, the number of guerrilla attacks remained high. The members of the "War Councils" at federal, state and district levels were kept busy with briefings on the progress of the war, the number and the location of the guerrilla attacks and the campaign to get the people, especially the Chinese, to back the war effort. The hearts and minds of the people had to be won if the guerrillas were to be defeated.

The Colonial Government's pressing problems were not simply military but also broadly political. They had to manage the political activities and seek to reconcile the demands of the different communities. After leading the AMCJA, Tun Tan launched the Malayan Chinese Association in 1949. Now called the Malaysian Chinese Association, the MCA is today a major component party of the ruling Barisan Nasional alliance. At the time I didn't think much of its chances. I thought it would be difficult for the Chinese, who were divided between the communists and the pro-Kuomintang Nationalists, to work together politically. Tun Tan was a very prominent Chinese and it was natural for him to lead the movement. He had considerable influence over the Chinese, even though, as a Straits Chinese, he could speak only Malay and English.

Irked by all this political strife, the British had appointed Malcolm MacDonald Commissioner-General for Southeast Asia in May 1948. He was able to bring a few of the community leaders together through the Communities Liaison Committee.

After Dato' Onn Jaafar left UMNO in 1951 to set up his Independence of Malaya Party (IMP), Tunku Abdul Rahman assumed leadership in August that year. The Tunku's reputation preceded him and most people who were politically active knew of him. He and his brother Tunku Yaacob were known in Kedah for trying to promote Malay small businesses and for their concern for the well-being of poor Malays generally. Besides being my brother's friend, I also came to know him when I had earlier invited him to watch a stage play by the Kesatuan Pemuda Melayu Kedah (Kedah Malay Youth Association).

144

During the protest against the Malayan Union the Tunku had voiced his objection to the proposal. He helped draft the petition by the Kedah Malay Association to the Colonial Secretary, registering the people's' protest. His heart was obviously in the right place with regard to Malay interests and aspirations and, accordingly, his assumption of the leadership of UMNO was generally well accepted.

The Tunku began to talk about independence for Malaya almost as soon as he took over. The British were displeased, to say the least. Their candidate to win over Malay support was now encouraging freedom from their rule. They had also wanted him to get UMNO to relax its view with regard to Chinese and Indian citizenship but instead, the party, with the Tunku at its head, rejected this intended policy outright.

One month after the Tunku became leader of UMNO, Gurney was killed in a guerrilla ambush on his way for a holiday in Fraser's Hill. A new High Commissioner had to be appointed, not just to deal with the new leadership of the Malays but also to implement the strategies worked out by Gurney and Director of Operations Sir Harold Briggs against the insurgents. The state of emergency had been extended and the plan to relocate the squatters to New Villages approved. But without a decisive High Commissioner, there was little chance of a victorious war, despite all the careful attention and planning.

In 1951, 531 civilians and 504 soldiers and policemen were killed. The British planters and miners again demanded the appointment of a "Supremo" to deal with the political and military situation. In February 1952, General Sir Gerald Templer arrived with comprehensive powers over the civil and military administration. He had a tough job — the political problems alone were highly complex and required an accurate combination of diplomacy and firmness. He also had to carry out and extend Gurney's plans for social and economic development. To win the support of the Malays and other races, Templer promised to hold elections for towns and municipalities, the states and finally, for the Federal Legislative Council. The last could result in self-government.

The British Government had at last realised the seriousness of the situation in the Federation. It promised powerful and continuing help in defeating the guerrillas and attaining the objective of a united Malayan nation. Templer had a productive, two-year tenure as High Commissioner. His term marked the turning point in the war against the insurgents as well as progress towards representative government for the Federation of Malaya. Templer's term of office ended in June 1954. Elections to municipal and town councils had already begun during his time, but the British were not yet ready for an elected Federal Legislative Council.

In 1952, elections were held for the Kuala Lumpur Municipal Council. This election saw UMNO working with the MCA for the first time, and the branch-level alliance of the two parties won a majority of the seats. But more significantly, none of the multiracial parties — including Dato' Onn's IMP — won any seats, which meant the formula for Malay/non-

Malay political cooperation seemed to be the most acceptable course to the different races. One of the most positive features was that in the coalition, parties did not lose their distinct ethno-communal or separate racial identities while working for the common good.

The Tunku was quick to appreciate its political usefulness. After the 1952 Municipal Election he worked hard towards broadening it on a nationwide basis. When subsequent town council elections were held, the new coalition, called the Alliance Party, did admirably and won most of the seats. The Tunku began to press for early elections for the Federal Legislative Council. The British Government was reluctant to let the locals control the council as this would effectively mean self-rule, so they refused to set a date for elections. Templer, however, had promised that there would be a democratic government in Malaya.

The Tunku went to the United Kingdom with T. H. Tan of the MCA, who was also Secretary-General of the Alliance. The Colonial Secretary, Oliver Lyttleton, refused to see them at first. But the Tunku knew a lawyer and soldier, David R. Rees-Williams, who had long served in Malaya but returned to England and had been elected a Labour Member of Parliament. Through the Rees-Williams' intervention, the Tunku saw the Colonial Secretary. But Lyttleton thought that it was too early for elections to be held in Malaya.

The Tunku came back disappointed but not defeated. He continued to pressure Templer's successor, Sir Donald MacGillivray, for elections to be held as soon as possible. Finally, the High Commissioner agreed and decided that elections would be held in 1955 for just 52 of the 98 seats in the Federal Legislative Council (the remaining members would be named by the High Commissioner). Misreading the local situation yet again, the British thought that it would be impossible for any of the Malayan parties to gain an absolute majority.

The Tunku protested and demanded a bigger number of elected members, if not an entirely elected body. He was finally persuaded to accept the 52 elected members but, in exchange, he managed to obtain one condition: that the party with the largest number of elected members would be consulted over the appointment of the nominated members.

At that time, the number of Chinese who were eligible to vote was very small. Moreover, the number of constituencies where they made up the majority was insufficient for the MCA to play a meaningful role in the election. In a bold step, the Tunku persuaded UMNO to give up Malay-majority constituencies to the MCA and the Malayan Indian Congress (MIC).[3] That UMNO agreed to it was remarkable. What was even more remarkable was that Malay voters supported the Chinese MCA and Indian MIC candidates, frequently against Malay candidates from the Pan-Malayan Islamic Party (PMIP).

Dato' Onn had dissolved his multi-racial IMP and instead set up Party Negara, a virulently anti-Chinese party. Together with the PMIP, Party Negara was expected to draw Malay votes away from the Alliance. Instead, and despite everyone's scepticism, the Alliance won an astounding 51 of the 52 seats that were contested. Left with no choice after this enormous triumph, the Colonial Government had to allow the Alliance under Tunku Abdul Rahman to form a government in Malaya.

Prior to this, the British had introduced a member system of government in which a few selected members of the nominated Legislative Council were given the responsibility of overseeing certain government departments and answering for these departments in the Council. The High Commissioner nominated to these positions prominent figures in the Malay, Chinese, Tamil and Ceylon Tamil communities who enjoyed some official confidence.

147

The Tunku, Dato' Onn, Tun Dr Ismail Abdul Rahman and Tun H.S. Lee had been among the members so appointed. Upon the Alliance's victory, these nominees were replaced by nominations made by the Tunku in the Federal Executive Council, of which the Tunku was Chief Minister.

The first phase of the Federation of Malaya had been initiated upon the end of the Malayan Union in February 1948. Now began the second phase, during which we would become a self-governing people. The British High Commissioner effectively remained the head of state; however, as Chief Minister, the Tunku was the head of government and he lost no time in showing his independence. One of his first announcements was to

---

3    The Malaysian Indian Congress was established in 1946 and was one of the founding member parties
     in the Alliance.

say that he was willing to meet Chin Peng, head of the MCP, to negotiate a ceasefire. In a radical move away from British policy, he also offered amnesty to the insurgents.

This rattled the British badly. They were completely against recognising the MCP, let alone seeing them play a role in Malayan politics. But the Tunku was adamant.

Together with Tun Tan and David Marshall,[4] the Singapore Chief Minister, the Tunku met Chin Peng and his right-hand man Rashid Maidin in Baling, in rural Kedah. Chin Peng wanted recognition for the MCP and the right to retain the arms they possessed. But the Tunku demanded the disbanding of the MCP and the surrender of all arms possessed by the guerrillas. Chin Peng refused and returned to the jungle to carry on the fight.

This meeting was a great victory for the Tunku. With one deft stroke, he proved to all that he was no British puppet. Henceforth Chin Peng and the MCP would be fighting against Malayans, not as freedom fighters of the country and its people. In effect, Chin Peng made the case as to why the British might still need to stay: to counter armed resistance and insurrection. For all his anti-colonial rhetoric, Chin Peng and his stubborn followers showed that it was the MCP that was now prolonging British colonialism. That put paid to MCP's charges that the Tunku and the new national political forces that he was leading were nothing but British puppets. It was Chin Peng who was now placed on the defensive. There was no place, the Tunku affirmed, for a party that used force and terror in the politics of Malaya. The Tunku's credibility as a leader of Malayans of all races was sealed and from that time on, the British had to take him and his quest for independence seriously.

But the Rulers were apprehensive about independence for the Federation of Malaya. They had regained their positions and had obtained the right to choose the *Menteri Besar* or Chief Minister of their respective states. Democracy as promoted by the British and espoused by the *rakyat* would put an abrupt end to feudal autocracy. The nine Malay rulers — who all had equal status — had been prepared to accept the British High

---

[4] A renowned criminal lawyer, David Marshall was the leader of the Singapore Labour Front and became the first Chief Minister of Singapore in 1955.

Commissioner as the head of state as he represented the British monarch. But an independent Malaya could accept neither the High Commissioner nor even the British monarch herself in that office.

India had had a similar problem soon after it became independent in 1947. It, however, resolved the problem of hereditary rulers by taking away their titles and reducing them to ordinary citizens. Dr Rajendra Prasad, a commoner, was chosen to be president. A commoner president breached no royal protocol after that. In Indonesia — especially in many parts of Sumatra whose traditional political systems were Muslim Malay sultanates rather than Javanese Hindu-Buddhist sacred states — this problem of protocol was solved by more drastic measures: murder. Royal families were assassinated, and the use of royal titles forbidden.

These developments posed the question: what would happen to the nine ruling houses if Malaya were to become independent? Could there ever be a commoner head of state? It may seem improbable now, but such a course of development was not unthinkable then. Earlier, UMNO had proposed a commoner Deputy High Commissioner, which was rejected by the Rulers. Much royal awkwardness was felicitously avoided when the 1955 elections installed a prominent member of the Kedah royal family as Chief Minister of Malaya. Still, the Rulers knew that it might just as easily have been a non-royal.

As Chief Minister, Tunku Abdul Rahman did not precede the Rulers in terms of protocol, but a commoner head of state was a different matter. Until these issues of protocol and status of the Rulers were settled to their satisfaction, they would not support independence. And if they did not, the resulting confrontation between the *rakyat* and the Rulers might delay independence at best and even cause prolonged political upheaval.

Meanwhile, the insurgency continued and the fight against the guerrillas might have lost momentum, and even focus, if indeed a confrontation erupted between the *rakyat* and the Rulers. Certainly, there were loyal feudalists among the *rakyat* who would throw their weight behind the Rulers at any price, yet the ardent champions of independence would not back down. The ensuing fight would drain important resources and undermine political resolve in the anti-guerrilla war. The fact that the Tunku was of royal blood reassured the Rulers that republicanism would not be espoused by the newly-elected government. Had it been headed by Dato' Onn or another commoner, the path to independence may not have been quite as smooth.

When the Tunku proposed that an Alliance delegation should go to the United Kingdom to demand independence, the Rulers also decided to send their own separate delegation along. Agreement regarding independence had yet to be reached. The two delegations went by sea so that they could meet and iron out their differences before they arrived. The Rulers named four *Menteri Besar,* headed by Datuk Panglima Bukit Gantang of Perak, as their representatives, while the Tunku headed the Alliance delegation.

Aligning their views was crucial. If the two groups presented differing views, the British would have pounced upon any disagreement as a good excuse to delay independence. Fortunately, during the sea voyage the two delegations managed to reach a common stand, which respectfully took account of the positions of both parties. In essence, while sailing to London, the Rulers' representatives and the Tunku as head of the elected Government resolved the problem of the head of state and the positions of the Rulers in the independent Federation of Malaya.

There would be a "Paramount Ruler" — known today in our Constitution as the Yang di-Pertuan Agong, or simply, the Agong — elected by the Rulers from among themselves for a term of five years to serve as a Constitutional Monarch without executive authority. He would be the living symbol, in Malay cultural terms and form, of our state and national sovereignty.

The Government, the two sides also agreed, would be based roughly on the Westminster model. There would be an elected Parliament and a Chief Executive or Prime Minister named by the Paramount Ruler from among the elected members, based upon the Paramount Ruler's judgment about who had the support of the majority of the elected members of the national legislature. The Prime Minister would be assisted by a Cabinet of Ministers. Meanwhile, each state would have as its chief executive a Chief Minister or *Menteri Besar*. He was to be chosen by the state's Ruler from among the members of the elected state councils, again based on which member held the majority's confidence. The Chief Minister would be assisted by a State Executive Council, nominated by the Chief Minister from among the elected members.

The independent Federation of Malaya would therefore be a constitutional monarchy with a parliamentary democracy. The elected government's term of office would be a maximum of five years, though a government may at any time request the Paramount Ruler to dissolve Parliament and hold a General Election for a new Parliament and government.

Armed with these ideas, the two parties were prepared to meet the British. The Federation of Malaya Constitutional Conference was held in London between January and February of 1956. The British remained reluctant but finally agreed that Malaya would be granted independence in 1957, "if possible". Otherwise, independence would be given in 1959. The later date was perhaps intended by the British to hold something back and give themselves one more card to play, should further difficulties and disagreements erupt between any of the key players in the new Malayan politics. Instead, it acted as an incentive for everyone to resolve their differences so that there would be no excuse for the British to delay granting independence to Malaya.

The Tunku returned to Malaya in a glow of triumph. There was a huge gathering in Malacca where the Tunku was accompanied by the Rulers' representative, the Datuk Panglima Bukit Gantang. There, the Tunku announced the results of the Independence negotiation. He told the crowd the British said that Independence would be granted in 1957, "if possible", but the *rakyat* rejected the caveat outright and demanded that Independence be given that year.

On 31 August 1957, at the stroke of midnight, the once-mighty Union Jack was lowered from a special flagpole erected in front of the Federal Secretariat building in Kuala Lumpur. So began the third and final phase of the Federation of Malaya, the culminating phase of *Merdeka* or full national independence.

On that day I was in Alor Star — travel was not easy at that time so I had decided not to go to Kuala Lumpur for the celebrations. Hasmah had also given birth to our first child Marina just a few months before. But even in Alor Star, buildings had been repainted to mark the occasion and the whole town was decorated with lights.

To be honest, none of us could fully understand what would come next, now that we were an independent nation. We expected a change of guard and the opportunity for self-government (even so, the Tunku had already been Chief Minister of Malaya for two years by then) but beyond that, we could not see what else would be different. The idea that it was now time to build the country did not occur to most people; in fact, there were many among us who doubted that we could make a success of Independence. I myself was unsure if we could tackle the complexities of government. How wrong we all turned out to be.

# Chapter 12:
## From Theory To Reality

After graduating in 1954 I returned to Alor Star for a short while before I was posted to the Penang General Hospital to do my housemanship[1] in medicine and surgery.

I was paid $400 per month for my post-qualification statutory housemanship training. The allowance indicated that I was not just being trained but was also serving the Colonial Government. I was therefore subject to restrictions imposed on all government servants, which included not being involved in either politics or business. Even though I was keen on UMNO, I accepted these terms without fuss because I knew the training would be invaluable. There is always a wide gap between theory and practice, and in medicine, it was sure to be very wide indeed.

Young doctors often tell stories of how gruelling housemanship is, and I can confirm how true these stories are. My work schedule included a 24-hour stretch of duty every other day for two weeks of every month. This was just for medicine — for surgery, I was on duty every other week. Night duty was especially onerous as patients came in at all hours. Housemen frequently got no sleep at all.

I doubt that patients got the best care under a doctor who had had no sleep the night before, but it was very good training for me. When the time came to set up a practice of my own, there was no telling the kind of hours I would have to work, nor the awkward times at which I would have to make house calls. My mother had been right: to be a good and dedicated doctor, you had to give up the luxury of sleep.

There were other costs and sacrifices. The houseman's allowance that year was increased by one dollar to $401. This lavish "raise" meant that we were exempt from having to contribute to the Employees Provident Fund (EPF)[2] and therefore our pay was not cut for this purpose. More to the point, the Government did not have to contribute its six per cent share on behalf of

---

[1] The equivalent of an internship.

[2] Malaysians working in the private sector contribute a percentage of their salaries to the EPF, which invests the money for contributors' benefit in retirement.

its employees to the EPF. We were now not pensionable for the houseman's year and were also not entitled to payment by the EPF upon retirement. That one-dollar increase was no gain for us, despite the extra dollar in our hands. The Colonial Government was very mindful of its money.

In those days, only Europeans had the honour of being specialists and we were in awe of them. One of the surgeons, who I remember only as Mr Campbell,[3] was famous for his ferocious temper. If the wrong instrument was handed to him during surgery, his response was to yell and throw the instrument onto the floor. Everyone was terrified of his fury and I would avoid assisting him when he operated. I did my best to stay out of his sight, though it was not always possible.

Later in Alor Star I worked under a Mr Frazer, who was mild and consistent where Campbell was wildly temperamental. Given the wrong instrument, Frazer would mumble his disapproval but would still try to use the instrument. I learnt far more from him than from Campbell. It had been drummed into us that surgeons (much like artists) were entitled to temper tantrums. One of the best surgeons in the UK was a Mr Hunter, who was also notorious for his temper. He used to say that since he had a heart condition, he would very likely be killed by the people who angered him. Apparently, he did die of a heart attack during one of his fits of temper.

154

I learnt one thing from all these tantrums, and that was *not* to lose my temper. It was difficult at first. Most people tend to react strongly to anything that they dislike, but I find that this annoys others and doesn't achieve anything. Certainly in Campbell's case, his violent temper didn't help him succeed in teaching us because we would run away from him. I normally went to the other operating theatre as I couldn't be seen to be doing nothing. So it was a tricky business.

I have since learned to walk away from anger — at least, I try to. Losing my parliamentary seat in 1969, for example, was painful, but what I felt was more sadness than anger. Rather than lose my temper, I try to reason things out. But it is hard to hold one's temper when others won't listen to reason.

---

[3] The tradition of addressing surgeons as Mr or Ms, not Doctor, is an entrenched part of British surgical practice.

I have learnt to be more deliberate. Calm, not anger, ensures effective action. Dramatic gestures don't work and are unnecessary. By and large, I think I have succeeded not to be like those ill-tempered men. Over many years, as a doctor and then a politician, I have interacted with an unusually large number of people every day and I was always able to get on with my staff, colleagues and friends — and even my enemies — without getting overly angry.

In the end, my main concern during those sleep-deprived years as a houseman was my inability to go to Singapore to visit Hasmah, who was still completing her degree. For one whole year I had to be satisfied with words on paper. Though these letters were precious and remain so to this day, they were no substitute for actually seeing her. I only saw Hasmah when I went for my convocation with two of my sisters in 1954.

Fortunately, I was deeply immersed in my work. I was keen on the practice of medicine, especially surgery. I hardly ever called the surgery registrar when I was on duty. I did most minor surgeries myself and I owe much to the hospital assistants who showed me how to deal with the cases and carry out those surgical techniques with finesse. I believe I am quite dextrous and this added to my enthusiasm. Of all the medical work, surgery gave me the greatest satisfaction. Unlike treatments using just medication, with surgery the results can be seen almost immediately. That suited my temperament because I like to see results. When I was only a young Medical Officer, I performed complex procedures such as amputations, appendectomies and intestinal resections.

155

In Langkawi,[4] I once had to operate on a strangulated hernia. The patient was the owner of the Hai Huat fishing company and he was brought in early one morning from Pulau Tuba, one of the Langkawi islands. There was no operating theatre in Langkawi Hospital then, only the examination table in the outpatient's room. I could have sent him to Alor Star by fishing boat, where he could go to the General Hospital, but the journey would have taken more than 10 hours and he was already in great distress. So I decided to operate in the outpatient treatment room on the examination table. I had no silk sutures and had to use catgut.

---

4     An island off the state of Kedah.

I thought it was quite a simple thing to do, even though I didn't have all the special equipment and materials. I was quite confident and the family obviously trusted me. I just told them that the operation had to be done. The patient survived and lived for many years after. His wife still sends salted fish to me whenever I go to Langkawi.

But my most harrowing experience took place when I was the Medical Officer on duty at the Alor Star General Hospital. It was a Friday and officially the weekend in Kedah, so all the surgeons and other doctors had gone to Penang. I had not expected any serious emergencies but then a woman in the maternity ward suddenly went into labour. She was almost full-term but the baby was not positioned at the birth passage. I had to make a decision right there that the best course of action would be to carry out a Caesarean section. Thankfully, I was assisted by Hasmah, who by then was my wife. As there was no sophisticated intravenous anaesthesia in those days, we had to drip ethyl chloride and ether onto a mask on the patient's face. It was all quite primitive and you had to be careful that just enough was given. After she was under, I made the cut. To my horror, I discovered that it was an ectopic pregnancy as the foetus had developed outside the uterine cavity. Ectopic pregnancies are very rare and few doctors would deal with even one case over the span of an entire career.

There was an awful lot of blood. I tried to tie up the blood vessels but I could not stop the copious bleeding. I made every attempt but the child did not survive and neither did the mother. They were the only patients I ever lost on the operating table while I was in government service. It was very sobering and deeply upsetting for me and Hasmah.

I knew the woman's husband personally — he ran a printing shop in Alor Star. I felt very bad for him and was very apologetic. The husband did not blame me at all but if it had happened today I probably would have been sued. Attitudes have changed considerably since that time, and litigation has become quite a regular recourse for those who feel wronged.

Perhaps this change is a good thing. But having to insure against malpractice has increased the cost of treatment. Doctors in America often refuse to treat accident cases or to volunteer their help when fellow passengers take sick on airline flights for fear of litigation. To avoid litigation they often order unnecessary and costly laboratory tests. The human touch has been lost and treating sick people has become just another business.

Overall, surgery gave me much satisfaction. My hands are still very steady though I am no longer qualified to practise, having been away from medicine for over 30 years now. I miss working as a doctor but it is surgery I miss the most. Having said that, I'm not sure I could manage or would like the kind of sophisticated surgery being done now using highly specialised equipment. For me surgery was a human skill and it enabled me to give much to others: life, recovery, restored health.

In 1957, the year of Independence, I left government service to set up my own practice. Many colleagues and friends advised against it but I went ahead. There were few private practitioners in Alor Star in those days and mine was in fact the first clinic to be established by a Malay doctor in the state. I called my clinic Maha Klinik, short for Mahathir and Hasmah, although my wife never joined me in private practice. She worked as a contract medical officer in the Government. For some reason she was never put on a pensionable scheme, so even though she worked for the Government for many years, she draws no pension now. I left my practice when I became a Minister and my partner Dr Mohamad Yaakob took over. Both he and the clinic are still there.

157

Although I was quite successful medically and professionally, I did not run my practice well. I left the management and the fee collection to two of my brothers-in-law, who would lend the clinic's money to friends. I made about $2,000 per month — not much, but more than I would have earned as a Government Medical Officer. They were paid a starting salary of $730 per month but by the time I joined, the yearly increment in pay was $30, so by 1957 I was getting $790. Private practice income, therefore, was a great improvement.

I was quite a popular doctor and the number of my patients — Chinese, Malays and Indians — kept increasing. I did not like to stop to rest as long as there were patients waiting. In the first few months it was possible to see all the waiting patients before breaking for lunch. I did not go home but had a quick lunch in my consultation room. Chicken chop was my daily fare and as soon as I finished eating, I would start seeing patients again because I felt guilty making them wait. I cannot understand how counter clerks can chat with one another and ignore the waiting public. When the number of patients increased I simply worked longer hours and after that, I would do house calls.

In one instance, a well-intentioned patient said he did not want to bother me too much because he was not suffering from anything serious. So instead of coming to the clinic, he decided to have me see him at home. It would have taken me 10 minutes to attend to him in the clinic; instead, I had to travel for two hours to and from his house. One can be killed by such acts of kindness.

As the years passed, I found myself stuck in my clinic for the whole day and long after other people had gone home. Once I got into my clinic at 9am I did not see daylight again for the rest of the day. My world seemed to consist only of nights. Even weekends were not mine, as I would make house calls to see bedridden patients. I played no games and hardly had time to go to the cinema. I was also not able to be involved in politics as much as I would have liked.

One unattractive aspect of a doctor's career is obvious but rarely mentioned — most of the people I came into contact with were sick. Some were dying, and some died in front of me during treatment. A close friend, my senior in school who was an athlete, died one day of a heart attack and I was called to certify his death. There was very little one could do for cardiac failure in those days. I was so affected by his death that I wept silently. Some of my friends noticed and I heard one of them remark that I was crying. But another countered him and said it could not be, because I was a doctor and therefore used to seeing people die. I did not disabuse him of this idea because I wanted to appear strong, but as time went by I found myself more and more prone to such breakdowns. It was a symptom of being burnt out, of having no release or let-up from the life of a doctor.

I generally feel very strongly about things. I try to control any show of emotion because I see it as a lack of manliness, but very often I fail. Even today when something affects me, I get a tight feeling in my chest and my voice breaks. When this happens during a speech, I choke and stop speaking. I feel betrayed by this weakness, by my own lack of a certain toughness and strength. This happens frequently when I talk or even think of the Malays and their failures. I get emotional and my tears well up. Hasmah tries to console me and says it is normal to break down when one feels disappointed or melancholic, but still I continue to feel ashamed that I cannot keep a lid on my emotions.

Ironically, I have a reputation for being tough, even ruthless. Maybe I am. If one wants to get things done one must be single-minded and determined. When I was Prime Minister, I wanted to redeem the honour of the Malays, Malaysians and Malaysia. I wanted to see Malaysia and Malaysians proving themselves to be as good as any other nation or people. From the beginning I knew that it would require a great sense of purpose and a willingness to fend off all challenges. It must have been these qualities that made me seem hard and uncompromising when I was Prime Minister, for nobody can succeed in politics if they do not have a tough skin. People would not know or suspect what lies beneath. What I did not want to show was how easily touched I was by tragedy and human suffering. When those feelings of compassion came to me in public situations, I would try to prevent that familiar choking and tightness in my chest.

159

A doctor is never far from the calamities that affect people. I have seen people, frequently relatives and friends I had known from when they were young and healthy, getting strokes and becoming unable to speak or move their limbs. Sometimes, you can read the deep sadness in their eyes as they try in vain to get their limbs to move and their lips to form words. The brain remains alive and active but the body is inflexible and unmoving. Their frustration is unimaginable.

Some died quickly, and in many ways, it was fortunate. Others would linger in this sad state for months and perhaps even years, cared for by their loved ones. For the patient, death must come as a relief. But for those left behind, the finality is staggering, even if you have strong faith in the hereafter. There is just no coming back.

These thoughts developed in my mind, probably because of my huge exposure to those who were ill and dying. Working day and night at my own clinic, depression slowly set in.

I thought of the inevitable deaths of the ones I loved, of my father and mother, the older members of my family and my friends. Invariably, I thought of my own death, of being struck with the diseases that my patients had. I thought of heart attacks and strokes and the helplessness that would follow. I grew more and more morbid.

I finally decided that I needed to take some leave. In 1960, I closed my clinic for a week to go to Hong Kong for a holiday with my wife. In those days no locums could be found. Not having someone to take care of my patients gnawed at my conscience but I had to get away or I knew I would have gone mad.

We had never been beyond Malayan borders other than to Singapore and a half-day trip to Haadyai in southern Thailand. Hong Kong amazed me. There were so many well-dressed people in coats and ties. Jeans and casuals were unknown then. I saw my first shopping complex at the Miramar[5] but most of the shops were two or three-storey buildings lining the streets. There were Chinese tailors running to and from the hotels with half-finished suits as they tried to meet their 24-hour deadlines.

I met a number of Chinese Malayan doctors who were working in Hong Kong and they took me to plush Chinese restaurants. They had formed a dining club to try new restaurants every week. They told me they never went to the same restaurant twice in a week, because there would always be at least one new restaurant in town. I could feel the vigour of Hong Kong keenly and I wondered whether Malaya would ever be like that.

The following year Hasmah and I decided to go to Japan, which was still considered an exotic place in those days. After the Japanese defeat in World War II, they were forced to adopt a democratic parliamentary system with a constitutional monarchy, like Britain. The Japanese had become Europeanised and they had long discarded their kimonos to wear coats, ties and dresses. But it was only a cosmetic change — culturally and intellectually, they were still very Japanese and very polite. In the event of a minor car accident, both drivers got out and bowed to each other before getting back into their cars and driving away. The Nissan cars they were

---

5    The Miramar is centrally located in the heart of Hong Kong's tourist and shopping centre, Tsim Sha Tsui.

using looked like poor copies of the British Hillman. There were old trucks and three-wheeled cars that rattled noisily along the poorly paved streets.

In the 1960s and 1970s, Japan was booming. It was making a surprisingly rapid recovery from the ruins of war. It was, in fact, becoming one huge factory, producing all kinds of manufactured goods and obviously beefing up its economy through exports. The dynamism was palpable. I still remembered the atrocities committed during the Japanese Occupation of Malaya, but I also had a growing admiration for the Japanese. I thought that if we could be like them in our sense of hard work, innovation and determination, what a country Malaya would become!

During our visit it was clear Japan was still in the midst of reconstructing after the devastation wrought by the Allied bombings. There were still a few wooden shops in the Ginza shopping district.[6] An elevated highway was being built from Tokyo to Haneda Airport in readiness for the Tokyo Olympics.[7] In those days few countries could afford or were eligible to host the Olympics but Japan had won the right to organise the Games in 1964. There was no great fuss, no dramatic reporting of rival bids to play host to the Games as, at the time, few countries saw it as a prestigious opportunity. But Japan had decided to host the Olympics to showcase its new economic strength and cultural integrity, and to symbolise its full return to international acceptability following World War II.

161

Japan was returning and Asia was again rising. Not everybody saw or could accept this, but some of us from Asia glimpsed this development and its significance, perhaps a little earlier than the rest of the world. Rather than feeling threatened or resentful, we admired what Japan was doing and, if it succeeded, we would be ready to learn from its example. What I saw during this trip, for example, left a permanent impression on me and influenced me when I became Prime Minister.

There was activity everywhere in Japan and roads and buildings were being constructed at a furious pace. Japanese industries were being revived and were already producing transistor radios and personal movie cameras. Our

---

6     Ginza is today Tokyo's most famous upmarket shopping district.

7     Japan was the first Asian country to host the Olympics in 1964. The country spent some USD3 billion on facilities for the Games.

embassy friends told us not to buy local products in Japan as their choice items were all set aside for export. The Japan of that time had not yet overcome its reputation for producing cheap and shoddy goods. We were witnesses to its first steps towards becoming the cutting-edge electrical goods and electronics giant that it is today. Now, Japanese products are innovative, highly-respected and prestigious.

We also visited Osaka on that trip, flying there on a propeller-driven plane. One of our reasons for flying was that we were told we could see the famous Mount Fuji on the way. The Japanese steward, in all earnestness, wished us a "good fright". Hasmah and I had a good laugh. The Japanese cannot pronounce "L" and invariably substitute it with "R". The results can be quite hilarious and we repeated "good fright" many times along the way.

When the steward announced that we were passing Mount Fuji we looked out the window of the aircraft. There were snow-topped mountains but none looked like the majestic Mount Fuji we had seen in picture books.

Then the passenger in the aisle seat next to Hasmah, who was obviously Japanese, quietly said to Hasmah, "Up there, Madame." Mount Fuji is 12,000 feet high. We were flying at only 10,000 feet in the small aircraft.

After our great amusement over having a good fright, we were now deeply embarrassed. There we were making fun of the steward, thinking that the Japanese passengers around us could not speak English. All through that time, our neighbour could clearly speak the language perfectly. But, even after hearing all the things we had said, he was good enough to show us what we had been looking for. After that, we learnt to be far more careful when speaking in front of foreigners.

Like Tokyo, Osaka was booming. With the help of a Japanese guide we toured the city and its outskirts. Even then, there were factories everywhere. A Matsushita factory was built right in the middle of a rice field. I remember thinking that that would not be allowed in Malaya as we are very strict about land use. Padi land would not be used for anything else other than for the planting of padi.

The embassy officials had told me that travel between Tokyo and Osaka by train was very pleasant as we could see more of the country. I was eager to take the train back from Osaka but could not get seats. Already, Japanese trains were carrying full loads of passengers.

I had a friend from the Takeda Pharmaceutical Company, a Mr Rio Yonemoto, who was sent by the company to meet us at Osaka Airport. It was then tiny with an ordinary building as a terminal. He told us that the Japan National Railway was planning to put a very fast train (to be called the Bullet Train) on the Tokyo – Osaka route. The current train trip took six hours; the new train would take just three.

But it was the trains at Tokyo Station that fascinated me most during that first trip to Japan. Hasmah and I stood just outside the station and watched the trains as they arrived and departed. As soon as one train left the station, even before its tail end was out, another would arrive. It was an endless stream and it was really quite breathtaking for I had never seen anything like it. The Tokyo train station must have been the busiest in the world. This impression was confirmed when I visited Europe later, as no European station showed such frenetic activity. Victoria Station in London had stationary trains and for long intervals there were no trains moving in or out of the station.

163

During my frequent visits to Japan in later years I never ceased to be amazed at the train service. Even on the train from Narita Airport to Tokyo, a distance of only 50km, I would pass more than a score of trains going in the opposite direction. When the Shinkansen or Bullet Trains passed each other in opposite directions at high speed, there would be a loud boom, probably caused by the two columns of air pushed by the trains hitting each other at the combined speed of nearly 600km an hour. Although the Swiss railway system is comparable, their trains are nowhere as frequent or as fast as in Japan. The French and Germans have also designed their own high-speed systems, but there are still not as many trains.

That scene of the Tokyo Station in 1961 implanted itself in my mind, never to be forgotten. For Malaya to have a similarly impressive railway was a dream.

Later as Prime Minister I tried hard to modernise the creaky Malayan Railways but I learnt that it could never be like the Japanese train system.

Still, I did manage to double-track and electrify the section between Seremban, south of Kuala Lumpur, and Rawang, north of Kuala Lumpur. The line to Port Klang was also double-tracked and electrified.

When I stepped down from office in October 2003, the Government was doing the same from Rawang to Ipoh. I had wanted something different: to my mind, the upgrading should have been done throughout the length of the country, beginning at Johor, our southernmost state, right up to the Thai border in the northern edge of the Peninsula. Through this, I wanted to make train travel popular again. Traffic on the highways, which was reaching the point of congestion, would then hopefully lessen. Perhaps people do not realise that trains are faster than aeroplanes for short journeys of 400km and less. Because they take you directly from one city centre to the other, the need to drive to and from the airport and to set aside time for security checks and airline check-ins are all eliminated.

A considerable amount of heavy freight, including car transporters and container carriers to and from the ports, can be taken off the road and be carried by train, further reducing highway congestion. Unfortunately, the Government which succeeded mine classified it as a "mega project", the subtext of which is "white elephant". The claim was that there was no more money to carry on with this track upgrade after my profligate ways. Nevertheless, I am glad that I stayed on long enough to modernise at least the short segment between Seremban and Rawang. Today the electric commuter trains are chock-full of passengers but the roads around Kuala Lumpur are still jammed. The rate at which multi-grade crossings are being built cannot keep up with the growth in the number of motor vehicles. Pollution in Kuala Lumpur is no longer due only to forest fires in Indonesia. It is caused by emissions from moving and stationary road vehicles. And the air quality in Kuala Lumpur is not going to get any better as under-priced foreign cars hit the roads.

These days as I have my breakfast on the veranda of my house at The Mines,[8] I can see ordinary passenger and goods trains, the electrified commuter trains and the wide-gauged Express Rail Link or ERL, which

---

[8]   The Mines is a residential area with a resort hotel and shopping centre, located about 25 minutes by car from Kuala Lumpur.

plies between Kuala Lumpur and the Kuala Lumpur International Airport, passing frequently in both directions. Some have said these trains were a waste of money, but I wonder how much it would cost to build these tracks and trains now — or later, when clogged roads will make travelling by car almost impossible. I try to imagine Kuala Lumpur without these trains and the Light Rail Transit System and I see only a big collection of stationary vehicles going nowhere.

In 1962, the year after we visited Japan, we took a three-month holiday to do a grand tour of Europe. There was still evidence of the widespread damage wrought by the war, but Europe was recovering fast. What impressed me about Europe was the grandeur of its cities. Despite the arrogance with which they had treated the rest of the world, the Europeans had undeniably built a great civilisation. They had built empires and extracted wealth from their foreign adventures. They had industrialised, engaged in trade with each other in Europe and with the rest of the world and achieved tremendous progress.

With this wealth they built cities where the streets were lined with beautiful, grand buildings. These were built hundreds of years ago in hard granite and other stone, while we in Malaya were still living in wooden houses easily destroyed by white ants or fire.

They have a sense of history, these Europeans. They build for the future, for the centuries to follow. They are careful to preserve what they already have and take pride in this heritage. The Palace of Versailles, for instance, was built by the Sun King, Louis XIV. His grandson Louis XVI lived a decadent life, not bothering that the population was starving. Eventually, the people revolted and the French Revolution saw him and his queen, Marie Antoinette, meet their fates at the guillotine. When we went on a tour of the Palace, the guide proudly pointed out the gilded panels and the long corridor of mirrors, the beautiful formal gardens and intricate fountains. It occurred to me that ironically, the French would have none of this to show if their kings and queens had not spent huge amounts of money on luxury. Yet the wayward ways of the royals are largely forgotten. Only their heritage remains. Although they may be strong republicans today, the French proudly preserve their feudal past.

Overall, our trip to Europe left me with questions that I was determined to resolve: why were they rich and developed? Why was their standard of living high? Could we be as rich and as developed?

In my childhood, I had regarded the Europeans as supermen, extraordinary people who could do everything that we could not do. But then the Japanese found a hole in their invincibility and proved that the Europeans could be defeated in war. My visit to Japan also proved that manufacturing and industry could be mastered by non-Europeans. Why, I wondered, couldn't Malays and other Malayans do the same?

I returned from these trips much refreshed. The depression had lifted and I was reconciled to my mortality. No one lives forever, so I decided to make the most of my time here. I spent time reflecting on what life was about. Was it just eating, drinking and being entertained? As a Muslim, I believe in the *akhirat*, the afterlife. But I simply cannot believe that Islam wants us to be insular and selfish, spending our lives to gain reward in the hereafter. Life could not just be about preparing for death.

166 Later, as I studied the Quran and the verified Hadith, I learnt that on earth one must contribute to the well-being of the Muslim *ummah*, or worldwide community of Muslims, and humankind as a whole. My spirits lifted and I could now see better how, as a doctor, I could contribute meaningfully to people's lives. My new insight enabled me to rethink my work, my life and how through them I might contribute something of value to something larger than myself.

I did not know it at that time, but another way would present itself in which I would be able to do something for people. When I returned from my trips to Japan and Europe, my mind was brimming with ideas. I brought back with me a new energy, spirit and enthusiasm. It was the vision of a Malay nationalist who was now committed to engaging with economic development, technical modernity and the most fundamental human issues as a Muslim whose thinking was grounded in authentic Quranic teaching. When I eventually became Prime Minister, this thrill of innovation and efficiency that I had glimpsed in Japan influenced many of my projects and policies.

# Chapter 13:
## The Tunku Makes A Proposal

In 1961 the Tunku took off on yet another project. To the surprise of everyone, including UMNO members, he announced almost casually at a Press conference in Singapore that the Federation of Malaya, Singapore, Brunei, Sarawak and British North Borneo[1] should join together to form a new Malayan Federation.

This caused a furore. Opposition came not just from within the territories involved but also neighbouring Indonesia and the Philippines. Indonesia basically did not want to see the Federation become bigger than it already was. The Indonesians may also have had their own ambitions for Sarawak and British North Borneo as an extension of their Kalimantan province. The Philippines had its old claims to North Borneo[2] and its grievances that the former Sulu Sultanate's rights over the area were not internationally recognised. Many in Singapore, meanwhile, wanted to go their own way. When the British proposed the Malayan Union and then established the Federation of Malaya, they had not included Singapore, nor had the Peninsular Malays pressed for its inclusion. The British wanted the island as a naval base and the Malays didn't want to include its many Chinese in their Malay-centred polity.

Among the first to support this proposal was Lee Kuan Yew, the young leader of the People's Action Party (PAP) in Singapore. Lee had always believed independence for Singapore would result in a communist takeover. The island's population was overwhelmingly Chinese while the Malay minority was mostly poor and had very little political or economic clout. There was hardly any agriculture in Singapore, only some small-scale pig-farming and insignificant small rubber estates. There were few opportunities for Malays to farm or own land. They could not even be fishermen, because fishing in Singapore involved wooden stakes driven into the shallow seabed, attached to big traps. These were costly and only the Chinese could afford them.

---

[1]  When North Borneo joined to form the Federation of Malaysia it became known as Sabah, and was declared independent of British sovereignty.

[2]  When the Philippines achieved independence it made no claim to the territory of British North Borneo.

When the British acquired Singapore from the *temenggong* (Johor's head of government) in 1819, they cared only for developing it as a trading post and a base for their naval forces to protect British interests and trade in the Far East. Very little was known of the Johor Malays living there except that they were mostly fishermen. The welfare of these people did not seem to have concerned the British at all. To provide the commercial infrastructure and support for their trade, they allowed for unlimited immigration of the Chinese. They also allowed in a few Indians to man clerical posts in the Government and their trading houses. The Malays eventually found work as syces or drivers, as orderlies, peons, office boys or manual labourers. This was British colonialism's preferred racialised division of labour. The extent to which they see it as natural is evident in their virulent condemnation, even today, of Malaysia's affirmative action to undo this economic hierarchy. British policy turned Singapore into a Chinese settlement. When it gained Independence it became a Chinese country in which the Malays ended up a second-class minority. Their *kampung* were broken up and, under the Housing Authority's ethnic integration plans for its new mass-occupancy high-rise dwellings, they were dispersed among the majority Chinese, making it hard for them to come together to protect their interests.

When the Malay Congress was held in 1946, representatives of Malay organisations from Singapore also attended. Following the founding of UMNO, Singapore Malays decided to set up an UMNO branch in Singapore. This proved a deft move because its links with the politically dominant UMNO in the peninsula earned Singapore's UMNO leaders recognition from the Chinese-based political parties, including the PAP. Lee's early plans for Singapore made it clear that he assumed there would be a merger with Malaya. When the Tunku proposed the inclusion of Singapore in a bigger Malayan Federation, Lee eagerly welcomed it. He even aspired to become its Prime Minister, something he knew was entirely possible because the Chinese would make up the biggest racial group in the Federation.

Yet although Singapore was part of Malaya historically and geographically, the Malays of the peninsula did not want the island included in the Federation. By right, Singapore should have been returned to Johor, or at least to Malaya, since it was originally part of *Tanah Melayu*. But the peninsular Malays had their future to think about. They did not object to the exclusion of Singapore from the Malayan Union proposal, nor did they voice any desire to include Singapore in the Federation before or after Independence. They were fully aware that Singapore's large and aggressive Chinese community would adversely tilt the delicate racial balance in the peninsula.

At the time of Independence in 1957 the Malays made up only slightly more than half the population of the Malay Peninsula. The Chinese made up more than 30 per cent of the population, the Indians about 10 per cent and the rest comprised a number of other racial groups. Feeding Singapore's population into this mix would increase both the percentage and absolute numbers of Chinese, making them the biggest community in the new Federation proposed by the Tunku. Inclusion of the natives of Sarawak, Brunei and British North Borneo might have reduced the overall proportion of Chinese, but it would not increase the number and demographic weight of the Malays. It would not affect the standing of the Chinese as the largest ethnic component in the proposed new Federation's population.

The Malay hold on Malaya was tenuous. Demographically, they had almost been outnumbered in the peninsula before World War II. Politically, their standing was weakened by the post-war MacMichael Treaties, which paved the way for the Malayan Union. When the Sultans signed over practically everything to the British, their Malay subjects banded together in protest. With their numbers and astute political tactics, the Malay people rescued the Rulers and restored the primacy of the Malays in the *Tanah Melayu*. Grouped and organised together, the Malays succeeded in forcing a change in direction. The Malayan Union and the MacMichael Treaties were revoked and a new Federation was formed instead, and on that basis, Independence was achieved. Throughout all these crucial stages, the Malays of the peninsula were keenly aware of the importance of numbers, of political demography. Being indigenous to the country and its definitive people was symbolically significant; but it counted for less in hard facts than making up the majority of the country. Consequently, they were hesitant about the Tunku's idea of a bigger Federation that would include Singapore, fearing that they would not remain the majority race.

They had already made a huge cultural concession by giving up the name of their beloved land, now officially called the Federation of Malaya. But the Malay people still referred to it by its emblematic Malay name, *Persekutuan Tanah Melayu* or Federation of Malay Lands. Earlier, the Malays had suggested a name for the new country, including the new component states. But *Melayu Raya* or Greater Malay Land was rejected collectively by the peoples of Sarawak, Brunei, British North Borneo and Singapore. Reluctant as ever to insist, the Malays acquiesced. The new Federation would be known as Malaysia.

But the risks faced by the Malays did not end there. The Tunku had not considered that the population of Singapore at that time was bigger than the combined population of Sarawak and North Borneo. The indigenous peoples made up about 75 per cent of the population in these two states and the Chinese were also about 75 per cent of the population of Singapore. But since its population was bigger, the Singapore Chinese easily outnumbered the indigenous peoples in Sarawak and North Borneo. Even if the majority populations in both states voted together with the peninsular Malays in solidarity against all others, the Chinese in Singapore would still be dominant. So the Tunku had miscalculated. He had assumed that overall, by including Sarawak, North Borneo and Brunei, the indigenous population would outweigh the Chinese population, thus preserving Malay primacy in the *Tanah Melayu*.

As far as it can be ascertained, the Tunku had not fully consulted anyone in UMNO about his proposal to expand the Federation. Certainly no proper study was done first — had UMNO done a feasibility study, things might have been different. There should have been full, open party discussions before any steps were taken. My own firm belief was that the British put the Tunku up to it, planting in his mind a pleasing but hardly workable idea, because they did not think their North Borneo colonies could survive as independent states. They feared Indonesia had further ambitions after it had demanded Dutch Western New Guinea and got what it wanted. Would Sabah and Sarawak, which they claimed as integral parts of their island province of Kalimantan, be their next target? The British looked to

Malaya and the Tunku to block any such move. Britain was fearful then, as were many others, of Sukarno,[2] who was the bogeyman of the region.

The Tunku eventually realised that his assumption was wrong. He tried to get the PAP to agree not to be involved in politics outside of Singapore, but this solution was highly untenable. In effect, he was asking for an understanding with the most powerful political party in Singapore at the time to limit its political ambitions to its own corner of the country. His request had no legal basis and would not be binding upon any other party that might come to power in Singapore. Not even the PAP felt bound to honour the understanding.

In 1964, the year after Malaysia was inaugurated, the PAP reached into the peninsula, appealing to racist sentiments in order to gain power over the new nation. The Tunku's negotiations with the PAP to confine itself to Singapore politics were not made known to UMNO members and mid-level leaders in the party divisions. The Malays in general were apprehensive about their ability to promote their interests and to gain real benefit from the enlarged Federation. They had given up their *Tanah Melayu* for Malaysia — what more would they be asked to give up to make Malaysia acceptable to the peoples of the other four territories?

171

Once Indonesia and the Philippines objected to the formation of Malaysia, it was too late for UMNO or the Malays to protest. We in Malaya could not object without appearing to support Indonesia and the Philippines. To prevent being accused of being disloyal, the Malays of the peninsula were forced to accept the risk of the Singapore Chinese tilting the balance of the races in the proposed Malaysia. Between risking charges of treachery and the potential threat of Chinese numbers, the Malays chose the latter. Yet the Chinese in Singapore, being mostly wealthy, were not used to the ways of the Malays. They knew them only as servants and as members of the poor labouring class of Singapore. By looking down on the Malays, they may also have underestimated the community's strength.

Brilliant lawyer that he was, Lee could not claim to have not understood the Constitution of the Federation of Malaya, which was to be the basis

---

2    Sukarno led Indonesia's push to win independence from the Netherlands and was the country's first President from 1945 to 1967.

of the Constitution of Malaysia. It included clear provisions for the special position of the Malays, which would surely be extended to the natives or indigenous peoples of Sarawak and North Borneo, and also the Singapore Malays. He would have noticed that the delineation of the Federation's electoral constituencies favoured the rural areas where Malays and other indigenous people lived. The urban areas may have had larger population concentrations but, partly for that reason, the number of urban constituencies was smaller. Mainly Chinese, these urban areas would have a proportionally smaller number of representatives to Parliament compared to the rural constituencies. So long as this fact was accepted, it would balance out the higher number of Chinese voters.

Not the kind of person to be content with a secondary role, Lee saw Malaysia as his chance to dominate a substantial nation and become its Prime Minister. The Singapore of the early 1960s was too small for him and his ambitions. Malaysia was a real country, not a city-state and to become Prime Minister of Malaysia would satisfy his ambitions, especially for power and a more than municipal role. The disparities between the Malays and the non-Malays did not concern him. He was counting on the Chinese in Singapore and throughout Malaysia to support his party and thus shoulder aside the MCA and UMNO. He denounced what he called Malay racism, but in expecting the Chinese to support him as a Chinese who would uphold Chinese interests, he revealed himself as a racist.

Apparently unaware of these undercurrents, the Tunku was satisfied with the support he got from Singapore and the Borneo territories for the creation of Malaysia. The refusal of Brunei to join was for him a small matter. He did not think that it would change the equation in terms of the mix of races. He expected the PAP and Lee to respect their informal understanding with him, which was not to meddle in the politics of the other states of Malaysia. The Tunku continued to believe that the Alliance would win huge majorities in those states and so rule the country as a whole, while the PAP would do no more than rule Singapore and represent it with a limited number of seats in the Federal Parliament. In the Tunku's mind, the PAP would never have enough seats in the Malaysian Parliament to form the government.

But Lee had no intention of accepting Tunku's views of what was good for Malaysia and of Singapore's limited place within it. The PAP was overtly a multiracial party but the Indians and the small number of Malays were just window-dressing. Effectively, it was a Chinese party. Moreover, as a Singapore Chinese, Lee appeared not to appreciate that there was a difference between the Singapore Chinese and the Chinese of peninsular Malaya, Sabah and Sarawak. The latter lived among ordinary Malays, had known Malay dignitaries — even royals — and had in some measure accepted, accommodated themselves to, and even practised elements of Malay culture. Living in peace with the Malays, they did not care to rock the boat. Initially, they had not been happy with the Malay opposition to the Malayan Union that denied them equal citizenship with the Malays. But when the communist insurgency was launched, the less extreme Chinese — who made up the majority — identified with neither the ambitions nor the violence of the communists. Instead, in 1949, they founded the MCA, to fight for better access to citizenship in the Federation of Malaya. On their behalf the MCA leader Tun Tan Cheng Lock championed the principle of *jus soli* or the common right to citizenship for all who were born in the country, regardless of origins and descent, to citizenship.

UMNO and the Malays had preferred *jus sanguinis* or citizenship by descent, through birth to at least one parent who was already a Malayan citizen. This criterion would have reduced considerably the number of Chinese Malayan citizens. But for the municipal elections in Kuala Lumpur in 1952, when UMNO and MCA made the momentous decision to cooperate, Sino-Malay political ties through the Alliance would not have been possible. By the time the Tunku proposed Malaysia, the Chinese of the MCA were quite comfortable working with the Malays of UMNO. And while non-Malay access to citizenship remained restricted until 1957, it was enlarged considerably in the following years. The Chinese of the peninsular states were not as receptive to the PAP's appeals, or to Lee's own views of Chinese political identity and action.

Shortly after Malaysia was inaugurated, Lee rolled out his plan for achieving power in Malaysia. He believed the PAP could oust the MCA from the Alliance and take its place. In his book *Looking Back*, the Tunku quoted from several of Lee's speeches and statements, all obviously anti-Malay. "None of the three major racial groups — Chinese, Malays and Indians — can claim to be more native to Malaysia than the others," he declared, "because all their ancestors came to Malaysia not more than 1,000 years ago." The Tunku countered by pointing to the history of the United States. The English people were the first people to settle there. When in 1776 the American colonies became independent, it was considered to be an "English" country. Thereafter, immigrants from Europe poured in and settled into the American Anglo-Saxon way of life. They accepted English as their national language and mother tongue and for a long time they did not question that only WASPs — white, Anglo-Saxon Protestants — could become President. Catholics were unacceptable until the swearing-in of John F. Kennedy.

In a limited, technical sense, Malays may be immigrants. Some anthropologists believe that they originated from South China long before recorded history. But that does not put them on the same level as the white Americans, Australians, New Zealanders, the Spanish and Portuguese of Latin America and others of recent overseas colonial settlement, as some would argue. No one thinks of the Malays as migrants in this sense. Those migrants who settled earlier in the peninsula saw the Malays as the definitive people, and without protest, adapted to the Malay culture and language. They accommodated themselves to what they found among the local Malays, and much of Malay culture was adopted by the Baba and Nyonya, or Straits Chinese, and incorporated into their own local Chinese way of life.

While in many countries immigrants with citizenship are officially regarded as formally equal to original citizens, they are often denied significant public posts unless they convert to the religion of the majority, who are considered the definitive people. Such discrimination is not grounded in law, but it is subtly practised. While everyday acts of prejudice may be nothing more than the turning of a blind eye or a deaf ear, their occurrence demonstrates the absence of honest equality even in those countries that boast of having achieved it. Malaysia has been no worse than many of the countries of the West that criticise its Malay-centric multiculturalism, and is decidedly better than many of them in providing and assuring a place under its sun for those of immigrant origins. Like many of Malaysia's Western critics, Lee failed to recognise that Malaya's accommodation of its non-Malay immigrant communities greatly reduced the force of Chinese grievances which he could exploit in Malaysia.

Braced with this attitude and ambition, Lee set himself on a collision course with the governing parties of Malaysia. In the 1964 General Election, he made his bid for leadership of the Chinese in Malaysia. His first step was to displace the MCA. The rallies he organised were attended by huge crowds of Chinese and the PAP's characteristic bullying tactics were displayed in full. People who tried to heckle the PAP speakers had powerful spotlights turned on them. The effect was dramatic and also decisive — no one dared raise objections at PAP rallies for fear of this intense embarrassment. But despite the huge numbers at its rallies, the PAP won only one seat in the 1964 elections. The PAP's attempt to discredit the MCA and replace it as UMNO's partner failed spectacularly. Its "Malaysian Malaysia"[3] campaign did not prove the winning formula that Lee expected.

The Malaysia proposal was initially not well received in Sarawak, British North Borneo and Brunei. In the end, the declaration of Malaysia's establishment had to be delayed by two weeks to confirm that there was sufficient local support in Sarawak and British North Borneo for joining the new federation. But it was the reaction of Malaya's neighbours, Indonesia and the Philippines, which proved decisive. The people of Sarawak and British North Borneo were divided. The Malays and indigenous Muslims generally favoured the idea of Malaysia. Other natives were ambivalent, while the majority of the Chinese were opposed. But no one wished to be a part of Indonesia or the Philippines. With the tacit consent of the British Government, though often not of the British officers serving in the two colonies, the Malayan Government set out to explain and win the support of the people there.

175

Large numbers of people from Sarawak and British North Borneo were brought to the peninsula and shown the progress made and the generally higher quality of life enjoyed by its people. The visitors were hosted at

---

[3]   This was in contrast to what the PAP alleged was a "Malay Malaysia", which was supposedly being imposed by the Alliance Government.

the best hotels and given tours of the sights and sounds of the mainland. Members of UMNO and the other Alliance parties acted as guides. This hospitality convinced most of them that being a part of the Federation of Malaysia would be beneficial. British North Borneo and Sarawak, they hoped, would become as developed as the states of the Peninsula. Brunei, however, decided not to join. Among other points of disagreement, its Sultan was not happy that Brunei's oil would be taken over by the central Malaysian Government.

President Sukarno of Indonesia had actually first welcomed the proposal, but he changed his mind and began to agitate against it. As the people of Sarawak and British North Borneo began to express support for federation with Peninsular Malaya, Sukarno launched his *Konfrontasi* or Confrontation against Malaya. While it was less than a formal declaration of war, it involved Indonesian military intrusion and aggression as well as diplomatic measures. A *Ganyang Malaysia* (Crush Malaysia) campaign was launched and anti-Malaysia sentiments were whipped up among the Indonesians. Indonesian soldiers crossed the border into Sarawak and parachutists were dropped into Johor. A key pillar of the Non-Aligned Movement (NAM)[4] ever since the Bandung meeting of 1954, Indonesia drew upon its international standing to mount a propaganda campaign depicting Malaysia as a "neo-colonial" project. Persuaded by its anti-colonial credentials if not its wild allegations, many newly independent countries sided with Indonesia. To counter this anti-Malaysia propaganda, a group of the younger Alliance members decided to set up a Malaysian branch of the Afro-Asian Peoples Solidarity Organisation (AAPSO). I was then a Member of Parliament and led the delegation to Ghana, where a conference of the AAPSO was to be held. The AAPSO trip was a relatively minor event in the bigger scheme of things but, as I discuss elsewhere in these pages, it was to prove a definitive mission in my own political journey.

Malaysia took its case against Indonesian aggression to the United Nations. Our Foreign Minister Tun Dr Ismail Abdul Rahman did an accomplished job in the Security Council, displaying Indonesian arms

[4] Founded in 1955, NAM is an international grouping of countries that consider themselves not formally aligned with or against any major power bloc.

captured by Malaysia. The developed countries, in particular the ethnically European (or "Old") Commonwealth countries, took Malaysia's side. But the behaviour of the Americans was puzzling. A key supplier of arms to Indonesia, they encouraged the republic to be more belligerent. We learnt later that the Americans were actually cultivating the Indonesian military, particularly the army. When Sukarno was later overthrown and General Suharto took over the leadership of Indonesia, the Americans and their corporations gained a strong client state in Southeast Asia. So, in time, they got value for money from their support of Indonesian opposition to the Malaysia proposals.

Added to the Indonesian Confrontation was the Philippines' claim over British North Borneo, which at one time had been part of the Sulu Sultanate. It had been ceded by the Sultanate to the British via the British North Borneo Company, which paid a fee every year. As political successors to the Sulu Sultanate, the Philippines claimed North Borneo as part of its national territory. Our response to that claim rested on the fact that when the British held British North Borneo, no demand was made that it be included in the Philippines. Neither was a claim made when — and since — the Philippines gained independence. On our side, we were prepared to pay what the British were paying.

But law and legal rights are one thing, politics and diplomatic advantage another. President Diosdado Pangan Macapagal appeared to be working with President Sukarno to frustrate the formation of Malaysia. The suddenly reactivated Philippine claim to North Borneo rode on the coattails of Indonesia's aggressive territorial expansionism, a stance adopted at the time to shore up President Sukarno's increasingly shaky domestic political position.

Responding to Indonesian and Philippine opposition to Malaysia, the United Nations then set up the Cobbold Commission[5] to assess the support for the proposed inclusion of Sarawak and British North Borneo in the proposed Federation among the peoples of the two states. Singapore had already carried out a referendum and the result was almost unanimous support

---

5   The Cobbold Commission was also responsible for drafting the Constitution of the Federation of Malaysia.

for joining the Federation. Although it was stipulated that the findings could not be announced until after the Cobbold Commission findings were officially revealed, the Government went ahead and celebrated Malaysia Day on the Federation's Independence day to the chagrin of the United Nations. The announcement was made two weeks later on 16 September 1963.

The beginning of the end of *Konfrontasi* unfolded around the time I went to the United States in 1965 as Malaysia's delegate to the United Nations General Assembly. Malaysia's Permanent Representative to the United Nations then was Mr Radhakrishna Ramani, a lawyer who was initially active in the politics of India and had once entertained hopes of becoming its Foreign Minister. I remember him suffering from severe insomnia. He apparently could sleep only once a week after an injection of a sleeping drug. New York, with its skyscrapers and the Empire State Building, then the tallest building in the world, fascinated me. But I also found it dirty, decayed and very depressing. Police sirens blared day and night. Men who seemed quite mad walked along 42nd Street, one of the major streets in Manhattan, shouting incoherently as they made their way.

While I was at the United Nations the Indonesian Communist Party attempted to seize power in the republic. Five top military officers were rounded up by a group of soldiers, murdered and dumped into a well. General Nasution, the Chief of the Armed Forces, escaped. From the subsequent counterattack by the armed forces, General Suharto emerged. He successfully defeated the communists and their sympathetic Air Force officers, but in the ensuing bloodbath nearly half a million people were said to have been killed. Very soon after, moves were made to end Indonesia's Confrontation against Malaysia. After Sukarno's Foreign Minister, Subandro, was jailed, Adam Malik took over. He was well-disposed towards Malaysia and even had Malaysian relatives in Perak. Contact was made between General Benny Moerdani, who later became Indonesia's Chief of the Armed Forces, and our Permanent Secretary to the Ministry of Foreign Affairs, Tun Ghazali Shafie, which led to an agreement to end the conflict.

But the Philippines continued to claim Sabah, as British North Borneo was renamed, and relations remained strained. Despite this tension the five countries of Southeast Asia — Indonesia, Singapore, the Philippines, Thailand and Malaysia — resolved in 1967 to form ASEAN, the Association of Southeast Asian Nations. The moving force behind this measure was Adam Malik. This was the beginning of the normalisation of regional relations which in turn provided a secure context for strong economic growth and development. The progress they achieved enabled the ASEAN members to raise their profile and project themselves internationally, and Malaysia has made the most of that opportunity.

So in the end the Tunku was vindicated. He succeeded in determining the development of his homeland and through his vision and initiative, the Federation of Malaya became Malaysia. It was a great achievement for the prince who had become a politician and leader by default. Like Malaysia, Singapore has also raised its international standing and profile under Lee and his successors — but not as part of Malaysia. Lee has come very far, but his reaching across the Causeway into peninsular politics came to nought.

# Chapter 14:
## The Bitter Thrill Of Politics

In 1958, after I had left Government service and set up my own medical practice, I was elected a member of the Kedah UMNO committee and headed its political sub-committee. I had differences with the Kedah UMNO chief, the late Tun Syed Ahmad Shahabudin, the same Syed Ahmad who had been sent to my house when we were schoolboys to study under my father's strict tutelage. He was a member of the Federal Legislative Council, elected in the 1955 General Election. It was my view that candidates for state and federal elections should have some educational qualifications, and at least be able to read and write. I was not the only one to think so and within the committee there was strong objection to those who did not have the educational credentials to become candidates. Syed Ahmad, however, disagreed and took the matter to the Tunku.

The Tunku decided that educational qualifications would exclude many UMNO stalwarts from contesting. Displeased with me, he ordered the Kedah UMNO political committee to be dissolved. When I got the news I decided to resign from the committee first, and when I was asked to contest in the 1959 General Election, I refused. I was still sore at being asked to dissolve the committee and at the stand the Tunku had taken.

As the 1964 General Election approached, many in the Kedah UMNO branch came to see me to persuade me to be a candidate for a parliamentary seat. They hinted that Tun Razak, the Deputy Prime Minister, wanted me to contest. I eventually agreed to contest the Kota Star Selatan parliamentary constituency, previously held by Tunku Kassim, Tunku Abdul Rahman's half-brother. The head of the UMNO division there was a well-to-do farmer, Haji Ali. Even though I was not a member of the division, there was no objection to my candidature as Tunku Kassim was not well and did not wish to contest. In those days — so unlike today — few would push themselves forward to become candidates for elections. As the division head, Haji Ali would contest one of the two state seats rather than a parliamentary seat in his constituency.

At this time my medical practice was still very popular. Although I was widely known as "the UMNO doctor", many of my patients were strong supporters of PAS. One of them was a very influential religious teacher in Pendang, which was in the Kota Star Selatan constituency. I made a point of going to see him to seek his support. He advised me to concentrate on my practice and warned me that my political partisanship might make me unpopular as a doctor. I told him that the purpose of my visit was to let him know that I was about to enter his territory. This is Malay courtesy — even when entering a forest, Malays always ask the spirits for permission first. I was adhering to the *adat*, but from his rather discouraging reply, I knew I would not have an easy passage in the elections.

Kota Star Selatan was a rural constituency of about 26,000 registered voters. On the night that I set out to campaign for the first time, I had to use an open four-wheeler to travel on the dirt track roads to a small rally. When I arrived I was greeted with laughter, which had me mystified and a little miffed. It turned out that, because the roads were unpaved, the vehicle in front of us had kicked up clouds of dust which covered our four-wheeler and all the passengers in it. In the light of the pressure-lamp, my face and hair looked completely white from the dust. My spectacles had protected my eyes, but when I took off my glasses to clean them, matters got even worse. I now looked like what the Malays call a *mawa*, a kind of masked gibbon with white furry rings round its eyes — I must have looked a sight. Though memorable, this was not the kind of impression I had intended to make. Today, most of those roads have been paved and there is very little danger of looking like wildlife.

It was a relatively quiet campaign in Kota Star Selatan. I was not very good at public speaking and still lacked the knack of rousing people, which to me felt artificial, too much like fishing for applause. Even now, when speaking in either English or Malay, I prefer using simple language. I do not consider myself erudite and don't seek to project a grand image. Instead of rich oratory, I am keen to make sure that people understand what I am saying — there is no point in trying to show people how brilliant you are when you are not. But over time, my public speaking improved.

In Kota Star Selatan, I was contesting against PAS, which as usual had a religious teacher as a candidate. UMNO had won Independence for Malaya only recently and the memory and appreciation of it was still fresh in the minds of the people. The FELDA[1] settlers in the constituency were grateful to UMNO for the 10 acres of land they were each given to farm and earn a living. The Chinese, who made up about 15 per cent of the voters, were wary of PAS's agenda. So too were the small Thai and Indian communities. Since they would not vote for PAS, support for me — as the Alliance candidate — was very strong.

With an 82 per cent voter turnout, I won comfortably with a majority of 4,210 votes. Though PAS lost, it managed to obtain 8,196 votes and was obviously a force to be reckoned with (this would be clearly demonstrated in the next election in 1969). I was at the counting centre when the results were announced. I could hardly believe that I was now a Member of Parliament, even though from the response I got during the campaign and from the number of people who had turned up at my *ceramah*, or small indoor talks, I had been somewhat confident that I could win. It was not a landslide victory but I was still very happy. At last, I could contribute effectively to the well-being of my new constituents. Over the years, the people of Kota Star Selatan wanted good roads and they got them. They also got electricity, piped water and schools. Elected representatives must take their positions seriously because the electorate has learnt the power it wields with its votes.

In Kuala Lumpur for the first Parliamentary meeting, I became aware of my new status when, during a pre-parliamentary briefing, I found myself in the presence of luminaries like Prime Minister Tunku Abdul Rahman and other Cabinet Ministers. Most of them did not know me of course, as I was new and just an ordinary backbencher. From where I stood, the Cabinet Ministers seemed in a class of their own. They had a plaque with the word "Minister" fixed above their car number plates and the national flag and party flag flew proudly from their front fenders. It left a great impression on me, and I thought what an achievement it would be to become a Minister.

---

[1]  Established in 1956, the Federal Land Development Authority (FELDA) is a government agency that manages the resettlement of the rural poor onto farms in newly developed areas.

The 1964–1969 term of Parliament would turn out to be a most eventful one. It saw the expulsion of Singapore from Malaysia, the end of Indonesian Confrontation, the fall of Sukarno and the birth of ASEAN. It also saw increasing tension between Chinese and Malays, which culminated in the divisive and tense 1969 General Election that nearly destroyed the country. It was exciting to watch all this history unfold before me in the Dewan Rakyat.[2] Playing a small part in it was even more fulfilling, and I was able to voice my ideas and opinions in the most important legislative and policy-making body in the country. I wanted to be an effective Member of Parliament for my constituents, to be a representative of whom they could be proud. I wanted to contribute in some way to the well-being of the country.

My medical qualifications did not go unnoticed. I was seated with two other senior doctors, Dr Megat Khas and Dr Awang Hassan (who later became the Governor of Penang) in the second bloc next to where the members of Government sat. Today that bloc is fully occupied by the members of the Cabinet, which is much larger now than it was then. Ordinary members now sit at quite a distance from the Ministers. Opposite me sat the Honourable Mr Lee Kuan Yew and three Singapore Members of Parliament. They were not quite in the Opposition area but they were lodged next to them. I do not think Lee approved of this seating arrangement.

Lee and I had a civil relationship, but it was never a friendship. In the period until Singapore left Malaysia in 1965, I had numerous brushes with him in the Dewan Rakyat. His demeanour usually seemed condescending and he appeared to want to deliver lectures to the House on what it and the Government should do. He would stand up with a clipboard in front of him, take off his watch, deliberately place it before him, and then proceed to talk down to the House. I listened carefully at first, but I got tired of his style of delivery. He adopted the didactic tone of a know-all schoolmaster, telling us all what we should do and pointing out all the "mistakes" we were making — it did not make for good listening. Sometimes, to keep the proceedings on track, and sometimes, just to be a nuisance, I interrupted by asking questions and seeking clarifications. Lee could barely hide his annoyance at my constant interruptions, but I noticed that he cut back on

---

2    The (lower) House of Representatives in Parliament.

his speeches. A number of other Members of Parliament thought he was arrogant and disliked him. Soon, other Alliance members got into the act and began to harass him, until he could no longer preach to the Dewan Rakyat.

Another very vocal Member of Parliament was D.R. Seenivasagam of the People's Progressive Party (PPP). Together with his brother, S.P. Seenivasagam, they made it very clear that they did not think much of the Malays. They were from Perak and represented the Ipoh and Menglembu constituencies, which they had won because of strong Chinese support. They had lived among the Chinese and reputedly could speak both Cantonese and Mandarin. Strangely, when the Barisan Nasional was formed, S.P. Seenivasagam, who had taken over leadership of the PPP after his brother passed away, joined the coalition and became a Minister in both Tun Razak's and Tun Hussein's Cabinets.

PAS attacked the Alliance with a different strategy altogether. Abdul Samad Gul Mianji, PAS member for Pasir Mas Hulu, made it very clear that he did not consider UMNO and its members to be proper Muslims. Other PAS members believed the same thing but they were less open about it. Abdul Samad had a very coarse, vicious manner of speech. He was eventually murdered in 1967 by unknown assailants in Kota Baru, near the PAS party offices. Other Honourable Members I often clashed with included the Member for Batu, Tan Sri Dr Tan Chee Khoon. He was from the Socialist Front but he mainly championed the rights of the non-Malays. It was obvious that he regarded the Alliance Government as a primarily Malay Government and he refused to accept that MCA and MIC represented the Chinese and Indians.

In 1965 I was given my first mission abroad. Tun Razak wanted Malaysia to be respected the world over by all nations, weak and strong, and also by non-governmental bodies. For that reason, he wanted Malaysia to become a member of the Afro-Asia Peoples Solidarity Organisation, or AAPSO, a non-governmental body that was largely anti-American, pro-communist and highly influential. Almost all the newly independent countries and those belonging to the Non-Aligned Movement were represented in AAPSO. During the Indonesian Confrontation, the republic had launched a diplomatic offensive to isolate Malaysia and show the rest of the world — especially the Afro-Asian countries — that it was a neo-colonial creation. At the organisation's conference in Algiers in 1964, Malaysia was strongly condemned although it was not a member and was not present. Wiser from this experience, Tun Razak wanted to change perceptions of Malaysia at the AAPSO conference in Ghana the following year. I was hastily drafted and made Chairman of the Presidium of the Malaysian chapter of AAPSO and was asked to go to Ghana to seek membership in the organisation. It was an honour and I was determined to show results.

The other members of the delegation were James Puthucheary (a lawyer who had been made persona non grata in Singapore and had been detained under Singapore's Internal Security Act); Tan Sri Lee San Choon, an MCA Member of Parliament; Tun Musa Hitam, political secretary to the Minister of Transport Tun Sardon Jubir; Wong Ling Ken of the PAP; well-known Malay journalist Tan Sri A. Samad Ismail, and C. V. Devan Nair, a former trade unionist and PAP Member of Parliament for Bangsar in Kuala Lumpur and a future President of Singapore. Even our flight to Ghana proved to be memorable, though not always for the right reasons. For one thing, I was briefly quarantined in Cairo for not having proper health papers. Also, the Ghana Airways aircraft was of Soviet make and vibrated a great deal. The pilots were Ghanaians but they had Soviet pilots sitting behind them who, it seemed, were instructing the Ghanaians on the job. It was not very reassuring, to say the least, but we managed to arrive safely in Ghana's capital city of Accra. After that experience we opted on our return journey to use Alitalia, which flew via Rome.

185

Ghana had gained independence in the same year as Malaysia. Its leader was the colourful and highly regarded Kwame Nkrumah, who believed strongly in non-alignment. When I arrived in Accra, I found that everything had been named after him. He seemed very popular but the shine wore off somewhat when I saw the tight security ring around him. My idea of a popular leader was one who mingled freely with the people, unafraid of being harmed by them. I know better now. In the midst of numerous supporters lurk assassins, as many democratic leaders have found out. Still, I never liked even the minimal security that the police insisted I needed to have as Prime Minister.

The conference was held in Winneba, a town almost 80km from Accra, where the ruling party had an ideological training centre. We had already spent some time in Accra meeting as many delegates as possible to lobby for their support for Malaysia to get membership. The Ghanaians, Egyptians and the Soviets were friendly but they asked us to get sponsors from among the African delegations. Many of them were still struggling for independence and most were supported and trained by the communist bloc. They were not inclined to support the supposedly pro-Western "neo-colonial" creation that was Malaysia and we found the going very tough.

In his opening speech, President Nkrumah called upon Malaysia and Indonesia to start roundtable talks. He said that the withdrawal of the imperialists from Southeast Asia was a prerequisite to successful peace negotiations. Neither Indonesia nor Malaysia, according to him, could divert resources sorely needed for development "into a conflict so easily avoidable". I welcomed this call for peace talks but insisted that the struggle to eliminate foreign bases in Malaysia could not begin as long as there were military threats from Indonesia. In a statement, the Malaysian delegation made clear that in order to reduce the military presence of the imperialists, "it is paramount that the danger of military invasion of Malaysia be removed". The statement also asked the delegates to help bring the weight of Afro-Asian opinion and moral influence to bear on the Malaysia-Indonesia dispute. It appealed for Malaysia's membership of the organisation. The Indonesians protested, claiming the presence of the Malaysian delegation was "completely illegal and intolerable". Yet one of the most telling arguments raised against our admission was made by the Viet Cong delegation, which condemned Malaysia's support for the American bombing of North Vietnam. Communist China and Indonesia threatened to leave the organisation if Malaysia was admitted. Faced with this condemnation and the threat by China and Indonesia, there was no hope of Malaysia being admitted. I had failed in my first mission abroad.

Upon my return, during a Parliamentary sitting, Dr Tan Chee Khoon questioned my involvement with AAPSO. He said it was inconsistent with the stand of the Alliance Government as the organisation was leftist and my designation as Chairman of the Presidium was typical of communist organisations. I explained that the Alliance Government respected differing opinions among its supporters, but I do not think I sounded very convincing. The reaction of the Tunku later proved how wrong I was about the Alliance's stance. Tun Razak, on the other hand, gave the delegation his vote of approval. Speaking during the same Parliamentary sitting, he said that Malaysia, while not a member of the conference, had sent representatives there to rebut Indonesian accusations. Three days later the Tunku, who had been in Tokyo at the time, returned and said publicly that he would never have agreed to the mission. He regretted that a Malaysian delegation had gone to Accra to attend the conference without his knowledge. He described the organisation as "a communist set-up established in Cairo for their own ends. It is being financed by Russia and communist China," he said, adding that, "they had never admitted us into the conference and I had no hope of it at all".

Yet the Tunku's disapproval of AAPSO and my visit to Ghana did not result in the disbanding of the local chapters. On 21 July 1965, I issued a statement in the name of AAPSO. Seizing on the apparent American support for Indonesia, my statement demanded that the Government, "carry out the re-examination of our foreign policy immediately". In essence, the statement demanded that the policy towards America and other Western powers be re-evaluated and made more realistic, consistent with our national pride and aspirations as an independent Afro-Asian nation. The Americans, the statement added, were unreliable friends who were motivated by their selfish economic interests. The progressive countries were the USSR, Yugoslavia, Poland and the Afro-Asian countries, and I pleaded for lasting friendship with the USSR and the People's Republic of China.

My statement as Chairman of AAPSO was clearly not calculated to endear me to the Tunku. Even then, my stand was not the same as his but was more in tune with that of Tun Razak's. The AAPSO incident may seem minor but it served to highlight the differences in the perceptions and views of the Tunku and his deputy, Tun Razak. Re-reading the reports today, I realise that I had often been unable to agree with the Tunku. On another occasion during my first term as Member of Parliament, I urged the Government to do away with Imperial Preference. This was a relic from the days of the British Empire when goods imported from Britain and other countries of the Empire attracted preferential duties. I urged the Government to stop this bias in favour of an Empire which — even then — was an anachronism. Here again I seemed at odds with the Tunku's thinking. Other Members of Parliament and most UMNO members did not seem to know about Imperial Preference, and did not appear to be interested. Unsurprisingly, I received little support on the matter. The Tunku did not see things in the same way, and neither did many of his UMNO loyalists.

I also remembered the Ghana mission vividly for another reason. At Winneba, we attended a ceremony where President Nkrumah was to unveil yet another monument to himself in the struggle for independence. Until the last moment, we were unsure if he would attend the ceremony. The Ghanaian chiefs, meanwhile, had all gathered at the foot of the monument, which took the form of a huge sword about 12 metres long, pointed tip down and embedded in a concrete base. Nkrumah arrived almost two hours late. The local chiefs gave speeches to praise and welcome him, and Nkrumah then made a long reply. When he was later overthrown all the monuments to him were pulled down and destroyed.

I realised then that people's adulation of those who are in power is rarely sincere — or permanent. Losing your position means losing the praise once conferred upon you. Successors, even if they are of the same party, do not wish the people to remember their predecessors. Many try in different ways to obliterate memories of the recent past. This is easy if the predecessor is disgraced, yet even if the predecessor willingly surrenders power, a successor may be uncomfortable if he is remembered too kindly.

As an elected representative, I felt it was important to raise issues that affected the nation, even if I did so at a personal political cost. During the Budget Debate in 1968, for example, in my first encounter with financial matters, I raised the problem of the devaluation of the British pound. Malaysia was in the vaunted Sterling area and its currency, the ringgit, (then still referred to as the Malaysian dollar), was pegged at eight Malaysian dollars and thirty cents to the British pound, which in those days was a strong currency. The US dollar, which was valued at three Malaysian dollars, was not yet the major trading currency of the world. Most of Malaysia's reserves were held in pounds, so when Britain decided in 1967 to suddenly devalue the pound in order to be competitive in the world market, we suffered losses. Prior to this, they had been under enormous financial pressure from the Swiss bankers. Despite this mounting pressure and our enquiries about the safety of our reserves placed with them, the British had explicitly denied any plans to devalue the pound. Too much the gentleman, then Finance Minister Tun Tan Siew Sin accepted their assurances, to our great cost. England was not known as "Perfidious Albion" for nothing, it would seem. Once the British succumbed to pressure and devalued the pound, the Malaysian dollar fell in value by 15 per cent and we lost a great deal of money.

Things were worse at the ground level, especially in the Malay rural areas. At that time the old Board of Currency Commissioners' paper currency was being phased out and new notes, issued by our own Bank Negara,[3] were being introduced to replace them. This process was quite advanced in the urban areas, but further afield, the old notes still predominated. Not trusting the banks, many village people had been holding their savings for years, mainly in the old Board of Currency Commissioners' notes. A problem soon arose — tied to the pound, those old notes were automatically devalued by 15 per cent. The new Bank Negara notes were pegged to the gold value of the US dollar and were therefore not devalued. The holders of the old notes, especially rural folk, lost heavily while others more exposed to the circulation of the new notes suffered fewer losses. Problems of trading simultaneously in both old and new money also brought many rural markets and businesses to a halt. Again the rural folk suffered badly, although there were also rumbles of discontent and demonstrations in some urban areas, especially Penang.

189

It was grossly unfair of the British not to inform us beforehand of their decision to devalue the pound. In the debate on 26 January 1968, I expressed my disagreement that devaluation would improve the economy of Great Britain. Tun Tan was also unhappy and mentioned it in a speech. In the Tunku's time Malaysia was still very pro-British so the incident did not affect bilateral relations. Yet, although the devaluation was conducted twice, Britain's economy did not improve. I learnt much from this episode

---

[3]   Bank Negara Malaysia is the country's Central Bank, and was established on 26 January 1959.

and the memory of it helped me in the late 1990s, when international currency traders attacked the ringgit. Again, experience would prove a great teacher. But the fees one must pay may be quite exorbitant and getting good value from the lessons may take much patience.

The real cause of the British economy's bad performance, as I pointed out to the Government, was the British workers, who did not seem to be as industrious as other Europeans. They went on strike very often, worked to rule and always demanded pay hikes without increases in productivity. They even demanded to be paid for merely watching machines doing their work for them. Even when the British economy suffered, the workers continued to go on strike. Pay increases were fine when British products were protected through the Imperial Preference system, as that assured them captive markets and sales. But once they had to compete in the open market with the Japanese, their industries soon imploded. They simply could not survive. Here too there was a lesson that Malaysia would have to learn.

Meanwhile, Dr Tan accused the Government of discriminating against non-Malays in appointments to senior government posts. Having done my homework, I knew that although Malays made up the majority of the Civil Service, the professional posts were largely filled by non-Malays. Of the 3,638 Division I and II posts that existed in 1965, the Malays held only 1,156. The per annum salary bill for Division I and II was RM34 million, of which Malays earned only RM11 million. Simple arithmetic showed that RM23 million was earned by non-Malays. In order to earn this amount, they would have had to dominate senior government posts. Dr Tan tried to say that racial origin did not matter as long as the candidates were Malaysians. To this I replied that if truly it did not matter, then why was he pointing out that in the Civil Service there were few Chinese and Indians? I went on to accuse the Labour Party of trying to deny the Malays, who made up more than half the population, even one-third of the senior posts in government. The fairness of this argument made an impression on a few non-Malay members of the Opposition and even some members of the non-Malay public. PAS, despite its usually moralistic manner, made no comment, and once again I was left to expose this truth alone. It made me unpopular with the Chinese and did not win me any more support from the Opposition Malays, which was to haunt me in the 1969 General Election.

My main concern, which was included in my parliamentary interventions, was the welfare of the Malays and their share of the country's wealth. By accepting the principle of *jus soli* as the basis of Malaysian citizenship, the political parties had essentially struck a social contract assuring the Malays a bigger share of the country's economic wealth. More than a million Chinese had been able to gain Malaysian citizenship but little Malay economic advancement had been registered. By the late 1960s the Chinese began to demand that this inter-communal social contract be ignored. As a Member of Parliament, I spoke at length and frequently on this issue, both in the chamber of Parliament and outside. Since the Malay Press gave me extensive publicity, I became regarded as something of a champion of the Malay cause. Although I made a point of distinguishing the MCA Chinese from the DAP Chinese, whom I condemned for being anti-Malay, the Chinese community as a whole regarded me as an unfriendly figure.

Their dislike was made worse by the PAP of Singapore. After my many clashes with the Honourable Lee Kuan Yew in Parliament, he retaliated by labeling me, together with Tan Sri Syed Jaafar Hassan Albar, as Malay "ultras", the intransigent Malay extremists. The label stuck. After that, anything I said, no matter how mild or reasonable, was regarded as extreme by the Chinese community. The labelling was a political ploy. It was intended to suggest that my views were extreme and therefore need not be considered on their merits, and that I would promote extreme views at any cost and in the face of all other evidence. Yet nothing that I said or did was extreme. All I did was to refute allegations that we Malays were taking things for ourselves, seizing what did not belong to us. Lee did not see himself as an extremist, or some sort of "non-Malay ultra", when, in commenting upon Malay poverty and its causes, he remarked that "it is not the Malays themselves who are backward, just their culture". I did not mind the Chinese attitude as long as I retained and gained the support of the Malays. After all, I thought, they were my real constituents, even if promoting their interests hurt my Chinese supporters a little. By my fourth year as a Member of Parliament, my popularity among the Malays saw me elected to the UMNO Supreme Council with the highest number of votes.

There was no money politics in those days. The Malays were much too poor to indulge in it. Besides, UMNO members were still fired by nationalist sentiments, so campaigning for positions within the party was not necessary. I myself did not campaign for the UMNO Supreme Council seat and I believe I received those votes because of my performance in Parliament and my obvious Malay nationalist credentials. In those days, election to the Supreme Council was held yearly. There was no factionalism, no rival camps, and UMNO members remained solid and united after elections. I had thought that as a member of the Council, I would be able to push through some of my ideas for improving the lot of the Malays. But to my great disappointment, the meetings of the Supreme Council under the chairmanship of the Tunku were a charade.

The Council did not meet regularly, for one thing, and when the Tunku did decide to hold a meeting, it rarely lasted more than half an hour. No serious matters were discussed. Held in the Tunku's residence at Bukit Tunku, their most important feature seemed to be the dinner that followed. Even at dinner nothing of import was discussed. Many Council members were adept at telling jokes and funny stories and there was always a great deal of laughter. Other Council members did not mind the meetings being conducted in this way, while those outside the Council were not aware of what went on at the residence and of the fundamental lack of political seriousness in the way UMNO addressed the challenges facing it and its supporters. Bonhomie and jokes were fine with me, but I would have been more comfortable had at least a few basic issues been highlighted and discussed.

My elevation to membership of the Supreme Council did gain me a place on the most important committee of the party, the political committee chaired by the deputy head of UMNO, Tun Razak. This committee worked on the problems of the Malays, whose disadvantaged social and economic position Tun Razak sincerely wanted to correct. Through this committee, I was able to contribute a few ideas. I believe Tun Razak took me seriously and tried to make use of my suggestions on education and Malay participation in business. My membership in the prestigious political committee further enhanced my status in the party — but not in the eyes of the Tunku.

In retrospect, I realise that my relationship with the Tunku had never been good. When I was still a student and active in the Kedah Malay Youth Association and the Kedah Malay Association, I had corrected the Association's draft of a memorandum against the Malayan Union, which had already been vetted and approved by the Tunku. I was given to understand that he was not too pleased. Then, when the Tunku decided to adopt the Perak State anthem, which was also a popular song called *Terang Bulan* (Bright Moon), as the national anthem, I joined a group from Kedah which went to see him to protest against this choice. The Tunku, who was resting in Port Dickson, refused to see us. Instead, we met with his close colleagues, Tan Sri Mohd Khir Johari[4] and Tan Sri Senu Abdul Rahman. They told us that the Tunku had made up his mind and there was no way we could change it.

There were other incidents which did not endear me to the Tunku, but I was not discouraged. Since my popularity was increasing, I thought that I would be considered at least for the position of Assistant Minister[5] when Tun Dr Ismail, then the Minister of Home Affairs, decided to leave the Government in 1967 due to health reasons. When an Assistant Minister was promoted to full Minister, a vacancy would fall open in the reshuffle. But mine was a hopeless dream. My name was never even mentioned in the speculation before the new line-up was announced. Had someone told me then that I would one day lead the country, I would have thought him quite mad.

Around this time, I sensed a change in the atmosphere. The Chinese were not as friendly to the Alliance as they used to be. They were demanding compensation for the atrocities committed by the Japanese during the war. Since the Chinese claimed that they had suffered the most, they believed they were entitled to "blood money" which should then be used to set up a Chinese university in Malaysia. This ran completely against the grain of the National Education Policy, where Malay was to be the sole medium of instruction at all levels. The idea of a Chinese university was anathema then to the Malays. Malay had been recognised as the national language

---

[4]   Tan Sri Mohd Khir Johari served in the Cabinet of three Prime Ministers. His last Cabinet portfolio was as Trade and Industry Minister in 1972.

[5]   From the 1960s, Assistant Ministers were called Deputy Ministers.

and a medium of school instruction ever since Independence. As 1967 approached, the question of the status of the Malay language became a matter of intense concern to most Malays. Driven by people such as Tan Sri Syed Nasir Ismail of the Dewan Bahasa dan Pustaka,[6] pressure was mounting to extend the 10-year "promotional period" for improving the use of Malay for another 10 years, or perhaps indefinitely. In that context, a proposal to create a separate stream for Chinese education to the tertiary level without requiring them to learn and use Malay simply ran counter to the political and cultural currents of the country. The relationship between the Malays and the Chinese, within the Alliance and outside, deteriorated further.

I became ever more convinced that the Chinese would not vote for the Alliance in the 1969 General Election. But I could not convey my concern to the Tunku, who was still calling himself the happiest Prime Minister in the world. He appeared to be quite unaware that Chinese sentiments had changed and that they had become disaffected. His Chinese friends probably assured him that all was well, when in fact it was not. Unconcerned, the Tunku stayed the course and called for elections only at the end of the parliamentary term. There was therefore no element of surprise in the timing of the elections, no wrong-footing of the Opposition, no forcing them to engage in battle on terms imposed by the Alliance. Then the Tunku made another mistake — he did not object when the Election Commission decided to allow the campaigning to go on for the maximum period of six weeks. Had he insisted on a shorter time perhaps things would have been different, if not in the results themselves then at least in the reaction to them. Instead, what took place was an eruption of pent-up feelings — of rage in some and jubilation in others — which might otherwise have been more constrained, less violent and destructive.

During those six weeks, the communal campaigning was vicious. Tempers frayed and inter-communal tensions mounted. All parties played on racial issues and the emotions they engendered. Each tried to outdo the other with increasingly racist statements at every successive campaign meeting. One Opposition worker and one Alliance party worker from Penang

194

---

6   Dewan Bahasa dan Pustaka, or the Institute of Language and Literature, is a Government agency that oversees the use of the Malay language in the country.

UMNO were killed during that period. The exhausting six-week campaign provided plenty of scope for relations to sour between the races and parties in the Alliance. Invectives were venomously hurled as each side tried to demonise the other. I felt the pressure in my own constituency, but since it was a Malay-majority constituency and I had retained my popularity with the Malays over the past five years, I believed I could still win even if I lost Chinese votes.

I thought my chances against my PAS opponent were good, because the strong antagonism between the Chinese and PAS would work to my and the Alliance's advantage. Non-Malays dreaded the Islamism of PAS, while PAS showed open hatred for the Chinese and Indians. The party talked of imposing Islamic laws on everyone irrespective of religion. UMNO, on the other hand, had guaranteed the rights of the non-Muslims, assuring them that they would not be subjected to Islamic laws.

But such reasoning did not take into account the powerful anti-Alliance and anti-Malay feelings that surged among non-Malays, especially the Chinese, as the protracted campaign continued. It seemed inconceivable that they would snub UMNO and the Alliance and register their disapproval of Malay political claims by casting their votes for PAS. I had won by more than 4,000 votes in 1964. Even if the Chinese voters, because of their suspicions of me as a so-called "Malay ultra", refused to vote for me this time, I thought I would still retain my seat. I believed that they would either abstain or spoil their votes if they wished to register their protest, but I did not anticipate that they might actually vote for an Opposition party they disliked so intensely.

If they did so, I would have had to double the number of additional Malay votes cast for me in order to win: 3,500 to replace Chinese votes withdrawn from me, and 3,500 more to make up for the Chinese votes which went towards PAS. That was an impossible gap to close. As it turned out, in the polling stations where the Chinese voters were in the majority, nearly all their votes went to PAS. I lost the election by just under 1,000 votes.

The same swing and pattern was seen elsewhere in Kedah. On his rounds during polling day, the Tunku was shocked to see Chinese voters in his constituency going to the booths belonging to PAS. Normally they would have given these booths a wide berth. Even though the Tunku won, it was with a reduced majority (3,504 in 1969 as against 11,647 in 1964). Other UMNO candidates including stalwarts like Khir, Tun Fatimah Hashim[7] and Tun Zahir Ismail[8] all won with much reduced majorities as well. Senu, then the Secretary-General of UMNO, actually lost his seat. A similar quake was also reflected in the national results. While the Alliance won the General Election, it was with a much-reduced majority. UMNO members were, to say the least, shaken.

Losing my Parliamentary seat hurt terribly and on the ride home with Hasmah, I could not help shedding tears. The taste of defeat was unfamiliar and it was painful. I was also angry at the Chinese, in particular the MCA, who I felt were responsible for my defeat and with it the undermining of my political future. I felt betrayed. I realised however, that the Chinese did not really want PAS to govern the country. They knew it could not win enough seats to form the Federal Government, but they wanted to serve notice on the Alliance Party that they should not be taken for granted. They had played a crucial role in all the Alliance's electoral victories so their demands should be given serious consideration. They wished to be heard, and were so angry that they were prepared to hurt to make this happen. I swore that I would never again cooperate with them.

As I returned home that night, I had no idea of either the coming violent aftermath of the election or the long-term political lessons that would be drawn from it and given form in the New Economic Policy. When it was eventually implemented, Malaysia would have a plan for redressing the problems of the Malays and a way to create social peace and equitable economic development. This would assure the non-Malays, especially the Chinese, that their own stake in the country and their prospects for economic advancement would not be diminished just so that Malays might enjoy support and progress. But much would have to take place first before this could happen.

---

[7]  Tun Fatimah Hashim was head of Kaum Ibu Malaya, later known as Wanita UMNO, for 16 years. She was the country's first woman Minister, and held the post of Welfare Minister from 1969 to 1973.

[8]  Tun Zahir Ismail was the country's longest-serving Speaker in the Lower House of Parliament, holding the post for six terms over 22 years.

# Chapter 15:
## Expelled

The Alliance won the 1969 General Election, but its members were shocked by its reduced number of seats, both at federal and state levels.

It also lost Penang to Gerakan, a party formed just before the polls by Tun Dr Lim Chong Eu's[1] faction of the MCA and an assortment of academics and politicians dissatisfied with the Government.[2] In Perak, the PPP increased its share of state seats considerably while the DAP and Gerakan defeated many MCA candidates in Selangor. In the end, the Alliance could not form the Government in these two states.

Had all the Opposition parties, including PAS, been able to come to a consensus, they could have formed a state government in Perak. In all the peninsular states except Johor — traditionally an UMNO stronghold — support for both UMNO and MCA had eroded badly. In Parliament, the Alliance won 74 out of 140 seats compared to 89 out of 100 seats in 1964. The majority was enough to form a government, but a weak one.

197

The Opposition parties were jubilant and did not hide it. They behaved as if they had won the General Election. The Chinese-based DAP and Gerakan, in particular, were elated by their success and wanted to celebrate on the streets of Kuala Lumpur. The police gave them permission to hold a procession in certain areas but they ignored the designated routes and deliberately headed towards the old Malay settlement of Kampung Baru.

Given the unusual level of tension during the long election campaign, the decision to allow this celebration was, in my opinion, unwise. Many non-Malays who predominated in the crowd made rude remarks and gestures. They taunted the Kampung Baru Malays with such cries as *Melayu balik kampung* (Malays, go back to your kampongs), and "This is our country now". What had started as a celebration was turning into something very different.

---

[1]  The founding President of Gerakan, Tun Dr Lim Chong Eu went on to serve as Penang's Chief Minister for 21 years.

[2]  This group included Professor Datuk Dr Syed Hussein Alatas, also a founding member of Gerakan, and author of the book *The Myth of the Lazy Native*. The book deconstructed conceptions of the indigenous people of Indonesia, Malaysia and the Philippines as lazy and unproductive.

The next day, May 13, the Kampung Baru Malays, joined by Malays from areas around Kuala Lumpur, mounted a counter-celebration. When the large crowd went out of control, Kuala Lumpur's fateful racial riots ensued.

Trouble had long been brewing and some of us had seen it coming. I had tried to alert the Tunku to the signs but he did not give me a hearing. In the two years leading to the 1969 General Election, antagonism between Malays and Chinese had risen sharply. The constitutional provision of certain privileges for the Malays and other indigenous people had been openly questioned by many Chinese as well as the PPP's Seenivasagam brothers. In their largely Chinese constituencies near Ipoh, they had strong local support against the MCA and the Alliance.

Around this time, 11 Chinese men were found guilty of treason and sentenced to death for their crime. Malay suspicion of the Chinese was further aggravated by the Tunku's decision to have these men's sentences commuted to life imprisonment after the case attracted condemnation and appeals for clemency from all over the world. The Tunku said that he had even received an appeal from the Pope. Many countries were abolishing the death sentence at the time, and they saw imposing the sentence for treason, rather than murder, as political and therefore unacceptable. Yet his decision, his readiness as ever to be unduly conciliatory and give way to Chinese demands, angered the Malay community and contributed to his growing unpopularity. I could identify with that sense of Malay disappointment myself.

198

Many Chinese also refused to serve in the armed forces or the police as they disliked spending time doing something that earned them little in return. The general feeling on the ground was that while the Chinese wanted the privileges of citizenship, they were unwilling to shoulder the responsibilities.

The PAP of Singapore also did its bit to increase Chinese dissatisfaction with the status quo, in which the Malays apparently wielded more political power than the other races. In the 1964 General Election, the PAP had used the slogan "Malaysian Malaysia", creating the subtext that the status quo meant a *Malay* Malaysia. The PAP clearly did not see the Malaysia they joined as a country for all Malaysians. The party lost the 1964 elections but continued to talk about a Malaysian Malaysia — even after Singapore was expelled. The PAP mantle was now draped over the DAP, a party formed by Malaysian Chinese members of the PAP. By persisting with the Malaysian Malaysia campaign, the DAP incited Chinese chauvinism and so helped stoke the fires of Malay racialism.

On their part, the Malays became emotional and argued their case poorly. Officials at the Dewan Bahasa dan Pustaka were always promoting the Malay language and urging everybody to speak it. They failed to point out that while Malay was designated the national and official language, other languages could be used freely, including for instruction in schools. Nowhere else in Southeast Asia was this permitted, let alone guaranteed by law.[3]

But the Chinese did not seem to appreciate these finer points and the fairness of the Constitution of Malaysia. Dr Tan, as well as the DAP leaders, harped upon Malay rights and privileges as if in Malaysia only Malays had rights and others had none.

Although the Malays are masters of political nuance, ironically, in argument, they often lack subtlety and emphasise the wrong things. They also take pride in themselves for all the wrong reasons. They like to emphasise their *ketuanan*, that is, their being masters of the country, even though they are not. The PAP never talked of the Chinese being masters of Singapore because they did not need to. Everyone knew this was the case.

The PAP wanted a "Malaysian Malaysia" because they knew that, without positive discrimination in favour of the Malays, the Chinese would dominate every field, including the Government. Even in Malaysia today, despite all the so-called privileges and opportunities enjoyed by Malays and other indigenous people, there are proportionately more educated and professional Chinese and Indians than Malays. In business, the Malays still lag very far behind. Thirty-six years after the NEP, they have managed to achieve only a 20 per cent ownership of economic equity when 30 per cent was the original goal. Yet as I have often argued, blaming others is not the

---

[3]   In most Southeast Asian countries, the law requires all citizens, primarily the Chinese minority, to adopt indigenous names. There is no such regulation in Malaysia.

solution; the Malays themselves must accept a good part of the blame for the community's under-performance.

When the May 13 riots broke out in Kuala Lumpur, I was on my way to the city by road. I was hoping to see UMNO colleagues and leaders to discuss why I had lost my Kota Star Selatan parliamentary seat. At Tanjung Malim, about an hour from the capital, I was stopped by the police who asked me to turn back.

I had expected something to happen, but nothing of the scale and violence of the riots. I feared that violence might spill over and the Chinese living in Malay-dominated states would be in danger. As it turned out, those living in rural areas among the Malays were not touched and the situation outside of Kuala Lumpur remained calm. There was no outward animosity and no confrontation from either side.

Tan Sri Abdullah Ahmad, who was then the political secretary to Tun Razak, said he had been horrified to witness a Malay man chasing a Chinese man and stabbing him. Malays outside of the city did not condemn the riots even though there was general anger in the community. But they were mindful of the Government's order not to take any action independently.

When I finally made it to Kuala Lumpur a few days later, the city looked like a war zone. I was shocked to see the extent of the damage. Many buildings had been blackened by fire and the skeletons of numerous burnt-out cars blocked the streets. Here and there, black smoke still rose as another building was torched. Officially, more than 100 people, mainly Chinese, were killed. The atmosphere was very quiet and strained. Other than the strong police and military presence, few people were to be seen and all the shops were closed. I thought it was the end of Malaysia as we knew it. Malays and Chinese, I thought, would never be able to work together after this. I even wondered whether I would ever dare go into a Chinese shop again.

The international Press wrote Malaysia off. Foreign observers had repeatedly predicted that the Chinese and Malays would not be able to live together. The Malays, they now declared, would seize power and rule the country without any democratic practices or pretences.

The Tunku was in tears. He could not understand how this could have happened. He blamed instigators, generally the communists, because in those days they were the main bogeyman. After he called for a state of emergency, Parliament was suspended and a special body called the National Operations Council (NOC) was set up under Tun Razak. There was to be a Cabinet under the Tunku, but for all intents and purposes, Tun Razak was to run the country. The Tunku had never been involved in actual administration, preferring to focus on policy. Tun Dr Ismail, who had left the Government in 1967, agreed to return as Minister in the Cabinet and as the number two man in the NOC.

By and large, the political parties that had indulged in racist rhetoric also came quickly to their senses. They denied being the cause of the riots but were all willing to help reduce the tensions. While in Kuala Lumpur I met Tun Musa Hitam, Sulaiman Alias, Abdullah Ahmad and the other young Turks, and discussed the political situation. We believed that the Tunku was to blame, that he had been so taken up with euphoria over the creation of Malaysia, he had failed to see what was happening on the ground.

While the Tunku was setting up the new Cabinet, Tun Tan Siew Sin made a public statement that the MCA would not join the Cabinet and the Government but would remain in the Alliance. Tun Tan felt that, having failed the Alliance, the MCA did not now deserve to be in the Government. This triggered heated discussion in the Press, especially the Malay papers, and among the Malay public. Asked to give my opinion when I was interviewed by telephone, I did not mince words. I said unequivocally that the MCA should not be in the Government. It had not supported the Alliance and its members (as in Kota Star Selatan) had even voted for the Opposition, including PAS.

I knew I was not helping matters but my anger at the MCA was strong and personal. They, I felt, were the reason I had lost the election. The bitterness of defeat, the knowledge that someone you regarded as your supporter had let you down, coloured my words. So I thought it only right that the MCA leave the Government.

It was this statement that drew the attention of the Tunku and made him decide to write to me. In a letter dated 6 June 1969, he said that I was not being helpful. My statement had made matters worse at a time of extreme tension when the country had not yet recovered from the riots of May. The trouble, he wrote, had spread to Sarawak and might recur in the Peninsula. He urged me to be patient and not to do anything until conditions were settled in the country.

I wrote back to him on 17 June, some 10 days after receiving his letter. When I read it now, I see that I was most intemperate in my language. It was not as if I was replying in the heat of the moment as I had deliberately given myself time to cool down. But I must have been fuming over my losing the election and the role played by the MCA and the Chinese in my defeat. The Tunku's request that I be patient and avoid doing anything that might worsen the situation only angered me more. If the partners of the Alliance were not ready to be honest with each other, I thought, we might as well do away with the coalition.

In my letter, I accused the Tunku of being the cause of the racial riots — and effectively of a coalition and even regime crisis — because he had been too soft with the Chinese. In particular, I wrote to him about commuting the death sentence of 11 Chinese men who had been found guilty of treason. I blamed him for listening only to the sycophants around him. In that letter, I wanted to tell him what people really thought of him. The Malays, I wrote, had been so insulted by the Chinese and Indians during the Opposition's "victory" celebration that they lost control of themselves and started to riot and kill people. Others may have been incited, but the culpability for their frustration rested with their leaders who failed to appreciate the feelings of the Malays.

To hurt him even more, I told the Tunku that Malays, whether from PAS or UMNO, hated him. I accused him of playing poker with his Chinese friends at the height of the crisis, when the Emergency was declared. The Chinese, I said, considered him naïve and of low calibre. The Civil Service, police and armed forces no longer supported the Government and now leaned instead towards PAS. I hinted that he might well lose control over the armed forces and once this happened, it would be near impossible to regain their respect. The people, I told the Tunku, thought it was time for him to step down.

In addressing the Tunku in this way, I knew I was courting arrest and detention. I mentioned in the letter the fate of Aziz Ishak, the former Minister of Agriculture, who had been sacked from the Cabinet and detained under the ISA for doing less than I had. But I also stated outright that I was prepared to go to jail for my views. Finally, I insisted that my statement on the MCA's not joining the Government was made in all sincerity. If the Tunku allowed the humiliation of the Malays to continue, there would be a worse price to pay.

It was my fervent hope that the Tunku would read my letter through and see the truth, no matter how bitter it may have been. I had given this letter in confidence to two of my friends. I needed their support and understanding so that, if I was indeed arrested, they would know why.

On hindsight, I was unforgiving and deliberately provocative in my letter. I could have been milder, but I wanted to hurt the Tunku, to shock him into realising all that he had been avoiding. I wanted him to know that he was the cause of all our nation's troubles. I now regret my harsh tone very much.

Yet I found it odd that the Tunku simply could not understand how racial tension could have arisen. When I knew of him in his younger days, when he was in the Kedah State Civil Service, he had always shown great concern about the Malays. But after he became Prime Minister and head of the multiracial Alliance, his views seemed to flatten and become one-dimensional.

Unkind as my letter may have been, I do not think I could have handled the situation differently, so great was my anger at that time. I had lost the election and was not in a position to influence the Government. While I was still a member of the UMNO Supreme Council, it was inactive. I was simply responding to the tumultuous Malay sentiments of that time. So many people were very angry with the Tunku, but none dared to do anything. I, on the other hand, felt the need to act. As far back as the Malayan Union crisis of 1946, when I moved a small group of schoolboys into public action, I had felt the same way: one may grumble endlessly, but it is action that can make a real difference, that can change the course of history.

Very quickly, the letter was reproduced and circulated throughout the country. I was in two minds about the letter being made public. On the one hand, it was good for people to know what I had written. On the other, there was the possibility that it would reflect badly on me, and might even cause action to be taken against me. I soon found out that there was considerable support for what I said and many people contacted me to express their agreement. But the letter's wide circulation caused great consternation among Tunku loyalists.

I received a phone call from Tan Sri Senu Abdul Rahman, who was at that time the Secretary-General of UMNO. He roundly told me off for writing such a letter and strongly suggested that I withdraw it. I told him I could not, as I had meant every word I had written. Besides, these were not just my views; what I said was the general view of the Malays and the Tunku needed to know what was happening on the ground, especially with regard to the Malays.

Senu said I had hurt the Tunku's feelings. He himself was angry because he, Khir and the Tunku were very close and had been friends since their time together in the early Kedah Malay nationalist group Saberkas in the 1940s. Apparently, at the time of my writing the letter, the Tunku was unwell and in hospital. My 17 June letter was handed to him only after he was discharged. On 30 June, he replied. In a seven-page typewritten missive, he pointed out that his letter to me had been couched in civil language but my reply had raised numerous issues with the intention of smearing his good name. He said I was wrong in thinking that he did not know what was being said about him. He "knew" of my activities with friends to overthrow him. He prayed and hoped I would realise the error of my ways.

He questioned my claim that I knew the views of the *rakyat* and said that no one had given me a mandate to speak on their behalf. He pointed out that he had intervened in the case of the 11 Chinese individuals because of world opinion. As to playing poker, that was his way to relax.

He referred to his service to UMNO and the Malay people, how he had resuscitated the party and restored our country's honour and independence. All was fine so long as the party was doing well, but the moment it faltered all manner of accusations were directed at him.

I was disloyal to the top leadership, he again said, and he knew of my plotting against him. But he still held power as head of the party and unless I withdrew from the Council, he would bring this matter up with its members.

I could have left it at that. But I was still angry. I still felt the Tunku's leadership had failed to alleviate the economic plight of the Malays, and even the Indians were doing better (although many of them were still among the poorest in Malaysia, there were also many in the professions — in medicine, law and engineering). I decided I should reply to explain why I had written my letter.

I apologised for my harshness, but there was no way to put things clearly without sounding harsh. I said I appreciated his service to UMNO. But had Dato' Onn not united the Malays from the various states, I pointed out, the demand for Malayan Independence might have come from non-Malays. They, not the Malays, would have led the movement and claimed the prize. Yet despite his immense service to UMNO and the Malays, Dato' Onn still had to leave the party when majority opinion so decided. Past service did not make a leader immune to the consequences of subsequent bad decisions.

While I acknowledged all the good services the Tunku had rendered to UMNO, it was time, I reiterated, for him to step down. It had to be that way, since nobody of stature would challenge him openly. Anyone who disagreed with him would find himself dismissed from the Cabinet, sent abroad, or even detained as Aziz had been. Had there been no fear of punitive action, I said, he would have been challenged long ago.

A meeting of the Supreme Council had already been scheduled for 12 July and my case would now be on the agenda. I told the Tunku that I knew of the meeting, and that I expected to be expelled from the council because no one would dare go against him and speak up for me.

On 11 July I went to Kuala Lumpur and met many of my supporters, including Professor Zainal Abidin Wahid, who was then a member of the academic staff of the University of Malaya. He and his friends within and outside the university believed that they could influence the Supreme

Council through a signature campaign. In the last General Election, Zainal had campaigned for PAS because he believed the Tunku had betrayed the Malays. Suddenly realising the possibility that PAS might win in my constituency, I had appealed to him in the midst of the campaign to intercede with PAS on my behalf. It was a futile and desperate measure. Zainal did not have much influence over PAS, but he had always been close to me, especially when pushing his Malay agenda.

Though he was able to get about 6,000 signatures, I did not believe that the campaign would change anything. But I accepted the massive document he gave me for submission to the Supreme Council. I arrived early on 12 July at Sri Taman, Tun Razak's residence, where the meeting was to be held. Some other members were already there. They advised me to withdraw my letter and apologise to the Tunku, but I reserved comment. Nearly all the Council members attended the meeting, and they included UMNO Ministers, *Menteri Besar* and Chief Ministers. The Tunku himself did not attend so in his absence, his deputy, Tun Razak, would chair the meeting. I appreciated the Tunku's choice not to be present to avoid any appearance of seeking to influence the decision of the Council. But in truth, I did not think his physical absence would have any bearing on the outcome. The Tunku was the President of the Council — anyone taking my side would effectively be stating a vote of no confidence in his leadership.

The police expected some trouble from some of my sympathisers so security was tight. Police personnel surrounded the residence and the roads leading to it were closed, except to members of the Supreme Council. The Press was kept away and there were no photographers present. I went in with the others when the meeting was called. The usual preliminaries were cut short and the subject of my sending my letter to the Tunku and circulating it to the public was then brought up. I was asked by Tun Razak whether I was prepared to withdraw the letter and apologise to the Tunku. I briefly explained the background of the exchange but made it clear that I was not prepared to withdraw my letter or to apologise. I was then asked to wait in the sitting room.

To this day I still do not know exactly what ensued at the meeting. Some members felt that expulsion from the Council was too drastic. I believe

Datuk Harun Idris was among those who cautioned the Council against dropping me. I had the weight of Malay opinion behind me, they said. The meeting lasted almost two hours. Outside in the lounge, I was restless. I knew I would be expelled, but I had already decided that if asked to recant, I would hold my ground. Doing otherwise would diminish my hard-won credibility, and anything I might ever say after that would be ridiculed. That I could not afford.

Before the meeting ended, Tun Dr Ismail came out to me in the sitting room. He asked me again whether I would be prepared to withdraw my letters and apologise to the Tunku. I confirmed my stand and he returned to the meeting. Shortly after, the meeting was adjourned and I was told that a public announcement would be made that afternoon. I believe they wanted to inform the Tunku of their decision first.

At 4.05pm the Minister of Information and Broadcasting, Tan Sri Hamzah Abu Samah, issued a 17-line statement by the UMNO Secretary-General declaring that "the Council considered the action of Dr Mahathir in distributing copies of the correspondence between him and Tunku Abdul Rahman, President of UMNO, which contained vitally important party matters and details which in view of the situation in the country should have been first discussed by the Council of UMNO" as a breach of party discipline and regulations. Accordingly, "the Council decided that Dr Mahathir has ceased to be a member of the Council as from that day". It added that the Tunku was not present at the meeting.

I did not protest or try to make a case for myself and simply went back to Kedah, relieved that I had been expelled from the Council, and not the party. In a telephone interview I said I would remain an UMNO member as I still believed in its struggle. Two days later action was taken to ban my letter along with five other documents which were being circulated. One was allegedly by a university lecturer entitled, "The Struggle of the Non-Malays", which was purported to have urged the Chinese to deprive the Malays of their rights and seize power in Malaysia.

Any person who was found publishing, printing, selling or distributing any of the six documents would be sentenced to a maximum of three years jail or a fine of $2,000, or both. Possession of these documents without legal grounds would attract a sentence of one year in jail or a fine of $1,000, or both. No reference was made to my obvious possession of copies of these letters.

Surprisingly PAS, which at that time had not yet joined the coalition, came out strongly in support of the Government. Hassan Adli, who later became a Minister in Tun Razak's and Tun Hussein's Cabinets, urged PAS members not to get involved in this "personal crisis". Gerakan, then an Opposition party, also supported the Government. This was less surprising as the letters could have been construed as stirring up the Malays against the Chinese. The statement was issued by Professor Datuk Dr Syed Hussein Alatas, the President of Gerakan, but the party itself was largely Chinese.

In an extensive interview in *Utusan Zaman,* a Malay paper, the Tunku alleged that there were groups stirring up hatred against him among university students. He regretted that his 17 years of good work had been shattered. He denied reports in the foreign Press that Tun Razak had taken over power from him, explaining that he was not well and could not shoulder all the responsibilities of running the country. Remarkably, he blamed the 13 May riots on the distribution of my letter (even though it was written after the incident).

While travelling to the states to meet the State Operation Councils, the Tunku talked of taking legal action against me to clear his name before he retired. The newspaper reported a power struggle within UMNO between the "ultras", meaning me and my supporters, and the leadership at that time.

This same allegation was also made by the Tunku in his book *May 13 – Before and After.* I was singled out as the author of a plan that others executed. He bitterly condemned the tone of my letter and its distribution and reiterated his strong belief in the MCA and MIC as partners in the Alliance. Even if there were only three MCA members, he said, he would still work with them. They would always be partners, whether they were big or small.

He accused the "ultras" of wanting the Malays and only the Malays to govern the country and immediately dismissed this as an unrealistic idea, since there were only slightly fewer non-Malays than Malays in the country.

On 27 September, after I had steadfastly refused to withdraw the letters, Tun Razak announced that, at a meeting of the UMNO Supreme Council chaired by him, it was decided that "Dr Mahathir is no longer a member of UMNO". Asked by the Press if I was expelled from the party, Tun Razak repeated, "All I can say is that he is no longer a member of the party".

So, I was finally expelled, just as the Tunku had threatened. The Opposition, especially the DAP, was overjoyed. Many Alliance politicians were disturbed and worried about possible consequences. Most Malays were angry but I think the Chinese felt I deserved what I got. Questioned repeatedly by the Press, I made it clear that I had no intention of joining any other political party. I also said that I would not appeal against the decision.

I had expected to be expelled all along so I did not feel any great loss at first. But I soon realised that I was now without a platform to influence events, especially the national agenda for advancing the Malay community. Now I would never be an UMNO leader, and, should elections be held again, I would not be nominated by the party or enjoy its support. I had become a nonentity, a person of no consequence. Finally, the truth sank in.

# Chapter 16:
## In The Political Wilderness

I was made persona non grata twice in my political career, the first time in 1969 and the second in 2003 when I stepped down as Prime Minister. But the harder of the two was my expulsion from UMNO. After five years as a Member of Parliament from 1964 to 1969, I had grown used to having frequent visitors to my house. But the constant stream of UMNO members and people from my constituency of Kota Star Selatan ceased abruptly after I was expelled from the party.

Still, I was not completely ignored and I received a number of invitations to give talks. The youth branches of the party's local divisions invited me to speak, not about recent events, but about politics in general and my views about the Malays, their predicament and how it might be remedied. It was a strange period, a kind of political pause or moratorium. The Tunku may not have liked people inviting me to speak but he did not penalise anyone for doing so. During the period of National Operations Council rule, ordinary politics and elections had been frozen so, for a while, the threat or fear of not being made a candidate just wasn't there. People in those days were not dependent, as so many are now, on government contracts that can be revoked. And the Tunku, I must say, rarely sought to punish those who were not on his side.

There were some brave souls, not UMNO members, just people genuinely concerned about the Malay *rakyat*, who came to see me. For example, there was Fatimah Hamid Tuah, a student activist who was well-known for publicising the cause of her father Hamid Tuah and his followers who were being displaced from their land at Teluk Gong in Selangor. She arranged for a number of students to visit me to hear my views on politics, particularly the plight of the country's Malays and the failure of national politics to address their needs.

No one else was championing the cause of the Malays then. Among the younger group in UMNO, there were some who shared my basic concern over the fate of the Malays but they were generally not as outspoken as I was. People such as Tun Musa, Abdullah Ahmad and Sulaiman Alias largely agreed with me, but they were reluctant to say so aloud. Mostly, it was ordinary Malays and students from the University of Science[1] in Penang who came to speak to me and to pray, asking Allah to protect me and give me guidance. But, with one or two exceptions, no UMNO members came to my new house in Titi Gajah in Kedah to discuss politics.

Needless to say I was disappointed, especially with my UMNO colleagues who had shared my views of the Tunku. It was painful to learn that I had so many fair-weather friends. Being deprived of our lively political debates also depressed me and only heightened my loneliness. Only later did I realise that this was my first taste of how easily you are abandoned when you are no longer "kosher". It did not hit me immediately then, but I recognised the return of this same feeling when I ceased to be Prime Minister. Colleagues started avoiding me and were clearly unwilling to discuss current politics with me. That, I suppose, is how the game works. It has a basic rule: never risk incurring the possible displeasure of those who can exercise power over you. I am largely reconciled to this behaviour, to this unappealing aspect of human nature, yet among the sea of people who no longer wish to know you, there are always those who remember and genuinely value friendship. They make everything — all the sacrifices — worthwhile.

211

Most of the people in my new neighbourhood of Titi Gajah were PAS supporters and one of them was a minor leader in the party. His son was unemployed and from time to time I used to help him out with a little money. The father would come to the house and we would argue about politics, but no matter what I said his faith in PAS never wavered. Yet, unmoveable though he was, our debates filled a void I felt very keenly.

When I was the Member of Parliament for Kota Star Selatan I befriended a rural leader who helped me get to know the villagers better. Manaf Abdullah or Pak Su Manaf (Elder Uncle Manaf) was a natural *kampung* leader who was very knowledgeable about the ways of the *kampung* people. His advice was invaluable to me as I had been born and bred in the town. We became good friends and when one of the State Assemblymen in my constituency died, I recommended him as a candidate in the 1969 General

---

[1]    It is now known as Universiti Sains Malaysia.

Election. He won, but when I later asked him to speak critically of the Kedah government within the State Council over some basic issues such as the failure of Government policy towards the Malays, he refused. He was too frightened. For me, it is important — even necessary — to stick your neck out if you believe in something, but I realise that very few people behave in this way. They much prefer to play it safe.

I was so upset with Pak Su that I cut him off after that. Looking back now, it is clear that I had expected far too much. He was a new representative of the people and it had been very unfair of me to ask him to challenge his superiors head on. It would certainly have blighted his future. How could I have expected it of him when even long-serving Ministers generally do not risk their political lives for a cause?

There was usually a car parked outside our home and I suspected it was the Special Branch, sent to keep a watchful eye on me. I knew I ran the risk of being detained under the ISA. The Tunku had often said to UMNO circles and outside the party that communists were influencing the Malay ultras. In those days the communist bogey was often used when the Government wanted to stifle the Opposition. Every day I expected to hear that knock on the door at 5am, with Special Branch officers waiting on the other side. I think they know you are at your weakest during those early hours. But it never happened.

About two months after my expulsion I decided to visit Kuala Lumpur and contacted my good friend Tunku Abdullah Tuanku Abdul Rahman, the Member of Parliament for Rawang. I usually stayed with him during my visits to the city. I yearned to see friends and political sympathisers from the group of young people with whom I used to associate. Tunku Abdullah told me that the situation in Kuala Lumpur was not very good. Tension was still high and houses were still being burnt. He warned me that I might be arrested if I came, but I decided to go anyhow and see what happened. Having the threat of arrest hanging over my head was simply too unsettling. I did not want to worry Hasmah so I did not tell her about these rumours.

The police knew of my intentions, as did a lot of people, and most of them were sure I would be arrested upon my arrival at the Kuala Lumpur railway station. Tunku Abdullah was at the station waiting for me that morning. None of my other friends were aware of my visit so they were not with him, but Tunku Abdullah was not alone. When I got off the train I spotted the first Malay Chief of the Armed Forces, Tunku Osman Jewa, who was the nephew of the Tunku, on the platform. I also saw a number of policemen. The sight of them made me a little nervous and I fully expected them to approach me. But they did not, so I got off the train and followed Tunku Abdullah home.

Later, after I had been re-admitted into UMNO, I was told that the Tunku had indeed wanted to have me arrested and detained. I found this out from the police themselves, as many of the most senior officers in those days were from Kedah. It was they who stopped him. I was relieved there were some in the police who seemed to be sympathetic. They advised the Tunku that arrest would only make me more popular and he would be more reviled by the Malays.

After that I visited Kuala Lumpur fairly frequently and always stayed at Tunku Abdullah's house. As far as I know, he never suffered any dire consequences for openly remaining my friend after my expulsion. He also remained close to the Tunku and to Tun Razak. He was one of the few who did not feel that he would fall out of favour because of his association with me.

213

But the Sword of Damocles still hung over me. An American visiting professor at the University of Malaya, Karl von Vorys,[2] a political scientist from Philadelphia, came to see me in Titi Gajah. He reminded me that detention, should it happen, might not be for just two years, which I had been prepared to face. It could be for a very long time, as the two-year detention order could be renewed repeatedly. It was then that the chill of fear set in. If I was detained indefinitely, I would lose all opportunity to influence the course of events. It would mean not being heard at all. It would literally mean being locked away and forgotten. The physical discomfort

---

[2]   Karl von Vorys wrote the book *Democracy Without Consensus* and played an advisory role in the Economic Planning Unit from 1968 to 1970 and in the early stages of the drafting of the NEP.

mattered little to me – that I thought I could endure. But knowing that people would no longer care about you because you have been obliterated from their memory, was truly frightening.

With no foreseeable entry back into mainstream politics, I kept busy with the business of making people well. I was also able to conduct minor surgical procedures at my clinic, including circumcisions. I was popular because I used local anaesthesia, whereas the local *mudin* or circumcision specialist used a cutthroat razor and no anaesthetic. I can personally vouch for the pain this can cause. To this day, I get people coming up to me and shyly reminding me that it was I who had performed their circumcisions. I sent more serious cases to the government hospital, as there were no private hospitals with surgical facilities in those days.

I made a lot of house calls and charged my patients very little. Someone even suggested that I could easily win elections by giving free treatment. But this was by no means the reason for my low charges. If I ever ran for office again, I wanted people to choose me because I could serve them politically, not medically. I treated people free of charge when I saw that they could not afford to pay. I believe most doctors do, except that nowadays the cost of medicine is so high that completely free treatment would make a big hole in one's pocket.

Time passed slowly, but not uneventfully. In 1971 Hasmah, who was working as the first woman Medical Officer in Kedah at the time, was involved in a car accident while driving to the hospital in Arau, Perlis. A motorcyclist turned into her path and, swerving to avoid him, she ended up crashing into a telephone pole before her car rolled into a padi field.

She remembers weaving in and out of consciousness before being able to wave to some passing villagers for help. A group of them happened to be nearby as they were literally moving a house to another location, a common *kampung* practice at the time. The first thing Hasmah asked them was if the motorcyclist was all right, but he had already fled the scene. They managed to get her out of the wreckage and into a taxi, which took her to the Kangar hospital. Once she was there Hasmah tried to call me at the clinic, but as it turned out, the telephone pole she had knocked down meant there was no way to reach me by phone. The taxi driver who had taken her to the hospital was kind enough to drive to the clinic and tell me the news himself. I put down tools immediately and rushed to the hospital.

When I finally saw her, Hasmah simply told me that she had been in an accident. She seemed very calm, so much so that I did not immediately realise how serious the accident had been. She managed to get away with just a cut on her forehead but she could have been injured far worse. I was very relieved at her escape. We had been married for 15 years by then, and I had been in the political wilderness for almost two years. I have always had the tendency to keep things to myself, even from Hasmah, mainly because I don't want to make her anxious for no reason. The decisions that are needed are usually mine to make. But during those years when I was out of UMNO, she made things easier for me by being supportive, sympathetic and understanding.

Hasmah and I both came from large families and we had wanted a large family ourselves. But we ended up stopping with four children of our own — Marina, Mirzan, Mokhzani and Mukhriz — and adopting three more. By the time Hasmah finished her housemanship and we were able to get married, I was 32, and that was considered to be quite old at the time.

Being a parent is a great accomplishment and it also feels like a windfall of good luck. Having children to care for also makes you feel immortal — you know that they are going to survive you, that they will have children of their own and that a part of you will always live on through them. I confess I wanted one or two of our children to become doctors themselves, but as it turned out, none of them wanted to.

When we had our children Hasmah was one of the few working mothers at the time, and since there were many occasions when we both pulled night duty, we were used to being unable to meet each other as often as we would have liked. The children were very young and seemed to accept that this was the way things were.

My wife thought I would want a son first but when Marina was born in 1957 in the Alor Star General Hospital, I was very happy. At dinner we would sit her on the high chair between us and on weekends in our free time, we would drive with her to Penang. Marina was always outgoing and independent. When she was about 13, we hosted a girl named Lauren Hess from the US under the American Field Service programme.[3] Lauren was about Marina's age and the two of them got along well with each other. I later met Lauren's parents in California and they expressed their wish to have Marina stay with them. I had now "inspected" their house, they said, and they hoped I would trust them. We sent Marina to stay with the Hess family for about three months when she was 16 years old.

She travelled alone and even went to school there, and when she came back I think she had picked up a few American ways. She wanted more freedom and wanted to study in Kuala Lumpur. I had a problem with that, and told her she would have to stay in Alor Star with us. Marina turned out to be a lot like me: argumentative, stubborn, opinionated and always believing she is right. She does not mind expressing her views and that makes things very difficult sometimes. Hasmah always said that an elephant could get crushed between two people who think they are always right.

Mirzan has always been much more quiet and retiring. At one point he sat for an examination that would qualify him to study in a private (i.e. public) school in England, under a programme designed to expose Malaysian children to a different way of life and culture. He thought he had failed the exams at first, and he was so upset that he just stayed in his room. But, as it turned out, he was one of the few to be selected, so he left to study there until he finished his 'A' levels. But he found it difficult making friends with his English classmates and he kept very much to himself while he was there. He eventually studied at a technical college in Brighton, before going to do his MBA at the Wharton School of the University of Pennsylvania in the US.

Mokhzani was very outgoing even as a young child — once, in kindergarten, he went up to a girl and told her, "You look gorgeous!" But he also had a tendency to hurt himself by falling down a lot. He broke a femur when Hasmah and I were visiting Europe in 1962, and after that, he broke his arm in an accident at the age of four. Still, it never seemed to dampen his cheery spirit.

---

3    Established in 1947, the American Field Service sends thousands of students and teachers to live and study in a foreign country in a programme that promotes understanding between different nationalities and cultures.

I was on a train on my way to Kuala Lumpur when Mukhriz was born. He could be quite irresponsible when he was young and he was not very studious at first. But after we sent him to Japan — where he learned to speak Japanese fluently — and then to the US to study, he changed and became much more serious in nature. I think he resembles me the most. Helping people seems to give him a lot of satisfaction, and he's much more of a politician than the others.

The first child we adopted was actually the daughter of one of my patients. It was common practice at the time for parents to ask others to nominally adopt their children by tying a black string around the child's wrist, but in this case, this six-year-old child was brought to our house so often that I eventually decided to bring her into the family properly. Her parents agreed. Her name was Aishah, but since it had become a tradition for all the children in our household to have a name that started with the letter "M", we re-named her Melinda. Melinda adapted quickly to our family, and the other children accepted her as their sister with no resentment. When she later married, she moved to Japan with her husband.

Much later, I adopted two children from Pakistan, a boy and a girl. During a visit to the country I had seen the local children wearing full traditional gear, and I had been so charmed that I knew I wanted to adopt one into our family. As it turned out, we ended up with two, Maizura and Mazhar.

Hasmah left the job of disciplining the children to me and I know I was often quite strict with them when they misbehaved. My own sisters had pinched me when I had misbehaved as a boy, and I remember once fleeing my father as he chased me around the house, to spank my bottom. I once used a ruler to spank Mokhzani, but I caught myself starting to get carried away and I stopped immediately. That's why I'm against teachers using canes in the classroom — there is a tendency to lose control when you are angry. That was the first and last time I used the ruler. After that all I had to do was bring it out and show it to the children, and that was enough. I even had a cane, although again, it was also more for salutary effect.

My wife would scold the children too but more often than not, she would take their side. Sometimes when I scolded the children she would tell me I was just as bad as they were. But it was important that they understood their mistakes. I wanted them to be disciplined, not to be spendthrifts, and to learn to be able to look after themselves. At the same time I wanted to be closer to my children than my father had been to me when I was a boy, so I worked hard to have an affectionate and relaxed relationship with them. That was something I had wanted from the very beginning, so despite my occasional harshness, my children did not grow up fearful of me. Mealtimes, especially dinners, were important because that was when we could all talk together.

As they grew older, my children did not always approve of the things I did during my political career or the people I associated with. They often told me that these people were making use of me, when really I thought I was the one who was making use of them. My children did not always share my political views either, but whenever there was a heated discussion I always clammed up because I did not want to quarrel with them.

Hasmah always said that my years out of politics between 1969 and 1974 were a blessing in disguise because it allowed us to focus on our new house in Titi Gajah, which we had moved into during the 1969 General Election. It was at that house that I tried my hand at boatbuilding to fill up my free time. There was a river behind our house and I wanted to go upstream to our small *kebun* or fruit orchard, where we grew rambutan[4] trees.

I ordered the plans from the US and modified them with the help of our neighbour, who was a contractor. I also read books to figure out how to work with fibreglass and build moulds. In the end I built five boats, each named after one of my children. I started with a small boat, then a racer, but the last one was a 26-foot cabin cruiser built from marine plywood. I sailed that one with my children from behind the house to Kuala Kedah, and then across the sea to Pulau Payar. The fishermen of Kuala Kedah were so frightened the boat might sink that several of them accompanied us on their own boats, just in case. On hindsight, the trip was certainly risky because I was not an expert boat-builder, and if there had been a storm we would have likely sunk. The boat, however, turned out to be very seaworthy and I later sold it to the Attorney-General, Tan Sri Abdul Kadir

---

[4] The rambutan fruit is palm-sized and sweet, but seems exotic to foreigners because of its hairy appearance.

Yusof, who sailed it all the way to Mersing in Johor. I found boat building to be a lot of fun, although I burnt my arm once on the exhaust of one of the boats. I still have the scar.

I did other things to occupy my time. In the workshop in the basement of our house, I followed instructions in a manual to make wrought-iron chandeliers and rods for hanging signboards. We had a hand-operated letterpress but I could never learn to do the typesetting properly. With a partner, I also opened a small shop that could do off-set printing work, duplications and other odd printing jobs.

I have always been curious about how things work. I dismantled clocks as a child in a bid to find out what literally made them tick, but had less success with putting them back together. I would stand for hours outside the window of the printer's shop near our house, watching the men inside work the presses. When I visited car manufacturing factories during official visits to Japan, I always wished they would show me how the car was made from the very beginning of the assembly line and not from the end, as they usually did. You cannot learn about things from back to front. I wish more people had this kind of curiosity, because I have found it to be very useful to me.

My interests were eclectic, and even included interior decorating. I designed our wedding bedroom, from the bed and kidney-shaped dressing table to the fabrics and carpets (the colour scheme, ironically enough, was a PAS shade of green). I designed the first desk I could afford to buy after I had become a Medical Officer.

Not everything I tried my hand at worked out perfectly and there were a few near-disasters along the way. I once tried my hand at smelting iron in my workshop in the house, just to see if I could do it. Nothing happened when I tried to light the gas the first time, but so much gas had already seeped out of the tank the second time I tried to light the fire that there was a small explosion. Nothing was damaged and I was not hurt, but I did not tell anyone about what had happened either.

As a medical practitioner I earned a bit more money than most other people, so when a friend could not operate a Mobil petrol station as he had no money, I bought it off him as an investment. I did not have the time to manage it myself however, and it was very badly run. In the end, the Mobil representative came to see me and said if I wanted to keep the petrol station I would have to give up my medical practice. I was not willing to do that so the station was taken away from me.

It was not the first time I had tried my hand at other things besides medicine and politics. When I was still a Member of Parliament in 1966 I experimented with being a property developer. There was one other Malay property developer at the time and I thought that if he could do it, there was no reason I couldn't either. I took a piece of land that my sisters owned and built 32 three-bedroom, semi-detached houses, giving my sisters a house each as payment for the land. The development was called Taman Malid, a combination of my name and that of my partner, Tan Sri Khalid Haji Abdullah. I did not make much money from Taman Malid, although I can claim to be among the first Malay property developers in the country.

Just before the 1969 General Election, I also got into the business of tin mining. My partner in that venture was Abdullah Gaffar, who everyone said was the only Malay who could cheat the Chinese. He had discovered tin-bearing land in Sintok, near where Universiti Utara Malaysia now stands, but the land was very rocky, which caused terrible problems for our tin mine. The rocks damaged the impeller so badly that it had to be replaced frequently. To solve the problem I invented a way of separating the rocks from the tin without the impeller. We built a road up to a sloping grill, where the lorries would dump the tin-bearing earth. We then used water jets, which caused the rocks to roll off and the tin to fall between the grill to the wooden receptacle below. Still, there were so many rocks that within a few days there was an enormous pile of them and it cost us money to move them. I ended up losing RM80,000, all the money I had made out of the Taman Malid deal, and we had to close the tin mine.

I wanted to know if I could make money out of these ventures, and when they did not go as expected I was sometimes angry at my partners. But these businesses proved to be good learning experiences, as were all my hobbies. I have always believed that if you want to learn something, you can always find the time to do it. Reading books on different subjects always helps, and I have never had any qualms about asking questions.

Politics, however, never strayed far from my mind. I was especially frustrated over the apparent lack of progress that the Malays were making. The country's professionals — the doctors, lawyers, architects, accountants — were mainly non-Malays. In the business sector, Malay participation was minimal — indeed hardly visible. While the Tunku was Prime Minister there were no serious attempts to increase Malay participation in the economy. For as long as he headed the Government, I knew that he would do nothing about this unfortunate state of affairs. But being on the outside, all I could do was swallow my frustration and anger. What was the use of *Merdeka* and self-rule, I asked myself, if we could not improve our unhappy and ever more desperate situation?

# Chapter 17:
## An Outsider's Lament

Speculation about the possibility of my re-entering UMNO after my 1970 expulsion never died down, especially when, asked repeatedly by the Press, I made it very clear I had no intention of joining any other political party.

But belonging to no party meant that I had no platform to air my views. It was deathly suffocating. I was also very angry. I could not bear to see how the Malays still lagged behind the other races in their own country. After more than a decade of Independence, during which they had been very much at the helm of the Government, they had made no progress at all. Surely more could be done to push them into the economic mainstream.

Under the Alliance's Independence "bargain", the Malays may have dominated politics but to me politics was not an end in itself. It was and is merely a means to achieve certain objectives. What good was having a Government dominated by Malays if they, as a whole, were poor, backward and not respected even in their own country?

They had agreed to share their homeland, their *Tanah Melayu*, with the Chinese and Indians. It may seem a small point now, especially to younger generations, but it needs to be emphasised that this was a great sacrifice on their part. UMNO had willingly forsaken the Malays in PAS, causing a split in their ranks, in order to work with the non-Malays. To secure its rival's share of Malay votes, UMNO could have worked with PAS and played up the Islamic issue. Had UMNO done that, it could have been strong enough to win elections and form the Federal Government solely on its own terms. But that would have alienated the Chinese and Indians and, governed in that way, Malaysia would never have been stable. That was the main reason why UMNO did not join up with PAS against all others.

UMNO's rejection of PAS was based on the belief that it was not a true Islamic party and that it could not help the Malay cause. UMNO had its own religious leaders, generally more open-minded than those aligned with PAS, and, unlike PAS supporters in those days, UMNO members were not drawn completely from the villages. The party appealed to well-educated Malays, people who were worldly and understood what the problems were.

But, more grounded in pragmatic political considerations than in religious doctrine, UMNO's rejection of PAS and the Malay-Islamist option still carried a heavy penalty. It meant that UMNO's bargaining strength with its partners in the Alliance was weakened by PAS's significant share of the Malay vote, so it had to depend in many ways on non-Malay support.

The dismal 1969 General Election results showed how this dependence on non-Malay votes could hurt UMNO. Still, the party would not forsake its non-Malay friends in order to get the support of the Malay supporters of PAS. But the cost of sustaining the Alliance's working arrangements between Malays and non-Malays and its need to satisfy non-Malay demands had meant that the Government had done very little for the Malays in the first decade of Independence. In many ways, while others had gone ahead, most Malays had stood still or fallen even further behind.

That was the source of widespread Malay anger and resentment that, at the 1969 elections and in its aftermath, they had vented against the Government and its leadership, personified by the Tunku himself. There was now no way of going forward without addressing those Malay feelings and the legacy of Malay disadvantages. This would eventually require a new political formula and a new kind of politics, which the Tunku's UMNO successors, headed by Tun Razak, would have to be brave enough to provide. This would have also offered me a way back into politics, but there was no way for me to know this at the time.

223

The political relationship between the Malays and non-Malays would repeatedly resurface in the years to come. Even though I pushed very hard for the advancement of the Malays, I always recognised the value of working closely with the Chinese and Indians. Yet in the eyes of many, including many foreigners, I remained the Malay chauvinist.

The more immediate problem I faced was how to say what I wanted to say and be heard. I had few choices as there was never any question of me joining another party or becoming an independent. I considered PAS a betrayer of the Malays and never once believed in their Islamic pretensions. PAS would never be able to build a truly Islamic state in Malaysia like those of the great age of Islamic civilisation. Nor would they be able to rule and develop the country. The party had no coherent plan or strategy for the betterment of the Malays or of the country. Since they had failed in the overwhelmingly Malay state of Kelantan where they held power, how could they expect to rule Malaysia, with its multiracial population and its complex federal structure?

I also blamed PAS for the split in the Malay ranks. There was no PAS when we were fighting against the Malayan Union, when politics was not yet financially rewarding. There had been no talk of setting up an Islamic state then. All the Malays, including those who were learned in Islam, had been united as Malays against the threat to the Malay people. At the time, UMNO had its *ulama* section or council, but they broke away from the party. By then politics held the promise of lucrative jobs and they feared that the more religious would not be selected as election candidates. Until they broke away to form PAS, the relationship between the *ulama* and non-*ulama* in UMNO was good as it was rooted in common concern for the Malays. When the Malays were united even Great Britain, with all its imperialist might, had to bow to their demands. But with the defection of PAS from UMNO, Malay unity was shattered. This was not a wise course of action or something that I could ever forget.

It was only after the UMNO *ulama* broke away to form their own party that they started to make references to an Islamic state. Those with an Islamic education obviously saw this as a good political gimmick; others, who were less educated, fell for it.

To further its own cause, PAS quickly learned to use symbols that Malays associated with Islam, such as the colour green. This enabled it to project its own cause as that of Islam itself — and to depict its opponents, especially UMNO, not just as mundane political rivals but as the enemies of Islam. In speeches and rallies, PAS members quoted from the Quran and it did not matter that most people in the audience could not understand. The crowd would be impressed when the speakers recited these verses to them and gave an interpretation on the spot. Nobody could be sure if they were accurate. Sometimes the speakers would leave out the part of the verse that carried the real message of Islam. PAS could elaborate its self-serving interpretations, always confident that no one in the audience would know the difference. They would tell stories purportedly from the Hadith, the sayings or deeds attributed to the Prophet Muhammad, which similarly could not be verified. PAS claimed that those who voted for them would go to heaven while those who voted for UMNO would go to hell since their cause embodied that of Islam and their opponents, in working against PAS, were enemies of Islam itself. This remains the party's message today, even if it now uses more sophisticated terms and phrases as well as modern technology to promote its cause.

As part of this strategy of identifying itself in the popular Malay imagination with Islam, PAS chose to label UMNO as *kafir*, or infidel, declaring that the party was not Islamic because it cooperated with non-Muslims. Years later I had a good laugh when, in the late 1990s, PAS decided to work with the DAP, the party that totally rejected PAS's Islamic state objective. It was unabashed hypocrisy.

Yet while PAS used Islam as a political tool, it never hesitated to obscure the good values that Islam teaches its adherents. These are values which, when understood and properly practised, would make Islamic states great, would produce great thinkers as leaders able to create and build entire civilisations. But I suppose if they really adhered to those values, PAS orators would not be able to use Islam as their primary political tool or label UMNO members infidels. Instead, they would have had to find ways to cooperate and strengthen the *ummah*. But how then could they hoodwink the electorate? How would they project their political cause and make it appear sacred?

225

Islam advocates the brotherhood of Muslims and urges Muslims not to fight against one another. If PAS really believed that, they would not have broken away. The party is largely made up of religious teachers in the village schools or *pondok* (huts). As revered teachers they shape the minds of their students, old and young, to accept what they say about Islam without question. They arrogate to themselves the title of *ulama*, the learned ones. They even assert that as *ulama* they are the successors of the Prophet, although they know very well they are just ordinary people with only some knowledge of Islam. The Muslim *ulama* of old were truly learned people who studied Islam thoroughly and wrote treatises on it. Most had no political motive. But today anyone who knows a little about Islam or who has graduated in Islamic studies claims to be an *alim*, one learned in Islam, and be a card-carrying member of the religiously erudite. Membership of the Malaysian Union or Association of Ulama can also make one an *alim*. No wonder Islam has acquired a thousand interpretations and is now divided against itself. Muslims of today are a very gullible and confused lot. The kind of *ulama* who align themselves with PAS and work through it feed upon that gullibility and cultivate that confusion.

PAS could easily have undermined our quest for Independence, or at least delayed it, had they done just a little better and prevented the Alliance from winning enough seats in the 1955 Legislative Council elections to form the Government. As it turned out, the newly-formed Alliance coalition of MCA, MIC and UMNO won 51 seats, giving it an overwhelming majority. Had PAS campaigned a little more astutely, it may well have forced the course of Malayan history onto another path. But PAS won only one seat, mainly because it declared that Malaya, with no industry to support it, was not yet ready for Independence. The party famously stated that Malays could not even make needles, much less run their own country. PAS also

tried to create fear in the Malay mind that the Chinese, with their wealth and superior education, would dominate an independent Malaya, leaving Malays to be their coolies.

In the 1955 elections PAS did not invoke Islam fully, focusing more on anxieties surrounding the question of independence. When it did use Islam in the 1959 General Election, the party took control of Kelantan and Terengganu. After forming the state government of Terengganu, PAS leaders began to quarrel among themselves. By 1961 several defected to UMNO and brought down PAS in the state. It recaptured Terengganu in 1999 but the state returned to UMNO rule in 2004. Quarrels between PAS leaders also led Kelantan to fall to Barisan Nasional in 1978. But in 1990 PAS recaptured Kelantan and remains in charge of its state government until today. Today the party's leadership is changing. More non-religiously trained leaders are becoming prominent, but it is still undoubtedly the religious teachers who hold sway.

My views on PAS clearly stated, I did decide to speak at a PAS campaign during the Kapar by-election in April 1971, when I was out of UMNO. My frustration at not being heard had festered to that extent. In my speech I commented on the softness of UMNO in dealing with the MCA and MIC. I pointed out that rich Chinese *towkays* were friendly with the top UMNO leaders and appeared to be influencing them.

It was a huge political risk, one that could have cost me what few ties I had remaining with UMNO. I feared my decision would anger my supporters in the party, so I took pains not to identify myself with PAS. I used the opportunity only to air my own views and I made sure that whatever I said that was critical of UMNO could not be construed as support or endorsement of PAS. It was a fine line to tread, but in the event, I did not lose the support of those in UMNO who regarded me as their voice in the campaign to change the leadership of the party.

Over 30 years later, my detractors among the UMNO leaders still delight in reminding the party that I once spoke at a PAS rally. What they seem to have forgotten is that soon after the speech, UMNO Youth, led by Datuk Harun Idris, came to persuade me to rejoin UMNO. The episode was forgotten after my return and I gained much support from the UMNO rank and file when I made bids for positions in the Supreme Council.

Although they provided me with a platform, PAS showed no inclination to have me in their party. They feared losing the Chinese votes that had helped them defeat UMNO in a number of constituencies, including my own, in the 1969 General Election. Their subsequent flirting with DAP years later was laughable but, in this sense, not surprising.

Meanwhile, Tun Razak heard that I had spoken at a PAS event and had criticised UMNO. He was probably informed by people hoping to elicit a negative reaction from him towards me. His response must have disappointed them. Instead of taking offence, he simply said that I was not an UMNO member and was therefore free to say what I liked.

I was not in contact with him at that time — in fact, I made no attempt to establish contact with any of the UMNO leaders — but I sensed that, in some ways, he held similar views to mine. I think he also knew that I was never angry with the party, just with the Tunku's leadership. I believed fiercely that the party was right in its philosophy and approach and that it was more than capable of attaining its objectives if there was a change of leadership and Tun Razak took over.

I still managed to keep track of developments within UMNO through the newspapers, from rumours and via a few party members who communicated by phone and sometimes met me. My mind kept turning to how I could make my views known in a widespread manner. The newspapers would certainly not publish what I said.

I remembered several articles I had written while I was still a Member of Parliament and began to sit down and write more of them, on different subjects that supported my ideas on the Malays and the possible solutions for their problems. I started sitting down for about an hour a day to put my thoughts down, and soon had enough for a book, which I decided to call *The Malay Dilemma*.

# Chapter 18:
## The Malay Dilemma

*The Malay Dilemma* outlines my political philosophy concerning the Malays. As early as my teens, I had noticed that Malays were not involved in businesses in the town of Alor Star, where I grew up. But for a few Indian Muslim shops dealing in spices and one Indian store which ground dried chillies, the retailers were mostly Chinese. They were involved in all kinds of commercial activity, from manufacturing gold and silver jewellery to selling books and tailoring. Chinese coffee shops were also everywhere, whereas Alor Star had only "one and a half" Malay shops. One was in Jalan Langgar and it sold Terengganu *songket*, a rich, hand-woven fabric, and brassware. The half-shop, which only took up half the space of a normal lot, was in Jalan Pekan Melayu and sold magazines and religious books.

*Pekan Melayu* means "Malay Town", but it seemed like a misnomer under the circumstances. At the time I thought the problem was a lack of premises, but I was to learn later that it was far more than that. Under the New Economic Policy (NEP), when premises were made readily available to Malays, the number of shops did not increase much.

Even at that young age I was troubled by the absence of Malays in commerce. Why could they not have at least a coffee shop in Alor Star? The problem continued to nag at me as I grew older, and I mulled over ways to get Malays into business. During the Japanese Occupation some enterprising Malays formed cooperatives and went into rice wholesaling. The leader was a former government servant who had acquired a shop-house in Jalan Regent, and, for a while, the business was reasonably successful. However, for some reason, it stopped when the British came back.

I thought that upon Independence, the Malay-dominated Government would remedy the situation, but nothing was done. Since 1947, I had been writing in the *Straits Times* about the plight of the Malays but besides earning a little pocket money for myself, my articles did not change the attitude of the Malays. When I became a Member of Parliament in 1964, I again wrote about the Malays. I showed my article to a friend, Khalid Awang Osman, a former Member of Parliament and ambassador, who became so excited that he made duplicates and distributed them among UMNO leaders and Malay intellectuals. Many of them commented positively and suggested that something should be done about the matters raised in the article. But nothing was.

The theme of *The Malay Dilemma* revolved around the position of the Malays — should they be content with being poor or should they attempt to take ownership of some of the country's wealth, even if this meant blurring the country's economic development? As indigenous people, I thought their plight deserved consideration. Mere independence would be meaningless if they derived no benefit from it.

To find the remedy, I sought to identify the deep underlying causes of Malay marginalisation from the modern economy and the reasons for their chronic underperformance. In *The Malay Dilemma* I blamed hereditary factors, poor educational facilities, inbreeding, chronic endemic diseases like malaria and tuberculosis, colonial government policies and practices for the poor performance of the Malays.

230 The New Economic Policy, launched in 1971, addressed most of these problems fairly well. Education is now made available to all, right up to tertiary level. Thousands of scholarships were created for a wide range of disciplines. I also observed that with more young Malays entering tertiary institutions and more marriages taking place outside the extended family, the problem of inbreeding between close relatives was considerably reduced. The general health of the average young Malay also improved so that they became physically able to study or acquire skills through training.

Prior to the NEP there were practically no Malays working as repairmen or mechanics. Now if the electricity supply or an air-conditioner breaks down, the electricians who answer your call are often Malays. It warms my heart to see them confidently hoisting their ladders and brandishing their tools to repair my air-conditioners. At our national car plant, Malays constitute the majority in every department. They design, make clay models, put prototypes together, test them, programme the assembly, and mass-produce the cars, acquiring these intricate and involved skills in less than 17 years after the NEP. The success of the national car proves my contention that Malays are capable of mastering all aspects of modern business. The outstanding accomplishments of the national oil company, Petroliam Nasional Berhad, or PETRONAS, is yet another example of sterling Malay performance. The biggest corporation in Malaysia, it is the only Malaysian company on the Fortune 500 list. It operates not only in Malaysia but in almost 40 other countries, competing with the oil majors, and is involved in every aspect of the petroleum industry, upstream and downstream.

The past 30 years have also seen many Malays appointed as senior executives in major foreign companies and banks. They have done very well, exuding self-confidence and are accepted as equals by their European and other Asian colleagues. Today, this once backward community occupies a broader area of responsibility than just business and commerce. The administration of the whole country is largely in their hands. Under the British, they had only held junior posts, but Independence, growth and democracy demanded highly skilled administrators and Malay officers rose to the occasion. Ours may not be the most efficient administration, but we are certainly one of the best-run former colonies in the world. Our reputation was so good that many developing countries sent their public-sector officials to Malaysia for training.

There are now Malay entrepreneurs and contractors who own billion-dollar companies and operate not only in Malaysia but also in many other countries. It is said that the Malays now have 20 per cent of the total wealth and shares in the country, which would suggest that our national goals, as well as my own hopes in *The Malay Dilemma,* are being fulfilled. But that view is misleading. Some 12 per cent of Bumiputera wealth is held in trust by various government institutions, which effectively insulate most Bumiputera to the real risks of doing business. They are not enterprising risk-takers but rather government-coordinated rentier shareholders. The attitude and mentality of the passive beneficiary is not the mental revolution that the Government wants to promote in the Malay and other Bumiputera communities, especially through the NEP.

Our towns and cities also do not reflect any obvious change in Bumiputera participation in business as the urban areas are still largely Chinese. The new buildings that are not Chinese-owned belong not to Malay real estate and property magnates, but to the institutions set up by the Government for the Bumiputera or simply to the Government itself, as state-owned and occupied buildings. The only visible change in our large cities that shows more Bumiputera involvement is the presence of Bumiputera employees in hotels, restaurants and shops. Prior to the NEP there were hardly any Bumiputera among the salespeople, waiters, cooks and other employees in the hotel industry. The Majestic Hotel in Kuala Lumpur and the Railway hotels were all operated and staffed by the Hainanese. This is no longer so today — Malay chefs, looking very confident and smart in their white headgear, cook both Malay and international cuisine with expertise and flair. While this is heartening, there are still hardly any Malay retailers in the towns and cities. The Government's efforts to attract Malays into the retail business through franchising have not yielded significant results.

The NEP has had its achievements, but they fall short of my hopes. This gap is worrying — it has already been nearly 40 years since the NEP was introduced, and Malay work attitudes and practices leave much to be desired. Why have the special efforts under the NEP failed? It is because of greed and poor money management. When Malays go into business, avarice overtakes prudence and good practices. They go into businesses in which they have no expertise and many fail to do due diligence. They borrow without assessing their creditworthiness, and want to live upon ungrounded hopes rather than sound, hard-headed calculation and self-discipline. Sometimes they even use company money illegally. Perhaps worst of all, they often use a portion of the borrowed capital for personal luxury consumption.

In *The Malay Dilemma*, and in many public addresses since then, I have tried to highlight the underlying problem in Malay attitudes, work ethics and work culture. These observations bear repeating. The key idea of the NEP was not to see Malays becoming disproportionately wealthy through Government help. The distribution of wealth in society at large needs to be equitable at all levels, including the very highest. Then and only then can antagonistic divisions along economic and racial lines be avoided. If there are wealthy non-Malays, there must also be Malays in the same income band. The goal of getting Malays to own 30 per cent of national wealth may not yet be achievable but a critical mass — at least — must be in the hands of Malays, distributed perhaps not equally, but fairly.

The trouble is the majority of the Malays have not yet learnt the uses of money. For them it remains merely a convenience, a means of exchange for buying or acquiring goods and services, and gaining status. Money is still not regarded as capital that can be managed and invested in order to earn more money. To them, money is merely for consumption, and not to generate more wealth. If the NEP is ever to overcome the original "Malay dilemma", the Malays will have to learn to manage wealth and treat money as capital.

In my book I blamed the social environment and the Government for Malay underperformance in the modern economy. Now, from fresh observations, I am convinced that much of the problem lies with the Malays themselves. Unfortunately, too many of them still refer to my original analysis and related solutions to overcome their disabling dilemma. Worse still, most Malays have come to think that the affirmative action instituted by the Government in the NEP is a recognition of their "superior" position as the indigenous people of this country. They claim that because they are the *tuan* or lords of Malaysia, this discrimination in their favour must be permanent.

This is the new Malay dilemma. Do we take the bull by the horns and tell Malays the truth, or do we refrain for fear of losing their political support? If the affirmative action favouring them is removed, the Malays will likely again become a deprived, dispossessed and marginalised community in their own country. But if we continue with it, we risk making the Malays a permanently dependent people, like the Native Americans. This is a malignant fate, but a different disaster from that which I highlighted in my book.

The NEP has helped the Malays to secure some of the country's riches for themselves without disrupting, too greatly, the overall economic picture or the rights and expectations of the non-Malays. Could the country have done better economically had it not been bound by the NEP solutions? Perhaps. The economy might, for a while, have registered a higher rate of growth, but social cohesion and political stability would have been in danger. This would have damaged investor confidence and slowed down the longer-term rate of economic growth. A strained and divided society cannot be home to a thriving economy, even in the narrowest of economic terms. The resulting and worsening antagonism between Malays and Chinese would very likely culminate in another May 13, and this second bout of violence may become even worse than the first.

Unfortunately, the protection and privileges accorded by the NEP may weaken the Malays further by lulling the next generation into complacency, thinking that the NEP's affirmative action will always be there for them to fall back upon. I have spoken about this danger many times, likening the NEP to crutches which, when used too long, would result in atrophy of the muscles. The NEP can make the users so dependent that their inherent capability regresses.

The argument that I originally made in *The Malay Dilemma* was that, for a variety of reasons, Malays submitted easily to their immediate environment, both physical and human. They like the easy way out and fail to rise above challenges. In time, a set of dominant cultural traits surfaced, which encouraged compliant adaptation and discouraged effort. With this, Malays stopped trying to adapt to changing circumstances but remained laid-back and compliant.

In time, this cultural orientation became a major impediment to successful Malay engagement with the modern world. This is because, under colonial rule, they were marginalised and were culturally demotivated. I had proposed in *The Malay Dilemma* a way to break out of this bind. The solution was to provide as many opportunities as possible and for the Malays to make the best of the chances given. How would they respond? Would they seize and make the most of the opportunities? Or would they take them for granted and enjoy them without serious effort? Would they treat these prospects as a temporary privilege or a permanent entitlement?

With the benefit of hindsight, we now know the answer: while some Malays and other Bumiputera have taken up the challenge, the majority regrettably have not. Now, what we appear to have is a new culture of indigenous entitlement. This new environment impedes rather than promotes the growth of modern Malay cultural, professional, economic and entrepreneurial competence. Far from supporting professional Malay capabilities and competitiveness, it dampens the desire to strive.

Still, I strongly believe that Malays have all the capabilities of other people. Take the Malay woman, for example. When I was a boy, women were confined to the kitchen and regarded as mere chattel or vessels for producing children. It was believed that they had limited intellectual capacity and would not benefit from education. Fortunately, in Independent Malaysia, girls were given the same educational opportunities as boys and the results have been amazing. Today, over 60 per cent of the students in our universities are girls, including Malay girls. Moreover, they now make up a big percentage of our professionals. In some of our hospitals, almost all the specialists are women. I do not think that women are inherently better — they have simply availed themselves of the opportunities to work and study hard. The boys, though equally capable, have not. The most recent surveys indicate that the boys are missing from the universities and the workplace. Could it be that they have grown complacent and more indulgent of leisurely pursuits? Among young Malay boys in particular, the *Mat rempit* phenomenon[1] has obviously contributed to this imbalance.

History has many examples of a backward people not only catching up, but outstripping those ahead of them. The Muslims were progressing at a phenomenal rate when the Europeans were still stuck in the Dark Ages. This state of affairs was not to last. Seeing the level of Arab skill and education, the Christian Europeans set out to acquire their knowledge. Unfortunately, at the same time, Muslims decided to focus their learning on religion and nothing else. In the end, the ignorant Europeans became stronger and culturally better endowed than the Muslim Arabs and, ever since then, Europeans have maintained their advanced status. The Arabs have made no effort to regain the knowledge for which they had once been famous. Had the abilities of the Europeans and Arabs been inherent, their relative positions and strength would never have changed. It was the value system developed by the Europeans and the rejection of Islamic philosophical and intellectual culture by the Arabs that resulted in this astounding historical reversal.

The Malays can also change their fate, but to do so they must face a new dilemma: to persist with the NEP would mean taking away the need

---

[1]  The term *Mat rempit* refers to motorcyle daredevils who race through the city streets at night, often in large groups.

to be self-reliant, yet abolishing it could weaken the Malays and undermine their political position in their own land. The Malays have a saying which aptly captures the predicament now facing the community: *Telan mati mak, luah mati bapak* (If you swallow, your mother dies. If you spit it out, your father dies).

There is a belief among most Malays that they will always rule this country since they make up the majority of the population. But this will not hold true if they are divided. If this happens, other interested parties will move into the power gap, making the dilemma of discerning Malays even more acute.

No one in Malaysia was prepared to publish *The Malay Dilemma* so I took it to Donald Moore, a publishing firm in Singapore. They were immediately keen and asked for all rights, including film rights. Making money was the last thing on my mind: I only wanted to be heard and so I signed everything they asked.

The book was a runaway success and was immediately banned by the Government. As with any banned material, it was soon in great demand and Malaysians would travel to Singapore to smuggle it in.

I fervently hoped that my ideas might now help shape the country as it searched for a new foundation and direction. I was told that Tun Razak asked the panel then drafting the New Economic Policy to read it. Whether or not they did I do not know, but several ideas I detailed in the book are similar to the recommendations in the NEP.

With this, my support among the Malays grew, but I was still adamant about not starting my own party. The Malays had hung together successfully during the time of the Malayan Union, and I had no intention of splitting the community further than PAS already had. Few people, especially Malays, thought this way. Perhaps they did not have the long perspective that comes with age, or the experience of watching the power of the Malays when united. Splintering the community seemed of no consequence to most.

At heart, I remained an UMNO member. It was the only party that I believed in. But I could no longer accept the Tunku's leadership and his simplistic belief that the Malays would always be content with jobs in the Government. I also did not like his being an Anglophile, or his devotion to the Commonwealth and all things European. It was not that I thought the Tunku was not "Malay" enough. Indeed, I deeply appreciated what he had accomplished in the past, when he had been instrumental in leading the nation to Independence. He was much more successful as a leader of a Third World country than most and whether or not he was the right man for it, he was the one who had done it. Dato' Onn, who should have been the one, went against the party and in that sense, the Tunku was much more adept politically. He structured Malayan and Malaysian politics to make his agenda acceptable to all communities, including the Malays themselves. But as the 1969 General Election approached, his easygoing policies became of great concern, not just to me but to other young Malays. They subjected him to unprecedented questioning, which was something that he was ill-suited to handle.

The Tunku seemed content to hand Malays civil service jobs instead of getting them actively involved in the economy. Moreover, considering how the British had tried to impose the Malayan Union on us, I thought the Tunku's subsequent pro-British stand was unacceptable. Where was the anger, the outrage, for what they had tried to do? What made it worse was that the British did not even care to treat him with due respect. When he had gone to study at Cambridge University he had been initially denied student accommodation, simply because he was not British. He had to contact his father, the Sultan of Kedah, before the university officials agreed to provide accommodation for him where the white students stayed. When the Tunku became Chief Minister, the British allocated him a broken-down house that leaked so badly he could hardly sleep at night. I could not understand how or why he was willing to forget all this. In short, in the Malay interest, I thought it was time for a change in Malay leadership.

So did many Malays, including many who honoured and respected the Tunku for his astute captaining against canny British obstruction during our pursuit of *Merdeka*. But he could not go on living on his past glories while the Malay future became ever more bleak and uncertain. That was why we felt he should go; the question was, when would he?

# Chapter 19:
# UMNO Opens Its Doors

Towards the end of his time as Prime Minister, it must have been obvious to the Tunku that he had become very unpopular. He somehow believed that I was responsible for the public's changed attitude towards him and that I was working with Tun Razak to get rid of him. This was the talk at the time among UMNO leaders; it has also been recently alleged by Dr K. K. Soong.[1] Certainly, our exchange of letters made it clear that the Tunku and I didn't see eye to eye. When you quarrel with someone, it is easier to write something down and send him a letter than to go to him and tell him to his face that he is wrong. But the fact that I "went public" with my criticism of him did not mean that I was scheming to overthrow him, as he seemed to believe. When the Tunku later publicly explained that he had been Prime Minister long enough and wanted to retire, he would continue to tell people that he thought his removal had been engineered by Tun Razak and those whom he described as communists.

In a Radio Malaysia interview on 26 August 1970, the Tunku said that there would be no change in government policy after he resigned. Perhaps he meant to provide reassurance of continuity, but I did not take it to mean that his successor Tun Razak would not change anything. Whenever a new person takes over the leadership of a country, policies must change. A new leader wants to show that he is different; he wants to leave his own mark on the nation. Occasionally, in an effort to show how different he is, he may dismantle the policies of the previous leader or try to highlight mistakes that had been made. He may want to show how much more in touch his Government is with the needs of the country and people.

This, of course, is human nature, but it is sometimes a dangerous course to take. Such changes may not embody a clearer understanding of how government is best conducted for the country's good. Yet a new leader may have the freshness of mind and spirit to correct what is evidently wrong or to inject renewed vigour into the pursuit of the previous Government's objectives.

---

[1]  In his book *May 13: Declassified Documents on the Malaysian Riots of 1969*, Soong alleges that the May 13 riots were not the result of inter-ethnic tension, but of an attempted coup by an UMNO faction.

I believed firmly that Tun Razak would be far more proactive than the Tunku had been in helping Malays enter the business and commercial world. I also believed he would alter the Tunku's very pro-West and pro-Commonwealth foreign policy. If these changes were made, particularly with regard to Malay participation in business, I would work very hard to try and rejoin UMNO.

Since the 1969 General Election, UMNO had not been officially active. But after Parliament reconvened in 1971 and the ban on politics that had been imposed after the 1969 riots was lifted, UMNO planned to have its General Assembly in January of 1971. At this meeting, new office-bearers would be elected. Generally, people welcomed this as a sign that things had settled down enough for the country to pick up political activities once again. Everyone — especially the Malays — now expected the Government to attend promptly to their dissatisfaction.

During the assembly the late Tan Sri A. Samad Ismail of the *Straits Times* newspaper, who had been a member of the AAPSO mission I had led when I was a Member of Parliament, wrote that the party was striking out on a new course. What UMNO would now do under Tun Razak would be quite different from what had been done under the Tunku, who had been very pro-West. Tun Razak wanted to be neutral and make friends with everyone. I was sceptical at first and held back because I wanted to see what changes and policies the new UMNO leadership would introduce.

In the assembly's party elections there was to be no challenge against Tun Razak as UMNO President and Tun Dr Ismail as Deputy President. They were already the Prime Minister and Deputy Prime Minister respectively. But there would be an open contest for the positions of Vice-Presidents and below.

Some UMNO divisions in Kedah and Perlis wanted to propose my name for the Vice-Presidency in the belief that it would help promote the ideas that I had laid out in *The Malay Dilemma*. But I was not even an UMNO member at that time, nor could I be certain that my plans to rejoin the party would succeed. When questioned by the Press, I pointed out that I was not eligible to contest and I appealed to UMNO divisions not to nominate me.

Shortly after I spoke at the PAS by-election at Kapar, UMNO Youth Chief Datuk Harun Idris came up to Kedah to see me, accompanied by his close associates Aziz Salehuddin and Yahya Zakaria. They tried to get me to sign an apology letter so that I could apply to rejoin UMNO. I wanted to return to the party very much, of course, but this was not the way I was going to do it. I felt I had nothing to apologise for — what I had done was to make statements that I believed were completely factual and reflected Malay sentiments.

I had always suspected that I had been expelled not at the wish of the party, but on the specific wishes of the Tunku. Of course there were some who may have wanted me out anyway — Tan Sri Senu Abdul Rahman and perhaps Tan Sri Syed Jaafar Hassan Albar, who probably saw me as an upstart, a pushy young politician who was not sufficiently respectful of the Tunku's leadership. But an apology was out of the question because it would mean losing all credibility. I was also not prepared to crawl back, resentful and humiliated. That would not be a return to the party, but a grudging surrender. Pressmen called soon after to ask whether I would apologise but I stood by my previous statement. That, evidently, did not endear me further to some leaders in the party.

In the meantime, the Government was working on a new, detailed policy to give the Malays and other Bumiputera a fair share of the economic wealth of the country. A team was set up to devise and implement an economic strategy, which later became known as the New Economic Policy or NEP. It was not immediately apparent how Tun Razak was going to achieve the NEP objectives but at least he made it clear that he wanted to correct economic imbalances. He was a pragmatist, not the blind slave of any particular ideology. He was prepared to borrow ideas and policies from anyone so long as they might serve the Malaysian interest.

I was heartened by Tun Razak's leadership, though the changes he made must have hurt the Tunku. These were necessary changes, but not any that the Tunku himself, with his hands-off approach to policy implementation, could have directed. Another aspect of the change in direction was foreign relations. Tun Razak made it clear that Malaysia was to be non-aligned and was to establish friendly relations with all countries, regardless of their ideology. The Tunku's extremely pro-West foreign policy was to be diluted.

At home, Tun Razak worked vigorously on the NEP. Its main feature and objective was to restructure the economy both to eliminate poverty irrespective of race, and the identification of race with economic function. It was clear that the latter statement meant Malay participation in the country's economic activities and non-Malay participation in the public sector. A study by the Prime Minister's Department of the ownership of national wealth found that 60 per cent of the country's economic wealth, as represented by share holdings in big corporations, was owned by foreigners, 30 per cent by the Chinese and the rest by the other races. The Malays and other Bumiputera owned less than two per cent.

It was decided to reduce foreign share to 30 per cent while the Chinese share was to be raised to 40 per cent and the Malay and indigenous share to 30 per cent. This approach was carefully balanced. The policy was to be carried out not by expropriating what belonged to the foreigners but by enlarging the economic cake. From the new growth, a bigger share would be apportioned to the Malays and the Chinese. The foreigners would have to make do with a smaller share of the new growth until their portion shrank to 30 per cent.

241

I was doubtful of this strategy at first. The Chinese share had to grow by only a third of what they already had. For the Bumiputera, it was a completely different story. Since they now owned less than two per cent, achieving the 30 per cent target meant that their share would effectively have to grow by over 1,500 per cent.

But I could see no other way. Taking away what already belonged to the Chinese and the foreigners would prompt intense resentment that would have slowed, not promoted, the country's growth. There would be less, perhaps very little, new wealth to redistribute. Despite Government assurances that non-Malay wealth would not be touched, a fairly large number of Chinese sold out and emigrated to Australia and elsewhere.

I was happy with this affirmative action policy because I always felt that unless the extreme disparity in wealth between the Chinese and the Malays was corrected, tension and animosity would never be erased. The last time that resentment surged to the surface, the 1969 riots ensued. For Malaysia to be stable and therefore politically and economically healthy, that economic gap had to be reduced, even if it could not be eliminated completely.

After my ouster from UMNO, I was interviewed by Leslie Hoffman, a well-known journalist from the *Straits Times*. His conclusion was that I was still maintaining my "hard line". I pointed out that the restructuring under the NEP had to involve some channelling of opportunities from the Chinese to the Malays. I qualified that by saying "…the authorities will have to deny some Chinese applicants places in the university and in the government service. Some Chinese who are qualified would not be able to get jobs or promotions in the Government service".

But I also added that "something as drastic as this is necessary if the situation is going to be changed in any permanent sense". Hoffman pointed out that *The Malay Dilemma* had made me very popular with the Malays and many young UMNO members regarded me as "the ideologue" of the "new order". Hoffman himself was not convinced by my ideas. He was one of those who thought there should not be any discrimination in favour of the Malays. Asked about the Alliance coalition, I said it was the best way for the Malays and Chinese to work together and I complimented the Tunku for this. But he had only concentrated on the top layer, leaving little cooperation on the ground. Still, I believed that only the Alliance formula would work.

The Press frequently sought my opinion of the Government and asked about my rejoining UMNO. My answers were always cautious. I noted that the new Government was more pragmatic but I was non-committal about my re-entry. The local English and vernacular newspapers as well as the foreign Press tried to pin me down on the subject whenever they could. I was good copy for journalists — I was controversial without being inflammatory. With my reputation or stigma as a pre-1969 "ultra" still intact, I was a convenient bogeyman for all those who were opposed to doing anything to redress Malay disadvantages.

These days the foreign Press still want my opinion on things happening in Malaysia. My not being in Government has not changed their attitude towards me. They still regard me as a Malay racist who jailed my deputy. No amount of evidence to the contrary will change this perception.

For my part, when asked a question I just state the truth as I see it. While it is the truth from my perspective, my viewpoint regularly clashes with the perceived wisdom of the day and the stand people take in general. When I was cast out of UMNO, people did not say I should be silent, that I had lost my right to speak and be heard. On the contrary, they wanted to know what I was thinking. After I stood aside as Prime Minister, things were strangely different. People seemed to think that I either had nothing more to say or I had no right to say it. This difference is largely due to the policies of Tun Abdullah Ahmad Badawi. I got back my voice only after he was forced to retire as Prime Minister.

In July 1971, an incident occurred which was misconstrued by many, but ended up working in my favour. I was invited to present a paper at an UMNO Youth Seminar in Morib, a town in southern Selangor. Tun Razak came to open the event. UMNO Youth was then under Harun, who had always supported me, and Tun Razak had raised no objection to my being there.

As Tun Razak was leaving the seminar, I was pushed forward by the jostling crowd around him. For the first time since my expulsion I met him face to face. Naturally, I greeted him and shook his hand. The Press snapped a picture and it appeared the next day on the front page of most papers. We had simply greeted each other but the picture suggested that a full reconciliation had taken place. Once more a whole flurry of questions was raised about whether I would rejoin UMNO. Tun Razak was smiling in the photograph but people made more out of it than they needed to. Still, for me it was progress.

I then delivered my paper on automation and unemployment. During the break the Press again asked me whether I would be rejoining UMNO. This time, I replied, "Slowly, slowly. Wait until next year".

My concern, even worry, for the country made me continue my criticisms of government policies, even after indicating that I would like to rejoin UMNO. I hoped the Government would take note and would act on some of my ideas so I accepted many invitations to speak at events. I often spoke about the urbanisation of the Malays. I believed they could only progress if they left their *kampung,* or if the *kampung* were developed into small towns. The Government subsequently spoke of the urbanisation of the Malays and other indigenous people.

As usual, I thought it would be easy. Malays would go into retail business and the towns would not be so exclusively made up of Chinese shops and businesses. This would bring Malays, Chinese and Indians together. I pictured Malaysian towns and cities where the businesses and shops would be evenly distributed among the races. In 1969, when the Malays rampaged through Kuala Lumpur burning shops and vehicles, they could be certain in most areas that all shops belonged to non-Malays, primarily the Chinese. But when the towns had shops and houses belonging to all races, things would be different. If Malays again torched shops in anger, they would also be likely to destroy what belonged to their own community. They might then think carefully before resorting to such actions.

Unfortunately, reality did not prove so simple. When Malays began migrating into the towns and cities, they did not go into the same businesses as the Chinese. Instead, they illegally occupied vacant land and built huts to live in that were actually worse than their former *kampung* houses. In these urban *kampung,* they started little shops in haphazardly scattered shacks made of zinc and timber, with plastic sheet roofing and extensions. These areas lacked proper roads and drains. Dirty water flowed from shops and houses onto to the earthen roads. There were flies everywhere. These squatter settlements quickly became slums, ironically located near skyscrapers of granite and marble.

Today, people in these high-rise buildings still look down on the rusty zinc-roofs and dirty alleys of the slums. And when these skyscrapers happen to be hotels, foreign visitors are given a full view of how the Malays live in a country where they exercise political power, where they dominate the Government, and where they like to think of themselves as the *tuan.* Malays often talk of *ketuanan Melayu*, but does living in zinc-roofed slum huts reflect their exalted position as masters?

In time, I came to understand why urbanisation led to an inferior quality of life for the Malays. Urban living is more costly. One cannot grow food or rear chickens and everything has to be bought. Without a reasonable income it would be difficult to survive. Besides, a migrant to the city leaves his family, his first-line social support group, behind in the *kampung*. He can no longer fall back on them for support or sustenance. Rather, it is the other way around: urban migrants are supposed to earn enough money to send some home. They must now adopt and adjust to a whole new lifestyle and culture, one that is rooted in the cash-based consumption of even basic living necessities. Cash is always scarce and hard to earn. Migrants to the cities either did not realise this before leaving the villages or else, in their eagerness to leave, they did not care.

Later when the Government built multi-storeyed flats for these slum-dwellers, they refused to move in, demanding single houses like those in the *kampung*. It was as if they imagined that they were still living in the village. They arrived from the countryside without the capacity to conduct any kind of business. They came expecting to get jobs but most available work was far from where they lived and travel always costs money. What they earned could not support an urban lifestyle. They started small businesses selling food, stationery, secondhand clothing and so on, but these businesses remained small and insufficiently capitalised. They rarely interacted with others and the mixing of the different races which I had envisaged did not take place.

Living in towns is not only about bright lights. It is about being skilled enough to be employed or to do business. It is about being savvy and understanding that the road to success is built upon hard work and discipline, even if you have to start small. It is about a willingness to adjust to a new way of living. Failure to do and be all these will result in a life more barren and deprived than in the rural areas they had left behind. The myth of urban living is that it is always a move up the economic ladder. The bitter and lasting reality is that it can be a descent into squalour.

When I see most urban Malays today I grieve, largely because they have not made the necessary adjustments. I had no idea that this would happen when I suggested that Malays move into the towns and cities. I was naïve.

Governments may plan but it is the response and behaviour of the people that determines the results. Yet the urbanisation of the Malays has not been a total failure. This is a topic which I will return to later.

Besides Malay urbanisation, I also spoke on other issues, usually at the invitation of UMNO Youth. I spoke against the excessive use of machinery because unemployment was high in those days. Machines often displace labour rather than absorb it in intensified employment and production. Our early attempts to industrialise had not been very successful. We tried the path of import substitution: manufacturing the products we usually imported but only for our own market. It did not work as there were no economies of scale. Since our domestic market was very small, everything we produced for ourselves cost much more. Nor did we team up with foreigners to acquire their advanced technology. Buying the latest expensive technology made no sense in producing for a small market.

We also tried to manufacture our own tyres, which seemed to be the right thing to do as we produced rubber. But we found that the cost per unit was high and the technology input low. In any case, we had to import components like wires and threads, and we soon realised that there was a lot more to making tyres than just having easy access to cheap local rubber. In the end, the tyres we produced were not even good enough for our own market. We could not export them, so we could not earn foreign exchange. Import substitution had been the favoured policy during Tun Razak's time and even earlier under the Tunku, although he never pushed it as hard as Tun Razak did. But that choice was not their idea alone. It was the dominant idea at the time in development economics, favoured by most leading international experts. It was the orthodoxy of the day — until it proved unsustainable, not just in Malaysia but worldwide. Our Malaysian experience disproved the belief that, if you have the raw materials, you can produce things more cheaply.

Nor did we seem adept at reading the job market and going where the work — and therefore money — was. Young *kampung* Malays did not want to follow in their fathers' footsteps to plant and harvest rice. Their education made them disdainful of agriculture without preparing them for other types of work. In the 1970s there was a shortage of labour in the rural areas, and at the same time there was a high level of unemployment. The young left the villages for the glamour of the city and few stayed behind to work the padi fields. The growing use of machinery in industries further reduced job opportunities. But at least the use of small Japanese-made hand-tillers and harvesters helped us overcome the labour shortage in the rice fields. I often joked, "Buffaloes are better. They reproduce themselves. Hand-tillers get old and useless and they don't reproduce themselves." Nor can you eat them as curry at village weddings!

Another talk I gave at the time was at the Institute of Southeast Asian Studies (ISEAS), a Singapore think-tank, on "Trends in Malaysia". They were very eager there to keep abreast of developments and new thinking in Malaysia and wanted me to talk about domestic political trends. Instead, I gave my opinion concerning defence issues. I chose to condemn the Five Power Defence Agreement (FPDA) which involved Singapore, Britain, Australia, New Zealand and Malaysia, and said it was worth less than a scrap of paper.[2] Some Australian leaders had said outright that they would not automatically come to the defence of Malaysia, so I could not see the point of such a pact.

It seemed to be a part of the United States policy in those days to contain China. All the pact did, I had said earlier at an UMNO Youth forum, was to identify China and the Soviet Union as our enemy, now and in the future. Those two countries would consequently look upon us with hostility. The US would gain from having another supporter in us. But what would we gain?

Countries belonging to the Association of Southeast Asian Nations (ASEAN) were initially solidly behind the idea of ZOPFAN, a Zone of Peace, Freedom and Neutrality,[3] which Malaysia promoted. But this needed the support of the United States, the Soviet Union and China at a time when the Cold War was still on. The US, which had its 7th Fleet in the Pacific, was the only country willing to support ZOPFAN. Both Russia

---

[2]   According to the Five Power Defence Agreement, created after Britain ended its defence guarantee of Malaysia and Singapore, the five countries would work together should there ever be the threat of attack against Malaysia or Singapore.

[3]   Malaysia, Indonesia, the Philippines, Singapore and Thailand are signatories to the Zone of Peace, Freedom and Neutrality to keep the region "free from any form or manner of interference by outside Powers".

and China simply ignored ASEAN's request to guarantee neutrality and peace in the area.

But no matter what I spoke about in those days when I was still an outsider, the Government never responded. As a political outcast and has-been, I suppose they thought I didn't deserve a reply, but I continued giving these talks and kept a keen watch on national political developments.

At this point, Tun Razak had begun to woo the Opposition parties to join the Alliance coalition. It was a deft move politically — what he really wanted to do was reduce politicking and focus on the NEP objectives. Tun Dr Lim Chong Eu, the Gerakan Chief Minister of Penang, had known Tun Razak during their days as students in England. They were good friends and had participated in the Malaysian Students Association there together. Tun Dr Lim had left the MCA because of his disagreement with the leader Tun Tan Siew Sin. It was essentially a struggle for leadership of the party, and Tun Tan had been backed by his father, Tun Tan Cheng Lock. Tun Dr Lim had no quarrel with UMNO.

At a meeting aboard a Malaysian warship off Penang, he and Tun Razak discussed Gerakan's possible entry into the Alliance. Tun Razak was able to persuade him to join, provided that the Chief Ministership of Penang remained with Gerakan and the party was given a seat in the Cabinet.

The MCA might well have objected to Gerakan joining the Alliance as it was really a Chinese party, not a multiracial one as it claimed to be. Besides, most of its members were ex-MCA, having left the party because of their disagreements with Tun Tan Siew Sin. Gerakan could also undermine the MCA by attracting its disaffected members and by eroding Chinese support for MCA Alliance candidates. Yet the MCA could also do the same to Gerakan. A conflict between the two parties could seriously hurt the coalition, especially in Penang.

But the MCA did not make too strong a protest. It was still, after the events of 1969, in a weak political position and in no condition to resist strongly. Both Tun Razak and Tun Tan must have realised this, so it was not hard for Tun Razak to persuade Tun Tan and the MCA to agree to Gerakan's entry — even though the Chief Ministership of Penang had, until 1969, been the preserve of the MCA.

Many Malays were disturbed by this acceptance of an Opposition party — and a Chinese one at that — into the Alliance. During a question-and-answer session at the Government Staff Training Centre in Petaling Jaya in February 1972, I was asked why the Alliance had formed a coalition with the Gerakan in Penang.

I was certainly not privy to the discussions and agreements between Tun Razak and Tun Dr Lim. Nevertheless, I defended the move. "It is not what party or which leader that is important," I said. "For the Alliance the most important thing is to serve the people. Without the Alliance in the Gerakan-led Government of Penang, the Penang people would not benefit from the Second Malaysia Five-Year Plan.[4] The Alliance Government's utmost and ultimate concern is the welfare of the people and not a certain party or party leaders."

So I found myself defending the Alliance even before I had rejoined it. I approved entirely of what Tun Razak was doing, as such a move was necessary to enable the Government to concentrate on economic development. I went on to explain that in Malaysia, no party which appealed only to communal sentiments could ever expect to form a central government. Neither could any party which forgets the racial origin of its members hope to succeed.

People thought, and many still think in terms of their own race, specifically its position and the opportunities it gets. The Malays felt their race was not getting a fair share of the nation's wealth. Whoever echoed that sentiment was bound to get support from the Malay community. The Chinese felt that they were being denied opportunities to make more wealth, to study in their own language, and so on. It was only natural as we are constructed or socialised to see race as the primary determinant of our own identity.

This is why the race card is so often played to inflame emotions and mobilise disproportionate support. The Alliance approach was the best choice because, as I said, "it is not too communal and yet its component parties have not forgotten their racial origins". The coalition's main problem was that it always needed to restrain and manage the communal inclinations it

---

4   Malaysia's agenda for national development is packaged and implemented in plans that each span five years.

was dependent upon. It ran the risk of being overtaken by the communal passions that it sought to overcome. It was and is a difficult balancing act. In the real world, and in politics especially, one must often choose not between one thing and another, but how to combine and satisfy both.

DAP and PAS were extremely communal while the leftist Parti Sosialis Rakyat Malaysia[5] wanted people to forget all racial differences. The DAP still claims to be multiracial but how plausible is that claim when it is dominated by Chinese leaders? Their criterion and argument for accepting non-Chinese is that all will ostensibly benefit from their fight for non-Malays as a whole. But the main beneficiary of their struggle is the Chinese community. The link to the DAP's predecessor, the PAP of Singapore, and its "Malaysian Malaysia" idea — which was supposedly for all Malaysians but which was really designed to benefit just one community — is evident.

Such is the way of politicians. They say seemingly harmless things but their objectives can differ greatly. I have a way of speaking bluntly which makes almost everyone uncomfortable. For instance, instead of playing the race card, I criticise the Malays openly. I know it makes make me unpopular but I hope they realise I'm actually trying to help. Sometimes harshness is necessary and I'd like to think that they recognise this.

Perhaps one day Malaysian politics will be a contest between highly functional and authentically multiracial parties. But for now, there are still disparities — too many and too obvious — among the races for this to happen. In Malaysia the race with the greatest numbers and economic influence soon dominates any supposedly multiracial organ or institution, no matter how noble or well-intentioned its formal guiding principles, and will accordingly ensure the interests of the majority are met first. The minority soon finds that the "fair deal" was a myth.

If the NEP succeeds in the long term, the country's Malays will feel more capable of competing with the Chinese and will have less fear of Chinese domination. The Chinese in turn would experience less discrimination.

---

5     Parti Sosialis Rakyat Malaysia was founded in 1955 and was inspired by Indonesia's fight for independence. It has since merged with Parti Keadilan (Justice Party), forming Parti Keadilan Rakyat (People's Justice Party).

A multiracial party at that stage would not be too particular about the racial origins of its leaders or fearful of domination by any one race. Unfortunately, I think it will be a long time before Malaysians reach that level and until then, a coalition of communal parties serves Malaysia and its multiracial people better.

The success of PAS and DAP in the 1969 elections, I went on to say, was not because the Chinese truly believed in them. It was because they were angry with the Alliance Government and they wanted to teach it a lesson — that their support should not be taken for granted.

At the end of my talk at the Government Staff Training Centre, I was also again asked about my possible return to UMNO. "I can't say whether I will return to the party," I replied. "Somebody might want me back, somebody else might not."

This was very shortly before my application to rejoin was approved.

At the time of that particular question-and-answer session, I was waiting for some sign of approval. I had been hearing all kinds of rumours but I am not usually the sort of person to pay attention to anonymous whispers. Sometimes, however, especially in moments of high anticipation, one cannot help it.

I had heard that there were powerful people who did not want me back in UMNO. They were angry over my letter, my refusal to apologise to the Tunku and the party, and they were particularly incensed at my statement to the Press that I would not crawl back. Even after Harun failed to get me to apologise, he still expressed a desire to see me back in the party. Journalists continued to speculate, many of them because they knew it would make good copy.

In June 1971, Tun Razak, in reply to a question from the Press about my rejoining the party said, "He (Mahathir) must apply through the proper party channels". This was in response to my own statement that "there is every possibility of my rejoining UMNO". Two days later, UMNO headquarters reiterated that "the party's door is open to everyone including Dr Mahathir bin Mohamad".

Perhaps Tun Razak saw me as partly responsible for the Tunku stepping down, giving him a chance to lead the country. In any case, it seemed clear to me that he knew that I had nothing against him, the Supreme Council or the other leaders of the party. People speculated that he was subtly trying to woo me, to co-opt my standing with the rank and file. I did not see things that way. I believed that he genuinely understood my concerns and recognised the principled nature of my stand towards the party and Malay political interest.

At first I thought "proper channels" meant joining a local branch of UMNO. Tunku Abdullah Tuanku Abdul Rahman told me his division, Rawang in Selangor, was ready to accept me as a member. So I joined the Rawang UMNO Division and Tunku Abdullah relayed the news to UMNO headquarters. Apparently this was not quite what Tun Razak meant by "the proper channels". Before I could rejoin I needed approval from UMNO headquarters. First I had to be vetted by the Disciplinary Committee, and if it made a favourable recommendation, the Supreme Council then had to approve it.

I accordingly applied once more through my old Kota Star Selatan division and on 6 February 1972, I wrote to Tun Razak explaining why I wanted to rejoin. I said I still believed in the party's policy and struggle. This time, no one insisted on an apology or that I recanted.

The crucial factor here was Tun Razak. Had he insisted on an apology, the others would have followed suit. In UMNO, if a leader is willing to concede, the others will usually not make an issue of things. So the Central Working Committee, also known as the Supreme Council, did not voice any objection except to refer my application to the Disciplinary Committee under Tun Dr Ismail, the Deputy President of the party and the Deputy Prime Minister.

I did not know Tun Dr Ismail well. He was very proper in manner, a taciturn person who was not given freely to open friendship with everyone. People within the party were scared of him. No one tried asking for favours because they knew they would not get any. The public also regarded him with a great deal of awe and respect. He was a medical doctor who had qualified in Australia and was from a well-to-do Johor family. His family and Dato' Onn's family were not on good terms, so he became involved in UMNO only after Dato' Onn left the party. Later, when I rejoined UMNO, his political secretary Wahab Majid told me that Tun Dr Ismail did not like me very much. Why, he did not know, but it did not worry me greatly. It was something I thought I could manage.

I knew that there was still a strong possibility that my application would be rejected outright, but I was not unduly anxious. I have always tried to adopt the philosophy that whatever happens to me happens, and that I would simply have to accept it. Now, at this stage, the fact was that there were people who liked me and those who did not. But there is never a moment in a person's life when he is liked by everyone. If there is, you are probably a nonentity, a person of little consequence or character. At the height of your popularity, there will always be someone who wishes you dead. Holding closely to that idea, I do not expect to be loved or supported by everyone.

I did not want to publicise my application because it would have been embarrassing if I were rejected, so I kept it as discreet as possible. Had I been rejected, I do not think it would have been the end of politics for me. There are many ways of skinning a cat. I have always employed what I later discovered was called "lateral thinking" — if I could not get in one way, I would try another. I would move sideways instead of seeking to bulldoze my way via a frontal assault. Consequently, I have almost always succeeded in finding some way of doing the things that I want. As soon as problems arise, possible solutions start spinning in my head. Initially they may not be perfect, but by making adjustments along the way I find that problems can be reasonably resolved, God willing. Still, the best-laid plan can go wrong. I never forget that while man proposes, God disposes. You make your plans and try your best. If you encounter problems you have to be flexible, analytical, and ready to try something else. This is the kind of modern sensibility that I have tried to encourage Malays to acquire and master.

My application went to the Disciplinary Committee. Among the members of the Committee were Tan Sri Syed Nasir Ismail, Tan Sri Syed Jaafar Hassan Albar, Tun Musa Hitam and Tan Sri Senu Abdul Rahman. Tun

Ghazali Shafie and Tan Sri Aishah Ghani, the Wanita Chief, were also Committee members but could not attend. The Committee met and approved my application and in the first week of March, the Central Working Committee endorsed the findings of the Disciplinary Committee. When informed of their decision I said, "I am happy to hear it. I hope to be able to serve UMNO in any way that is possible for me".

The politicking began immediately.

Syed Jaafar offered to step down from several posts in the party — including the Central Working Committee — to make way for me, so that I could play a more significant role. "It is better," he said, "[that] I sacrifice my position in the party to give a chance to a much younger man".

I said straightaway that it was not necessary. My return to UMNO should certainly not result in Syed Jaafar or anyone else withdrawing. I said I would wait my turn and any membership of the Central Working Committee should be determined by the annual General Assembly to be held in June. A few days later I was reported to have had "a verbal battle" with Syed Jaafar. At the time I thought that the Press was exaggerating but on hindsight, perhaps they knew better than I did.

Syed Jaafar's offer may have been made in good faith but that does not explain why, when I later became Deputy Prime Minister, this UMNO strongman showed extreme displeasure and tried to get UMNO Youth, of which he was chief, to go against me. Still, this Press drama did not detract from the happiness I felt at being in UMNO again. I looked forward to playing a significant role in its affairs and, through it, to serve the Malays and Malaysia. The feeling of emptiness that had descended upon me when I was cast out of UMNO was lifted.

# Chapter 20:
## Into The Deep End

On 8 March 1972, I was readmitted into UMNO amid a flurry of headlines. I was very happy that my years of isolation were finally over and being back in the party that I believed in so strongly was invigorating. The possibilities seemed limitless as I might now once again contribute to the party, perhaps even to the Government. Best of all, I was with friends and colleagues again, like-minded people with whom I had had many passionate discussions about politics. That was something I had missed very much during my years of being an outcast.

As it turned out, it was to be an eventful year not just for me but for the country as well. Tun Razak had taken over the premiership from the Tunku and I felt he was going to introduce policy adjustments in keeping with our independent national status. We did not need to be so tied to the British and the West as we had been when Tunku was at the helm. We would also be tackling the intricate details of some basic Malay problems more seriously.

My readmission into UMNO was well covered in the Press. At that time, the *Straits Times* was still a Singapore paper, owned by the Overseas Chinese Banking Corporation and run by British expatriates. Famed even then for his searing candour, journalist Tan Sri A. Samad Ismail wrote a very encouraging piece in the Malaysian edition about my return to what he called "a new UMNO". The article focused largely on his observation of my character during my years away from the party. Even now, I feel self-conscious quoting from it, but I do so to show the atmosphere in which my re-admission into UMNO took place.

Samad correctly said that my dispute was never with the party: "Throughout his days of separation from the party," he wrote on 22 March 1972, "he carried himself with dignity and detachment…He denied rumours that he was planning to form a political party or had plans to join another political party. 'There is enough disunity among the Malays without me making it worse,' he had said…his quarrel was not with the party but with its past. But the chapter with the Tengku [Tunku] was closed and Mahathir never revived it.

"... His was the voice of a section of the people yet to be satisfied with the changes envisaged for them by a new leadership," Samad continued. "But Mahathir played his part with diffidence. He could be a thorn had he wanted to. If he was a source of embarrassment it was not of his own making. He was not petty; he addressed himself to a larger audience, standing by the sidelines, aloof from party squabbles. He was critical without being hostile."

I had never been particularly close to Samad so I was pleasantly surprised by the article. But later, when I was Minister of Education, he wrote a nasty piece about me which I felt was blatantly unfair. When I rang him up to register my protest, his reply was characteristically curt: "If you don't like it, you can tell Tun Razak".

The other Malaysian-owned vernacular papers were equally positive. The Jawi-script *Utusan Melayu* had a cartoon of me as Superman flying in towards a crowd of welcoming UMNO leaders. That was more than a little over the top and it embarrassed me greatly. I also knew it would cause those who disliked me, including several veteran UMNO leaders, to resent my return even more. Still, despite its exaggeration, I appreciated the show of support.

UMNO was to hold its annual assembly in June of that year and new members of the Supreme Council were to be elected. There were many who wanted me to be on the Supreme Council — my staunchest supporters even began to propose my name as a candidate for one of the three Vice-President's posts.

This aggressive approach to pursuing party and political positions was something new. Prior to this Malays often refused to be nominated, even to be Members of Parliament, saying modestly that they were not qualified. That gentle attitude generally lasted only until people realised that when you become a Member of Parliament or a State Assemblyman, you also become *Yang Berhormat* (The Honourable) and get an allowance, even if you don't have any qualifications. Then the rush was on! To become an office boy a person needed some educational qualifications but none was required — even now — to become a representative of the people, a lawmaker or even a Prime Minister.

These days, the desire for prominent positions and their accompanying high status has become rife among Malays. Status-seeking is a pervasive obsession of modern Malay society. Malay culture, notably middle-class and urban Malay culture, has become more individualistic, competitive, egoistic and materialistic. Even people who have done little want to become Members of Parliament and, once elevated, very few are prepared to step down. When I resigned as Prime Minister, several of my long-serving Ministers said they would follow suit, but in the event, almost none did.

These days, incumbents are also challenged all the time. Everybody wants to be an UMNO Vice-President. This may be the democratic thing to do, but I doubt that we yet understand the fundamental workings of democracy. In a democracy you support the winner. You may run him down during a campaign and you may vote against him, but once the votes are counted you close ranks and throw your weight behind the one who wins. This way the party and the country remain united and strong. Today however, there is no functional democracy in the party, so the whole game has changed.

Also, in UMNO, members continue to support their own candidates long after elections have been held. Candidates for party positions continue to pursue their opponent, whether he is defeated or not. If he is defeated, he is shamed and forced to defend himself, and by asserting your own power, you show how pitiful the loser's position can be. If he has won, you undermine him by obstructing and frustrating him at every turn. This pattern does not make for a strong party. Ultimately, it weakens the Government, its capacity and authority. The higher up you go, the worse it is. If there is a contest at the Deputy President's level and there are two or more candidates, the losers and their followers will refuse to support the winner. A splinter group may even form, as indeed happened after I defeated Tengku Razaleigh Hamzah in the 1986 party elections.

In a democracy, it is crucial for people to accept that there will always be winners and losers. That is why I sometimes felt that there should not be a contest at certain levels, for certain positions in the party. People either genuinely did not understand how elections worked, or they simply did not care. The good of the party is regarded as secondary — what matters is individual ambition.

257

During the Tunku's time, even though the UMNO rank and file were unhappy with him, no one would have challenged him or his Deputy or even the three Vice-Presidents if the incumbents were still in position. This is a strong trait in the Malay culture. Typically, it is unwritten, even unspoken. This same time-tested culture of respecting those who hold positions and deferring to their right to hold such offices gave UMNO great strength in its early years.

So, despite the insistence of my supporters, I felt it was too soon for me to run for Vice-President. It was not in keeping with the party tradition that I valued and was likely to antagonise the incumbents and other older leaders. I hesitated a great deal but in the end, support from the divisions, especially those in the north, was very strong and voluble. It was hard to resist.

The incumbent UMNO Vice-Presidents at that time were Tun Ghafar Baba, Tun Sardon Jubir and Tan Sri Syed Nasir Ismail. Tun Ghafar was a grassroots man, while the other two enjoyed great stature as party leaders who had been on the scene since the founding of UMNO. The decision to contest would have been an easier one if at least one of the incumbents withdrew. Then there would be a vacancy to fill and a contest would have to be held. But none did, so any new candidate would appear to be challenging all of the incumbents. To offer such a challenge would be a gross departure from UMNO's ways at the time.

Finally, a month before the Assembly, I succumbed to the pressure from my supporters and agreed to contest the Vice-President's post. It was a thin line to walk. I did not want to disappoint them, but I also knew I had to be careful as I would be unpopular if I were seen to be too ambitious. Going for the Vice-President's position would hardly be considered a modest move.

I did not think I would win so I hedged my bets, but not going for broke undermined my bid. I lost that election for Vice-President. Tun Sardon, Tun Hussein Onn and Tun Ghafar were elected instead. Tun Hussein's success was telling as he had left UMNO with his father, Dato' Onn, when the latter formed the Independence of Malaya Party in 1951. Apparently Tun Hussein was now fully rehabilitated in the eyes of UMNO members. Everyone knew that Tun Razak had engineered his return to the party, so no one questioned Tun Hussein's political loyalty.

I was not too disappointed about losing as I did not think it would affect my future. Instead, I felt vindicated as I obtained the highest number of votes as a member of the Supreme Council. UMNO can be quite subtle in some ways. The voting results indicated that the rank and file did not feel I was ready for the Vice-President's post. But they wanted to show their support through a big vote for me as an ordinary member of the Supreme Council.

For someone who had returned to UMNO only three months earlier, I felt I had done very well. Now I was again going to be in UMNO's decision-making body. My anticipation was heightened because I felt sure that under Tun Razak's leadership, the Council would no longer be the rubber-stamping body it had been during the Tunku's presidency.

Tun Razak and the Tunku were completely different personalities. The Tunku had been imperious and would simply announce major decisions without any prior discussion. Tun Razak, on the other hand, valued discussion. Even during the Tunku's time, when I was a member of the political committee headed by Tun Razak, he invariably made sure that we contributed, deliberated and planned. He was much more acquainted with the rank and file and they did not feel the same remote awe towards him that they did with the Tunku. Consequently, Tun Razak did not seem as distant. Initially, however, I myself felt that he was such a great personality that I had difficulty addressing him. It felt almost like addressing royalty. But slowly, I began to remind myself that he was not a royal.

259

I came to admire Tun Razak immensely. He understood administration, planning, and implementation, and so he understood what he needed to do for the Malays and the country. During his term as Prime Minister, he focused on rural development, something he initiated during the Tunku's time. His foreign policies were also different from the Tunku's. Tun Razak was less Western-oriented and was more inclined towards non-alignment and establishing diplomatic relations with every country, irrespective of ideology or system of government. He established relations with China and many of the Eastern Bloc countries, and he even visited the Soviet Union and China. The Tunku never set foot in the latter. I am not sure he ever visited Russia.

After my election to the Supreme Council I was invited to speak to numerous groups within and outside the party on many issues, particularly those relating to the problems of the Malays. I tried to advise the Malays on how to maximise the benefits of the Government's New Economic Policy. I felt that unless people were properly guided, the opportunities would be wasted. Later events were to prove me right.

As Prime Minister, Tun Razak recalled Parliament in February 1972 in order to validate the laws passed in the interim period when Parliament had been suspended and the country had been ruled by the National Operations Council (NOC). There were amendments to the Constitution which required the support and approval of two-thirds of the Members of Parliament. Whereas before this the Constitution could be debated freely in and out of Parliament, with the new amendments there were certain "entrenched" clauses which could not be debated or challenged. The most important provision was that Malay would be the official language of the Government, but other languages (Chinese and Tamil) could be used for non-official purposes, including in education as the medium of instruction in the Government-assisted national-type primary schools. No other country in Southeast Asia allowed — or indeed allows — this linguistic latitude.

The other entrenched provisions included the special privileges of the Malays and the preservation of the rights of the Chinese and Indians as citizens, which also could not be questioned. Whereas during British rule the Chinese and Indians could be repatriated and their citizenship annulled, the Constitution forbids such action by the independent Government.

I thought the no-debate provision was a good move to prevent rabble-rousing and the fomenting of conflict between the Malays and Chinese. The Constitution is a well-balanced document. Close scrutiny shows that when something is given to the Malays, something is also given to the other races. While Islam is the official religion of the Federation, non-Muslims are guaranteed the freedom to practise their own religions. Malay may be the official language, but other races are free to speak, learn and publish in their own languages.

These are rights which are rarely noticed, especially by Malaysia's international critics. Many observers don't seem to realise that in countries like Indonesia, the Philippines and Thailand, you are not allowed to use Chinese in schools. While some like to point unfavourably to what was accorded to the Malays, implying that there is discrimination in their favour, they never mention the parallel rights accorded the non-Malays. Ever since Independence in 1957 our Constitution, while designating Islam the official religion, ensured that other religions may be practised freely. There can be no forced conversion of anyone to Islam. The Shariah laws here cannot be applied to non-Muslims.

Europeans in particular should note this last point since during the colonial period, forced conversions to Christianity by the Spanish and others were common. The British colonialists were more subtle. They did not force conversion through policy, but they made it easy for their Christian missions to open schools and hospitals and to use them as platforms to preach. In some instances, scholarships were preferentially awarded to those who converted to Christianity.

261

The Constitution also made provisions for Malay reserve land. This is often seen as legislated discrimination against non-Malays but the reality is otherwise. Since Malay reserve land can only be sold to other Malays, prices tend to remain low, as Malay purchasing power is low. But should the reserves fall into non-Malay hands for whatever reason, prices shoot up. The higher prices then would preclude the land from being bought back by the Malays. Should a Malay subsequently reacquire this land, that land would revert to being Malay reserve, losing value for economic exploitation. Effectively, these plots then become non-Malay reserves. Just as there is a duality of legal-religious space for Muslims and non-Muslims so that only Muslims are subject to the Shariah, so too are there two spatial zones for Malay and non-Malay land, two distinct land markets where different land values and prices prevail.

Malay reserve land can be excised and sold if it is found to be tin-bearing, for example. An equal-sized piece of land must then be identified for conversion to Malay reserve to replace the excised land. This land need not be tin-bearing, or hold any resources at all. This was a provision made by the British, so that Malay Reserve Land Laws would not prevent them from acquiring Malay reserve land to mine for tin or to open up rubber plantations. They appeared to want the Malays to own land, but they did not want the provision of the law to prevent them from acquiring land suitable for their economic exploitation. So Malays ended up with guaranteed access to the least economically valuable land. That is how the Malay reserve areas took shape and evolved.

The Malay Reserve Land Laws were put in to institute some degree of protection. Their rationale was that if there were no such reserves, the Malays were likely to sell most of their landholdings. At the same time, the rigid provisions of the law prevented them from exploiting the economic potential of their land through joint-ventures with non-Malays, using their land as capital or leasing the land for a fixed period while ensuring that upon the lease's expiry, the land would revert to Malay ownership.

It is bizarre that many Malays seem to think that Malay reserve land is a recognition of their being "masters" of the country. This is disgraceful. Indigenous people should not have to live on reserve land. The Native Americans of the US do live on reserves but no one regards it as a privilege. Indeed, it is an open acknowledgement and a powerful statement on how they cannot compete with other Americans.

The Malay Reserve Laws should be nothing more than an interim measure, and at best, temporary crutches. The real solution lies in learning how to manage assets such as these lands and to develop business skills. Malays should not be isolated from competition but enabled to compete. But mastering these skills requires the right attitude.

This is where value systems come into play. Values shape personality, action and economic development. That is why I keep emphasising the importance of maintaining and also modernising our systems of Asian values. If you understand the value of what you have, be it material or ethical, you will not readily part with it. But to maintain one's material and moral stake in the world requires strength of character. That is why we need a broadly based group of well-educated and well-to-do Malays in Malaysia. But they must make the effort — so long as they keep seeking the easy way and looking for effortless means of getting rich quickly, they will never be able to make gains from their assets. It is easy to sell what one has been given — including land — and then live off the money until it is finished. After that, Malays will become paupers in their own country in the long run.

In the past, most Malays lived along the rivers where there was plenty of fish and other food. Life held no great challenge. If life is easy, you have no reason to try too hard to improve. Immigrants do not have things so easy and they must work hard to raise themselves up. These are the basic ingredients of the immigrant mentality. The Chinese immigrants came here because in their time, life was difficult in China and they were prepared to come here to work hard and compete. They found the Malays easy to beat in all fields and, unused to competition, the Malays retreated before the Chinese onslaught. They would have sold all their land to the Chinese had there been no Malay reserves.

Nevertheless, Malay reserve land actually leads to a larger problem. Overtly, the Constitution seems to protect the Malays but in reality it does not. It debilitates them, making them very dependent and disinclined to stand on their own. But it is hard to suddenly abolish the long-established Malay reserve land system. If that were to happen, the Malays would lose far more than they could ever gain. It is hard to throw away a crutch or give up a benefit when one has adapted to its presence and come to take it for granted. This, too, would in time become the problem of the NEP.

The Constitutional amendments of February 1972 were passed with a good majority because the Sarawak United People's Party (SUPP) had joined the Alliance, giving the coalition control of 98 votes out of 144, a clear two-thirds majority. In addition, Gerakan, with seven members, and the PMIP with 12 members, also supported the amendments. The Alliance had now regained the strong position it had lost in the 1969 elections.

I continued to have doubts about the implementation of the NEP but I had not reckoned with the ingenuity of Tun Razak. He proposed that every state set up an economic development corporation to engage in various wholesale and retail businesses allocated to the Malays. I was appointed a Director of the Kedah State Economic Development Corporation and was also elected Vice-President of the Kedah Malay Chamber of Commerce.

The President was Hanipah S. Alauddin, a prominent Kedah businessman and a close friend. Unfortunately, he died in October of 1972 and with his passing, I took over as President of the Chamber. Hanipah was also a Senator, one of the two the Kedah Government was entitled to appoint. In December, the Kedah State Council proposed that I also take Hanipah's place as Senator.

The State Economic Development Corporations, or SEDCs as they came to be known, were in theory a brilliant mechanism for realising the NEP. The Malays needed capital and know-how to take advantage of the opportunities created by the NEP. Tun Razak decided these state units would go into the big industries like timber, mining and rubber plantations. Individual Malay entrepreneurs would then be brought in later when they had accumulated capital and business savvy. It was already clear that simply allocating shares to Malays was a problem, as they would not hold on to them. As with other assets given them, they would sell their shares almost immediately to non-Bumiputera for a quick profit. The SEDCs had to hold these shares for them to ensure the Malays retained their stake in the future.

But once the SEDCs had built up their business, they were disinclined to sell the shares to Malay individuals. Instead, they tended to behave like government departments. They were run by civil servants who allocated timber and tin concessions to the SEDCs; the few Malays who were already privately operating in the business or who wished to apply for timber or tin concessions found themselves competing against the SEDCs and were denied the opportunities. Yet despite being favoured by the Government and at times given monopolies, the SEDC-owned businesses often failed.

When I was invited to sit on the board of the Kedah SEDC, the responsibilities of the job were not clear. Business activities in Malaysia were not that dynamic or varied in those days. The construction and housing industries had hardly begun, there were no supermarkets or restaurant chains, and roads and other infrastructure projects were few and far between. The share market was insignificant and most companies were privately-owned and small.

The Kedah SEDC therefore decided to develop the state's natural resources. Kedah had never been rich in tin nor was its forest land extensive. Of all the states, Kedah had been the most intensively cultivated. It was a "rice bowl" state. As elsewhere, the Chinese in Kedah had a near monopoly on timber extraction and ownership of the open-cast tin mines, although a small number of Malays were involved. The entry of the state corporation meant that almost all new forest concessions were now swallowed by it. This was not quite in keeping with the spirit of the NEP, but there was no arguing with the civil servants and Malay politicians who were on the boards of the state corporation and its subsidiaries.

Malay timber concessionaires who competed against the SEDC usually lost. In future, this would be the main grouse of Malay businessmen against the NEP. Invariably, their own prospective business opportunities were seized by the state corporations against which, repeatedly, they would find themselves competing unsuccessfully. Meanwhile, the Chinese also lost most of their concessions to the state corporations. But since these corporations had no experience in operating timber concessions and had no logging machinery, they had to sub-contract to the Chinese to do the actual extraction and market the timber to mills — which also belonged to the Chinese. The corporations seldom made profits. It was the sub-contractors who did best under these arrangements.

Similarly in Pahang, Majlis Amanah Rakyat, or MARA, the successor to the Rural and Industrial Development Authority,[1] obtained huge forest concessions. However, poor management meant no additional wealth flowed to the Malays. At one time, the timber cut down was piled up in the forests, as it allegedly could not be sold. Some of these precious logs, it was reported, were simply burnt.

There can be no excuse for this. If you cannot sell the timber in one form, common sense dictates that you try to sell it in another. If you can't sell the logs, you need a sawmill or you must turn the logs into laminated plywood or fibre boards. It is crucial to learn how, so that you can understand how much return you can get on your investment. But the officers involved were

---

[1]   The Rural Industrial Development Authority (RIDA) was the original agency that sought to promote Bumiputera participation in the economy by setting up rural or cottage industries.

mostly administrators with no business experience. They were asked to extract timber and this they did. To do anything else would require directions from the Government, not just the management, and government directives take time as only the topmost men can make decisions. Sadly, the timber was not a priority for them and so the logs got burnt. The old-fashioned public service attitude is hard to uproot. It is a mindset that prefers to do nothing and maintain a "clean" copy-book, than to take the risk of making a mistake. And if that attitude is entrenched at the upper levels, which lower-level functionaries, no matter how much initiative they may have personally, are likely to go against it? In the public service it would be a fatal career move.

A Canadian timber company was engaged to help MARA, and expensive logging machinery was imported to modernise operations and improve efficiency. But the human resources on the ground were less sophisticated and the MARA officers directed the logging operations by radio from their offices in Kuala Lumpur. Not unexpectedly, they failed, despite the Canadian technical input.

Elsewhere, the story was roughly the same. At the time I rejoined UMNO, these failures were unknown to me and the public. We were all very excited that the NEP was going to correct the imbalances between the wealth of Malays and non-Malays, so we pushed on with the SEDCs. Good intentions seemed sufficient, and their successful implementation was taken for granted.

I had continued with my medical practice while observing the performance of the NEP and waiting for the General Election. To increase Bumiputera shares in the corporate sector, it was decided that companies, especially new companies, should allocate 30 per cent of their shares to the Bumiputera. At the time a number of new companies were being floated on the stock exchange. Almost immediately after the Initial Public Offer, share prices would appreciate. Those who were lucky enough to be allocated such shares immediately sold them. It was like getting free money. Naturally, there was a rush for these IPO shares. I applied for shares to the Ministry of Trade and Industry, not for quick resale but to hold as an individual and contribute to the Malay stake in the country. I was very disappointed upon receiving a reply that the shares were only for the Bumiputera who had registered with the Ministry. The officer gratuitously informed me that I could apply for the non-Bumiputera shares in the usual manner, that is, by filling the application forms which came with the company prospectus printed in the newspapers. The number of non-Bumiputera applicants was naturally huge. I later learnt that about 10,000 Bumiputera applicants had registered with the Ministry.

Yet, true to past form, few of them kept the shares they were allocated. Most sold them to non-Bumiputera buyers to cash in on the initial price appreciation. They would then repay the banks the money they had borrowed to acquire those shares and pocket the difference. This, of course, did not help increase the percentage of shares in the nation's wealth held by Malays. Had the profits from their sale been reinvested to expand existing businesses or to buy more shares, that might have been defensible. But mostly, the money was spent immediately on luxuries, which gave them the symbols of status in modern Malay society. The cycle would then resume, and shares acquired would again be sold. The Bumiputera regarded this as a matter of right and not as a way to increase their stake in the nation's wealth. Everyone watched with eager anticipation for new public offers. The objectives of the NEP seemed to be of little concern to the beneficiaries and even to officials.

267

The NEP was actually a sound policy which would have reduced the disparities between the Malays and the non-Malays. But too many Malays abused the special treatment accorded them and the NEP achieved only minimal success. In fact, as the Malay recipients of this largesse sold to the Chinese, this particular exercise actually *increased* the disparity between the communities. The Government was trying to help make a success of the policy to correct the imbalances, but all that the Malay beneficiaries could see was an opportunity to enjoy a short-lived windfall. They could not have cared less if the NEP failed and were not concerned about the larger picture. It was very frustrating. They managed to find a way to abuse everything devised to help them improve their economic situation. The Government might put wealth and shares in their hands, but doing so was futile without changing the familiar old Malay mindset.

There were, of course, some successes. Today there are Malay contractors who can go abroad to build complex infrastructure projects. At home they have gone into manufacturing, producing components for cars. A number have emerged as successful bankers. The papers carry the names of successful Bumiputera executives who often command high salaries, and some even manage large multinational corporations abroad. But the success rate is low considering the concerted and consistent efforts of the Government. Here again the exception proves the rule. Those who have succeeded have done so not simply because opportunities and resources came their way but also because, when such chances came, they showed themselves capable of creating a new mindset.

To remedy Malay disadvantage and to raise the level of Malay initiative and entrepreneurship, what we need is a carrot-and-stick approach. When I was Prime Minister, I often gave talks at Bina Negara (nation-building) camps. I would spend two straight days on my feet, talking from morning to night, trying to explain what being successful required. Wise words fell like water upon a duck's back. Rather than hear what they needed to accept, many

preferred to say why it was unpalatable. Age-old Malay habits reasserted themselves. During question-and-answer sessions, participants preferred to give their own explanations for Malay failures and to suggest that my arguments and recommendations were faulty. Presented with an idea or when challenged to do things differently, their response was to argue why they should not, and why Malays could not.

For me, the formula is easy. First, do not be too greedy. If you are, you tend to rely on practices that only focus on making money. When one does that, one may not be too particular about ethics and legality.

Many commentators say that the NEP should be updated and indeed in some way, its successor policy, the National Development Policy[2] (NDP), attempts this. But I think perhaps it is *people* who should be developed so that they might benefit from the economic opportunities created for them. If we simply revert to the NEP with full force, if handouts are given without

---

[2]  The Government unveiled its National Development Policy in June 1991 after the NEP had expired. Poverty was redefined according to relative criteria, and a new emphasis was given to creating employment and placing a greater reliance on the private sector.

a second thought, they will again be abused to no public benefit and will damage Malay competence and dignity.

At the time of my rejoining UMNO in 1972 none of this was yet clear to me or others. After my one failed attempt, I did not try to buy Bumiputera shares again. Instead I sought to play a more active role in the party and the Government. Two months after I was elected to the Supreme Council, I was appointed a member of the newly-formed Higher Education Advisory Council.

After that appointment, I wrote to Tun Razak offering my services in any other capacity. I suggested that I should take over the running of Malayan Railways as I had some ideas about how to turn it around. Instead, in November, I was made the Chairman of the Food Industries of Malaysia (FIMA), a government company involved mainly in the pineapple canning industry. I accepted the challenge and set out to be a very active Non-Executive Chairman. I could not be satisfied merely to preside over a board of directors.

While I had no experience managing a multi-million dollar company, during the Japanese Occupation I had run a few small businesses, including a coffee shop and selling rice and bananas. There was, in addition, the experience of running my clinic. With what I understood about "the bottom line"; that is, the importance of making a return on the investment, and reserving some of the profits for the next round, I set out to achieve all these for FIMA.

The Pineapple Cannery of Malaya (PCM), FIMA's main subsidiary, had two pineapple canneries and a can-making plant. The marketing was done largely through a joint marketing company that had been set up by the Malaysian pineapple canneries but operated from Singapore. The canneries also marketed directly to certain customers abroad. I do not think PCM expected a CEO when I was appointed its Chairman, but that was what they got. I wanted to see things for myself. I had some general ideas about what was wrong with the management and what remedial measures needed to be taken. Mainly, the real cost of management and production had to be studied. My instinct told me that in this regard the current management was not too careful. This was confirmed when I discovered the General

Manager's travelling expenses. He was already drawing RM8,000 per month, a princely sum by the standards of the time; when I became Prime Minister in 1981, my monthly pay was also RM8,000. On top of that, the board had budgeted RM100,000 per year for his travelling expenses. The General Manager would try to use this by the year's end, whether the travel was necessary or not. I immediately put an end to this practice and decided that the GM was to travel only when it was considered necessary.

I made my first visit to the pineapple cannery in Pekan Nenas (Pineapple Town) in Johor on 25 January 1973, and I was met by a picket of 200 of the 900 workers of the plant. Although I was shocked, I went up to the picketing workers and asked them what they were protesting against. They were contract workers who did not earn monthly wages and their pay was very low, less than 40 sen per hour. They should really have been getting at least RM150 a month, or twice to three times what they were receiving. I had not yet been officially briefed, but I promised that I would look into their complaints. They cheered and broke up the picket 15 minutes after my arrival.

When I visited the storage area accompanied by the managers, the floors were sticky and slippery with syrup dripping from leaking cans. The managers were supposed to practise FIFO — first in, first out — when the cans were ready to be taken to wholesalers. But apparently this was a principle they adhered to rather casually.

Workers were taking cans from the easily accessible top pallets, where all the new products were stored. The cans on the pallets below remained there, untouched for months. After some time, some of the cans which were defective would explode due to fermentation of the contents. The syrup that oozed out dripped and drenched the cans below. These in turn would rust and eventually burst as well. The syrup flowed downwards from pallet to pallet, spoiling each layer as it went. Naturally, most of the stored pineapple was not saleable and needless to say, the condition of the store was terrible.

I asked the manager what he did with the useless products. The manager looked at the storekeeper, who was not able to answer immediately. Finally he said, "We get rid of them". I asked him how. Again, there was a pause.

Finally he said, "We bury them".

"Where?" I asked.

"Outside," he said.

We went outside and I was shocked to see huge holes cut in the chain link fence and tyre marks on the ground. "What is that?" I asked. This time there was a longer pause and I felt that perhaps we were on the brink of solving the mystery.

Then someone said, "The lorries come in that way".

"But why?" I asked. "There is a proper road leading to the store".

Finally, I got the explanation. Lorries apparently backed in at night through the holes in the fence and pallets of good canned pineapple were loaded onto them by thieves. We had security guards but they were afraid to stop these robbers. They were apparently fearsome thugs with machetes, who threatened to kill anyone who got in their way.

It was like a bad comedy. There was no sense of responsibility and nobody checked or audited the running of the company. To say I was horrified is an understatement.

The practice of the cannery was to allow the employees to take at least one case of canned pineapple with their wages every month. They could sell the cases to the shops in Pekan Nenas and hawkers could often be seen selling the canned pineapples on the roadside. But what was being sold was not necessarily from the employees. A great deal of stock was actually the stolen cans from the stores. No attempt was made to mend the fences or to stop the lorries from loading and taking away the stolen cases of pineapple. I ordered the fences to be mended and asked the security guards to stop any further attempts to steal from the stores. Remarkably, no *parang* or machete attacks ensued.

I implemented a number of other measures at the cannery. Even though there were more employees than we needed, I did not sack anyone as that would have created uncertainty and resentment. Instead, I allowed for natural attrition and did not replace ageing workers when they retired.

Doing things this way takes time and costs a little money, but in the long run it has no demoralising effects.

On another occasion while walking through the factory I saw a large number of can tops scattered on the ground near one of the passages. I asked the executive accompanying me what they were doing there. "They look good to me. Are they condemned?" I asked. The man's lips began to tremble, then he actually fainted and fell to the floor. The others quickly lifted him and lowered him down to lie on the cemented passageway. He recovered soon enough. I learnt later that they had been selling can tops to another factory. They were thrown on the ground to be collected as unsuitable can tops by the lorry collecting rubbish.

Meanwhile, relations between management and the workers and union leaders were bad. The workers often sabotaged the company by putting silver paper from cigarette boxes into the cans during the manufacturing process. Once, a Canadian consumer even found a lizard inside a can. The consequences were terrible for the company as whole containers had to be condemned. Getting rid of canned pineapple in North America was difficult as there was no place to dump it. In the end the containers had to be shipped back to Malaysia at additional expense and the consumer in Canada had to be heavily compensated to prevent bad publicity. The losses incurred went well into hundreds of thousands of ringgit. The workers did not realise that they were just shooting themselves in the foot by ruining the basis of their own livelihood. We might have had to close the factory and dismiss them all. Thankfully at least, the Press did not get hold of the story.

At that time there were trade unionists who believed that government operations like the Malayan Railways were there not to make money but to create jobs. The Government was apparently supposed to set up these operations and keep pumping money into them, even if these enterprises constantly lost money. The services that they were created to provide were regarded as secondary. This kind of faulty socialist thinking was very prevalent at that time in England where many British industries had to shut down. That's why the workers at PCM did not care. They thought they would be employed no matter what. Better yet, if the Government was afraid of them, they would pay more wages. It was a confrontational attitude. But is there really a winner in the end?

I sought the support of the President of the Union of Workers in the Government Canneries, who was a good man. I listened to his complaints and, as any union leader would, he exaggerated the grievances of the workers. But some of his complaints regarding the management were genuine. I met the committee of the union and had long discussions with them. I decided to entertain their legitimate complaints, to agree to better wages and allowances, and so on. I did not revoke their privilege of getting cases of canned pineapple with their wages. I gave pep talks and explained how necessary it was for them to cooperate and help the company to cut its losses. Sabotaging it by putting lizards in cans could result in the company closing down.

They were stunned by this notion, even appalled. They worked under the firm belief that the cannery was set up to create jobs for them. It was a government company where profit was not supposed to be the motive. They believed they could do what they liked and the cannery would still remain open. I told them that the Government might accept some losses, but if they were too high even the Government would have to stop the bleeding. If the company did well, then they stood a better chance of making more money. But salary increases should be accompanied by greater productivity. If salaries increased but the Government kept losing money, there would be a time when logically, the operation would have to be shut down.

273

The workers were also voters in that constituency and some of them hinted that UMNO candidates in the elections may lose their seats if the workers lost their jobs. But it was an idle threat. Most of the workers were UMNO members anyway, and in Johor, UMNO was powerful, with practically no opposition. PAS had very few supporters there. I believed the people would continue to support UMNO and so I confidently called their bluff. I was right — the Barisan Nasional[3] won the next General Election in 1974 easily. But even before that I had managed to win the union and the workers over to my side. The union leader became a good friend and I was always able to

---

[3]   The Barisan Nasional, or National Front, was formed in 1973 as a successor to the Alliance.

get his help and support whenever there was an industrial problem within the company.

Later, I would take the same approach with Malaysian Airline System (MAS) when I was Deputy Prime Minister. The union tried to sabotage the company and planes were tampered with until they could not take off. I told them I would close down the national airline, and I did. The DAP called me a thug but that did not matter to me. These were national assets and one simply did not tamper with planes and make demands on a company that was not doing well anyway.

I was willing to shut it down permanently if that became necessary. The airline trade union in Australia backed the MAS workers and began refusing to handle MAS planes. I responded by telling them that when Australian planes came to KL, we would make sure their planes would not take off. After that Qantas stopped flying here. People had to learn the limits of what they could demand. When the other party becomes unreasonable, I am also prepared to be very unreasonable. It does not come naturally, but it comes with the job.

Back at PCM, I also checked on the whole process of producing the canned pineapple, beginning with the grading of the fruit. From the lorry, the fruits were thrown into three baskets according to grade. The man throwing the fruits seemed an expert on grading, but after they had been sorted, I checked the fruits and found that the grading was not properly done. Grade A fruits were at times classified as B or C, while C-grade fruits could be found in the A basket. The quality of the fruit going into each can was uncertain. Putting the first-grade fruit into second- or third-grade cheaper cans caused the company needless financial losses. When lower C or B Grades went into Grade A cans, customers might complain or simply not buy Malaysian canned pineapple.

The basis of the cannery's problems was that it was run by an ex-civil servant who treated it like just another government department. He gave no thought to cutting costs and making a profit. Every year FIMA would submit a budget to the Government and Treasury would approve allocations for the year. Audits were carried out by government officials, but they were not familiar with business accounting and did not scrutinise accounts properly. They did not probe the causes of the factory's repeated losses because government departments do not expect to make money. In those early days, few government officers could adjust to the novelty of doing business and making profits. They thought it was normal to allocate funds every year to these new government companies. Effectively, they were injecting new capital every year with no return. No business can expect the gift of yearly capital injections or assume them as an entitlement. Businesses either use internally-generated funds or they borrow, and debts constitute a cost of doing business.

My time at PCM was also made memorable by my encounter with Hajjah Fatimah, the canteen operator. She was a colourful character, very strong-minded and very influential in Wanita UMNO, the party's women's division. She ran the canteen profitably, but there were many complaints from the workers about the quality of the food. I thought I could deal with her by terminating her contract, but it was not that easy. When I visited the cannery the next time, she was there waiting for me. She was a formidable woman who did not pull her punches. She explained quite forcefully that she was not making much from her business because the company did not pay enough for her to provide good food to the workers. In addition, the workers owed her a lot of money.

I decided that it was probably wiser to make a friend of her than an enemy. Besides, she was willing to change and accept some of my suggestions. I admit to being biased in her favour because she was the leader of Wanita UMNO in that constituency. Also, since it is somewhat like my own way of dealing with things and people, I can appreciate the straightforward approach in others, if they are reasonable. I am always prepared to listen to others, because I believe that a person who listens learns, and a person who continually talks learns nothing.

I would later benefit much from my close friendship with her and she ran the canteen quite efficiently after that discussion. When, much later, Johor UMNO proposed that Hajjah Fatimah become a Senator, I had no hesitation approving it. Mak Aji Fatimah as she was known to all, was a character and a firm friend until she passed away in 1998.

When I was appointed to the Cabinet after one year of managing PCM, I did not give up my chairmanship. But I was no longer able to spend as much time as I had earlier to oversee operations. I never really turned the company around but it did make a profit of RM2 million in 1978 when I was still in charge, although I had by then become Deputy Prime Minister.

Though it was difficult to get things right, it was an invaluable experience for me. It gave me a chance to be directly involved in managing a big business and international negotiations. I learnt about the importance of knowing details, a lesson valuable in the running of a business — or indeed a government. PCM taught me the need to provide clear instructions and the importance of follow-ups and of reporting back on work done. Never assume that things are done simply because decisions have been made.

During my time at the cannery, I was also involved in negotiating the price for the supply of tin-plates from Japanese companies. On one visit to Japan I went to the Kawasaki Heavy Industries Steel Rolling Mill in the Chiba Prefecture. I was fascinated by the massive plant, which was about half a kilometre long. The steel rollers flattened the heated steel blooms into thin sheets, which were then rolled into a coil at the end of the line.

Steel mills are usually very difficult to keep clean but the Japanese kept their mill spic and span. They built their plant in such a way that if you wanted to inspect it, you could walk along an elevated walkway and not get in the way of the operations. Everything was in its right place and the process was almost completely automated. Seeing that was an education in itself.

The visit influenced my thinking greatly when I became Prime Minister. I realised that you had to have a system or process in place before you could get anything done. The common assumption is that all you have to do is make a decision and then send it to administrators to execute. But from that visit, I realised that it was crucial to ask if people knew what they were supposed to do. I took the trouble to set up for the administration a process with desk files, flow charts and manuals of procedures.

At about the time I was appointed to FIMA, I was also made Chairman of the Council of the National University, or Universiti Kebangsaan. Once, I was scheduled to chair a meeting of the University Council to be held at the university itself. The students were quite restless then and the university staff learned that some students intended to hold a demonstration when I was at the campus. They suggested we change the venue, but I demurred as it was not my way to hide.

Although the meeting was at Universiti Kebangsaan, the demonstrating students were from the Mara Institute of Technology (ITM). Their leader was Halim Arshat, the student president of ITM. He had failed the compulsory English examination but he wanted the Institute to exempt him from the requirement because his failure was due to his union activities. The Institute had refused.

When I came out from the council meeting, I was surrounded by hundreds of students. I allowed them to lead me up the steps of the library, where they proceeded to hold a kangaroo court. I was asked a number of questions, such as why English was a compulsory language. I told them that it would be in their best interest to master a language like English, and I answered the rest of their questions to the best of my ability. Soon they had nothing else to ask and they began to complain about the poor conditions at the ITM campus. I agreed to go with them to see the facilities and found their complaints to be justified. The furniture was broken and needed either to be replaced or repaired. I promised to take it up with the authorities.

As events turned out, Halim Arshat never did pass that examination and he left the Institute to join PAS. He turned out to be from my new constituency of Kubang Pasu and in 1978 he stood against me. He lost by a big margin.

Time passed very quickly. I was busy with my medical practice, attending meetings of the Senate, managing PCM and giving talks to UMNO groups. I was also invited to give talks by various other groups in Malaysia and as well as some in Singapore.

Soon there was talk about elections. Despite the aftermath of 1969 and the two-year suspension of ordinary politics, Tun Razak appeared to want to maintain the practice of holding the General Election at five-year intervals. Strictly speaking, the five-year period should have begun with the first sitting of Parliament in 1972, so Tun Razak could have waited until 1977. But he chose to hold the elections in 1974 instead, as if the first sitting of Parliament had been in 1969, the year the last elections had been held. That choice made its own positive statement: it expressed a desire to return to normalcy, and indeed, to set aside any notion that normalcy had ever been affected by the events of 1969. It would also help to validate his leadership as he had inherited his position from the Tunku without going through a General Election. Tun Razak's plans would be for a return to a new political normality, not the one that had imploded in fire and bloodshed in May 1969.

I did not lobby to be a candidate, but something told me that I would be given a seat to contest in the 1974 elections. It was, at least, what I hoped for: to get back on my feet and return to the national political arena.

278

# Chapter 21:
## Up The Political Ladder

By the time the elections were held, the aftereffects of the race riots of 1969 had all but disappeared and the gloomy predictions about Malaysia had been proven wrong. Foreign newspapers and news magazines had said that the riots spelt the end of Malaysia; even Tun Dr Ismail had said at the time that this was the end of democracy in Malaysia. But we had not only survived, we had also gone on to hold elections and restore democracy. It would not be the last time we would prove the doomsayers wrong.

Tun Razak had done a good job with the National Operations Council. The country had been in despair when the riots broke out, but with Tun Dr Ismail as Home Affairs Minister and the number two man at the NOC, calm soon returned to Kuala Lumpur. Tun Dr Ismail was most certainly the right man for the job, making it clear that anyone, regardless of who they were, would be arrested if they broke the law. That put a stop to the rioting and the torching of buildings by irresponsible Malay youths. Business picked up, people were able to go about their work without fear, and the races intermingled once more.

279

One of the methods the Government used to bring the races together was to hold durian[1] parties. The Chinese loved to eat durian, perhaps more than the Malays. Sometimes they could not wait to go home but would open the thorny fruit at the roadside stall to eat it. It was thought that a durian party would be irresistible to the Chinese and would bring them out. The Government in Selangor duly organised these gatherings and issued an open invitation to people of all races. Everyone, including the Chinese from the New Villages, came out and gorged themselves.

The Malays and Chinese had been at loggerheads over a number of issues before the riots, but now the so-called Malay privileges seemed to be less of a point of contention. The Malays also appeared to have accepted the founding of Tunku Abdul Rahman College, which was to be largely owned and operated by the MCA in place of the proposed Chinese university.

---

[1] People either love or hate this pungent, thorny fruit, but it is one of the most popular fruits in Malaysia.

Much of the credit must go to Tun Dr Ismail, who had retired from politics earlier because of throat cancer. But after the riots he volunteered to come back, and was immediately made deputy head of the NOC. After taking over the premiership, Tun Razak appointed Tun Dr Ismail Deputy Prime Minister. He will always be remembered for being a good one.

When he became UMNO President and Prime Minister, Tun Razak embarked on a mission to bring all the political parties together, and he succeeded. He believed that politics should not be allowed to undermine a country's development. All the new parties which had joined the expanded Alliance — renamed Barisan Nasional, or the National Front — were getting on well, whether they were Chinese, Malays, native Sabahans and Sarawakians, or Indians. Members of Parliament representing the Malay and Chinese communities were also seemingly reconciled with the new situation and the New Economic Policy.

The Barisan Nasional was established with a clear blueprint for viability and its success was no accident. Tun Razak made sure that this coalition was rooted in certain principles, one of which was the fair sharing of political power and economic wealth. The unwritten, perhaps even unspoken rules were simple: never expect to get everything you consider to be yours. Always expect to give up something so that others are also willing to make sacrifices. That is what sharing is all about. A committed willingness to share will reduce conflict, and the resulting stability promotes growth for each party's share.

Prior to the 2008 General Election, the Barisan Nasional coalition was always strong enough to achieve at least a two-thirds majority at every General Election. This was important because if any party pulled out, the Government would not fall or be held to ransom. In a two-party coalition, on the other hand, when the minority party pulls out the Government would fall. Then the minority party may team up with the Opposition to form a Government. In a coalition of numerous parties, however, the party that pulls out will not reduce the majority of the Government to below 50 per cent. The defecting party will be in the Opposition. This acts as a deterrent against internal indiscipline.

There have been weaknesses and the Barisan Nasional is not always united. For example, the Chinese parties would look after Chinese interests and knowing the kind of strength they have, they could make demands and others must try to meet them halfway. But if they refuse to accept the solution offered and a break-up of the coalition takes place, they stand to lose as much as everyone else in the ensuing instability.

Under Tun Razak, the Barisan Nasional's new coalition members included former Opposition parties such as SUPP in Sarawak, Gerakan in Penang, PPP in Perak, and even PAS for a time. Their willingness suggested that they and their supporters wanted to put the animosity which had led to the 1969 riots behind them. This left only one Opposition party, the DAP, which, despite a good showing in 1969, was much weakened after the other parties joined the coalition. Thus from the ashes of the 1969 riots rose a powerful coalition capable of bringing stability and growth to the country.

Fresh from a successful state visit to China in 1974, which marked a turning point in Malaysia's foreign policy, Tun Razak decided to hold elections to show that the race riots had not affected Malaysia's commitment to democracy. It was five years after the last General Election in 1969; in other words, we were right on schedule. Malaysia's leaders, headed by Tun Razak, may be justly proud of the country's stabilisation and the restoration of democratic elections. Few countries have been able to return to democracy after enduring riots and a consequent switch to authoritarianism. There were voices which urged the retention of the NOC Government, but the majority supported the end of emergency rule.

After I was re-admitted into UMNO I had been appointed a Federal Senator by the Kedah State Legislative Assembly. It was a position I was happy to have, but compared to being a member of the *Dewan Rakyat* or House of Representatives, it was not very satisfactory because a Senator has less influence than a Member of the Lower House. Although you can use the appointment as Senator to become a Minister, it looks like a backdoor entrance into the Cabinet. In the Senate there was no Opposition because Senators were appointed by the Federal and state governments, and all these governments, including Kelantan at that time, were held by the Barisan Nasional. There was no challenge and so, bored, I spent my time irritating the then Transport Minister Tun Sardon Jubir by asking him silly questions to make the Senate proceedings livelier.

But now it was time to face the 1974 General Election. I was persuaded to give up my old constituency of Kota Star Selatan, which I had lost in 1969. Its boundaries had been changed and it was given to a PAS candidate, as the understanding was that Barisan Nasional parties would field candidates for the seats they had won in the last election. I was not aware that I was initially earmarked for Padang Terap, a constituency in northeast Kedah. It was poor and sparsely populated, but UMNO members from the constituency of Kubang Pasu had other ideas.

When they learnt that a PAS member had been fielded for their constituency, a group of them, led by the father of the divisional head Osman Aroff, rushed to my house one night to ask me to be the Barisan Nasional candidate instead. UMNO had always represented Kubang Pasu, and they did not want that to change.

This was indicative of the general attitude that UMNO members had towards PAS. Although UMNO leaders wanted PAS in the Alliance, there was some unhappiness among the rank and file about the party's inclusion. The quarrel among party members at the grassroots had become personal and they were not going to make up and be friends just because they were now both in the same coalition. They distrusted one another deeply and the idea of having someone from PAS represent the constituency was anathema to the Kubang Pasu UMNO Division. That was why they engineered my candidature to replace the proposed PAS candidate, Haji Shaari, who in 1964 had lost to me in Kota Star Selatan.

Fanatically loyal to their party, PAS supporters have always been rigidly disciplined. If their leaders decide that a candidate, even a recent defector from UMNO, should be supported, they give him their full support. PAS members know that their party will not abandon them. Even in constituencies which they know they have no hope of winning, such as those in Johor and Selangor, PAS makes sure to field a candidate so that its supporters in the area have someone to vote for. They want to make sure that no PAS supporter votes for UMNO, even by default.

I readily agreed to the suggestion to contest in Kubang Pasu, not knowing that I was supposed to contest the Padang Terap seat. They relayed the news to UMNO headquarters, which approved the switch. In preparation I resigned as Senator. Kubang Pasu was quite a large constituency, bigger than Kota Star Selatan. Hasmah worked in the area and I had lived there for a time, so I knew the people there. I thought I had a good chance of winning the seat because PAS was on our side and could therefore not field a candidate against me. There would, if at all, only be a weak independent candidate to face.

On nomination day I turned up at the Jitra District Office where I was to register as a candidate. From a distance I saw Ghazali Ya'acob, a former police officer, who probably was there to register as an independent candidate. Ghazali looked very surprised to see me as he had expected to see someone from PAS. Once he realised that I was the Barisan Nasional candidate contesting that seat, he decided not to stand. No other candidates registered, so I won Kubang Pasu uncontested — much to the chagrin of my supporters, who had been looking forward to an exciting time campaigning.

In Malaysia political parties enjoy a good election fight. There is the natural excitement of preparing for a campaign: posters must be put up, *ceramah* (small election rallies) are organised, and money is liberally spent on cigarettes, food and drinks for the campaign workers. No contest literally means no fun and no allowances, so the celebration over my uncontested victory was quite subdued. The best I could do for my campaign workers and supporters was to take them all to a local coffee shop where we had a good lunch. Yet despite everyone else's disappointment, I was quite elated. I had won the seat without a fight and could now give my time to campaigning for UMNO candidates elsewhere.

Winning Kubang Pasu meant a return to Parliament, whose doors had been closed to me for the past five years. I relished the chance to participate once again in the debates and to speak on important national issues. There was a lot that I wanted to say and I got my chance sooner than I expected.

In October, shortly after the elections were over, Tun Razak unveiled his new Cabinet and named me Education Minister. I had been hoping to be made only Deputy Minister, but Tun Razak apparently thought I was experienced enough not to go through the usual process of holding a junior post before becoming a full Minister. A lot of people felt that my political rehabilitation was proceeding too quickly and that my rise through the party ranks was unprecedented. As a member of Cabinet, I was now at the very centre of decision-making in the Malaysian system of Government. I believe there was some resentment, but it was not too apparent.

I was in Alor Star when I got the news of my appointment from Bakar Mohd Nor, the Secretary to the Cabinet. He contacted me and said I was required to attend the swearing-in ceremony a few days later. In Malaysian politics, the Education Ministry has always been seen as a very important portfolio, as those who held the position were thought to have a higher chance of eventually becoming Prime Minister. Tun Razak himself had previously been Education Minister, as had Tun Hussein. But this supposed path into the Prime Minister's office is far from certain. Although Tun Abdullah Ahmad Badawi, the Prime Minister who succeeded me, was once a Minister of Education, there have been several who held this post who did not make it to the nation's highest office.

I was surprised by my appointment but the education portfolio suited me well. I had always had strong opinions about education, and that must have been well known. From the moment I first became involved in UMNO politics, I was chosen to head education committees. I was a member of the Council of the University of Malaya in 1966, chaired the Committee on Higher Education when Malaysia had only one university, and was involved in the founding of the Malay-language Universiti Kebangsaan. Upon my return to UMNO I was again made the Chairman of the Malaysian Higher Education Advisory Committee. I was reminded of how much importance my father had placed on education, for himself when he was a boy and later for his children. I also remembered my own long-held belief that a good education was an open door to the world, to upward mobility.

As Education Minister, I had to face problems almost immediately. Students began staging demonstrations on a massive scale in Kuala Lumpur in 1974, alleging that people were starving to death in Baling, a town in my own state of Kedah. I had earlier attempted to address their concerns at a student forum at the University of Malaya. There had never been a widespread food shortage in the country, I had told them, nor would our culture of sharing allow us to let our neighbours starve. But the students had already made up their minds to protest and demonstrate against the Government. Urged on by Datuk Seri Anwar Ibrahim, then the leader of *Persatuan Bahasa Melayu Universiti Malaya*, the student organisation that promoted the use of the Malay langauge, students descended in full force upon what is now Dataran Merdeka, our Independence Square. They marched and carried banners, condemning the Government for not caring about the starving people in Baling, and they forced the police to cordon off parts of the city. Left to themselves the students may have started a riot, but as Education Minister I was more concerned about their not studying.

With Tun Razak and the then Home Minister Tun Ghazali Shafie, I pondered upon how to stop the demonstrations and get the students back to the universities. My main contribution was to suggest that the police use canes rather than batons when confronting the students. I feared that the batons might crack skulls and cause permanent injury, even death, whereas a cane could only hurt. It would be painful but it would break no bones. Besides, it would be humiliating, making schoolboys of university undergraduates. It was very effective and from then on, the police used canes rather than batons when dealing with students and other demonstrators.

The demonstrations stopped soon after Anwar went to the police station to try and get the arrested students released. Instead, he himself was arrested and detained under the Internal Security Act. The students remained restless and Tun Razak was very concerned. I assured him that I could handle the situation. Among other measures, I introduced amendments to the University and University Colleges Act 1971, which greatly contributed towards restoring order in the institutions of higher learning.

Students, academics and intellectuals have roundly condemned me for introducing the amendments, which they consider undemocratic and repressive. They say the Act now dampens the civic-mindedness and intellectual activity of students and curbs their freedom of speech. They claim that the Act has resulted in young Malaysians becoming less creative and failing to grow into good leaders.

I really do not think so. To me, education is so important that nothing should be allowed to impede it. A leader experienced in demonstrations is not likely to be able to handle the complex machinery of Government, where management skills and diplomacy are required. Many revolutionary leaders fail completely to stabilise and develop their countries. In the end, they resort to strong-arm methods and show intolerance towards any opposition, the very ideas they fought against.

My view has not changed. Students who indulge in demonstrations and violent politics cannot devote enough time to their studies. Malaysia is still a developing country and we need to have good, educated people to drive and sustain our development. For this reason, vast public funds are poured into education and even then, only the lucky ones are admitted into universities. Whether they are on scholarships or not, much of the expenditure on education is borne by the public.

During my time it cost RM50,000 to finance a medical student for just one year. That is equivalent to the annual pay of a senior civil servant. When someone goes overseas for a Master's degree, the Government spends RM1 million of taxpayers' money on that person. Would the public be pleased to know that government scholars are spending their time demonstrating instead of studying? True, governments may need to be prodded and even exposed to agitation, but whoever wishes to do this should do so in his own time and at his own cost. The public has a right to know that its money is being well spent.

Malay students in particular must not waste time and public money because their numbers have always been small and for that reason they must study harder. They are given ample opportunity to study, not simply to encourage their own personal upward mobility but to help balance the unequal development of the different races in Malaysia. The NEP's objectives will never be achieved if we fail to produce enough well-educated Malays, yet if those NEP objectives are not achieved, the Malays will be the first to complain. The University and University Colleges Act can be repealed once students are mature enough to understand that they are there to acquire knowledge, improve themselves and contribute to the development of the country. Perhaps it is now timely to consider whether it might be relaxed a little.

With the demonstrations over, I turned my attention back to my priorities as Minister. These were to increase the opportunities for higher education — especially for Malays who could not afford to go abroad to study — and to place more importance on the sciences rather than the arts. Science had a lot more to do with the work we faced, for at that time we needed engineers, doctors, architects and others with professional degrees. We had to start by literally forcing students into the science stream. Those who achieved a certain level of results were simply moved there. It was not a popular decision and there was a lot of resentment, especially from Malay parents who feared their children would now face more difficulty in passing their examinations. It was far easier in the arts stream, from which you emerged with a Bachelor of Arts degree after three years at university. Parents could take pictures of their children in that all-important graduation gown, mortarboard and tassel, which they could then proudly put on display in their houses.

But the reality was that apart from a career in the administrative and education services, graduates from the arts stream were practically unemployable. They were certainly not suited for the business field. The Government had assumed that with a BA, graduates were intelligent enough to carry out administrative work. That assumption was not completely wrong, but they still had to be trained to be administrators and managers.

I was very much involved in getting Malay to be used as the main medium of instruction in schools. I believe that a common language can contribute to nation-building, a sense of identity and unity among people of all races. It was always my intention to have students proficient in Malay as well as in English as a second language. Malaysian students should at the very least be bilingual, while most Chinese and Indian students will naturally end up being at least trilingual. But when we switched to Malay, most Malays came to think very misguidedly that English was irrelevant. They ceased recognising its importance and stopped studying it. These days most of our Malay-educated graduates cannot speak or write even a simple sentence in clear, correct English.

We have long started seeing the effects of this attitude. When we recruited our Malay graduates into the Civil Service, for example, we found that most were not able to function properly because their English language skills were so poor. In the service they were required to meet foreigners, negotiate with them and participate in conferences. We do not even have Malay interpreters fluent in English, an essential international conference requirement as poor understanding or misinterpretation can be disastrous. No one may fully understand what important documents state. Worse, and even more dangerous, they may nonetheless think that they do. Officers lacking a command of language that is equal to the tasks they face become frustrated because they cannot argue with clarity and force. In the end, they develop an inferiority complex.

I had long worried about the quality of education in Malaysia. The creation of public and private higher education institutions increased tremendously to meet fast-growing demand. To ensure that proper international standards were maintained, "twinning" arrangements with established foreign institutions were encouraged. Twinning reduces cost as the early years can be done in Malaysia while only the final year or last two years are done abroad. The degrees awarded would then bear the names of the respective foreign institutions. Such twinning arrangements also helped us overcome the problem of not having enough places in local universities, which already suffered from a shortage of teaching staff. Significantly, it mostly benefitted non-Malay students, who could better afford the cost of private education.

As Education Minister I was rather unpopular with the teachers — unfairly so, I thought. They were always asking for better pay and former Ministers of Education had tended to accede to their demands. When I was Prime Minister, I remember being furious when one Education Minister approved increased allowances for teachers amounting to RM90 million a year without clearing the idea with the Cabinet first. It threw the whole salary scheme into disarray when other government servants in different ministries, but of the same level and in the same Civil Service category, demanded similar allowances.

During my schooldays teachers valued their jobs. They were highly respected and were considered learned people. Even if a teacher was in a Malay primary school, he was thought to be much better informed than the rest of the people from the *kampung* and even the towns. But today, almost anyone can become a teacher. Unfortunately, our culture these days adheres to mediocre standards. We do not like anyone to stand out, so whoever works too hard or shines too much is unlikely to be appreciated by the community. As the Japanese like to say, if you see a nail standing out, you hammer it in.

There is of course some basis to the teachers' complaints of overwork, but teaching is a special profession. It is a calling with very different demands from any other profession or corporate job. It is about shaping the young to face the adult world. It involves a great deal of work outside of school hours, including supervising extracurricular activities. But teachers keep comparing themselves to people in other jobs. In Malaysia today, job opportunities are abundant. In the days when there were fewer jobs, you would have been glad to be a teacher or indeed, to have any job at all.

The first thing I did when I became Minister of Education was to call together all the heads of the teacher training colleges and give them a long lecture about the need to work hard and be dedicated. After that impassioned plea, all they said was that the pay was not sufficient. I could not give them more than other government employees of comparable status because that would only cause other employees to demand for more. Since that day their pay has been revised many times, but it has never been enough. I had always thought I might inspire people but over the years I have found that I cannot. I have given talks to UMNO Youth about commitment, about the evils of corruption, and so on, but when it comes to question time, their questions are always about something else. I have given special talks for hours on how people can achieve success and be counted among the most advanced in the world, but my audience would inevitably dispute my views and the session would end up in confusing arguments. My frustration levels would shoot up after these sessions.

Overall however, I do not think I did too badly as Education Minister. I was able to calm the universities down and get them to function once again as places of higher learning, not political agitation. More students studied the sciences. More attention was paid to the national schools. And with the twinning arrangement, poorer students who could not get into local universities because of the quota system now had another option.

Meanwhile, important changes were taking place in UMNO. With the death of Tun Dr Ismail in 1973, Tun Razak appointed Tun Hussein as the new Deputy Prime Minister. Some party leaders were unhappy with this choice as Tun Hussein had been an outsider for a long time. He had remained associated with his father and the other political parties the latter had formed. Since Tun Hussein's return to UMNO in 1969, he had never been prominent as a politician and was regarded simply as an ordinary party member. Now the feeling arose that it was Tun Razak, his brother-in-law, who had ensured his spectacular rise through the ranks. The party and public reaction to Tun Razak's announcement of his Deputy, as I recall it, was hardly enthusiastic.

For my part, I thought Datuk Harun Idris would have made a better Deputy Prime Minister. He was certainly much more of an UMNO type of leader, popular with the activist youth wing and widely regarded as a Malay nationalist. But he had run afoul of Tun Razak, and as things turned out, the appointment of Tun Hussein as Deputy Prime Minister was to prove fateful for my own political future.

# Chapter 22:
# A Dream Delivered, A Mentor Dies

Becoming a member of the Cabinet in 1974 marked a new stage in my political career, but it also closed one door to me: the practice of medicine.

Until then I had been both a politician and a doctor. It had not always been easy juggling both lives, especially since Hasmah was then also working as a rural Medical and Health Officer. We were often only able to see each other at dinnertime. Even then, the nights did not go undisturbed. Earlier, when she worked as a Registrar at the Alor Star General Hospital's maternity ward, the telephone in our house would ring so frequently that I once pulled it out of its socket in sheer frustration.

After 20 years as a doctor I had to leave that world behind me; for good, as it turned out. The rule is simple: once you become a Cabinet member, you must give up all your other activities to prevent any possible conflict of interest. I had some regrets. I have always liked working with my hands so I knew I would miss the satisfaction that surgery gave me. I would also miss being able to ease other people's pain and cure their illnesses, but I consoled myself by saying that I would now have the chance to help more people throughout the country. My patients were very encouraging, and told me that I was going from treating them to treating the ailments of the nation. And while I had grown to love medicine, I felt that I was now moving to my true vocation.

As a young man I had thought that law would be the best platform to launch me into politics, but I discovered that medicine had taught me many lessons about what it takes to be a good politician. One of the earliest things I learnt as a medical student at the King Edward VII College of Medicine, for example, was how to conquer my fears.

I had grown up afraid of death. When we were children, our elders had told us stories about ghosts and monsters coming after us as a way of making sure we would all come home before dark. It worked, and by 7pm all of us would run home, afraid that monsters would get us if we stayed out too late.

At school I was afraid to look at drawings of human skeletons. When I went to university, I walked past the anatomy lab during the first day of lectures. Even the sight of bodies covered with white sheets sent chills down my spine. The idea of handling those bodies was even more frightening. Strangely, it had not occurred to me that as a medical student, this was exactly what I had to do. All I had thought about was becoming a doctor, a person who could cure illness and bring people relief. Dissecting dead bodies was the last thing on my mind.

I summoned all my strength to overcome this fear, something I had practised from a young age. When I was a boy I had been afraid of dogs. I had been brought up to think of them as ferocious animals, an idea that was confirmed when a friend of mine was attacked and bitten by one. When I was about 12, during a visit to my uncle's house, his dog started to chase me and I ended up running into the outdoor bathroom and slamming the door shut after me.

My uncle later told me that I should not have run but should have stood my ground and faced the dog. He also taught me that pretending to pick up a stone from the ground was usually enough to scare the dog away. The next time a dog approached me I remembered his advice. I gritted my teeth and resisted my usual urge to turn and run. I remained where I stood and stooped as if to pick up a stone. This time, it was the dog that ran away.

Back at the medical college, the day I realised I had to handle the corpses, I actually thought of giving up medicine. I wrestled with this fear until I remembered that even the girls would have to do the same thing. I had the idea that girls must naturally be timid and scared of the same things that scared me, but oddly enough, it did not seem to bother them. Indeed, no one talked about being afraid of dead bodies.

Ashamed of myself, I decided I had to overcome my fear. I went to the lab where the second-year students were being introduced to anatomy and asked one of them to uncover one of the corpses. It was a Chinese man and he smelled strongly of formalin. I put my hand on the cadaver. It was cold to the touch. I told myself it was dead and could do me no harm. Slowly, by facing my fears, I managed to reach a point where dead bodies no longer frightened me.

In my second year I had no qualms about handling and dissecting the human body. In those days students at the medical college were able to buy an entire human skeleton, real bones and not plastic imitations, as study aids. I bought my bones from some senior students. We would carry them back with us when we went home for the holidays, and sometimes customs officials who opened our bags would be startled to find them filled with human bones. I even developed the habit of taking a skull to bed with me as I struggled to remember the names and the routes of cranial nerves. I would fall asleep with the skull in my hands, and when I woke up the next morning it would be there in my bed, grinning at me.

Much later, when I was doing post-mortems in Alor Star, I had a policeman standing next to me when I was cutting up the body of a murder victim. He was there to make sure I was dissecting the right corpse. The standard procedure is to cut open the body and pull out all the organs to examine them for disease. To do this, you must have strength and be able to withstand the smell. I hadn't even probed the wound fully when the poor policeman toppled over in a faint.

These amusing anecdotes aside, this closeness to death kept me free of the temptation to abuse power for material gains. This was another important political lesson: in the end, you have to leave everything behind. As someone said, there are no pockets in *kain kapan* (funeral shrouds). Everyone, rich and poor alike, end up just like the deceased patients I encountered almost every day when I was working in the hospitals and as a private doctor.

Some doctors end up becoming insensitive to the death of their patients and other people, even colleagues and friends. But it was impossible for me to remain untouched as death is so final. There is no return. The only way to face your mortality is to believe that what you do in life will matter even after you are gone. You must have faith to face death. With this in mind, I was determined to live a full life. I wanted to get married and have children. Later, as I studied religion more and more, it became clear to me that life was a gift that had to be valued. It became much easier to become reconciled to my mortality and my exaggerated fear of dying slowly disappeared.

What became more important than worldly wealth was to maintain my good name: not because I wanted to be admired but because I did not want to give my children and grandchildren any reason to be ashamed of me after I am gone. I think I have done the best I can. My conscience is clear, although there will always be people who will smear my name. I have long accepted this but in my mind, I will not leave behind a legacy of shame.

My training as a doctor also helped me to approach problems in a rigorously methodical and logical manner, another skill that would help me in politics. Doctors must go through a process of taking a full medical history, listening carefully to the symptoms, and also do a physical examination, followed by whatever laboratory tests may seem necessary. All this information is collated and, one by one, unlikely diseases and possibilities are eliminated. Additional tests may be done. This is how one arrives at a diagnosis, and once that is made, appropriate treatment can be prescribed.

When faced with political or administrative problems I always apply the same approach. The solution may not always be right but mid-course corrections can be made as problems arise. The results from this methodical way are seldom entirely negative.

294     During the currency crisis of 1997-1998, when the value of the Malaysian ringgit was plummeting, we were told that our problem was our mismanagement of the economy. I refused to believe this as only months earlier, the International Monetary Fund (IMF) Managing Director Michel Camdessus had praised Malaysia's administration. I had to find out exactly why the crisis was happening: to identify the causes, or aetiology as we say in medicine. In politics as well, if you can remove the causes you may be able to overcome the problem. And as in medicine, standard formulae may not always work. Sometimes, outwardly similar occurrences of the same problem in different places may be due to different causes. The IMF apparently believes that all financial problems can be overcome simply by reducing expenditure, achieving a surplus, increasing interest rates and bankrupting inefficient businesses. The IMF merely looks at the numbers, caring little that bankrupting such companies can have far-reaching social repercussions. Although I have no clear evidence of it, there seemed to be something of a hidden agenda to prevent upstart nations from becoming established economies.

Only later did I learn the great difference between the principles of law and those of medicine. Lawyers are trained to look at every case from the perspective they are engaged for, that is, for their clients or against their adversaries. Doctors, by contrast, must view a patient's problem from all sides in order to reach a correct diagnosis. If a lawyer is defending someone, it is his job to obtain and present evidence — and even find loopholes in the law, if need be — that may free his client, even if he knows the person is guilty. But to cure a patient, doctors must set aside all preconceived ideas and correctly identify the disease and its causes. Lawyers by professional necessity are partisan in their thinking. Doctors are, or at least must strive to be, objective and seek the truth. Politicians must do the same if they are to discover the root causes of problems affecting policies, development plans and election strategies, and deal effectively with them.

Medicine also helped me to understand people better, to appreciate what ails them and what might meet their needs. Other professionals may meet hundreds, even thousands of people in their line of work. But the difference is that all kinds of people go to see the doctor when they are vulnerable. When you are visited by such a wide section of society and are privy to their most private vulnerabilities, I believe you come away with a better insight into human nature.

My patients did not tell me only about their medical problems, but also about the poor conditions of their villages, about how their children could not go to school, and about their worries over the year's padi (rice) crop. Doctors are trained to listen. It may be tedious but you learn if you listen, and by the same token, you learn very little if you only talk. That is why I was able to sit through innumerable political and other briefings throughout my career in the Government — interjecting or questioning only when necessary.

Understanding people is vital when you are a politician, especially in a democratic system when you continue in office only if you are voted back in. The policies and solutions that you propose must not only be good; they must also gain popular support from the people. This is not as easy as one might think. Establishing a medical facility in a rural area, for example, might seem like an idea that will earn you the support of the constituency.

But there will be tussles over location, contracts, and whether to employ external or local workers. A great deal of discontent may soon arise. To be right and at the same time popular is often not possible.

When we decided to build the Muda irrigation scheme[1] for example, which brought water to 250,000 acres of padi fields, it was to help the people there to double their yearly production of rice. It cost RM400 million, equal to about RM1 billion today. Everyone should have been reasonably satisfied, but PAS politicised the issue and said the land should be allowed to rest instead. They also told the community that with the scheme, their sarongs would always be wet, an idiomatic way of saying that they would always have to work. They said it was not what God had intended for them. This kind of rhetoric is very effective with *kampung* people. Despite what the scheme was meant to achieve, it also made some unhappy because it meant they had to surrender some land through which the canals would be dug. Whatever compensation was paid was never enough.

I left medicine with the belief that my training as a doctor had made me a more capable politician. Hasmah continued working as a Medical Officer even after we moved from Kedah to Kuala Lumpur when I joined the Cabinet. She remained with the Public Health Institute until 1979, after I became Deputy Prime Minister.

In 1975, less than a year after I had become Education Minister, UMNO held its party elections. I had contested in 1972 and although I had lost in my bid to become one of the three party Vice-Presidents, I did manage to secure a seat on the Supreme Council with the highest number of votes. Now, I was once more expected to contest the post of Vice-President. Close party colleagues urged me to put my name forward as a candidate and since support for me seemed widespread, I agreed.

Party elections in those days were very different from now. Campaigning was not carried out as aggressively and it usually consisted of merely calling on people. I noticed that for ordinary members of the Supreme Council, your chances would improve if your name appeared at the top of the list of candidates. Party members had the habit of going down the list and ticking

---

[1]   The Muda irrigation scheme is located in Kedah and came into operation in January 1970.

off the names of candidates they were familiar with first. Only after that would they consider the rest, also in top-down order. This method meant that invariably, a few good candidates would be left out simply because they were near the bottom of the list and there were no more places left for them. For the Vice-Presidency, however, the number of candidates was always smaller so the voters were more inclined to go through the whole list and make considered choices.

Nowadays, campaigning for positions in the party always involves money. The 1986 UMNO election is a good example of when money was used lavishly to win votes. It might be said that this was the start of large-scale money politics, and since then it has become a feature of all UMNO elections. Despite all the vehement denials, I know this is true. In 1993, when Datuk Seri Anwar Ibrahim challenged Tun Ghafar Baba as Deputy President, I had reliable information that a lot of money also changed hands. But when I asked the division heads who later became members of the Supreme Council whether they had received any money, they were silent.

Unfortunately, my attempts to stop this practice were unsuccessful. The biggest problem was I could not take action on the basis of hearsay. The person who receives the money must cooperate by revealing who gave it to him, and this would rarely happen. Occasionally, with some evidence I was able to take the matter all the way up to the disciplinary committee. Even then it was hard to prove the charge as money also changes hands to prevent the evidence from surfacing. Because corruption is not easy to prove, the only way to handle it is to reject it.

It is sad to see the change in UMNO. I have spoken to groups within the party and told them money politics will destroy them and eventually the party itself. But in their minds, what they do is not money politics. For example, they argue that if people need computers, why should *they* not be the ones to provide them? I suggested that they give the computers to the party headquarters which would then distribute them, not just to their own constituencies but to others who were also in need. The idea met with all-round disagreement. The local leaders insisted that there was nothing wrong with giving away the computers themselves. Clearly what was paramount to them was not the needs of the people but the political credit that comes with these acts of charity. As Muslims they must know that when giving charity, "the right hand must not know what the left hand is doing." There is merit in being anonymous when giving *sedekah*, the charity that all observant Muslims who can afford it are enjoined to give. But they also know as politicians that such largesse creates a sense of indebtedness and obligation that can later be translated into political support or votes.

During the 1975 party elections I did not campaign personally, but my candidacy was enhanced by the fact that I was already a Minister and was considered a champion of the Malay cause. My chances were also boosted by Tun Razak's political secretary, Tan Sri Abdullah Ahmad, who made sure that the Prime Minister's speech at the General Assembly mentioned the names of three people who were deemed to have done well: Tengku Razaleigh Hamzah, Tun Ghafar and myself. UMNO members viewed this as Tun Razak's endorsement of our candidature and all three of us emerged winners.

I defeated my old ally Harun by 47 votes. He had helped to engineer my return to the party and I did not think my beating him for the third Vice-President's post would sour our relationship. The following year, Harun was charged with corruption and imprisoned. He was apparently a model prisoner while he served out his sentence. I tried to have his case reviewed by the Pardon's Board when I became Deputy Prime Minister, but failed. When I became Prime Minister in 1981, the Board conducted a review and recommended a full pardon. He came back into politics and turned against me, working very hard to get me defeated by Tengku Razaleigh in the 1986 party elections. Much later, one of his sons wrote me a bitter letter. In it, he said the family believed I had sabotaged his father's chances of winning in the 1975 election for Vice-President. Clearly, all my efforts to help him were not appreciated.

I remember that I was not in the hall when the names of the new Vice-Presidents were announced, as it was never my habit to wait around for the results. My attitude was always philosophical: if I win, I win, and if I don't, I don't. Had I lost, I would have been disappointed of course, but neither did I think it decent to show too much exuberance in victory. It was only a little later in the day when I walked into the hall and heard the delegates clapping that I knew I had won. I had come in third among the winners, with Tun Ghafar and Tengku Razaleigh ahead of me. They were both senior party members who were much closer to the UMNO leadership, so mine was not a bad performance for someone who had been sacked from the party and readmitted only three years earlier. But I did not realise the full significance of this success then.

Around this time, I had other growing concerns. I had come to regard Tun Razak as a mentor and protector. He had defended me from the Tunku's anger after I led the AAPSO mission in 1965. It was he who suggested that I run as Member of Parliament for the Kota Star Selatan seat in 1964, and again he who nominated me to UMNO's all-important political committee. As a committee member, I would go to his house for long, in-depth discussions, and that contact allowed me to grow even closer to him. His confidence in me seemed to increase after I helped to deal with student demonstrations when I became Education Minister. I like to think that he regarded me as someone who was willing to act and a person he could rely upon.

But at this point his health was failing. Even in 1973, just after I had returned to UMNO, when he came for a meeting with state-level party officials in Sungai Petani I could see immediately that he was unwell. Still, he continued, even though it clearly took a great effort.

I learnt a lot from Tun Razak. He was a doer. The Tunku had left almost all the administrative tasks of running the Government to him, and he understood that preparations had to be carried out before plans could be implemented. He was a sincere leader who truly wanted to do something for the country and the Malays. His tendency to favour me was apparent to everyone in the party and naturally caused some jealousy. There was talk about my being his blue-eyed boy, but still I found myself unable to be too familiar with him. We did not socialise, but in all matters of politics I had grown to rely on his judgment and support.

One day in 1975, we were at a function at Parliament House shortly before he was supposed to fly to London. I was among the last to take my leave. Just before I did so, Tun Razak called me aside. He had visibly lost weight by then, but I was still taken aback when he told me that he was suffering from a blood disease and would be seeking treatment in England. He probably told me because he felt that, as a doctor, I would understand. I was very distressed by the news. Shortly after I saw him off at Subang International Airport, I called his doctor and learnt that he was in the advanced stages of leukaemia. I knew then that he was not going to recover. There was no effective treatment for cancer. One might hope for remission, but even then the disease would return.

Later, I learnt that many of the people who surrounded Tun Razak were planning to visit him in London. I considered this unwise. He badly needed rest and I was concerned that they would disturb him. But many of his closest friends did go and I heard that they tried to keep his spirits up by persuading him to have new suits made and to dine on roast beef and Yorkshire pudding at Simpsons-on-the-Strand, his favourite restaurant. I hope their presence did give him some cheer because, despite medical treatment, the cancer did not go into remission. Tun Razak died in London at the age of 54 on 14 January 1976.

Hasmah and I had just returned from vacationing in Indonesia when we heard the news. For me it was devastating, a personal tragedy. The public was shocked by the news of his death, as few people knew how seriously ill he had been. Even most of Tun Razak's political colleagues had not been aware of the true state of his health. Ministers and senior Government officials gathered at Subang International Airport when his body was brought back home one evening a few days later. Many in the crowd were crying. I myself could not stop my tears from flowing as I watched the casket being lowered from the aircraft. For a long time after, I would feel a tightness in my chest every time I talked about him. I remember that the newspapers described the public's reaction as "an outpouring of grief". That sums up how many of us felt.

Without him, undeniably, my future in politics seemed less bright. I had lost my protector. While I may never rise beyond being a Minister, so long as Tun Razak was the head of the Government, I could be sure that he would listen to my views. I did not know what Tun Hussein, the new Prime Minister, thought of me. Under him, could I still remain confident of being heard? That remained to be seen.

Tun Hussein was more aloof than Tun Razak and did not make friends easily. On my part, I always had trouble pushing myself forward and this may have added to my difficulties. The only consolation was that nobody else seemed close to him either. Tun Hussein took charge after Tun Razak's death and immediately seemed to be under tremendous pressure. He was known to have a short fuse and people were usually careful not to tell him anything that might make him angry. On one occasion he lost his temper when his aide-de-camp could not be found. To be fair to Tun Hussein, his ADC was not very good at his job and had a habit of disappearing. His patience sorely tried, Tun Hussein shouted at the man when he finally turned up.

The lobbying and campaigning for the now vacant post of Deputy Prime Minister went on for several months. At one point, Tengku Razaleigh called Tun Ghafar and me for a meeting to discuss who should be appointed the next Deputy Prime Minister. He suggested that since we were the three Vice-Presidents of UMNO, the choice should be confined to us. Tengku Razaleigh's family members had a history of dying relatively young, so he suggested that he should be given the chance to be Deputy Prime Minister. In the end, however, the three of us agreed to approach Tun Hussein and put forward the idea that he make his selection from among the three Vice-Presidents.

Frankly, I did not think I had much of a chance. I was the Vice-President who had won the position with the lowest number of votes, and was also still stuck with the image of being a Malay "ultra". This made me popular with Malay voters, but caused some worry in the Chinese community. As Education Minister I had clashed with Chinese educationists, while the MCA still remembered how I had blamed them for the Alliance's setback in the 1969 General Election. A man who was perceived as anti-Chinese was not likely to be welcomed as the heir apparent to the leader of this multiracial country, for in effect that is what the Deputy Prime Minister would be. The foreign Press was also vociferous in their criticism. They simply could not conceive of me as a leader of this nation. Their dislike of me never abated and I was to be their *bête noir* (or at least their *sawo matang* or brown-skinned bogeyman) throughout my political career.

The day Tun Hussein was supposed to announce his choice of Deputy Prime Minister, I went to see him to tell him that I was going to Kluang in Johor to visit a school. Perhaps I was hoping that he would indicate something, that he would ask me not to go as he would be announcing my appointment as Deputy Prime Minister. But he was stony-faced and said nothing. Disheartened, I left him and took the car to Kluang. I went to the school and was given the usual briefing, after which I inspected the facilities and talked to the teachers.

Sometime during the course of my inspection, my bodyguard came and whispered that I had been selected as Deputy Prime Minister. I was at a loss for words. The State Education Officer, the Headmaster and the senior teachers crowded around, congratulating me. The State Education Officer suggested that I cut short my visit and return to Kuala Lumpur, which I did. It was a long drive. At the border between the Federal Territory and Selangor I enjoyed the first privilege of my elevated status: the police outriders were waiting and they smoothly fell into place and escorted me as Deputy Prime Minister to my Ministry of Education office in Federal House.

I decided to go and see Tun Hussein to thank him, but I could not do so immediately as he had a prior appointment. When I finally managed to see him, it was at the Deputy Prime Minister's office as he had not yet moved into the Prime Minister's office. I thanked him profusely but he seemed quite cool. I cannot even remember him smiling when I shook his hand, but then he was not a demonstrative man. I learnt later that the Press conference during which he had announced his decision had not gone well. There had been a loud gasp, almost a groan when he named me Deputy Prime Minister, followed by a flurry of questions about why he had chosen me. The questions suggested that they did not think much of his choice and I think he was rattled by that. He closed the Press conference by saying that he hoped and prayed that he had made the right decision.

The reporters were not the only people disturbed by the news of my appointment. Hasmah's colleague at the Public Health Institute told her about the announcement before I had a chance to tell her myself. She locked herself in an empty room and cried. She told me later that she was upset because she was worried about the amount of work and the burden of responsibility that had now fallen on my shoulders. After she had calmed down, she left the Institute and returned to our house in Petaling Jaya, where our neighbours started knocking on the door to pass on their best wishes and congratulations.

I cannot say my fellow party Vice-Presidents were happy about Tun Hussein's decision either. Tun Ghafar, who had received the highest number of votes in the VP contest, was upset enough to resign from the Government. He went into business after that. I tried to soften the impact of his leaving and said he had planned on leaving anyway, but I do not think that went down very well with him. The truth was that Tun Hussein did not know Tun Ghafar very well and perhaps did not consider him well qualified. As for Tengku Razaleigh, Tun Hussein remembered very well how, as Finance Minister, the prince had bypassed him to deal directly with the Prime Minister. I believe I was chosen by default, as Tun Hussein's "least worst option", and not because of any particular virtue that I may have had.

There were many lessons to be learnt. I thought that as Deputy Prime Minister I would be high enough in the hierarchy to be free of any direct opposition. That was, of course, very naïve. The party's Youth Chief Tan Sri Syed Jaafar Hassan Albar, who was a very senior member of UMNO, was so dead against my appointment that he travelled the country to campaign against me. I think he believed I did not deserve the position because of the way I had opposed the Tunku in 1969, and because I was still a relatively junior member of the party. But he found out that his own youth members did not feel the same way. Feeling secure about the level of support I had in UMNO, I decided not to respond to his campaigning. Nor did I hold this against him or his son, Tan Sri Syed Hamid Albar, who was appointed by me to my Cabinet for many years and was Foreign Minister when I retired.

I did not enter the office of the Deputy Prime Minister with a comprehensive set of ideas about what I wanted to do, and this was just as well. I was soon to discover that it would not be the experience I had expected.

# Chapter 23:
## From Education To International Trade And Industry

My children were completely unfazed by my promotion. We had to move from our house in Petaling Jaya into the official residence, which was quite small for our relatively large family. Tun Hussein had been living there and had extended it slightly, but there was still not enough room for all of us. The old colonial house had been built for British officers, who of course did not have their children with them. Since there were only two big rooms upstairs, I had to partition the space carefully so the children would be comfortable. I ended up converting the bathroom, which was sizeable, into Marina's bedroom. The three boys had to sleep in one room and I created a dining area by constructing a platform above the staircase. Meanwhile, my daughter Melinda slept in a converted storeroom.

The children did not seem to mind the lack of space, since they were largely away and only came back to stay with us during the holidays. There was no change in their attitudes either — they had the same friends and went on with their usual activities. There was no added security for them and when they travelled, they never told people who they were. When Mokhzani later went to Tulsa, Oklahoma, in the US to study, he befriended a young Colombian boy who was his roommate. By then, I was already Prime Minister. One day, in preparation for my visit, the US Secret Service came and examined the room. The boy was startled beyond words and wondered what on earth was happening. Mokhzani finally had to tell him that his father was the Prime Minister of Malaysia.

By becoming Deputy Prime Minister, I had already gone further than I had ever expected when I first became a politician. Still, I could not completely give up the life of an ordinary citizen. I liked and still like to drive and do my own shopping. I disliked protocol intensely and often had to instruct my bodyguard not to push people aside or ask them to get out of my way when I was out in public. Sometimes I deliberately ignored the path cleared for me and instead would walk in another direction. Once, during a visit to the Smithsonian Museum in the US, the hefty six-footers in my security detail insisted on surrounding me completely so that as I walked around, all I could see were their huge backs.

I understood why security was necessary — should anything happen to me, the security officers would have been blamed. But the only time my personal security was actually breached was on 28 July 2006, when, as a result of local political rivalries, I was blasted in the face with pepper spray during a visit to Kelantan. Despite that incident, my feelings about security and protocol have not changed and I am happiest when I can walk about and speak to people without any hindrance.

My appointment as Deputy Prime Minister also entailed moving from the Education Ministry to the Ministry of International Trade and Industry (MITI). It was suggested that heading the Education Ministry was not consistent with my new status as Deputy Prime Minister. For my part, I believe some who were wary of my continuing rise in UMNO feared the consequences of my retaining my old portfolio. The position of Minister of Education was powerful in the party because many Malay teachers were UMNO members and, in those earlier times especially, they exerted a strong influence in the party, especially during the elections.

I realised this only later, but at that time I had no reason to suspect anything and thought people were only trying to be helpful. I also felt that, as the new Deputy Prime Minister, my eventual candidature for Prime Minister was now becoming more certain. Switching Cabinet portfolios therefore seemed unlikely to affect my fortunes greatly. In any case, staying on at the Education Ministry would not have helped me because I had not made any effort to establish closer contact with the teachers.

I found MITI to be very invigorating as I had always been interested in business, particularly in encouraging the climate and environment for its growth. Besides, I had often wondered why some people and some races seemed to succeed in business while others just could not manage it.

When I took over I discovered that Approved Permits (APs) to import reconditioned foreign cars were being given to Malays because they were unable to get into the business of selling cars. The principal agents for the major vehicle manufacturers and distributors were not willing to appoint

Malays as dealers or sales agents for their cars. Nor could Malays import cars, as by agreement with manufacturers, the sole agents controlled all imports. But secondhand cars did not come under the control of the sole agents, so APs could be given for the import and sale of reconditioned secondhand cars. This was how Malays could get into the car-selling business, as reconditioned secondhand Japanese cars, for example, were almost as good as new and had a strong market.

Unfortunately, the Malays who were issued the APs did not import the cars themselves. They sold the permits to the Chinese, who did the actual importing and selling. The profits were so substantial that each AP would fetch as much as RM8,000. As Malay applicants could get as many as 10 APs a month, they could make as much as RM80,000. Only a few of them, however, did the actual honest work of importing and selling motor vehicles.

When I came to the Ministry, I stopped APs from being given freely to those who had no evidence that they were importing and selling the cars themselves. I had our staff check whether these applicants had showrooms and if they did not, I instructed the staff not to issue the APs. Loud protests followed. The individuals concerned wanted to demonstrate against me, but I called their bluff and they backed off. Doing this was politically risky as many of them were UMNO supporters and employees at the party headquarters. Some Malays were, however, above-board. Individuals like Tan Sri Nasimuddin Amin of Naza Motors, who passed away in 2008, had showrooms but they were in the minority. I was willing to give any number of APs to applicants like these.

There was another category of people I gave APs to: those who wanted to import cars that were not already being brought into the country. Under this permit, each person was allowed one car in a lifetime and it had to be for his own use. Usually these were very expensive prestige models and not too many of these APs were given out. Malaysians living abroad could also import the cars they had been using. The AP system is a sound one and it did help a few Malays to break into the automotive business. Eventually, when the national car company Proton began to produce cars, more Malays were able to set up agencies to sell Proton.

Soon after I retired, I was to disagree with the way the Ministry was giving out APs to those who I suspected were not conducting legitimate car businesses. This led to a falling out between me and the then Minister Tan Sri Rafidah Aziz, which the local Press front-paged for weeks. In all fairness, she was very good at what she did and was promoted to the post precisely because of her ability to perform. But she was intolerant of criticism and, unlike most Malays, not afraid of being blunt. During Cabinet meetings, nobody dared to criticise her because they were wary of the heated arguments that would invariably follow. If you criticised her, even courteously and in good faith, her retort was always to point out how much worse you yourself were. It was all very unpleasant. For my part, I kept her in the Cabinet because she was an able negotiator and wasn't afraid of anyone. Because of this, she was able to obtain favourable terms for Malaysia in many trade agreements. Not without reason did those on the international trade scene call her "Rapid Fire Rafidah".

But there were occasions when she agreed to conditions which were not in our favour. The most glaring case was for countries under the ASEAN Free Trade Agreement (AFTA) to reduce taxes for motor vehicles that had 40 per cent local content. At the time, Proton had 90 per cent local content, so naturally the price of Proton cars was higher because of the built-in costs of design and development. When I discovered this, I was concerned that we would not be able to sell Proton cars either locally or in other ASEAN countries. I told her to inform AFTA that we needed to postpone the date of implementation from 2003 to 2005.

Today, because of that AFTA agreement, there are huge numbers of foreign cars in Malaysia, but only a few Protons in Thailand or other ASEAN countries. Our inability to compete is largely because we do not have the economies of scale. There are ways of overcoming this, but the Proton management at that particular time had not found the answer. They also apparently do not have the capital despite the huge cash reserves the company had earned earlier.

The Thai automotive industry consists largely of assembling foreign cars. Admittedly, they use components made in Thailand, but they only need to have 40 per cent local inputs to benefit from the AFTA agreement. These are crucial economic issues which the public does not know about, or does not care to know. Contrary to what critics said, Proton was a profitable venture that helped in the development of engineering capabilities in the country. But it now needs a miracle to survive. The misuse of APs and under-declaration of import prices of foreign cars have played a large part in its unfortunate decline.

When I was Minister for MITI, I tried to encourage foreign investments with Malaysian participation. The idea was for foreign investors to bring in funds so that there would be a net capital inflow. Much later, when I was already Prime Minister, I learnt that little capital was brought in since much of it was borrowed locally.

Nevertheless the increase in foreign investments helped to create jobs and so lowered the unemployment rate, which was high at the time. Our approach differed from those of Japan and Korea, where the preference was for acquiring foreign technology for investment by the locals. We did not have local entrepreneurs with the money or the willingness to invest in industries they were not familiar with. It was only after many years that Malaysians acquired the knowledge and industrial skills to invest in manufacturing. Thus it was through FDI that we succeeded in converting our agricultural economy into an industrial economy and eventually solving our unemployment problem.

Industrialisation in Malaysia began under the stewardship of Tun Razak. I helped to speed the process by actively promoting it myself and introducing a climate that was friendlier towards investors. I led many investment promotion delegations to Japan, Europe and America. Investors came in droves once they heard about Malaysian stability, our easily trained workforce, low inflation rates, our liberal attitude towards the expatriation of profits and generally good financial administration. In those days, other newly independent countries were unwilling to allow foreign involvement in their economies.

Malaysians were less sophisticated then than they are now. They certainly did not possess the aggressiveness that is sometimes necessary in business. They preferred to sell their products to Singapore, which then acted as a distribution centre and made a tidy profit marketing products obtained from Malaysia. They exported those same products — like orchids — to other countries, or sold processed raw materials back to Malaysia for a much higher price. Singapore agencies invariably included Malaysia as part of their own territory. It was my fervent desire to see Malaysians do the marketing themselves, as there was so much to be gained from cutting out the middleman.

In the beginning, when I went looking for foreign investments and new markets, I found that it was difficult for foreign investors to accept Malaysians as their partners. The only company that responded — very much earlier in the 1960s — was National, the Japanese electronics giant. National had aggressive plans to expand and it was willing to accept certain conditions in order to do so. The company wanted to sell its products in Malaysia so one of the conditions we set was they had to give us a share of the business. They eventually set up a factory in Subang Jaya, a suburb near Kuala Lumpur. Later we did away with the requirement for Malaysian participation if the products were meant for export.

It took time to introduce Malaysia, as few people had heard of our country then, and far fewer knew where in the world we were. Many thought we were in Africa. In New York, we arranged for Citibank to sponsor a seminar on investment in Malaysia, and we also had other banks and organisations join as sponsors. They agreed as they had branches in Malaysia and there was a possibility they would receive a piece of any resulting foreign investment. These seminars were very well attended. Once we experimented by bringing in a trade unionist to try to explain the labour situation, but he ended up talking about the need for good pay and better working conditions. Although his underlying principle was acceptable — that as investments increased wages would also increase — talking about these issues certainly did not encourage investment, without which the demand for labour would drop. Consequently, wages were not likely to rise. I had to drop the idea of bringing in trade union leaders as speakers as their militant approach served neither the country's interests nor their own.

I am pragmatic in such matters, as Tun Razak was. Like him, I was willing to borrow ideas from anywhere, even from the communists. One of the communist ideas that Tun Razak borrowed was having five-year plans for Malaysia's development, as he believed it would be a useful mechanism for speeding up development. But we also believed that the basis of communism — that workers should own all the means of production — was not logical or practical. The facts were glaring — workers in capitalist countries were better off than in communist countries. Owning the means of production had not benefited them.

Equality is a fine principle, but as an economic practice it is flawed. In a workers' government, the workers would want better deals and wages for themselves and this would result in costs going up and profits going down. If everyone is a worker and the country produces luxury goods, who would buy them? You would effectively impoverish the local market and would have to sell the products to wealthy people in capitalist countries.

During a trip to Venice I was shown an antique table that was beautifully made and embedded with pearls and precious stones. Why were people able to make such costly things in the old days? Because there were very rich people who were able to buy them. In any society, there are inevitably the wealthy and the poor. If everyone was rich, wealth would be made quite meaningless. Purchasing power is what counts, and this is determined by what money can buy. If everyone, including the workers, have to be rich, then the cost of production and therefore the cost of goods and services would be high. The purchasing power of everyone would be low.

As the country grew wealthier, our imports also grew. We tried to get the best from our trading activities. Learning about the offset programme, we insisted that big suppliers to Malaysia give us something extra to sweeten the deal. When we bought Sukhoi fighter planes from Russia, for example, we also asked them for help to train Malaysian astronauts. When MAS purchased aircraft, we insisted that the suppliers also sourced aircraft components from us. This was how we got into the manufacturing of composite parts of the large commercial aircraft manufactured by Airbus. The value of the parts came to hundreds of millions of dollars. Today the company Composite Technologies and Research Malaysia is regarded as a very competent manufacturer of aircraft parts.

As Minister of Education I had rarely travelled outside of the country, but at MITI, I had to visit many industrial countries to promote Malaysia as a location for investment and a centre for trade in Southeast Asia. This gave me the experience to deal with foreign officials and business people. The lessons I learnt were invaluable when I later became involved in foreign policy and international relations. My duty in MITI was to find new markets, and I went to many parts of the world that were unknown territories to us at that time. I had realised that Malaysia was too small a country to support large-scale industries and we needed foreign markets for our goods. In order for Malaysia to export directly, without going through Singapore merchants, our businessmen had to find potential markets and trade with those countries. The effort yielded results and today Malaysia is a big trading country with exports of over USD100 billion. At one time it was the 17th biggest trading nation in the world, although it has since fallen to 25th place.

I learnt many lessons during my time as International Trade and Industry Minister, but even as I felt that I was making some headway in my new portfolio, it was my position as Deputy Prime Minister that proved to be unexpectedly frustrating.

# Chapter 24:
## Frustrations Of Being Second In Command

Being made Deputy Prime Minister meant much more than just having added responsibilities and authority — it also marked the first time that I had any reasonable certainty of one day becoming Prime Minister. As the heir apparent, you are perceived to be head-and-shoulders above other members of the Cabinet. I assumed that Tun Hussein would hold office for at least as many years as the Tunku had, so I concentrated on fulfilling my duties as Tun Hussein's deputy and establishing the best relationship I could with him.

It was not easy. I served with him for five years and we were never as close as I had hoped we would be. Tun Hussein did not open up readily and his interaction with people was rather stiff. He was a serious person and though he had a dry sense of humour, he was not the type to crack jokes and laugh. Tun Razak had been much more relaxed and had laughed more and enjoyed company, though he was not given to joking. Tun Hussein was more of a loner.

I too did not make friends easily, nor was I in the habit of telling jokes and laughing heartily with him. It was always strictly business between us and I did not meet him unless it was to discuss something official. The only one who seemed to be able to get his personal attention was Tengku Razaleigh, who had always been skillful at getting close to whoever was Prime Minister. I sometimes had to gain access to Tun Hussein through Tengku Razaleigh and this was not something I appreciated. It did not enhance my position as Deputy Prime Minister. Still, for certain matters in which Tengku Razaleigh was also involved, I had to use this approach. At other times, I had to make use of the Secretary to the Cabinet, Tun Abdullah Salleh.

Tun Hussein had had quite a colourful and varied career. He had been in the Johor Military Forces before the Pacific War and, together with Tun Ibrahim Ismail, who later became the third Malay Chief of the Armed Forces of Malaysia, was sent to Dehradun in India to train as a military officer. He joined the British Army during the war and served in Egypt before being selected to join the British forces set up to invade occupied Malaya and fight the Japanese. Tun Hussein landed in Morib as part of the assault force, but the Japanese surrendered before the British could attack. After he left the army, he joined Johor's administrative service. When his father, Dato' Onn Jaafar, became the head of newly-formed UMNO, Tun Hussein became the leader of the youth wing.

As Prime Minister Tun Hussein was a very principled man and there was never even a whiff of corruption or scandal around him. He was a straightforward leader, but many UMNO members could not quite forget that he had left the party for 17 years to join his father's Independence of Malaya Party.

Many people joked about his habit of underlining words and sentences in the papers he studied. He would go over the documents again and again and in the end he would have underlined every sentence in every paragraph in different colours. He worked very hard and always took his files home in the red box-like containers provided by the Finance Ministry. There could be as many as 12 such boxes and they were all carried home in the evening, then back to the office in the morning. Cabinet meetings under him were serious, drawn-out affairs that sometimes went beyond lunch and continued into the afternoon. He was meticulous and his style, painstaking. He attended to details carefully and dealt with issues in depth.

He had a frail constitution so he had to take as many as five days' rest upon his return from official travels abroad. Between this and his thoroughness when dealing with his paper work, he had little time to visit the rural areas and meet UMNO divisions and branches. He missed out on opportunities to build popular support this way but there was always a great deal of respect for him among the UMNO rank and file and the people in general.

Two years after he became Prime Minister, Tun Hussein pulled off a political coup that dealt a blow to PAS. In the aftermath of the May 13 riots in 1969, PAS had joined the Barisan Nasional and had co-operated quite closely with UMNO and the other parties in the coalition, including during the 1974 General Election. But it was not long before many UMNO members began to doubt PAS' sincerity and suspect that it was using its position in Government to strengthen the party.

Then PAS President Datuk Asri Muda, who was Minister of Rural Development, started turning FELDA settlers from being UMNO supporters into members of PAS. When he visited FELDA schemes he would arrange popular theatrical plays that outwardly featured religious themes, but which actually promoted PAS and its ideas. In his own remarks to the settlers, he obliquely suggested that UMNO was not as religious as PAS. These people were very easily swayed by arguments apparently based on religion, especially when Arabic words were used.

After the 1974 elections, there was disagreement over who should be the next *Menteri Besar*, or Chief Minister of Kelantan. Since the former *Menteri Besar*, Asri, had now joined the Federal Cabinet, he was ineligible. The Barisan Nasional proposed PAS moderate Datuk Mohamad Nasir to replace him, a choice that did not please PAS. He had long been Asri's deputy as Chief Minister and, with PAS too, relations between the top man and his number two had often been awkward. Some PAS members saw Nasir as too open and too close to UMNO. A friendly person, he related easily with UMNO leaders and PAS did not trust him because of that. He was also a very upright man who frowned upon any deliberate misinterpretations of Islamic teachings to favour PAS.

Nasir's investigations into the former state administration under Asri led to civil unrest in Kelantan and prompted PAS to call for his resignation as *Menteri Besar*. Nasir's investigations were driven not by any political agenda, but by his character. He was thinking not about PAS and its partisan interests, but about what was right. He could not tolerate corruption. I myself attempted to work out a compromise and tried to get them to set aside their personal differences to give priority to the interests of the party, theirs as well as the Barisan Nasional. Both sides should have known that in cases of serious impropriety, legal action would have to be taken. As the situation deteriorated, Tun Hussein eventually declared a state of emergency and imposed federal rule on Kelantan.

On 8 November 1977 the Bill to place Kelantan under federal rule was tabled in Parliament. PAS opposed this Kelantan Emergency Act and instructed its members to vote against it. As in most parliamentary systems, the Barisan Nasional used the party whip system to maintain discipline, especially on major issues. PAS's defiance of the whip, therefore, amounted to repudiating the Barisan Nasional coalition. This indiscipline merited serious action and PAS was expelled from the coalition.

After three months of federal rule under a civil servant, Tan Sri Hashim Aman, state elections were called in Kelantan in February 1978. PAS contested all 36 state seats but won only two. Barisan Nasional won 23 seats and Berjasa, the party Nasir founded after quitting PAS, took 11 seats.

The split in PAS gave UMNO the opportunity to regain a state that PAS had controlled since 1959. Its defeat was so severe that it was thought that PAS was finished as a political party. For Tun Hussein as Prime Minister and President of the Barisan Nasional, this was a major achievement — he had returned a state to UMNO rule and rid the ruling coalition of incompatible elements.

Tun Hussein and I had our disagreements, but one which escalated into some harshness and raised voices took place just days after he appointed me as his deputy. It was over the corruption case against the UMNO Youth chief, Datuk Harun Idris. I had always regarded Harun as a Malay nationalist, and for this reason I respected him. I thought the case against him was not justified and should have been withdrawn.

The underlying issue had to do with the financing of a world heavyweight boxing match between Muhammad Ali and Joe Bugner. Harun was keen to bring this event to Kuala Lumpur but Tun Razak had advised him not to proceed. People whose opinions Tun Razak valued were complaining that the fight was not properly managed. But Harun went ahead anyway, and afterwards it was claimed the money collected was not fully accounted for. Harun denied that anything improper had happened.

There may have been more at stake here than simply a dispute over the financial accounts of a sporting event. Harun was directly involved with the organisation that staged the event and he sought to raise his own profile by his personal association with it. Harun, I thought, was showing his hand and signalling, much too early, his ambitions to become Prime

Minister. That prospect would not have pleased Tun Razak. Had Harun contested against Tun Hussein, Harun would likely have won because he was a grassroots man and very popular. I too supported him because it was he who went all out to bring me back into UMNO.

A way out was offered to Harun: that he would be made Malaysia's Ambassador to the United Nations, which would have removed him from the local political scene for a while. But he refused, so the prosecution's case against him went ahead. He gambled and lost, and ended up paying a high price for refusing to be sidetracked from politics and his obvious ambition to become Prime Minister.

I had in fact expected Tun Razak to choose Harun as Deputy Prime Minister, but he had chosen Tun Hussein instead. When Tun Hussein had been the Minister of Education, Harun had led an UMNO Youth delegation to see him. It is said that Harun's manner during the meeting was appallingly rude. He emphasised his arguments by pointing his index finger at Tun Hussein, a gesture that, for Malays, is completely unacceptable. Tun Hussein never forgave him for that episode.

By the time Tun Hussein had taken over as Prime Minister, Harun had been indicted but not yet jailed. I thought Tun Hussein would act strategically and garner political goodwill by not proceeding with the legal action against Harun. Thinking that he would at least be open to the idea, I met with him and suggested dropping the case. Strictly speaking, it should have been the Attorney-General's decision, but the truth was the entire case was political. And in those days, the Prime Minister had a say in everything.

I was totally unprepared for his reaction. He flew into a rage and shouted, "This man is a criminal. I intend to jail him whether people like it or not". He then went to a huge safe in his office, took out a thick stack of files and threw them on the table in front of me. "You can look at these files if you want. It's all in there. He is a criminal and he deserves to be jailed." The intensity of his anger was terrible to behold.

I was dumbstruck. I had imagined that, as Deputy Prime Minister, my opinions would now be listened to and considered, whatever the case. But apparently Tun Hussein thought differently. Once he began shouting I could say nothing, so I simply nodded.

What most affected our relationship, however, was his cautious decision-making style. Though being the Deputy Prime Minister meant having a lot of clout, in the end you could only do the things you wanted if the Prime Minister agreed with you. In my case, I was discouraged because I often did not get that support. One of my biggest frustrations involved our staking a claim to an island in the South China Sea. Unlike other islands, which are little more than underwater reefs, Amboyna Cay has trees and enough land for a runway. It is also geographically situated closer to Malaysia than to Vietnam. Several other countries, including China and the Philippines, wanted to claim this member of the Spratly Group of islands.

At first, Tun Hussein agreed with my plans to claim Amboyna Cay for Malaysia, but the following week he changed his mind, believing that our claim might provoke a confrontation with the other countries. I believe one or two other Cabinet members agreed with me but they did not say so openly. To this day, I am certain that Amboyna Cay could have been ours if Tun Hussein had not revised his decision.

The issue may seem a small one but it was most important, especially in the light of subsequent debates about the finite and diminishing nature of the world's available natural resources. We don't know what resources may lie beneath Amboyna Cay and its vicinity, especially now that we have developed the technology to drill deeper into the seabed. Some people have since claimed there is oil there. In any case, the island is closer to Malaysia than to any other country. It is only 130km from Sabah and Sarawak. By claiming it as part of our territory, we also lay a claim to a large part of the sea around it.

By right all those adjacent islands and the many atolls should belong to us because they lie within our continental shelf. We put up marker monuments on all these islands to denote that they are part of Malaysia. In the end, Amboyna Cay was occupied by Vietnam. They put their troops there and we chose not to contest their claim. The problem with these claims is that you have to maintain a continuing physical presence to enforce the claim and make it credible.

After we lost Amboyna Cay, we identified Layang-Layang, also known as Swallow Reef, and it was agreed that we put men there. One week the Cabinet agreed, and the next week Tun Hussein again decided that we should not make this claim, for fear of war with Vietnam. That same year, when I became Prime Minister, the first thing I did was to put people on Layang-Layang and to begin developing it as a small base and a tourist resort.

Another point of contention between me and Tun Hussein was the construction of the North-South Expressway, which I proposed to the Cabinet. At that time it would have only cost us RM6 billion to construct the 800km expressway, which was relatively cheap. For that amount of money we would have been able to build a four-lane dual-carriage expressway from Johor Baru to Bukit Kayu Hitam on the Thai border. That made good sense to me, even though there were not so many cars on the road at that time.

I had seen what highways had done for Japan and the US. I also remembered how in Standard Two, my teacher told the class that when the railway line was constructed between Penang and Padang Besar, new townships and villages had sprung up all along the line. It seemed clear to me that a North-South Expressway would encourage the same kind of development. The same pattern had been seen in the Malay Archipelago in the past. When a port was built where the products of the hinterland could be gathered, ships would come from all parts of Asia to buy those products, to sell and exchange other goods, and so create an entrepot port. That was how Malacca became great, as did Sri Vijaya[1] and Majapahit[2] before it.

But Tun Hussein scrapped the highway idea. I managed to revive it only when I became Prime Minister, and today all along the North-South Expressway you can see development on a huge scale, unfolding on both sides. There are factories, housing estates and business parks. The highway has contributed much to the growth of Malaysia's economy. By the time we were able to start building it, however, the cost of construction had

---

[1]  Historians believe that Sri Vijaya was a great maritime kingdom that was situated in southeast Sumatra and lasted between the seventh and thirteenth centuries.

[2]  Majapahit had its capital in East Java and was the last of the Malay Archipelago's great Hindu empires.

gone up considerably. We decided to privatise it but we had to subsidise the project to bring down the capital cost. Otherwise, toll rates would have been prohibitive.

On another occasion, I suggested setting up a Federal Territories Ministry. Kuala Lumpur was our only Federal Territory at the time and I believed the city needed attention. I already had the habit of driving around the city to look at things like landscaping, lighting and the condition of the road dividers. I hoped very much I would be chosen as Federal Territories Minister so that I could implement my ideas for KL. Tun Hussein did create the Ministry, but appointed himself Minister. Sadly, he did not have enough time to focus on this portfolio and I think if I had been in charge, changes would have taken place much earlier. Still, it is very pleasing to see that KL is a very different city today. Road dividers now have flowers and plants and there are well-kept gardens under the monorail, which I had insisted upon.

By and large, most of the other Ministers minded their own business and busied themselves with their own ministries. But from the time I had been Education Minister, I had always looked at the Cabinet's responsibilities in totality. Too many suggestions, it now seemed, were coming from me. It was not that I was impatient, but I did have a strong sense that things were moving too slowly. I wanted quicker development to push the country forward. At this time Tun Hussein seemed overburdened with work and I once offered to take on anything he did not have time to handle. He looked at me and asked, "Don't you have enough work to do?" Again, it was not a response I had expected. I have never felt my work to be a burden. Yet, in contrast to Tun Hussein's characteristic deliberation and caution, I had so may ideas about what could be done to speed the development of Malaysia. But I was not able to act on them.

At the back of my mind, I always had to consider what Tun Hussein would say and how he would react to my ideas. I could not do things that I believed he would not like. When one is not in charge, one must learn to curb bright ideas and ambition. It is the politic thing to do.

Despite the lack of encouragement, I was able to introduce a number of initiatives as Deputy Prime Minister. There was the Malaysian

Administrative Modernisation and Management Planning Unit, or MAMPU, which looked at ways to improve the Government's efficiency and productivity. MAMPU was created as a unit under the Prime Minister's Department, but I was able to guide it and make good use of it.

I had visited commercial offices and had noted that their layouts were changing, as senior officers no longer sat in rooms away from the rest of the staff. The staff had cubicles where the partitions were low enough for everyone to be able to see one another. In effect, because no one could hide, they had to be seen to be working. It seemed a much better way to organise an office and I thought there would be merit in bringing that style to government offices. When I became Prime Minister, one of the changes I made was to have a glass panel fitted into the door to my office. It served a dual purpose — anyone wanting to see me could see if I were free, working, or seeing someone. At the same time, the staff knew I could see them and they kept to schedule, with much fewer attempts to sneak off early.

I was also able to restructure salaries and the grade system for Government staff. Prior to this, salary adjustments had been made haphazardly, and allowances that were given distorted the pay structure. Ministers were liable to suggest pay rises under pressure by their staff because they wanted to appear generous, but these changes created great dissatisfaction and unhappiness among other civil servants of the same grade, whose salaries had not been adjusted. It also caused disgruntlement among those with higher salaries to start with, as they found that their juniors were earning almost the same salaries as they were.

What was needed to disentangle the mess was a comprehensive salary revision scheme that would apply to all government servants. It took me several months to devise one. First I had to establish a rationale for pay, and I eventually decided that a person's salary must be sufficient to cover food, clothing and shelter for someone of his status in the Government. The higher up you go, the more you would spend on these three items, the higher the salary would be. Lower income groups also had to earn enough to pay for these essential needs. The other established principle was one of seniority: an employee is regarded as more senior based on qualifications, years of experience and level of responsibility, and this had to be reflected in his salary.

I also felt that employees of the same grade had to be paid the same salary, no matter which Ministry they were in. If Officer A is on par with Officer B in the salary scheme, when you push Officer A up, then you must do the same for B. Otherwise there would be endless complaints. But even if you do this, Officer C, who is below A and B, would wonder why he is now earning so much less than the other two. Because of all these inherent difficulties, and taking into account human feelings, changes in salaries must be total and the relative positions of the employees in the government hierarchy must be maintained.

However, even this system was not without its flaws. It remained difficult to adequately compensate services that had grown in importance. The technical services, for example, complained bitterly that their greater contribution in the age of technology had been ignored. But there was little that I could do. Even the Civil Service Unions were not willing to recommend better pay for the technicians and technical assistants. While drawing up the new comprehensive salary scheme I decided to do away with cost of living allowances, incorporating them into the salaries instead. This was a cost to the Government as it would be taken into consideration when calculating pensions. Once we had decided on the scheme, it could not be altered. Allowances to individuals could not be given out unless they could be truly justified. For example, we gave certain allowances to pilots because of the inherent risk of flying. We also gave special allowances to certain professional officers including doctors, because otherwise they would leave the service.

Today, salaries for civil servants are once again being adjusted on an ad hoc basis. The Government also gives cost of living allowances to those who live at least 25km away from KL. That has caused many to want to live out of the city so that they can claim the allowance. But there is really no rationale for this. Living in rural areas may mean spending on transportation but in urban areas, the cost of living is usually higher. If allowances are to be given, then everyone should be entitled. And unless a thorough cost of living study is undertaken, there in no justification for differentials in pay.

Another item I looked at was the pension scheme for retired civil servants. Calculating a retired Government servant's pension was taking a very long time, up to three years in some cases — pensioners were actually dying before they even received their first payment. The delay was due to the lack of information on the pensioner's service. He may, for example, have owed the Government some money, and the Pensions Department would want to deduct this from the monthly payment. The concern and conscientiousness was certainly to be admired, but the fact remained that the delays were hurting old and often sickly people.

To allow payments to be made on time, I asked the Pensions Department to get the employees to provide relevant information about themselves a year before they retired. Six months after that, they would have to provide additional information. This ensured that by the time they were pensioned off, the necessary data had already been processed and payment could be made immediately. In any case, I requested that full pensions be paid the first month after retirement. If there was money owing, it could be recovered by deducting future payments. The Government, I reasoned, would not be bankrupted because of the small sums involved in overpayment.

While I was working on this I thought of my father, who had drawn a pension of RM90 until he died in 1962, having been a pensioner for 30 years. People were now living longer and with the increasing cost of living, the amount they received as pension would not be sufficient for long. So I decided that pensions should be revised with each salary revision. I am proud of our pension scheme and believe it to be the best in the world. We have compared it to other schemes in developing and developed countries, and most of them do not bother with revisions. In many cases they also only last for 12 years after a person has retired, while our system makes sure there is a derivative pension that goes to the wife and the children until they reach a certain age. We want to take care of those who have served well and given their best years to the Government.

But we always remember that unlike most pension schemes in other countries, ours requires no contribution from the employee. It is the Government that must set aside the money. Some people take it for granted that there will always be money, but that is not so because the cost of living is always going up and life expectancy is increasing. That is why younger civil servants today can opt out of the pension scheme and go for the Employee's Provident Fund, the contributory retirement scheme created for the private sector.

Even as I worked to push my ideas forward, I faced political threats that were rooted in events within UMNO in which I was directly involved. Unhappy with Tun Razak's decision to engineer Tun Hussein's return to the party, several UMNO leaders had accused Tun Razak of being influenced by alleged communists such as Tan Sri Abdullah Ahmad and Tan Sri A. Samad Ismail. It was believed by some that these people were leftists who influenced Tun Razak not to follow the Tunku's pro-British and pro-Commonwealth policies.

The moment Tun Hussein took over as Prime Minister, the then Home Minister Tun Ghazali Shafie decided to arrest Samad, Abdullah Majid and Abdullah Ahmad, accusing them of being communists out to influence the leaders of UMNO. Tun Ghazali was a very powerful Home Affairs Minister and he cut a fearsome figure. People have asked me why I thought he may have done this. Some believe that it was to get back at Tun Hussein and myself as successful "upstarts" who had leapfrogged over others, including many loyal and long-serving veterans in the UMNO hierarchy. Perhaps Tun Ghazali held those he had arrested responsible for the eclipse of other powerful party hopefuls — himself included.

These former leftists were said to have influenced Tun Razak. I tried to argue against this idea, but Tun Hussein was more willing to listen to Tun Ghazali. Tun Hussein talked about how many communists had tortured and killed people, but neither Abdullah nor Samad had ever engaged in such activities. Despite my efforts, all Tun Hussein promised to do was to review the situation after six months.

Those who were arrested had been close to Tun Razak, who had liked to surround himself with younger people, myself included, and discuss issues with them. Tun Ghazali had not been one of those people. I myself would have been arrested had I not been Deputy Prime Minister. The effect of these arrests was chilling, and they cast suspicion on Tun Hussein and me for harbouring communists.

After six months, I spoke to Tun Hussein to try and secure the men's release but once again he refused, saying that Abdullah Ahmad would likely be attacked by soldiers for being a communist. I did not believe our soldiers would behave that way, but in the end, these men remained under detention. When I became Prime Minister, I ordered their release. I do not think this made Tun Hussein happy at all. Certainly he became even unhappier when Harun was pardoned.

Tun Ghazali did not stop at trying to associate me with alleged communists. Just days before I became Prime Minister, Tun Hussein came to my office — incidentally, for the first time — to tell me that my political secretary, Siddiq Ghouse, was going to be arrested for being a spy for the Soviet Union's KGB. Tun Ghazali, he said, would show me the evidence. Officers from the Special Branch soon arrived and showed me pictures of Siddiq allegedly meeting with a representative of the Singapore High Commission. I do not remember seeing any pictures of KGB agents.

I could have objected to the allegations. I had never suspected Siddiq of anything; indeed he seemed like a very ordinary person. But neither did I know for sure that he was not involved in spying. Siddiq was detained for almost two years. Having an alleged KGB spy work in my office could have been held against me. However, these incidents did not undermine my political career as they could have, had I, or rather my political views and commitments, not been better known. Within the party, I was still seen as a nationalist who struggled on behalf of the Malays and that lent me a certain amount of protection. Ironically, in the past, this reputation worked against me among the non-Malays, who had always regarded me with suspicion. Now, it was my armour against baseless accusations among Malays.

Still, I was not about to let non-Malay uneasiness fester and as Deputy Prime Minister, I think I was able to gradually gain their confidence. With the profile that I had, I could finally show them that while I was pro-Malay, it did not mean I was against the other ethnic communities. It was just that I firmly believed elevating the Malays' economic wealth would be good for them as a community, and the country as a whole. Spreading the wealth could only lead to a healthier economic future.

I began receiving invitations to talk to members of the Chinese Chambers of Commerce, and groups of Chinese educationists. My Chinese colleagues in the Cabinet also took the trouble to reassure their constituents that I was not anti-Chinese. It became clear to most of my detractors that I was doing nothing to take away the wealth of the Chinese. In fact, the increased foreign investments I was bringing into the country as Minister of International Trade and Industry boosted the activities of Chinese businessmen.

Meanwhile, I also looked to strengthening my position in UMNO. When Tun Razak died, Tun Hussein became acting President of the party. But as he still held the substantive post of Deputy President, I could only remain Vice-President until party elections were next held. Tradition qualified me as a candidate and I was fortunately unchallenged when I submitted my name for the Deputy President's post in September 1978.

Almost nine years had passed since I had been expelled from the party. While I had harboured hopes of returning to UMNO during my years of political exile, I had never imagined that I would rise to the second highest position within the party less than a decade after my expulsion. When I stepped back to look at myself then, I was amazed at how quickly I was moving up, overtaking several senior politicians along the way. I put it down to hard work and good luck. I did not know then that more changes were in store for me, and that they would take place just a few short years later.

# Chapter 25:
# Reaching The Top

Tun Hussein was generally not a very healthy man; he was also a very heavy smoker. I remember a meeting we had at Dewan Tunku Abdul Rahman in Jalan Ampang in Kuala Lumpur, where many people were smoking. As the hall was air-conditioned all the smoke was trapped inside. It reached the point where I could hardly breathe and had to peer through the haze of smoke to see someone's face. I turned to Tun Hussein to ask him to tell everyone to stop smoking — only to see him lighting a cigarette.

In January of 1981, Tun Hussein informed the Supreme Council that he was going to London to undergo a coronary bypass operation. I was away attending the third Organisation of Islamic Conference meeting in Taif, Saudi Arabia at the time, so I did not see him off before he left.

He remained in London for two months after the bypass, and during that time I took his place as Acting Prime Minister. Tun Hussein did not recover fully from the operation and when he came back to Malaysia, he was still very ill. I gave instructions to everyone, including Ministers, to let him go straight to his car after getting off the plane. I did not want people to shake his hand or otherwise bother him, as this could prove to be a strain or expose him to infection.

It was while I was Acting Prime Minister that I launched the Heavy Industries Corporation of Malaysia Berhad (HICOM)[1] as the Government vehicle that would oversee and implement our industrialisation efforts. I also started introducing ideas about Islamisation and the need for Malays to get serious about the future of the country. I was still mindful of what Tun Hussein would say, but that period turned out to be good training for me because things were about to change.

Shortly after he returned to work, Tun Hussein held a meeting at his residence in Seri Taman. At the end, he pulled me aside and told me that he was not able to carry on. All the others had already left and there were only the two of us standing at the door. His face showed his depression. He

---

[1]    Incorporated in 1980, HICOM merged in 1996 with Diversified Resources Berhad (DRB) to form DRB-HICOM, the biggest industrial conglomerate in Malaysia.

said he was not well, that anything could happen, and so he wanted me to take over as Prime Minister. It was a startling but very short conversation which could not have lasted more than a few minutes.

I knew he was ill, but I thought he would continue as Prime Minister at least for a while longer. I repeated my earlier offer to take on some of his work so that he could have time to recover and carry on. But he refused, saying that he had already decided he should step down. I did not tell anyone about our conversation, not even Hasmah. My greatest fear has always been that revealing confidential news may jinx the potential result. Tun Hussein, for example, could have easily changed his mind. But it became clear that he was firm in his decision when he announced his stepping down at his UMNO division meeting in Johor Baru in May 1981. There, he also said that I would be taking over as Prime Minister. The news came as a shock to the people gathered there that day. He repeated his decision at the UMNO General Assembly on 26 June 1981, and when he stepped down as Prime Minister on 16 July, I was sworn in the following day.

I do not think the public realised how he had never fully recovered from the bypass. Back then they had little information about heart operations since none were done in the country. But they knew that it involved having your chest opened up and being placed on a heart-lung machine. It was frightening, to say the least.

When Tun Hussein took over from Tun Razak many people, especially journalists, had asked me whether things would be different. My reply had been that there would only be a difference in style, not objectives. This held true when I became Prime Minister as well. I believe that Tun Hussein did not agree with many of my policies, particularly my belligerence towards the British. This was not his style at all. He was not confrontational and disliked being blunt.

I can understand why he was not happy with me. But if as Prime Minister I had asked for his advice, my fear was that he would say something that I would not be able to follow and this would have been a sign of great disrespect. I did, however, go to see Tun Hussein at the former PETRONAS office at Dayabumi because I felt I needed to explain to him why I did what I did about several issues. He was adviser to PETRONAS at that time. He did not say much during our meeting and I left with the feeling that he did not fully approve of some of the things I was doing. For my part I sincerely believed that what I was doing was for the good of the country. And so I went ahead with the changes I had planned for Malaysia's accelerated industrialisation, and a foreign policy which was less pro-West and pro-Commonwealth.

Malaysia was beginning to experience a swift and sharp change from an agricultural to an industrial economy. I had been to Japan, Korea and European countries and seen the industries that they had there. The workings and the running of modern industry were no mystery to me and I knew that if we truly wanted to, Malaysia too could industrialise. All that was needed was the willingness to learn and work hard. There would be mistakes and failures — that was a given. But corrections could be made and eventually the cost of these mistakes would be recovered from the growth and development that industrialisation would bring.

Malaysia had long had import-substitute industries but these had not brought about meaningful industrialisation. With that, I decided it was time to develop our own heavy industries, a necessary step towards becoming a developed country. There would also be numerous spin-off effects, which would make supporting industries viable. Heavy industries would have to be serviced and supplied with raw materials, component parts, engineering and technological support, and the manpower to operate heavy equipment and machinery. These were all services we could learn to provide given proper training, which in turn meant more employment opportunities. In agriculture, the number of people you can employ is limited, but that is not the case in industry. For one, it makes for much more economic use of land. One acre of agricultural land can feed one family, but that same acre, given over to industry, can provide 500 jobs and generate wealth many times over.

We also needed technological know-how to build our industries. For this, I looked back to how I had become a doctor. As a young boy I had thought of it as a fantastic, unattainable profession, something I would never be capable of. But I did become a doctor, by working hard and taking all the necessary steps. Applying this to the technology we needed, it became clear that it was a question of identifying clearly what you wanted to do, and then being willing to work hard to attain it. I am a firm believer in success being the end result of these actions. There is a link between means and ends, between effort and outcome, between knowledge and success.

I chose to focus on heavy industries because I believed developed countries had become less efficient in this area and their costs — particularly labour costs — were too high. We would also be dealing with readily available raw materials. I identified the heavy industries that we should pursue: a steel mill to be built in Terengganu, a tin plate mill, a car factory and a cement plant in Langkawi. I thought of establishing the tin plate plant because of my experience managing the Malaysian Canning Company. Malaysia was using a lot of tin plate for its growing food industries. The steel mill that was proposed would consist of a direct reduction plant and an electric arc smelter to produce billets and blooms to be used for producing construction steel. That was to be the first stage. Section mills and other downstream products would be added later.

I did not think we would face too many problems establishing these industries if we gave them enough careful thought. As part of the purchase agreement the suppliers of the plants would train our people to operate them. But I overestimated the Malaysian capacity to learn how to operate a major industry. Apart from managing and operating plants, a lot of experience is needed in order to deal with any bugs and problems with the machinery.

At the time it was built, the cement factory was the best in the country. It was located by the sea on the island of Langkawi, off the northwestern coast of the Peninsula, close to the limestone hills which were to be quarried for the plant. The other raw materials and products could be transported economically by ship. Unfortunately, the factory was sold off during the financial crisis in the late 1990s as the market was poor and it had stopped making money. It was not a matter of mismanagement, but if you don't have deep pockets to weather the bad periods, you will always lose. Now it is owned by the French company Lafarge and is doing very well. People later asked why we built a dusty cement factory on a tourist island. The truth was Langkawi was not yet a tourist destination when we made the decision. When it became one, great care was taken to minimise the dust. The people of Langkawi also enjoyed employment in the cement factory at a time when there were almost no hotels to provide jobs.

When the demand for cement was low during the recession, I asked the Public Works Department to use cement for building roads. Fourteen kilometres of road leading to the Datai Hotel in Langkawi were built with cement. Many rural roads were also built with cement during that time, even though it was more costly than tar roads and more difficult to repair.

The tin plate plant was also eventually sold off. It was a joint-venture with the Japanese, who had a minority share but still participated in the management of the plant. I do not know who was responsible but someone arranged the sale, which more or less amounted to a transfer of Government shares to the private sector. Contrary to general belief, I did not always know everything that went on in Government. But I accepted blame if things went wrong as that is the proper way when you hold a high position. Because of the sale, the Japanese partner was no longer able to help manage the plant, even though they were still holding on to their shares.

We discovered that one of the shareholders was using the company for his other deals, which led to huge losses. This was when the Government decided to step in and buy the company back. We made sure the Japanese partner would have a bigger say in the management, and with their expertise, we managed to turn the company around. Today it is doing very well and even has a branch in Vietnam.

The industry venture that gave me the most trouble was the steel mill, run by a company called Perwaja. We first tried working with the Japanese to use a system of direct reduction, that is, burning off the oxygen to produce pellets from ore and scrap which were free from rust. The pellets would be mixed with more scrap and melted in electric arc furnaces to make billets and blooms. These in turn could be made into construction steel. Careful management rather than high technology was needed here. The Japanese Direct Reduction Plant failed, but they compensated us fully while leaving the plant they had built intact.

I knew something about steel making but not enough to be able to rebuild a failed plant. I had to consider other systems of direct reduction which were in use at that time. Finally I agreed to a Mexican system by Hylsa which modified the plant. To cut a long story short, Hylsa put things right and the plant was able to function. But if costs were to remain low, skill in management and operations was needed. Unfortunately, the manager appointed by HICOM lacked this skill — and much more.

I was flabbergasted to discover that he tried to run the mill from Kuala Lumpur and, needless to say, we lost a good deal of money. I decided to get a new Managing Director, a man called Tan Sri Eric Chia whom I had first met in the late 1960s. He had been introduced to me by a fellow Member of Parliament and friend of mine, Lim Pee Hung, whose father had owned the first motorcar dealership in Alor Star. Chia was a Straits-born Chinese who spoke Malay well. He was also a successful businessman and I had earlier appointed him to be a member of the Board of FIMA. At a time when few Chinese were more than small shopkeepers, Chia was running UMW, an engineering company, and was producing component parts for the heavy machinery he was importing.

331

He was a pioneer of local manufacturing and I was impressed with his ability to produce heavy parts for road rollers and track vehicles. I saw in him someone who was innovative and willing to try something new.

When Chia took over Perwaja, the plant was in bad shape and was dirty and untidy. He turned it into a spotless workplace, much like the factories I had seen in Japan. Any breakdown of the electric furnace or other machinery was handled quickly, enabling the plant to keep running. He also set up storage facilities and a sales centre in Kuala Lumpur.

Perwaja's previous management had used lorries to dump scrap iron on wasteland next to the factory. The scrap often included sharp pieces which, even after being buried in the soft earth, would cut the lorries' tyres to shreds when they drove in to dump more scrap iron. Replacing the tyres cost the company a lot of money. Chia decided to cover the dumpsite with cement and from then on, made sure the scrap was piled neatly away. It was amazing how much money this saved.

Chia also infused a new spirit among the workers, arranging for them to undergo physical training and motivation courses. He supplied them with uniforms, improved their pay scale and ranked them according to their performance. He also provided small, thoughtful touches like supplying the workers, who were mostly Malays, with dates to help them break their fast during the month of Ramadan. They became more motivated and dedicated at their jobs, and seemed to genuinely enjoy working under him.

As the head of Perwaja, Chia became a part of the business delegations I led to several countries, including Chile on my first trip to South America in 1991, where he negotiated successfully to buy iron ore. Chia then decided to expand and buy a section mill, i.e. a plant that would produce I-beams and H-beams that were used for the construction of steel frames. He told me that the plant was produced by Danieli of Italy for Iraq, but there was a ban on such exports to that country. I agreed to the purchase after he convinced me that we would be able to get it cheaply. The plant was built in Gurun in Kedah. The truth was that locating the plant there was not a good idea logistically because it meant moving steel ingots and blooms all the way from Terengganu. The finished products would also then have to be transported from Gurun to other parts of Malaysia for use or for export. But I must admit that his decision to locate the plant in my home state swayed me, because I wanted to see more development take place there.

He also showed me steel fabrication machinery that would bend construction rods for pillars and other ferro-concrete structures. Before that the rods were being bent manually and the vertical and horizontal parts were tied with wires by hand. Using the new machines, the steel rods could be shaped accurately and welded to vertical rods at intervals. They could also be fabricated elsewhere according to specifications and then delivered to the worksite.

Chia was also responsible for introducing a number of small steel industries. For example, he brought in machines that could be set up in a house in the *kampung*, and the villagers literally just had to turn the machines on to produce nails. I thought this was something that could help villagers go into small-scale industries.

Overall I thought he was doing a good job at Perwaja, but I do know that he often rubbed people the wrong way. Chia always talked good sense, but he could be abrasive and this sometimes got him into trouble. During one of his trips through the US, the Immigration officers did not like the way he answered their questions and detained him. He was handcuffed, shackled and thrown into a police van along with common criminals. He asked to be given time to get his insulin jab for his diabetes but they ignored him. He was only released after prolonged questioning.

I was shocked when people started accusing Chia of embezzling funds from Perwaja.[2] Although he was a friend I did not defend him, because if the allegations were true then I felt that he had let me down. As it was, when the UMNO leadership asked me not to campaign for the Barisan Nasional in Terengganu during the 2004 General Election, they told me it was because the people in the state associated me with Chia.

When he was alleged to have numbered bank accounts in Switzerland where he kept the money, I spoke to the Swiss President when I was there on an official visit to help Malaysian authorities gain access to information about Chia's dealings with the Swiss banks. There was a long, drawn-out legal battle and in the end, the court found that prosecutors had not been able to prove Chia had taken any money from the company. After the court decision, I'm afraid I made no effort to meet him, which is something I regret now that he has passed away. After the court case was finally over he practically disappeared from the scene. I think he was brokenhearted over the whole case. It had dragged down his reputation and career as an up-and-coming industrialist.

333

In between developing these industries, I also had to make sure that Malays were participating at all levels. As far as possible, I wanted these industries to be run by Malay executives so that they could gain experience. They were usually drawn from our government officers, as the Government was usually the biggest, if not the only, shareholder of these ventures. Some government officers learnt quickly and were able to adjust to the ways of the private sector, but many retained their bureaucratic ways and were

---

[2]  Chia was brought to court on 10 February 2004 and charged with misappropriating RM76.4 million from Perwaja Rolling Mill and Development Sdn Bhd.

unable to make quick decisions when needed. PETRONAS, for instance, went through a very difficult period before the officers seconded from government departments acquired management skills.

Making these industries successful was a matter of finding the right people with the right management skills, or at a more fundamental level, with the right attitude to learning. Managing a manufacturing industry is very difficult and there was no substantial industry in Malaysia at that time that we could take our lessons from. We went for foreign investments because we did not have locals who were willing to take the leap. Locals wanted to stay within their comfort zones. When there is no competition in the mix, it is easy to get away with low quality, bad management, dirty processes and inefficiency. But in a competitive environment, you must always be on guard. You have to look for ways to improve your product and be more cost-efficient. If you do not, you can be very sure that your competitors will be doing exactly that. Tax protection may provide some comfort but it should not make things too easy and discourage effort. It should certainly not cultivate bad attitudes and habits.

Overall, towards the end of my premiership, I was satisfied with the state of heavy industries in Malaysia. Things could have been better but we at least had engineering skills we did not have before. That was one of the main aims of the automotive industry: to develop an expanding array of industrial skills and a national repertoire of technical competencies, not simply to produce components and machine parts and to fabricate items using steel and aluminium. Today the engineering industries have spawned a number of new products such as cranes, turbines, electric motors, workboats and ships and so on, which can help increase Malaysian exports.

With proper training, Malaysians have acquired manipulatory skills very quickly and very well. Their Asian hands and fingers are small and this seems to help them do delicate work and assemble small parts easily. Before automation was used in the assembly of microcircuits, Malaysian workers did this with great efficiency. Even the boys and girls from the villages who would have worked in rice fields could acquire great skills in manufacturing. It is a matter of discipline. The Japanese remarked that Malaysian workers were second only to them, which was high praise indeed. We did not even know that we had these skills until we threw our people into the deep end. We had to teach them the hard way, by just doing it.

Yet one problem bothered me a great deal. While we may possess skill, our work ethic left much to be desired. I always noticed a big difference between the people we sent to Japan under the Look East policy[3] and those who studied elsewhere. Those who went to Japan were very dedicated and hardworking. Japanese manufacturers in Malaysia snapped them up when they returned home because of their good work habits and mastery of Japanese. It was the same with those trained in South Korea.

I believe that the key to the Japanese work ethic can be seen in their traditional tea ceremony. At the deep cultural level, it seems part of the training process because the ceremony follows a very precise method of handling the beautiful bamboo implements used. When you have a culture that is so refined, right down to the finest details, everything grounded in that culture is likely to be equally neat and precise. When the Japanese erect a pillar in a building, they wrap it immediately with protective material so that it does not get damaged by workers carrying heavy items. The culture of thoughtful precision may slow things down at first, but speed is achieved very quickly because good procedures and practices are established from the start. When the Japanese decided that they must produce high-quality products, they were able to do so and still maintain their low cost. The amount produced over a given time did not diminish and eventually the profit margins grew bigger.

335

Malaysians are producing a much better quality of work than before. If we were prepared to improve our work culture just a little, we would do very well indeed. The Koreans once lagged behind the Japanese but they were prepared to work hard. Today Samsung produces goods which, in terms of quality and innovation, can compete successfully with Sony of Japan while maintaining relatively low prices. When you cultivate the right work culture, its values and attitudes spread outwards beyond the workplace and are eventually integrated into daily life. Some worried that this would erase our overall cultural orientation and religious identity, but it has not.

---

[3]  The Look East Policy emphasised looking to Japan and South Korea as models of national development rather than to the West. See Chapter 28: Looking East.

# Chapter 26:
## From Ideas To Action

Most newly-elected leaders spend their first day in office coming to terms with the vast dimensions of their position and responsibilities. I spent my first day as Prime Minister in the Deputy Prime Minister's office, figuring out how to put together a Cabinet. I did not plan on making major changes, but I knew I needed to shuffle a few Ministers around.

After my swearing-in ceremony, I had taken the car back with Tun Hussein to the office so that he could say goodbye to the people he had worked with for five years. There were many sad faces among the staff who lined up to bid him farewell. After he left, they crowded around to congratulate me. I had decided to retain his general staff, keeping only my personal secretary and political secretaries for myself. I usually did not change personnel as it took time to get to know new people, and I disliked the period of adjustment.

Tun Hussein's departure from the building symbolised the beginning of my new office. I was the Prime Minister now, and I was alone. I made my way to the Deputy Prime Minister's office, where I had a discussion with then Chief Secretary to the Government, Tan Sri Hashim Aman, on how to go about appointing Ministers. Although the Ministers from Tun Hussein's Cabinet had already been sworn in during his time, I thought it proper that continuing Ministers should take the oath once again together with those newly appointed to the Cabinet. I doubt whether oath-taking really means much but it is a part of procedure and cannot be ignored.

Even as I mulled over the choice of Ministers for my Cabinet, I was anxious to get on with my work. Having the authority of the Prime Minister was important because it meant you could achieve things you otherwise could not. I was, for example, itching to do something about the neglected appearance of Kuala Lumpur, so when Tun Hussein stepped down and relinquished his positions, including as Federal Territories Minister, I was finally able to make some of these changes.

For example, I wanted to get satay[1] to be sold in proper shops like in American franchised restaurants, instead of roadside stalls. When I was still the Deputy Prime Minister the Datuk Bandar[2] (Mayor) had been able to get Tun Hussein not to approve the idea. The reason given was that if satay was sold in restaurants, the hawkers who were selling it on the roadside along Jalan Campbell (now Jalan Dang Wangi) would protest because it would mean a loss of business.

It was an example of the typical Malay mentality — growth and the upgrading of business were alien ideas. If they had been hawkers a thousand years ago, they expected to be hawkers for the next thousand. Satay was hawker food, hence only the lower classes of people would eat it in zinc sheds erected on the roadside. People who go to restaurants, so the thinking went, should eat other food like steak and chicken chop.

I believed the business of the hawkers would not be affected as the restaurant would be patronised by people with slightly more money to spend and who wanted a more congenial ambience. With the country's wealth increasing, there would be more and more people like these who wanted to eat satay but did not necessarily relish the idea of sitting in a zinc shed.

337

Once I had the authority of the Prime Minister I decided to move immediately with what I had planned for Kuala Lumpur. A shoddy capital was not something I was going to tolerate. It would reflect badly on both the quality of the Government and Malaysians alike.

I was aware that there was corruption in City Hall, so I issued an open warning that I would come down hard on anyone involved in shady deals. I knew it was not easy to stop the rot, but following my warning the Datuk Bandar resigned. I was able to appoint a new one and to impress upon him the need for greater efficiency and speed in processing applications for licences or permits. When applications were delayed, applicants would be tempted to offer inducements. Obviously, if there was no delay, there

---

[1]  Marinated skewered meat that is then grilled, satay is a popular Malaysian meal and a signature part of our cuisine.

[2]  Kuala Lumpur got its first Mayor when it was given city status in 1972.

would be less corruption so speeding up bureaucratic procedure was given priority throughout my stewardship.

You do not need to be an architect or landscape artist to have ideas about improving a city. For my part, whenever I travelled to other cities I would make note of how they were well-ordered, cultured and clean. I did not see why Kuala Lumpur could not be the same. There cannot be anyone who would not want to live in beautiful surroundings — surely it is a natural desire. And with these observations and thoughts, I decided to make suggestions on how to keep the city clean.

For one thing, I had noticed something strange about our street lamps, most of which appeared unlit. When I looked closely, I discovered that the lamps had transparent plastic covers. The covers were not fitted tightly enough and insects, attracted by the bright light, were able to get in. Over time the heap of dead insects obscured the light bulb completely. I pointed out the problem to the Datuk Bandar and soon enough the covers were cleaned, and more importantly, kept clean. Small things like these reflect the way people work. The workers attending to the lamps had done nothing on their own initiative and had to be told what to do. I also told the relevant Minister that the lamp posts should be spaced regularly, a small visual cue that we attended to details.

Of course, having the Prime Minister see to these things is like using a sledgehammer to kill a mosquito. But it is important that interest is shown by the most senior man so that those below him will be less inclined to be negligent. I contacted the Datuk Bandar directly on all matters including the collection of rubbish and the water supply. I had recommended Tan Sri Elyas Omar to fill the post of Datuk Bandar, admittedly because I knew him personally. Perhaps this was wrong. The Chief Secretary to the Government normally makes a recommendation and I would have the opportunity to reject the nomination. But I was new and not fully aware of all the procedures and protocol.

In Alor Star, before I became a Member of Parliament, I had worked closely with the UMNO committee overseeing the town council. I checked records and discovered that people who were long dead were still drawing salaries. No one else was looking into these matters. Throughout my term as Prime Minister I insisted on looking into details, in "taking care of the pennies". Contrary to the saying, the pounds may not always look after themselves, but the big picture is less liable to get damaged if you guard the details.

I also had some ideas about the implementation of the NEP. It was a crucial pillar of the Government's policy and had to be executed flawlessly. But it was not just the NEP — it was everything. Now I could no longer lean on anyone, for the ultimate responsibility of running the country was mine alone. The buck stopped at my desk and it was intimidating. Off and on throughout that first day, I had to remind myself that I was the Prime Minister and I kept pondering how I had reached this position. It had all been very sudden and even now, I do not think that many in Malaysian politics have had that same experience.

I was still living in the Deputy Prime Minister's residence as I did not want to move to the residence of the Prime Minister, which was then in Lake Gardens. I planned to convert it into a memorial for Tun Razak, my mentor and the first Prime Minister to live there. I did not want to live in the Tunku's old residence either as there was not enough room for a family, so I decided to move into the house of the CEO of London Tin after the company was acquired by the Government. As Deputy Prime Minister, I had been given a fairly big car, an old British-made Daimler limousine which reminded me of British colonial governors. Though it was very dignified, I did not want to look like a British officer. These were the days before Proton so I decided to use a Japanese Lexus, which I continued using when I became Prime Minister. They also gave me two additional outriders and two Special Action Unit plainclothes officers, or UTKs.[3] Six members of my security detail were also armed.

339

One of my first acts as Prime Minister was to release 23 political detainees, including Tan Sri Abdullah Ahmad and Abdullah Majid, who had been Deputy Ministers under Tun Hussein; the newspaper editor Tan Sri A. Samad Ismail; Kassim Ahmad, then Chairman of Parti Sosialis Rakyat Malaysia, and several MCA Members of Parliament and executive

---

[3]  The Unit Tindakan Khas (UTK) or Special Action Unit is the Royal Malaysian Police's second special forces. This unit carries out SWAT (Special Weapons and Tactics) duties and undercover missions.

committee members. Among the group were also DAP Members of Parliament Chiang Heng Kai and Chan Kok Kit; 11 members of the Pertubuhan Angkatan Sabilillah and six others, including three women. Yet, for some reason, during my entire tenure as Prime Minister I was often accused of detaining political prisoners under the Internal Security Act (ISA). The ISA was more frequently used during the time of the three earlier Prime Ministers against politicians and alleged communists.

I could not have Tun Ghazali, who was still Home Minister, detaining people under vague charges of being communists, so one of the most important things I did with my first Cabinet was to move him to the Ministry of Foreign Affairs. After all, he had been the top civil servant there for about 10 years before joining the Cabinet in 1970. He explained to the public that it was a normal transfer and he was happy to be in the Foreign Affairs portfolio. I put Tun Musa Hitam, the new Deputy Prime Minister, in the Home Ministry, which continued to hold a great deal of power.

Otherwise I retained most of Tun Hussein's Cabinet. I also promoted certain Deputy Ministers, including Tan Sri Sanusi Junid[4] and Tun Abdullah Ahmad Badawi, who were made full Ministers. All this was done on the basis of merit, not because of any personal relation to me. The Press had asked me why certain Ministers were moved and I said "they need a change of atmosphere", which drew considerable laughter.

As I had decided the Prime Minister and Deputy Prime Minister should hold the Defence and Home Affairs portfolios respectively, I moved from the Ministry of International Trade and Industry to take over Defence. Tun Musa relinquished the Education portfolio when he took over Home Affairs. A month earlier, Tun Musa, who was by nature confident and capable, had contested the post of Deputy President in the UMNO elections. He and his rival Tengku Razaleigh had gone for broke so when Tun Musa won, Tengku Razaleigh said he would leave the Cabinet. Both men had given an undertaking that they would continue to serve UMNO

---

[4]  Tan Sri Sanusi Junid was a Supreme Council member who went on to become UMNO Secretary-General and then Vice-President. He was President of the International Islamic University from 2001 until 2008.

but when Tengku Razaleigh decided not to join the new Government, I felt his choice was not in accordance with his pledge to continue to serve the party. I persuaded him to stay in the post he had held in Tun Hussein's Government and retained him as Minister of Finance, a decision that would later cause me much difficulty.

My philosophy in politics is that the winner does not take all, nor does the loser lose all. I did not want Tengku Razaleigh to feel that he had lost everything. Although he had lost in the party election, I knew he had many supporters in UMNO and I did not want to alienate them. I went to considerable trouble persuading him to come back as I wanted the party to close ranks after the bruising campaign.

My efforts and Tengku Razaleigh's subsequent return greatly annoyed Tun Musa, who wrote to me to complain that I had retained his rival as Minister. Naturally, he did not want a political rival in the Cabinet — that is politics. You try to drive out your enemy because you do not know when he will rise up and challenge you again. Contrary to what some believe, I did not bring Tengku Razaleigh into the Cabinet to keep Tun Musa in check. I made sure he was a Cabinet member because I believed he had the ability to do the work. He had, after all, been the Finance Minister under Tun Hussein and I did not see why I should discriminate against him. If I could put up with him, others should be able to do the same. In fact, I dropped Tengku Razaleigh only much later in 1987.

341

But in 1981, I recognised that both he and Tun Musa were backed by substantial numbers in the party. If I had dropped one, I would have lost his supporters. It was a fight between figures of almost equal stature and popularity so, to keep the party intact, I had to find a place for Tengku Razaleigh.

My way during that first year was filled with hazards that tested my mettle as a politician as well as a leader of the people. In 1981, the second world energy crisis, which began in 1979, had pushed up global oil prices and thrown the US economy into recession. When US domestic interest rates went up, the ripple effects were felt all over the world. In Malaysia, it forced down the prices of our primary commodities, rubber and tin.

Our export markets shrank drastically. We also did not have enough foreign direct investment (FDI) coming in. At the time, Malaysia depended a great deal on FDI because the locals were not yet capable of starting modern industries.

We were also still an agricultural country and depended heavily on rubber, palm oil, and tin. The annual Malaysian crude palm oil (CPO) output was only 2.8 million tonnes in 1982 and, as such, government income was very low. To impress the severity of the situation upon everyone, the moment I became Prime Minister I cut my pay, the pay of Ministers, and that of senior civil servants by 10 per cent. It was a largely symbolic move, since the amount of money saved was insignificant. There was no expectation that poor workers should do likewise. Needless to say, the response — and the result — was very disappointing. Ministers and civil servants were unhappy and the pay cut did not have the desired effect on the Congress of Unions of Employees in the Public and Civil Services (Cuepacs) either. I thought that they would be willing to make sacrifices during bad times; instead, they issued a statement saying that they would not give up even one ringgit.

It was in this testing climate that my first Budget was tabled in Parliament. This all-important financial plan also had to take into account the global economic situation. The Government had to cut public service expenditure and place several state-owned enterprises under close watch. At the same time, we had to push for heavy industries like steelmaking and cement production. For this we had set up the Heavy Industries Corporation of Malaysia, HICOM.

Still, despite the recession, I wanted to implement many new ideas. I wanted to introduce new ethics and change old ways of thinking, but I did not find fertile ground for these notions. When I introduced Islamic values, many thought I was trying to create an Islamic state in the harshest sense. It took the non-Muslims some time to realise that this was going to bring absolutely no harm to them. Some Muslims thought that I had become a fundamentalist and was trying to outdo PAS. For most people, being a fundamentalist means becoming an irrational extremist. I hold a different view —Islam preaches peace and moderation. So a Muslim fundamentalist should really be a learned moderate who avoids giving trouble to anyone.

New ideas, especially those introduced at a time of economic and political change, need time to take hold and produce results. Years may pass before one can tell if an idea is good or not. When Japan was experiencing a prolonged recession, I was asked by a few Japanese individuals how they could overcome their problem. They used to change their Prime Minister every two years and I pointed out that each Prime Minister would try to revive the economy. But they all failed because they had hardly begun to implement the plan they had devised before they would be out of office. The new Prime Minister would not want to proceed with his predecessor's plan. He would want to have his own strategy so that he could leave his mark on Japan's history, but he would not have the time either. It was only when Prime Minister Junichiro Koizumi stayed in office longer, from 2001 to 2006, that Japan recovered.

It may seem ironic but one thing about Japanese culture that left a great impression on me was their concept of shame. It was something that my mother had also taught me when I was growing up: if you did anything wrong, it would not just be morally objectionable but also shameful. I have always been afraid of being shamed. To talk of the success or the achievements I intended and then to fail, for example, would cause me enormous shame. I noticed this same attitude among the Japanese, which is why they always try their best to succeed. They too *takut malu*, or fear being shamed. The old Japanese custom of *seppuku* or *hara-kiri* was based on this age-old notion.

This abhorrence of shame is related to the attitude that I wanted Malaysians to acquire: the attitude that we should not make ourselves, or permit others to make us, feel inferior. To put ourselves beyond that risk, we simply had to do our absolute best, always. If we did, we would be recognised and respected in the international arena. I wanted us to become proud of who we were, but, rather than simply taking pride in what we had managed to do already, to keep striving and go on improving. Other Asian countries had done it, so why couldn't we?

When I make a decision I like to see it through, and one of the most important decisions was to claim Pulau Layang-Layang, which I had wanted to do since I had been Deputy Prime Minister. Layang-Layang is a submerged reef in the middle of the South China Sea. It is part of the Spratly Islands and is located about 300km northwest of Kota Kinabalu in Sabah. I have already related how Tun Hussein was disinclined to claim Amboyna Cay. I thought this was a big mistake and a great loss, but I was determined to have a presence in the South China Sea. I instructed the Navy to build a tangible symbol of our possession of the Layang-Layang reef, even though it was not a real island and only a tiny part of the reef could be seen above water level at low tide. Once a makeshift hut was built, I visited the island in 1983 with senior Navy Officers and decided to spend a night there.

I remember how seasick the helicopter pilot was, sleeping on the navy ship in rough seas. But he was fine as soon as he took off. The tide was high and at first he could not find any place to land. Finally, he decided to set the helicopter down in shallow water close to the hut. Fortunately we could wade through the thigh-deep waters to reach it. As I have confessed earlier, I did not know how to swim. Together with me on this first trip was Tan Sri Ibrahim Mohamad of Promet, a company which built oil rigs and platforms. I wanted him to see the place and suggest how we could reclaim it and station our troops in more comfortable accommodation. The hut was a shaky structure of wood and a storm could have blown it away, but our Navy personnel had been staying there so I felt reasonably safe. After I stayed the night, I made the decision to build a proper base so no one else would claim Layang-Layang.

Starting from that humble hut, we were able to create an island with a runway for aircraft and a hotel for tourists keen to dive in the beautiful clear waters of the South China Sea. The coral atoll rises vertically more than 2,000 feet from the sea bed. I am not a diver but I was told the cliff formed by coral is one of the world's most beautiful diving sites. We also eventually reclaimed five other reefs and our men are now stationed there.

I was very satisfied with this outcome. We are not a warlike nation but we must claim what is ours. In the past Malay states lost many islands simply because they had no means to survey and oversee their domains.

They merely acquiesced when others occupied their territories. Today, islands such as these are very important as their natural beauty or access to resources may generate income. When I was Prime Minister I was keen to visit all these outlying islands. Malaysia's westernmost point is Pulau Perak, a bare granite and marble outcrop in the Strait of Malacca. It is a perfect location for observing the traffic plying the Straits. From the Spratlys claim, I learnt a very important lesson: that something which may at first appear useless may later turn out to be very valuable.

# Chapter 27:
## How Government Works

I was well aware that the public was not very happy with the services provided by the Federal and state governments at the time I became Prime Minister. The local authorities generally failed to provide quality service and to look after the areas they were directly responsible for. Of course, the public was never — and will never be — completely satisfied with what the Government does. Improvement is measured by comparison to the situation immediately before, and usually even after changes are made, the carping criticisms begin again. Therefore, there must be continuous effort to improve services and utilities.

Malaysian towns and cities were generally not very presentable and only inadequate attempts were made to keep them clean, to beautify them, and to have proper landscaping. Public utilities did not function well either. The Civil Service personnel were often curt and unfriendly, and many projects were not carried out properly and on time. I spent the early months of my premiership thinking about this problem. I had been in the private sector, even though I was actually only managing pineapple canneries and a tin-can plant. But what I learnt there was invaluable: unless proper detailed instructions and practical training are given, work will not be carried out according to plan and quality and efficiency will be compromised.

When instructions for a given task were issued, I wondered whether government officers and other staff really understood what they had to do. Should the construction of a house or a hotel be proposed, for example, what would be the correct procedures to follow? What would each officer have to do to enable approval to be given for the hotel to be built and operated?

Upon investigation I found that the procedures were murky — not deliberately so, but because they were not organised. The officers concerned were not fully knowledgeable about what they had to look for in the applications they had to approve. A natural succession of events would then follow: if an officer found something wrong with the application or was uncertain how to proceed, he would simply put it in his Keep In

View tray — and they all seemed to have big KIV trays. The applicant, meanwhile, would not be informed. Not wanting to annoy the officer, the applicant would wait for a considerable length of time before he dared to make any enquiries. Only then would he be told what the mistake was.

He would then correct the mistake in all the six copies he had submitted and return them to the department. Another officer was likely to find another mistake and would again set the application aside, and the whole rigmarole would repeat itself. It explained why at times it took two or more years for a building approval permit to be issued. Applications were also frequently lost, causing more delays.

There was very little construction taking place in Kuala Lumpur when I took over and this was simply due to bureaucratic delays and inefficiency. In 1981, the tallest buildings were the Federal Hotel and Merlin Hotel. None of the three or four then existing "skyscrapers" was more than 20 storeys high.

I decided to introduce a few innovations to speed up Government work and render it more productive. The first was for each department to produce a Manual of Procedures to enable every officer to know what steps to follow for each task at hand. The manuals were to include workflow charts for easy reference. Such systems and processes are important to ensure that no necessary steps are left out. It reminded me of the checklist that airplane pilots go through before takeoff, and which I myself used when I learnt to fly. Airplanes are very unforgiving — if you do not carry out the right actions in the right sequence, you may lose your life.

347

Based on this sound practice, I thought that if a checklist was provided then the administrative officers would not overlook or omit any of the steps. The applicant should also have such a checklist so that both parties could keep track of the process.

To ensure each officer knew his own role and his job for a particular task, he was to be provided with a desk file. This would tell him what to look for, what to check and approve or reject. He would also know from the workflow chart whom he was supposed to receive papers from, and to whom he should forward them after his section of the procedure was completed.

Needless to say, if there were grounds for disapproval, he would have to inform the applicant after he had checked everything that was within his area of responsibility. This needed to be done after going through the whole application and identifying all the errors. Where possible, all the other officers involved should check to see all that was wrong. Then the applicant should be informed of their decisions and asked to correct all the defects and deficiencies.

I had several discussions with the Chief Secretary and he was persuaded to adopt my suggestions. I believe the manuals, workflow charts and desk files were prepared by each department. Whether it was because of this or not, I don't know, but the fact is that the cities and towns of Malaysia began to sprout innumerable buildings, skyscrapers and large housing projects — creating the impression of rapid growth and prosperity. All other infrastructure projects including expressways, water supply facilities, ports and airports were also constructed far more quickly than before.

I could not use technical language in conveying the processes, because I did not have time to study the art and science of administration in books written by experts. Many of the innovations I introduced were the result of my observations and of turning things over in my head.

For instance, when I realised that Cabinet decisions were not being carried out properly, I suspected that the officers did not really understand what the decisions meant. As a rule, Cabinet decisions were conveyed to them through the minutes of Cabinet meetings, which, for obvious reasons, could not contain all the details of the discussions. Frequently, only the decisions were recorded and passed on to the officers. They were then expected to know the objectives of the Cabinet and to figure out, with no guidance, how to implement them.

Unfortunately, the decisions often lent themselves to several interpretations. Sometimes the officers disagreed with the Cabinet decision, not having heard the supporting arguments and why other possible proposals had been rejected. They could even end up implementing what the Cabinet had rejected.

I once had the idea of building a tourist attraction near Menara KL, or KL Tower, that would resemble Rome's famous Spanish Steps. I thought we could have steps leading down from the tower that would be lined with kiosks that sold souvenirs and snacks. The Public Works Department immediately responded by sending a team to study the Steps. But they could not find the Spanish Steps...because they were sent to Spain.

To avoid such incidents, I made it a requirement for Ministers to hold a post-Cabinet meeting with their staff later that same day. Ministers would then be able to clearly explain the Cabinet's decisions to the officers, and could answer and clarify any doubts so that civil servants would carry out what the Cabinet had decided, with a forgivable margin of inaccuracy. Along the way the officers could find that certain things simply could not be implemented. They were given some leeway to modify the decision, but they were not empowered to change or reverse the decisions completely.

Bureaucratic procedures are necessary. But if officers are simply given a free hand to do what they think should be done, then the administration would be chaotic. They will do what suits them best, which may or may not be what the task itself was about, or what the Government or the people wanted as a whole. That is human nature. Were it all to be left to the discretion of the bureaucrats, people would never be certain what to expect, and in the face of uncertainty, corruption becomes ever more common. Corruption aside, bureaucrats like to follow and uphold bureaucratic procedures, often, it would seem, for its own sake. Unfortunately, bureaucratic procedures tend to expand, often in order to cope with various possibilities of misinterpretation and to ensure that procedures are duly followed. To avoid such error and confusion, the administration tends to add new conditions and procedures. The number of procedural hurdles that an applicant must cross continually increases. In many cases the approvals take the form of licences which have to be issued by certain departments, authorised by certain officers. Quite naturally, the issuing authority becomes powerful, and abnormally so.

There are laws against corruption and the Anti-Corruption Agency (now the Malaysian Anti-Corruption Commission) investigates and takes action. But in the fight against corruption the best method is to have a checklist of the requirements to be fulfilled and to determine the time needed to check and approve or disapprove each application.

To set up a hotel for example, used to require more than 200 different approvals, permits and licences and each took considerable time to be issued. There was also the idea that one should not make a decision until another officer has made his decision, and even if this is not as prevalent today, decisions are still not made as quickly as they should be. An officer only needs to be concerned with his own responsibilities. If the conditions are met, then he should give the approval, irrespective of the decisions of other officers. Since numerous copies of the application are required, each officer can work on his own copy. After each officer has scrutinised his copy and recorded his decisions, the most senior officer can check the entire application and inform the applicant as to whether he has been successful, or whether he needs to make corrections or changes.

There is no mystery to reducing bureaucratic procedures, but attempts at doing this invariably meet with resistance from those who stand to lose their authority. We tried to set up one-stop centres, but they did not work because senior officers would not or could not be present. They would send junior officers who invariably said that they could not make decisions until they met with their seniors. It would take ages for this meeting to take place, and even then the senior officer would usually not make an immediate decision.

Very often, it is corruption that causes the bureaucratic system to break down. I realised very early on that it would not be easy to act against corrupt officers. Even if they could be taken to court, the case may not stick. In 1981, soon after I was made Prime Minister, I issued a strong statement saying that I would take action against corrupt officers. Following this, a number of officers decided to take optional retirement. The statement obviously had a salutary effect and I believe there were fewer blatant attempts to extort money from people who did business with the Government.

One issue that arose frequently during my term was the increasing level of corruption within society as a whole. It has always existed, of course, but in Malaysia it is not as institutionalised as in some countries, nor is it an ingrained part of our administrative culture. The civil service and staff know that corruption is a crime and are careful not to indulge in it, at least not openly.

Monitoring was crucial to ensure that work was carried out properly, without money illicitly changing hands. The original idea about the role and responsibilities of the Cabinet was that it should confine itself to decision-making based on the papers prepared by the civil servants in the Ministry. But where possible, I required Ministers and senior civil servants to oversee the work themselves. They had to visit worksites and offices and check on progress. If too many projects were going on at the same time, reports accompanied by photographs would be sufficient. I myself required such reports to be provided to me at regular intervals. Every now and then, I would visit worksites and meet the supervisors and engineers. Following this I would inform the Cabinet and give them my comments. It helped to keep the Ministers and other officials on their toes.

After a decade as Prime Minister I found that Cabinet decisions were still not being properly implemented. I had asked my Ministers to oversee the implementation of our decisions but, as I did not make it an absolute requirement, many Ministers left matters to their officers.

This was poor management. Officers were handicapped in many ways — they had difficulty gauging how much they could modify Cabinet decisions to suit the situation at hand. If they wanted to make reports to the Cabinet about the difficulties they faced, their only avenue was through the Minister or Cabinet papers. Not being able to present matters in person compromised the accuracy of the picture and in the end, the Cabinet decisions remained a dead letter.

Because of this, in the early 1990s it was decided that Cabinet Ministers were obliged to be hands-on and oversee the implementation of Cabinet decisions themselves. The advantage was that they had more authority and could modify somewhat the decisions of the Cabinet to make their implementation possible, and if necessary, they could report directly to the Cabinet and seek new directions. Officers may not have liked this because it amounted to interference in their work, and it may have seemed to them that their authority was being undermined. It was up to the Ministers to be judicious and apt in the handling of relations with their staff.

One obvious example of the importance of being directly involved was that of Port Klang, the principal port of Malaysia. During the colonial era, the British developed a port in Selangor which they named Port Swettenham, after one of their High Commissioners. There was already a port in Penang and of course there was Singapore, a full British colony which also served as the principal naval base of Britain in Southeast Asia.

The British did not want the Peninsular Malay states, which were not really British colonies, to compete with Singapore. Commercially the island had already grown into the largest entrepôt port for the whole of the Malay Archipelago. Consequently the British decided that Port Swettenham was to be just a feeder port for Singapore. To ensure this, the British charged higher railway freight rates to Port Swettenham than to Singapore, even though Singapore was further away. This guaranteed that Port Swettenham would always be unable to compete with Singapore.

After Singapore's separation from Malaysia, it built up its port until it became one of the 10 major ports in the world. At times it even ranked first. Singapore had obviously gained much from its port operations and it became the hub for moving goods throughout the region, using Malaysia and Indonesia as its hinterlands.

Before I became Prime Minister, the Government decided to develop Port Klang, the former Port Swettenham, into a major port for ocean-going ships. New wharves were built north of the original jetties which served the old port (these jetties are now referred to as the South Port). We also added more wharves west of the old port, increasing the capacity of Port Klang considerably.

As was my habit, I would drive to the West Port[1] area when it was under construction. I have always been fascinated by the metamorphosis of bare land into housing estates, industrial estates, highways, bridges and other structures. The building of West Port changed swampland into a modern deep-water port and after its completion I would drive there to see the ships which the port was to serve. For months on end, I saw only a few ships using the port. It seemed that all that work had wastefully produced a barely-used

---

[1]    Opened in 1995, West Port is the biggest private seaport in the country.

facility. In the early 1990s the Cabinet asked the Minister of Transport to get information on the number of ships and containers handled by the Malaysian ports. For standardisation and statistical purposes, containers were measured in twenty-foot equivalent units. (TEUs). I was shocked that by the end of the 1980s, all the ports of Malaysia put together handled only 1 million TEUs. Singapore, with two harbours, was at that time handling 12 million TEUs. I wanted to know the reasons for this great disparity. It seemed that Malaysian ports still served only as feeder ports for Singapore, and that the majority of the containers originating in Malaysia did not even use Malaysian ports. They were going to Singapore by road or rail to avoid double-handling, that is, loading up on ships at Port Klang and unloading in Singapore for reloading on ocean-going ships there.

Big ocean-going container ships did not come to Port Klang because it was said to be uneconomical. Malaysian containers would be waiting at the Singapore port for them, and they would unload Malaysian containers at Singapore for overland or sea transport to Malaysian destinations.

It did not make sense. Port Klang was a deep-water port and could handle the biggest container ships, which at that time carried a maximum of 5,000 containers. All the money spent to make it a deep-water port was wasted because only small coastal container ships of shallow draft would use it. The Cabinet instructed the Minister in charge not just to find out why, but to personally promote Port Klang to the big shipping companies. After ensuring that the port administration was efficient, he went to the headquarters of major shipping companies in several countries and persuaded them to use Port Klang, pointing out the advantages in terms of cost and so on.

Slowly at first but then more quickly, Port Klang began to be used by the big shipping companies and their ocean-going container ships. Today Port Klang's North Port and West Port together handle more than eight million TEUs. The new port of Tanjung Pelepas in Johor also handles more then five million TEUs. Together with other Malaysian ports, total TEUs being handled is now more than 10 million. The lesson learnt by the Cabinet was that when Ministers got personally involved in the work of their Ministries, impressive results could be obtained because they had stature and clout.

Despite this, there was still much that needed to be fixed. We still received reports of schools and hospitals remaining uncompleted years after work had been started. There were still problems in the bureaucracy, many structural bottlenecks and procedural obstacles to clear. Frequently, businessmen and other members of the public would complain about the officers in the Government. Their complaints alerted me to the continuing and intractable nature of certain problems of governance, of ensuring systematic rather than episodic administration.

It may have seemed like a straightforward problem. All a Minister had to do was issue a directive and show that action was being taken. In truth, however, it was a very delicate matter. People expected the Ministers, whom they had helped to put in their positions, to intercede on their behalf. They wanted to see results, perhaps even a little drama. Certainly, the Ministers could not ignore their complaints, but on the other hand, punitive measures doled out publicly on civil servants would have had adverse effects. The elected Government requires the cooperation of the permanent service. Antagonising them could well result in them withdrawing their cooperation in subtle ways, and their capacity to do damage to the Government is considerable. Still, the *rakyat* had to be heard and their cries for assistance attended to.

I found that the best approach was to talk to officers privately. The *rakyat* may not have been happy with this but no one likes a public scolding. Humiliation aside, it would not produce the required results. It was a lesson that I myself learnt because before I joined the Government I was openly critical of Government officers. After I became Prime Minister I recognised that there were many angles to consider and I was very careful in the way I dealt with the service.

One way to be proactive about identifying problems was to note them in writing. I always carried a small notebook to jot down things I observed and wanted to raise in the Cabinet, or directly with the Ministers concerned. I encouraged the Ministers to do this also, as memory can be flawed. At Cabinet meetings, the first one to two hours would be devoted to the points jotted down in our notebooks. Issues were resolved and many of the innovations made in Malaysia were the results of these notes made whenever I travelled abroad or at home, or anytime an idea came to my mind.

From the start I decided to oversee the whole Government and its work, and not just restrict myself to matters in the Prime Minister's Department. Likewise, I expected Ministers to be directly in charge of their respective portfolios as well as take an interest in Government as a whole. Public criticism of other Ministries was sternly discouraged, but during Cabinet meetings each Minister was free to point out problems in other Ministries. We believed in collective responsibility and so it was the duty of Ministers to point out any shortcomings. Quite often a Minister may not notice anything wrong in his own Ministry that is glaringly obvious to others. When I was Minister of Education I scrutinised all the papers of other Ministries and I did not hesitate to comment on them and to participate in the discussions of every Ministry during Cabinet meetings. Unfortunately, one or two of my Ministers were resentful of comments or criticisms directed at their Ministries because they believed they were always right.

In my time, Ministers were occasionally unable to attend Cabinet meetings and would send their deputies instead. But this did not seem right to me. Much to the disappointment of the Deputy Ministers, it was decided in 1983 that an absent Minister should delegate his responsibilities to another Minister. These acting Ministers, however, should not make drastic changes or decisions and should only ensure that the Ministry was carrying out its usual work. If problems arose, they should be put aside until the return of the Minister. If they were urgent, they should be reported to the Cabinet immediately. Only rarely, I found, could decisions not wait for the responsible Minister to come back. Along with the rest of the improvements made to render the Malaysian administration more efficient, the hands-on involvement of the Ministers helped to speed up Malaysia's development progress and economic growth.

The most powerful figure in the Malaysian system of administration is the Prime Minister. This is not ego, it is fact. From this fact stems many implications — if the Prime Minister is observant and willing to listen to the complaints and suggestions brought to him, and then to make firm decisions, then Malaysia will grow and prosper rapidly. Because of the structure of government, much depends on this one person, in Malaysia at least.

When I led the party in elections I openly campaigned not just for victory, but for a two-thirds majority. I told the electorate that only a strong Government could deliver on the promises made. Although the Barisan Nasional which I headed lost three of the 13 states at different times, that is, Kelantan in 1990, Terengganu in 1999 and Sabah in 1984, I never failed to get a two-thirds majority in the Federal Government.

The reverse side of the same coin is that once a Prime Minister heads a powerful Government, a culture of feudalism — marked by deference and flattery, patronage and access-brokering, client politics and favour-seeking — tends to take over. The party seldom ever criticises him. Even when the leader makes mistakes and his judgment seems faulty, there is little criticism other than that made by the Opposition. In the party, everyone usually rushes to show support and to express sycophantic loyalty to the leader. Advertisements and signboards show how close the leaders are with the Prime Minister, and the mainstream media refrain, voluntarily or otherwise, from criticism and instead find reasons for publishing fawning praise.

Recognising this, one of the things I did during my tenure was to forbid the use of my name for buildings, roads, schools and so forth. As far as possible, I tried to prevent the personality cult that so easily develops around strong leaders. I did not allow my picture to be put up in offices — although I know it was anyway — and I told Ministries inviting me to functions that they should not give me gifts.

I did not even want to have my name used in conversation, but that was impossible to avoid because by and large, people enjoy name-dropping. At one time, I even tried to put a stop to the congratulatory, thank-you advertisements that regularly appeared in newspapers if I opened or launched anything. But then the newspapers complained because they lost a great deal of advertising revenue.

In the final analysis, Malaysia's civil service and administrative machinery is, I believe, better than that of most developing countries. One of the most important indicators is efficiency in tax collection. In many countries taxes are not collected properly. In some cases, the taxpayer negotiates with the tax collector as to how much he should pay. Apart from resulting in the full amount not being collected, the negotiations inevitably lead to corruption. It would be naïve to think that all Malaysians pay the full amount of tax due, but the amount of tax collected is quite considerable. However, sometimes officers do make life very difficult for companies. They have been known to remove books for closer examination and keep them for weeks, even months. Naturally, business cannot go on as usual.

During my 22 years in office, I often received complaints about tax collection but what many Malaysians may not know is that the Inland Revenue Board (IRB) is strictly independent. I could only make general criticisms, but I could never mention any company specifically because that would be interfering with the operations of the Board.

Yet the IRB loves publicity. People they raid may not actually have done anything wrong, but the Board appears and carries off truck-loads of documents, all in the presence of the media. The targeted company, however, loses crucial business credibility.

Just before I became a Minister in 1974, the Inland Revenue Board raided both my clinic and my house. They took away the stubs of old chequebooks and concluded that I earned more than I had declared. I tried to explain that some of the money deposited into my accounts was cash from party headquarters for elections. I had to deposit it in my accounts before I could distribute it to party workers, but none of this made any impression on the income tax officers.

There were also crossed cheques from people who did not have bank accounts and who needed my help to cash the cheques. I deposited these cheques in my accounts and issued cash cheques to various people. When I was raided, all the crossed cheques were regarded by the tax officers as earnings, and I had to pay tax on them. Again all explanations fell on deaf ears and I ended up having to pay RM130,000, a princely sum for me then. The department officers hinted that if I disputed their assessment I might have to pay three times the amount due if the courts found me in the wrong. And there was no telling what the courts would decide. In the end I had to pay about one and a half times the amount due in instalments which was only completed long after I became Deputy Prime Minister. I also learnt that if I forgo payments due to me for whatever reason, I still have to pay tax on the money I do not receive. Because of this experience, my natural sympathy lies with people who complain about the IRB. But the Board generally did a good, conscientious job.

Thanks to them and to the Customs Department, the Malaysian Government has always had enough money to pay the salaries and the cost of development projects without much borrowing. We were also always able to tide over financial crises that came our way because we were financially strong. Most other countries would not have been able to do what we did.

# Chapter 28:
## Bersih, Cekap, Amanah

We launched the *Bersih, Cekap & Amanah* (Clean, Efficient & Trustworthy) campaign in 1982 for use in the first General Election after I became Prime Minister. I wanted to hold the election early to legitimise my position as leader, and we needed a good slogan to point to the changes which we thought should take place during my leadership. We decided that change was needed in three areas: cleaning up corruption, and promoting efficiency and trustworthiness.

This was a part of our continuing process of raising standards. Traditionalists like to say, "This is how we did it 100 years ago, 1,000 years ago". The Malays, especially, are bound by *adat* or tradition because it makes them feel safe. They dislike change. But I always believed that things could be done differently, and that value systems determine the success or otherwise of an individual, a community or a nation. While the values of a community or nation develop naturally, they can also be deliberately inculcated, and the best way to do this is for the Government to practices these values.

With the campaign, things began to move. This was one way of reducing corruption. As I mentioned in the previous chapter, to build a hotel then needed 200 separate approvals, and it took years to get them. The anxious applicant, knowing that time meant money, would resort to bribery to speed things along. Soon officials learnt that it was worthwhile to delay processes, a habit that had to be broken.

Hoping to lead by example, I practised the values we promoted and resisted any attempts to corrupt me. It involved controlling greed. As Prime Minister I was already receiving an adequate salary but the Government also provided me with comfortable accommodation, paid my electricity and water bills, gave me cars and aircraft for my trips and allowances for my travels. I had everything and I did not need anything more. But of course my detractors still considered me corrupt. However, my conscience is clear.

Corruption cannot be completely eradicated, but it can be reduced. By reducing the number of approvals needed and requiring them to be given out quickly, corruption became more difficult. To speed up the process whenever a complaint was made, I would personally make repeated enquiries. This sometimes led to accusations of cronyism but if I did not intervene, there would be delays and opportunities for corruption. I finally decided it was better to be accused of cronyism or corruption than to tolerate delays. At least things would get done.

It was the same with foreign investment, which encountered many difficulties after the Industrial Coordination Act (ICA) was introduced. The ICA, which was meant to ensure that a 30 per cent share of all investment was in Bumiputera hands, was already in place by the time I took over. The minimum investment, which was subject to the 30 per cent share was very small, a capital sum of only RM100,000, but instead of ensuring Malay participation in companies with foreign investments, the ICA ended up affecting Chinese-owned family businesses and purchasers of property, which naturally did not want strangers involved. To avoid appointing Bumiputera partners, proprietors would subdivide family businesses in an attempt to reduce capital in each part to below RM100,000. Later we increased the threshold to RM250,000 but even that proved too small. In the end, we abolished the requirement for Malay participation in the purchase of property for rental or other commercial projects. The ICA was just not practical — it caused much resentment, evasion and dishonesty, and it did not benefit the Bumiputera.

The ICA would have done better to monitor and promote the participation of Malays in partnerships or public limited companies, where the shareholders were members of the public. Malay participation had to be genuine and involve putting up the necessary capital. If they could not, then exemptions could be given. The ICA covered so many areas that investors and buyers of property, both local and foreign, felt harassed and as a result nothing could move and commercial activities stalled.

The officers responsible for implementing the policy were at first inflexible and I had a tough time convincing them that this was not the way to implement the Act. Eventually, they concurred, albeit very reluctantly. They still felt they had to painstakingly examine every investment, which was time-consuming and cost businessmen money. Delays inhibited investment and economic life as a whole. The economy was not doing well in those early years of my premiership and the ICA made recovery very difficult.

By 1984, at the height of a severe economic downturn, I completely rescinded all Bumiputera and other local ownership requirements in certain cases. Foreign investment was simply not forthcoming and needed to be encouraged, so the Government stipulated that if the product was for export, there was no need for local participation in the business. As a result, Intel and Bosch — international companies which did not sell products to locals — came in. It's important to be consistent and business-friendly and the Government must listen to foreign investors and try to resolve their problems, and not make things harder for them. Without their investments, there would be no jobs or economic growth and the Bumiputera would not get anything either.

When it came to *amanah,* or trustworthiness, our Government officers were generally reliable, though many lacked a sense of urgency. One officer remarked that while his signature helped a businessman to make millions, he still received the same salary regardless of how many documents he signed. So why rush or seek to be prompt? When it was explained that civil service salaries were paid from taxes collected from business, and that greater profits meant more revenue for the Government and possibly pay increases for its civil servants, attitudes changed. Later, when we introduced the concept of Malaysia Incorporated, the Government officers were more ready to serve the private sector.

361

As approvals for construction became easier to get, cranes appeared all over the city. Cement mixer lorries became a common sight and construction of high-rise buildings was seen everywhere in Kuala Lumpur. Papers were no longer lost and applicants dared to make enquiries if there were any delays. So omnipresent were the cranes that at one time, I thought that the Coat of Arms for Kuala Lumpur should include a crane. Even today cranes are part of the Kuala Lumpur skyline, and the city's construction seems to go on endlessly, come rain or shine. From the insignificant capital of a little-known country, Kuala Lumpur is now a large metropolis comparable with other modern cities elsewhere in the world. In this transformation, our new Government slogan played a role.

In retrospect, even the most cursory look at Kuala Lumpur and the rest of Malaysia today shows what the *Bersih, Cekap & Amanah* campaign has done for the country. It was not the only thing responsible for Malaysia's development, but it did change our administration for the better, refocusing official attention, energies and thinking. It reduced corruption to a certain degree and it accelerated development.

In Malaysia today, it is actually faster to build or repair a house than in England, where all sorts of obstacles are put in the way and everyone has to have a say — about the environment, about the traditional façade, and the like. It took the British Government and local authorities 13 years to approve the construction of the fifth terminal at Heathrow Airport, for example. Our Government and administration may not be the most efficient in the world, but they have improved considerably since the first two decades of Independence — and they are better than those in many countries, developed and developing.

The campaign was not just an election slogan, although it began as such. Slogans do help but they must be used sparingly. Too many slogans not only bore people; they expose the sloganeers to popular ridicule, the last thing that competent, change-oriented governments need. This has been the sad experience of so many developing countries and slogan-addicted regimes. By themselves slogans achieve nothing, and the more of them you devise the less effective they become as a whole and individually. Slogans are important only as shorthand for the realities they represent or promote.

At Independence, Kuala Lumpur was a town of about 300,000 people. When I took over, there were almost 500,000. Today there are more than two million people in the Federal Territory proper, and more than one million at its periphery. The population of KL actually increased four times, much faster than the national growth rate. People are also more well-to-do, and even the squatters have become better off as new housing is made available to them.

I remember a KL squatter area that I visited after a fire. I noticed one home had a Mercedes, some had two cars, and their fridges were bigger than mine, though I think they were using them for business. Of course, some of them were very poor, especially the Indians. The Malays were different — if they were allocated a low-cost house they would rent it out and continue to stay in a squatter hut. To them, living like squatters approximated living in a *kampung*. Still, they are at least changing in their outlook. Today many live in high-rise flats, and in time, the squatter slums in Kuala Lumpur at least will disappear.

There was some unhappiness that the old easygoing ways had to end. I used to call City Hall every week to find out how certain projects were progressing. Later I asked them to report to me directly, complete with pictures and progress reports. This practice of close monitoring helped to get everyone to work, the Ministers included.

In the past, unspent budget allocations for the various Ministries and Departments would be used up at the end of every year for what was called "Christmas shopping". They were determined to use up all the funds allocated to them for the year; how else might they ask for increased funding, or to resist cuts, for the next year? Public servants try not to return funds because doing so implies that they are inefficient or too generously funded in the first place, so they will do just about anything to show that all their allocations have been spent. Often, it was said, they bought useless things, inappropriate equipment or gadgets that quickly became obsolete after hardly any use.

When I assumed office, I announced that this practice would have to end and that funds had to be spent only on approved projects. Departments had to budget to cover only what they felt reasonably confident they could do. Budgeting, I insisted, would not be guesswork; it had to be more precise. I looked over their shoulders all the time and usually drove around on weekends to visit worksites. Rubbish disposal and landscaping were of special interest to me. They say the devil is in the details and I was determined to deal with this devil.

A later slogan stressed leadership by example, and as the highest leader in the country this slogan was meant more for me than anyone else. The other leaders were the Ministers, the administrative heads and also the party heads. But if the slogan was to be meaningful, I had to provide the example.

It was decided that Government staff should clock in in the morning because I saw how casual they were about coming to work and leaving in the evening. Many came any time they liked and would leave one hour before the working day came to an end. When clocking in was made compulsory I made a show of punching the time-clock myself, and I kept it up throughout my years in office. When we moved to Putrajaya, the new federal administrative centre just south of Kuala Lumpur, they introduced an electronic card and I lost mine. But I was always in the office at 8.30am and I left only at 6pm. I also insisted that those functions I had to attend at night ended at 10pm.

Then it was decided that we would all wear nametags so that the members of the public would know who they were dealing with. Making complaints against officers was easier after that. As usual, I wore the tag first and then everyone followed suit. This was standard practice in Malaysia until the slogan "1Malaysia" was introduced.

As Prime Minister I was given a huge Daimler limousine as my official vehicle. After our national car manufacturer Proton produced the Perdana, a 2,000cc saloon, I began to use that instead. I got the Ministers to use this Proton car but many senior officers felt that they deserved a Mercedes. I did not force them to change. So in Malaysia, during my time, Ministers used cheaper cars than senior civil servants. I think they still do, even the Prime Minister.

When I was President Jacques Chirac's principal guest at the French National Day Parade, I was given a small Renault car as they don't make big cars in France. The French could have given me a Mercedes or Cadillac, but they gave me their own car. Even President Chirac came in a Renault. There is a lesson for us, and everybody, in this — regardless of size, be proud of what you have.

I was also invited to be President Zia Ul Haq's principal guest at Pakistan's National Day Parade in 1995. I was escorted by very tall horsemen who wore smart uniforms. Even though "small" may be "beautiful", I thought that Malaysia should have a similar unit in the army because we had reached a stage where we could afford to look grander. Now there is a special cavalry unit in the Army which provides an escort for the King when he rides in a horse-drawn carriage. They also do guard duty at the Istana, the King's royal palace and official residence in Kuala Lumpur. Foreign tourists like taking pictures of the mounted guards in their red tunics.

Leading by example was a strain on me but it was worthwhile. I learnt how to fly to encourage young Malaysians to do the same. After I began horse-riding, equestrian clubs were started all over the country. In Kuala Lumpur alone there are now eight equestrian clubs and our riders have won in many international events.

When I was in Chile in 1991 I was honoured with the Key to the City of Valparaiso, and during the ceremony the Chileans sang their national anthem. It is a stirring tune, and we Malaysians were impressed. There and then we decided to sing our national anthem *Negara-ku* (My Nation) and from then on, we would sing whenever it was played. Doing so gave us a strong sense of being Malaysian and roused our patriotic spirit. I always felt exhilarated and this was where the beauty of leadership by example came in, for when I started singing, everyone else sang as well.

Apart from the obvious changes there were many subtle differences too. When the slogan *Malaysia Boleh* (Malaysia Can Do It!) was introduced, Malaysians became more ready to undertake new challenges. They climbed Mount Everest, sailed solo around the world, swam the English Channel and walked across the Antarctic and the Arctic.

I sought to show that the same rules applied to everybody, even the Prime Minister. As citizens we all had to observe the same code, and follow the same regulations. In 1982, I removed the difference in time between East and West Malaysia. Before that, Sabah and Sarawak were ahead of Peninsular Malaysia by half an hour, putting them in the same time zone as Hong Kong and China. The internal time difference was inconvenient and it meant offices opened and closed at different times in different Malaysian cities and towns. Besides, the world was now generally divided into hourly time zones; very few half-hour zones remained and adjusting the time when traveling was often confusing.

I remember telling Lee Kuan Yew about this when I visited Singapore. The Japanese produce world clocks with time zones for the principal cities, and it is easier to use these clocks if the difference between home time and local time is one hour. Many people think time is fixed by God and cannot be changed. Day and night are determined by God, but giving time to it is a human invention. During British rule, 7am in the Malaya was signalled by one strike of the gong because it was 1am in England. During the Japanese Occupation, Tokyo time, which was two hours ahead of Malaysian time, was used. Among other things, this forced the amusement parks to close very early.

Some regions like the Caribbean have only one time zone and a great distance between its eastern and western areas. As a result, mornings are very bright in the east while it is still very dark in the west. And Jakarta, despite being well to the east of Kuala Lumpur, lags behind us in time. There, the mornings are very bright but dusk begins around 5pm. Russia, which stretches for thousands of kilometers east to west, maintains five to seven different internal time zones. Official communication between Moscow and the Russian Far East cannot be easy since working hours vary so greatly.

Standardising time between the eastern and western parts of Malaysia has given us very important benefits. It has meant that many of us in the Peninsula must get up and go to the office just after sunrise, but we have more time in the evening for sports and recreation. Most importantly, standardisation gave all Malaysians, in the east and on the peninsula, the feeling that we really do belong to the same country. And since we adopted Sabah/Sarawak time, they did not have to change and were given no cause to believe that peninsular requirements were being imposed upon them. All of Malaysia, not just Sarawak and Sabah, now share the same time zone as the major commercial and political centres of East Asia.

Though I succeeded in streamlining time, in my years as Prime Minister I was unable to establish a standard Malaysian weekend. Since the time of the British the non-Federated Malay states had their weekends on Friday. This, I think, was a reaction to the introduction of Sunday as a rest day in the colonies of Penang, Malacca and Singapore and the four Federated Malay States. The British, being Christians, would go to church on Sundays. The Malay Sultans naturally assumed that a weekend should be a holy day, a day for prayers. Since Muslims have their congregational prayers on Friday, they chose Friday as their weekend and Thursday replaced Saturday when work stopped at midday.

Among Christians, Sunday is regarded as the Sabbath when strict believers are not allowed to work or play, but most Christians may just ignore this religious injunction. The Jews regard Saturday as their Sabbath and they too are not supposed to work. But today Sunday is just a day off, the work-free weekend. It no longer has any religious significance or connotation, so many non-Christian countries also adopt the Sunday weekend without problem. Malaysians, too, generally regard Sunday as part of the weekend without religious associations. When independent Malaya decided to retain the Sunday weekend, the five former unfederated states retained Friday as their day off. Where Sunday is the weekend, Muslims are given time off to go for Friday prayers.

The Quran is very clear that Friday is not the Muslim Sabbath as after the congregational Friday prayers, they should go about their work. Unlike Jews and Christians, they are not forbidden to work. If they do not have a work-free day on Friday, it is not a sin. Choosing Friday as a day of rest was a decision made by people who wanted to emphasise the difference between Islam and Christianity. I prefer the Sunday weekend because working when nobody else is in their office in the rest of today's globalised world is inconvenient and unproductive, a definite disadvantage. It would be far better to conform to world standard practice.

Eventually, towards the end of my term in office, Johor and then Perlis decided to make Sunday their weekend. But Kedah, Kelantan and Terengganu still refuse to fall in line.

Everybody, from the Prime Minister to the ordinary citizen, should do their jobs as best they can and not primarily for monetary consideration. We all need to contribute to developing the right attitudes and work ethic that can sustain a successful nation. To see the results of your work taking shape is far more rewarding than any financial compensation. There are those who may not care much for the development that took place during my stewardship. Still, it gives me intense satisfaction to see Kuala Lumpur grow, to see the majestic Twin Towers, the well-planned administrative capital of Putrajaya, the North-South Expressway, the electrified double-track trains, the Kuala Lumpur International Airport, the city's Light Rail Transit, the development of our beautiful holiday island of Langkawi, and much more.

# Chapter 29:
# Looking East

Before the Japanese invasion of Malaya, we had all believed that Westerners were superior, cleverer and all-powerful, which conversely meant that we believed all non-whites, including Asiatics (the word "Asians" was not used in those days), were somehow inferior.

My early travels to Japan, however, convinced me that Malays and Malaysians could learn a great deal from that part of the world. By the time I became Prime Minister, Japan had become a great industrial power and South Korea was emerging as an industrialising country. It did not take long for me to decide that Malaysia should look to these countries as models of national development, and this was how the Look East policy was formulated and launched.

I was mystified by the initial reaction to the policy, which was negative. Malaysians, including civil servants, suggested that it was ridiculous to model ourselves after Japan. They believed it made more sense to look at Europe, which was far more developed. Was it not more logical, they said, to go straight to the source rather than indirectly through the countries which had learnt from Europe?

But what they forgot was that Europe had over 200 years of slow development. The Japanese had only just become industrialised and the problems and hardships they had faced and overcome were still fresh in their memory. I did not completely disregard the West's experiences and many contributions — they still had a lot to teach us, but it is always better to learn from people with recent experience. While there was not a single living European who remembered the Industrial Revolution, there were any number of Japanese and Koreans who still recalled vividly how hard and costly it had been for them to acquire Western industrial know-how and to manage industrial plants.

Even in the 1980s, many people still did not think much of Asians. Most Europeans still held a very superior attitude. They were always talking down to us and insinuating that our ways were primitive and therefore wrong. When I introduced the Look East policy, many people believed it was connected to our Buy British Last policy,[1] but that was quite another matter and the two had distinctly different objectives. As for the Look East policy, it simply seemed more logical to look at Asian countries which were doing well. Its rationale had nothing to do with my not being trained and educated in England. Had I been educated in England and then visited Japan, I imagine I would have been even less inclined to look to the West for ideas about our own industrialisation.

When I visited England in 1962, one year after my trip to Japan, the British were still very undecided about joining the European Economic Community, the predecessor to the European Union. British workers were perpetually on strike at that time and productivity was very low. There was less reconstruction going on in London than in Japan and some of the areas that had been bombed during World War II had still not been cleared. Britain did not look at all as if it was rebuilding itself, certainly not the way Japan was.

On that trip, I was invited to the house of Sir Richard Winstedt, a highly regarded Malayan Civil Service officer, who had looked after my sister-in-law Saleha when she was studying in England. Winstedt had written a number of books about Malaya and Malay culture. I met his nephew over lunch and remarked that British workers seemed lazy and were always asking for less work and more pay. I said that there was no way they could compete with workers in other countries, especially in Japan. I had a strong feeling that he did not like what I said.

I do not have anything against workers and their unions, but reason tells me that more pay and less work reduces productivity and competitiveness. The Japanese on the other hand, worked very hard. Even their protests, or strikes, were held *after* working hours. It may seem funny, bordering even on the ludicrous, but there is a very sound logic beneath it. If it is done in their own time, workers will strike only over genuine issues which they feel strongly about. They will not go on strike over frivolous issues to see if some unwarranted advantage may be achieved.

---

[1]  I introduced the Buy British Last policy three months after I became Malaysia's Prime Minister. It stipulated that government departments had to consider other options before buying any British goods or services. I explained that the policy was prompted by, "Britain's lack of appreciation of the millions of pounds we have been pumping into the British economy through fees and living expenses of our students in this country."

If no work is done, no money is made. And if no money is made, claims and petitions for increased pay cannot be met. I concluded very early on that it was their work ethics — their intense dedication to their work — that enabled the Japanese to recover from the war so quickly. For that reason the principal aim of the Look East policy was to emulate how the Japanese worked. In his book *Made in Japan*, Akio Morita, the founder of Sony Corporation, recalls the founding of Sony and how, in the immediate postwar years, Japanese workers were willing to work for just a ball of rice with some soya sauce. The West would call this exploitation but the Japanese workers knew that Japan was poor and that it had to rebuild its industries. They were working not for individual gain, but for the country, and they understood that lifting the country from its depths would eventually result in better lives for them. Sacrifices had to be made, and they were made without complaint. The country did well and today Japanese workers are among the highest paid in Asia.

The Japanese system of employment was completely different from the European and also the Malaysian systems. They provided lifetime employment for their workers. When companies get into trouble in Europe or the US, one of the first steps taken is retrenchment, now euphemistically referred to as "downsizing". Dismissed workers then register themselves as unemployed and may then collect dole from the Government.

This makes scant economic sense. Dole payments in some European countries are ridiculously high. Upon dismissal a worker may be paid up to 90 per cent of his last drawn pay, so the more highly paid the employee, the larger the dole payment. Obviously, one can live quite comfortably on 90 per cent of one's previous pay and this fact inevitably leads to abuse of the unemployment relief system. People may simply choose to remain unemployed, imposing great strain upon government funds. The dole neither encourages workers to seek an early return to work in a different job nor encourage investment in new enterprises. It simply forces up the cost of labour to all employees and is a powerful disincentive to economic growth and development.

The dole system (that is, unemployment benefits) depends on the revenue received by the Government. When the economy is doing well, revenue is higher and the need to pay dole is less because unemployment levels are lower. But when the economy experiences a downturn and Government revenue falls, that is when more workers will be unemployed and dole payments will increase. In a recession, when revenues diminish greatly, dole payments will increase so much that they become a big strain on the Government at a time when it needs to spend more to help the economy recover. The dole is not really a good system.

When Japanese companies were not doing well, they did not sack workers, choosing instead to redeploy or create work for them. The Japanese devised a variety of measures to retain their workers. The workers received these benefits in return for their loyalty to the company, while the company, assured of the commitment of its hard-working employees, could plan, recover and prosper. Unfortunately today, Japanese workers are no longer loyal to their companies. They no longer want lifetime employment, and prefer to hop from job to job.

Admirable though lifetime employment was, I did not think that Malaysia could afford this same system. We have no dole for the unemployed, and they usually have to depend on their families to sustain them. This makes them uncomfortable, so they would make an effort to find jobs. The Government on its part tries to create as many jobs as possible. Creating jobs, especially by implementing policies that encourage the creation of private sector work opportunities, is the proper role of government. That was why when Malaysia invited foreign investment, we did not insist on immediately collecting taxes. We were prepared to forgo taxes if the investors created jobs for our people. In our view, no one who was prepared to work should remain unemployed. In fact, the Government was so successful in creating jobs that there are now more than two million foreign workers in the country. We cannot ourselves meet the demand for labour that our economic development has generated.

Before the war, there were a number of Japanese shops in Malaysia that specialised in selling cheaply-priced Japanese products. One was a good quality pencil sharpener, which I bought when I was about seven years old. At the time I assumed that it had been made by Europeans, probably the British, but when I turned it over I saw "Made in Japan" engraved on the blade and I was surprised that an Asian country could produce such goods. In those days Japanese products had a bad image because they were generally of poor quality. The British wanted to perpetuate that stigma so it became British policy for Japanese goods to be marked with "Made in Japan" to discourage sales.

Yet even in those days, it was apparent that the Japanese were quite innovative. Their mechanical toys may not have been durable, but they were ingenious. A propeller-driven toy plane would fly round and round, suspended by a cord. I remember seeing a bamboo blade with a spiral launcher that could fly through the air. The Japanese also made toy pop-guns and balsa wood planes which actually flew. The ingenuity of these toys was rooted in the technological creativity and innovation which was the basis for Japan's postwar emergence as a great industrial giant. Soichiro Honda, the founder of Honda Motor Co. Ltd., was not a trained engineer but an ordinary bicycle mechanic, yet he developed an entirely new kind of engine for small motorcycles. When he first exhibited it in the UK, British engineers were quite astounded as the engine was finely engineered and resembled a watch mechanism. When Honda started to produce small cars, the British had a good laugh. Now, they said, the Japanese would know that making cars was not like making motorcycles. But in the end it was the Japanese who had the last laugh.

The sudden Japanese defeat of the British army proved that the Europeans were not the only ones with the capacity to produce guns, motor vehicles and even aircraft. The war broke the spell that the White Man had over me. I had not thought that an Asian country could ever defeat the Europeans. At that time I had not yet heard of the Japanese naval victory against Russia in 1904 at Port Arthur in Southern Manchuria. The retreat of the British forces in front of my eyes shocked me, but such was my faith in the White Man that I did not think what I was witnessing was the total defeat of the British — the beginning of the end of the Empire and imperial domination. I believed they would soon come back. My experience with inferior Japanese goods, no matter how ingenious they may have been, did not conjure images of a resurgent Japan setting new standards for the whole world.

Looking East did not mean simply looking at Japan and South Korea's capacity for manufacturing, but rather what lay beneath their success. What were the social and cultural foundations of their newfound strength and competitiveness? One factor, clearly, was their work ethic, which consisted of working very hard and taking pride in their products. They were also very nationalistic. Among the practices that we could learn from the Japanese, I also thought, was how they organised their companies. They had their *zaibatsu*, huge Japanese conglomerates that were set up long before other people began talking about conglomerates. The *zaibatsu* usually included a bank, which would finance the rest of the conglomerate. The bank officers sat on the boards and were involved in the running of the corporation's various businesses. This close involvement is no longer permitted, but the practice served Japan well while it lasted because it provided an internal source of funds for use in rebuilding the huge pre-war industries. I was also struck by Japan's approach to technological acquisition: first copying, then modifying and improving technology to meet new needs as they went along, and eventually developing original technologies and products of their own.

More than just a willingness to make sacrifices, Japanese workers displayed other qualities that were well worth emulating. Generally, the Japanese are so thorough and meticulous that one wonders why Japanese goods were so inferior in the past. Perhaps it took them time to apply their traditional meticulousness to modern industrial activities and processes. Whatever the reason, these days the Japanese abhor poor quality. They have integrated into their culture an insistence on the importance of creating and producing the best products. These do not just involve modern electronic devices; even when working with bamboo they produce superior quality goods, products of great aesthetic style, precision, taste and appeal.

For example, they slice bamboo into very fine pliable strands and then weave them delicately into baskets or containers of all shapes which can withstand rough handling. The bamboo sets used for their tea ceremony reflect their attention to minute details. The shape of the stirrer, for example, is retained even after repeated use. They give this same attention to their industrial products. Everything fits precisely, with the narrowest possible gaps between the parts. No wonder those British engineers with their conventional outlook and standards saw the precision of Honda's motorcycle engines as more appropriate to watch-making than automotive engines. It was the same with all Japanese products and was not unique to one person or industry. This was a deep, pervasive and fundamentally cultural attitude — the core, so it seems, of an entire value-orientation.

I was able to convince most of the Cabinet members that a Look East policy would be good for Malaysia, but there were some who were not fully convinced. The Deputy Prime Minister at the time, Tun Musa Hitam, did not care much for the policy. But when you are the Prime Minister, you have a lot of clout and the capacity to use it. As Deputy Prime Minister in Tun Hussein's Cabinet I found that my ideas were not usually entertained but now, it was mine to decide. Though he was entitled to his view and to argue for it in Cabinet, ultimately Tun Musa's lukewarm support did not affect the policy.

Before long the policy took hold. We used to send all our students to Europe — to Britain in particular — but now the Civil Service devised programmes to send them to Japan and Korea and provided tuition to overcome the language difficulties. Some of our local firms also sent their workers for work experience in Japanese factories and to acquire their superior work ethic. Proton sent a large number of workers and factory managers to work in Mitsubishi factories.

The moment the Japanese Government heard about our Look East policy, they responded by offering our students places in their universities, and scholarships. The war was only recently over, memories were still fresh, and sentiment against the Japanese was still present among many Malaysians. So when I said that Malaysia should "look east", I suspect Japan felt some relief that the Malaysian Government did not display the animosity it may have expected. To demonstrate my belief in the Look East policy and in the spirit of leadership by example, I sent my son Mukhriz to study there, although I insisted that he should not be given a government scholarship. In the 1980s my son-in-law joined a Japanese firm, and he and my daughter lived and worked in Japan and learnt to speak Japanese fluently. Looking East was not just a theoretical stance or public policy on my part. I practised it and my family lived it.

I wrote earlier about how central the concept of shame is in Japanese culture. A people with such intense feelings about failure will do anything to avoid it. Like military defeat, failing in business or being branded producers of poor quality goods also creates a sense of shame. This is a deep, perhaps unique, anthropological feature of Japanese culture and character. Japanese employees, it is said, are reluctant to go home early as this may give their neighbours the impression that they are not being given enough work, or are not highly valued by their companies. A wife would be highly embarrassed to have such a husband.

The Japanese sense of shame is quite distinct in that it differs from what is common elsewhere in the world. They freely bathe naked in their communal pools of water from hot springs. Whole families do this together quite unabashedly. Whether this lack of shyness or shame in exposing one's body is admirable or not, I cannot say, but I do not think we need to copy this aspect of Japanese culture in order to achieve their level of success. For the Malays nothing is more shameful than being seen naked. But producing poor quality products is not regarded as shameful.

The Japanese outlook on life is amazing to behold and can be discerned in many activities, large and small. Their perfectionism is perceptible even, perhaps especially, in their cooking. I like tempura, a Japanese dish of prawns, fish and all kinds of vegetables, dipped in very light batter and deep fried. It is eaten with soya sauce and ground radish, or fine salt.

Eating tempura is even more enjoyable when you sit at a tempura counter watching the cook at work. What fascinates me is how he goes about the process of cooking. He is never still. He shells the prawns, straightens them and arranges them side by side neatly in a plastic container or plate. He trims the different kinds of vegetables, cleans them, cuts them carefully to uniform lengths and lays them down in a row on another plate. Then he prepares all the other items for frying, and arranges them methodically.

Next he cleans the part of the counter he used until it is bright and shiny, with not a scrap of waste or dust visible. The deep frying pan is cleaned and polished. The batter is carefully mixed with perfectly measured amounts of flour and water, and the gas fire is turned on to give the right temperature. He then arranges the plates in front of the diners and places pieces of absorbent paper on each one.

The frying is precise — the batter must be a light golden colour. When done, he picks up the fritters with a pair of long chopsticks and drains the excess oil. Then he places them neatly on the absorbent paper on the plates in front of the diners. Next to each plate is a small cup-like vessel for the tail of the prawn to be deposited. The prawn heads that were laid aside before the frying are then dropped into the batter, picked up carefully and fried. When they are done, he picks them up one by one, placing one on each plate.

This is the joy of eating tempura — such a simple dish becomes so much more appetising because the cooking is done so meticulously, so tantalisingly before you. And the hefty bill is paid without demur. The Japanese have developed the cooking of food in front of the customer to a fine art, part cuisine and part entertainment.

I relate this because the Japanese tempura cook exemplifies the Japanese attitude towards work. There is always something to be done and they are never idle. The gleaming stainless steel kitchen and cooking utensils are washed and wiped after each use, so that they shine and appear not to have been used at all. Everything in the kitchen is arranged neatly. Waste is removed from sight immediately and the plates and absorbent paper are changed before they get unsightly. The cook greets his customers politely. When he has finished, everything on the table is tidied up and rendered spic and span once more. Then, with a polite bow, he takes his leave before going to serve other customers. When this fine approach to work is applied to the production of industrial goods, the results are no less appealing and are equally precise.

I believed that if Malaysian workers could be made to develop that Japanese work culture as an integral part of their habits and work routine, their work would yield products of comparable quality. Our people have the capacity and the aptitude, but they also need to have the culture and the right attitude towards their work.

When I appointed a Japanese CEO to Proton, he managed to implant some elements of the Japanese work culture among Proton workers. They would come to work early and form groups to discuss the work they had to do and the targets they should set for themselves for the day. They would begin work right on time. Sure enough, the quality of Proton cars improved considerably. The Japanese CEO turned the company around.

When reconstructing their country after the war, the Japanese Government worked very closely with the private sector. Often, civil servants would join the big Japanese corporations after retirement as senior executives. They would know their successors in the government offices personally and presumably could make easy contact with their former juniors in the civil service. Whether they used this to promote their companies or not, the fact remains that in postwar Japan, during the country's period of phenomenal economic growth, there was close contact and cooperation between the Government and Japanese corporations.

Competitors in Europe and America were not happy with the success of Japan's penetration of the international market. Japanese goods were rapidly displacing Western products and international contracts were going to Japanese firms. Looking for some reason to condemn Japan, Western critics singled out the close cooperation between the Japanese Government and their private sector. They applied a derogatory label to this, calling it Japan Incorporated, implying that the country was not observing good business practices, perhaps even implicitly likening Japanese industry to their own notorious organised crime syndicates, the Mafia.

Yet close cooperation between government and private corporations had been common in Europe for centuries. The British and Dutch East India Companies were strongly supported by their respective governments. Even pirates used to get the imprimatur of the Government. And when European companies were hampered overseas by local authorities, their governments never hesitated to invade and even colonise their trading partners to ensure security of supply for their trading companies.

Even today, European corporations get strong support from their governments. Their diplomats often speak well of these companies, and support them during bids for contracts. The pressure that their governments exert to open up targeted countries in the World Trade Organization is another example of their government/private-sector cooperation. Among other things the Western governments are now pressuring the governments of developing countries to open up government procurement to their companies. This is surely an example of government-private sector cooperation. Yet those Western critics maintained that the Japanese Government's support of the private sector was grossly unfair and unethical. They strongly implied — but only when their competitors resorted to it — that the practice was incompatible with free trade and free competition. I studied Japan Incorporated and its workings to find out why Japan adopted this strategy and why it was condemned by its competitors. I concluded that there was nothing wrong with close government and private-sector cooperation. Private sector activities generate wealth for the country, create jobs, and fill the coffers of the government through taxes. In helping the private sector, the government is helping itself and promoting the economic development of the country. Best of all, while the government need not invest any capital, a percentage of the profit would still accrue to it.

In 1983, our Government officially adopted the Malaysia Incorporated concept. By doing so we undertook that the Government would consult the private sector regularly before formulating policies and drafting laws affecting the country's economy, in particular those governing investments, incentives and taxes. The private sector was to participate in the promotion of the country for investment and trade and its people were to join Government delegations visiting foreign countries for this purpose. At home the Government would actively help Malaysian businessmen and companies to achieve profitability. Because of our NEP objectives, Malay and other Bumiputera businessmen were given special attention. During business forums, I would explain that the Government was not being altruistic when helping the private sector. Apart from acknowledging that the private sector plays a role in enlarging the economy and developing the country, the Government, I frankly admitted, was interested in their profits because 28 per cent would be collected as corporate tax. But, unlike some, our Government was not lazily collecting unearned rent from the business sector. It was working hard with business for its share of the profits — together with various other taxes it collects when business is active.

The labour unions were also brought into the Malaysia Incorporated concept. During the financial crisis of 1997–1998, a special consultative body called the National Economic Action Council[2] was established. It included representatives of the private sector and the workers' unions. A smaller executive committee was also set up, again with private sector members. As I will describe later, it sat daily to monitor the economic situation caused by the devaluation of the Malaysian ringgit and to propose remedies. Working together and by conscious effort, the crisis was overcome. Cooperation between the public and the private sectors in Malaysia was unsurpassed by any other country.

But cooperation between the Government and private sector under the Malaysia Incorporated concept came under heavy fire from detractors, especially foreign journalists. They accused the Government of cronyism. But there can be no doubt that the Malaysia Incorporated concept resulted in rapid growth of the economy and contributed greatly to the development of the country. Europeans believe in competition, in tests of strength or skills for solving all conflicts. Theirs is what some have called an "agonistic" culture — one that loves and thrives on contests of strength and will. They believe that in any competition whoever emerges as winner is right and is entitled to the spoils. I, too, subscribe to this "fight-to-death" mentality if I am made to do so, but bankrupting businesses does not help anyone. Moreover, it creates social problems. If at all possible, one must find a way to achieve a win-win result, which is the opposite of the European "winner takes all and woe be to the loser" approach. Malaysia Incorporated was designed and adopted to pursue this kind of win-win situation. Our Government has always preferred to help companies overcome their problems if the fault was not due to them, rather than leave them to wither and die, such as when international currency traders undermined Malaysia's economy. Both the Government and private sector gained from the cooperation, and workers and national development benefited.

Of course, the Look East policy was not a one-way exchange. The Japanese also benefited as they became familiar with Malaysians, with our officials and politicians. The practical truth is that you do not do business with those you do not know. When British Prime Minister Baroness Margaret Thatcher decided to charge full fees for our university students in the UK, we

---

[2]  For a more complete explanation of the National Economic Action Council's functions, see Chapter 52: Currency Crumble.

stopped sending our students there because of the expense. I told Baroness Thatcher that she was making a mistake — when our students returned from England as engineers or other professionals, they would naturally recommend British goods and services in the course of their work. If we sent our students to Japan, they would of course recommend Japanese products instead. So by raising the fees, the UK would save a few million pounds but it stood to lose a great deal of business for decades to come. Inevitably, the Look East policy gave Japanese companies an advantage in Malaysia.

Some people were unhappy that many Japanese companies won big construction contracts during this time, but it was simply because they were very aggressive and impressive. We did not favour them especially, but they convinced us that they could do the job. They had the capacity to do the work, their bids were low, and execution was excellent. Besides, there were at the beginning very few capable construction companies owned by Malaysians. When I had just taken over as Prime Minister, the retaining wall on which the wharf was built at Kuantan Port collapsed because it had been built into very fine sand. Ironically, it was built by a Dutch company. Since the Dutch had amassed such enormous experience over the centuries building and maintaining their system of dykes and sea-retaining walls, behind which a large part of their country shelters, one might have expected them to do a first-rate job. But our trust was misplaced. When we sought remedies for their neglect after the wall collapsed, we discovered the company had been dissolved and had disappeared. We could not be left with a half-completed project, and the Japanese were the only bidders who undertook to bring in expert university professors to study the situation and who would give the Government a guarantee. Others dared not take on the project. The guarantee was for seven years but the retaining wall has now lasted more than 20.

Without the Japanese, we also would not have learnt how to build a car. They were initially reluctant to be involved, but eventually we managed to persuade Mitsubishi Motors to help us. At first, most components of the Malaysian car were Japanese, but we eventually mastered all aspects of the automotive industry: design, production, marketing, and technical innovation and development.

Still, no one should ever expect a 100 per cent transfer of technology. We ourselves do not transfer all of our palm oil and rubber technology to others. When foreigners come to Malaysia looking for the best rubber clone, we do not give it to them. A great deal of research and money had been poured into this area and we cannot be expected to give it away gratis. Intellectual property belongs to those who found and developed it. By the same token, we cannot get the formulations for medicinal drugs developed by foreign companies so as to produce our own brand without paying a high price for the rights.

It was the same with the Japanese. They gave us access to some things, but not everything. Perhaps they will never be willing to sell the intellectual property, no matter how high the price offered. They have their own interests and their advantaged position, which they have earned for themselves by their own efforts, to protect. That is business, and that is the way of the world.

I am realistic, not resentful. I do not expect others to help me get the better of them. To expect otherwise is unrealistic and irrational. In doing what it did for us, Mitsubishi was not acting altruistically as there also had to be something in it for them. But through our arrangement, we learnt a lot. A similar principle is applied with regard to foreign investment. Investors are attracted by such factors as our low-cost labour and on our end, we like having them here because of what they bring: technology, investment, job creation and generally, the strengthening of our economy.

In the case of Proton, when we could not get all the technology that we wanted from Mitsubishi, we bought British sports carmaker Group Lotus Ltd[3] and later we bought the Italian motorcycle company MV Agusta.[4] Lotus helped us to develop our own engine and we had great plans with Agusta. In recent times this last venture has taken a bad turn, reducing our access to technological innovations relevant to automotive production.

---

[3]   Proton and its key shareholder, Tan Sri Yahya Ahmad, collectively bought an 80 per cent stake in Lotus in October 1996.

[4]   Proton bought a 57.75 per cent share of MV Agusta for 70 million Euros (about RM350 million at the time) in July 2004, then sold it to an Italian company called Gevi SpA for just one Euro (about RM5) the following year. Harley-Davidson went on to buy Agusta for RM355 million.

We would have sent more of our young people to Japan but unfortunately, the number of places was limited. There also should have been a substantial trickle-down effect from those who went after their return to Malaysia, but that did not happen to the extent that I had hoped it would. Whether that was because our people who returned were unable or unwilling to pass on what they had learnt in Japan, or whether their numbers were insufficient to create the critical mass capable of engendering widespread attitudinal and cultural change within the industries where they worked, I do not know.

Most Malays are inclined to take the easy way. If they can get somebody else to work for them, they will, rather than get their own hands dirty by doing it themselves. Unfortunately, that is not the way to learn. There was a government-run carpentry school in Alor Star in the immediate postwar years. At 4pm sharp, the students, most of them Malays, would down tools and leave. They expected someone else to deal with the rubbish they left behind. If no one was detailed to do this, their attitude was that it was just too bad; after all, they were not paid to clean up. Relations with fellow students or workers were usually poor. There was no teamwork, no pride in their workplace, no dedication to good work standards, practices or products. The Japanese, by contrast, valued teamwork and cleanliness. In their factories, each shift of workers would stay behind for a few minutes after working hours and clean the premises so that the new shift could begin work in a tidy environment. The Japanese are taught that the next shift is their customer, and as customers they must be well treated.

People ask if I was disappointed that Japanese discipline did not catch on here. Yes, of course I was. Failure can often be traced to a lack of discipline, which in turn leads to poor dedication to work and low productivity. And low productivity affects cost and profitability. Once when I was in the Ministry of International Trade and Industry, I looked out the window at 3.30pm and saw many of the staff leaving. When I asked why, I was told they were leaving early because they wanted to avoid the traffic jam. But you are paid to work — the difficulties encountered are something that should be expected. They come with the territory, they are part of the job, of working life itself. I was not inclined to indulge such unprofessional attitudes, which was why I introduced clocking-in and clocking-out as a standard practice for all our civil servants.

Our workers are also not loyal in the sense of staying with one company throughout their lives. They hop restlessly from one employer to another in order to improve their earnings. They do not try to improve the quality of their work and increase productivity in order to be promoted to higher positions and earn higher income. Being loyal to one employer was until recently a Japanese trait. It ensured that one always tried to do one's best for the company. The employee's interests and fate were so closely tied with the company that this was the rational way for the worker to improve his position and income. It was a kind of "selfless selfishness": the worker served his own interest through the company making profits, not through withholding work to get better pay, as often happened elsewhere under other industrial systems. This attitude contributed greatly towards Japan's recovery. How gratifying it would have been to see Malaysian workers develop this same sense of loyalty as a result of the Look East policy. We would today be much more developed than we are.

The attitude of European workers towards work is quite different. They are not company-oriented but individualistic and display little loyalty to their employers. They do not give of their best to help their company to succeed. Even when the company is in dire straits, they make demands which only create greater difficulties for the company and impose added costs on it when it can least bear them. That is why today, so many products are no longer made in Europe. We did not look to Europe for our industrial model. Their work ethic had undermined their industrial strength and would not be beneficial for an industrialising Malaysia.

Under the free trade system, business has to accept the challenges of competition and, to win, the product or the service offered must be of high quality and the price must be reasonable. Very high wages and other benefits for workers unaccompanied by improvements in quality and productivity affect production costs. Any test of strength between unions and employers will be disruptive and must carry a cost, even though it may result in the workers demands being met. But unless the increased cost is accompanied by higher productivity, the business may fail. Any such victory is pyrrhic, as the workers may end up not winning better pay but losing their jobs and livelihoods.

By and large our Malaysian union leaders are quite reasonable, but when they go to International Labour Organisation conferences, they interact with European union leaders who usually urge Malaysian trade unionists to demand more pay and better working conditions. They imply that Malaysian workers are victims of capitalist exploitation. On some occasions, I was able to argue that the European unionists were probably not concerned about the wellbeing of our Malaysian workers. Behind the offers of support, they were probably concerned with protecting their own jobs. If Malaysian workers were less demanding, if there was greater industrial peace and factory-floor goodwill, investments would flow more rapidly towards Malaysia. We might then attract more European investments and, in time, some of their markets as well. The European workers and trade unions would then lose their jobs. But if Malaysians workers are too demanding there would be less foreign investments and the jobs would stay in Europe.

Outsourcing is an important means of lowering the cost of production. Its popularity has grown enormously simply because outsourcing components from lower-wage countries greatly reduces costs. To stay attractive to investors, Malaysia must maintain both a comparatively lower wage level and industrial peace. Disputes should be settled through negotiation or arbitration, not strikes.

The standard of living can be kept reasonably high and can steadily improve by controlling inflation. This was the route taken by Malaysia. We have never abandoned price controls for essential goods, not even long after the war was over. One Malaysian ringgit can buy in Malaysia what one US dollar can buy in the US. Lower wages need not necessarily lead to lower standards of living.

Malaysians of all classes have a tendency to blindly emulate European ways, so our trade unions do not always act in ways that are appropriate to the Malaysian cultural and business contexts. Some think it makes sense to go on strike, to punish employers as European unions like to do. In my arguments with trade unionists who were demanding pay rises, I had to convince them that we simply did not have the money that Europe had. It took me a long time to reach a state of amicable understanding with

Cuepacs. Before that, the union under the leadership of its President T. Narendran was always threatening to go on strike. Perhaps he sincerely believed that the damage to the Government from industrial action would be so bad that their demands would be met. Consequently, relations between the Government and the union were strained. Remembering my experience with the Malayan Pineapple Cannery Union, I decided that I had to establish a better relationship with the unions, both in the public and private sectors. I spent many hours talking to the leaders of Cuepacs and the Malaysian Trades Union Congress, explaining the problems faced by the country. I could see how things looked to them from their position, and I accepted the legitimacy of some of their demands and assented to them. In the end the confrontation between employers and unions was replaced by rational, even friendly, relations. Here, too, antagonistic mindsets and attitudes had to be replaced by a commitment to allow both sides to benefit. As a result, there are far fewer strikes in Malaysia than in other countries, developed and developing.

This, I firmly believe, is the Asian or Eastern way of dealing with conflicts. Strikes, working to rule, go-slows and picketing were common in Malaysia before because people thought that those were the only ways to settle labour disputes and protect workers. But such actions lead to low investment, poor job creation, arrested development and low wages — the complete opposite of the workers' own aspirations and agenda. So, who do such actions serve? Not the workers, not the employers, not the development process, nor the Malaysian people, economy and state. It is not a win-win formula but it is a no-win for everyone.

Western writers often assert that there is no such thing as Asian values as they hold that all values are universal and their values are the universal ones. I believe otherwise. Certainly there are universal values, but there are also strong and well-grounded Asian values which contribute to Asian customs and traditions that affect their behaviour. It is my unwavering belief that Asians do not believe in violent competition and crude tests of strength as so many Europeans seem to do. Those methods of resolving conflict are disruptive and destructive. War, for example, is a test of strength, the ultimate test, and it is clear from so many horrific events, past and present, that the winner is not always the just and righteous party. Very often an evil force wins simply because its capacity to kill and its ability to destroy are greater than its adversary's. Certainly, Asians have also gone to war, but never as frequently as Europeans. The reason for this difference lies, I believe, in Eastern or Asian values.

Before the Look East policy, Malaysians used to think of themselves as incapable of doing anything better than others. We used to feel very small when interacting or merely being in the presence of non-Asians. Our self-esteem was rock bottom and I felt that something had to be done. To liberate the captive Malaysian mind, we had to prove to the people, the *rakyat*, that they could do what others could, just as well, and perhaps even better.

Twenty years ago, if you told a Malaysian company to build a power plant in Saudi Arabia, it would have been a pie-in-the-sky remark. When we wanted to build the Federal Highway from Klang to Kuala Lumpur, we awarded the contract to Mitsui, a Japanese company. We had to bring the Japanese in just to build a road. But today Malaysians are building roads, refineries and power plants all over the world. In the past, the best talents in Malaysia for building roads were the Indians, but today we are building roads in India. Things have changed a great deal since we adopted the Look East Policy.

My Japanese friends have asked me whether I am still looking East, still looking at them during their prolonged period of recession. I told them yes — you learn not only from the successful ventures of others, but also from their mistakes, how they face hardship and how they overcome setbacks. There is always something to be learnt from capable people, from resourceful societies and tenacious cultures.

The Japanese had been doing very well for decades after the war. Apparently, whatever systems or policies they adopted worked well for them. Then overnight, quite inexplicably, they seemed incapable of managing their economy. They floundered into a recession and their government and people seemed incapable of countering and then reversing the downturn.

What happened? After studying the inability of the Japanese to recover, I concluded that they had lost faith in their own systems, the systems which we had adopted. Somehow they felt that what they were doing was wrong, perhaps because of the comments of Western critics. They seem to have abandoned the systems that had worked for them in the past for new ones suggested by European so-called pundits. Worse, they made a sudden transformation, forgetting the disruptive impact of rapid change. This triggered Japan's prolonged recession. Recovery demanded coherent policy that was consistently pursued, but with its frequent changes in administration and bewildering policy reversals every year or two, consistency was precisely what Japan did not get.

Despite Japan's setbacks, Malaysia decided to stay with its Look East policy, to continue to apply Japanese work ethics, to adopt selected aspects of Japanese culture such as its value commitment to work, orderliness and excellence, and to implement our Japanese-inspired Malaysia Incorporated concept. There were deliberate attempts in 1997-1998 to impoverish us by devaluing our currency, but we survived and regained our capacity to grow. We did so, as I shall recount later, by refusing to make the strategic mistake that Japan, perhaps heeding too dutifully the voices of its foreign critics, may have made.

Looking East also meant looking at Korea and China. We had noticed that Korea was rapidly industrialising and we wanted to know why they had achieved noticeable success. So we sent some of our students to Korea. Our observation was right. There is something about the Koreans that has enabled them to catch up and in some instances even to outstrip the Japanese.

Today, Korea has become a fully industrialised and developed country. Their products have found acceptance worldwide, including in the United States. Korea's performance convinced us that the Look East Policy was right. Despite some setbacks we refused to lose our nerve, or to doubt ourselves and our chosen direction. Even though we were under pressure, we chose not to implement policies that might have been held in high esteem overseas but which were not in our own interest to adopt. Perhaps we learnt from Japan about the need to pursue one's own path into economic prosperity and cultural modernity. To do so, we were not prepared to sacrifice our dignity or our sovereignty, our mastery of our own fate. If today Malaysia is less of a Third World country than what it was when I became Prime Minister, it is because we made the right decision to turn our gaze to the East.

# Chapter 30:
## The Europeans[1]

We live in a Eurocentric world. Whichever way we turn we see evidence of European dominance of the world. What we hear and what we think are largely influenced by the perceptions and thinking of the Europeans.

Yet we, non-Europeans, know very little about these people who play such an overwhelming role in every aspect of our lives. What we do know about them is what they tell us about themselves. Naturally, try as they might to be impartial, what they tell about themselves is biased. They cannot help but see themselves in the light they would like others to see them.

There is, as far as I know, no major works on the anthropology of the Europeans studied and written by non-Europeans. Neither Asians nor Africans nor any others have provided us with a non-European perception of the Europeans. There may be some academic studies but certainly they are not as well-known as the anthropological studies by Europeans on various non-European races or tribes.

We must know the people we are dealing with if we are to interact with them. This is even more important today than in the heyday of the European empires, the time when the European nations physically owned almost the whole world.

They have given up their empires but far from losing their influence over the world, they are more influential than ever. They effectively control international politics, the international economy, modern knowledge and information, the sciences and technology, ideas and ideologies, languages, systems and methods of doing things, including modern administration of countries. They are militarily powerful — exerting hegemony over the whole world and extending even into outer space. In fact nothing happens in the world which is entirely divorced from and unconnected with the Europeans.

---

[1]    "Europeans" is my shorthand for those commonly described today as "white Caucasians" and can be grouped together according to shared histories as well as broad similarities in culture, language and experience. I also include those of ethnic European origin who have colonised other countries, for example Americans, Australians and New Zealanders.

It is amazing that we should know so little about the people who have physically, mentally, emotionally and even spiritually, played and still play such an important role in our lives.

Non-Europeans really need to do very extensive studies about the Europeans to do justice to the subject, to be authoritative and to enable us to compare our present European-dictated views of them and our own original views about them.

I decided to write this chapter on the Europeans largely to meet my own needs largely. I am deeply conscious of the Europeans' influence over my own thoughts and ideas and I feel a need to be independent of them if I want to achieve a more correct analysis of their influence on me personally and on my country and people. Though necessary, this chapter on the Europeans is far from adequate. But what I write represents my own independent perception of the Europeans with whom we must come into contact in the course of our private and public lives. People may think that like the Europeans, I would be biased because I have always wanted to view the Europeans from my own racial angle. I admit that this may be the case. Even then, it would still be useful as my views would be contrary to the conventional image of the Europeans.

To really know the Europeans, there is no better way than to study their history. Firstly, we should know that the Europeans, like the other peoples of the world, were initially divided into tribes. Some, like the Germanic peoples of Northern Europe and the Latins of Southern Europe, were truly European in the sense that the first evidence of their existence was in Europe itself. The eastern Slavic people originated from Central Asia. These Slavic tribes migrated west and settled down in Eastern Europe.

Over the centuries these three principle ethnic groups acquired a common basic culture but their European identities were actually geographical, i.e. they were Europeans because they inhabited that part of the world recognised as the European continent.

These three tribes, initially nomadic, had roamed all over Europe, sometimes settling down when conditions were good. In the process of their initial nomadic life they came to confront each other over the land they chose to settle. Consequently the history of these European tribes, and the nations they later set up, is full of wars.

We read about their wars from before the Common Era until now. Not a year passed in the past four millennia when there was no war among the European tribes and nations. Because of the constant need to fight each other, the Europeans became very highly skilled in warfare. They built impregnable castles and walled towns and developed ever more effective weapons.

The Europeans would always covet the lands of their neighbours far and near. When they became powerful because of the weapons they had developed or through newer ways of fighting, they would become aggressive and make war against others.

They glorified war and the killing of their enemies. Warriors became their heroes and would be immortalised through their legends and writings. They invented all kinds of ways to lionise and perpetuate the memories of these warrior-heroes. They not only erected statues and monuments, they also embellished them with eternal flames. Elaborate memorial ceremonies would be held on anniversaries to keep the warrior spirit alive and to persuade their people to fight to the death in the interest of their tribes or nations.

They have developed the most effective war machines. Their armed forces are well organised with groups of increasing sizes under officers of different ranks wielding ascending orders of power and authority. They coin command words for every action to be taken. Their huge armies move and act with precision. In fact, they call their armed forces, "war machines".

The Malays had their first taste of this when the forces of the Sultan of Malacca met those of Alfonso de Albuquerque. The Sultan's army was far bigger and he had war elephants. But to this day we do not know who the commander-in-chief was, who his subordinates were and their ranks. Against their rabble hordes the Portuguese forces were puny. But they were better organised, better armed, disciplined and well trained in the skills of fighting. The Sultan's forces, despite the elephants, were no match for them.

Malacca was defeated and occupied. But more importantly, the Europeans established their superiority in the eyes of the Malays for centuries after.

As a by-product of their wars, the Europeans developed their concept of competition. Everything must be settled through competition. As in war, the winner or victor is right. Thus very early the Europeans subscribed to the belief that "might is right".

The idea that competition will not only establish who the winner is but who is right pervades the thinking of the Europeans. All their games are based on this belief. An early game was jousting, in which the contestants riding on horses would try to unseat each other using a long lance. Since then more and more games have been invented and all would involve competition. The winner is then venerated.

An old way of settling conflicts was duelling to the death. That it was usually the more skilful who would win, did not matter. The winner just had to be right.

Likewise, in English common law courts it is usually the more skilful lawyer who gets his client acquitted even though he knows and others may know that the person acquitted was guilty.

In disputes between workers and employers, the competition is about finding who would suffer more and eventually give in. Who is right or who is wrong is not the point. If the unions can inflict damage on the business and force it to give in then the conflict would be regarded as resolved. The process is unimportant: that much damage is suffered by the employer and the business itself is of no consequence. Winning in industrial action is all that counts.

This belief that competition will settle all is also seen in business. Companies and businesses are often bankrupted in order to determine who the winner is and who should then be able to carry on unchallenged. Government must not interfere. Like gladiators, the winner takes all. The loser is left to lick his wounds, that is, if he is allowed to live after his defeat.

However, Europeans also have many redeeming characteristics. They can be very caring. They can be dedicated to the truth in science. They can be absolutely honest and considerate. They can be strongly dedicated to justice and fair play.

They are forever trying to improve things, never satisfied with whatever they have. In the governance of nations they have come up with many systems. Those who care to study the Europeans and their thinking as to the best forms of government will notice that the Europeans would be initially enthusiastic with the system they had in place. However, disenchantment sets in sooner or later and they would then start designing a new one to replace it.

And when they adopt the new system they would insist that it is the best, the most perfect. They would not only practise the system but would want everybody else to do the same. Many who refused would be killed, forcing the survivors to be more ready to accept the new ideas.

Thus it was that the Europeans became disenchanted with their absolute monarchy and replaced it with republicanism. Finding that it was not as perfect as they believed it to be, they came up with socialism, and then communism. Then they discovered that these ideologies did not deliver the equitable societies they had hoped for. Seeing that capitalists were doing better, they discarded their egalitarian ideas in favour of capitalism. Through all these, millions of lives were lost in promoting and subsequently discarding the different ideologies and governmental systems.

Not content with killing their own people in order to spread their beliefs, they would go to war with other countries and invade them with the same purpose. Yet later they would again become disenchanted with their current system, would devise a new system and would fight and kill to spread their new beliefs. Currently they believe that democracy, the free market and a borderless world will create heaven on earth. Again they invade countries and kill people in order that democracy and its accompaniments be accepted by all. But already they are seeing disaster in their own countries as the free markets wreak havoc on their finances. In time, we can expect them to introduce a new system and woe betide anyone or any country that refuses to accept their latest brilliant idea.

Europeans will continue to believe they know best what is good for the world. The idea of a world that is not Eurocentric is repugnant to them. That is why they are worried that a new power in the East might arise to displace them, spelling the demise of Eurocentrism.

I have described the character of Europeans as briefly as I can. But it is not out of place to relate incidents and revolutions in European history which illustrate their behaviour.

Firstly, it is obvious that Europeans are different from Asians and Africans. For millennia the Europeans were confined to their small continent. But the Greeks, who I believe to be more Asian than European, went beyond Europe to invade Asia. But they were eventually assimilated by the peoples of the countries they conquered. Other than the Greeks, the European tribes of Europe never got out of Europe for centuries.

The Asians had very early reached eastern Europe where they settled down and built new nations. Later the Turkic Asians and the Mongols also reached Europe, to pillage and to rob the cities. But after their raids the Asians preferred to return to Asia, although some did indeed extend their domains into Europe.

It can be truthfully said that Asians discovered Europe first. European discoveries of non-European continents came much later, after the Arabs, the Turks and the Mongols had already invaded Europe. Columbus crossed the Atlantic and Vasco da Gama rounded the Cape of Good Hope very much later to find that there were other continents besides Europe.

But European attitudes towards their discoveries were different from those of the Asians. As has been pointed out earlier, the warlike Europeans always coveted what belonged to others. If they had the power to seize it for themselves they would do so.

Thus when the Europeans sailed to the new continents they did so in armed merchantmen. They were keen to trade but they distrusted the people they wanted to trade with. Whereas the Indians, Chinese, Arabs and the peoples of the Asian archipelagos sailed in unarmed ships with their trade goods and exchanged these goods among them, the Europeans did not care for the entrepôts set up for this purpose by the people of the Malay Archipelago.

They always wanted to secure the supply of trade goods which they were anxious to procure. Having come in armed merchantmen, they demanded to be given land to set up fortified trading stations at strategic points. They wanted trade agreements for monopolistic rights. And finally they simply conquered their trading partners to ensure supply. Thus empire followed trade.

Europeans acquisitiveness knows no bounds. Having been used to fighting each other in Europe in the quest of more land, the Europeans naturally resorted to wars when simple trade was slow and frustrating to their greed and acquisitiveness.

The Indian sub-continent and Southeast Asia were conquered through trade, when unscrupulous traders gave support to pretenders to local thrones and then extracted treaties from them for exclusive rights.

The Malay Sultans were persuaded to give up the administration of their states simply by bribery. They were offered substantial political pensions, palaces and Rolls-Royce cars if they signed agreements to hand over to the British the administration of their states. A clause in the agreement made the British administrators, called Advisers or Residents, de facto rulers of the states simply by stipulating that their advice, when given to the Malay Rulers, must be followed. The Rulers were paid from revenue collected in their states, and so were the numerous British expatriate officers, thus spending not a single penny of their own money. With the power and authority they gained for themselves, the British were able to ensure that the wealth of these states accrued to the British Government and their business people.

And all these were obtained without shedding a drop of British blood. Literally, the Malay Sultans and their subjects had to pay the British to become their masters and overlords.

In other parts of the world a few bottles of whisky were enough to exchange for vast stretches of land; Manhattan Island was obtained in this way. And when the local inhabitants became troublesome and refused to give up their land, force was used to evict them. The natives usually did not have the capacity to defend their land. Their forces were just unorganised irregular warriors armed with primitive weapons like bows and arrows, spears and machetes.

The European forces were well organised, well trained and they were equipped with muskets, guns and cannons. Later they invented the Gatling gun, a machine gun capable of mowing down the native warriors by the hundreds and thousands.

In these unevenly-matched wars, the natives invariably lost. Tens of thousands of them would be killed. Whole tribes would be wiped out. Genocide was carried out everywhere, and today we can no longer find many of these tribes.

The natives, much reduced in number and decimated by new diseases, would be confined to reserves which effectively served as prisons for these once-free people who roamed the plains and forest. In North America, the bison, the principal food of the Indians, was almost completely wiped out by white settlers clearing the plains for their plantations and farms.

396  In South America there was much intermarriage with the Amerindians, resulting in large populations of mestizos. The Indian languages and cultures were displaced by European languages and cultures. Most were forced to convert to Christianity.

In Australia the aborigines were treated like wild animals who could be shot on sight. The Maoris of New Zealand were forced to sign the Treaty of Waitangi and gave up their beautiful islands to the European invaders.

The blacks of Africa were partially wiped out but they were so numerous and prolific that a very substantial number survived to fight for freedom later. But their territories have been so torn up and divided between numerous European nations that they can now no longer be identified with the original tribes living there. And so the different Africans living in their artificially-created countries frequently fight each other, using the weapons they buy from European arms merchants.

Wherever they went the Europeans created demographic chaos. Peoples of different races were thrown together without regard for the rights of the indigenous people. A divide-and-rule policy kept the races apart. Yet when these people demanded for independence, the indigenous people, usually less well-off than the immigrants, were forced to give citizenship rights to all and everyone. Failure to do so would prolong their serfdom to the European colonisers. Even if the different racial groups were to accommodate each other the Europeans would continue to harass them with demands for them to be more democratic, uphold all kinds of human rights and generally force the weaker races to give in to the stronger on the principle of equal rights, regardless of the inequality created by the European colonisers themselves.

Where the Europeans could not gain total control and maintain their superior positions, they would leave time bombs in the form of racial incompatibility. Thus the countries achieving freedom from European rule would become unstable and incapable of growth and development. Many would remain in a state of civil war long after the Europeans left. Their instability would provide excuses for the Europeans to continue interfering in the affairs of these nations.

That is the world the European imperialists left when they apparently abandoned colonialism. Almost all the ex-colonies have failed to achieve stability and growth. Most have become basket cases, and the Europeans then label these countries as "failed states". The impression created is that these countries should never have been given independence. They should have remained colonies of the Europeans.

After the Europeans had been forced to dismantle their empires they started to make a bastion of their continent. They have now consolidated their position in the world with the creation of a United States of Europe, now known as the European Union. Already individually powerful, their coming together has made them even more powerful. Now once again they are ready to take on the world. Together with the North American Europeans, the Europeans will continue to be the centre of the world.

World War II once again demonstrated the superiority of the Europeans in war. This war determined what the world should look like. Victory somehow divided the Europeans into Eastern Europeans and Western Europeans. A Cold War then ensued and like it or not, the rest of the world had to become a part of this European confrontation. They had to take sides and suffer the pains of someone else's war.

Western Europeans had always regarded Eastern Europeans as somewhat inferior. The arranged marriages between members of their royal families improved relations a little. Then during the 1917 Russian Revolution, Tzar Nicholas II, who was related to the British royal family, was murdered. Relations between Britain and communist Russia became strained. Although Russia sided with the Western Alliance during World War II, the moment the war was over the Western Alliance broke off from the largely communist Eastern Europe headed by Russia.

Unwilling to openly wage war against each other because it would again mean destruction for Europe, West and East fought a Cold War through their proxies. The West claimed a right to emplace its nuclear missiles in Turkey just across the border from the USSR. The Russians then decided to have their missile based in Cuba, just next to the United States.

Both sides moved to the brink of a nuclear war that could have destroyed the whole world. But at the last moment the Russians agreed to abandon the Cuban base if the United States would give up its Turkish missile base.

398   The Cold War went on for decades. Non-European countries were forced to align themselves with one or the other of the protagonists. Proxy wars were fought in third countries to test each others' weapons, and their willingness and readiness to go to war. But each time the principal protagonists pulled back, they left the proxy countries devastated.

The cost of this confrontation was enormous and it was a drain on the coffers of both. Finally Mikhail Sergeyevich Gorbachev, the President of the USSR, realised that the East was worse off than the West and decided to put an end to the wasteful war.

The world heaved a sigh of relief when the European Russians could no longer sustain the confrontation. The Eastern bloc crumbled and the USSR itself disintegrated into independent states. The Cold War ended.

The Americans exulted and declared that it was the end of history. The democratic capitalist free market had triumphed. There would be eternal peace as the Western Europeans headed by the United States established a new order for the whole world to be enforced by the United States of America with its mighty military capacity.

Then suddenly the world realised that a new and more powerful European monster had risen from the "ashes" of the Cold War. This monster wanted to impose its will on the whole world. This time there would be no other power to restrain or check it in any way.

This power resides with the United States of America but it is essentially ethnic European in origin and character. It is the same old European imperialism manifesting itself in a new form. Its objective is still dominance over the whole world.

Its onslaught against the non-Europeans would encompass all areas of human activity, from politics to the economy and to social systems. Everything prescribed by Washington must be accepted and practised by all the world.

It was not so very long ago that European countries were ruled by dictators. The last to go were those of Portugal and Spain. Except for Greece, the European countries had all adopted democracy as their political and administrative system. Now it was the turn of the non-European countries: accept and practise democracy or face the might of the European powers. That the Europeans themselves took more than 200 years to adopt and adapt to the democratic system is no reason why other countries should take that long. They must become democratic now, immediately. They would be helped by the Europeans through whatever means available.

The recalcitrant countries found themselves attacked by specially-trained and financed rebel guerrillas seeking to overthrow their governments. Frequently civil wars would break out, and over prolonged periods these wars would bring death and destruction to the countries involved.

Excuses are then found to justify European military invasion of these countries. In the name of democracy and freedom they bring even more suffering to the people. But still the attempt to bring down recalcitrant governments and install puppet regimes goes on. Millions are killed, millions more wounded and maimed, and whole countries devastated in the name of democracy and freedom.

In other cases, leaders were assassinated in order to force a regime change. Sanctions against countries would deprive the innocent inhabitants of food and medicine. Children would die of malnutrition and lack of medical treatment. But, said one American Secretary of State, it was worth it.

Their love for war is terrible. Huge sums of money would be spent by them on inventing, developing and perfecting ever more powerful weapons and killing machines. The ultimate is the nuclear bomb. Tens of thousands of these weapons were produced and stored for future wars. A small number of these nuclear bombs and warheads would be enough to destroy the whole world and wipe out the human race. Still the development, production and storage of these and other weapons would go on. That nuclear weapons cannot be rendered harmless does not matter. The human race has to live with the fear of being wiped out by nuclear war either by accident or deliberately.

The art and science of war would be constantly upgraded and improved. It was the Europeans who first clothed their soldiers in uniforms, equipped them with ever more lethal weapons, organised them in patrols and squads, battalions and brigades and army corps. Their soldiers were drilled into perfect killing machines which would be ready to fight anyone they were ordered to. Theirs was not to reason why: theirs was to do or die. That is their motto.

Their naval and air forces are similarly organised to execute their missions precisely and unthinkingly. They are currently thinking of war in outer space and are organising their forces for this eventuality.

The European military forces which were launched against their enemies through the ages were so successful that all the countries of the world adopted the organisation, the training and the weapons used by the Europeans.

When the Europeans introduced Special Forces, the Commandos, whose training includes creeping up to an unsuspecting enemy and slitting his throat with a knife to avoid making noise, the rest of the world followed suit.

Much as I deplore their belligerence, the Europeans are geniuses at planning, organising and implementing. They are very systematic. They develop detailed blueprints for the construction of everything they wish to produce. Using the blueprints they, and others now, can produce the same thing as accurately as the planner at great speed and in huge quantities. Mass production is a European invention.

By contrast, the Balinese build beautiful and perfect houses without any plan. They achieve excellent results. But anyone else wanting to build the same building will have to be apprenticed to the original builder. This limits the spread of the skills to others. Truly the European way is best. No one learns architecture from the Balinese. Everyone has adopted the European system.

The blueprints can be used in the design of the smallest engineering product to an aircraft or a ship of any size.

Methods and systems are the Europeans' gift to the world. Because of this the administration of large corporations and populations is made possible. By the same token, the destruction on a massive scale of people and economies is also possible.

401

The contributions of the Europeans to modern civilisation are enormous. In fact, modern human society is largely organised and administered through European methods and systems.

Before the coming of the Europeans, the administrative systems of the nations of the world were by absolute monarchies in form and practice. The monarch owned everything. All revenue and all sources of revenue including natural resources belonged to the monarch. The bureaucracy was dedicated to serving and upholding the monarchy and the enforcement of law and order to protect and sustain the monarch.

The laws were usually not codified and their administration was arbitrary, usually at the pleasure of the monarch. In some cases the ruler actually presided over royal courts to determine the guilt or otherwise of the accused person. Not guided by written laws, the judgments were often made according to whim. Punishments were usually harsh: death or indefinite imprisonment. There was no appeal and the death sentence would be carried out immediately.

Muslim monarchs would sometimes provide courts where judges would apply Muslim laws. But the laws were not properly codified. There were books on Muslim laws written by Muslim jurists, but they served only as guides. In most Muslim countries the laws were not legislated systematically.

The system of courts presided over by judges who based their judgments on written laws was introduced largely by Europeans. Initially the courts were just as bad as those found prior to the introduction of the rule of law. But gradually the Europeans improved the standard of judgments and miscarriages of justice happened less and less frequently.

As with other European practices and systems, the rest of the world has adopted, if not the whole legal and judicial system, at least elements of it.

It is the same with governments and administration. Most governmental and administrative systems used around the world are based more or less on the systems developed by the Europeans. The divisions into Ministries, each headed by a Minister, which in turn are divided into departments and other units headed by officers of increasingly lower grades, are also of European origin. The increasing levels of seniority are linked to increasing areas of responsibility until finally the Chief Minister or Prime Minister or Executive President presides over the whole government.

It is the same with businesses. Starting from privately-owned companies, where the organisation is headed by the owner or senior partner, business organisations have become more and more complex as they grow into ever larger corporations and conglomerates. To oversee the management would be the Board of Directors presided over by a Chairman or President. Running the company under a professional Chief Executive Officer would be a variety of officers, some, like the accountants, with special functions.

I have always admired European astuteness in devising systems and methods. It enables their administration or management to grow really big and still be able to make things happen the way the head desires.

There are many other systems invented by the Europeans to enable them to control their worldwide empires. They are not foolproof or perfect but are certainly better able to function than the personally-owned and managed businesses which developed in the non-European countries, especially in Asia where, should the founder-owner die, the whole business would collapse. European-style business organisations last long after their founders have died.

For all these contributions towards the management of the increasingly complex world of politics, economy and societal organisations, the world has certainly much to thank the Europeans. Nevertheless the Europeans have their weaknesses and it behoves the non-European world to know as much about the Europeans as possible to distinguish between what schemes, ideas and systems initiated by the Europeans should be followed and what should be rejected.

As a good example, the world should scrutinise the banking and financial systems which were the creations of the Europeans. We now know the systems are based on fraud. They have survived for a very long time. But finally, the balloon has burst and the whole fraud has been exposed.

The Europeans will undoubtedly invent another system or will modify the present system. Will this again be based on fraud? Knowing the Europeans better now, the world must look askance at whatever solution the Europeans come up with.

I had hesitated to include this chapter in my memoirs. It can be taken as confirmation that I am anti-European. It may hurt the feelings of my European friends. But I also feel that there is a great need for people to know the real Europeans, or at least Europeans as seen through Asian eyes. I also think that Europeans should know what non-Europeans really think about them. Examine all the great problems faced by the world in history and today, and we will find none that does not involve Europeans directly or indirectly.

For these reasons I think this chapter is truly necessary.

# Chapter 31:
## Anwar Joins UMNO

Datuk Seri Anwar Ibrahim joined UMNO soon after I became Prime Minister in 1981. I was surprised that he wanted to join our party as his involvement with the Angkatan Belia Islam Malaysia (ABIM),[1] or the Muslim Youth Association of Malaysia, and his public statements, made him a natural ally of PAS.

But I thought that it was to his advantage to join UMNO because he would not make much headway in politics outside of the party. He would most likely have languished permanently in the Opposition, which would not have been what he wanted. On my part, I thought he would be useful to UMNO. For me the party came first, and as long as anyone could contribute to the party, even if the person disagreed with me, I would not stand in his way.

It is commonly believed that UMNO made the first move to recruit Anwar but this is not true. For a long time, UMNO had been a big and successful party and did not need to solicit for members. To join the party was a privilege. Over a period of several months, a number of people had come to tell me that Anwar was keen to join UMNO. So I agreed to meet him.

Our first meeting was at my office. That was the first real interaction we had with each other with no one else present. He wanted to join the party so he was most accommodating and did not behave in a way that would cause him to be rejected. When I asked why he wanted to be a part of UMNO, he said he now subscribed to the party's struggle. He admitted that ABIM's leadership was critical of his decision and wanted to know why he wanted to join UMNO. He had told them he wanted to convert UMNO to ABIM's views and influence the Government from within. His agenda, he said, was to turn the Government into an Islamic one and joining the party was the most effective way of doing so. He was smart even then. He managed to convince ABIM, and so he made the transition without cutting off his ties with the association. Later I was to learn that he could even convince opposing parties that he agreed with them all.

---

[1]  Angkatan Belia Islam Malaysia was founded in 1972 and supported Islamic revivalism and the foundation of an Islamic state in Malaysia.

His idea of changing the party from within did not worry me as I believed I could handle him. In any case, I felt that if he joined PAS instead he could have won in elections and would probably help it attract members away from UMNO. In other words, outside UMNO, he was potentially a thorn in our side. There was also a positive side to his joining us: as a youth leader with a fairly big following, he had many contacts among young leaders worldwide. His brand of Islam did not alienate him from youth leaders of other faiths, yet Muslim youth leaders and other Muslim activists seemed to think he was a great Muslim leader.

In Malaysia, his leadership of ABIM ensured him a good following and that could be to UMNO's advantage. Among Malaysian Muslim groups, ABIM was unusual. It was active in helping young Muslims to pursue knowledge, spread the teachings of Islam and do charity. Although it was hardly friendly towards UMNO or the UMNO-led Government, it did not appear extreme. Anwar's joining UMNO might soften ABIM's stand against the Government or at least blunt it slightly.

With his Islamic credentials, I hoped Anwar would add credibility to UMNO's claim to be a champion of Islam. Having made up my mind to accept him and finding no strong opposition among my colleagues, I arranged for him to sign the membership forms in my office. Anwar formally joined UMNO in 1982. I made a Press announcement from my office. My decision to use government premises for party business was criticised by Tan Sri Dr Tan Chee Khoon, the retired leader of Parti Keadilan Masyarakat Malaysia (the Malaysian Social Justice Party) or PEKEMAS.[2] He was known nationwide as Mr Opposition. I responded by pointing out that it would be a charade if I were to go out of the office for the signing and then go back into my office to see Anwar, as I always saw visitors there, whether political or non-political.

405

I had known Anwar's father, Datuk Ibrahim Abdul Rahman, a staunch UMNO member and Member of Parliament when I myself was also a Member of Parliament between 1964 and 1969. I thought that, at heart,

---

[2]  Tan was a founder of Gerakan but formed the multiracial Malaysian Social Justice Party in 1972 after Gerakan joined the Barisan Nasional Government. In the 1974 General Election, however, he was the only member of his party to win a Federal seat. The party effectively disbanded when he retired in 1977, and most of its members joined the DAP.

Anwar was an UMNO man. He had even been my supporter when I was at odds with the Tunku in 1969-1970.

Anwar also had qualities that could contribute towards UMNO's standing among intellectuals. He was well-read and could quote many philosophers and thinkers, from Sun Tzu to Malik Bennabi. His command of the Malay language was excellent and he was fond of using literary language in his speeches. Though most of his terminology had people reaching for their dictionaries, his style of speaking impressed them no end. He was also able to mingle with academics within and outside the country. I genuinely thought he would be an asset to the party, so I was inclined to back him.

Some UMNO members, however, were worried and felt threatened by Anwar. During Tun Razak's premiership, these people had worked hard to counter Anwar's anti-establishment activities. Led by Tun Abdullah Ahmad Badawi, this group included Datuk Abdul Aziz Shamsuddin, my former political secretary who later became a Minister.[3] I do not think Aziz ever reconciled himself to Anwar's UMNO membership and both he and Tun Abdullah thought that much of what Anwar said was just posturing. Anwar's future father-in-law, Datuk Dr Wan Ismail Wan Mahmud, was also among those who were strongly against him. At that time, Wan Ismail worked with a psychological warfare unit and was a strong supporter of the Government. When I heard that he objected to Anwar marrying his daughter Wan Azizah, I had a talk with him and persuaded him to relent. This was before Anwar joined UMNO.

The first disquieting sign came when I formed the Cabinet in 1982 and appointed Anwar as a Deputy Minister. He came to see me, expressing disappointment that he had not been made full Minister. I was startled. "There are so many who are senior to you. How can I appoint you?" I asked. I also told him that no one had ever jumped from being a critic of the Government to becoming a full member of the Cabinet in such a short time. Besides, he had only just joined UMNO — senior members would have been deeply offended if his elevation to a ministerial rank were to take place so soon. I had already given him a very high position by

---

[3]   Datuk Abdul Aziz Shamsuddin became Minister of Rural and Regional Development in 2004 before losing his Federal seat to Khalid Abdul Samad of PAS in the 2008 General Election.

appointing him a Deputy Minister and to complain over the appointment was unprecedented, and, I felt, unbecoming. At that time I did not realise the extent of his ambition. Perhaps I should have learnt then how deep it went and his strong resentment when his plans were frustrated.

Another display of Anwar's ambition came at the party election in 1982, when he decided to contest for the top post in UMNO Youth. The head then, Datuk Suhaimi Kamaruddin, liked to hang on to the leadership position of any organisation he headed. When he led Gerakan Belia 4B Malaysia (4B Youth Movement Malaysia),[4] for example, he kept changing the rules so that he could continue to lead.

I backed Anwar's bid but Suhaimi rejected the idea of stepping aside for him. I had a rather ugly contretemps with him, but he still insisted on contesting against Anwar. Suhaimi lost his position and became very bitter. In 1987, he backed Tengku Razaleigh's challenge against my leadership, which I will deal with in a later chapter.

From then on, Anwar made clear that his ambition knew no limits. He clearly wanted to rise in the UMNO hierarchy as quickly as possible, as that alone appeared to be his objective when he joined UMNO. I quickly realised this but made no attempt to curb him, as I knew that he had the qualities to make a good leader. It seemed prudent to have someone in line, ready to take over from me.

However, becoming the head of UMNO Youth did not satisfy him for long. Soon after, he wanted to become an elected Vice-President of the party. As head of the Youth wing, he was already *ex officio* a Vice-President. The heads of UMNO's main sections, excluding the recently-formed Puteri UMNO,[5] enjoy that rank automatically. Through Tan Sri Megat Junid Megat Ayub, then a Deputy Minister under me, I learnt that Anwar wanted to hold the post in his own right. I told Megat that Anwar should be content with his current position and allow others the opportunity to move up. But in the end, because he was very insistent, I allowed him to contest for the post.

---

[4] Gerakan Belia 4B Malaysia, formed in 1966 to provide for a national youth movement, has served as a proving ground for UMNO youth leaders.

[5] Puteri and Putera UMNO were formed to attract greater youth participation in the party.

Why did I support him? Why did I not stop him from contesting? Actually I did not support him. But I did not stand in his way either. Was there any way to say no? Some people perhaps saw my allowing him to contest as a sign of my approval. It was less than that. It was not an endorsement — there were simply no grounds for me to stop him. But I did tell Megat that I thought Anwar's move was not proper and that his impatience was not in good taste. However, it did not go against the rules.

There are three elected vice-presidential positions in UMNO. They are very senior positions immediately after the President and Deputy President, who by convention would become Prime Minister and Deputy Prime Minister respectively. Because the Vice-President is just one step from becoming Deputy Prime Minister, there would usually be a fierce contest for this post. It is the level at which people try to prove their mettle and establish themselves as potential contenders for the second and then top position in the party. I personally know how bruising these contests can be, especially if none of the incumbents is prepared to stand down and so create a vacancy. I myself contested one of those three positions against all three incumbents in 1971/1972 and lost.

408

I never spoke to Anwar about his own wish to enter this contest. That I did not stop or discourage Anwar had nothing to do with my attitude towards him specifically. That was simply my way and personal inclination in general and I seldom tried, as UMNO President, to influence party elections. If I did involve myself it was with a general, not a personal, objective. In contests for specific party positions I chose to be hands-off. I did not like to back a loser and then have to work with the winner.

But I was aware that while I myself did not place much store on such things, many UMNO members saw my neutral stand as an endorsement as they put a high premium on traditional Malay etiquette and precedents. Still, Anwar's impatience to rise must have appeared unseemly to them. Partly because of his religious credentials, Anwar was quickly able to build a power base within the party and when he became Education Minister, he ingratiated himself with the Malay teachers and their union. They became his loyal supporters. Before Malays became more dominant in the business sector in the 1990s, it was teachers who had considerable influence in

UMNO and were considered to be a major power bloc in the party. They also had close contact with Malays on the ground, with the voters in the villages and in the Malay urban areas. They were in touch with popular Malay sentiments and aspirations.

When Anwar wanted to win people over, he could be very polished and charming. He could win over the strongly religious Arabs while being friendly with die-hard, anti-Arab Jews. He was not seen as a Muslim extremist. Even after his 1999 convictions for corruption and sodomy, many Muslims continued to believe in Anwar and his version of what happened to him. In this sense, Anwar is quite a remarkable man. He is amazingly persuasive and knows how to convince people of his sincerity.

To most Muslims, he appeared very pious and even before he joined UMNO, he had built up a considerable international Muslim following. One member of the staff at the Saudi Arabian Embassy in Kuala Lumpur, I recall, thought rather poorly of me, but changed his attitude towards my stewardship after Anwar joined the Government. Anwar cultivated people and knew how to win their support. He had travelled a lot when he was a youth leader, meeting Afghans, Pakistanis and many well-known Muslim and non-Muslim youth leaders. He made it a point to meet and talk with them. He appeared to be all things to all people. Anwar also befriended people like Paul Wolfowitz, then the neoconservative US Deputy Secretary of Defence and a strong supporter of Israeli aggression against Palestinians and Iraq.[6] Anwar also courted the international media, presenting himself as a liberal who was against many of the practices of the Malaysian Government, of which he was himself a member. He dangled the promise that things would change once he took over.

409

People would come to tell me that he was trying to gain personal popularity, especially with the UMNO rank and file. He visited the party divisions and branches often but to a certain extent, I thought this was a natural thing to do. All politicians seek to ingratiate themselves with people to gain popularity. When he became Deputy Prime Minister and UMNO

---

[6] A US politician who served in the Ronald Reagan and George W. Bush administrations, Wolfowitz was also US Ambassador to Indonesia before serving as World Bank President until June 2007, when he was forced to quit over allegations involving the undue promotion of the bank's employee Shaha Riza, who was his girlfriend.

Deputy President, I thought his contacts with the UMNO division leaders were useful. One day, he would take over the leadership. When he did, he would need these party connections to help him lead UMNO and the nation effectively.

For many years, we had a good personal relationship. He took up horse-riding because I did, although he proved to be an impatient rider. Before he learned to ride properly, he started galloping. He fell and nearly broke his neck and had to be hospitalised. Later he was to claim the police had injured his neck.

Before he became Deputy Prime Minister, I would take him with me on my official trips abroad. On the plane we would talk and discuss politics and religion, topics which were of interest to both of us. He was very knowledgeable and appeared to be religiously committed, performing his ablutions and praying even while flying. He struck me as a very impressive and pious man. He was one of my strongest supporters and always said the right things. There is no doubt that there was a special aura — a charisma — about him and I was perhaps affected by that.

One of our UMNO customs is that on the evening of Hari Raya, the Eid ul-Fitr festival, after all the visitors have left the Prime Minister's residence, he visits the Deputy Prime Minister. Such visits among Muslims are intended to remove misunderstandings and to renew goodwill and amity for the coming year. This is the practice of Muslims everywhere and is especially valued by Malay and Malaysian Muslims. Given the complexity of the relations between Prime Minister and Deputy Prime Minister (as my own experience with Tun Hussein showed), it is particularly important that trust be reaffirmed between our party's and nation's two topmost leaders. Yet between Anwar and myself there was no special need to build goodwill or heal wounds. Anwar's family was very close to mine. His wife, Datin Seri Dr Wan Azizah Wan Ismail, would prepare the northern dishes that I liked, and she and Hasmah got on very well together. I liked Azizah, who had a charm of her own. Even after we parted ways I cannot think of her as a political opponent or as someone I had quarrelled with. I understand her decision to stand by her husband.

Anwar was also very hospitable. During the fasting month he would set aside many evenings to break fast with lots of people at his house. I noted that he always invited the *Menteri Besar* from all the states on these occasions. I never did that, thinking it would be a great inconvenience for these outstation people to come all that way just for a short dinner. The Government would have to pay their travel expenses, but Anwar must have felt that it was good public relations and politically profitable.

After gaining the party's vice-presidency, Anwar was still restless. His next quest was for the position of Deputy President. The Deputy President, he knew, also becomes Deputy Prime Minister. In the past, however, the incumbent had seldom been challenged. That happens only in extraordinary times, such as 1987 when I and Tun Ghafar Baba, as Prime Minister and Deputy Prime Minister, were both challenged by Tengku Razaleigh Hamzah and Tun Musa Hitam. By challenging the then Deputy, Tun Ghafar, Anwar was not only violating party tradition but also revealing his impatience to get to the top. When he came to see me about his intentions, I pointed out that it was inappropriate to challenge Tun Ghafar, my nominee for the post of Deputy Prime Minister. I asked him not to stand. For a while, he seemed to heed my words and he did not campaign. But when I criticised some UMNO leaders in Terengganu for staying on too long and not giving a chance to young aspirants, he interpreted my advice there to mean that I wanted older leaders like Tun Ghafar to step down. He assumed the challenge would be in accord with my views, and so without asking for my permission, he began his campaign.

How he managed it I do not know, but more than two-thirds of the divisions nominated him for Deputy President. Even divisions known to be Tun Ghafar's strong supporters failed to nominate him and it became obvious that Tun Ghafar would lose. Seeing the situation as hopeless, he chose not to contest and Anwar won uncontested.

I did not want to remove Tun Ghafar but what would have been my excuse if I did not appoint the new Deputy President of UMNO to the Deputy Prime Minister's post? I have always considered and followed the wishes of UMNO. For example, in 1993 when the party elected Tun Abdullah, the former Prime Minister, as a Vice President of UMNO, I brought him back into the Cabinet even though he had supported Tengku Razaleigh against me in the 1987 UMNO elections.

Later I was informed that Anwar was very active in cultivating support for himself among UMNO divisions and urging them to criticise me. Even then, I told myself, as he was going to be the next Prime Minister, it did not matter. I wanted to maintain a good working relationship with him, so I was prepared to overlook his impatience regarding my retirement. It is hard to fault a politician for being ambitious, tireless, and forward-looking. Perhaps Malay society now needed such leaders and more of them. We had come a long way from the Tunku's easy affability that had so troubled me in the late 1960s. Perhaps that was a good thing, and Anwar's aggressive approach exemplified the new Malay politics.

As I said when Anwar joined UMNO, many senior members of the party did not like him because he posed a threat to their own ambitions. Anwar and Tun Abdullah did not get on well because when Tun Abdullah was a civil servant, he had been tasked by Tun Razak with countering Anwar's leadership of Muslim students and youth. With Anwar's rapid rise in UMNO, he became a threat to Tun Abdullah's leadership of the Penang state UMNO. Tun Abdullah's fears became reality when Anwar became Deputy President and replaced Tun Ghafar as Deputy Prime Minister. Anwar quickly displaced Tun Abdullah as the Penang liaison head of UMNO and Barisan Nasional.

With time I noticed that Anwar's criticism of the Government, especially with regard to alleged cronyism, was becoming more open. He would speak against this abuse of public trust, spicing his words with veiled hints that it involved me. He condemned cronyism in principle, which I applauded, but his words were double-edged. His rhetoric offered a morality play in which he was Good, while whoever he opposed was Bad. When he spoke out against cronyism at the top, to whom was he alluding if not to me? Above me, and above him, there was no one else. Moreover, by condemning cronyism as he did, he suggested that he never indulged in it himself. It was a clever strategy to deflect attention from his own cronyism. Senior UMNO members warned me that he was up to no good and that he was not loyal to the party. After ousting Tun Ghafar, they said, his next target was me. But I was not worried. I did not think he would succeed and was very confident of my own position.

Uncomfortable as the situation had become, I thought I could handle it and I doubted he would get enough support if he turned against me. While I still saw Anwar as an effective leader, I felt that his desire to oust me was premature. But my confidence in myself and my chosen direction has always allowed me to live with disagreement, with people who think and act differently from myself. Perhaps I was being over-confident, but to me it is important that all factions be accommodated within the party. If you remove one leader, another will surely step forward to take his place. There is no guarantee that he would be less ambitious and problematic than his predecessor. You would still have to deal with him. If Anwar were to challenge me, I knew he would have supporters and that might weaken UMNO, but I was prepared to handle all that.

A number of people close to me — people who had no stake or interest in politics — also told me what they saw and heard about Anwar. They were not put up to it so I had no reason to question their motives. By then, all sorts of stories were being circulated and encouraged. Some of these rumours of corruption and cronyism against me reached the Press. Eventually, to put an end to those allegations, I had to publish the names of all the people who had won government contracts when Anwar was Minister of Finance. The list showed that many of those who won negotiated contracts were his friends and members of his family. There were also one or two of my family members and people connected to me, but their contracts were considerably smaller. Crying "Thief!" is a good ploy to divert attention from yourself and that was precisely the strategy that Anwar employed and, I am afraid, continues to employ.

Publicly, as I have noted, Anwar cut an impressive figure. He also made an impact upon American and Western journalists with his seemingly liberal ideas. He arranged for United States senators and congressmen to visit Malaysia every year, paid for by funds he had set up. These senators and congressmen believed him to be a liberal, democratic politician and liked him. At the same time he maintained his contacts with many Muslim activists in the Islamic world. All this groundwork came in useful later;

these connections and that enviable reputation stood him in good stead when he was later tried and convicted on criminal charges in our courts. They believed his story that he was framed so as to prevent him from becoming Prime Minister.

No doubt the Americans thought that he would make a better Prime Minister than I — a number of their leading newspapers and business journals said so. I was abrasive and had never been liked by the Americans. Still, I tried to please Anwar by seeing the visiting senators and congressmen and participating in the seminars he had arranged. And why not? I did not question his objective of inviting the Americans to Malaysia every year, presumably so that they might get to know Malaysia better. When action was taken against him for breaches of our criminal law these people all condemned me and demanded his release. The price of his international popularity was something my Government had to deal with later when he was arrested and tried on criminal charges, and when he claimed that it was he who dealt successfully with the currency crisis.

At home, some UMNO leaders whom he did not like or who were close to me began to complain that, as Deputy Prime Minister, he was making life difficult for them. One Chief Minister was accused of having an affair with a schoolgirl. He claimed that the Deputy Prime Minister had directed that the case be given wide publicity. In the end, the Chief Minister lost his position.

In 1993 the then Inspector-General of Police, Tun Mohamad Hanif Omar, came to see me with evidence of Anwar's sexual misconduct. It was so serious an accusation that I thought it simply could not be true and may have been part of an outlandish plot against him. I did not suggest that any action be taken, but the police, as is their practice, continued their surveillance. No more reports came to me until 1998 when, as I will return to in a later chapter, the evidence was so compelling that I had to act.

Meanwhile, Anwar's attempts to force me to step down became more and more obvious. Even though I was not too concerned, relations between us were becoming strained and I was beginning to have doubts that he would be a good leader and successor to me. But I had to carry on as if nothing was happening, just as I had when things became difficult with Tun Musa. That is how I deal with people — I don't accuse them of anything, I just carry on.

When Tun Musa went against me, I thought he only harmed himself because he became unpopular within the party. Later, I was willing to have him back and I didn't protest when his supporters wanted him to return as Deputy Prime Minister and Deputy President of the party. That had proven to be the right strategy. Now, with Anwar, I took the same view and approach. Anwar remained his disarming self and behaved as if nothing was happening. Meanwhile, I heard that there were Cabinet members who were going around saying unpleasant things about me. Yet despite what he and his allies were doing and the underhand methods he was using, Anwar retained a reputation for religious piety and uprightness.

I kept my doubts to myself. I felt confident that should he mount a direct challenge to my presidency, I would still be able to defeat him. As things turned out, my plans to step down after the Commonwealth Games in Kuala Lumpur in 1998 were thwarted by the assault against the Malaysian ringgit by international currency traders in 1997-1998. No matter what my personal plans were, I could not stand down under those circumstances. I could not leave at a time when the country was facing a major crisis. I thought it was my duty to put things right first. This was especially so because Anwar, as my successor, seemed unable to deal with the situation. He had followed the IMF formula and the situation had become worse. Unless corrective actions were taken the country that my successor would inherit would go into economic depression.

# Chapter 32:
# Realigning Malaysia In The World

When I assumed office, few people had heard of Malaysia or even knew where it was. When a Malaysian abroad told people where he came from, the next question was always, "Where is that?" For a long time foreigners thought Malaysia was in China, in the Himalayas, or even in Africa, confusing it with Malawi or Madagascar. Everyone knew Indonesia, Thailand, the Philippines and Singapore. Even Vietnam was better known, largely because of the war there. Malaysia, a Southeast Asian country just like the others, was the least known, and that made attracting tourists and investors very difficult.

This ignorance about our country was not surprising as Malaysia was not in the news much in its early years. Nothing spectacular had happened in our struggle for Independence, which was negotiated rather than won by force of arms. There was no long saga of bloodshed and strife of the kind that journalists and their editors love to report, as had been the case in the protracted pursuit of independence by Indonesia and Vietnam in our region, or Algeria and Cyprus closer to Europe. Our new nation had initially been called the Federation of Malaya, the successor to what many people knew as British Malaya. It was not too difficult to connect the two. But later it became Malaysia, the new name adopted after Sabah, Sarawak and Singapore joined the already independent Federation of Malaya in 1963. Singapore's separation from Malaysia in 1965 briefly attracted international media attention, as did Indonesia's Confrontation against the enlarged federation between 1963 and 1965. But overall, we remained a low-profile member of the international community, not known by most foreigners.

In the late 1960s our Ministry of Foreign Affairs had an allocation of only about RM14 million. We had diplomatic relations with very few countries, mainly those in the Commonwealth. Both the Tunku and Tun Razak had been pro-Western in their policies, although Tun Razak did pay wider attention to the rest of the world, as his state visits to the USSR and then China in 1974 showed.

When he became Prime Minister, Tun Hussein essentially followed Tun Razak's policy as he did not have much time to change things. At heart he was still very close to the West, but he upheld the principle of non-alignment, which Tun Razak had embraced. Tun Hussein was a peaceable man who was wary of causing anger towards Malaysia and always tried to avoid conflict. He mended fences with Brunei, which had accused Malaysia of helping anti-establishment Bruneians during Tun Razak's time.

When I took over I decided to review and change our foreign policy. I felt we should ignore ideological differences and be friendly with everyone. My first priority was building stronger relationships with the member countries of ASEAN as they were our close neighbours, and whatever happened to them would affect us. In any case, ASEAN was formed not as an economic community like the European Union, but in order to avoid conflicts between neighbours, such as when Indonesia launched its Confrontation against Malaysia and the Philippines claimed Sabah. I was determined that conflicts between Malaysia and her neighbours should be avoided through good relations with ASEAN countries. At a time when national sentiment in Malaysia ran strongly in the opposite direction, I even sought to establish good relations with Singapore after it separated from Malaysia.

417

The second priority was the small countries of the Pacific and Africa, followed by Islamic countries, and only then, the Commonwealth. I made moving the Commonwealth down Malaysia's list of foreign relations priorities very clear when I chose not to attend the biennial Commonwealth Heads of Government Meeting (CHOGM)[1] in Melbourne in 1981 and again in New Delhi in 1983. Sir Shridath Ramphal, the Commonwealth Secretary-General, and many others tried to persuade me to attend but my answer was always the same: I needed to see other countries first.

The world powers and the European countries came last. To the East, I regarded relations with Japan and South Korea as most important. Later, when the People's Republic of China stopped aiding Malaysian communist insurgents, I hastened to develop strong relations with that giant nation as well.

---

[1]  Every two years, Commonwealth leaders meet to discuss global and Commonwealth issues, policies and initiatives for the group.

I began pursuing these new priorities by paying visits to the member countries of ASEAN, with the exception of the Philippines. Wanting to establish good relations with Indonesia, our biggest ASEAN neighbour and the closest in terms of ethnicity, culture and language, I made a point of visiting Indonesia first. President Suharto received me and Hasmah at Halim Perdanakusuma International Airport with a few members of his Cabinet. I inspected a guard of honour with the President and we then drove together to the guest house behind the Merdeka Palace. Lining the streets along the way were large portraits of myself and President Suharto. The President was a good host and conducted me to the very door of my suite, wishing me a good stay and politely telling me that if I needed anything, his protocol officers would see to it.

Then I visited Thailand, where General Prem Tinsulanonda, the Prime Minister, received me at the military section of Don Muang airport. Again there was a guard of honour and after inspecting it, I was driven to the guest house with General Prem. We held discussions on bilateral issues and were entertained with a lavish dinner, followed by a special Thai dance performance in which the friendship between Thailand and Malaysia was the theme. I was satisfied that relations with Thailand would be good, and General Prem was particularly friendly.

I did not visit the Philippines because the problem of their claim over Sabah had not yet been resolved. The practice then was for the leaders of Malaysia and the Philippines to meet only during ASEAN or other international conferences. It was not until General Fidel Ramos was elected President that he visited Malaysia unofficially. This visit broke the ice but official visits were still not made as their claim to Sabah was still extant. Our differences could not be resolved as Filipino legislators saw it as a good issue, one that could always win popular support for the champions of the return of Sabah to the Philippines. Their politics are so divisive and fragmented, that no Philippine President has ever been strong enough to drop the claim. So the claim remains alive to this day. But at ASEAN meetings, we were cordial and we did not let the issue sour our personal relations.

It was only in Singapore that I experienced a very unusual kind of protocol. As a visiting head of government, I was only greeted by a protocol officer at the entrance to the Prime Minister's office and was then required to wait in an adjacent holding room until the Prime Minister was ready to see me. I was made to wait for about 15 minutes and felt very sorely used. This was not the proper way to greet a foreign visitor of equal rank. Whether this is their routine procedure for all heads of government, I do not know, but I thought that if this was good enough protocol for Singapore, it should be good enough for Malaysia when receiving the Singapore Prime Minister. So when Lee Kuan Yew, and later his successors, came to Kuala Lumpur, I followed his precedent. I always received other heads of government at the main door; we also accorded them a ceremonial welcome at Parliament House, complete with a military guard of honour.

On that first visit I made to Singapore, there was no state dinner nor were there any formal speeches so far as I can remember. I also paid a courtesy call on President Benjamin Henry Shears, who had been my professor of obstetrics and gynaecology at medical college in Singapore. We spoke for about 20 minutes before his aide-de-camp entered the room and said that the President had another appointment. I took the hint, got up and left.

Talking to Lee Kuan Yew was a one-sided affair. His style of conversation, like his manner of addressing the Malaysian Parliament when he was a member, was to lecture his listeners about what was right and what was wrong. But during our discussion, I came to realise that he did not know all that much, especially on technological matters. I remember one occasion when he mentioned that he had just come across a new process of desalination. But it was not new at all and had been used generally for years.

As related elsewhere, I had often crossed swords with Lee, dating back to the time when we were both Members of the Malaysian Parliament. Our opinions were usually diametrically opposed to each other. Our relationship then was proper, professionally appropriate for political opponents, but never very friendly. Still, as Prime Minister, I worked hard at trying to resolve our various problems with Singapore but found them unresponsive.

When it came to the West, I was faced with other foreign policy expectations. The US Ambassador to Malaysia was already planning my visit to Washington DC, immediately after I took office, presumably so I could pay homage to Ronald Reagan, the new President. He told me how difficult it was to get an appointment with the President and apparently expected me to appreciate what he was doing to arrange this visit. However, I directed Wisma Putra[2] to inform the United States Ambassador I was not going to Washington any time soon. Not surprisingly, I did not see the Ambassador again after that.

Had I gone to Washington, I would have been just another Third World leader going to beg for aid. I was not going to ask for anything and had already decided that Malaysia would not plead for anything. If we had no money, we would simply cut our spending. Malaysians had to show that we had self-esteem.

I wanted to show the great and powerful nations that as far as I was concerned, Malaysia did not care about their size or importance. So, after visiting the ASEAN countries, instead of the US I went to Fiji, Tonga, Western Samoa, Papua New Guinea and the Maldives. These may be small countries but I was not thinking of the economic, trade or diplomatic benefits of visiting them. I simply believed in making as many friends as I could. As things turned out, their support often proved useful later, especially in their votes in the Commonwealth and at the United Nations. I also felt that there would be genuine hospitality and appreciation of Malaysia's interest in them. A Malaysian leader can never visit Washington with such expectations. But I must admit that when Datuk Seri Anwar Ibrahim, as Deputy Prime Minister, visited Washington he was given a red-carpet welcome.

Very early in my administration I started the Malaysia Technical Cooperation Programme, whereby we invited many developing countries to send their people here for training. They had long expressed an interest in the way we were developing our economy, particularly in how we were attracting foreign direct investments. They were also curious about how we set up our administration, our diplomatic service and the production-sharing agreements which PETRONAS, our national petroleum company, had concluded with the major international oil companies.

---

2    Wisma Putra is the office that houses Malaysia's Ministry of Foreign Affairs.

All this, I maintained, was cooperation, not aid. We insisted on the word because this programme allowed our countries to work together in a spirit of mutuality and cooperation, not inequality and manipulation. We were not giving aid, as we were a Third World country ourselves. Nevertheless over the years we have spent millions of ringgit on this programme, which has helped us make friends around the world. We have also reaped the benefits of helping them. After training their diplomats, for example, our delegates and businessmen would often meet friendly faces at international meetings or when visiting their countries. When we wanted to do business in Africa, it became easier for Malaysians because African officials were familiar with us. I asked our Foreign Affairs Ministry to have our ambassadors concentrate on business and trade opportunities, and not just on the politics of the countries to which they were accredited. Whatever their ideology, we wanted to be friends with them.

We also had no wish to interfere in their domestic affairs. In Myanmar, for example, where the military dictatorship has drawn much criticism from other countries, what good would interference do in the long run? The situation must be remedied by the people of Myanmar themselves. It must be their own work or it will mean little and will not last. Perhaps we had learnt this lesson from the big powers, who offered aid but with strings attached. In the end, the client states hated them.

Other governments may look down on smaller, less developed nations and cannot see what is to be gained by being friendly with them. We were not completely altruistic in our motives but we believed in our slogan, "prosper thy neighbour", when helping them and our friends to thrive. When these countries prospered, we were able to trade and do business with them.

At the Non-Aligned Movement (NAM) meeting in Belgrade in 1989, I was approached by Sir Shridath Ramphal about setting up a smaller, more effective group of developing countries. He also approached five or six leaders from South America, Africa and Asia. The NAM group was too big. At its biennial meetings leaders made country statements, but it was unable to attend to any of the problems of the South in a meaningful way. So Sir Shridath suggested that a group of 15 developing countries drawn from Asia, Africa and South America might be better able to discuss in-depth the problems of the developing countries and perhaps hold dialogues with the G-7 (now G-8)[3] highly industrialised countries.

I liked the idea and agreed to organise the group, which led to the inaugural meeting of the G-15 in Kuala Lumpur in 1990. It was attended by Malaysia, Indonesia, India, Iran, Sri Lanka, Argentina, Brazil, Chile, Venezuela, Colombia, Algeria, Egypt, Nigeria, Jamaica, and Zimbabwe. The Latin American countries were lukewarm in their support but the Asians were enthusiastic. Discussions were substantial and focused mainly on trade between the developing countries and economic development. This Group was later known as the South-South Group.

However, the G-7 refused to recognise the G-15 as a group that represented the South or as the voice of the developing nations. That was, of course, their choice, which they did not have to justify — they merely ignored the G-15. When Indonesian President Suharto went on our behalf to Tokyo for the G-7 meeting in 1993, he was kept waiting and eventually did not even get to see them. This behaviour is typical of developed countries. They preferred dealing with the Group of 77,[4] which included many small and weak countries beholden to them. Whatever efforts made to present the views of our group at G-7 meetings, to point out how its past decisions had adversely affected the developing countries, were fruitless. There was no interest and no response.

France's President Jacques Chirac was perhaps the friendliest of the G-7 leaders towards the countries of the South. I myself knew Chirac well, so when France was scheduled to host a G-7 meeting, I wrote to him. Chirac decided not to invite the G-15 as a group, but did invite certain leaders from among the countries of the South. I was one of those who attended the G-7 meeting in Evian in 2002. During one of the sessions, I was able to point out the damage done to developing countries like Malaysia by the Plaza Accord.[5] Strengthening the yen by almost 300 per

422

3   The Group of Eight (G-8) is a forum for Canada, France, Germany, Italy, Japan, Russia, the UK, the US and the European Union (although the EU does not have the right to host or chair a meeting).

4   The Group of 77 is an informal grouping of developing countries that cooperates to promote its collective economic agendas at the UN. As a coalition, the Group also works to give itself a stronger negotiating platform in the UN.

5   In 1985, France, West Germany, Japan, the US and the UK signed the Plaza Accord that agreed, among other things, to depreciate the US dollar in relation to the Japanese yen.

cent increased the yen debts of the poor countries accordingly, and this was grossly unfair. The poor countries were effectively made to pay to solve the financial problems of the rich countries, especially the economic costs of the imbalance between the Japanese and US currencies. We, who could least afford it, were made to pay the price of rescuing the dollar. I even tried to talk to the Japanese about our problem but they could do little about it. In the end, the Plaza Accord cost them dearly too. They won a place as a key player in international finance but at the price of forfeiting their competitive economic edge. The cost of their exports rose and the long Japanese economic recession began shortly after. The underlying structural imbalance between the US and Japanese economies was not remedied. The Japanese could do little to help anybody, even themselves.

After I stepped down as Prime Minister, the G-15 continued to meet. The membership had grown to 19 but it continued to be called the G-15. Its thirteenth meeting was held in 2006 in Havana, Cuba, on the sidelines of a NAM conference. Raul Castro, brother of Cuban President Fidel Castro, spoke in support of the Group as a guest, as Cuba is not a member. Despite the opposition it encountered from the G-7 nations, the G-15 Group did enhance South-South cooperation.

Malaysia's change of tack did not endear us to the developed, ethnically-European countries of the Commonwealth. Certainly their Press became more and more unfriendly. Even when Malaysia prospered during my stewardship, I earned no credit and instead came in personally for a lot of criticism and outright condemnation for my style of running the country. I was described as a dictator. It must have been galling for them not to be able to show up our failure after Independence like many other former colonies of theirs.

In response I decided to be tough and critical of the ethnic Europeans, which was not difficult to do as they provided critics with ample cause. I felt strongly about their unfairness, their overbearing attitude, their self-righteousness, and their habit of being quick to use force on the weak. Our own independent stand attracted worldwide attention, especially among developing countries. However, I did not want to lose them as a market either, since they were rich and we had a lot to sell to them. Despite our criticisms of their governments, I found that their business people still liked what Malaysia had to offer. They did not always support their own governments' policies. They knew Malaysia well and realised that a lot of what was said about Malaysia by their media and their governments was inaccurate. Thus, our policy of being business-friendly paid off.

My natural inclination is always to adhere to Malay *adat* or etiquette, but I would have got nowhere in my negotiations with industrialised nations had I been self-effacing. *Politesse* is a two-way thing; practising courtesy towards those who are deaf to its subtle tones is fruitless. I never minced words and soon got a reputation for being uncharacteristically blunt for an Asian, and a Malay at that.

When I addressed the United Nations General Assembly for the first time in September 1982, I chose to speak about Antarctica. A number of the developed countries had claimed tracts of the continent, and there was no one there to struggle against these colonialists. Antarctica is truly *terra nullius*, a land that is inhabited by nobody and which accordingly can be claimed by anybody. I saw no reason why those powerful countries should claim even uninhabited land, any more than the right to grab — as they did in the imperial age — inhabited land and dominate over the "natives". Uninhabited land should belong to everybody, to the world community. If there are resources to be extracted then the whole world is entitled to benefit. Antarctica, I resolved, should be a global common. For me it was a matter of principle.

A number of countries, mostly the rich ones, had entered into an Antarctic Treaty. It did not take into consideration the rights of the poor countries, which could not afford to even reach that remote frozen continent. Accordingly in 1983, Malaysia launched its opposition to the Antarctic Treaty, which supposedly regulated the activities of people on that continent. I again raised the issue at the seventh NAM summit in New Delhi, India, in 1983 and asked for a review of the current legal regime that governed Antarctica. The response was lukewarm. For most NAM countries, Antarctica itself was not of pressing concern and they were slow to recognise the general principles involved. They felt that rich countries exploiting oil and mineral resources there would not affect them.

We saw things differently and established the Malaysian Antarctic Research Programme in 1999. We made no claim but merely tried to involve Malaysians in research work on the continent. We succeeded in generating international interest in this cold continent and nowadays, no additional national flags are planted there. Exclusivism has been replaced by talk about common concerns and research cooperation. Malaysia's Antarctica policy has been vindicated and the agreement that there should be no mining or oil exploration and production there has been upheld. Having raised this question of Antarctica, I developed a curiosity regarding the continent and wanted to see it for myself. In 2002, before I stepped down as Prime Minister, I visited Antarctica and it was an experience which I will never forget.

It is a cold and lonely place, consisting of land covered by thick layers of snow and ice built up over thousands of years. Nothing seems to grow there, and the only inhabitants we saw were the penguins, seals and birds. To land and walk upon that icy ground was strange. The water was so cold that, if you fell in, you would die within minutes. We travelled around on a Zodiac inflatable boat wearing life-jackets. Once, the captain brought our ship alongside an iceberg so we could touch it. Then the crew put out a ladder and we walked onto the iceberg, careful not to step onto the thin patches for fear of falling through into the sea.

The roughest part of the journey was crossing Drake Passage, the 800km-wide expanse of open water where the Pacific and Atlantic Oceans meet between Cape Horn and the northern coast of Antarctica. Here, the enormous force of the Antarctic Circumpolar Current surges. For two days out and another two days coming back, the sea was very rough. Sleep was impossible as you simply had to cling hard to your bed. Hasmah never got up from hers, as the boat was so unsteady that she was constantly seasick. She was not the only one. I was fine, however, and was able to move around and eat.

Throughout my term in office, I continued to use my official international visits to signal Malaysia's changed foreign policy priorities. After I visited the island nations of Oceania, I decided to visit the Islamic countries. Malaysia had not yet made much progress in its development, but we were already quite well known in that part of the world because our first Prime Minister, Tunku Abdul Rahman, was instrumental in the founding of the Organisation of the Islamic Conference, or OIC.[6] I was received politely in all the countries except for one, which I will not name. That country refused to set a date for my visit. Apparently it had something against me, although I never discovered what it was. Later however, when Malaysia had demonstrated its capacity for both stability and rapid growth, and had begun to voice the views and feelings of Muslim countries and Muslims worldwide, I was invited by that country to receive an award as a Muslim leader.

The Arab countries were not yet as rich as they were to become later but, like many other developing countries, they saw no particular need to be close to Malaysia. Only the Kuwait Investment Fund was active in Malaysia then but even they pulled out after some time. The Arab countries looked up to Europe and America and seemed to believe that the Europeans were supermen who could work miracles. European countries and their business people always have an advantage when dealing with Arab countries. Even Japan found difficulty convincing these countries that it could do what the Europeans could do, and do it better.

It must be admitted that at that time, Malaysia did not think much of the little states which dotted the Persian Gulf either. They had only just discovered oil but they still had the appearance of overgrown fishing villages — their gleaming new glass towers had not yet been built. My visits to these small emirates were driven by no immediate economic considerations, but stemmed solely from my policy of friendly engagement with all Islamic countries.

Of the Islamic North African countries, I visited Egypt, the only Arab country with a large population. Cairo fascinated me. I did little official business there but did go on a tour of the Aswan Dam and Luxor, with its spectacular temples and tombs. I had flown over the Nile River several times and was much impressed by the greenness of the land on either side. The two strips were of uniform width and they stopped abruptly where the

---

[6] The Organisation of the Islamic Conference (OIC) was established in 1971 to unite the global Muslim community and promote its political, economic, and social interests.

desert resisted cultivation. I understood then why the Egyptian civilisation was possible and why it prospered. The people had learnt to irrigate the land in order to grow grain and other crops. Not needing to gather and hunt for food, and with ample agricultural produce, the Egyptians could turn their minds and attention to improvements to their way of life and the acquisition of knowledge. All the early civilisations had developed along river basins, the most remarkable of which, apart from the Nile, were those in the valleys of the Tigris and Euphrates, the Indus and the Yangtze.

When I went to Mali in 1982, I noticed the River Niger flowing through Mali's arid land just like the Nile in Egypt's desert. I wondered why the people living on the banks of the Niger did not cultivate the land the way the Egyptians did. After our Ambassador to Mali told me that he had grown Malaysian vegetables and plants there and that the land was very fertile, I decided to help the Malians make use of their land to enrich themselves and develop their country. Malaysia set up an agricultural station and sent agriculturists to grow vegetables and breed goats. Clearly the River Niger valley could be developed like the Nile Valley. Unfortunately, the Malians did not show a keenness to develop their agricultural potential. Between geographical fact or environmental potential and rational economic action, something else intervenes: culture and values. These, I had learnt, had enormous consequences that had to be addressed in the case of the Malays. Perhaps something similar was occurring with the Malians. After three years, the Malaysians came back and the station was neglected.

We were more successful in Malawi, where we also set up an agricultural station. We showed them how to make use of the water from Lake Victoria and cultivate their land. They had this huge freshwater lake that, strangely, they did not use. Having no tradition of agriculture, they did not establish a civilisation like that of the Egyptians. To do that takes a certain kind of people. The Malays too, lived on the riverbanks which provided water, fish, and transportation, and while they developed agriculture, it was not a great agrarian civilisation. Yet our own *alam Melayu* (Malay world) cousins in Java did: not in the coastal areas connected to international trade but in the interior. The reasons for this difference in pre-colonial development trajectories are factors that we must ponder and probe if we are ever to fathom the heart of the Malay dilemma.

By the time I stepped down as Prime Minister, I was told that the agriculture station we had created was better accepted by the Malawians. Whatever the initial cultural inhibitions, it seems they can be overcome.

In those days few people believed that Asia and Asians might provide development models for other countries — certainly not Malaysia, which, it was assumed, would never be anything more than a backward, Third World country. That, anyway, was the prevailing attitude at the time. I realised this when I invited a few African leaders in the Commonwealth to visit Malaysia. They showed no interest; apparently, there was nothing for them to see or to learn from another Third World country. But I was convinced otherwise. Even in the late 1980s, Malaysia was already moving ahead of most other developing countries.

I decided to attend the 1985 Commonwealth meeting in the Bahamas in order to get to know the leaders of the African, Caribbean and other developing countries which were members of the Commonwealth. At the Bahamas meeting, the Prime Minister Sir Lynden O. Pindling was embarrassed by the Opposition holding a demonstration on the road the delegates were to take to a state dinner. An attempt was made to bypass the demo by taking boats but, somehow, it did not work out.

These small island states should learn from Singapore, where the Opposition was not allowed to lift up their heads. There would never be such a demonstration in Singapore. But these small states were so much under the critical eyes of the European members of the Commonwealth and nearby US that they had to put up with political instability and poor development in order to prove their democratic credentials.

In 1987 I attended the Commonwealth meeting in Vancouver. I had earlier decided that the only way to get the leaders of the countries of Africa and the Caribbean to visit Malaysia was by hosting the Commonwealth Heads of Government Meeting. At the Vancouver meeting, Malaysia made a bid to host the 1989 CHOGM. I think Sir Shridath and many of the delegates regarded Malaysia as the prodigal son who wanted to return. They were therefore quite enthusiastic about our desire to host the meeting and gave their full support.

On our side, we wanted to show that Malaysia could be a good host. This was going to be the first big international meeting for us and we did not want anything to go wrong or to fall short in any way. I insisted that we plan properly, looking into every detail. We carried out several dry runs to detect any shortcomings.

We gave our retired ambassadors the task of welcoming our guests, many of whom they knew. A senior ambassador was chosen to direct and manage the whole conference. Dinners and entertainment for heads of government and spouses were arranged. Traditional dancers and a choir from the Yamaha Music School practised hard to display the full range of Malaysian talents.

The 1989 Malaysian meeting would also choose a new Commonwealth Secretary-General to take over from Sir Shridath. I was to preside over the election. There were two contestants: Malcolm Fraser, a former Australian Prime Minister, and Chief Emeka Anyaoku of Nigeria. The Chief won. As soon as the result was announced, Fraser left Malaysia for home. As host, I presided over the conference as well.

This was also where I used a prompter for the first time when delivering a public speech. Some of the government heads congratulated me on my ability to deliver a long speech, apparently without reference to my notes. I did not disabuse them of the idea but I found it strange that so many people in the political spotlight then were not aware of the prompter and other technological possibilities. Generally, the conference went very well and the delegates congratulated Malaysia for the well-organised and efficiently-run meeting we had staged.

Following our hosting of the Commonwealth Conference in 1989 and my attendance at subsequent conferences, I formed good relationships with the heads of government of the African and Caribbean states. Their visit to Malaysia in 1989 convinced them that a Third World country could develop and prosper. After seeing Malaysia's achievements and the prosperity of its people, many made repeated personal visits to Malaysia or sent their Ministers and senior officials to exchange views and experiences about governance and development. In time, we agreed to hold frequent dialogues on administration, planning and development. This later led to the

Langkawi International Dialogues[7] and the Southern African International Dialogue,[8] which consolidated Malaysia's relations with the countries of Africa and the Caribbean. The dialogues were attended by many African heads of government, including those outside the Commonwealth. Caribbean countries usually sent representatives and they held their own Caribbean Dialogues to exchange ideas and regional experiences.

These initiatives advanced Malaysia's foreign policy objectives of becoming close to other developing countries. Malaysians, including Malaysian businessmen, were welcomed there so when business opportunities narrowed in Malaysia, our people could turn to these small countries to find work and to trade. Malays who had long relied on the award of government contracts now proved that they could find opportunities and do business in these countries as foreign contractors and service providers. They had come of age internationally and our good relations with other developing countries enabled them, and Malaysia, to prove their capabilities.

I had made a point of developing friendly relations with Japan, South Korea and China. Japan helped us greatly through investments and support for our Look East policy. Today many Malaysians have studied and been trained in Japan and South Korea, where they acquired not only knowledge and skills but the work ethic that underlay the success of those two countries. The South Koreans provided us with the latest model of how a backward country could make tremendous leaps towards becoming a great industrial nation. We learnt a great deal from them about industrialisation.

China was not yet an open country when I visited it in 1985, when Deng Xiao Peng[9] was in charge. Lee Kuan Yew had once told me that we should not fear China because it was a poor and backward country. He was aware of our fears of the Chinese desire to spread the communist ideology in Southeast Asia and our belief that the American "Domino Theory" would

---

[7]  The Langkawi International Dialogue (LID), first held in 1995, promotes partnerships between Commonwealth leaders, businessmen, social groups, civil servants, and other professionals to enhance collective socioeconomic and business development.

[8]  The Southern African International Dialogue (SAID) encourages smart partnerships and networks that can lead to the development of southern Africa.

[9]  Deng Xiao Peng's reforms helped turn China into a market-oriented economy by encouraging, among others, private enterprise and foreign investments, and changing the focus of local industry to the production of everyday consumer goods.

be proven right as one country after another would fall to the communists. What I saw in China when I stopped over in Shanghai and Beijing on my way to North Korea when I was Deputy Prime Minister had convinced me at the time that Lee was right.

We had problems at first with China's support of the mainly Chinese communist insurgents in Malaysia, but as China gradually withdrew its backing, relations between us improved. Deng had visited Malaysia when Chou En-Lai was President and I was still Deputy Prime Minister. He had wanted to talk to Tun Hussein, but the Prime Minister asked me to meet him instead and the two of us ended up having a very long, private discussion. Deng was interested in the development of Malaysia and asked innumerable questions about our economy and our industrialisation policies. I answered as best as I could but some of the details he wanted stumped me. He asked how many tons of steel Malaysia produced, which I didn't know. Deng proved to be pleasant and very curious about every aspect of how we had developed our country.

When he succeeded Chou En-Lai, he opened up China and formulated the socialist market philosophy. I became convinced China was going to be a great economic power and that Malaysia must develop good relations with it, ideological differences notwithstanding. We were familiar with the diligence, skill and enterprise of the Chinese in Malaysia. If a few million of them could be so successful in a foreign environment, how much more successful might the 1.3 billion people in China be?

In the early days of communist rule, too much emphasis had been placed on ideology. But as Deng himself had often said, "it does not matter whether the cat is black or white, as long as it catches the mouse". He was pragmatic and favoured what worked and it did not matter to him whether the practices were ideologically proper or not, as long as China developed. And develop it did — by leaps and bounds — astounding the whole world.

Whether we liked it or not, we had to live with China as our neighbour. I had never liked the US policy of containing China as it caused great tension in Asia and boded no good for Malaysia. We did not care to have the United States Pacific Fleet in the region to protect us from Chinese aggression, and I did not think China was going to invade us. So what was the need for the US naval force here? China had long been an imperial nation, yet it had never indulged in systematic conquest and colonisation as the Europeans did. On those grounds, I decided, we should not fear China. Instead we should be friends and support its integration with the rest of the world.

I struck up good relations with Chinese leaders, in particular with President Jiang Zemin. Malaysia's goodwill and support are well-known to most informed Chinese citizens. China has now become the world's factory, churning out all kinds of manufactured goods which are very quickly achieving world standards. Their per capita income is below that of Malaysia but their population makes China a huge market. Malaysia is China's biggest trading partner in Southeast Asia and our trade volume continues to grow. I hope our China-friendly foreign policy will continue. We must not fall into the American trap of regarding China as a potential enemy. When you regard a country as a potential enemy, you can be sure that that country will regard you as its current enemy.

Besides China, we also established diplomatic relations with other countries in the communist bloc. I visited the USSR when Mikhail Gorbachev was President. As part of my itinerary I went to Tashkent in Uzbekistan. I also visited Yugoslavia, Romania and Hungary before they decided to give up communism. In the East I visited Vietnam, and as Deputy Prime Minister I had visited North Korea. I was, therefore, well acquainted with communist countries.

I noticed that the communist countries were not as well-developed as the capitalist, free-market nations. There was a certain uniformity about their buildings and cities and the multi-storeyed flats of the workers looked the same everywhere. I was told of a Muscovite flat-dweller who visited Leningrad (now St Petersburg) and after a good dinner and some vodka, casually took a bus to what he thought was his flat and was surprised to find a woman there. The lady was equally surprised and told him it was not his flat. Only then did he remember that he was in Leningrad and not Moscow. The flats all looked the same. There was a happy ending because he married the woman.

I visited steel mills and factories in communist countries and found them shabby and old, while their products were unimpressive. I soon decided that communist countries were not good development models for us. But when it came to weapons, aircraft and tanks, these were quite impressive. Their military equipment may not have looked as good as what others had to offer but it worked just as well, so when we decided to buy fighter jet planes, we turned to Russia.

This decision upset some of the top brass in the Royal Malaysian Air Force as they had been trained in the US and regarded the Russian planes as inferior. Without my knowledge, they decided to buy the F18 fighter jets from the US as well, with part of the allocated fund. By the time I got to know about it, it was too late to change. They suggested that the F18 would complement the MIG-29, which we already had, but we later learnt that the Americans refused to release the so-called source codes, without which the F18 could not be flown in combat. After paying them their price, they don't fully deliver what you have paid for. Worse, you make your ability to defend yourself subject to their approval.

433

This is the problem with the Americans — they want their defence industry to make money and be commercially successful. So they are eager to sell their arms. But they also want to retain control over their use, even after the buyer has taken possession and duly paid for them. Similarly, when we wanted to sell our old, American-built, F5E fighter aircraft, they insisted on deciding who could buy them. In the end we could not sell them as there were no approved buyers; the only countries interested were on the US's prohibited list.

What they did to the Pakistanis was even worse — they took their deposit money and then decided that Pakistan was not the kind of country to which they should sell warplanes. They refused both to deliver the planes and to refund the deposit. Making oneself dependent on such countries is risky.

That is why I took so long to visit the US, which I only did in 1984, three years after I became Prime Minister. Once I decided it was time to go I was determined that I would be properly treated as a Malaysian leader. I was told I would meet President Reagan and have discussions with him, followed by lunch and then a meeting with the Press in the Rose Garden.

There would be no dinner. Anwar, as Deputy Prime Minister, received better treatment than I did when he visited Washington DC. But I did not mind as my visit there was part of a bigger foreign itinerary. I visited Canada first, then flew in a presidential plane from New York to Washington DC and took a helicopter from Dulles Airport to the grounds of the White House. I was told that Blair House, the usual residence for visiting VIPs, was being renovated so I had to stay in a hotel. They provided me with two huge identical Cadillacs to confuse potential assassins, which amused me. While leaders in this great democratic country lived in fear, in Malaysia I could walk freely among my fellow citizens in the supermarket to do my shopping. Reagan's Vice-President George H.W. Bush hosted a dinner for us. I also met several other members of Reagan's administration but nothing of significance resulted from the visit.

I visited Washington DC a second time in 2002 when George W. Bush (Bush Junior) was President. As with my earlier trip, I was told it would be good for Malaysia's relations with the United States. I had always been critical of US policy, but some officials thought it would be a good thing if we appeared not to be too hostile against the US. I decided to try and see whether we would gain anything. This time the visit was arranged by private individuals, much to the chagrin of our Ambassador in Washington DC and Wisma Putra. Led by Tan Sri Megat Junid Megat Ayub, a long-serving Minister who had left the Government, a small group of Malaysians had held discussions with the American Heritage Foundation regarding Malaysia's relations with the United States. They concluded that my visit to Washington DC would help America to understand Malaysia better. I do not know whether my visit achieved this objective — afterwards I certainly could not stop criticising the United States, especially after the US attacked Afghanistan and Iraq.

Bush Sr had been a much more likeable person and a good host, but I had never seen such blatant disregard for world opinion as was shown by his son's rough-riding administration. It was as if the rest of the world did not exist. The US apparently could do only one of two things: totally disregard the rest of the world in the pursuit of its own agenda or use its military might, or the threat of it, in seeking total domination of the world. Until it realises that powerful though it may be, it is still a part of this world and it has a need to work with others, the US will be so isolated that it will effectively be sanctioned by the rest of the world.

The younger Bush also won the presidency in a most unbecoming way, chosen by the courts rather than by the people. That would have been unbecoming in any country that calls itself democratic; but from a country that parades itself as democracy's main custodian and practitioner, the election of Bush by the courts was astounding. But more astounding still was the decision by the American Congress and Senate to allow for the torture of prisoners by the Bush administration, apart from detention without trial for indefinite periods.

This President actually lied publicly in order to go to war against Iraq. That war had already killed, maimed and traumatised hundreds of thousands of Iraqis, destroyed towns and cities, and plunged the country into a brutal civil war. Yet, in the face of world condemnation, Bush insisted that it had all been a great success. "Mission accomplished," he claimed. What mission? What accomplishment? He used the presence of weapons of mass destruction as an excuse for invading Iraq and these were proven to be blatant lies. Yet, unfazed, Bush claimed he went to war to remove Iraqi President Saddam Hussein and make Iraq a democracy. But despite his lies and his failures in Iraq, he was re-elected by the American people for a second term. As I have often stated, people get the governments they deserve. The blame is not Bush's alone but also that of the people as a whole who re-elected him and continued to assent to his deceptions and violence.

Everything that the US did increased my dislike of that great nation. When I was young I was very pro-US; I admired the Americans in every way. They fought well in the Pacific War and I believed that their atom bombs saved Malaya from the scorched earth tactics the Japanese were planning should Allied forces land in the Peninsula. At that time, I did not really understand the horrors those diabolical bombs caused in Hiroshima and Nagasaki. After the war our people looked up to the Americans, but later we were puzzled by them. Malaysia did not understand US support for the Indonesian armed forces during the Confrontation; only later did we realise that they were working to bring down President Sukarno. This is a CIA specialty — engineering regime changes. But since it resulted in a regime that was friendlier towards Malaysia, we did not greatly mind this interference in the domestic affairs of a neighbour.

The United States Peace Corps was also a hit in Malaysia and they showed a softer side to that country. But no sooner had the Cold War ended than the world's saviour turned into a monster. The United States would now stop at nothing to ensure its total world hegemony.

How the Americans could ignore the blatant lies told by their President and then vote him in for a second term, I cannot understand. But he was not alone. Tony Blair and Prime Minister John Howard of Australia told the same lies and were also re-elected. But when I told Britain's *Guardian* newspaper in an interview that I had lost faith in democracy, it reported that I had lost faith in the Commonwealth. I do not know if the reporter was hard of hearing but I do know that the Western Press is forever trying to undermine the credibility of leaders they don't approve of.

I know quite a number of Americans, both in business and in government. Many Americans are family friends and they are good, well-meaning people. But they are unusually ignorant about the world. For most of them, the world consists of the US and only the US, which is why they call their national baseball competition, confined entirely to their own country, the World Series. If individuals think that they are the only ones who exist in this world, that limitation in terms of knowledge may be due to mental illness or aberration. For people who could think up of a borderless, globalised world, their gross mental block is amazing. When it happens to a whole nation, this is even more astounding. Yet it is these people who are now in a position to rule the world. The prospect is truly frightening.

As with the United States, I did not immediately make an official visit to Britain. When in 1982 I visited Britain unofficially, Baroness Thatcher met me at the Malaysian High Commission. Despite all our high-level meetings, relations with Britain after we gained our Independence were never smooth. When Baroness Thatcher made an official visit to Malaysia, she became upset over my speech in which I said that Malaysia had no hang-ups regarding our past as a British colony. I pointed out that there was a very British setting in the very heart of Kuala Lumpur for we had maintained the very British Selangor and Lake Clubs, the cricket grounds (now partly taken up by our Dataran Merdeka or Independence Square) and St Mary's Anglican Cathedral next to it.

Yet personally, I got on well with Baroness Thatcher and I greatly regretted the way she was ousted by her party, to be replaced by Sir John Major. She had done wonders reviving an exhausted Britain; she looked upon her country as I look upon Malaysia. We both wanted our countries to succeed. His successor very quickly lost to the Labour Party.

Before Tony Blair became Prime Minister, he paid me a visit at my official residence near Hyde Park in London during one of my trips to England. I rather liked him — he was youthful and full of ideas about rebuilding Britain as a major player in international affairs. He asked quite a number of questions about Malaysia. The next time I met him he was already Prime Minister. After defeating Major, Blair hosted the Commonwealth Conference in Edinburgh in 1997. Malaysia was facing the currency crisis at that time and I made an appointment to see Blair to ask for his support to get the IMF to stop the unfair impoverishment of Malaysia through currency devaluation. But he was less than forthcoming. I suspected he knew he could not influence the IMF to do anything, so I let it pass and came back to work out my own solution. By then I knew that I could not rely on anyone outside our country to help solve our currency problem.

With a standing invitation to call at 10 Downing Street whenever I visited London, I met Blair there several times. Once we talked about Saddam Hussein and I tried to caution Blair against using force against him. I pointed out that when President Hafez al-Assad of Syria died, he was succeeded by his son, who was a much more approachable man. Saddam would not live forever, I said. But Blair responded that Saddam was still young and the "world" could not wait for him to die before putting an end to his depredations.

The British had always been more knowledgeable and experienced about the Arabs and the Middle East than the Americans. They should have known better the dangers of taking a simplistic view of the Middle East and its problems. I had therefore expected the British Government to be less belligerent than the United States. Before the Iraq invasion, Jack Straw, then the Foreign Secretary in Blair's Cabinet, visited Malaysia. I asked him point blank why Britain was associating herself with Bush's aggressive policies. Straw replied that Britain wanted to influence the US to be less belligerent. But as things turned out, it was Britain that was influenced by the US. Perhaps that is the nature of things: the dog wagged the tail, not the reverse. For reasons known only to them, the British allowed themselves to be dragged into a quagmire from which they could not extract themselves. For this, Blair must bear the blame. As for me, I lost my respect for him. I now regard him as a war criminal who should be tried as the German and Japanese leaders were tried and punished after World War II.

The early 1990s saw a period of great political and social change worldwide. Communism had fallen by 1991 and the Cold War was finally over. A new era had begun and there was much rejoicing. Some claimed it was the end of history. Some said a new world order was taking shape. It was certainly new, but was it better? Yugoslavia was violently torn apart as Slovenia and Croatia broke away. Then Bosnia-Herzegovina endured a terrible war as the Serbs committed genocide against the Bosnian Muslims. The world did nothing to help as it watched 200,000 Muslims being slaughtered on TV.

What was happening to the Muslims in Bosnia greatly upset me. In full view of NATO troops the Serbs were conducting ethnic cleansing and nothing was done to stop the massacres. One video clip showed an angry British officer yelling at Serbs who had just burnt down a house with the occupants inside. "What kind of people are you?" he shouted in disgust. But his was a lone anguished voice, not an official government policy or part of any concerted world action. The worst case was in Srebrenica, where Dutch troops moved away from the Bosnians they were supposed to be protecting, allowing the Serbs to openly slaughter 12,000 Bosnian men and boys. The women were gang-raped.

When the United Nations finally decided to send troops there, Malaysia sent the biggest contingent. Our troops had to endure very cold weather but they did not have to fight anyone. They were located in a valley with the Serbs camped above them, but the Serbs left them alone and did not attack the Bosnian villages nearby. We were able to protect the locals, some of whom I believe were Croats. While the fighting was still continuing I visited our troops there, mainly to thank them for their brave service. Though their quarters were cramped, I could see that their spirits were high. I did not see the Serbs but I was conscious throughout that they were on the ground above us and could have lobbed shells into the camp at any time.

Then the Europeans made the bizarre decision not to provide arms to the Bosnians on the grounds that, should the Bosnians be able to defend themselves, more people would be killed. Apparently it was better if only Bosnians were killed. This, we thought, was morally wrong. So we decided to provide them with some light weapons. That may have contravened United Nations orders but at this point the Bosnians had no means to defend themselves. We provided Russian-made missiles which could be fired from a cannon that the Bosnian Muslims already had. Other Muslim countries also provided aid, but to this day Bosnians still think that Malaysia was the country that helped them the most.

What the Serbs did was unimaginably cruel but what the Europeans did was equally appalling. European countries that make up NATO like to lecture us about human rights but their inconsistency is shameful. If a dog gets stuck in a drain, they spend time and money to rescue it. A whole town may become concerned over the fate of one dog. Yet they refused to help innocent people who were being killed.

Malaysia's foreign relations were reoriented during my 22 years as Prime Minister, and the many changes that were implemented have given Malaysia a high profile on the world scene. Today, it is no longer an unknown country "somewhere in China, Africa or the Himalayas". It is even looked upon as a Third World leader. Many have come to Malaysia to learn how an agricultural country could evolve into an industrialised one and how, despite its multiracial and multi-religious population, it was not only able to remain stable but to develop and thrive. They marvelled at our infrastructure, reliable water supply, nationwide electrification and the expressways crisscrossing the country.

Malaysia now has many friends throughout the world. I was gratified recently when a lady who had visited Yemen told me how proud she was to be a Malaysian when she was there. The owner of a restaurant where she was having a meal asked her where she was from. When she said Malaysia, he and his customers had nothing but good things to say about the country. He even refused to let her pay her bill, and said he appreciated what Malaysia had done for the Muslim world, and for its support of Palestine.

Some say to be a big frog in a small pond is no great achievement, but we have proven that even a little frog in a big pool can thumb its nose at the largest, most powerful toad. That it can has not only been gratifying to us, but has also vindicated our foreign and national policies and has brought us self-respect and pride, and given us a sense of accomplishment. Malaysia has shown that a well-intentioned policy of engagement, cooperation and practical involvement with small countries can prove far more beneficial and successful on the international stage than a policy of antagonism, aggression and domination as practised by world powers. There is no need to toady to the powerful.

I am a doctor.
With Hasmah on my graduation day.

With new graduate, Dr Siti Hasmah, one of our
first Malay women doctors, 1955.

Riding is one of my passions.

Hasmah and I during the early years of our marriage.

Doting parents with our first-born, Marina, seen here at two weeks, 1957.

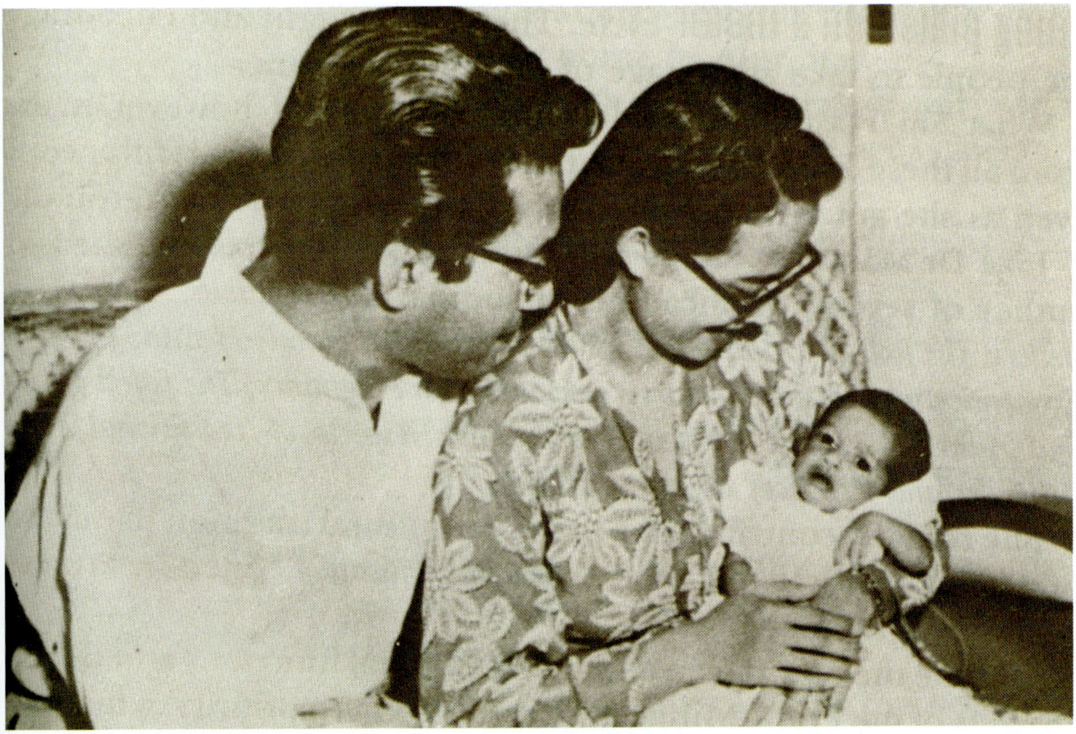

Breakfast with Hasmah at Sri Perdana. With us are Maizura and Mazhar.

Indulging in another favourite hobby, woodcarving, at our Bukit Tunku home.

Making *nasi goreng* (fried rice).

Carving a Bombardier Challenger in our Bukit Tunku home.

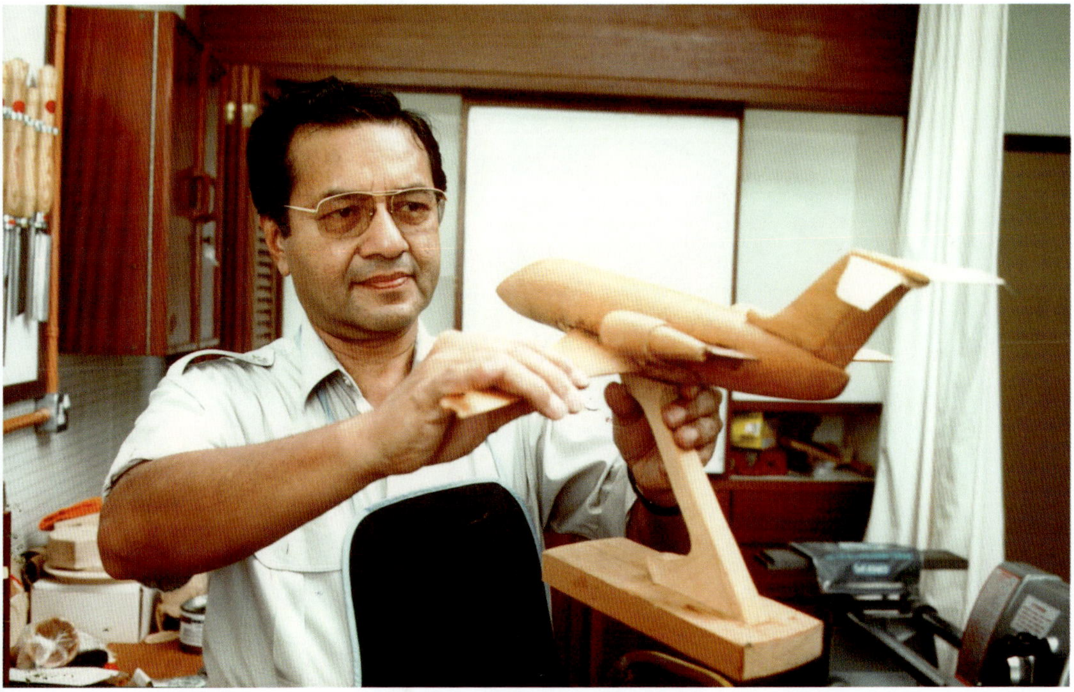

Sailing in the Mediterranean.

Getting a feel of a South African helicopter at LIMA, Langkawi, 1991.

My 100th day as the fourth Prime Minister of Malaysia in October 1981.

With Hasmah in the Antarctic, February 2002.

A nation grieves. Tun Razak's casket arriving at Subang Airport, 1976.

On my favourite horse, Don Lois, in 1994.

One more for the album with Hasmah.

Praying in front of the Kaabah while performing the umrah.

At the Putrajaya launch site, circa 1996.

Riding in Argentina.

On my favourite horse, Don Lois, at the Putrajaya Equine Centre.

Swearing in as Minister of Education as my mentor Tun Abdul Razak looks on.

After 22 years – leaving the Prime Minister's office in Putrajaya, 31 October, 2003.

Hasmah stands behind me as I leave office after 22 years, 31 October, 2003.

Hugging Tun Hussein after he hands over the party leadership and premiership to me at the UMNO General Assembly in June 1981.

At the UMNO General Assembly with party president Tun Hussein.

Guiding Tunku Abdul Rahman at the UMNO General Assembly, September 1985.

With Tunku Abdul Rahman at the launch of the Regional Islamic Dakwah Council of South-East Asia and the Pacific (Riseap) at Parliament House in June 1982.

With Tunku Abdul Rahman at the UMNO General Assembly.

My last official address as Prime Minister at the closing of the 2002 UMNO General Assembly.

One of my saddest moments, announcing my resignation
at the closing of the 2002 UMNO General Assembly in June.

Testing an electric-driven boat in Mitchell, England. (1998).

Trying out a classic electric car in England.

Yet another test drive, this time the electric buggy in Mitchell, England.

Clean-up campaign on Jalan Munshi Abdullah, Kuala Lumpur. Leadership by example.

Making a school visit as the Minister of Education, 1975.

Showing off my *teh tarik* skills at a family day event.

In Langkawi with Datuk Azhar Mansor on his return from a solo round-the-world sail on the *Jalur Gemilang*, 1999.

Getting a taste of padi planting in Perak, 1984.

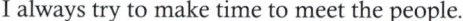

Moving house, kampung-style, during our Semarak campaign in Kelantan in March 1988.
The house was for a widow.

I always try to make time to meet the people.

Launching the 2000cc Proton Perdana, yet another national pride, July 1998.

Visiting the Antarctic with Tan Sri Law Hieng Ding,
Tan Sri Syed Hamid Albar and Datuk Seri Najib Tun Razak.

Driving with pride – the first Proton Saga in July 1985.

With the winners of the Petronas Malaysian Grand Prix, 1999.

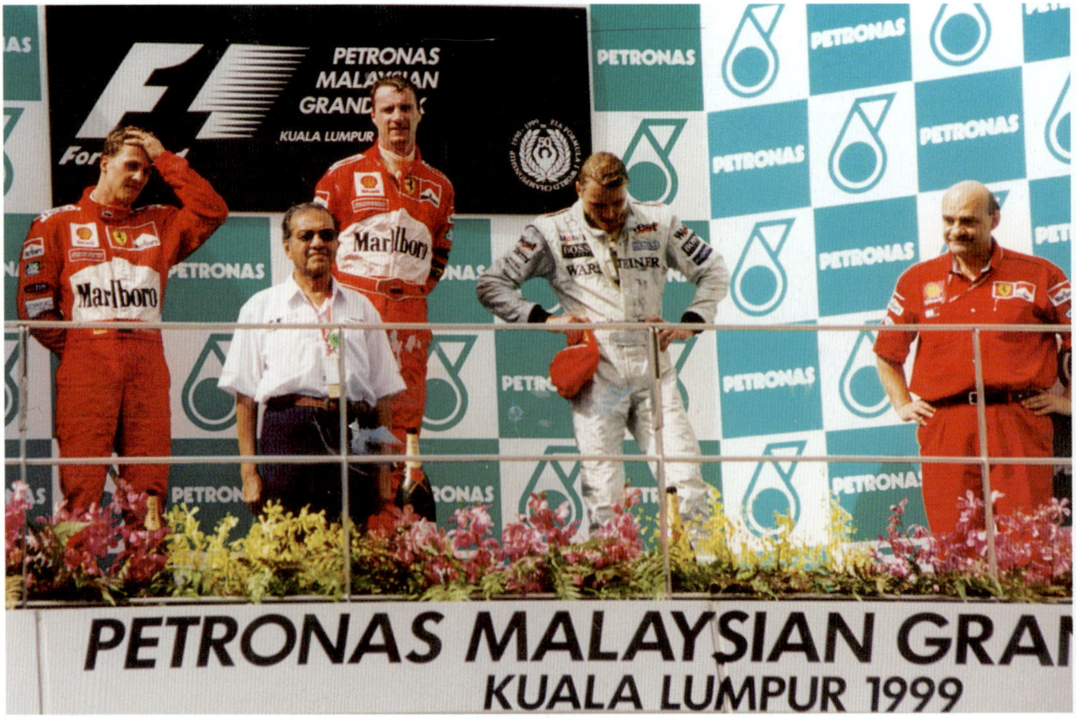

PETRONAS MALAYSIAN GRAN
KUALA LUMPUR 1999

Addressing an assembly in front of the new Ministry of Finance building, Putrajaya, September 2002.

Greeting Baroness Margaret Thatcher at a dinner in her honour at Sri Perdana,
Kuala Lumpur, April 1985.

Launching of the Modenas motorcycle in 1996. On my left is the late Tan Sri Yahya Ahmad.

Receiving Baroness Margaret Thatcher at the Malaysian High Commission in London.

A truly great leader and humanitarian, South Africa's Nelson Mandela
on his visit to Malaysia in November 1990.

I visit Sri Lanka.

At the Apec meet in Shanghai, China in October 2001.
With, from left, Indonesia's Megawati Sukarnoputri, Japan's Junichiro Koizumi, South Korea's Kim Dae-jung, New Zealand's Helen Clark, Brunei's Sultan Hassanal Bolkiah and China's Jiang Zemin.

Singapore's Lee Kuan Yew and wife greeting me on my first official visit to the island republic in 1981.
Ours was a civil relationship, never a friendship.

At the G-15 Summit in Cairo, 2000.

With China's Premier Jiang Zemin in Beijing, 2003.

With Nelson Mandela after receiving the South African Award in Capetown.
Our abhorrence of apartheid was a joint crusade.

With President Bill Clinton in Washington.

President George W. Bush plays host at the White House, 2002.

Hasmah and I with Turkish Prime Minister Tayyip Erdogan and wife, Emine.

Yasser Arafat's visit to Malaysia.

More photo taking in the Ukraine, 2002-2003.

Doing the honours in Germany with then Chancellor Gerhard Shroeder.

In the Ukraine, 2002-2003.

Watching an aerial display of the Sukhoi S-25.

G-15 meet in Kuala Lumpur.

Greeting the troops in Konjik, Bosnia-Herzegovina in July 1994.

Visiting our Malaysian contingent in Konjik, Bosnia-Herzegovina
with Armed Forces Chief General Tan Sri Hashim Aman in July 1994.

ASEAN meet in Brunei.

With Pope John Paul II at his apartment in the Vatican City in June 2002.

# Chapter 33:
## The Malaysianisation Of Companies

It seemed outrageously wrong to me that, when Malaya became independent in 1957, practically all the big tin mines and rubber estates in the country were owned by British companies and listed on the London Stock Exchange (LSE). Perhaps some nominal tax was paid here but it was clear that much of the profit flowed to the UK. At that time, about 80 per cent of our wealth and export earnings came from tin and rubber. Had the earnings stayed in the country, our people would obviously have been more prosperous.

Established during colonial times, the major companies trading in our country continued to belong to foreigners after Independence. Land had been sold or leased to them at very low rates, hence their great profitability. But there were no corporate taxes under the Colonial Government, which meant most of the profits they made and whatever taxes they paid went straight into the British metropolitan economy. Yet they would never have made their money without their favoured access to cheap (five ringgit per acre) Malayan land. Malayan tin and rubber had kept a financially-strained Britain and its empire economically prosperous for much of the inter-war years of the twentieth century. The departing British colonialists had thought that an independent Malaysia would never be governed properly and would suffer chronic financial problems. At Independence, a British head of the Prisons Department voiced his misgivings about the jails being as well-managed as they were under British gaolers.

The Government of independent Malaysia felt that something needed to be done to maximise the returns from our own main assets for our country. I decided to be more aggressive about re-acquiring what should have belonged to us but I could not nationalise foreign holdings, as many other countries had done when they gained their independence. That would have had an adverse effect on the foreign investment that we needed. The only choice, then, was to buy back those major wealth-generating assets. We wanted an orderly transfer of ownership from willing sellers to willing buyers. We wanted those companies back — partly for the profits they would generate for us once we owned them and partly for reasons of national pride.

When we first sought to buy back Malaysian companies, we met with open hostility. But the way we went about making our bid revealed a sophistication no one suspected Malaysia had.

Permodalan Nasional Berhad or PNB, our National Equity Corporation, was keen to add big plantation companies to its portfolio. We had already bought London Tin Corporation in 1972, the biggest tinmining company in the world, and we now also set our sights on the big plantation companies. The Guthrie Group,[1] now part of Sime Darby Berhad,[2] was one of them. After the acquisition of London Tin, there was some resistance to Malaysian purchases of the shares of the big plantation companies. To succeed, we had to devise strategies to avoid being thwarted by British authorities.

We ruled out negotiating to buy shares from the biggest shareholders as we did not believe they would sell if it meant Malaysians would gain control of a major British plantation company. It had to be a hostile takeover — several parties would have to buy shares in coordination, striking as soon as the London Stock Exchange opened in the morning. That was what we did in what came to be known as the Dawn Raid.

442

The plan was masterminded by Tun Ismail Ali, a former Governor of Bank Negara and Chairman of PNB, who also happened to be my brother-in-law. A taciturn man who did not suffer fools gladly, he was the ideal person to carry out this very complex operation in London, far from familiar ground. Under his direction the foray into the market was well coordinated. As soon as trading opened on 7 September 1981, the Malaysian team swooped in and mopped up the shares, acting in concert but initially appearing to act separately. Under British stock market rules, once we had acquired 30 per cent of the company's shares we had to make an open offer to buy the rest of the shares at the same price. By noon, Malaysians had acquired controlling shares in Guthrie plantations and at that point, we made a general offer to purchase the remaining shares.

---

[1]  The Guthrie Group was Southeast Asia's first trading company and pioneered rubber and oil palm plantations in Malaya.

[2]  Sime Darby Berhad is one of Malaysia's biggest multinational companies with interests in plantations, property, motor, heavy equipment and energy and utilities. It is also one of the biggest listed oil palm plantation groups in the world.

The 30 per cent equity threshold requiring that an offer be made for the rest of the shares was designed to deter individuals from getting control of public limited companies. But the Dawn Raid was to prevent interested parties from denying us this control. Our Dawn Raid has subsequently been quoted repeatedly in the standard accounts of how stock markets are managed. But after the raid, the LSE changed its rules. To make such surprise acquisitions nearly impossible, a trader acquiring as little as five per cent of the shares had to make a public announcement of his holdings. That made it almost impossible for us, or anyone else for that matter, to gain control of a public limited British company through share acquisition. The LSE and its favoured inside players did not want to be so easily caught ever again, but Malaysia had already made its mark. We had forced them to take account of us as serious players in their tricky game.

I was elated by the success of our Dawn Raid and the acquisition of Guthrie, but the British Press was furious. They and the British business community condemned our legitimate acquisition as back-door nationalisation. Their rage distorted their reasoning: on the one hand, they insisted that we could not nationalise as this was not done in a free capitalist economy. Yet they also effectively said that we could not buy shares either, if this resulted in us gaining control of an expatriate company. We were apparently not allowed to do anything to acquire the assets that they had held for so long and so lucratively. It seemed that they could not accept that we should manage and be master of our own assets. The era of colonial rule may have ended, but colonial-era thinking was alive and well in London's stock market and financial Press.

443

We did not simply seize assets that we believed were ours, as other nations had done. We wanted to do what was right, because we had been told that if we unilaterally nationalised such overseas-owned assets, foreigners would no longer invest in Malaysia. But how long could we let foreigners control the biggest industries in our country? Arguments that we were not competent or qualified to run these enterprises simply did not apply anymore.

There were no technical or technological barriers, as oil palm estates were not so sophisticated that they were beyond our abilities to manage. Growing oil palm and extracting the oil was not the most complex of processes and we could accomplish both without foreign expertise. In fact, by the time we bought Guthrie, we had mastered the business completely. We were ready to welcome foreign investors who had new know-how we could learn from and use, but the owners of the plantations at the time of the Dawn Raid no longer brought anything new to the industry or to Malaysia. They had nothing to teach us any more. Besides, they had already got back their money many times over on their investments. How much longer would they continue doing so? To go on enjoying those profits without further raising the industry's technological level would have been indefensible, nor could it be justified on business entrepreneurial grounds. Foreign control of our key agro industries had reached the end of its historical road. That, and not the staging of our Dawn Raid, was the real basis of the grief and wailing we heard from the British Press and the industry's former owners and investors.

This defensive reaction by the British did not endear them to us. When governments or their agencies can change market mechanisms at will, the market cannot be regarded as free. Our experience with the London Metal Exchange, which permitted British speculators to renege on their undertakings, makes nonsense of the claims of impartiality and fairness of the market mechanism. The so-called free market is not free at all. The time would come, in 1997-1998, when I would be ready to break market rules and employ unconventional methods in dealing with international institutions and mechanisms. By then I had learnt that the market's rules and international financial structures were not devised to achieve fair trade. They were concocted to lend dubious legitimacy to the rich countries and their giant corporations in their efforts to grasp the wealth of the poor and to re-establish their old economic hegemony.

The Dawn Raid greatly strengthened our confidence and we were no longer treated as people of no consequence. We had proven ourselves to be resourceful players. While the new five per cent rule barred us from buying more companies in the same way, acquiring major strategic corporations was something we would continue to do.

The private sector also entered the fray. The late Tan Sri Lim Goh Tong, a self-made billionaire and one of Malaysia's richest men, decided to buy an old British plantation company, Harrisons and Crosfield.[3] He was a remarkable man. He had come to Malaysia as a penniless 20-year-old from China but went on to transform Genting Highlands into a successful mountain-top casino resort just outside of Kuala Lumpur. At the time of his death in 2007, he owned Resorts World, a fleet of cruise ships, plantations and other major assets. When he went to London to complete his purchase of the plantation company, he caused quite a sensation.

Reporters, photographers and TV cameras buzzed around him, ready to record his statements and answers regarding his acquisition of Golden Hope and Harrisons and Crosfield, both large companies set up early during British rule in Malaya. But Lim could only reply to their questions through his interpreter. He only spoke Chinese and bazaar Malay and did not look like a corporate raider. Yet he was able to outwit the best brains in the business.

In the mid-1960s Malaysian students used to fly back and forth from Britain on chartered flights operated by the British. Seeing the opportunity to make money, some Malaysian businessmen bought a Boeing 707, intending to charter it out for Malaysian students. Malaysia had freely given landing rights to British charter flights but Britain now refused to allow the Malaysian charters to land in the UK. While Malaysia did not then have its own international airline flying between Malaysia and the UK, the British Overseas Airways Corporation[4] flew into Kuala Lumpur as it pleased. But when the Malaysian Airlines System (MAS) was set up, no satisfactory reciprocal arrangements could be struck and only a limited number of MAS flights could fly into London.

When I was studying in the English-medium school during the British colonial period, I was always taught about sportsmanship, that noble sense of fair play that was supposedly characteristic of the British. In this spirit, they would never take advantage of an opponent's misfortune and would ensure that competition would always be fair and just. I was impressed by

---

3   Harrisons and Crosfield was a British trading company that united a number of small estates in Malaya into Golden Hope Rubber Estates, which eventually became Golden Hope Plantations Berhad.

4   The British Overseas Airways Corporation became British Airways in 1976.

this idea and decided to display that same noble quality in my own actions. But my belief in the British sense of fair play had by now almost vanished. The people I had put on a pedestal, the people I had regarded as my role models, had proven to be far less than what I had imagined.

Despite all this, we managed to repatriate Malaysia's foreign-owned industries and even to acquire high-profile British companies such as Laura Ashley, Lotus, and Crabtree and Evelyn. Today many British retail companies are owned by Malaysians. However, we would also learn many other hard lessons about the management of our assets and finances. In the 1960s, as a producer of raw materials, we suffered from the instability of market prices and the continual relative lowering of commodity prices against the cost of the manufactured goods we had to buy. We were essentially trapped in a downward spiral, and kept having to sell more and more tin and rubber at ever lower prices in order to buy fewer and fewer of the manufactured goods we needed. Even when commodity prices went up our earnings could not compensate for the increases in the prices of the manufactured goods we needed.

Internationally, the prices of tin and rubber were not allowed to be dictated by market forces. The United States, for example, held huge stockpiles of these commodities. They would release their stock into the market, causing available supply to outstrip immediate demand. Prices would then fall, even plummet. In this way, they could buy our raw materials on the cheap, produce manufactured goods, and sell them back to us at high prices.

When I was Member of Parliament in 1965, I argued with James D. Bell, the US Ambassador to Malaysia at that time, about how their General Services Administration[5] stockpile was being used. It was not fair, I said, for the US to depress tin prices, which Malaysia's economy depended on so heavily. He replied that it was important for the US economy to keep commodity prices low. He maintained that the strategic use of their commodities stockpiles was legitimate, and that we just had to accept it. That the US did not depend on tin the way Malaysia did, left him unmoved.

---

[5] The General Services Administration is a US Government agency that oversees the operations of federal departments by implementing cost-cutting policies and providing products, transport, and communications.

At one stage as Prime Minister, I had to send an unofficial team consisting of Tun Daim Zainuddin,[6] who held no Government position at the time, and Tan Sri Alex Lee[7] to intercede with the stockpile managers. They warned the Americans that our unemployed tin mine labourers would join the communist guerrillas if they had no income. This strategy succeeded in stopping the stockpile managers from releasing the tin into the market. It was a small but important coup, one that could not be publicised at that time.

Then we had to contend with the tin market in London, which, of course, was not managed by Malaysians. On the London Metal Exchange (LME), where tin was bought and sold, prices were fixed by the buyers and sellers. Malaysia had no say whatsoever. The LME allowed speculation and short selling, which gave rise to gambling and deliberate manipulation. Those entering into such contracts had the incentive to make or help the commodity's price to fall or rise. The advance selling of non-existent tin — of virtual or hypothetical or prospective supplies, rather than physical tin already held in hand — for future delivery is harmless enough in itself. But heavy, aggressive forward selling to push the price down creates a notional surplus without producing any tangible extra tin. This fictional surplus of tin in the market forces the price down. This affected the earnings from tin in tin-producing countries like Malaysia.

After they had forced the price down, the sellers would buy tin to be delivered at the higher, contracted price at which they had agreed to sell, when prices had been higher. Traders obviously stood to make great profits by this dubious practice, but depressing the price of tin in this way hurt Malaysia badly. Needing money from the sale of our tin, we had to sell what we produced at the prevailing, manipulated market prices. The lesson here was that the market is not an impartial and impersonal, price-setting mechanism but an arena for strategic, even covert and illicit action, and furtive manipulation by those powerful and devious enough to get away with it.

447

---

6     See Chapter 39: Daim becomes Finance Minister.

7     The late Tan Sri Alex Lee was the son of Malaysia's first Finance Minister, Tun H.S. Lee. A lawyer by training, Alex Lee was also a politician who held several Cabinet positions until he decided not to seek re-election as a Member of Parliament in 1995. He was also a key figure who helped Malaysia win her bid to host the 1998 Commonwealth Games.

I had only just become Prime Minister when tin prices tumbled. I knew little about the tin market and about short selling and was resigned to see Malaysia's economy experience low growth. Then a friend, H.M. Shah, a businessman from Malacca, brought a Swiss metal trader named Marc Rich to meet me. He told me that he could reverse the downward trend in tin prices by buying up the tin being sold in the market. He explained all about short selling and convinced me that if the sellers had no tin they would be unable to deliver when the time came. If Malaysia had physical tin and others didn't, they would have to come to us to get it, on our terms, when the time came for them to deliver. They would have contracts to fulfil, and meeting a contract is a sacred obligation to businessmen, whatever the cost since the price of a ruined reputation is always greater. It would become at that time a seller's market. If Malaysia refused to sell them the physical tin or they refused to pay the price asked, the sellers would not be able to fulfil their contracts and would be in serious trouble.

If Malaysia also bought up tin for sale once the short sellers had pushed prices down, they would be in even greater trouble. We would be in a position to hold back the physical tin and demand whatever price we liked. We would be able to name a price higher than the depressed buying price we had paid and so profit both ways, as both seller and buyer. We would sell at a high price the tin delivered to us at the lower contracted price. At one stroke, we would make a considerable profit. As a result of our new ability to sell at a price set by us, tin prices would rise and eventually settle at fairer, more realistic levels.

It sounded like a good and practical idea to me. We were not going to corner the market, which is a practice that is frowned upon by the international community. We would not be trying to buy up all the tin or create an artificial scarcity that would drive the price up. We already had the physical tin. It was ours — we produced it and owned it. Yet the speculators' price manipulation operation was killing our major source of income.

The agreement we made with Rich was that he would make only limited purchases on our behalf. Any buying that goes beyond the agreed amount to be spent would require approval from our Treasury. Unfortunately, Rich did not abide by this agreement and he bought huge quantities for future

448

delivery without our permission. When we learned of his excesses we became alarmed and tried to stop him. But by then, he had committed us to big purchases. Still, we felt we were on firm ground. Since we actually had the physical tin, the people who sold tin to Rich and others would have to buy tin from us when they needed to deliver. We could demand a good price from the short sellers. But when the time came for the sellers to deliver the physical tin, they accused us of trying to corner the market. The LME sided with the commodity traders and ruled that the sellers could renege on their contracts and had no obligation to deliver.

This blatantly unjust ruling by the LME ensured that tin prices would remain unduly low. It was a decision in favour of manipulated, not fair, prices. We could not do anything to Rich either, and we later learnt that we were not the only ones he cheated, as he had also managed to con the US Government's Inland Revenue. We lost some RM600 million on the exercise, a huge sum in those days.

We came in for much criticism from both the foreign and local Press, who accused us of trying to corner the tin market. The Opposition also attacked us for misusing government funds. The LME was the British institution for buying and selling tin and other metals and our contracts under that system were legitimate and properly concluded. But it would have cost them a bomb in terms of money, power and reputation — so they ruled against us simply to save their market players.

Next to the tin debacle, our foreign exchange trading was the second mistake we made in the management of the country's finances. In September 1985, the Organisation for Economic Cooperation and Development (OECD)[8] countries met in secret at the Plaza Hotel in New York to correct the huge trade imbalance between Japan and the United States. They decided to revalue the yen and the European currencies against the US dollar. That agreement became known as the Plaza Accord. But the strong yen caused consternation among developing countries. Malaysia had sizeable borrowings in yen because of the low Japanese interest rates and the accord meant that the value of that debt in Malaysian ringgit would almost treble.

---

[8]   The Organisation for Economic Cooperation and Development involves 30 countries who adhere to the principles of representative democracy and a free-market economy.

Had we held our reserves in yen, there would have been few problems. Bank Negara, our central bank responsible for managing our reserves, accordingly decided that it could not be caught holding devalued currencies, particularly the US dollar. It therefore set up foreign currency trading operations which traded only in the currencies of developed countries, principally the US dollar, German Deutsche mark, Swiss franc, the yen and pound sterling. The bank also set up currency trading offices in London and New York, manning them with experienced personnel who worked in shifts round the clock. They did quite well, making good profits. Every central bank is involved to some extent in this kind of currency trading to protect its reserves. This is one way to manage the country's currency and protect its value against the uncertainties of the world monetary system.

In the early 1990s many believed that, because of European integration, Europe was soon going to overtake the US as the strongest economic power. Everyone expected the US dollar to crash again, as it did following the Plaza Accord. But Denmark refused to ratify the Maastricht Treaty[9] and the European currencies faltered. Our currency traders had large holdings in several European currencies and we lost money. We were not alone as many currency traders, individuals and companies, had wagered on the European currencies appreciating after Maastricht.

Anwar, our Finance Minister then, faced a barrage of questions from the DAP. Tan Sri Jaafar Hussein and Tan Sri Nor Mohamed Yakcop, Governor and Deputy Governor of Bank Negara respectively, took the blame and resigned. That was simply the honourable thing to do, not an admission of guilt or wrongdoing. They had not acted improperly — they had simply taken a risk and lost. It took us about 10 years to recover from those losses. Our attempt to trade in foreign exchange may have proven to be an expensive failure, but as always, we were able to mine a valuable lesson that would help us a few short years later, when the ringgit came under international assault.

---

[9]  Signed in 1992, the Maastricht Treaty led to the creation of the European Union and the euro.

# Chapter 34:
# Constitutional Amendments

Another important matter that needed urgent attention in the early days of my administration was the way Bills in Parliament became law. There were flaws in the system which required changes to the Constitution.

The Malaysian Constitution is the result of an agreement reached by the representatives of the Malay Rulers and an Alliance delegation led by Tunku Abdul Rahman, then the elected Chief Minister of the Federation of Malaya.

The two delegations were due to discuss with the Colonial Office in London the future of the Federation, principally its Independence. The Rulers were apprehensive over their status and role in independent Malaya and decided that they should be involved in the negotiation for Independence by the Alliance Government of Tunku Abdul Rahman. Hence, their delegation.

The wily Tunku decided that the two delegations should go by ship so that they could have time to iron out differences between them and present a united front to the British Colonial Office. In this the Tunku was so successful that they were able to fly to London when their ship reached Ceylon (Sri Lanka).

Essentially, it was agreed that independent Malaya would be a Parliamentary democracy with a constitutional monarchy. Obviously both sides had as their model the British system, which had successfully retained the monarchy while giving legislative and executive powers to the people via an elected Parliament. Republicanism, which had been the choice of India and Indonesia, was never considered by the Malayans.

However, the British Constitution is unwritten. Malaya could not allow such an important law to remain unwritten. It was agreed that an independent commission would be set up to recommend to the Rulers and the elected Government a constitution in keeping with the understanding between the Rulers and the democratically-elected representatives of the people.

It must be remembered that the Malay states were absolute monarchies when they invited the British effectively to rule their states. The Malay states had no provision for citizenship. The only people recognised as the people of these states were those designated as the subjects of the Malay Rulers. These were mainly the indigenous Malays and the Malays from the Malay Archipelago (Gugusan Pulau-Pulau Melayu) who chose to migrate and settle in the Malay states and were Muslims.

The delegation agreed that the Malay states should federate and become a single country. Each Ruler would continue to be the head of his state but in addition, a King would be chosen by the Rulers from among themselves to preside over the federation. The King as well as the Rulers of each state would be constitutional non-executive heads. When finally the Constitution was accepted by all parties, the provision was for the King and the State Rulers to act on all matters on the advice of the Prime Minister and the Chief Ministers (*Menteri Besar*) of the states. On only three matters may the King and the Rulers act on their own and they are:

a)  the appointment of the Prime Minister (or state Chief Minister),
b)  the dissolution of Parliament (or State Legislative Assembly),
c)  the requisition of a meeting of the Conference of Rulers concerned solely with the privileges, position, honours and dignities of their Royal Highnesses.

It would seem that the division of roles and power of the King (and the Rulers) and the representatives of the people was clear-cut. But in practice the King and the Rulers held significant authority and power which could negate the democratic principle of government by the people.

This is because the assent of the King (and the Rulers) to all decisions made by Parliament must take the form of a signature appended by the King (and Rulers) to the documents concerned. If the King chose not to append his signature, Parliament could be frustrated. There was nothing in the Constitution to provide for this contingency.

Although the Malays had accepted democracy, they were and still are very feudal in their thinking. They find it extremely difficult to say "no" to their Rulers. Although they may consider some requests made by their Rulers as not being right, the Malay *Menteri Besar* and Prime Minister would find it extremely difficult to say so. The easy way out was to accede to the royal request.

If they turn down the royal command, it is likely that their relations with the Rulers would sour. Yet the Prime Minister, *Menteri Besar* and other senior officers of the administration need the cooperation (and consent) of the Rulers in the course of their work. Should the Rulers withhold their cooperation, work could become difficult if not impossible. The impasse could present many administrative problems.

Over the years it was seen that the non-official activities of the Rulers might also create problems embarrassing to the Government, and may also be difficult to resolve. Although it was not mentioned in the Constitution, it was felt that Rulers should not be involved in business. Tunku Abdul Rahman made this clear and so did Tun Hussein. This is because most businesses involve dealing with Government officials and the officials would find it difficult to reject any request from the Rulers, especially when they are state officials.

There is also the possibility of business people "partnering" with the Rulers or making use of them to get permits and concessions. Where there are other business people competing for Government projects or licences or concessions, it would be difficult for officials and even politicians to be evenhanded. They would be forced to favour the King or the Rulers.

Then there might be disputes between business partners and the Rulers. At such times the immunity conferred on the Rulers could frustrate the processes of law.

Every now and then young members of royal families would be involved in fights and assaults. Even Rulers themselves might be involved. Where grievous hurt has been caused, it is unfair to the victims when they cannot resort to redress through the courts. In most cases such incidents would be covered up and would not be reported in the Press. The police would feel powerless to act. But the people would know anyway and there would be much public resentment. When immunity is conferred on the royals, it is expected that they would not abuse it. But the fact is that in Malaysia they do, even if infrequently.

Then there are royals who interfere with the administration, including in appointments to senior posts. There have been cases of royalty tampering with political matters. The Government would be placed in a dilemma. Led by Malays, the tussle faced by Government leaders was always between Malay respect and subservience to royalty and the need to do what is right. At the same time, Malay politicians felt constrained because any overt show of disrespect for the Malay Rulers would cause a lot of Malays to be resentful towards them (the politicians). Disrespect or seeming disrespect of the Rulers by the Government or leaders can result in accusations of wanting to do away with the monarchy, or wanting to convert the country to a republic.

Politicians have always been aware of the strong feelings of the Malays in favour of the royals, and in particular the persons of the Rulers. Ordinary citizens are usually not aware of any wrongdoing by their Rulers. Even if they are, they do not seem to mind, especially when it does not affect them personally.

454

The Constitution says that the King must act on the advice of the Government as represented by the Minister entrusted by the Cabinet, usually the Prime Minister. But, as pointed out above, it does not say what the action of the Government would be if the advice is rejected or ignored. During the Colonial period, British Advisers actually interfered in the appointment of successors to the Sultan. The Constitution of independent Malaysia provides for no such interference by the Government. Yet there might be cases where the suitability of a candidate might be questionable.

In the case of the promulgation of laws, the Constitution clearly requires the assent of the King in the form of his signature before a law properly legislated by Parliament can become operable. If he refuses, can anything be done to uphold the right of the representatives of the people to make laws? Can it be said that Malaysia is a democracy if it is the King who eventually exercises the right to validate and approve its laws?

Although the Constitution provides that the King may refuse to appoint as Prime Minister anyone representing the majority of elected members, this can easily be remedied by the elected members passing a vote of no confidence in whoever is named by the King. But now we know that the

King or the Sultan can effectively frustrate the leader of the majority party by insisting on the appointment of the Rulers' own candidates.

The majority party should be able to reject the Ruler's choice simply by passing a vote of no confidence in him when the legislative body is convened. But Malay custom and respect for the royals can prevent this from being done. Thus Malay custom and feudal attitudes can actually override the Constitution. This is not healthy.

When I took over as Prime Minister in July 1981, I was determined to get along with the Rulers and especially the King. The practice in Malaysia was for the Prime Minister to have an audience with the King every Wednesday before the Cabinet met. The King was given a copy of all the papers, including the minutes of the previous week's meeting for him to read, study or peruse so that he may be able to comment or ask questions on the Cabinet papers. Often the King would not have any question or comment to make. But the meeting also enabled the King to raise any matter, personal or official, that he may feel a need to.

I will not relate here the specific issues that were raised by the six Yang di-Pertuan Agong I served. Suffice to say that a number of these items did put me in a quandary. Despite the provision or the tradition that the King acts on the advice of the Minister (i.e. the Prime Minister) representing the Government, the opposite was sometimes the case. The Prime Minister on several occasions had to accede to the wishes of the King. There had even been cases where another Sultan was able to influence the King.

It is for this reason that I discussed with my Deputy, Tun Musa Hitam, about how the elected representatives of the people, i.e. Parliament, should be the final authority in determining the legitimacy of Acts of Parliament. The King should still append his signature to the laws passed by Parliament, but should he fail to do so for whatever reason, the laws would still come into effect after a period of time. All the other rights of the King, such as the appointment of the Prime Minister and the dissolution of Parliament, would remain with His Majesty.

I thought there should be no difficulty in getting the amendment to the Constitution through as the King would normally accept the advice of the Prime Minister.

After the 1982 General Election and the setting up of the new Cabinet, Tun Musa, who was reappointed Deputy Prime Minister, expressed the view that if we wanted to amend the Constitution to return the rights for law-making to the elected representatives of the people, we should do it as soon as possible after the election. This would prevent the amendment from becoming a fresh issue at the next election. Besides, the 1982 General Election strongly confirmed public support for the Barisan Nasional and my leadership of the party and the Government.

The Attorney-General was tasked with the drafting of the amendments to be made to the Constitution. It was to be quite simple as all that was needed was to provide for all Bills, which had gone through both Houses and been approved as drafted or as amended, to be submitted to the King for His Majesty's signature. If for any reason the King fails to append his signature, the Bill would be regarded as law after a period of 15 days.

Basically the amendment simply formalises what was already being practised, i.e. the King approves and signs into law the Bills, on the advice of the Prime Minister or any Minister authorised to advise the King. Since the Prime Minister heads the Government which had proposed and obtained the approval of the Parliament, his advice on the amendment would be in accord with the spirit of the Constitution and therefore should receive the King's assent.

The British monarch also acts on the advice of the Minister authorised to get Her Majesty's signature. The British Constitution is unwritten but I have not read about any British monarch refusing to sign any Bills of Parliament. But in Malaysia, written laws are needed to legitimise any act by the Government or the administration. Since there is no provision in the Constitution should the King fail to follow the advice of the Government, it was felt desirable that the Constitution be amended to provide specifically for this eventuality.

We needed to be clear about this as it would be an embarrassment to the Government if the King refused to take the advice of the Prime Minister. The Government could not afford to face an impasse in the administration of the country. Accordingly, an amendment was made to Article 66 (5) of the Constitution so that if a Bill in Parliament which has been passed by both Houses failed to get the signature of the Yang di-Pertuan Agong, it would be considered as having been signed by His Majesty after 15 days had elapsed and would be regarded as having been duly passed.

The amendment to Article 150 provides for the Prime Minister, if he is satisfied that a state of Emergency has occurred and the safety or the peace of the Federation or any part of it is threatened, to advise the Yang di-Pertuan Agong, who must accede to that advice, to declare a state of emergency and make an announcement to that effect. The amendment to the Eighth Schedule also provided that if any state law is not approved by the Rulers after 15 days, then it too would be considered as having been approved by the Ruler and would become law.

In August 1982 both Houses of Parliament passed the amendments to the Constitution, and the Act was duly submitted to His Majesty the Yang di-Pertuan Agong. The Sultan of Pahang was then Agong and he decided to consult his brother Rulers. This was because the amendments applied also to the State Governments and their Rulers.

Sadly, the Rulers all disagreed with the amendments. I was left with the task of persuading them and, if that failed, I had to negotiate with the Rulers. I felt strongly that somehow the amendments must be a part of the Constitution.

I had good relations with the Agong then, but he would not go against the expressed wishes of his brother Rulers. His failure to take my advice to sign the amendments highlighted the very weakness that these amendments were designed to address. But at the same time, any law that affects the position of the Rulers in whatever way must have their consent.

I enlisted the help of Tengku Tan Sri Ahmad Rithauddeen, a Minister in the Cabinet who was the brother-in-law of the Raja of Perlis, but it was to no avail. The future Sultan of Perak who was then Lord President of the Supreme Court, Raja Azlan Shah, also interceded but again failed. In the meantime, the Rulers were conferring with each other unofficially. It seems they were conscious of the mounting feelings against them. They wanted to work out a solution.

I felt a need to explain the situation to the people. Public meetings were held and I explained that the amendments were not meant to do away with the monarchy, nor make the country a republic. It would not affect all the other provisions of the Constitution, including the special position of the Malays and the Bumiputera, the position of Islam as the official religion of the country, and of the other religions, etc. Generally the people were very supportive and wanted the Rulers to give their assent. We had to be careful not to allow excesses in their criticism of the Rulers. But there were some, and the Rulers were not put in a good light.

There were also dissenting voices even from within UMNO itself. The former Secretary-General of UMNO, Tan Sri Senu Abdul Rahman, circulated a letter against the amendments. Tunku Abdul Rahman advised that the Government and the Rulers should seek agreement through discussions and negotiations. PAS was also against the amendments and was bent upon making an issue of it.

The people were getting agitated and I felt that a solution had to be found soon. The trouble was that the amendments as passed by Parliament needed to be signed into law even if the Rulers wished to change it. There had never been a case of a law that had not been rendered operational being returned to Parliament for amendments for whatever reason.

Then the Yang di-Pertuan Agong went away on leave. According to the provision in the Constitution, the Deputy Yang di-Pertuan Agong would act in the King's absence. The Yang di-Pertuan Besar of Negeri Sembilan, who was the Deputy King, was made acting King. I knew the Yang di-Pertuan Besar well. Besides, his younger brother Tunku Abdullah, the Tunku Panglima Besar of Negeri Sembilan, was a close friend of mine. I prevailed upon Tunku Abdullah to talk to his elder brother on the need to settle the problem quickly.

I had received a note from the Rulers which gave their views on the amendments. They felt that 15 days was too short a time and they suggested that it should be 60 days. If the King did not sign after 60 days then the Bill would be returned to Parliament. Parliament would then review the Bill, taking into consideration the objection of the Agong. If Parliament felt that the Bill should be amended, it could do so. If not the Bill would be sent back to the Agong. If after 60 days the Agong had not signed the Bill then it would be considered as having His Majesty's consent and would become law.

The Rulers also disagreed with the amendment to Article 150 on the right of the Prime Minister to declare a state of Emergency. They also objected to the amendment requiring the Rulers to sign into law any Bill presented by the state Governments within 15 days, failing which the law would be regarded as having been assented to by the Ruler .

I had an audience with the Deputy King at Istana Tetamu where he was residing during the period he was acting King. After prolonged explanations about the importance of the amendments being signed by the Agong, and after undertaking to make the amendments as proposed by the Rulers, the Deputy King signed the original amendments.

I was much relieved. The incident proved the need to make the amendments. In future, should the King refuse to sign into law any Bill, the way out would be very clear, i.e. after 60 days of the Bill not being signed by the King, it would be referred back to Parliament. Parliament may or may not amend it before sending it back to the King. Sixty days later, whether the Bill had the King's signature appended to it or not, it would be considered as having had his assent.

It was an incident which I would not like to go through again. I hastened to repair my relations with the King and the other Rulers. I must say the Rulers were generous and prepared to forget the incident. The Kings who succeeded the Sultan of Pahang got on quite well with me, and my work as Prime Minister was in no way hampered. They gave their full cooperation.

Then came another incident which forced me to amend the Constitution again. This time it was to partially remove the immunity of the Rulers.

The case involved a Ruler slapping a member of the public, a hockey coach. Apparently the Sultan was incensed by the Malaysian Hockey Federation banning his son from playing for five years. The coach, David Gomez, was summoned to the palace where he was allegedly slapped. He lodged a police report in which he claimed the Sultan had assaulted him.

I and my Cabinet colleagues felt this was not right. It is true that the Rulers had immunity before the law but it was assumed that they would not abuse this privilege. The rights of the citizens to seek legal redress needed to be maintained. People would not be comfortable if they could be assaulted by the Rulers with impunity. The incident took place in 1993, 10 years after the previous amendment. I was not keen to have another contretemps with the Rulers but I felt it was my duty to ensure the citizens of this country were protected by the law.

The immunity conferred on the Rulers was really to free them from any liability in the performance of their official duties. It should not extend to personal acts which were not in any way connected with the performance of their duties. Malaysians as a whole respect and honour the Malay Rulers. Usually they avoid criticisms of royalty. Even the Government would try to cover up serious misdemeanours committed by the Sultans. The occasions when the Government had to do this were few and far between, but certainly some involved serious cases. I will not elaborate on this but I know that if ordinary citizens were to commit these acts, they would be charged in court and if found guilty, would be very severely punished indeed.

The unfortunate thing is that other members of the royal families seemed to think their royal status also conferred immunity on them. There were cases involving assault against members of the public by children of royalty. Out of respect for the Sultans concerned, the police and other officials would try to hush up such cases. But when a citizen actually made a police report and this received much publicity in the Press, the Government could not be seen to ignore the matter. The Cabinet discussed this issue at length and concluded that the immunity of the Rulers should be better defined so that incidents such as that involving the hockey coach would not happen again.

There was also much talk about royalty being involved in business. As mentioned earlier, such involvement was thought unbecoming of the Rulers and they should therefore not lend their names to business ventures. This is because when their names are connected with a business, Government officials would find difficulty in applying the normal criteria before approving or rejecting the application. This means that others in the same business would be discriminated against.

Their involvement in business may also lead to the Rulers becoming liable for debts or losses incurred by their enterprises. If the Ruler failed to honour his commitments, legal redress would not be available as he was immune to court action. Many felt that if the Ruler wished to be involved in business, then he must be liable for any breach of trust or laws like everyone else. There was also always the possibility of business people making use of the Ruler as a front for activities that breached the law, such as operating illegal gambling establishments.

The assault incident mentioned above involved one Ruler, but it would not be possible to provide a law that did not apply to the other Rulers as well. I felt certain that the other Rulers would not feel happy. From the experience with the previous amendment to the Constitution regarding royal assent to Bills of Parliament, I anticipated a lot of resistance on the part of the Rulers. Nevertheless, I asked the Attorney-General to draft the necessary laws for presentation to Parliament.

Essentially the amendments provided for three things.

Firstly, for the immunity of the Rulers to be limited to the performance of their duties as constitutional Rulers. Should they breach laws in their personal capacity, they would be liable for court action.

Secondly, should a Ruler make an appeal to the pardons board at Federal or State level, the Ruler concerned should not sit and chair the board. Another Ruler selected by the Rulers Council would preside.

Thirdly, members of Parliament or state councils may not be subjected to charges of treason if they speak regarding the wrongdoings of the Rulers during the course of their debates in Parliament or state councils.

On 10 December 1992, Tun Ghafar Baba tabled the amendments regarding the constitutional rights of the King and the Rulers for First Reading in the Dewan Rakyat. The amendments contained the three items mentioned above.

The Rulers reacted immediately. While Raja Nazrin Shah, who at that time was the acting Ruler of Perak, said that the rights of citizens and their freedoms must be protected, the other Rulers disagreed. They held an unofficial meeting in Alor Star and in Negeri Sembilan to discuss the amendments. A meeting of the Barisan Nasional Council was called on 12 December and it was decided to hold a special sitting of the Lower House of Parliament to amend the Constitution as planned.

In a meeting on 9 January 1993, the Rulers requested for time to consider the amendments. Several more unofficial meetings were held by the Rulers to discuss them. The people were getting agitated by talk that the Rulers would not agree to the amendments. Well-known Malay writers and intellectuals had a meeting at the Dewan Bahasa dan Pustaka and issued a declaration urging the Rulers to be conscious of the wishes of the people.

I found it necessary to explain at length that the King and the Rulers would retain their immunity when performing official work. The Act was only concerned with any action by the Rulers in their personal capacity, which may involve assault against individuals or other criminal acts or breaches of the law.

The Act would also prohibit any proposal or resolution to abolish the system of Malay Rulers. Such proposals would constitute subversion and would be punished under the Act as treason.

Many public meetings were held to explain to the people the provisions in the amendments, especially on the worries of the Malays that we were going to abolish the institution of Malay Rajas and make Malaysia a republic. On 17 January, together with Deputy Prime Minister Tun Ghafar Baba, Minister of Finance Datuk Seri Anwar Ibrahim, and Attorney-General Tan Sri Abu Talib Othman, I met six of the Rulers unofficially to try to find a solution to the impasse. In the meeting, the six Rulers appeared to agree with the Bill.

Parliament met on 19 January even though the Rulers refused to give their consent at the last minute. After I presented the Bill, the Barisan Nasional members and some Opposition members thumped the tables in a show of support. The Bill was passed with the DAP, the PBS of Sabah and four independent members voting with the Government. I must admit I was reluctant to have the Bill passed without the Agong's signature although there was provision for this. The debate in Parliament saw many members vehemently demanding that the Rulers must be prevented from going against the laws of the country.

I remember Tun Hussein Onn, during his tenure of office, being very unhappy with some of the Rulers and he informed the Cabinet that he would have a special meeting with the Rulers to advise them against doing anything against the laws of the country.

Following the passage of the Bill in Parliament, there followed a period of strained relations between the Rulers and the Government. Semangat 46, the party led by Tengku Razaleigh Hamzah, condemned the Bill and Razaleigh spoke against it in public.

Of the Rulers, the Sultan of Kelantan was the most vehemently opposed to the amendments. At one stage, the Cabinet decided to withdraw unofficial privileges for the Rulers. Tunku Abdul Rahman urged the Government to meet and discuss the matter with the Rulers so as to reach an amicable settlement. The Tunku must have remembered his attempt to stop the Rulers from being involved in business.

Anwar spoke at many public gatherings criticising the Sultan of Kelantan for trying to help his uncle Tengku Razaleigh and Semangat 46. He urged the Sultan to find some other way to help his uncle.

Eventually, there were signs that the Rulers would agree to the amendments. The Sultan of Pahang, who was scheduled to chair the meetings of the 159th and 160th Conference of Rulers on 11 February, said he believed the problem would be settled at the meetings. It seemed that the Rulers wanted a say in the composition of the special court which would hear cases against the Rulers. The Government felt that it could concede on this matter.

The usual practice was for the Prime Minister to accompany the Agong on the second day of the Conference of Rulers. On 12 February, Tun Ghafar accompanied the King. All the Rulers were present except the Sultan of Kelantan, who asked the Sultan of Kedah to represent him.

The meeting unanimously agreed to the amendments after being assured that certain changes would be made to the text of the Bill. This was to be done during the committee stage of Parliament's sitting. A joint statement was made by the Keeper of the Rulers' Seal and the Attorney-General to the effect that the Conference of Rulers had agreed to the amendments.

On 25 February the Sultan of Kelantan contested the validity of the Conference of Rulers' decision. His Royal Highness wrote to the Attorney-General on 3 March that he would challenge the decision in court.

On 8 March, a special meeting of the Dewan Rakyat was held to debate amendments to the Bill which had been passed by Parliament during the 18 to 20 January sittings, which had not received the assent of the Yang di-Pertuan Agong. At this sitting, Semangat 46 members were absent. PAS members did not vote. But DAP and PBS as well as four independents voted in support of the amended Bill.

This was the first time that members of the Opposition voted with the Government. It was a measure of the general feeling of members of Parliament and the people on the need for confining the immunity of the Rulers to their official duties only. Of the 173 members present, 167 voted for the amendment.

The amended Bill was sent to the Agong, Sultan Azlan Shah, on 16 March and signed by him on 22 March. The Bill was sent to the Speaker of the Dewan Rakyat, Tun Mohamed Zahir Ismail, who informed me that it would be gazetted as soon as possible.

I felt much relief and so did all the leaders of the Barisan Nasional component parties. Anwar said that "one lesson to be learnt from the episode is that the issue was not entirely confined to the abolition of the Malay Rulers' legal immunity in their personal capacity. It concerns the understanding and maturity of all quarters involved with regard to the real meaning of freedom and the rule of law."

Then Opposition Leader Lim Kit Siang welcomed the King's assent to the Bill and hoped "this particular chapter of the Rulers' issue" would be closed. The DAP National Deputy Chairman, Karpal Singh, also described the royal assent as the closing of another chapter. " The issue is now closed and is effectively now law," he said, adding that the Government should forward the Bill to the Government Printers as soon as possible for gazetting as an Act. He said, "The law must be fairly applied to all Rulers, irrespective of whether the present Government leaders have good relations with them or not."

Since the amendment to limit the immunity of the Rulers became law in 1993, there has been only one case for the special court to hear and deliver a judgment. This case did not involve any bodily harm to anyone. It was a civil suit. One can claim that the law has been quite effective. Now there is a suggestion that the law be annulled, that the Rulers be given back their total immunity. Among those who voiced this opinion are the very people who as leaders in the Government and the Opposition spoke strongly and voted in favour of the amendments.

Laws often look ineffective in preventing some crimes, but the moment the laws are annulled, one may see a sharp increase in the incidence of that crime.

Whatever the case, the amendments were necessary at the time and for the reasons I have mentioned, and the Government then was also formulating many new policies to enhance social justice for all Malaysians.

465

# Chapter 35:
# Equitable Affluence

The disproportionately small share of our national wealth that the Bumiputera held was a matter that concerned me throughout my political career. As I mentioned earlier, a study conducted by the Prime Minister's Department in 1970 on the distribution of wealth based on share ownership found that Malays and other Bumiputera, who made up some 60 per cent of the population, owned less than two per cent of shares in public listed companies. The Chinese, who made up slightly less than 30 per cent of the population, owned 30 per cent of the shares. Sixty per cent was owned by foreigners, mainly Europeans, who had founded large public limited companies controlling rubber plantations, tin mines and trading houses from colonial times. The remaining shares were owned by Malaysian Indians and other Malaysian nationals.

Based on these and other findings, the Government under Tun Abdul Razak Hussein had formulated the New Economic Policy (NEP), whose objectives were both to remove the identification of race with economic roles and functions and to eradicate poverty irrespective of race. The second of these two aims is hardly noticed and most Malaysians, not to speak of our overseas critics, seem to think that the official "leg up" was exclusively for the Bumiputera via the economic function. But all the poor had to be helped. To save the country from experiencing the dire consequences of widespread poverty, the situation of the Malays had to be dealt with earlier and more thoroughly as they made up the majority of the poor. It would not look good if poverty among non-Malays was eradicated first, leaving only the Malays among the poor in the country, as was bound to happen if the same amount of attention was given to the non-Malays as to the Malays. But poverty eradication among the non-Malays was certainly not neglected.

The first of those two NEP objectives entailed engineering the redistribution of wealth among the races so that it would be more equitable. Malays and other indigenous people, it was decided, should hold 30 per cent of the corporate wealth, the Chinese and Indians 40 per cent (up from the previous 30 per cent) and foreigners reduced to 30 per cent. The NEP was not about the expropriation of existing wealth and its transfer from old to new owners, but about the creation and allocation of new wealth. If the economy could grow significantly, much of the fruit of that new growth could be allocated to the indigenous peoples. This entails discrimination in the allocation of new opportunities to the have-nots as against the haves. But how else can we balance the end results if the haves must get an equal or even greater share of the new opportunities?

In practical terms, this would mean allocating more opportunities, licences, permits and contracts to the Bumiputera and fewer to the non-Bumiputera. We were aware that the sense of deprivation would still be felt by the non-Bumiputera, but by comparison, it would be far less than that caused by expropriation. Their existing wealth would not be taken from them; but their entitlement to new wealth and economic opportunities would be less than for Bumiputera. They would have to accept that while the property that they already had was a legally-protected entitlement, they could not expect to have unrestricted access to wealth opportunities in the future as they did before if we were to reduce the disparities instead of exacerbating the inequities.

Distributing company shares to the Bumiputera seemed simple enough. The shares to be distributed would come from Initial Public Offers or, when a company was expanding or restructuring, when new shares would be issued. Thirty per cent of these new shares would be allocated to the Bumiputera so that their shares in the corporate sector would increase over time. Simple arithmetic would show that if the balance of the shares went to the non-Bumiputera, the 70 per cent that they get would actually increase the disparity. Strictly speaking, if the Bumiputera share of the corporate sector were to be increased to 30 per cent from two per cent, their share should be bigger than the allocation to the non-Bumiputera. But at no time were they allocated more than 30 per cent. From the beginning it was realised that the Bumiputera had no capacity to take up even the 30 per cent due to them. They lacked capital. There had to be other ways of enriching the Bumiputera.

That, at least, was how we envisioned the plan would work. But almost as soon as the Bumiputera were allocated the shares, they sold them, mainly to the Chinese who were prepared to pay more than the issue price. Since during good times almost all IPO shares appreciated in value upon being issued and would continue to appreciate for some time, demand for the shares was high and Chinese speculators were always ready to buy them. For their part, the Bumiputera were happy simply to make easy money from the initial capital gains. Since many Bumiputera borrowed money from the banks to acquire their shares, they were eager to pay off their loans. This they did by disposing of their shares while making a little profit from the sale. Sometimes the Chinese who wanted certain offered shares would pay, in effect, a commission or fee to the Bumiputera who would front for them. Upon allocation, they would take the shares over from their nominal owners and pay those Bumiputera their fee for providing that service.

Obviously this sale of shares for upfront profits frustrated efforts to increase Bumiputera ownership of corporate wealth. In fact this practice increased the disparities in wealth ownership between the Bumiputera and the non-Bumiputera. If this continued to happen, the NEP would prove to be a spectacular failure. Politically, this would be disastrous as the envy of the Malays over the ever-increasing wealth of the non-Malays would create tension and might destabilise the nation.

But it was not only company shares which were being sold upfront upon allocation. The Bumiputera were also selling contracts, licences and permits immediately after they were allocated.

Actually they had no choice. They had no capital, management skills or understanding of the businesses that came their way for them to raise capital and carry out their own business. When they tried, their inexperience resulted in their businesses failing. They would then default on their bank loan repayments. They actually ended up poorer than before they started. A small number of them succeeded somehow. A decision had to be made whether to give more opportunities to these successful Malays or to keep on giving to the others in the name of fairness. In the end it was decided to continue giving opportunities to the successful ones without neglecting those who had failed and were likely to continue failing.

Mulling over this dilemma, I recalled a method of investment that I came across when I was Minister of Education in the 1970s and had to oversee the affairs of the Tunku Abdul Rahman Foundation. A charitable trust, it was administered voluntarily by a Chinese businessman, who invested the money in shares on the Kuala Lumpur Stock Exchange. In those days business was good, so he made decent returns from dividends on his investments. He would periodically sell the shares he held for capital gains and then reinvest the proceeds in other promising shares. The fund grew under his management. It seemed to me that a similar trust should be set up by the Government and the Initial Public Offer of company shares should be allocated to it rather than to impecunious individuals.

The Bumiputera could then invest in this trust fund which would be allocated the 30 per cent shares meant for Bumiputera. This trust would not sell off the shares for immediate capital gains. Instead, it would earn dividends which could be passed on to the Bumiputera investors. The fund could judiciously buy and sell shares to benefit from the movements of share prices.

Investing in stock markets requires skill and experience. A unit trust manager would be better able to determine what shares to buy, when to buy and when to sell. By investing through unit trusts, investors would not be directly exposed to the ups and downs of the share market.

Share ownership was new to most Malays. They did not value it as much as the ownership of landed property or gold ornaments. It took a long time before they considered ownership of shares as an appropriate and strategic way of holding wealth. Share prices, however, may fluctuate violently while gold and property values change less dramatically. Cash was also a way of storing wealth, but inflation could erode its value. Malays used to save money in cash because it was something tangible. Ready money was something they could understand, but not how the purchasing power of their savings was reduced over time by inflation.

Many Malays also looked askance at fixed deposits because they saw bank interest as *riba,*[1] which is *haram* or forbidden to Muslims. The Muslim

---

[1]    In Islam, *riba* is forbidden because it is considered to be profit that is gained without effort or risk.

objection to interest is that it involves no uncertainty, so all Islamically-acceptable borrowing must take the outward form of a business venture in which there is shared risk. But the stock market was, for them, simply too risky. Not understanding its volatility, they were loath to invest in shares. They lacked the necessary knowledge and confidence to entrust their wealth to its uncertainties.

In 1960, on a holiday to Hong Kong with Hasmah, I read about unit trusts in the *Hong Kong Standard*. To reduce the risk of private investment in companies, unit trusts were set up and were managed by professionals. Managing large sums of money, they minimised risk by spreading their investments wisely and judiciously among different business sectors and among different companies operating in the same sector. With their knowledge of the market and their access to expert market intelligence, professional fund managers were believed to be less likely to make bad investments. When they saw that a company was likely to fail, they quickly sold the shares; when they received information of impending developments that would enhance a company's performance, they bought shares. To me that sounded like a good way to invest, so in the early 1960s, I put a small amount of my own money in one of the Hong Kong unit trusts. Sure enough, the unit price appreciated. Not having any long-term strategy, I sold off my shares and made a small profit. I was behaving like the Malay that I am.

I must admit that despite the profit I made, I did not invest again in those Hong Kong unit trusts. That was my last investment, until I bought 200 shares in Malayan Tobacco. Of course, I am against smoking. During the Japanese Occupation, I had no money to buy cigarettes but I vowed that when the British returned, I would buy a pack of Rough Rider cigarettes and start smoking. It was stylish and macho — everyone was doing it. But when I lit up my first cigarette and inhaled, I choked and got a horrible taste in my mouth. My reasons for opposing smoking are now less personal, and are based on medical knowledge and the public interest. But I bought the Malayan Tobacco shares long, long ago — before I became a Minister — and I still have them. I own no shares in any of the companies listed on the Malaysian Stock Exchange. I did buy shares in our own national unit trust scheme — the Permodalan Nasional Berhad unit trusts — when it was launched as well as in the other state-owned unit trusts every time they were launched. I bought them because I was expected to, and the management wanted me to be seen to support them.

Faced with the problem of Malays selling off their shares upon being allocated, it occurred to me that we might set up a unit trust management entity to buy the NEP-mandated Bumiputera share allocations and then sell units to individual Bumiputera investors. If they wanted to sell them, they could only do so to the unit trust managers. In that way, the shares would not be sold to the non-Bumiputera but would remain with the unit trust managers, who might sell the units to other Bumiputera or hold them in the trust until there were Bumiputera buyers. The units bought back by the managers could still earn dividends. The managers might sell them for capital gains as the market rose, or to avoid losses as the share prices depreciated. Some shares might fall in value, but the spread of the investments would cushion the fall. Only in rare cases, when the whole market collapsed, would managers make an overall loss on their investments.

I wrote to the Governor of the Bank Negara, Tun Ismail Mohamed Ali, asking him to look into the setting up of a unit trust to take over shares allocated to the Bumiputera. The returns from investments should be such that they would be more than from investments in fixed deposits at the banks.

Tun Ismail set up a working group which eventually proposed a complex, three-tier arrangement that practically guaranteed the investors would never lose money. Yearly returns on investments would be more than the interest on fixed deposits. The Government initially provided the Yayasan Pelaburan Bumiputera (the Bumiputera Investment Foundation) with RM200 million in seed money. The foundation would then set up PNB and finance it to buy shares allocated to the Bumiputera. The shares would be transferred to a unit trust management entity (the Amanah Saham Nasional or ASN), and the units would be sold to the Bumiputera at a fixed price of RM1 per unit. The buy-back price would also be RM1 per unit. The unit trust holder could sell back the units at any time, but only to PNB. In the meantime, he would earn dividends based on the units he held.

The Ministry of International Trade and Industry then allocated more than RM2.5 billion worth of shares to PNB, all intended for the Bumiputera. PNB bought over plantation giant Guthrie Corporation for RM1 billion, sold off its non-plantation businesses and made RM600 million in profit. It also acquired Harrisons Malayan Plantations (re-named Golden Hope Plantations), London Tin (renamed Malaysian Mining Corporation Berhad), Kontena Nasional Berhad, United Motor Works and Kompleks Kewangan Malaysia Berhad. When it was set up, ASN was open-ended, but it grew so big that a second unit trust company was launched, the ASB, or Amanah Saham Bumiputera. By 1990 ASN and ASB had 4.3 million unit holders between them. Dividends paid amounted to RM4.15 billion, with a RM2.52 billion special bonus allocated to ASN unit holders.

PNB succeeded in more ways than just ensuring that shares allocated to the Bumiputera remained with them. A campaign to get them to invest in unit trusts was launched and it included education about the share market, its functions and how it could be a way of saving money. In the process, the Bumiputera began to understand more about the modern economy, the function of money as capital, the management of capital and the ways that it may be raised for business purposes. They also learnt about how banks functioned and how and when they should borrow. Previously, they borrowed from *chettiars* or Indian moneylenders, usually providing their land as collateral. Not knowing how to use the money they borrowed prudently, they frequently lost their collateral. They often had no plan for repayment. Usually they borrowed to fund things which gave no return, such as weddings. They expected to repay their loans from their normal incomes, and very often they would not be able to service the loan or pay the principal.

When the Government began encouraging Malay investment in shares, it had hoped to create a nucleus of a growing Malay investment community. But fears were expressed, and soon confirmed, that even if this approach were to work and people did not sell off their recurrent share allocations for fast profits, too much of the NEP's benefits would accrue to too small a group of Bumiputera investors. Most poor Malays would remain strangers to the benefits of unit trust investment. This problem needed attention so PNB was careful to give the poorest people an opportunity to invest and benefit from the economy's heartening growth. They made a special provision so that for as little as RM10, people might already own units in the trust. For that RM10 investment, they would be allotted not 10 but 100 units, all to be paid for from the gradually accumulating dividends. Knowing that they too held a share in the nation's top businesses and companies gave new pride to the poor.

In 1996, after some years of successful operation, it was decided that Malaysians of Thai origin should also qualify to buy the units. Next it was decided that Portuguese Eurasians should be eligible as well. Finally, a special unit trust fund was created for all Malaysians, including the non-Bumiputera. It soon became clear that the Thais, Eurasians and other non-Bumiputera had bought more units per head than the Bumiputera. While there were more Bumiputera unit holders, their average holdings were smaller and their total investments did not reflect their numbers. Were the Bumiputera less investment-oriented? Or did they just lack funds to invest compared to the non-Bumiputera? Perhaps, with newfound confidence, they were now investing elsewhere. It would have been useful to know.

While our policy of encouraging investment among Malays was perhaps not the success that we had expected, it was not a total failure either. At least the Bumiputera were now saving more than they had before. More significantly, perhaps, the people who ran unit trusts learnt a lot about finance. To those who complain about our opening the trusts to non-Bumiputera participation, one must reply that it would not have been fair to keep them out forever. We were initially using government money, money that belonged to all Malaysians.

We find that Malays regard the unit trust as a kind of savings bank. They would redeem their shares whenever they need money, as for example when going on pilgrimage. If they have some money to save they would buy unit trust shares. This is not bad because this way the money would be earning some dividends and to a certain extent would counter the depreciation of their savings due to inflation.

As of 2008, the number of PNB unit trust account holders stood at 8.9 million, up from 840,000 account holders in 1981. PNB invests in the international equity market and provides training in investments and scholarships for higher education. PNB has also given out dividends totalling RM60 billion to date and has invested in more than 300 companies. Most Malays, I fear, neither recognise nor appreciate this. Perhaps it is human nature to appreciate change only if you know how things were before. Our young people do not. They know only what came after so they don't see any difference. What they do see, they take for granted. But older Malays should know better and perhaps they can still help the younger generation to understand.

The success of the PNB unit trusts led to other organisations and states setting up unit trusts. Even Majlis Amanah Rakyat (MARA) operates unit trusts for the Bumiputera. But all these other unit trusts value their units according to the value of their investments. If their investments show no great rise in share price or dividends, people are inclined to sell their units back to the managers, who must take on the loss since they do not guarantee a buy-back price. These fund managers are not as popular among Malays and Bumiputera as the unit trusts operated by PNB.

Many states tried to emulate PNB's success and set up their own funds, guaranteeing big earnings for the unit holders. All went well for some time. But during the stock market collapse triggered by the devaluation crisis, the value of the state share funds dropped. For a while their units had inadequate backing, but when the unit holders wanted to redeem their shares, the state funds were unable to even pay the prices at which the shares were bought. Many investors lost faith in these state-operated unit trusts. During the downturn, they paid no dividends. They are doing better now because the value of their shares has improved, but it took many years before the market recovered and the share prices regained their original value. Thankfully, the problems with state funds have now been largely resolved.

As a form of affirmative action, public investment trusts are unique. The governments of many developing countries have since tried to emulate PNB because they see a system that yields steady and predictable returns, but few have succeeded. It is a model that seems particularly suited to the conditions of multiracial countries. In Malaysia, it has been the instrument to bring together the money-making capacities of the Chinese and the public-mindedness and capacity for public administration of the Malays, for the benefit of all Malaysians.

Our Malaysian managers have since acquired much knowledge about business. Whether they can successfully apply this knowledge in their private business after they leave fund management is still uncertain. One of them did, and failed, blaming the Government for his failure. But the funds have succeeded in improving the knowledge of Malays about business in the modern environment and have ensured that they hold substantial shares in the corporate sector. Apart from the huge number of scholarships given for higher education — well over 100,000 — which have enabled poor Malays and Bumiputera from all over the country to gain tertiary and professional qualifications, PNB has registered great achievements in its core activities. The majority of its unit trust account holders are now better off. They were not rich or even well-off when they started to invest. This simple fact refutes charges that the NEP benefited only the rich, or the cronies of the Prime Minister. Besides, their numbers run into millions and they cannot all be the rich cronies.

Ownership of the units is fairly and widely distributed. Those with more money cannot buy up large numbers of units as every fund has a maximum number that a unit holder can own. The NEP is about equitability at all levels. The unit trusts cannot achieve this. Reducing economic disparities among races means not just equal poverty but also equal wealth. All communities must have equity in wealth also. Methods other than the unit trusts had to be devised to ensure equitability among the middle class and the rich. That is why we developed such a wide range of initiatives in education, including scholarships and training, together with opportunities and assistance to set up businesses, such as capital and affordable premises.

PNB has undeniably contributed much towards giving the Bumiputera a permanent and beneficial stake in the corporate sector. In doing so, it has gone a long way towards solving the nation's core problem — the issue of inequity in ownership of corporate wealth. The disparities that plague us now are the legacy left by the Colonial Government's construction of a plural society, characterised by ethnic separation and a marked, racially-defined division of labour. The British created that problem over the 80 years they ruled this country; those who criticise us for trying to correct the imbalance should remember that the imbalance is not of our own creation.

There is still much that we need to do to repair the damage that was left to us. But what we have already done, under our NEP and through PNB, is momentous. No other affirmative action scheme anywhere in the world has, to my knowledge, worked better, and Malaysians ought to be proud of this achievement. We need apologise to no one.

# Chapter 36:
## Islam And Islamisation

I was born a Muslim and I was brought up as a Muslim child. Very early on, I learnt to pray and to fast. My mother and a tutor taught me to read the Quran though I received little explanation on the contents.

My faith was strong and my belief unquestioning. Islam was my religion and I could not visualise being anything else except a Muslim. I just could not imagine any Muslim forsaking his religion. He may not be much of a practising Muslim but his commitment to Islam surely could not be shaken.

My house was surrounded by houses and shops where people of other faiths lived and worked. In front of my house was a Chinese shop which had an altar facing the entrance. Before a portrait of a deity were placed bowls filled with sand with joss sticks stuck into them. Off and on, I would see the old women with joss sticks in hand praying to the deity.

When we were poor during the Japanese Occupation, we had Indian Tamils living under our house. They had no altars or carved gods but I knew they would pray to gods installed in their temples.

At school among my classmates was a Eurasian boy who was a Catholic. Of course when I went to university to study medicine, my classmates were of many faiths.

My knowing all these people from other religions, and being friends with them, did not undermine my own faith. But I never talked to them about religion. Instinctively I knew that we might get into arguments which might affect my relations with them.

Islam was and is to me a religion that tolerates the existence of other religions and their followers. Later when I began to read translations of the Quran in Malay and in English, I found that there is a full verse which proves that I was not wrong in my assumption regarding the attitude of Islam towards other religions.

The verse in the Quran, from *Surah Al-Kafirun* or The Unbelievers reads:
"Say: O ye who reject Faith!
I worship not that which ye worship,
Nor will ye worship that which I worship.
And I will not worship that which ye have been wont to worship,
Nor will ye worship that which I worship.
To you be your religion, and to me mine."

In another verse the Quran states that there is no compulsion in Islam (*Surah Al-Baqarah,* verse 256).

In Malaysia we may not be applying what is regarded as Shariah law in every case to avoid injustice. We do apply other laws but by upholding justice for everyone in this multi-religious country, by keeping the nation free of conflict and instability, we are following the teachings of Islam. Similarly our tolerance of other religions is also in keeping with the teachings of Islam. Indeed in everything that the Government has done, Islamic principals were upheld.

478     Therefore we have every right to call Malaysia an Islamic country.

Islam and the Islamisation of the Malaysian administration were not causes of contention before. What is a fact is that during the period when Malaysia adopted Islamic values and declared itself an Islamic country, there was peace and stability and the country developed and grew as never before.

Unfortunately many "learned" Muslims are not quite happy with tolerance as taught by the Quran. They would like Islam to be stricter, more severe and violently opposed to other religions. In fact a very learned mufti once told me that other than Islam, there was no religion. I found this very disturbing. Although the religion that is recognised by Allah is Islam, there are many references in the Quran to the religions of Moses and Jesus. In fact, in the passage from *Surah Al-Kafirun* quoted above, reference is made to the religions of those who do not accept the "faith", i.e. Islam.

I studied the history of religions and I discovered that invariably, over the passage of time, the interpretations of religious teachings would change. We know that the Christians had broken up into three major denominations, the Orthodox Eastern Church, the Catholic Roman Church and later on, the Protestants. But the break-up did not end there. Various religious scholars and prelates set up their own particular sects based on their own understanding and teachings. I will not comment further about the Christian denominations, as my knowledge about them is inadequate.

In Islam the same thing has happened. The Prophet brought only one Islam embodied in the verses of the Quran and the true sayings and deeds (the Hadith, or traditions) of the Prophet.

But today we have numerous sects of Islam with each claiming that the others are not Islam or not quite Islam. In fact such are the differences in their teachings that they often fight wars against each other.

The emergence of these sects may sometimes be due to charlatans wanting to gain from the gullibility and ignorance of some of the followers of the faith. Such has been the success of these opportunists that their followers go so far as to proclaim them as prophets, or even the Mahdi — the Messiah who is believed to reveal himself as the world comes to the Day of Resurrection. That these people have always been proven false has not deterred others from making similar claims from time to time, and from gathering followers who believe passionately in them. Incidentally, even among Christians there still are similar claimants and their followers have been known to commit mass suicide on the day they believed the world would come to an end.

But many of the founders of Islamic sects were great religious scholars who genuinely believed that they were giving the true or the correct interpretations of Islam. But because their interpretations and teachings differed so much from each other, they could not all be right.

Differences in the interpretations and teachings are only to be expected since these learned ones are after all only human, with all the frailties of humans. Their understanding and interpretations were therefore subject to these weaknesses.

They may not intend to cause the conflicts and separations into sects, and they often modestly implore their followers not to be fanatical about their teachings. But the followers are often far more rigid than their teachers and might not accept any other teachings as Islamic.

With the passage of time the fanaticism of the followers and the tendency to amplify and add to the teachings would be such that the differences between the sects would become irreconcilable. Any one of the followers trying to lessen the rigidity in their beliefs, or trying to reconcile the teachings of others (or even to observe the injunctions of Islam against schisms) would be regarded as disloyal renegades if not heretics.

And so today we see Muslims divided into innumerable sects, each with its own interpretations of Islam. The worst division is between the Sunnis and the Shiites. Within these two sects there are sub-sects and followers of different imams. The adherence of the followers is very strong and uncompromising. Self-sacrifice is a strong trait as is fighting for their beliefs. Shiites are more prepared to die for their beliefs than are the others. The belief is that such a sacrifice will be well rewarded in the afterlife.

The Sunnis are more numerous then the Shiites but they are less fanatical in the practice of Islam. But the animosity against the Shiites is nevertheless very strong. Violent attacks by Shiites against Sunnis invariably meet with similar violence by the Sunnis. At one stage the Shiites were not allowed to perform the Haj in Mecca by the Saudi authorities.

Islam is a tolerant religion but, as I said, some of the learned interpreters of Islam are not quite happy with it. They and their followers would like the religion to be much more intolerant, rigid and strict. This is especially so in the attitude towards non-Muslims. The yearning is to impose Islamic practices and laws on non-Muslims by force if possible. This does not endear Islam to non-Muslims, and their rejection of Islam is thereby made stronger. In other words, intolerant behaviour, extreme rigidity and fanaticism, which are contrary to the teachings of Islam, have not only given Islam a bad name but have prevented the spread of the religion.

The early Muslims were much more lenient and accommodating towards non-Muslims. This is why Christianity and Judaism thrived quite well in Muslim countries. In fact such was the Muslims' tolerance of the Jews that whenever the latter were persecuted by European Christians, they would flee to Muslim countries in North Africa and the Turkish-ruled regions in Eastern Europe.

By contrast when the Christian Spanish re-conquered Spain, the Jews as well as the Muslims were given the choice of converting to Christianity, being put to death, or being expelled from Catholic Spain. That is why a large number of Jews followed the Muslim evacuees to North Africa.

It is worth noting that despite Iran being apparently extremely Islamic, there are still Jews living in Iran and their synagogues are protected by the Government. The Jews are even represented in Parliament. The Iranians, despite their enmity towards the Israelis and Americans, seem to practise what is enjoined by the Quran with regard to peoples of other faiths.

But elsewhere in the Muslim world today Jews are not welcome. This includes Malaysia. When I tried to help the peace process in Palestine by allowing Israeli schoolchildren and an Israeli cricket team to visit Malaysia, I was soundly condemned by Malay Muslims. Yet in the Quran it says that when an enemy offers to make peace we should respond positively.

But the intolerance is not confined to non-Muslims. We are also critical of fellow Muslims in the performance of their religious obligations and rituals. Despite the Quran saying that Islam is not meant to be a burden to the faithful, many Muslims want to make it a burden. They reject the flexibility of Quranic teachings regarding minor prohibitions and the performance of certain rituals.

We are enjoined to pray five times a day. But if the learned in Islam can have their way, we would have to add to the five prayers various other prayers and recitations so that the prayers would be prolonged. Most of these additional rituals and recitations are optional but the learned ones would like to make them compulsory.

As an UMNO politician I had to contend with the religious quotations of PAS speakers. They were very impressive, quoting the verses of the Quran and immediately translating and dramatising them with very colourful Malay.

I learned to memorise some of the more frequently quoted verses and their Malay translations but I was at a disadvantage. My Arabic was not fluent enough even when the verses I quoted were correct.

I began to study the Quran more thoroughly, reading the Arabic text and then the Malay or English translations. I found that the interpretations made by the politicians, while being more colourful, were often not quite accurate. Often only half the verses were quoted.

While doing this I became more interested in reading the Quran because knowing the Malay and English translations made the study more interesting. Soon I was reading through the whole Quran several times in order to know what really were the fundamental teachings of the religion. Until then what I knew about my religion was what my tutors and teachers had taught me. They focused on certain passages only and on those verses which I had to learn by heart for my prayers.

It was really an eye-opener reading the Quran in a language I understood. The religious teachers were quick to point out that the translations of the Quran were not really the Quran. But then I pointed out that when they taught me they also translated Arabic into Malay so I could understand. According to their own arguments, their translations were therefore also not the words of the Quran, not truly the Message of Allah.

Later I was to learn that even those whose mother tongue was Arabic could not on their own truly understand many of the passages in the Quran. They still needed interpreters and what they understood was what the interpreters understood. And being human the interpreters, no matter how learned they may have been, might still have understood wrongly or differently from others, and consequently their teachings might not have been similar — or even be contradictory — to each other.

I assumed that the reason why the Muslims had been divided into different sects was because the understanding of these interpreters differed and their teachings differed accordingly.

Yet we need interpreters if we are to understand the teachings of the Quran, more so if Arabic is not our mother tongue or we just do not know the Arabic language well enough. I therefore accept that the translations of the Quran into Malay and English, while they cannot be regarded as the Quran itself, are still as acceptable as the Islam taught to me in Malay.

However, the verses of the Quran are divided into two fairly distinct categories. These are the *Muhkamaat,* the verses whose meanings are clear and unambiguous and do not lend themselves easily to different understandings and interpretations.

Then there are the *Mutashaabihaat* which are not clear or direct and may take the form of allegories or parables, opening themselves to varied and sometimes contradictory interpretations.

The clear *Muhkamaat* verses can be understood quite easily, even if one does not speak Arabic, provided someone translates the verses. They are simple and direct, and almost everyone translates them with no detectable difference from others. Thus the Quran says "A Muslim is a brother to other Muslims". It cannot be misunderstood or interpreted to mean anything different. The Quran also says "A Muslim must not kill another Muslim". Again it is very clear.

Yet we see Muslims fighting and killing other Muslims. Are they not transgressing? Surely they must be. But they declare that their adversaries are not really Muslims and therefore they are not killing Muslims and are not going against the injunctions of Islam.

There are other clear verses which enjoin Muslims to honour promises and undertakings, to be honest, not to accept gratification, to acquire knowledge, to be prepared to defend the *ummah* (the global Muslim community), to care for orphans, to divide inheritance in the prescribed way, to accept offers of peace, to judge with justice, not to allow hate to influence decisions, not to use force to convert, and many, many more which should not only guide the way of life of a Muslim but make an honourable and upright man of him. He should also become successful in his endeavours in life, but he should not forget the afterlife when his behaviour in life will be judged and where he will be punished or rewarded for what he has done.

Islam, as many Muslims will repeat, is "a way of life". It is not just a "faith" but a comprehensive guide to how a Muslim should live. By living the prescribed way then his afterlife, his *akhirat,* would be as good as is promised in the Quran. The "Way of Life" is about everything that he does and not just the performance of rituals.

Since the *Muhkamaat* verses are clear and unambiguous, their understanding and interpretation should not differ and therefore they should not divide Muslims. But as illustrated above in the case of a Muslim killing other Muslims, despite this clarity, the wicked and the misguided will still kill by claiming that their adversaries are not "real Muslims" or are not Muslims at all.

Another problem arising from differing interpretations is the tendency to stress the literal rather than the substance of the message.

The Quran is emphatic about the need to read (*Iqraq*). When one reads one will certainly acquire knowledge. Thus the early Muslims obeying this injunction read everything they could lay their hands on in order to acquire knowledge.

Since there was at the time of the Prophet nothing much written about Islam, and since the injunction to read did not restrict the material that was to be read, the early Muslims apparently read the works of the Greeks, the Indians, the Chinese and the Persians. To do this they must have learnt the relevant languages. We do know now that early Muslim scholars reproduced the scientific findings and the numerical systems of the peoples concerned. More than that, they carried out their own studies and research and added to the body of knowledge in many fields. It was Muslim scholars who pioneered astronomy, algebra, the study of disease and medicine, celestial navigation, and more.

For centuries Muslims were well ahead of other civilisations in their mastery of the sciences, medicine and mathematics. But around the fifteenth century of the Common Era, new interpretations began to be spread, saying that *Iqraq* referred to the reading and the acquisition of religious knowledge only.

Only the study of religion would gain merit for the scholars. All other studies or fields of knowledge would earn no merit. The people who gave this interpretation were those who had studied religion in depth. Naturally they must have been inclined to regard their particular discipline as having the utmost importance.

Whatever the reason may have been for this emphasis on the exclusive study of religion, the fact remains that the study of other fields of learning by Muslim scholars started to decline around the fifteenth century. Over time, Muslims became very ignorant about these subjects.

Incidentally just when Muslims were rejecting the study of science, European Christians, who were then living in the Dark Ages, noticed the superiority of Muslim civilisation and decided to acquire the knowledge of the Muslims. Christian priests learnt Arabic and studied scientific and other books in the great libraries of the Muslim world.

The end result was the regression of the Muslims and the rapid advancement of European Christians after the knowledge they had acquired was translated first into Latin and then into the other European languages. This made knowledge available to lay people, not just priests as had been the practice of the mediaeval Church.

As Muslims regressed due to lack of knowledge in the sciences, they became weak and incapable of defending themselves. They could not improve their defences with new weapons and strategies, and one by one Muslim lands were lost to the Europeans with their better weaponry.

Such is the effect of faulty interpretations of Quranic verses, such as that regarding *Iqraq*. Indeed, some declared that *Iqraq* did not even mean "read", but fortunately they are in the minority.

But there are other interpretations of the Quran which have led to Muslim regression. The Quran enjoins Muslims to have the capacity to defend themselves. For this the Quran mentioned the possession of war horses. The Prophet had war horses and other weapons of the time with which to defend the community.

It is unfortunate that the literal interpretation of this verse has resulted in Muslims ignoring the importance of defensive capacity. Instead they emphasise the literal possession of war horses, and weapons used by the Prophet, as the tradition that Muslims must follow. Had they stressed defence they would have strengthened their defence capacity by upgrading their weaponry the way their European enemies had.

The neglect of the study of science and mathematics contributed to the inability of Muslims to invent and develop new weapons. In the end, they were forced to procure their weapons from their detractors, and their capacity to defend themselves as enjoined by the Quran deteriorated completely.

Again it can be seen that even when a verse in the Quran is clear, the interpreters of the verse can miss the real message, opting for the literal meaning. The sad state of Muslims today, their inability to defend themselves, must be due to the wrong emphases in the interpretations of the teachings of Islam.

486   The Quran gives further guidance which is often misinterpreted or misunderstood to the detriment of Muslims. It is only right that, in facing problems or threats, Muslims should seek succour through prayers appealing to Allah.

The teachers of the religion stress the need for prayers, for appeals to Allah during any difficulty or threat. But what is not stressed is the injunction in the Quran that Allah will not change your situation until you make the effort to change it yourself.

That we should try to help ourselves is very important. Prayers alone will not help us except in cases where there is nothing at all that we can do for ourselves. But it is very seldom indeed that we are so completely helpless.

The present dire state of Muslims is due at least in part to them doing nothing or very, very little for themselves beyond praying for help from the Almighty. The 1.3 billion Muslims must be among the richest people in the world because Allah has bestowed on them untold wealth from oil resources. But can they say that they have made use of the wealth to help themselves overcome their present situation?

Clearly they are not following the injunctions of the Quran to help themselves first if they desire the help of the Almighty. Blaming others will get them nowhere for they cannot really expect others to take action to save Muslims when the Muslims are doing practically nothing to save themselves.

There was a time when I felt confused about Islam and its teachings. Studying scientific subjects when I was in the university, I found myself questioning some of the teachings of Islam.

Islam, apparently more than any other religion, requires believers to accept everything as articles of faith that may not be questioned. At least that is the teaching of the learned in Islam. Just believe whatever we are taught. Do not ask questions. But as a scientist I was taught to seek proof in everything. What I found in science frequently seem to contradict the teachings of my religion.

In medicine everything is explained in a logical way. Everything is reasonable and easy for the human mind to accept. Diseases are caused by tiny organisms, or by the malfunction of the human body. To cure an ailment you have to rid the body of the noxious influence. You kill the germs or you excise the diseased parts. You can succeed and the patient is cured, or you can fail and the patient will die.

You may pray and appeal to the Almighty for help. But you must give the prescribed treatment if you want the patient to get well again. If the patient is going to survive he will survive whether you pray to Allah or not. After all, non-Muslims also get cured. In fact, Muslims actually look up to non-Muslim doctors to cure them.

I was confused and disturbed. I just could not bring myself to reject faith. Yet what I observed could not be explained by religion, by the Islam that I believed in.

My religious teachers strongly objected to the idea of rationality or reason in religion. They wanted me just to believe. They wanted me in fact to accept what they said as the Word of God. I was not to argue. I had to simply believe.

But my enquiring mind refused to just believe. Surely the words of Allah must be rational, must be based on reason. Religion cannot be just about performing rituals. There must be reasons for everything, for God has given Man the capacity to think. To think is to reason. It could not be that there should be no reason in our faith.

For a long time I tried to find reasons for the miracle of life. Science taught me all about the bodily functions; our having to eat, to breathe, to rid ourselves of bodily waste, etc. But why should we live at all if in the end despite eating and breathing, we would still die?

Even as I studied biology, chemistry and physics in my first year at university I mulled over the fact called the miracle of life. Then slowly it dawned on me that science could not explain "why", it could only explain "how" things were the way they were.

We are told that we breathe in oxygen from the air to oxygenise the blood in the body, which in turn oxidises the cells of the tissue to enable them to live. The cells then pass into the blood the waste from the oxidation process in the form of carbon dioxide and other waste which are then expelled through the lungs, kidneys or the nether end. This way the organism, the creature, or the human being is able to live.

But why should this be so? The process described above is about "how" the body oxidises and generates waste, but it does not answer "why" this process gives life to the organism.

Why oxygen? Why not chlorine or some other gas? Science will explain that chlorine would poison the body. Science explains at length the process by which chlorine kills living organisms. Every time I asked why something behaved in the way it did, whether it was a living process or a "dead" one, invariably the answer explained only how the process took place.

In the end I was forced to conclude that there was a power which determined why everything happened the way it did. Scientists call it "Nature". But what is Nature? Why does it determine things the way it does?

I concluded that in identifying the power of Nature, scientists were trying to avoid admitting that there is a power which they could not explain that determined everything that happened in the world. This power determined even the laws of science and the way they govern every action and reaction.

I concluded that "Nature" must actually be God or Allah, the Almighty, the power that determines everything that governs the behaviour of all things on earth and beyond.

The power is far greater than what we have been taught to believe. We now know that the universe, with its stars (suns) and its myriad constellations, is far bigger than we had earlier been taught to believe. We know of the vastness of space such that it takes light years to travel even within each constellation.

Yet here on Earth everything is made up of electrons, protons and other particles that are so small, so tiny, that we cannot see them. These particles determine the properties of a given substance and its behaviour. At the molecular level, they can be so loosely packed as gas that objects can pass though them, but they can be so densely packed as solids that they resist vigorous efforts to change their physical shapes.

489

The power that creates this immeasurably huge universe and these tiny atoms, electrons, protons and other subatomic particles; the power which determines their properties and behaviour; the power that creates life and the chemical, physical and biological processes that are entailed; the power that governs everything from the smallest to the immense vastness of the universe must be a power that is really beyond human comprehension. That Power must be the Creator, God, Allah. If we do not believe in there being a Creator, we cannot explain why everything happens the way it happens in the universe. We would just be lost, unable to understand why things are the way they are.

I was relieved to discover this. Now I knew the limitations of science. Science explains how things are, and a knowledge of science can yield many practical uses. But that is as far as science can go. The moment science is asked to explain why things are, there is and there will be no answer.

Our scientists are now "creating" life through cloning by using stem cells, etc. They have succeeded and they can tell you how they did the things they have done. But when asked why it is possible to clone, to create new life, they have no answer.

What they have done is nothing more than harness the behaviour of living things as ordained by God, by Allah. After all, every one of us can create life. We do that through the miracle of birth. We can explain how the sperm fertilises the ovum, but again we cannot explain why. Why don't humans lay eggs? This process can create life just as well. But we are conceived in the womb of a woman. Had Allah wished that Man should procreate through the process of laying eggs, what would we say? We will explain how the eggs are laid, fertilised and hatched. But we would not be able to explain why the conception is not in the womb of a woman as it is now. All we can say is that it is God's Will.

Gradually at first, but more rapidly as I learnt more about the physical, chemical and biological processes of science, I regained my faith.

490    My faith became stronger than before because I now knew what the early Arab Muslims did not — that the power of Allah is far greater than they thought, that it extends into millions of years in time, and that it governs a universe that is unimaginably enormous. Science cannot negate the power of the Creator. Science cannot displace faith. Therefore there is nothing to fear from learning science. The study of science should not undermine faith. It will in fact strengthen it. There is therefore no reason why Muslims should not study science.

I regard this fact as very important because one of the reasons for the backwardness of Muslims is their ignorance in the scientific field. Attributing all phenomena to the Will of Allah is correct, but by not studying the "how" of science, we are unable to make use of Allah's creation for our betterment.

The greatest disservice done to the Islamic civilisation is the conclusions and teachings of the learned ones that Muslims should not study science because it is secular and not religious. Almost immediately after such teachings, the Muslim civilisation regressed and eventually Muslims became weak and incapable of defending themselves.

Worse still, the learned ones attribute this regression merely to Allah's Will. They ignore the injunction that Allah will only help the *ummah* if it makes the effort to help itself first. Surely the acquisition of scientific knowledge will give Muslims the capacity to defend the *ummah*. When they fail to do this, then their prayers will not be answered.

Of course there are things that can be done even now. But despite the bounty Allah bestowed on Muslims they have done nothing for their defence, and their well-being. And yet Islam is very clear on the need to perform what is categorised as *fardhu kifayah*, the injunction which requires that Muslim communities must have among them individuals whose ability and actions will serve in the defence and promotion of the welfare of their communities and of Islam itself. If there is no one capable of these things then the whole community must be regarded as having committed a grave sin.

In my understanding the availability of good administrators, doctors, engineers, soldiers and leaders will absolve the Muslim community of many sins. These people are actually fulfilling the injunctions of Islam.

Whereas prayers, fasting, the giving of alms and performing the Haj give merit to the individual, the provision for the needs of the Muslim community earns merit not just for the individual but also absolves the community of common sins.

491

Unfortunately, Muslims and their religious teachers stress more on *fardhu `ain* the performance of prayers, fasting, alms-giving and the Haj, than on *fardhu kifayah*. Yet nowhere in the Quran or the true Hadith is it said that "*fardhu `ain*" which earns merit only for oneself is more important in the afterlife than *fardhu kifayah*.

Muslims know very well that soldiers who die in the defence of Islam or the Islamic community are regarded as martyrs (*shahid*) and are promised places in heaven. If this is so then those involved in providing for the defence and well-being of the community must be regarded as earning as much merit for the afterlife as those who perform the various rituals and who study the religion, lead prayers and recite the Quran.

The territorial defence of the community is not done just by soldiers but by those who work in the defence industry, by researchers, developers and producers of weapons of defence; by the whole administration, in fact. Provided that they all do their work sincerely and properly, then they must be considered as performing *fardhu kifayah* and are deserving of the same merit.

Of course if they fail in their duty, if they are corrupt, then they would be committing grave sins and deserve punishment in the afterlife.

My study of the Quran has been extremely useful in providing guidance in my personal life and in carrying out the tasks entrusted to me as leader of my country, and I felt that others too should benefit from it. If the whole of Malaysia is peopled by the "rightly guided", then Malaysia must become a great country. It would help banish the general belief that Muslim countries cannot become developed the way non-Muslim countries can. Perhaps there is an element of ego but that does not detract from the fact that their work makes Islam a respected and strong religion.

When I decided to give more meaning to the constitutional provision that Islam is the official religion, I did not mean that all the different peoples of Malaysia must become Muslim. All we wanted was that Islamic values be imbibed by Malaysians without the need for them to even believe in Islam. And so it was that in my second year as Prime Minister I declared that the Malaysian Government would be guided by Islamic values.

There may be differences in the value systems of those of different faiths in Malaysia, but I did not think that the differences would be that great or that many. By and large good Islamic values are the same as those that are regarded as good Western values or the so-called Universal values. If they seem to be different it is not due to the teachings of Islam, but rather to the interpretations made by those who feel a need to be different. There are of course certain Western values which are incompatible with Islam, especially those which have evolved in modern times. But even non-Muslims in Malaysia would want to reject these values.

Even as a young boy I had felt unable to understand why Muslim countries seemed backward and weak by comparison to the countries of the West. It cannot be because of the teachings of Islam; the true teachings as found in the Quran and not as interpreted by some religiously learned people.

The fact is that there was a time when the Muslim countries were more advanced than the West.

I read that the Muslim settlers in Andalusia in Spain were much more advanced in agriculture than the Europeans of that time. They built viaducts to carry water from the mountains to irrigate the land. They were skilled in construction as evidenced by the Alhambra in Grenada. They built roads for travellers and merchants. They had hotels for the merchants, complete with compounds for their camels and horses. They had markets for itinerant traders and permanent shopkeepers.

They sailed the high seas and crossed deserts guided by the stars. Arab merchants traversed the vast Indian Ocean to trade and exchange goods with Chinese and Indian traders at Southeast Asian entrepot ports.

Their towns and cities were well laid out and their mosques reflected their skills, their understanding of physics, and their appreciation of beauty. Their armies were well organised and powerful, as were their naval forces.

Everything pointed to the superiority of the Muslims and their civilisation. Yet they were still ardent Muslims, strictly adhering to their religious duties, and they were learned in their religion. Their scholars studied the religion deeply and wrote tomes on the various aspect of Islam even as they excelled in the sciences, in mathematics, in astronomy and in medicine.

The world at that time respected Islam and the Muslims. They did so because of the success of Muslims in every field.

Being a successful country is not unIslamic. A country will be unIslamic only if it ignores the teachings of Islam. And the teachings of Islam say nothing about being failures in this world in order to gain merit in the next.

At the general meeting of a non-Muslim political party in 1996, I declared in a speech that Malaysia was an Islamic country. The non-Muslims did not object because they knew that since its founding the Muslim majority which dominated the Government had been fair and just to them. But there are some Muslims, even in Malaysia, who believe that the only thing that would qualify a country as a Muslim country is if we decapitate and chop off the hands of criminals.

But that is an arbitrary criterion. The Quran advocates an Islamic community and not an Islamic country. In the Quran it is not the punishment that is stressed. Indeed Muslims are enjoined to forgive and be merciful. In verse 45 of *Surah Al-Maidah* the Quran says that those who forego the right to exact retribution, will have their sins forgiven. Clearly Islam is merciful and forgiving. Above all, justice is what makes a community Islamic.

# Chapter 37:
## Introducing Privatisation

When socialism and communism were on the ascendancy, nationalisation became the byword. It was the standard recipe for national development — it was believed that if the state owned the means of production, all profits would go to it and not to middlemen or selfish private interests. The resulting wealth, undiminished by predatory businessmen, would then belong to the workers' government and would be fairly and equally expended on every citizen. But that approach did not work for a number of reasons so the pendulum swung back, and the idea of privatisation or denationalisation began to be considered seriously once more.

Malaysia had a few state-owned businesses but none were doing well, so we began to think of running these businesses as private corporations. The main difference between private and state enterprise was the profit motive. Whereas the whole of the profits from nationalised businesses would go to the Government, in the private sector the profit after tax goes to the owners or shareholders, and also to the management and employees via their salaries and wages. With profits as their incentive the owners, workers and managers would work harder. The advocates of private initiative claimed that this was the way to advance the enterprise and achieve profitability.

495

There was really no model of privatisation at that time for Malaysia to copy and we had to devise our own methods. We were concerned with what would happen to the workers who were government employees. So to ensure that the workers did not lose because they were no longer on government pay and pension, we placed conditions on privatisation.

First, the employees should have the option to stay on a government salary scheme if they wished. Should the government scheme be revised upward, they would be entitled to the revised pay even though they were no longer government employees. But if they chose to be on the company's pay scheme, they might enjoy the bonuses that are paid when a company does well. They would also enjoy any revision of pay by the company. However, once they decided which scheme they wanted to be under, they could not switch back. If they chose not to join the privatised entity at all, they would stay with the Government but would take on other jobs. They might also choose to leave altogether, in which case they would benefit from a voluntary separation scheme which would entitle them to a lump-sum payment. But they were not to be dismissed simply to reduce the privatised entity's costs. Certain personnel, however, had to remain with the Government to do supervisory work.

We first decided to try out our privatisation model with the Telecoms Department. The department's services were not efficient and it often took two years for applications for telephones to be approved. There was also evidence of corrupt practices. The Government had to allocate almost RM200 million yearly to run the department and that allocation kept increasing. The Government also earned practically nothing from operating the telephone and the telegraph services.

As a first step, the department was made into a corporation in 1987 called Syarikat Telekom Malaysia Berhad (STMB), Malaysia's first privatised entity. Its assets, in installed capital equipment, were given a nominal value and transferred to the corporation. The estimated capital was divided into shares of RM1 and the company was listed to enable investors to take them up, although the Government retained 70 per cent of the shares. Officers from the department seconded to the company were no longer subject to Civil Service General Orders or rules in the conduct of their work.

Service improved almost immediately, earnings shot up and very soon the company was making about RM300 million a year. The Government not only profited from the dividends but also no longer had to pay the annual RM200 million allocation to the old Telecoms Department. Of course, the Government also saved on the wages and salaries which had been paid to Telecoms Department employees before.

New telecommunications technology was just taking off at the time and fax machines had made the telegraph obsolete. Under these circumstances, a government department would have taken years to decide what to do. The company, on the other hand, made a decision to install the fax machines quickly and allowed private ownership of the machines. Other innovations followed and the company responded rapidly. Today's telecommunication businesses are among the most profitable money-earners, especially after wireless cellular phones became ever more versatile, popular and widely used. The telecoms company was able to cope with new challenges posed by the increasing versatility of wireless communications. Even when new private companies were licensed, the largely Government-owned STMB could hold its own in competition with them. Its share price rose and the performance of the company enabled it to borrow from the banks for expansion.

The use of land lines and copper wires has been reduced by wireless technology and even fibre optics are no longer as important now as they once were. The earnings of the telecoms company improved with each new technology and technical application. Adopting commercial practices, it promoted its services, something that a government department which monopolised service would never have done or even considered necessary. Privatisation resulted in better service, better pay for workers and new sources of income for the Government, where before the Government literally had to subsidise the service. The number of employees on government payroll was also reduced, with considerable savings.

The Government continued to act as the regulator and licensor, as new technologies had to be scrutinised before adoption to ensure they were not used for illegal purposes. When the colour printer was introduced, for example, some Ministers objected, fearing they might be used to make counterfeit currency notes. The Cabinet wanted to license the machines, but the usage would have been so great and diverse that licensing and control measures would only have hindered the adoption of this new technology. Despite the risk, it was decided to allow the machines to be imported and sold freely. After all, the machines could also counterfeit notes outside the country. Today colour pictures can be duplicated and then transmitted anywhere in the world within seconds and picture quality keeps improving. Whatever the abuses and criminal applications, the usefulness of the machines and the business they generate far outweigh the possibility of abuse. New advances in technology continue to give rise to new uses. Telecommunications companies must keep devising new applications quickly to increase their business and profits, and to maintain market share and survive. Unburdened by bureaucratic delays, they are able to respond quickly. As private companies they know and live by the truth that time costs money, and that delay can be fatal.

Government offices would not be able to cope with this challenge as people in different departments would want to have their say in the decision-making process. Delays would drag on. These would not cost those officers anything — a government officer apparently stood to gain nothing from the earnings that the decision might generate or sustain any loss from the delay in making decisions. It did not matter to them that the approved innovation might result in an increase in government revenue and promote the country's development. Once absorbed into the Consolidated Account, where all government revenue was consolidated, the added profits would be practically untraceable. Other government priorities would likely have a stronger claim on the money. Civil servants who held any proposal's fate in their own hands are not motivated as they have no personal interest or stake in reaching a good decision quickly.

Another reason that forced us to consider privatisation was that the public demand for utilities and services far exceeded our means to deliver them — specifically the Government's financial and manpower capacities. Waiting for the Government to set aside the funds needed would always mean a delay in providing the necessary utilities and services. Inadequate services would impede the country's economic growth and development and would also generate public discontent and anti-Government feelings.

We next turned our attention to the road system, which needed to be improved by replacing the old winding roads with expressways. Traffic volume was increasing and the narrow, two-lane roads could no longer cope. Good roads, we believed, would stimulate business and speed up the development of the country. I reasoned that if we built an expressway from the north to the south of the Peninsula, new towns would also grow and new businesses would be generated because of improved transportation of goods and employees. But the Government lacked the money to build this highway. If at all, we could only do it very slowly, over many years, and the country's development would be impeded.

Tolls were largely unknown in Malaysia then. In former times, to travel up the East Coast you had to cross a number of rivers by punt-ferry. At each, there was a charge for every vehicle. But people did not remember that, or else they saw the payment as a fee or gratuity rather than a toll. There was one bridge in Perak which was tolled. The PAS government in Kelantan also had to charge a much-resented toll for use of the bridge it built in the 1960s across the Kelantan River at Kota Baru. So Malaysians had some experience with paying tolls.

Motorists may not like having to pay tolls but I believed that users should pay for better roads. If the Government were to build a free road, then people not using the highway would have to pay the cost through other taxes. This would be unfair to the majority of the motorists who might never use the highway. We also needed to improve the roads in the cities and towns where cars would pass several times in a day. Tolling there would be difficult so expressway users would also be using the toll-free urban roads built by the Government. It seemed to me that they should at least pay for something. I felt that paying to drive on wide, six-lane highways with dividers was a fair compromise. Besides, if they liked they could still use the old toll-free roads. They may save on toll payment but the wear and tear on their vehicles would still be a cost to them, apart from having to use more petrol on the winding, longer, old roads.

The Cabinet agreed that the North-South Expressway should be privatised but few contractors were interested in attempting something so new. Eventually a group of Malay contractors was persuaded to build and operate the expressway. They would take on the project, they said, if they could be convinced that it would be profitable. They pointed out that if the Government set the toll rates, the project might not be viable. On its part, the Government feared that high toll rates would be met with protests from motorists and the general public and the Government would lose popularity. We insisted that we should fix all toll rates and they should be low. To ensure that the contractors and the operators would not lose money on the construction work, we agreed to transfer the completed sections of the new road to the operator for free, that the needed land should be acquired by the Government, and that a soft loan be given to the highway company to enable it to make a profit even though the toll rates were low.

These were not subsidies to the company. They were, in fact, subsidies to the road users to ensure they would not have to pay high tolls. If the rates were too high motorists might not use the highway and the project would fail. The cost of failing would be huge to the company and the Government alike, so it was far more preferable to subsidise the highway users by lowering the construction cost. The traffic volume was also crucial because it had to grow at a certain rate to make the project viable. If it did not, then the Government would have to compensate the company. If on the other hand it grew higher than projected, then the Government should have a share in the extra earnings.

Construction on the North-South Expressway began in 1988 and progressed in phases until it was completed in 1995, 15 months ahead of schedule. It now stretches for 772km from Thailand to Singapore. The North-South Expressway was initially a success, but the 1997 financial crisis affected its income and the Government had to take over the company. Now it is profitable again.

As proof of its success, once the North-South Expressway was completed the private sector clamoured to build other tolled highways. Malaysia now has the best road system in Southeast Asia. Relieved of the need to build highways, the Government was able to improve urban and rural roads. The elevated highways in the cities and towns are largely public freeways. Rural roads now cover the whole countryside. But for privatisation, these would not have been possible to build. We now have urban tolls as well but the charges are minimal and many people use them on a daily basis, Motorists now regard toll payment in the same way as paying for fuel.

Once the principle of privatisation was accepted, the Government examined all its facilities and functions to consider the possibility of their being transferred to the private sector. Power generation and supply, water supply, post offices, the national airline, the automotive industry, and many other government functions and companies were eventually privatised. Some were only partially privatised while others were merely corporatised, as was the case of the Institut Jantung Negara (IJN), or the National Heart Institute. Still others were limited to outsourcing services to the private sector. A few government-owned companies remain. Of these, PETRONAS is the largest and it is the exception that proves the rule, for it has managed to prove that a 100 per cent, Government-owned company could also succeed. It has done so largely because it is not run like a government department but like a commercial entity with little public interference.

Some companies inevitably failed, especially during the 1997 recession and financial crisis. But by and large, privatisation has succeeded in Malaysia and the country owes much of its rapid development to it. Ports which handled only a few hundred thousand containers annually when they were government-owned now handle four or five million containers a year. Their expansion to cope with this increased demand no longer needed government funding. The work was paid for from earnings or, if money was borrowed, the ports were able to pay off those debts from their earnings.

Granted, the Government sold assets at much lower prices than their theoretical market value. But these assets were not earning us anything — they were old and had been acquired or installed a long time ago. We might have sold the properties on the market but this would only have increased the cost to the privatised company. Had we transferred these assets at market value, these businesses would not have been viable, and a failed business is of no use to the Government. Should it involve an essential service such as electricity supply or telecommunications, failure entails an even greater cost to the country and people as a whole. The privatised entity must be viable and the public must not be made to pay high charges. If the sale of government assets at below market value is seen as providing a subsidy, it is a subsidy to the public.

Many people think that privatisation is a capitalist evil, but we turned to privatisation because nationalisation had been repeatedly proven to be a socialist mistake. Even the communist countries have turned to the private sector for economic rejuvenation. Nationalisation did not work because of a lack of incentive. All too often, bureaucracy tended to protect itself, and not to advance the substantive purpose which it was established to promote. Without the profit motive, no extra effort was made to improve services and earn bigger profits. While having to support its non-performing or resistant bureaucratic management, the Government also had to make allocations for running the company and even subsidising its activities. Government-run companies are often managed like government departments. Frequently the Government had to provide allocations of funds in the annual budgets.

Privatisation does not guarantee success but is more likely to provide better services at lower costs. It releases the Government from having to shoulder the cost of running the company, and reduces government staff and staffing costs including salaries, wages and allowances. Often the Government can quickly recover its financial support through the taxes on the company's profits and the profits of its subsidiaries. These profits may be so big that to reject privatisation on ideological grounds would be really foolish.

Another criticism of privatisation is that it has benefited the Government's cronies. This charge is difficult to refute simply because whoever receives any privatised project is immediately perceived and branded as a government crony. The logic of the accusation is circular and self-fulfilling. If every privatisation exercise is proof of cronyism, the only way to forestall that accusation is to refuse to privatise anything. But without privatisation, the Government could not have supplied all the services and utilities that our rapidly-growing economy and population needed. We simply did not have the money to do that ourselves and borrowing has its limits and problems. In the end, privatisation was the only way to go.

502

The big privatisation project, however, is not for everybody — it must go to people who have the capacity and a proven record of success. The requirements of the NEP further reduced the number of eligible companies. An open tender may seem like the correct thing to do, but choosing between bids is never easy. Eager to win the tender, bidders are prone to under-quote. Yet if the project is not awarded to the lowest bidder, there is a great hue and cry, including accusations of foul play and corruption. In the end, the Government must use its best judgment. It must find a way to award contracts and privatisation ventures to people who have the capacity to carry out the projects, will succeed, and will be able to relieve the Government of some of its burdens rather than add to them by failing. It must also seek to secure a fair price, one that will give the contractor a reasonable return from the contract.

We introduced the negotiated tender procedure in which a few companies were asked to submit a tender. The one selected according to predetermined criteria must then hold negotiations to reduce the cost and to ensure that the specifications are met. Once a bidder has performed well it is difficult not to consider him again for other projects, especially those in the same category. Unfortunately, despite meeting all the criteria, when he gets this new contract, he is perceived as a government favourite or crony. In an attempt to avoid this accusation and from a sincere desire to distribute opportunities fairly, projects were frequently given to incompetent bidders who subsequently failed. Many hospitals and schools have not been completed years after the time specified in the contract. We eventually learned to rely upon people who had a good track record, even if the Government was accused of cronyism. I would rather face such accusations than risk failure, which invariably cost the Government more.

Tenders also posed another problem — as soon as one bidder submitted his tender, three or four others would make almost identical bids, suggesting that tender documents were leaked to interested parties. The first bidder may lose out when others submit more competitive figures, so bidders became reluctant to submit their tenders to the relevant office. They insisted instead on submitting them directly to the relevant Ministers. This ensured that, if other bids were forthcoming, they would be different and not modified clones of the initial bid. Yet the practice of submitting tenders to the Minister rather than the department posed its own problems, as it encouraged further accusations of favouritism, cronyism, and establishing a political inside-track. Passing the bid to the officials, as some chose to do, would not insulate the Minister from suspicion. These charges were inescapable but we could not be deterred by them. There was work to be done and decisions to be made.

I suspect that foreign criticisms of Malaysian privatisation were largely due to the policy to allow only Malaysian companies to take part. Had we allowed the big foreign corporations to bid and acquire the privatised entities, there would have been few critics.

Whatever arguments or criticisms are offered, there can be no doubt that without privatisation Malaysia would not have developed as quickly as it did. The country's development was phenomenal. Over 30 years or so, it was transformed from a rather poor agricultural country into the world's 17th biggest trading nation, with 82 per cent of total exports of over USD100 billion made up of manufactured goods. Malaysia's infrastructure is comparable to that of developed countries and includes a network of first-class highways that crisscross the country and reliable electricity and water supplies.

After I stepped down, new criticisms were levelled against privatisation. These were political in character. An article in a local paper announced that the former head of the national power authority was against the privatisation of power generation. That this person was head of power generation and distribution when Malaysia suffered one of its worst nationwide blackouts[1] was not mentioned. That incident caused our manufacturing industries to lose hundreds of millions of ringgit as sensitive processes suddenly stopped. Industries also demanded compensation. Following this breakdown in the electricity supply, the Government issued the first licence to an independent power producer (IPP). Unfortunately, the government negotiators were not familiar with drawing up power supply agreements with IPPs. They followed a US model which included a Take or Pay clause: a certain payment had to be made to the IPP whether or not the national power company sourced power from it, and that IPP made huge profits as a result. We did try to renegotiate the agreement but the IPP company refused. Subsequent agreements on power off-take from IPPs did not have this provision.

Sometimes the private sector itself proposed totally new projects. We kept an open mind in such cases and considered giving our approval if the proposal was good and did not involve any special government allocations. One of these projects was the ERL, or Express Rail Link from the new Sentral Railway Station to the new Kuala Lumpur International Airport. Malaysia's old railway system used a metre-gauge track, but the ERL proposed to use broad gauge. The new airport would be about 50km by road from the city centre, and travel time would be quite long. A fast train seemed like a good alternative. It was built entirely from private investment and has proven to be a success since it was launched in April 2002. The fare is reasonable, and the convenience of checking in at the Sentral Station in Kuala Lumpur made it very popular.

504

---

[1] On 3 August 1996 the entire Peninsular Malaysia suffered a blackout. It took almost 14 hours to restore power to all affected areas.

The Government had to bear the NEP in mind throughout the complex privatisation process. Privatisation could provide Bumiputera businessmen with the opportunity to leapfrog quickly into big business. While at times they leapt over some non-Bumiputera companies, many non-Bumiputera themselves also enjoyed opportunities from the privatisation programme. To achieve NEP targets, more of the Bumiputera had to benefit from privatisation but this too attracted criticism. But still we had no choice — we had to balance the business successes between the two groups and also between economic imperatives and equitable distribution, all integral and essential parts of our national development. The Bumiputera with the ability to do the work were awarded privatisation projects and since there were not many of them, the NEP appeared to be benefiting only a few Bumiputera, even though there were far more non-Bumiputera in big business. To increase and consolidate the Bumiputera foothold in big business, we had to build upon those few — upon the strong, the capable and proven achievers. The criticisms were not convincing as they were political and not grounded in any reasoned analysis of our national development strategy.

505

Close analysis shows that even when large projects were awarded to a Bumiputera, the non-Bumiputera benefited as they received much of the sub-contracts. Yet when the projects were awarded to the non-Bumiputera, the Bumiputera got almost nothing, save for a handful of small supply contracts. We cannot blame the non-Bumiputera for not sharing their projects because most of the Bumiputera have simply not made any serious effort to become good sub-contractors.

My argument here is not motivated by any intention to support the Malay side. Rather, the facts show that, in addition to getting privatisation projects of their own, the non-Bumiputera also benefited greatly from the contracts that were awarded to Bumiputera contractors. Critics who assert that the NEP shut off opportunities for the non-Bumiputera refuse to acknowledge the fact that non-Bumiputera enjoyed much of the spin-offs.

Accusations of political cronyism were sometimes aimed at the personal level — against the Prime Minister and other Ministers — and sometimes generally, against UMNO. Charges were often made that the companies awarded privatisation projects were linked to UMNO, the core party of the coalition government. In its early days UMNO needed funds for its operations and created several companies under nominees that were supposed to represent the party in investments and contracts. The returns on these investments were not very good. Frequently, due to carelessness, the party could not prove that the shares or the companies or even the land involved belonged to UMNO. When the nominees died, their children often refused to acknowledge UMNO's claims. That was all long ago. Companies that were awarded privatisation projects often donated money to UMNO for elections, but they were not the only ones. Many companies donated to the party at election time. Often, so they tell us, they also donated to Opposition parties. To be prudent, the business world must hedge its bets, covering all bases and winning goodwill from all sides in the political arena.

But what those businesses gave had nothing to do with their being linked to UMNO. Many felt grateful that the UMNO-led Government had created a good business atmosphere and provided opportunities for them to make money. They gave because they were grateful, and because they hoped that the party would win again and continue to lead a business-friendly government. This is not uniquely Malaysian. Donating to political parties happens everywhere. I believe that in the United States, Britain and in other developed countries, political parties are all supported with funds from big business. Subscriptions from members or supporters would never be sufficient.

Political parties cost money, elections even more, and funds have to be raised somehow. We hear of peerages being sold in Britain by the New Labour Government, and perhaps the Conservatives did the same. In the United States donors may be appointed as ambassadors. Defence contractors know that their only customer is the government and their lobby is very powerful. What, one wonders, are all the "K Street" and Capitol Hill lobbyists in Washington DC doing if they are not lobbying for the interests they represent? One presumes that the vast lobbying industry there earns its keep, whether or not the nation's political leaders preach democracy and clean and transparent governance to the rest of the world.

To blame Malaysia's Government for favouring party-linked companies is discriminatory, another instance of double standards. We believe in being business-friendly. This is not a sin, especially when doing so ensures the delivery of needed services and better standards of living to its people. That is why we adopted the Malaysia Incorporated concept. We did so because we always have a stake in the success of the nation's companies: 28 per cent of company profits come to the Government as corporate tax, which means we cannot be indifferent to how business is faring. Business success stimulates the economy as a whole, promoting its growth and generating further tax revenue.

Privatisation led to competition among companies and while this was good in principle, excessive competition could lead to failure. Charges for services can be lowered to attract clients and market share, but if the charges are too low then the company cannot earn sufficient profits. We did not like companies to fail as it then became our problem in several ways. The Government collects no taxes from failed companies. Often it must also pick up the pieces, work out an alternative way for the delivery of essential services, deal with the human fallout of company failure, and, if the company is a recently-privatised one, suffer political consequences as well.

When a company is bankrupted it also tends to drag others down. Workers lose their jobs and sub-contractors also incur losses. Loans may turn bad and the banks too may be affected. It is difficult to appreciate the effect of one company being bankrupted on the community and overall economy. If a large number of companies are bankrupted, the devastating effects are soon felt by everyone and by the nation. If that can be avoided, or if corrections can be made, there is no reason why even one functioning or remediable company should be allowed to go under. We are now seeing the effect of companies going bankrupt in the economy of the United States.

Malaysia has been accused of bailing out companies, but a revived company can contribute towards the well-being of the owners and employees and will pay taxes to the Government. The idea that inefficient or struggling companies must immediately be closed down is short-sighted as the implications are bad for other companies and the economy as a whole.

Once it goes, the surviving companies face reduced competition and may be able to make more profits. What they do not do is to help overcome the social and economic problems resulting from the failed company's closure.

That burden is carried by abandoned employees, their families, society in general and the Government. Governments have to choose the best course of action in such situations and bailing out a failed company may be the best option economically. It can certainly serve the interest of social justice and hence the sustaining of social cohesion — a consideration that can never be far from the mind and priorities of a Malaysian government, given the special character and vulnerabilities of Malaysian society.

The critics of Malaysia's bailouts, however, would not hesitate to support that same strategy if their own companies failed. In 1998, the Long-Term Capital Management Company (LTCM) in the US, for example, was unable to repay the huge loans it had raised for its hedge funds operations. The rich bankers who had themselves invested in LTCM got their banks to bail out the company. Even the US Government applied pressure on the banks to bail out LTCM.

As recently as September 2008, George W. Bush's administration asked Congress to approve a USD700 billion financial package to rescue US companies such as mortgage firms Fannie Mae and Freddie Mac. Again, double standards. Some operators are simply too big to be allowed to fail and those who gamble through them must be protected. Malaysia and its Government, by contrast, are not that big. We have to concern ourselves only with the fate of our 22 million people, plus a couple of million more who flock to our shores and our industrial work sites in search of employment and sustenance that their own countries cannot provide for them. We, it seems, are not that big not to be allowed to fail. Unlike LTCM and its investors, our country is expendable.

Privatisation has not been an unqualified success, though in public life, few things ever are. In some cases the Government had to re-acquire privatised companies but by and large privatisation has contributed enormously to

GDP growth and saved funds for budget allocation to other important development initiatives. It has actually increased government revenue from taxes and dividends.

For the private sector, on the other hand, privatisation has stimulated the start-up and growth of big companies. Their management skills have improved, enabling many of these companies to undertake major projects abroad. This is a great achievement and it is also a decisive argument against critics of our privatisation policy. The situation that these companies face in foreign countries is totally different from the social and political environment they are used to in Malaysia. There they cannot rely on friendly government Ministers or cosy, long-standing, personal relations with key bureaucrats; nor can they expect to deal with the same laws and practices which they are familiar with at home. They must prove themselves and earn their success on alien ground.

These corporations have turned Malaysia into a showcase of what a developing country can be and can achieve if it has a good private sector. Many developing countries have taken heart from what we have accomplished, have seen our approach as a model to follow, and have shown a decided preference for Malaysia when looking for models for their own development efforts.

# Chapter 38:
# Revving Our Engines

While privatisation helped us to speed up the process of development, I decided it was time to pursue another, related dream. I did not just want to see more Malaysians driving cars — I wanted them to be driving cars that we had built ourselves, as accomplishing that would be a great step in our development and industrialisation. Since the 1960s, Malaysian companies had been assembling foreign passenger cars. I thought we could do more, going from assembling completely knocked down cars (CKD packs) to producing our own car.

Before we look at the rationale for producing a national car, it's worth noting certain features of our culture and character. Malays and most Asians are traditionalists — they like to do what their forebears had been doing in the past. Generally they don't like change. This is true both of their preferred lifestyles and of what they produce. If their forefathers used a wooden plough of a certain design, then they would produce and use similar ploughs without making any attempt to improve on the design or production methods.

510

I noticed very early on that Europeans were the exact opposite. They like to improve on everything. In Malaysia, the *orang asli* or aborigines build their houses on stilts. To enter the house they crudely hack steps into a straight tree trunk. The Malays improved on that and made better steps from planks with the ends inserted into slots cut in two planks, but then went no further. The Europeans, on the other hand, invented lifts and escalators to better the already good staircases they had.

The Europeans have integrated this search for improvement into their culture. To them, there is always a better product to be made and a better way of making it. Today they have research facilities devoted to improving all their products and production methods. Some Asians have now adopted this European attitude and are doing even better, but Asian traditionalists generally dislike change. In the contest between the traditionalists and the progressives, it is clear that the progressives have won. Their ideas have prevailed and have contributed greatly to their progress.

When we decided to build the national car, we did not aim only to learn about automotive engineering but also hoped to adopt the progressive attitude of continuously wanting to improve our products. We wanted to build and improve not just motor vehicles but attitudes, work practices, and the whole culture. Once we started producing the national car, we focused immediately on improving its design, capacity and power, and overall quality with each new model. By doing all this, we were able to keep up with progressive societies.

The seeds of this dream were planted in 1964, when I went to New York City for the first time as a member of a delegation from the Malaysian Youth Council to the World Assembly of Youth. I remember looking down from the airplane as we came in to land and seeing endless streams of cars moving to and fro on the roads around the airport. I had never seen anything like it, not even in Japan or Europe. It seemed as if a third of the population of the United States must be sitting in a car at any given time. To me all those cars represented wealth and development, and I thought it would be marvellous if we in Malaysia could have the same thing. Today we do, though I never thought we would.

Before we could build our national car, we had to look carefully at procedures. When I was running FIMA, I got to know many Japanese businessmen and I had to travel to Japan to negotiate the purchase of tin plate for can-making. They took me to visit the Kawasaki steel mill, in the Chiba Prefecture near Tokyo, where steel plates, each one about a quarter of a kilometre in length, were made and rolled into coils — almost without workers. It was impressive. This was clearly a good example of modern technology. Later I visited automotive plants. I remember thinking that if we could master assembly techniques of cars, producing them would not be beyond us. I knew it would be difficult but I did not really appreciate the level of complexity it would involve. Besides, my persistent belief that we could achieve anything if we really wanted to gave me the impetus to go ahead with this venture.

Building a Malaysian car really meant maximising its local content. I wanted Malaysians to learn about engineering, a crucial component of the manufacturing industry. I did not believe we could ever consider ourselves a developed country if we were merely consumers of industrial products from other nations. I did not want us to be like most developing countries, which may be very rich but unable to produce anything for themselves. The world is full of would-be cosmopolitans with a taste for all the finest modern products, but who have no ability to produce them or even understand how they are made. This kind of superficial modernity did not appeal to me as it could not provide a secure future for our people.

The idea of producing a national car did not receive much support initially. There were the usual cynical, defeatist remarks that we would never manage it. The Opposition, the Press and some economists were pessimistic about our prospects. Opposition politicians said that it was not for a developing country to build cars, and that we were leapfrogging ahead without having the money or the engineering and management expertise to do it. They wanted us to remain as we were — a vulnerable agricultural country. There were even a few disparaging remarks from members of my Cabinet.

I anticipated that negative reaction because I knew the Malaysian mind and how Malaysians like to stay in their comfort zone. They would not consider producing a Malaysian car as it had never been done before. I at least expected the support of my Deputy at the time, but it seemed Tun Musa was not happy with the idea either. He did not say it in so many words — he did not need to — but I learnt about his sentiments nevertheless.

Our foremost cartoonist Lat[1] drew a cartoon which showed the Malaysian car with the roof of a Malacca bullock cart. To me, that cartoon captured our mentality perfectly. It depicted the mental block our people had, an inferiority complex that needed to be overcome. Unless you take calculated risks, you will never know whether you are capable of achieving anything. I had been brought up to be careful with money and I was certainly not going to throw government money away on anything frivolous.

Those negative comments and the opposition I faced simply hardened my stand and made me more determined than ever to build the national car. Being Prime Minister enabled me to push my ideas through. The first

---

[1]  Datuk Mohammad Nor Khalid, or "Lat" as he prefers to be called, was a crime reporter at the *New Straits Times* before an editor accidentally discovered his talent. He has since become Malaysia's best-loved cartoonist.

Malaysian carmaker, Perusahaan Otomobil Nasional Berhad or Proton, was established on 7 May 1983 as a joint venture with Mitsubishi Motors (MMC) and Mitsubishi Corporation. Their participation in the equity ensured their support for the project. Mitsubishi was not the best automotive company of Japan but they were the only ones willing to entertain and become involved in my idea of a national car. I never once considered the Europeans or the Americans as they were already losing their market share in Malaysia and elsewhere.

Prior to proposing the project to MMC, I had talked to Daihatsu, the maker of small cars in the Toyota stable. But they were interested only in having us produce their cars and did not want any alterations to be made to their models. That was hardly my idea of a Malaysian national car. I appreciated the need to move step by step, but in the end Malaysia had to have the capacity to design and build our own cars. We had to start boldly.

Mitsubishi was more accommodating than other makers, but I doubted that they would want us to have the full capability to build cars which might compete with theirs. But so long as they were working with us as partners, they were prepared to withdraw their cars from the Malaysian market so we would not compete directly against each other. This loss of the local market actually worked to their advantage. In the early stages, much of the car included Mitsubishi design and parts and the returns on Mitsubishi's investments were high. They earned a bigger profit per car simply from supplying the engines and transmissions than they would have from selling a complete Mitsubishi car in Malaysia. With Proton capturing 80 per cent of a rapidly-growing car market, the gains for Mitsubishi from the Malaysian national car project were substantial. Later, when I wanted to build a small car, Daihatsu became very cooperative after seeing how Mitsubishi had profited from the national car project. The second national car now outsells Proton.

513

I was not overly ambitious though. During the 1964 General Election my constituency was provided with a small Toyota car. It was quite basic with little refinement, and it was cheap. Although in those days Toyota could not match what was being produced in Europe, I thought we could take the blueprint of that car and make some cosmetic changes before we produced our first car. Mitsubishi Motors conducted a survey of the Malaysian market and their recommendation was for us to produce more sophisticated cars of 1,300cc to 1,500cc, which were the most popular in the Malaysian market.

Proton's first model, called the Proton Saga, was launched on 9 July 1985. The name of the car came from saga seeds, which are so uniform in weight that they were once used to weigh gold. We expected our car to be as perfect and as uniform as the saga seed, but to be frank, the standards of the first Proton Sagas were not really up to the mark. HICOM nominated the first CEO, a local, but he had virtually no experience. When the cars did not meet the standards set, he simply lowered the specs. Though the permissible gap between the doors and the central pillars was initially set at three millimetres, for example, he reduced the standard to five millimetres. The public did not notice it but the Japanese supervisors did. There were also some small mechanical failures, though I think we did not do too badly for first-timers. I kept hoping that those initial teething problems would disappear, but the car was not selling well. At one stage Eon Berhad, the principal distributor, refused to take further delivery as it had too many cars in stock.

At that time our national automobile market was only 50,000 units a year. Proton was producing 25,000 units but the motoring public did not think it wise to replace their Japanese cars with a Proton, despite its lower price. The company was losing money — if it failed I would be in for a lot of criticism. Not even government supporters would spare me and the Opposition would have a field day. I knew I had to do something, so I decided to move out the Malaysian CEO and bring in the Japanese to manage the factory. The Malaysians would learn from them as understudies.

Mitsubishi Motors agreed to loan one of their experienced executives and in accordance with Japanese business practice, we had to pay him a substantially higher salary, in addition to paying his salary in Japan. It was very expensive but it proved to be a wise decision. During the four years that Proton was under Japanese management, the quality of the cars improved considerably and by the first year, we had turned the company around. But the most important contribution of the Japanese was to introduce Japanese work ethic and practices. Our workers did not become as good as theirs, but our productivity and standards improved considerably.

I believed we could do anything, provided we were prepared to learn. The Japanese obviously knew something that we did not, which is why they succeeded in the automotive industry. It was not just a matter of technology — a superior work ethic and sound ideas were needed to make our industries succeed. It was the Japanese who introduced *kaizen* and the JIT, or Just in Time system. The first entails striving continuously to improve both the way we work and the quality of products. Just in Time involves planning the workflow and schedule so that the parts are produced and delivered just when they are needed, rather than having large but idle warehoused stocks, which are subject to deterioration and pilferage. This saves financing costs and storage space. Although automation and robotics could improve production, we had to be judicious in opting for them because such machines were expensive. In many instances, we stayed with manual labour to lower our cost.

The new Japanese manager reported Proton factory's performance every quarter to me. I always knew how much money was being spent, what problems they were encountering, and how sales were going. I also visited the factory often, but even when I did not, I knew how things were getting along. That kind of close monitoring was not really a Prime Minister's job but I felt I was responsible. If Proton failed, I would be blamed, and besides, I was fascinated by the manufacturing process.

The manufacturing of cars was perhaps the first industry to adopt mass production techniques, the result of which was a huge reduction in cost. Mass production requires large volume and a properly programmed assembly process. The first step in car manufacturing is to produce the stamped parts. Step by step, the parts are put together to make up the body until finally, the engine, transmission, control and instruments are fitted. Amazingly, a fully built-up car would emerge from the other end of the assembly line, tested and duly certified. Visitors to the factory were fascinated by what went on. An overhead walkway allowed them to look down upon the workers as they assembled the cars without getting in their way. I think these visits helped to orient the minds of the young towards industry, including the discipline of the industrial workplace and production. Since Malaysia had long been an agricultural country, this reorientation was essential. It was fundamental to the process of cultural change that we were hoping to catalyse through the national car project.

Once the Japanese had the factory running properly we put Malaysians back in charge of management. Clearly our Malaysian managers had learnt a lot from the Japanese and we no longer needed to call in Japanese support, even though production levels were now far higher than before. At one stage we were producing 200,000 cars a year, and there were regular model changes as well. Our Malaysian engineers and designers rapidly acquired the full suite of skills in all phases of design, prototype production, testing and finally, mass assembly. Between 1983 and 2000 we acquired all the necessary technology of the automotive industry. But it is a sector that is constantly evolving. We needed new input all the time, so we acquired Lotus Engineering of the United Kingdom, famous for sports and racing car engine development. This helped us with our own engines, but even that was not enough. The Germans and Japanese were constantly improving their cars and unless we kept up with them, we would lose even the Malaysian market.

Some comment is necessary here about industrialisation and protectionism: there were Malaysians who were ashamed that our country protected its national car. Perhaps they imagined that other countries did not protect their industries and their economies, but the truth was these countries, particularly the developed ones, had more extreme protectionist policies, especially in the early stages.

I grew up with the British Empire's Imperial Preference, which was a blatant and unscrupulous protection policy for British products. Today developed countries apply tariff and non-tariff barriers to shield their products from competition. The US protects its agricultural products with huge subsidies and competing imports are subjected to stringent quality control. This is hypocritical. It is disguised protectionism. Malaysian palm oil was long declared injurious to health so that the US soya bean oil industry could be protected. Ironically, it was soya bean oil that was eventually shown to be dangerous to health. But condemnation or labelling works — long after palm oil was declared safe, US citizens still would not consume it as their rejection of the product had by then become second nature.

The US also imposed high emission standards on imported cars, especially after Japanese cars began making serious inroads into the American market. But the Japanese were equal to the game and produced cars with better emission standards than were required. The Japanese themselves and the Koreans are skilled in protecting their own markets. Until very recently, very few foreign cars could be sold in their countries.

Malaysia is a developing country with a small domestic market, which means nothing that we produce enjoys economies of scale. To industrialise, we needed to protect our infant industries. Accordingly the national car was protected by a lower excise duty than import duty on foreign cars. As a result Proton's share of the Malaysian car market grew rapidly and at one time hit a high of 80 per cent. No one really complained because they were used to paying high prices for imported cars. The Government did not lose out either as higher sales of Proton and an expanding market earned it increased revenue.

In a globalised world — with borderless cash flows — protective tariffs were questioned and forcibly modified. The rich industrialised countries wanted free access as they sought to penetrate the markets of the developing countries. Globalisation gave the raw materials of the poor countries no competitive advantage, but the manufactured products of the rich would enjoy lower tariffs. Proton should have been able to export more cars, but we were high-cost producers since our industry was still small. We could not compete with cars from Korea and Japan and gained nothing at all from the lowering of import duties following globalisation.

For this reason, I often spoke out against globalisation. Eventually many developing countries saw the crafty ploy behind the rich countries' pro-globalisation rhetoric, but the rich were not to be frustrated in their endeavours to exploit the markets of the poor. They proposed supposedly mutually beneficial Free Trade Agreements between nations outside the World Trade Organization framework. Among the first countries to enter into an FTA was Singapore. For Singapore, which is already a free port, the FTA cost them nothing. They did not have to give up any tax. But the

FTA between Singapore and the United States was held up as a model to the other ASEAN countries. They were told that if they did not enter into an FTA with the developed countries, they would lag behind Singapore. Beguiled by the prospect of increased exports to the rich countries and to each other, the ASEAN countries fell over each other to enter into free trade agreements. ASEAN even came up with its own FTA, whereby national goods from member countries could enter one another's markets with minimal or no tax.

But the catch was in the definition of "national". When ASEAN decided that any product with only 40 per cent local content would be classified as "national", foreign manufacturers immediately moved into low-cost ASEAN countries and began to produce cars with the minimum level of local content to take advantage of "national" status for their products. With its 90 per cent local content, Proton cars became more expensive than Japanese, German, French and American cars manufactured in the other ASEAN countries. The export of Proton into the car markets of the ASEAN countries was made quite impossible.

Clearly, developing countries cannot industrialise without some form of protection. I had proposed the production of a national car because I believed it would be protected, at least until its production volume was high, the local market had grown and economies of scale had been achieved. After that, the protection could be reduced gradually. But while the rich were allowed to protect their agricultural products, we were not allowed to protect our infant industries.

Initially Proton cars only had about 18 per cent local content, but the Government pushed for an ever-increasing level of locally-manufactured, component parts. We were prepared to lower taxes to help as we knew we could not do everything ourselves at first. The drive train (engine and transmission), for example, had to be sourced from Japan, but over the years we were able to make more and more of the parts in Malaysia. The 100 per cent local content level would now be technologically feasible if we could only increase our volume of production. But we cannot, because at the moment the domestic market is simply not big enough as we must share it with foreigners. The obstacle is due to the currently unfair rules of international trade. When the Japanese started their automotive industry the local market was theirs entirely, which gave them the necessary volume. It was the same with South Korea, which made sure that foreign cars were not imported. With their bigger population they maintained that advantage for a long time, ensuring they had a strong local market base.

Every country, rich or poor, protects its economy and its industries so Malaysia is doing nothing different when it seeks to protect its national car. Malaysians should stop feeling ashamed of this. Whenever something is proposed by rich countries, no matter how impartial and benign their proposal may sound, one can be sure that it is for their benefit. When they speak in favour of globalisation and a borderless world, when they propose that protection be removed, it is so that they will benefit, not us.

Proton has gone on to produce a number of other models, including the Waja, which was the first locally-designed car, the Satria, Gen 2, Wira, Iswara, Arena, Perdana and Juara. Each model can cost as much as RM500 million to develop and produce, but my favourite is still the first, the Saga. When it was launched in 1985, I drove a dark blue Saga over the Penang Bridge. I remember the look on people's faces — they were proud to see a national car on the road and many of them gave me the thumbs-up sign as I drove past.

It gave me immense pleasure to drive the Saga that day, especially over the 13.5km-long bridge, which we had officially opened in September of that year. In the past 20 years this dual-carriageway bridge has become one of the most recognisable landmarks in Malaysia. Linking the island of Penang to the rest of the Peninsula, it remains one of the longest such bridges in the world. It is integral to the dream of seeing Malaysia as a country with not only a thriving automotive industry but a strong network of bridges and highways to serve the travelling public. We paid RM800 million to build the bridge, which is not much in relative terms, but traffic has grown so much since then that we now need to build a second bridge.

The Government had invested only RM480 million to set up the Proton factory in Shah Alam before it lent the company an additional RM800 million. Proton has since repaid the loan so the Government's own investment in Proton amounts to only RM480 million. The tax collected from Proton in 10 years, on the other hand, added up to RM18 billion, which means the Government's investment in Proton yielded a return of more than 3,000 per cent. And because of Proton, more Malaysians have been able to buy cars. That is a major accomplishment, not just of industrialisation but also in transforming the lifestyle of contemporary Malaysia.

When Proton built a second, state-of-the-art manufacturing and assembly plant in Tanjung Malim in Perak in 1996, it was able to foot the RM1.8 billion construction bill without having to borrow from the Government or banks. The facility is 60 per cent automated and has 180 precision robots and 2,000 workers. The national car project has come a long way in the 23 years since the first Proton plant was built. It has also led to the establishment of over 200 small engineering companies, many owned and operated by Malays. Proton helped us to realise the objectives of stimulating Malaysian engineering industries and the NEP objectives of getting the Bumiputera into business as well.

But Malaysians like to run down their own cars and make them out to be worse than they really are — that is the Malaysian way. Scorn is easy and generously dispensed, but recognition and appreciation only grudgingly accorded. We should be very proud of what we have done, as even other countries are amazed at what we have accomplished. But instead, Malaysians say the cars' designs are not good, the roof is too low, and so on. I simply do not understand this — we seem to have lost pride in our abilities and insist on running down everything that we do. We proclaim that others are better than we are, and their products and achievements superior to ours. It is the old inferiority complex again.

If our cars are as bad as some people say, how did we manage to sell them overseas? We have even sold cars in established markets like Europe. We don't sell many units and we don't make money from this market, but it still proves that we are able to build cars of world standard.

But I must admit that the quality of our cars has deteriorated lately. I was very depressed when I learnt that the Gen-2, which is being marketed in England, was being offered to the public for a deposit of just one pound. That is a painful climb-down from the time when we first exported our cars to England, and they won prizes in the Birmingham Motor Show.[2] Proton used to employ a German firm that checked the cars to ensure they were of world standard, but the new management has dispensed with the services of this company, perhaps to save money. I am told that our overseas sales are now smaller than before, but I have no means of verifying this claim,

Proton sales in the local market declined sharply when the Ministry of International Trade and Industry issued thousands of Approved Permits or APs to import foreign cars. Most of those cars were from countries which do not import Proton. Worse, the importers of foreign cars grossly under-declare their landed price to minimise payment of duty. Proton has found it very difficult to compete with the resulting influx of Korean and Japanese cars. Instead of retaining its 80 per cent market share, Proton's share is now only 40 per cent. Even Perodua, the second national car, sells more.

Perusahaan Otomobil Kedua Sdn Bhd, or Perodua, launched its manufacturing plant on 1 August 1994. I had not planned to have a second car manufacturing company, but I believed there would be a good market for smaller cars, which Proton was not interested in building. I had approached Proton with the suggestion in the early 1990s, but the company believed that such a car would only compete with their existing models. They offered a series of excuses until I grew frustrated and gave up.

521

I then turned to Daihatsu, with whom I had spoken when I first thought of producing a national car. When they saw Proton's success they were quick to take up our proposal to build a small car based on a 660cc mini car they had produced. They now agreed to change the appearance of the car they had originally designed. Perodua's first model, the Kancil, had a tiny 660cc engine, but it was a neat little thing and remains popular. It is also my favourite of all Perodua cars. It did not compete with the Proton cars because the Kancil was seen as a second family car. The same plant is used to assemble Daihatsu cars, which means more revenue for Perodua. The company has since put out other models, like the Rusa, the Kembara, which is the country's first four-wheel-drive vehicle, the Kenari, the Kelisa, and most recently, the Myvi.

---

[2]   Proton won two gold medals and one bronze at the International Motor Exhibition in Birmingham, UK, on 18 October 1988. It won two more gold medals there in 1990, and two more again in 1992.

In 1995 Tan Sri Yahya Ahmad[3] bought a controlling share in Proton, changed its management and oversaw the company's continued progress. After he died tragically in a helicopter crash,[4] Tengku Tan Sri Mahaleel Tengku Ariff,[5] who had been appointed CEO, kept managing the company and helped it to accumulate cash reserves amounting to RM4 billion. After the two car projects were successful I decided we should have a national motorcycle as well. When I spoke about this idea to Yahya, he was very enthusiastic as he was a Kawasaki motorcycle dealer. We went to see the Kawasaki plant and spoke to the management, who agreed to help us manufacture a Malaysian motorcycle. That started Modenas, which was also an engine manufacturing company. The plant was built in Kedah and Kawasaki taught our people to build this motorcycle using quite a lot of automation. This too proved to be a successful venture.

The tax on imported motorcycles is very low, so Modenas had to be very good to compete in the market. They wanted to produce a scooter and other products as well. A motorcycle is basically a small engine with two wheels, so by extending the application you can produce things like lawn mowers, electric generators and outboard motors. Modenas has not yet started in that direction because they still have not exhausted the potential of building motorcycles. They started with the four-stroke motorcycle, which sold very well and was exported to other countries. I even spotted a few on a Greek island when I was there on a holiday. They can now design and test scooters and three-wheelers. With engineering, you can develop many different devices if you just learn to apply the technology.

For me, Modenas completed Malaysia's engineering industry. We started with nothing but we now had saloon cars, a mini car and motorcycles. The next logical move would have been the production of small engines; in fact, that was our intention when we bought a 58 per cent share of MV Agusta Motors, the Italian motorcycle manufacturer, for 70 million euros in 2004. Honda and BMW had started with motorcycles and now they also

---

[3] Tan Sri Yahya Ahmad became Director and Chairman of Proton and was President of DRB-HICOM, Proton's holding company. During this time he oversaw the latter's acquisition of some 200 transportation and automotive companies, including the Lotus Group of the UK.

[4] Yahya and his wife Rohana Othman died in a helicopter crash on 8 March 1997, near Kuala Lipis in Pahang.

[5] Tengku Tan Sri Mahaleel Tengku Ariff was Chief Executive Officer of Proton from 1997 to 2005.

produce motor cars and small engines for generators and outboard motors. But people who do not understand engineering could not appreciate the rationale of buying Agusta. In 2006, the new management of Proton sold the company for one Euro and just two years later, Agusta's new owners sold it for some USD109 million.

We have since gone into the aviation industry as well, another area that I hoped would yield engineering expertise and skilled workers for the country. The most successful local company in this field is Composite Technology Research Malaysia (CTRM), which is the main tenant in Malacca's Composite Technology City. CTRM has won more than RM1 billion in contracts to produce composite component parts for major aircraft manufacturers such as Airbus, BAE Systems and Bombardier Aerospace. It also produced the Eagle 150B, a single-engine, two-seater light aircraft. Today we are also able to manufacture flight simulators and our own unmanned aerial vehicles, all to world-class standards. We have pilots too — I once flew on a Boeing 747 from Kuala Lumpur to London, and discovered that one of the pilots came from Kodiang, a small town in my constituency of Kubang Pasu in Kedah. The town was regarded as one of the most backward places in the state, where the people eked out a meagre income by planting padi. No one thought that someone from this village could become a B747 pilot.

When it comes to aviation, Malaysia's showpiece event is the biennial Langkawi International Maritime and Aerospace Exhibition (LIMA), which we first held in 1991. I had fallen in love with Langkawi since I worked there as a doctor way back in 1956, and I wanted to promote the island. This meant we needed to hold some activities that would literally force people to go there. I read about the air show in Oshkosh,[6] USA, where people go every year with small aircraft, some of them homebuilt. I decided to have a small air show featuring small aircraft, since Singapore already had an air show with big aircraft. We would also hold the show in between the years of Singapore's event, to make sure there was no overlapping.

---

[6]   The EAA AirVenture Oshkosh is a seven-day-long air show and is one of the leading experimental aircraft exhibitions in the world today, drawing 10,000 to 15,000 aircraft each year.

The Government did not have the resources to stage LIMA so I turned to a businessman, Yusof Manan. Yusof, who was educated in Germany and could speak German, put the show together with his brother Datuk Radzi Manan. Interest in it was great from the very beginning and soon companies were asking to bring in military aircraft, which we agreed to readily. Then someone suggested holding a maritime show simultaneously, and that's how LIMA was born. I worried at first that those early promises to bring in aircraft would fall through, because transporting them was an expensive business. But the turnout of participants and visitors at that first show in 1991 was very good.

Although we had been concerned at first about possible competition with Singapore's air show, the truth was Langkawi had an advantage in that it did not have a busy airport and it was surrounded by sea. That meant aircraft manufacturers could conduct their aerial demonstrations throughout the day without interfering with commercial flights or flying over built-up areas.

The show also received support from some strange quarters — there was Russia, for example, which had hardly ever participated in air shows before. The Russian contingent was perhaps the biggest at LIMA 1991 and they came with aircraft such as the Sukhoi and the MiGs, which most people had previously only read about. The Russians themselves had never been to a place like Langkawi and they were very excited. Malaysia eventually bought their MiGs, which was the first sale of Russian aircraft in Southeast Asia. The Russians went from being a secretive country to one that was keen to sell their aircraft and technology. Their participation was a special draw for LIMA.

We also had support from South Africa, which has a very big aircraft industry, developed when sanctions were applied against them for their apartheid policy. The Red Arrows from the British Royal Air Force, one of the best aerobatic teams in the world, were also with us from the start. Their aerial displays were a daily highlight at LIMA, and everyone would come out of the indoor exhibition area to the tarmac to watch them.

We attracted warships from different countries for the show's maritime component. In any case, naval ships often sail to different countries as part of their exercise. They welcomed the invitation to participate in LIMA where they could promote the sale of their ships. Of course, Malaysian ships came in full force as well.

I had not planned LIMA to be so established and so grand, but it quickly grew by itself. I always made sure I spent at least three days at LIMA and saw all the exhibits, watched the aerial displays, inspected the ships and interacted with all those involved. I wanted to show the Government's support, but I was also personally interested in the aircraft and engineering technology that had gone into manufacturing them. It was very satisfying when Malaysian companies were able to show the progress of their aero-engineering capabilities. Malaysian aerial services, components and simulators attracted a lot of attention and sales.

Just as I had hoped, Langkawi benefited greatly from LIMA, which became one of the most important features in its events calendar. In the beginning there were not even enough taxis to handle all the visitors to the island during the show. We actually built a 200-room hotel in two months to accommodate the personnel of foreign air forces. Still, this was not enough and local visitors ended up having to sleep in mosques. The island's growth after that was phenomenal. We built hotels and kept lengthening the airport's runway, until it was long enough to handle a 747. In 1991 we had tents to house the participants' booths, but for the second LIMA in 1993 we built a permanent hall for the exhibition.

By 1995 we had to double the size of the hall and increase the parking space for visiting aircraft, of which there were hundreds. It was a scene that Langkawi never expected to see. Today I'm the adviser to the Langkawi Development Authority and I love to see how things have grown. Land has become so valuable that some people have been able to sell their property for RM1 million per acre. The island's biggest town, Kuah, is now five times the size it used to be, and you can even see buildings there that you won't see in Alor Star. There are many restaurants selling foreign food and one of the most beautiful hotels in the world is now operating in Langkawi.

The locals also benefited — they operated restaurants and food outlets and found good jobs easily. With the proceeds from the sale of their land they built modern houses, bought cars and now travel to the mainland frequently. In fact, their standard of living is higher than that of the rest of Kedah state.

LIMA's participants did not come to Langkawi expecting immediate sales, only a chance to promote the capabilities of their aircraft and helicopters. Still, sales and the number of defence contracts signed at LIMA were quite healthy. But that has since changed. LIMA 2005 was not that successful because people have begun to lose interest. Participation was down and even the Red Arrows did not come to perform their aerobatics anymore.

People sensed that the Tun Abdullah Badawi Government was not as keen to promote the show, and unless that changes, LIMA's popularity and relevance will continue to dwindle. That would be a shame, not just because of all that the show has been able to achieve but also because many Malaysians look forward to it. It is their chance, once every two years, to see the best and most expensive planes in the world go through their paces.

The automotive and aerospace industries complemented the other manufacturing industries in the conversion of Malaysia from an agricultural country to an industrialised one. Today, with fewer opportunities for business in the country, Malaysian engineering companies are able to bid for contracts to build and also to operate engineering facilities in foreign countries. If we had not made the effort to acquire engineering know-how through the national car project, our people would not be able to tide over the slowdown in Malaysia's economic expansion.

# Chapter 39:
## Daim Becomes Finance Minister

One man I've known and worked with for many years has long been a source of fascination for many people. They describe Tun Daim Zainuddin as an enigma, and that description fits him perfectly. He is seemingly a reluctant politician, yet he has played a crucial role in Malaysian politics. He guided Malaysia's economy during its most difficult years but did not stay to savour the success of his policies. He resigned but remained at the beck and call of the Government, contributing his ideas and criticisms freely without fear or favour. When he was recalled he willingly came back to serve, and when the time came again for him to resign, he just as willingly gave up his high post as Minister of Finance — no histrionics, no tears and apparently no grudges against those who had vilified him.

I knew Tun Daim's family before I met him. Their house was further up Seberang Perak where I lived. His eldest brother Senawi was a close friend of my brother-in-law Abdul Ghani so I got to know him as he often came to see Ghani in my house. When I organised the Kesatuan Pemuda Melayu Kedah (Kedah Malay Youth Association), I persuaded Senawi to become its Treasurer.

I first heard about Senawi's younger brother when I became a Member of Parliament. Tun Daim had started a salt farm, but it had failed. Then he went into housing and he did very well. I had a housing project myself in Alor Star and despite my poor management, I made some money. Tun Daim must have made a lot because his project was big and he managed it far better than I did. In fact, I believe he was among the first Malay millionaires.

He was close to Datuk Harun Idris, then the *Menteri Besar* of Selangor. Harun approved his application for land in Kuala Lumpur. The value of land was not so high in those days and the property boom had yet to come, but when it did Tun Daim prospered and was grateful to Harun. Yet in time Harun fell foul of Tun Razak Hussein and Tun Hussein Onn, and when Tun Hussein became Prime Minister, he proceeded to have Harun charged with corruption. When it was clear that Harun was headed for jail,

Tun Daim came to see me. I was the Deputy Prime Minister at the time and he thought I could intercede with Tun Hussein and get him to be more lenient towards Harun.

Tun Daim was very casually dressed for our meetings — no necktie, just an open shirt and slip-on sandals. He was very precise about what he hoped I should do. I listened and then explained to him that I had already interceded and all I got was to have the files on Harun thrown at me. Tun Hussein had erupted when I spoke about Harun and it was clear that he was not going to change his views if I brought the matter up again.

Tun Hussein appointed Tun Daim a Senator in 1980. He proved to be an enormous help when I became Prime Minister the following year and had my first brush with the United States. As I related earlier, the US's General Services Administration was releasing its stockpile of tin into the market and this was depressing the already low price further. Official representations to the US produced no result. At that time Malaysia's two main exports were tin and rubber, so a fall in their prices inevitably had a dire effect on Malaysia's economy and Government revenue.

Tun Daim, who did not hold a Government position at the time, suggested that I send an unofficial team to talk to US officials. I was sceptical. Who in Malaysia knew senior US officials well enough to meet with and persuade them? But I decided to give the suggestion a try and authorised him to go to Washington DC, accompanied by Tan Sri Alex Lee. The Americans initially proved unbending and did not care if Malaysia suffered economic problems. Moreover, the tin stockpile operation was not crucial to their economy. Only canners would suffer if tin prices went up and, since all canners worldwide would incur higher costs, their relative competitiveness would remain unaffected, whatever the price of tin.

Then Tun Daim played his surprise card. He pointed out that lower tin prices would affect the livelihoods of labourers in the mines, who might on that account be persuaded to join the communist insurgents then harassing the Malaysian Government. At that point, the US officials began to listen. Their ignominious defeat in Vietnam was still fresh in their minds and American fear of the communists was quite pathological. By invoking that fear, Tun Daim managed to stop the release of the United States tin stockpile. As his mission was unofficial, his activities in Washington DC remained publicly unreported but I was impressed that he had been able to contact and persuade decision-makers in the US Government. That he did so as head of an unofficial delegation convinced me of his versatility. Later, he was also instrumental in bringing the "Buy British Last" policy to an end.

When I decided to call a General Election in 1982 to validate my accession to the highest post in the country, I decided that Tun Daim should give up his Senator's seat and contest a seat in the Dewan Rakyat. I wanted him to be available should I need him for a post in the Government.

Tun Daim contested the Kuala Muda constituency in Kedah after Tan Sri Khir Johari, a veteran Cabinet Minister who had been a Member of the Federal Legislative Council and then Member of Parliament since 1955, decided not to contest. Although Tun Daim was not in the local UMNO division, there was no objection to his being a candidate and he won the seat quite easily against his PAS opponent.

He made no greater effort than was necessary to win the seat, which was typical of his style as a politician. He did not like to waste effort, to do any more than was required to ensure his position. He had other priorities and other claims on his attention and energies. Being a Member of Parliament was not his aim but was simply a means to secure the position to pursue his far-reaching, strategic objectives. Yet, he was well-accepted by his constituents. He has always been charitable and generous and liked to build mosques. He also always helped the party's local division with his own money. But Tun Daim never tried very hard to be popular with people. He always did what he wanted, what he considered right. Campaigning was also not his style and he didn't do much of it.

Initially I invited him, as a new Member of Parliament, to take over Bank Bumiputra or to head the large cooperative Ko-op Bersatu, but he declined both positions. Instead, he agreed to take over Fleet Group, which controlled the newspapers in the *New Straits Times* stable.

After the 1984 UMNO General Assembly however, I moved Tengku Razaleigh Hamzah to the International Trade and Industry portfolio, which left his former position as Minister of Finance vacant. I had no hesitation in appointing Tun Daim to the post. As expected, he was reluctant at first, but I would not take no for an answer. He had made enough money for himself, I thought — now he should give his time to the people and the Government. The economy was not doing well at the time as foreign debts were high and a number of banks were facing scandals, crises and failures.

Some people questioned the suitability of my choice and many suggested that I was favouring a friend. But I could not appoint a total stranger. I had to know the man who was to take over one of the most important Ministries in government. With his business experience, I felt fairly certain that he would be able to handle the work, and there were few others who were inside or close to UMNO who knew about business or finance.

When Tun Daim took over the Ministry of Finance, Malaysia's foreign reserves stood at only RM9 billion but its foreign debt was RM20 billion. During his time he had to tackle the Bumiputra Malaysia Finance (BMF) scandal involving Bank Bumiputra Malaysia Bhd (BBMB). The bank lost RM2 billion in Hong Kong, where it lent huge sums to the Carrian Group of Companies. In a bailout, the Government had to sell Bank Bumiputra to PETRONAS, which was chosen simply because it had the money.

The BMF fiasco resulted in a number of prominent Malay businessmen being charged with fraud. These included Datuk Hashim Samsuddin, Lorraine Esme Osman and Dr Rais Saniman (BBMB's former Executive Director, former Chairman and former alternate Director respectively). But BMF was not an isolated case. Tun Daim had to resolve a number of other banking and financial problems as Finance Minister: Perwira Habib Bank, Supreme Finance, First Malaysia Finance, Kuala Lumpur Finance, Kewangan Usaha Bersatu Bhd (KUBB), and the Cooperative Central Bank were all in trouble and Tun Daim took them all on.

He also began to cut back the Government's expenditure, revising or slashing allowances for Ministers and senior civil servants. He even wanted to end the pension scheme but this I resisted. He also accelerated the privatisation of Malaysia Airlines, Tenaga National, the North-South Expressway, the Telecoms Department, MISC, HICOM, Port Klang

Container Terminal and many others. Even Malayan Railway was offered to private entrepreneurs for RM1.

This offer was once quoted by Datuk Seri Kalimullah Hassan, a former editor-in-chief of the *New Straits Times,* as a justification for Proton's sale of its shares in Italian motorcycle company MV Agusta for one euro. But it is not the same. The buyer of Malayan Railway would not be able sell the assets because he still had to operate the railway service. He would have to settle the debts of Malayan Railway which was quite big, let alone make any profit. It was a public offer but there were no takers. In the case of Agusta, where no public offer was made, the sale may have relieved Proton of having to carry Agusta's debts but it certainly would not recover the cost of buying the company. Had Agusta been retained it could have been turned around, if the management had known what needed to be done. As we now know, the buyer of Agusta was able to sell off Agusta together with its debts for USD109 million.

Meanwhile, although Tun Daim spearheaded the privatisation of many public agencies, the Government wanted to have the last say should anything extraordinary happen. For this reason it retained a Golden Share, giving it the right to literally stop the sale of the company without Government approval. The listing of the shares of these privatised companies increased the market capitalisation of the Kuala Lumpur Stock Exchange (KLSE). At that time, the KLSE and the Singapore Stock Exchange operated as one, but share trading at the Singapore Exchange was greater because of its efficiency. This cost Malaysian stockbrokers money and limited their operations and prospects.

531

Tun Daim decided that the stock exchange should be split and I had no objection. I did not see why they should not become independent when our currencies were going separate ways and parity was impossible. The split resulted in a huge increase in the volume traded on the KLSE. Since many of the counters previously traded in Singapore were Malaysian, the Singapore Exchange faced possible decline. In response Singapore introduced the Central Limit Order Book (CLOB), an over-the-counter trading facility for dealing specifically in Malaysian shares. We eventually had to take action against CLOB when it undermined Malaysian share prices during the 1997-1998 financial crisis.

Tun Daim habitually came to see me with a list of the problems he had to tackle, together with his proposed solutions. I would listen to him and ask a few questions before giving my approval. Once I agreed, he would go, leaving me sure he would be able to resolve the problems. He never outlined a difficulty without offering a suggestion as to how it might be overcome. He was generally successful but he could be unfeeling about removing people and bringing in his nominees as part of his solution. Soon people began to talk about those they considered his proxies. He did not seem to care about what was being said and just went ahead with whatever harsh measures he had decided were necessary.

Tun Daim's austerity programme, however, started to slowly yield results. Government borrowings were reduced and some debts were even pre-paid. The economy began to pick up. In 1985 the growth was minus 1.6, but in 1986 it was back to plus 1.2; in 1987 1.4; in 1988 8.9; in 1989 9.2; in 1990 9.7, and 1991 8.7. Foreign debt — which had been high between 1980 and 1984, peaking at +70.3 in 1981 — was much reduced. In 1985 it contracted by 14.2 per cent and by 18.9 per cent in 1986. It experienced growth between 1987 and 1990, as new development was funded by fresh borrowing, but declined again by 5.5 per cent in 1991.

Tun Daim also made many parties happy when he resolved problems at the United Malayan Banking Corporation. UMNO Youth under Datuk Suhaimi Kamaruddin had objected to this bank being sold to Multi-Purpose Holdings (MPHB), the investment arm of the MCA. With 51 per cent of the shares, MCA would control the bank even though Pernas owned 30 per cent of the shares. Tun Daim negotiated with Chang Ming Thien, the founder of the bank, and it was agreed that Pernas should increase its shares to 40.68 per cent, while MPHB would limit its share ownership to 40.65 per cent. The rest of the shares would be placed with a company approved by the Government. With this settlement, UMNO Youth was mollified.

Throughout all these events and despite his obvious success in rehabilitating the nation's economy, Tun Daim came under a lot of criticism. His disposal of his personal and his family's assets came under attack. When he was made Chairman of Fleet Group, the company purchased Faber Merlin, in which Tun Daim was supposed to have shares. Prior to this, Faber had bought Tun Daim's Buluk Malwi property, but that was in 1977, long before he became Chairman of Fleet and certainly before he became Minister of Finance. That did not stop people from accusing him of making a big profit from selling his property to Faber Merlin, which had been acquired by Fleet Group when he was the Chairman.

Tun Daim was also blamed for the Maminco losses on the London Metal Exchange and BMF problems, which unfolded before he became Minister of Finance. The links he had with Malay businessmen, who became prominent during his time as UMNO's Treasurer, were also cited against him. Tan Sri Wan Azmi Wan Hamzah, Tan Sri Halim Saad, Datuk Samsudin Abu Hassan, and Tan Sri Tajuddin Ramli[1] were all close to him. The accusation was that they were his proxies, holding shares in all the big privatisation projects for him.

Recently Tajuddin accused me and Tun Daim of forcing him to buy shares and a controlling interest in MAS. I have checked newspaper reports of the time. Far from feeling coerced, it is obvious that Tajudddin was elated over his purchase. He wanted to swap his Malaysian Helicopter shares (a company with two aircraft) for MAS shares (a company with well over 60 aircraft). The Government rejected his plan and asked that he pay in cash instead, which forced him to borrow RM1.8 billion. He was therefore not coerced by the Government to buy the shares, but was forced by his own modest collateral to borrow heavily.

Although I was Prime Minister at that time, I never got involved directly in the actual sale. I do remember wondering how Tajuddin would be able to buy the airline and when I asked Tun Daim, he explained that Tajuddin's telecommunications company Celcom (Malaysia) Berhad was doing well. As for allegations that Tun Daim later forced Tajuddin to save the Government with the bailout of Malaysia Airlines, the idea is ridiculous. Tun Daim was at that time no longer the Minister of Finance. And while the Government did lose money in currency trading, that loss was not

---

[1]  Tan Sri Wan Azmi Wan Hamzah founded Land & General Bhd; Tan Sri Halim Saad was the Executive Chairman of Renong Bhd, which controlled the UEM Group; Datuk Samsudin Abu Hassan's business interests are largely based in South Africa, and Tan Sri Tajuddin Ramli was the former Executive Chairman of Malaysia Airlines.

about to bring it down. The Government's capacity to recover was far greater than that of any public or private corporation.

I found myself having to defend Tun Daim every now and again but he himself seemed unfazed. Once the *Far Eastern Economic Review* reported that he had been paid USD5 million to switch the supplier of engines for Malaysia Airlines' planes. He did not even bother to respond to the allegation.

People constantly talked about him having financial interests in the companies run by his cronies. This was especially so once privatisation was under way. Those who got the big privatisation projects were his protégés, often people who had worked under him in the Urban Development Authority. Yet, undeterred, he went ahead with the privatisation projects and many of his protégés were the beneficiaries. For my part, I wanted to use privatisation as a way for Malays to leapfrog into big business. I was in no position to evaluate the applicants as I did not know them. Their qualifications told me little about them. So I had to leave the choices to Tun Daim, his expert knowledge and his keen judgment, both of business prospects and of people.

Perhaps he did choose people who were close to him, and so ended up being accused of using them as his proxies. Could he choose, and recommend to the Government, people he neither knew nor trusted? I assumed he appointed them because he knew them and believed them capable of taking on big jobs. After all, I had chosen him as my Minister of Finance because I knew him.

I have myself often been unfairly accused of impropriety, so whenever someone was accused of wrongdoing I always demanded proof. Until I was satisfied that there were valid grounds, I refused to take any action. Tun Daim wanted to resign from the Government in October 1990, but I prevailed upon him to stay. Eventually however, the number of accusations became so overwhelming that I could no longer discount them.

I never found proof of any wrongdoing but I had to act to stop myself from being accused of staging a cover-up. My problem was made worse because Tun Daim simply refused to defend himself. Perhaps sensing my embarrassment, he eventually offered to resign as Minister of Finance in 1991 after presenting the Budget in December of 1990. I reluctantly agreed. But I kept my options open and made it clear that I would call him if I needed his advice or participation in any way.

Naïvely perhaps, he had thought that Datuk Seri Anwar Ibrahim, who replaced him as Minister of Finance, would seek his advice. But Anwar never did. The recovery and rapid growth of the economy which Tun Daim had engineered continued after he retired. Malaysia's GDP was growing at above eight per cent from 1988 and it seemed that this growth would go on forever.

But in 1997 the currency traders struck and the economy collapsed. Malaysia suddenly became very poor as the ringgit lost 50 per cent of its value. Imports became very expensive but our exports did not earn much to compensate. Foreign buyers of Malaysian products insisted on benefiting from the lower production costs due to our devalued currency.

Fortunately, Malaysia did not have heavy foreign borrowings, so it was not under pressure to seek the help of the IMF. Yet Malaysia's problems were compounded by the fact, described elsewhere, that Anwar allowed himself to be influenced by the IMF and the World Bank. He decided to adopt the IMF formula for overcoming the financial crisis, cutting back on government expenditure to achieve a budget surplus, raising interest rates, and increasing non-performing loans by shortening the default period from six months to three months.

The National Economic Action Council (NEAC) set up in 1998 — with members from Opposition parties, trade unions, the private sector and academics — proved too large and unwieldy to devise and oversee a response to our dire situation. With the currency depreciating every day and the economy imploding, I decided to work with a smaller team to monitor the situation on a daily basis. Tun Daim was among the people I appointed to this team. Anwar, as Deputy Prime Minister and Minister of Finance, sat on it as well. Later, when Anwar was indicted, Tun Abdullah Ahmad Badawi, as the new Deputy Prime Minister, became a member.

Tun Daim attended the daily morning meetings and his contribution was invaluable. I tested the idea of currency controls on him and asked for his support, and although he was not very vocal, he did not object, which was good enough. Once Anwar left the Government I had to act as Minister of Finance but I found the task burdensome. I just could not scrutinise all the papers as thoroughly as I should have, so I decided to ask Tun Daim to rejoin the Government. To give him some formal standing, he was made Special Functions Minister. One of his duties was to sit on the new economic and currency watch committee, which actually had no legal status. I just wanted a brains trust I could depend on. Some of its members were Ministers, some were not. Special Functions was a very vague title, but Tun Daim's purpose was mainly to give advice.

He oversaw the implementation of the currency controls and dealt with the shareholders of the trustee companies used by CLOB. The shareholders were not allowed to dispose of their shares. With the stabilisation of the currency, fixed at RM3.80 to the US dollar, our economy recovered faster than those countries which had submitted to IMF control. The KLSE main index crept up from 262, its lowest during the currency crisis, to well over 800 in one year. With that, market capitalisation increased considerably and both the companies and the banks were less threatened by the high percentage of non-performing loans.

Despite his help, the old criticisms that had plagued Tun Daim in the past soon returned. He was repeatedly accused of lining his pockets and taking kickbacks from contracts. No clear evidence was ever produced, but once again the whispering grew louder and more spiteful. People came to see me to complain about him, and when I demanded evidence, they could produce none. Yet I could not easily defend him. Exculpatory evidence was no more easily found than the incriminating variety. I could produce no solid grounds for his defence. I never spoke to him about this because I knew what his answer would be.

Tun Daim, as usual, ignored all the talk about him. He must have heard the rumours but he chose not to reply. When the talk got to be too much and I could not bear it anymore, I arranged for him to resign. In the end what worried me were not only the rumours of cronyism but also tales of his supposed disloyalty. He was supportive during the financial crisis, at least in front of me. But Datuk Abdul Ghani Othman, the *Menteri Besar* of Johor, told me Daim called a number of the other *Menteri Besar,* telling them not to support my idea of currency controls. Since nobody else came with similar complaints I just discounted the story. But when it had all become too much, I didn't accuse him of anything but sent word through a mutual friend that I wanted him to resign.

Tun Daim immediately wrote the letter and came to see me. He never mentioned what our friend had told him and only said that he wanted to resign. He had always said that he would step down any time I wanted him to do so and, true to his word, when I asked him he never questioned it. This was the second time he was stepping down. I did not like dropping people because it caused such upheaval and I did not like having to face emotional explosions. I tried to cushion their impact by working indirectly, through intermediaries. But it did not always work.

I knew he would not become destitute if he were no longer a Minister. When he joined the Government the first time, he was already a millionaire. He was wealthy when he left the Government then and I knew he was wealthy now when he was leaving a second time.

He was getting older, of course, and could look forward to a good life in retirement. I did not bring him back to balance him against Anwar, as many people believed. I admired his business acumen and his strong sense of purpose. One thing about him that I didn't like, however, was his closeness to Lee Kuan Yew. At one time Lee wrote a letter to me saying Tun Daim was a good man and should be retained. Lee even attributed the currency controls to Tun Daim, though he had actually not been very keen.

Tun Daim and I remain friends to this day and I am invited to his *buka puasa* (breaking of the Ramadan fast) gathering in his house every year. On one occasion, he invited Hasmah and me for dinner at his palatial home and when we arrived, I was delighted to meet some very old friends. Soon more old friends arrived, one even in a wheelchair. Tun Daim and Toh Puan Mahani, his wife, wanted to celebrate my birthday with my friends and colleagues, to talk and reminisce, and generally to relive the good old days. The party was wonderful and everyone had a good time, although I also felt a little saddened that many of my old friends and colleagues could not be there.

On both occasions, Tun Daim never made a fuss about having to resign from Government. He is not a politician, he is a businessman, and so he never cared much whether or not he was a Minister. He was there because he could contribute. Tun Daim rendered great service to the nation — that is what I like to remember when I think of him.

# Chapter 40:
# A House Divided: Team A & Team B

As Prime Minister I was often described as having a dictatorial style and being intolerant of opposition. But if that were true, why did I face so many challenges within UMNO? I was also always ready to reconcile with the very people who had tried to overthrow me, and even went on to choose one of them to succeed me as party leader and Prime Minister when I voluntarily retired. Dictators, by the way, don't retire — certainly not voluntarily.

Perhaps the most serious challenge I faced came during the 1987 UMNO General Assembly, when my former deputy Tun Musa Hitam teamed up with Tengku Razaleigh Hamzah to force me out of the party presidency. Tun Musa had resigned as Deputy Prime Minister the year before, though he still held the position of Deputy President of the party. Tengku Razaleigh had been the favourite for that post in the 1981 UMNO General Assembly that saw me formally elected as party President, but Tun Musa had managed to garner enough support to defeat him.

I had hoped that Tun Musa and I would have a good working relationship, better than the one I had with Tun Hussein Onn when I was his deputy, but the honeymoon period during our so-called MM or 2M administration did not last long. He did not give me the support I needed to push through key initiatives such as the national car project, and he was unhappy that I had chosen to retain Tengku Razaleigh in the Cabinet. Still, I was surprised when he sent me a letter in 1986 to say that he was resigning as my Deputy in Government and in the party.

UMNO Supreme Council members urged me to allow a delegation of party members to meet with Tun Musa in England, where he had gone after his resignation, to persuade him to return to the Government and to continue to be party Deputy President. They wanted to avoid a split in the party. A dictator might not have agreed to Musa's return as it was clear that he was impatient about taking over the Presidency and the Prime Ministership from me. But I respected the members' wishes and agreed to let a delegation of senior Supreme Council members go to London to see him. He agreed to remain as Deputy President of UMNO but refused to rejoin the Government headed by me. I had to appoint Tun Ghafar Baba as Deputy Prime Minister. For the first time, the UMNO Deputy President was not also the Deputy Prime Minister.

Tun Musa was expected to stage a comeback but I was not prepared for what he did next. He travelled to Davos in Switzerland to meet Tengku Razaleigh, who was attending the World Economic Forum, and persuaded him to contest the President's post in the next party election while he would defend the Deputy President's post.

I found this alliance to be mind-boggling — just before he resigned, Tun Musa had written me a letter expressing his disappointment that I had chosen to keep Tengku Razaleigh in the Government as Minister of International Trade and Industry. The two men had long been political rivals, and I think it was an indication of Tun Musa's dislike of me that he now seemed willing to serve under his erstwhile enemy to bring me down. He seemed to believe in the adage that the enemy of your enemy is your friend.

With Tun Musa working openly against me, I had to get Tun Ghafar to contest the post of party Deputy President. In UMNO, the Deputy President also becomes the Deputy Prime Minister. Tun Musa's choice to remain Deputy President while Tun Ghafar was the Deputy Prime Minister was therefore anomalous, and to regularise the situation, Tun Ghafar had to become Deputy President. It was simply easier if the same person held the posts as the thinking of UMNO would be clearly reflected in the Government. Of course, if Tengku Razaleigh and Tun Musa won, that anomalous position would be resolved too but differently — but to leave things as they were was untenable. Should Tengku Razaleigh win and Tun Musa lose or Tengku Razaleigh lose and Tun Musa win, there would be problems also. It was important that the challengers either won together or lost together.

With the battle lines drawn, UMNO members were now forced to take sides. The Press labelled us Team A, while Tengku Razaleigh and Tun Musa's group was Team B. There must have been residual tensions between those two new allies, given their past rivalry, but during the campaign they worked closely enough and were able to win support even from within my camp. They were ably helped by Tun Abdullah Ahmad Badawi, whose dislike for Datuk Seri Anwar Ibrahim — his rival for power in the Penang state UMNO — was intense. He had never quite accepted Anwar's joining UMNO and becoming a government Minister. Years earlier, when Tun Abdullah was a government officer and Anwar a firebrand campus leader, Tun Razak had given him the task of ensuring Anwar was cut down to size. There was therefore no love lost between them.

Tunku Abdul Rahman, the first Prime Minister who had retired and then been out of active politics for 17 years, openly supported Team B. While I did not follow their campaign closely, I heard that the Tunku even let them hold meetings on his property under the guise of religious gatherings. The Tunku was sympathetic to that side simply because Tengku Razaleigh had lobbied him. Besides, Tengku Razaleigh had always been his favourite — even though they came from different royal houses, their common background had given Tengku Razaleigh special access to him. To fund Team B, I was told that Tengku Razaleigh sold his racecourse property to the Sultan of Brunei, for RM14 million.

We also heard that Team B spent about RM20 million on their campaign, with most of the money provided by Tengku Razaleigh himself. Team B's campaign issues were simple: they said I was dictatorial and spent too much money on silly projects like the national car. Proton was not doing well at that time as the standard of the models being produced was not of the quality we had hoped for. The car company's initial struggle seemed to lend weight to their claims. They also circulated a photograph of me with a Chinese lady who they alleged was my Singaporean wife. In fact, she was the wife of an old university classmate, and the picture had been taken at their daughter's wedding.

In the beginning we appeared to have the support of the majority. Of the 120 UMNO divisions, more than 80 nominated me while fewer than 40 nominated Tengku Razaleigh for President. Confident that I would win hands down, I saw no great need to campaign. But Anwar, who was the head of UMNO Youth at the time, was not so certain. He knew his fortunes were tied with mine and if I lost, he would likely be dumped.

He urged me to campaign seriously and he started bringing groups of UMNO division committee members and other party stalwarts to my house for me to answer their questions and lobby for their support. Yet I found campaigning for myself very awkward. I had won the posts of Deputy President and then President without having to contest against anyone. When I had made a bid for the Vice-Presidency in 1972 and 1975, I did not campaign either. Now I found that I had to promote myself to advance my own cause when self-praise had never been easy for me. I still find it embarrassing and always avoid doing so if I can. Instead, during these meetings at my house I talked about the problems of the Malays and Malaysia and how they might be solved.

Some of the people Anwar brought to my home were frank, to the point of being rude. They criticised my appointments and choice of candidates. One lady, an ordinary member from Pahang, condemned me for appointing an Indian Muslim as Senator. I remember being taken aback by her forthrightness and lack of regard for a substantial community which needed to be represented.

542

Another person who came to these meetings was Datuk Mazlan Idris, who was a Pahang State Assemblyman at the time. He had been a loyal supporter of mine, but when Team B approached him and promised to make him *Menteri Besar*, he switched over to their side. What he did not realise was that several people had already been promised the same thing. Mazlan was an educated man — he had a university degree in business — but that did not prevent him from seeing a *bomoh*, or witch doctor, to increase his wealth. He believed that placing money under the bomoh's wet *sarong* cloth for three nights would multiply the money several times over. That belief cost him his life, because the *bomoh* he went to see was the notorious Mona Fandey, who later murdered him in 1993.[1]

On the campaign trail I was careful not to promise anyone anything. When you expect to win, as I did, you do not make promises which you know you cannot keep. This is a tactic you use only if you are desperate to win and you do not care what happenes afterwards. I believed I would

---

[1] Mona Fandey was charged and convicted of murdering Mazlan in 1993, and was executed on 2 November 2001.

win, and with a good majority. Party members, I thought, would see that Tengku Razaleigh and Tun Musa were old enemies who were now joined in what was nothing more than an opportunistic alliance. They could not really work together — that would surely be clear to sensible UMNO delegates and members.

Party members cast their votes on 24 April 1987, a Friday. Voting had to be halted halfway for members to attend Friday congregational prayers, but Team B supporters used the interval to campaign. They were seen following targeted delegates to their hotels, even into the toilet, and I was told that a lot of money changed hands.

The Team B campaign was clearly effective as the voting results did not reflect the stand taken by the divisions at the nominations stage. Towards the end of the day, Anwar called to quietly inform me that the voting was very close. Team B, he said, was so confident of victory that they had already started celebrating. The news that the outcome was uncertain worried me enough to prepare myself mentally for whatever might happen next. I had long ago learnt that if you want something too much you can hurt yourself badly if you do not get it. It was a lesson I had been taught as a young student, waiting in vain to get a scholarship to study law when all my other friends were already leaving to study abroad. I had always been prepared to resign as Prime Minister and UMNO President. From the outset, I accepted that eventually I would have to step down — no political career could last forever. But I had been Prime Minister for only four years and there was still a lot to do. I needed to stay on to complete my work.

543

Two hours after the phone call from Anwar, we finally received news that Tun Ghafar and I had won. I defeated Tengku Razaleigh with 761 votes to his 718, a difference of only 43 votes. Tun Ghafar defeated Tun Musa by only 40 votes. Ready to accept defeat, I was relieved that I had won. But I was certainly disappointed by our thin margin of victory.

Still, it was a win. Team A's candidates also won the majority of seats on the Supreme Council and two of the three Vice-President's posts. Tun Abdullah won as Vice-President for Team B. In the wake of the elections Tengku Razaleigh resigned as Minister of International Trade and Industry, as did his fellow Team B member Datuk Seri Dr Rais Yatim, who stepped down as Foreign Minister. I also dropped three Cabinet Ministers and four Deputy Ministers who had joined Team B: Datuk Shahrir Abdul Samad from the Welfare Services Ministry; Datuk Abdul Ajib Ahmad from the Prime Minister's Department; Tun Abdullah from the Defence Ministry; Deputy Minister Tan Sri Abdul Kadir Sheikh Fadzir from the Foreign Affairs Ministry; Deputy Minister Datuk Seri Radzi Sheikh Ahmad from the Primary Industries Ministry, Datin Paduka Rahmah Osman Deputy Minister from the Transport Ministry, and Datuk Zainal Abidin Zin Deputy Minister from the Energy, Telecommunications and Posts Ministry. I felt justified in removing them — they had not supported me and so would not be able to work with me as Cabinet members.

It is UMNO tradition for all problems and challenges to be resolved within the party, but it soon became clear that Tengku Razaleigh was unwilling to accept defeat. On 25 June, about two months after the party election, 11 Team B members filed a suit at the High Court to nullify the results of the General Assembly. Their contention was that members from 53 UMNO branches were not properly registered and their votes were accordingly invalid. I had heard earlier about their suit but did not believe they would proceed. Even if they did, this was, I thought, just a minor internal problem that the courts would dismiss. At most, they might order that the challenged UMNO members be disqualified and the votes recounted without them.

But Team B wanted the courts to require UMNO to hold its entire party elections once again, on grounds that the votes of the unqualified delegates could have determined the final election result. I must admit that the possibility of another election worried me. I saw it as an unhealthy development because ambitious people would spend even more money to buy votes. Taking a party matter to the courts was also, in my view, not right as the matter should have been resolved internally. Tengku Razaleigh's outside recourse made me lose respect for him. Following this episode, a new party rule was introduced so that anyone who took UMNO to court would lose his or her membership.

Tunku Abdul Rahman, meanwhile, continued to be open about his support for Team B. I wrote a letter to him to say that expressing his support publicly was not helping. He responded by saying that he thought holding another election was the right thing to do. I was aware of the irony of the situation and of the similarities between this correspondence and the one I had with the Tunku, just before I was expelled from UMNO. This time however, after he answered my letter, I decided to keep quiet.

Before the case went for judgment, the court granted a two-week postponement to allow an UMNO committee to try to resolve the dispute. Team A and Team B attempted to negotiate an out-of-court settlement but Team B insisted that another party election be held. They felt certain that, given more time, they would get the required number of votes in a new election. I too believed they might, especially since their method of persuasion was money. Holding the election again was not something we could accept; it would mean conceding everything the other side wanted. In the end, we had no choice but to let the court decide the case.

What happened next took everyone, including Team B, by surprise. High Court judge Tan Sri Harun Hashim dismissed the UMNO 11 suit, but ruled that under Section 12 (3) of the Societies Act, the existence of unregistered branches meant that UMNO itself in its entirety was an illegal party. His decision came like a thunderbolt. Never in the history of any country known to me had a judge decided that the ruling party was illegal. UMNO was not a small party — we had more than two million members and more than 2,000 branches. How could we ensure that every branch fulfilled every regulation to the letter? To condemn the entire party because a handful of members may have erred did not seem right. One must accept and respect court decisions but the reasoning in this one seemed unfair and unjust to me, even capricious. It was not a decision that I would say served the country well.

As soon as UMNO was declared illegal, the party's assets were frozen. These included the UMNO buildings and corporate shares. We were in a state of flux at the time and as the party's treasurer, Tengku Razaleigh had not yet given us a full account. When he did much later, it was to tell us that there was nothing in the party's coffers. A story started circulating that, denied access to the party's funds, we did not even have enough money to buy paper for the offices in UMNO's headquarters. The truth was we were not that badly off. Our monthly expenditure at the UMNO headquarters was quite small; only during parliamentary elections would we spend more money. We had no debts and even our building had already been paid for.

The problem was less UMNO's assets than its political identity. The leaders of Team A — myself, Tun Ghafar and a few others — knew that we had to move fast to retain control of its name. UMNO was a brand to which we had to lay our claim by registering our party before Team B did. It was now a race between Team A and Team B to register a new party that could pick up from where UMNO had left off. The old party had been condemned by the court so the new party had to be distinct from it, legally different and new. At the same time, it had to ensure that it would still own UMNO's name, its history and its assets.

We submitted an application to the Registrar of Societies on 9 February 1988 to establish a party called UMNO 88, but it was rejected on the grounds that the old UMNO had not yet been officially de-registered. Team B's application was also rejected, for the same reason. We re-submitted our application on 13 February and it was approved two days later. The new party, called United Malays National Organisation (New) or UMNO Baru, applied to become a member of the Barisan Nasional coalition on the same day. I had proposed changing the structure of the new party to make a small number of members responsible for all decisions, as I felt that its vast membership had made UMNO unmanageable. But others objected, insisting that UMNO Baru had to be a mass movement like its predecessor. Only mass participation, they argued, would ensure mass support.

Ever since that time some strange theories have circulated about this whole episode. I have heard people say that I let UMNO's deregistration go forward because I saw it as a chance to set up a new party, made up only of members who were loyal to me. To support this theory, some alleged that it was UMNO's lead counsel Datuk Gopal Sri Ram who drew attention to the section of the Societies Act that the judge cited in his decision. Others suggested that I did not fight against deregistration hard enough, since UMNO only offered a one-page response to the Registrar of Societies' show-cause letter.

For my part, I could not have known whether our lawyer influenced the judge or not. If he did in that way, it was certainly without our knowledge.

As for not protesting UMNO's deregistration strongly enough, we did not want a prolonged appeal process. We just wanted to get on with the administration of the country. That was the responsibility of being in power, which our adversaries did not have. Without the administration's duties to attend to, Team B could spend its time upon legalities, technical niceties and desperate politicking. For us, once UMNO was declared illegal, the most important thing to do was to register a new party which could be identified with UMNO. We succeeded in claiming that political inheritance and ensuring its historical continuity stayed in our hands.

Once the battle for UMNO was over, I concentrated on healing the rifts that had emerged within the party and ensuring that as many members as possible of the old UMNO now registered with UMNO Baru. Getting people, especially our Malay constituents, to accept UMNO Baru did not prove difficult. Over the course of about a year, we travelled to all the states to re-introduce the party, gather popular support, and ensure party leaders were in touch with the grassroots. We explained that UMNO Baru was essentially the same old party, with the same principles and the same struggle as the UMNO they had always known and supported. We also used identical flags and symbols, and made sure that "Baru" was shown in very light print in our letterheads. Eventually, people stopped using the word altogether and it was dropped completely from the party's name. It was important that we be the UMNO that everyone knew and remembered. If we were UMNO in every way, then our former UMNO members would come back and join as members of the new party. If we were seen to be something else, they might hold back.

The new party was open to everybody, even those who had stood against me. I always believed that I had no right to stop anyone from serving the party simply because they chose not to side with me. So I admitted into UMNO Baru everyone who wanted to join, including those who had thrown their lot with Team B — among them Tan Sri Syed Hamid Albar, Abdul Kadir Sheikh Fadzir and Tun Abdullah. After some hesitation, Tun Abdullah was among the first to apply to join UMNO Baru. I thought he had behaved in the most peculiar way during the contest between Team A and Team B. He had been a second-tier, Team B leader and was widely regarded as Tun Musa's follower. I remember that at one point, I campaigned in Tun Abdullah's constituency of Kepala Batas in Penang. He chose to share the platform with me that day and managed to give a speech that favoured neither team. It made me wonder which side he was on. I suppose he was hedging, in case I won.

Not everyone in Team B, however, wanted to join UMNO Baru. Tengku Razaleigh went on to form a new party called Semangat 46 (Spirit of 46), recalling the year that UMNO was established. Tun Musa and Tun Abdullah stayed out. With his long political experience, Tengku Razaleigh knew that UMNO's success was grounded in part upon its Malay support and its working coalition with MCA and MIC via the Alliance and the Barisan Nasional. He decided to adopt the same approach — he knew that so long as the various Opposition parties contested against each other, the split in the votes of those against the Barisan Nasional would always result in the Barisan Nasional winning.

He therefore persuaded PAS and DAP to cooperate with his party and field only one Opposition candidate against the Barisan Nasional in every constituency. They would share the constituencies between them just as the Barisan Nasional did, and would support one another's candidates. But PAS supporters found supporting DAP anathema while the DAP found PAS repugnant. Still, PAS and Semangat 46 supporters cooperated quite well. The main beneficiary of their cooperation, however, was PAS — Semangat 46 won very few seats and it quickly became clear that the Opposition coalition benefited PAS mainly through Semangat 46 votes. DAP also gained from Semangat 46 support, but PAS and DAP votes were insufficient to help Semangat 46 in contests against UMNO candidates.

After two general elections, Semangat 46 leaders realised that they were not getting anywhere through their pact with PAS and DAP. Several of its members who still had friends in UMNO made the first move to get Semangat 46 back in the UMNO fold. In this way, members did not need to endure the isolation and anxiety of making an individual choice. I thought it was a good idea, and a timely one too. Splintering the party had weakened UMNO and accepting people back would be good for it. I was willing to let people who had opposed me to come back into UMNO, and even gave them positions within the party. I realised that each had his own following and it was important that they bring their followers back with them. One could only do so by giving them face, by accepting them without recrimination or humiliating them.

That was my view, but not everyone in UMNO felt the same way. Many were still angry and the idea that we should re-admit a group that had caused so much trouble and turned against the party was distasteful to many UMNO Baru leaders and members. A few felt they could never work with Semangat 46, especially as the re-admission of a former Semangat 46 leader to an UMNO division could cause insecurity for that division leader. But I had to look at the big picture. Splinter groups could do a lot of damage in constituencies where the margins were very narrow. Even small numbers could make a big difference in an election. I could never forget that I had lost in 1969 because, though few in number, local MCA members refused to vote for me and voted instead for PAS.

The return of Semangat 46 to UMNO, however, still did not give Barisan Nasional victory in Kelantan in the 1999 General Election. PAS is a tough adversary to dislodge. How I feel about some of their leaders is one matter but I respect and admire the tenacity of their rank and file. Their followers support the party and its candidates because of an intense personal commitment, not because they receive lavish material rewards. It is a pity, though, that their trusting loyalty is so blindly and uncritically given. Working out how to sever that bond has always been one of UMNO's biggest political challenges.

Tengku Razaleigh and I spoke together in a public rally in Kelantan as a demonstration of reconciliation on 3 October 1996. Seven years after Semangat 46 was formed, we now spoke of the need for Malay unity and to strengthen UMNO, and of the importance of our now working together towards that objective. The month before that, Semangat 46's Supreme Council had decided that the party would be dissolved and that its 400,000 members would join UMNO. I knew there would be problems in the transition process and that many would find it difficult to forget what had been said at the height of the Team A-Team B split. These included Tengku Razaleigh's allegations that we had cheated our way to victory in the 1987 party elections.

But it was worth having them come back. I knew I could work with them, as I could with anyone who had something to contribute to the party. I even considered re-appointing Tengku Razaleigh to the Cabinet, but after he gave an interview to the *Far Eastern Economic Review* magazine that was very critical of me and the Government, I had to change my mind. Past disloyalty could be understood, forgiven and overlooked, but not a continuing lack of loyalty and discretion. Had Tengku Razaleigh been more patient, he would probably have taken Tun Musa's place as Deputy Prime Minister and eventually become Prime Minister.

As for Tun Musa, I held no animosity towards my former deputy. Even after he left UMNO I treated him well and appointed him to several posts, including Malaysia's Special Envoy to the United Nations with Ministerial rank in 1990 and later as Chairman of the Malaysian Human Rights Commission in 1999. I did not see any reason to deny him a role in the Government. After the failure of Team B, Tun Musa distanced himself from both sides and remained independent. But I saw his decision not to join Semangat 46 as a signal that he did not want to be in opposition to UMNO.

When Team B members joined UMNO Baru they were even offered the chance to return to their seats on the party's Supreme Council. Some critics said this was a calculated move on my part to soften my tough and unyielding image. That was of no concern to me — I was, I thought, as tough as ever. But when I believe an action may be good for the party, I will not hesitate to take it.

At heart, former Team B members were all really UMNO people. That was the truth behind the lifting of the ban against their rejoining the party. We had been separated from one another by our personal loyalties to different individuals, but our driving political objectives were the same. It was important to give a place to everyone who supported UMNO's struggle and principles.

I have always maintained that UMNO belonged to all Malays, and that any Malay who subscribed to the party's objectives has a right to join. From its inception UMNO Baru thrived; it was further strengthened when most of those members who briefly defected to Semangat 46 returned to their political home.

# Chapter 41:
# Ops Lalang

Shortly after the split in UMNO, I experienced one of the lowest points in my career when the police arrested and detained more than 100 people under the Internal Security Act (ISA). The police swoop, called Operasi Lalang (also known as Ops Lalang, roughly translated as Operation Weeding) began in late October of 1987 and would prove to be a permanent blot on my time in office.

I never favoured using the ISA and could never forget that in 1969, I myself had been a likely candidate for detention without trial by the Tunku's Government. At that time the thought of being detained indefinitely had been frightening. I made my dislike of the ISA clear by releasing more than 20 detainees as soon as I became Prime Minister. I intended later to modify and reform the Act, if not abolish it altogether .

I told Tun Musa Hitam, my then Deputy Prime Minister and Minister of Home Affairs, to tell the Inspector-General of Police (IGP) very early in my premiership that I did not intend to use the ISA. How then could I have allowed Ops Lalang, the biggest such police operation in Malaysian history, to happen just six years later?

The relationship between an elected government and the permanent administration is very delicate and complex. The Royal Malaysian Police is a professional body and it understands that it is subordinate to the elected government. But it also has the duty to advise the Government on the security situation and the action that may be needed to address it. Normally, the Minister responsible heeds this advice — only in exceptional circumstances is it ignored. But if the Minister were to regularly disregard the advice of the police chief, he would soon find working with his highest security adviser very difficult. The final decision is still with the Minister and the Government, but their decisions must be based on a proper assessment of the police reports provided to them.

I had often wondered in the past why the police, and for that matter the armed forces and the civil servants in the administrative services, agreed to submit to the elected Government. Ultimately, we had no way of enforcing our decisions on them. In Malaysia we do not have palace guards who are absolutely loyal to the leader to ensure Government decisions are obeyed. Our largely ceremonial guards are provided by the police and the armed forces who take orders from their superiors. In the final analysis, these superiors obey because they agree to do so, because they recognise the elected national leadership as a legitimate one. They also accept the legitimacy of the mechanism of democratic elections from which the national leadership, headed by the Prime Minister, emerges.

Elected leaders depend not only upon the specialised services which the police and army provide and the physical force that they wield. We are also dependent upon the continuing agreement and readiness of the police and armed forces heads to recognise us and accept our decisions and directives. We must therefore establish good working relationships with them and with the police in particular, because it is they who are most responsible for the security of the leaders and the country. Disregarding police advice is not something a leader may do lightly or with impunity.

Sensitive to these rather delicate power relations, I was careful from the outset to develop good relations with the IGP, the Chief of the Armed Forces and the Chief Secretary to the Government. In his own way, each could do much harm to my administration if he chose to. That none had ever done this in the past and had always been loyal did not mean they might not behave differently in future. I was mindful of military coups that periodically convulsed other countries and knew I could never allow a situation to get to a stage where those with the guns in Malaysia might toy with that idea. The later emergence of the al-Maunah group, which attempted to stage a bizarre coup against the Government in the year 2000, and other Islamic militants have shown us that some junior officers and other ranks did not always believe in being professional. While I might insist that my views prevail, I also had to take the advice given to me seriously, especially when it came from our most senior police officer, the IGP.

In the year that Ops Lalang took place, the Government had been weakened by a series of political rifts among the UMNO leadership. Tun Musa had earlier resigned as Deputy Prime Minister, a decision that led to the Team A-Team B showdown that split the party. The court case that followed weakened the Government further. I had always felt that a strong government was needed to keep Malaysia stable, while a seemingly fragile government would only tempt the extremists to test its determination. Following the party and legal upheavals, I was seen to be heading a very weak government and my detractors seemed to think that a slight push might suffice to topple me. Apart from this, the economy was also not doing well and the unemployment rate was increasing.

In this situation extremists promoting Chinese language, culture and education soon began to raise various contentious issues, at times provocatively. The Chinese educationists began by protesting the appointment of Chinese teachers who had not been educated in Chinese-medium schools to senior posts in the Primary National-Type (Chinese) Schools. The issue was soon taken up not only by the Opposition DAP, but also the MCA and Gerakan, the Chinese-backed parties in the Barisan Nasional Government. Among those condemning the appointments was Tan Sri Lee Kim Sai, the Deputy President of the MCA. A heated meeting was held in a temple attended by the Chinese educationists, numerous Chinese community NGOs together with leaders of the DAP, MCA and Gerakan.

Other issues raised included the proposed development of the Bukit Cina Chinese cemetery in Malacca and the failure of the MCA's Deposit-Taking Cooperative, which left many Chinese feeling that the Government should come to its rescue. The DAP also held demonstrations over the issue of changes to elective Chinese and Indian Studies subjects introduced by the University of Malaya. A memorandum against the official National Culture, which declared Malay culture to be the core component of our emerging national culture since the mid-1970s, was also proposed. In other words, racial rhetoric in the public arena was growing quickly and was becoming dangerously heated.

Predictably many Malays, particularly in UMNO, were incensed. Malay university students held an illegal rally. A Malay march through the Kampung Baru area of Kuala Lumpur, the scene of many of the worst clashes of May 1969, raised Malay temperatures and non-Malay fears. Both PAS and UMNO began to accuse Christian churches of the mass conversion of Malays. UMNO prepared to stage a mass rally of 500,000 people on 1 November 1987 to demonstrate the strong support that the Government enjoyed, but, wary of the deteriorating situation, we chose not to permit the rally. Tensions increased even further when a Malay soldier, for reasons that still remain unknown, ran amok and fired his M-16 in Jalan Chow Kit in Kuala Lumpur, killing a Malay and two Chinese.

In these rapidly deteriorating circumstances, the police felt that a repeat of the May 13 riots of 1969 was more than likely. The IGP advised me that pre-emptive arrests under the ISA had to be made quickly if public order was to be maintained. Agreeing to follow the IGP's recommendation meant having to overcome my own conscience. The essence of the ISA is prevention — it does not wait for something to happen, for a situation to develop until it becomes criminal and can be subjected to action in the courts. It would have been too late if we had simply waited for things to get worse and people to get killed. While I agreed to the arrests and detentions, I thought only a few ringleaders would be taken in. I even met several DAP leaders and assured them that they would not be detained.

But the arrests had only just begun and were far from over. To my chagrin the police went on to make wholesale arrests. They took in Members of Parliament from all the political parties including UMNO, Chinese educationists, and prominent personalities from non-governmental organisations (NGOs). Among those arrested were Sim Mow Yu, a Chinese educationist who wanted Chinese to be recognised as one of the official languages of Malaysia; Dr Chandra Muzaffar, a prominent political scientist and human rights activist; and Datuk Paduka Ibrahim Ali, an UMNO politician with a reputation for jumping from one political party to the next. Altogether, 106 people were taken in. Within a week, the police released more than 50 of them and after two months, only 33 remained under detention. But the figure that everyone remembers is still 106.

When I was finally told of the total number of arrests, I was flabbergasted. But I could not countermand police orders. I also had to accept responsibility and fully support the action taken by the police. In time, the Government issued a White Paper explaining the full background, the dangerous tensions between the races and the need to take drastic action.

Besides the arrests, we also revoked the printing press and publishing licences of three newspapers: *The Star*, an English-language daily, *Sin Chew Jit Poh*, a Chinese-language daily, and *Watan*, a weekly newspaper published in Malay. We felt that these newspapers had been stoking the fires of racial sentiments by playing up certain issues, encouraging the Chinese community to agitate against the Government. The incident with the Malay soldier who ran amok, for example, was made out to be some kind of Malay attempt to kill the Chinese.

I was not informed beforehand that the newspapers would effectively be shut down. I knew the worldwide fraternity of journalists would condemn us and give Malaysia a bad name. But I had to trust the police to take all appropriate measures, based on the intelligence they had in hand.

The whole world was watching us, and it was said that I was now showing my true colours as a dictator. There was no way I could explain my role in these mass arrests and Ops Lalang became an indelible black stain on my time in office. All accounts of my years as Prime Minister of Malaysia are coloured by Ops Lalang. It frames all descriptions of my overall political character and career, while the epithet "authoritarian" appears without fail in all my detractors' assessments of me. Even though I did not use the ISA against Datuk Seri Anwar Ibrahim later, reports invariably suggest that he too was detained without trial. That he was duly tried in a court of law has always been ignored.

But mine was not the only reputation that was marred by Ops Lalang. Public trust and confidence in the police force was also damaged. Many felt they had acted excessively and had done so because I had given them carte blanche to do as they pleased. Rumours circulated that the police tortured prisoners and ill-treated foreign workers held under detention pending repatriation. This was not true but our detractors made full use of it.

The NGOs had also begun looking into the situation of illegal foreign workers detained by the Government, and the Press highlighted cases of deaths of those detained in police custody. They demanded to see the conditions under which detainees were kept. When they were allowed to do so, they condemned the Government and the police in particular for the poor condition of the detention facilities.

No one could contest the grounds of detention when the ISA was used — not even the courts could question the detention order that the Minister of Home Affairs approved. But somehow, several lawyers managed to serve writs of habeas corpus, claiming wrongful procedures, and when they were produced before the courts, many detainees were released. A few were immediately rearrested by the police, who by now had prepared proper detention papers. They were right to do so, of course, but their actions did not improve their image in the eyes of the public.

Members of the Government never publicly criticised the police, but the Cabinet was quite concerned. We discussed the image problem and the need for the police to be given a free hand within the law. We knew that there could be bad hats among them, but we did not believe there was anything systemically wrong with our police force.

There is no truth to the allegations that the Government gave the police carte blanche in the running of their affairs, but disciplining the police is not an easy matter. Chastising them publicly is not an option. Most members of the police force are Malays who in particular do not take kindly to a public dressing-down. If they have to be scolded or punished, it should be done out of the public eye. Our police accept being scolded in front of their fellow policemen. However, taking the police to task publicly, playing up their failures in the Press and making fools of them benefits no one. If I had anything to say to members of the police force I would speak to the IGP. He would take up the matter with his officers, who would discuss and decide upon the best way to take corrective action or to mete out punishment. Theirs is a disciplined force and they are likely to correct their ways if the problem is properly handled.

Our police force has no political agenda of its own. Its personnel are there to serve the elected government and they will even obey orders that to them may seem unwise. The Government would have to do something terrible and illegal before the police as a force would show reluctance to obey. Yet well before its senior officers do this, the rank and file might make their own unhappiness felt in subtle ways, and whatever they may or may not do can affect the performance of the force as a whole. That kind of foot-dragging and resistance would not serve the security and stability of the country.

Some critics of Ops Lalang argue that there never was a crisis. They are wrong. Others argue that there was a crisis but that it was exaggerated and politically manipulated by the Government, UMNO and myself. They too are wrong.

More reasonable critics recognise that there was a genuine situation but that the Government's response to it was excessive and disproportionate. They may be right. But these critics comment from the sidelines and with the detachment of hindsight. The Government did not have these advantages. We were faced with a situation and the responsibility for managing it was ours. The downward destructive cycle was already well-advanced by the time we chose to cancel the UMNO rally and the arrests began, and a descent into chaos and a possible return to the street violence and destruction of 1969 seemed imminent. Malaysians would not have forgiven us, nor should they, if we had taken insufficient or ineffective measures and allowed the cycle of violence to take over. Who would want that on their conscience? Not me!

It is hard to know at such times what is required and reasonable, what is disproportionate and excessive. We had to act, and we did. In retrospect it seems that we clamped down too heavily. But we have learnt a lot from what we all went through: we the Government, the police, the political parties of both the Barisan Nasional and the Opposition, the NGOs and the ordinary citizens who long for a peaceful life and look to the Government to provide them with social stability.

While some may disagree, Malaysia is a democratic country. One of the principal features of a democracy is the separation of powers between the Legislature, the Executive and the Judiciary. Yet this separation cannot be total or the nation would constantly be pulled in different directions. There must be some understanding among them and also coordination of the work that each centre of power does. Each must know its own proper domain and where its limits lie. Each arm of government must know its role and how far it may go before being accused of overstepping its operational limits.

In late 1987 I had to suppress my own personal doubts and feelings; I had to recognise the role and expertise of the police and defer to their exercising their appointed role in our system of government. No doubt Ops Lalang proved a black mark in the administrative history of Malaysia. But it taught us a good lesson. If we have had no more such operations since Ops Lalang, it was because we all learnt a great lesson from it, both the Government and the people.

# Chapter 42
# The Judiciary

Malaysia's judicial system was inherited from the British. The founding fathers of the country saw no reason why it should be changed. It had worked quite well during the colonial period although there was discrimination in favour of the British – their nationals could not be tried by local judges. But since the cases involving them were few and far between, the discrimination was hardly noticed. Those who did, did not think it was unusual because the British were a race apart. They were the privileged colonial masters.

After World War II there were also no cases involving British or other European nationals. Certainly to my knowledge there were no European prisoners in Malayan prisons.

The law in independent Malaysia of course applies to everyone equally. There is no racial discrimination. The Constitution is the basic law and this is accepted by all. Should there be a need to amend the Constitution, the provision for this is in the Constitution itself.

559

By and large Malaysian legal and the judicial systems have worked well. The Government understands the role of the Judiciary and the separation of powers between the three pillars of the Government, i.e. the Executive, the Legislature and the Judiciary.

When I became Prime Minister I was the first non-legal man to hold the post. The first three were all trained lawyers and were educated in England. They of course knew about English Common Law, which had been accepted by Malaysia. Not being a lawyer, my knowledge of the law and the legal system was not on par with theirs. In fact Tun Mohamed Suffian Hashim, one of the most distinguished Lord Presidents of the Supreme Court, did hint at my inadequacy.

Not being trained as a lawyer, just as I was not trained as an economist, resulted in my having some unorthodox views on the administration of justice in Malaysia. The strongly held view is that a judge or his judgment must never be publicly criticised on pain of being charged with contempt of court. But on the other hand a judge may, in the safety of his court, comment or even disparage others including the Government. I did not think this was quite right.

Then there is the question of an issue being *sub judice*. When a case is before a court, comments on the case are not allowed. This seems fair enough. We do not want to have a public debate which often amounts to a public trial via the media, as often happens in the Untied States for example.

But then when cases drag on for years and years, the image of the parties concerned can be seriously damaged with no means of redress. Often the people involved, the accused, the prosecutors and counsel, and witnesses, could already be dead before the case was concluded. Besides, human memory is short: witnesses cannot be expected to remember accurate details of what happened on a particular day ten years ago. As a result justice may not be done.

Truly justice delayed is justice denied. But sometimes judges themselves are the cause of the delay. Instances where Malaysian judges fail to provide written judgments are common.

560

The Government could blame everyone else except the judges when delays occur or some miscarriage of justice takes place. Yet judges are also human and when they do wrong and they do not correct themselves, the Government, as a representative of the people, should be able to do something.

In my early days as Prime Minister I was perhaps less discreet and must have publicly exhibited my frustrations with the Judiciary. Once in Cabinet I jokingly quoted Shakespeare's *Henry VI* in which Dick the Butcher famously says, "The first thing we do, let's kill all the lawyers." Of course I had forgotten the actual words. What I said was "the first thing we do is we hang the lawyers."

Cabinet proceedings were supposed to be secret but somehow the lawyers got to know about what I said. They all, including a few members of the Judiciary, thought that I hated lawyers.

Although I knew a lot of people in the Government and outside, I must admit I was never close to the members of the Judiciary. If I held receptions, including *buka puasa* (breaking fast during Ramadhan), the only judge I invited was the Lord President. Except when the Lord President presented his list of judges for promotion, I never discussed court matters with him. Some of my friends had become judges but after I became Prime Minister I never met them. Maybe they felt that I was too proud after my elevation.

The general impression was that I was against the Judiciary. I was frustrated at times, yes. But I was not against them even though many decisions of the courts did not favour the Government I was leading.

Before my time the decision of the Minister regarding detentions under the Internal Security Act could not be questioned in a court of law. But clever lawyers got around this provision by presenting writs of habeas corpus questioning whether all the procedures involved in detention under the ISA had been followed. The court had found some failures, trivial though they may have been, and ordered the release of some detainees. Since then there have been many such cases, even though the enforcement officers have been more careful. Effectively, the provision that the decision of the Minister is not to be questioned by a court has been rendered quite meaningless.

561

Many other decisions were made against the Government, but the Government respected the court's findings. There was never any attempt to interfere with the courts.

However, even judges must admit that they are human. As human beings and as citizens of the country they have their own feelings. They many not be involved in politics but they must have political sympathies. This may influence their judgments.

There was a case of a judge deciding on a matter involving an accident in which a minor leader of a certain political party had his car damaged. Everyone knew that the leader was in the wrong. Yet the judge decided against the other person, claiming that he himself saw the accident. He the judge was clearly a witness and should have excused himself. But he did not because, so people believed, he was in favour of one party against the other.

Yet no lawyer dared to challenge the judge and point out that as a witness his judgment was biased. They dared not challenge him because they may have to appear in his court later and he might find against them.

Judges are supposed to be aloof and impartial. But quite often they seem to show favour for a variety of reasons, including political and personal.

The most celebrated case happened during my tenure. It involved me as the candidate for party President in the 1988 UMNO Elections. I had won with a small majority although all indications prior to the elections showed that I had the support of the majority of the divisions whose delegates were eligible to vote.[1]

The loser, Tengku Razaleigh Hamzah, took the case to court alleging that the election was illegal because a handful of the 2,000 plus branches did not hold their meetings properly. These branches were therefore illegal and their delegates to the General Assembly had no *locus standi*.

The judge decided that UMNO was an illegal party. This put not just the party but the whole Government into a difficult position. Strictly speaking I had been made an independent Member of Parliament and was no longer head of the Barisan Nasional coalition.

The Opposition could have challenged me except that they knew any vote of non-confidence against me in the Lower House would not have succeeded. So I was able to continue as Prime Minister even though I was not the leader of any party or Chairman of BN.

I was forced to re-register the party as UMNO Baru (New UMNO) and we held a membership drive to rebuild the party nationwide. Tengku Razaleigh chose not to join UMNO Baru but to form his own party, Semangat 46 (Spirit of '46). There was a scramble to get the members of the defunct UMNO to join either of these two new parties.

In the end, most of the defunct UMNO members joined UMNO Baru including the majority of the Members of Parliament. UMNO Baru applied and rejoined the Barisan Nasional, and I reclaimed my position as Chairman of BN.

Truly the decision of the courts to declare UMNO an illegal party created a lot of trouble for me in particular and the Government as well. I have every reason to be sore with the judge. I *was* sore, but it has never been

---

[1]    For the full account of that election, see Chapter 40: A House Divided.

my way to hold a grudge against anyone for long. Just as many who had tried to pull me down were reappointed Ministers in my Cabinet, the judge concerned, the late Justice Tan Sri Harun Hashim, was promoted shortly after the affair.

In the immediate aftermath of the bitterly-contested UMNO elections of 1986, a number of contentious legal matters came before the courts. These included the decisions in the Raphael Pura and John Berthelsen case over the right of the relevant Minister to exercise his due discretion not to renew the visas of foreign visitors and employees; the disputes over the amendment of Article 146 of the Constitution that allowed the Attorney-General, rather than the judges, to determine at what level of jurisdiction cases might be heard; the cases over the awarding of the North-South Highway contracts to UEM (at that time called United Engineers (Malaysia)); the case that led to the declaration that UMNO was an illegal party; and several others. In all these cases the authority of the Government was questioned by the courts and except for one, the courts decided against the Government.

The details of these cases and their possible interrelations with one another will be pondered over by legal and political historians of the future. I can say, however, that there is no connecting line of motivation that can be drawn between these events and the legal decisions and confrontations that led to Tun Mohamed Salleh Abas's dismissal as Lord President. But it is worth noting that in many of these cases Tun Salleh generally found for the Government whenever he was involved in any of them.

In some notable instances where the decisions went against the Government, he issued dissenting minority opinions calling into question the legal basis upon which the judicial majority had chosen to reject the Government's case. It was also significant that it was not Tun Salleh but Tan Sri Harun who delivered the remarkable judgment that the entire UMNO party was an illegal organisation.

I therefore had no quarrel with Tun Salleh. He had always been fair in cases involving the Government. In two important cases – the contempt of court charge brought against me by Lim Kit Siang and the injunction Lim sought against UEM – Tun Salleh was one of the judges who found in favour of the Government and myself, as opposed to three other judges who did not. Again, when the Supreme Court struck down an amendment to the Criminal Procedure Code allowing criminal proceedings to commence in the High Court (as opposed to the Magistrate's Court) on a writ from the Attorney-General, Tun Salleh's judgment dissented from the those of the presiding judge and two others.

I was not aware at the time that he had already made two speeches against me and the Government. One was the address he gave upon receiving the Honorary Doctorate of Letters from the University of Malaya in 1987, and the other was a speech that he made in 1988 to launch a Malaysian legal publication entitled *Law, Justice and the Judiciary: Transnational Trends*. But these speeches did not initiate the action subsequently taken against him. Rather, it was the result of a letter he wrote to the Yang di-Pertuan Agong.

To cast more light on the following account, one must understand the odd relationship between the rule of law and the Rulers in the Malaysian context. As we know, there was no democracy in the Malay states prior to Independence – there was only feudalism, where the ruler had the power of life and death over citizens. Thus it was that Hang Tuah, the legendary Malay warrior, was sentenced to death by the Sultan. There was no law prescribing this punishment for his alleged crime of having an affair with one of the Sultan's wives. Until 1993, the Rulers enjoyed immunity before the law under Article 181 of the Constitution.

But after the amendments of 1993, the relation between the Ruler and his subjects was made clear by the provision in the Constitution protecting the rights of everyone before the law.

People intending to commit a crime know what the consequences are: the idea of doing away with absolute monarchy is to remove the arbitrariness of punishments.

The power of the Malay Rulers and the Agong to punish citizens directly has been transferred to the courts. Yet, in Malaysia and especially among the Malays, the Ruler still wields considerable influence, being backed by strong Malay traditions or *adat*. I must admit that I too find it difficult to ignore *adat*. As much as possible I would try to avoid personal confrontations with the Rulers. But if I had to, I would resort to formal action through Parliament to prevent abuses by royalty.

By tradition, the Prime Minister sees the Agong every Wednesday morning before chairing the Cabinet meeting. This was mostly a matter of courtesy, but occasionally the Agong would give his opinion of the Cabinet papers or bring up matters which he felt the Prime Minister needed to know. At one such meeting in early 1988, the Agong showed me a letter that Tun Salleh had written to him, complaining about the noise that was being made in the course of repairing the Agong's private residence near Tun Salleh's own house. The Agong felt insulted – it was not in keeping with Malay custom to write a letter of complaint to a Ruler, much less the King. A very senior officer of the Government should seek an audience and politely mention the matter. But Tun Salleh had not only written the letter, he had also forwarded copies to all the other Rulers, a move the Agong regarded as an attempt to pressure and embarrass him.

He then insisted that I remove Tun Salleh as Lord President, a decision he noted in the margin of Tun Salleh's letter.

Although strictly speaking it was the Agong who appointed the Lord President and, according to the Interpretations Act he should have the right to dismiss his appointee, the Cabinet on the advice of the Attorney-General believed that the provisions of the Constitution on the removal of the Lord President and judges could not be ignored. We had therefore to set up a tribunal to hear the case against Tun Salleh. This was tricky as we had to take into consideration the sensitivities of the case. Besides, the Interpretations Act did not apply to the Constitution, according to legal authorities.

The Agong's annoyance only increased when Tun Salleh wrote a second letter, this time complaining about government interference with the Judiciary. Again, he sent copies to the other Rulers. In this second letter he complained that the Prime Minister had made:

".... various comments and accusations ... against the Judiciary, not only outside but within Parliament. All of us (the judges) are patient and do not like to make the accusation publicly because such action is not compatible with our action as judges under the Constitution. Furthermore such action will not be in keeping with Malay tradition and custom .... As such it is only proper for us to be patient in the interest of the nation."

He continued,

"Other than that, accusations and comments have brought shame to all of us and caused us mental anguish to the extent that we are unable to discharge our functions in an orderly and proper fashion. We all feel ashamed because we are not able to avoid being looked (down) upon by those who do not understand our position under the Constitution."

What the tribunal would decide would be anybody's guess. Should it favour Tun Salleh we would have an embarrassment on our hands. The Agong would not be pleased. But if his dismissal was made necessary by the tribunal's finding that he had not behaved properly as a senior member of the Judiciary, the onus would be on the Government to take the necessary action. That would not look good either.

I thought it would be best if the case were to be settled without resorting to a tribunal. The publicity regarding the removal of the highest judge in the country would not be good for the Judiciary or the Government. It would certainly not be good for me. So I decided that I would try and persuade Tun Salleh to resign on his own.

On 27 May 1988 at a meeting in my office, I asked Tun Salleh to consider resigning instead of being removed from his position. I told him of the Agong's request and his agreement to the setting up of a tribunal. Tun Salleh agreed and offered his resignation in a letter dated the following day. In it, he wrote : "To avoid embarrassment all round I have considered the matter and I have decided that it is better in the national interest for me to retire immediately after taking all leave due to me, that is 96 days and the leave is to commence from today." The tone of his letter did not reflect any anger and I heaved a sigh of relief. But before the day had passed, Tun Salleh withdrew his resignation and indicated that he would rather face the tribunal and clear this name.

Tun Salleh demanded that the tribunal be made up of his peers. We obviously could not find enough former Lord Presidents, but those chosen were either former senior judges or those still sitting on the bench. Tun Hamid Omar, who by then was the Acting Lord President, chaired the tribunal. The other members were former judge Tan Sri Abdul Aziz Zain; former judge and Speaker of the Lower House Tan Sri Mohamed Zahir Ismail, and the Chief Justice of Borneo Tan Sri Lee Hun Hoe. To ensure Tun Salleh had a fair hearing, two foreign judges were included: a Sri Lankan named K.A.P. Ranasinghe and the highly-regarded judge of the High Court of Singapore, T.S. Sinnathuray.

In the event, Tun Salleh refused to appear before the tribunal and gave two reasons for his objection. First, he alleged that the tribunal was not properly constituted. Second, he claimed that the Queen's Counsel he had engaged to represent him was barred from participation. The tribunal therefore had no choice but to listen only to the Attorney-General's presentation and use it to make its decision. Even as the tribunal was sitting, Tun Salleh tried to stop the proceedings through an ex-parte motion for an order of prohibition against the tribunal on constitutional grounds, to prevent it from deliberating and making recommendations to the King.

As Tun Salleh's attempt to stop the proceedings of the tribunal through the ex-parte motion was not heard by then, the tribunal sat and deliberated over the evidence presented to it.

The tribunal heard the case on 29 June and completed its proceedings the next day. As Judge Datuk Ajaib Singh postponed hearing the ex-parte motion to 4 July – because the Attorney-General could not be present – Tun Salleh applied for a temporary stay order at the Supreme Court to prevent the tribunal's report from being submitted to the King. Tan Sri Wan Suleiman Pawanteh, Supreme Court Judge, immediately convened and led a five-judge bench to hear the case. The five were Datuk George Seah, Tan Sri Azmi Kamaruddin, Tan Sri Eusoffe Abdoolcader, Tan Sri Wan Hamzah Wan Mohamad Salleh and Tan Sri Wan Sulaiman. It was quite clear they had a predetermined idea and came together to approve the stay order. The acting Lord President's approval was not sought as was required, and the judges arbitrarily postponed the other cases they were due to hear.

As judges, the five-men bench ought to have used proper legal channels to refute or reject what the Government had done. They could have registered their protests as individuals, or they could have become appellants and had other judges listen to their case.

Instead, they chose a way which seemed like they wanted to use their position to frustrate the work of a legally constituted tribunal.

On the same day this group came together, Ajaib Singh heard the Attorney-General's presentation, with documents showing the King's views regarding the suspension of Tun Salleh. Ajaib Singh then dismissed Tun Salleh's application for prohibition.

It was not the first letter (regarding the noise caused by repairing the Agong's house) but Tun Salleh's second letter of complaint – this time against me – that was entered as evidence in the Attorney-General's presentation to the tribunal. Perhaps there was some sensitivity about the first letter which prompted the Attorney-General's decision. In any case that was what he did. He also cited the two speeches by Tun Salleh about me and the Government as evidence of misbehaviour by the Lord President. I had never heard or complained about these speeches. As a result, the case for the removal of Tun Salleh appeared to be initiated because of his remarks against me. That in fact it was the Agong who instructed me to remove Tun Salleh because of the first letter complaining about the noise seemed to have been completely ignored.

I had never spoken or written about this line taken by the Attorney-General implicating me because, for a long time, I believed he had used the first letter with the Agong's instruction when presenting his case to the tribunal. In the course of writing these memoirs and in my explanation to Matthias Chang, my former political secretary who was one of the lawyers who vilified me for what he believed I did, I suddenly realised why the lawyers and the judges were so much against me. They thought it was because of what Tun Salleh said against me that resulted in his dismissal.

I recently called the Attorney-General at the time, Tan Sri Abu Talib Othman, and asked him where was the first letter. He said it was with the Government. I can have no access to it now but I am prepared to swear on the Quran that it was the letter and the instruction from the Agong which caused action to be taken to remove Tun Salleh Abbas.

On 8 August, Tun Salleh was found guilty of misconduct and, following the tribunal's recommendation to the King, was formally removed from office. A second tribunal was then set up to investigate allegations of misconduct by the five Supreme Court Judges. This tribunal was made up of Datuk Edgar Joseph Jr., as Chairman, M.D.H. Fernando from Sri Lanka, P. Coomaraswamy from Singapore, Tun Mohd Eusoff Chin and Tan Sri Lamin Mohd Yunus. The outcome was that Wan Suleiman and Seah were removed from office. Under normal circumstances they would all have lost their pensions, but upon appeal by the Attorney-General I approved their being paid full pensions, including the derivative pensions due to them.

Lawyers and the foreign Press regarded the removal of these judges as proof that I had undermined the independence of the Judiciary. However, the removals were done in the manner prescribed by the Constitution, and it was the tribunal that made the decision. Action taken against the Lord President was founded on the improper letters to the Agong and Tun Salleh's speeches. Also crucial was the fact that it was the Agong who commanded that Tun Salleh be removed. However, none of this is believed.

In his book *May Day for Justice*, Tun Salleh took pains to explain his belief that my audience with the Agong never took place: that I had lied to the Attorney-General, who in turn repeated that lie to the tribunal. He also pointed out that the date in my letter to the Agong, 1 May 1988, was a Sunday, and not a Wednesday, when the audience with the Agong had taken place. Perhaps the date was wrong. It often happens in the courts and elsewhere that an incorrect date is given to an event. But it is too simplistic to imagine that just because the wrong date is given, the event never took place. Besides, the letter may have been typed on a day before I met the Agong.

I could never have had the Agong become a witness to confirm the details of the meeting as this would not have been right. The Attorney-General had Tun Salleh's letter of complaint with the Agong's notation in the margin. But as has been pointed out, the first letter was not produced as evidence before the subsequent tribunal for reasons that are best known to the Attorney-General, and he is in a position to verify whether or not the letter existed.

Because I view certain actions by certain lawyers (particularly those involved in politics) with some animosity, people often assume that much of what I have done in public life that touched on legal issues has been motivated by a desire to get back at the legal community as a whole and cut them down to size. Many people, especially lawyers themselves, seem happy to encourage that idea. The trouble with their view is that it simply happens to be wrong. I have criticised doctors, even though I am one. My criticism of the Malays is well known. It does not mean I hate them. I always believe that when something is done which is wrong, someone needs to tell the person concerned.

Some incredulous readers will ask why, as an elected Prime Minister of this country, I was prepared to dismiss the Lord President, the highest judicial officer in the land, simply at the Agong's behest and on his personal demand. I had after all been tough on the Rulers and I had taken actions which were not to their liking. I had publicly clashed with Their Royal Highnesses. I could have blankly refused the command of the Agong.

But I did not. I had taken the letter and showed it to the Cabinet and asked them what they thought of it. I cannot remember anyone advising me to ignore it or to appeal to the Agong to do anything else.

I asked the Attorney-General, and as far as I can remember he talked about the procedures as given in the Constitution. I write all this now not to shift the blame to someone else. The final decision and the responsibility for initiating action against Tun Salleh was mine.

To many modern Malaysians, the fact that a Prime Minister should accede in that way to the Agong's demand may seem not just undesirable but also improbable. But that is the truth as to what happened. This account of how it happened is not offered to exculpate me, nor is it provided in an attempt to avoid responsibility and lay the blame upon others. It is related simply as an attempt to explain what really happened at the time.

I expect the members of the legal profession who had never been friendly towards me will find this story totally unbelievable. But that is their right. It does not alter the facts. Many see only what they wish to see. When what is placed before their eyes seems not to be in keeping with their preconceived ideas, their perception of things, the tendency is to reject it. For me that is simply human nature and it has to be accepted.

Labels carry much weight with the public, especially political labels. Once, when I was called a "Malay ultra", everything that I did – however harmless – would be regarded as extreme. Later I was branded a legal vandal, an accusation that stuck and will likely stay with me for the rest of my life.

In Tun Salleh's book, he refers to the case of Alfred Dreyfus, the Jewish officer in the French Army who was accused of being a spy and condemned to exile on Devil's Island. It was Emile Zola, the great French writer, who fought for Dreyfus's vindication, beginning with his famous newspaper article entitled *J'accuse*. Because of Zola, Dreyfus was rehabilitated. If Tun Salleh thinks of himself as the unfortunate Dreyfus, he should be happy that there are so many Zolas among his brother lawyers. For the vilification against me I expect no Zola.

571

# Chapter 43:
## Matters Of The Heart

I first felt a slight pain in my chest about a month before I had my heart attack in 1989, but I ignored it. I was at Genting Highlands, attending an alumni meeting of the King Edward VII College of Medicine. Many of my classmates and their children were there and everyone was having a good time. I was watching them when the young people pulled me on to the dance floor. As the dance went on I began to feel breathless and pain in my chest, but they stopped after I sat down. The next day I went horse-riding and again experienced the same breathlessness and pain. I didn't want to admit to myself that it might be a heart attack and so I told no one, and simply hoped it would go away. Even if you are a doctor and you know the signs and symptoms, you don't want to admit that you might have a problem.

In those days I didn't have regular medical checkups. I do however remember going for an extensive medical examination in London on a doctor's advice after having a slight blood pressure problem. It was a real nuisance as the checkup took a long time and I was forced to wear a small ECG machine that bulged from my waist. I had to attend a dinner with the machine strapped to my body and it looked like I was carrying a gun.

A month after the Genting party, I had dinner at a Thai restaurant at The Mall with Hasmah and Marina's husband to celebrate Mokhzani's birthday, even though he wasn't there. There should have been four of us but Marina didn't turn up, so there were only Hasmah, Didier, Marina's husband at the time, and myself. We had ordered food for four and I ended up eating most of Marina's share — perhaps as a result of wartime deprivation, I dislike wasting food. When we got home, I began to feel pain in my chest and breathlessness that this time refused to go away. I tried lying down and sitting up but the pain remained just as severe. Hasmah called up a specialist friend of ours at the Kuala Lumpur General Hospital, my former classmate Dr Jimmy Eapen. She described my symptoms over the phone and Jimmy came over immediately. He diagnosed a heart attack or cardiac infarction, but needed to return home to get his portable ECG machine.

When it confirmed his suspicions, I was immediately sent to the hospital. I felt well enough to walk but they insisted I use a wheelchair.

I should have known that it was a heart attack as the symptoms were classic. My history of chest pains and breathlessness after the exertion of dancing and horse-riding also fit. Heart attacks are also precipitated by worry, by long journeys or by having too much food during a meal, and I did eat too much food that night. I should not have brushed off the pain the first time I felt it and should have admitted to myself that I was having a heart attack.

I was admitted into the Kuala Lumpur General Hospital on the night of 17 January 1989. There, Datuk Dr Robaayah Zambahari confirmed that I had had a heart attack and gave me an injection to relieve the pain. She told Hasmah to call our family, which made us realise how serious the situation was. She also called Tun Ghafar Baba, then the Deputy Prime Minister, waking him up from his sleep to tell him what was happening.

After completing the standard checks, they decided that I needed an angiogram. Coincidentally, Dr Simon Stertzer, a heart specialist from California, was in the region and he was asked to be present for the procedure. He and Dr Robaayah concluded that I had had an infarction and needed a bypass. They gave me a choice of either going to the US for the operation or having it done in Kuala Lumpur. Without hesitation, I decided I would have it done here. I had to have faith in our Malaysian doctors and knew that if I didn't make an example of myself, no one else would have confidence in our medical service. Previously, all our VIPs had gone abroad, but I knew that Datuk Dr Rozali Wathooth had performed these operations successfully at the Kuala Lumpur General Hospital. He had already left Government service to work at the Subang Jaya Medical Centre, but there were other heart specialists at the General Hospital, including Tan Sri Dr Yahya Awang. I knew that Dr Yahya was quite experienced and I decided to entrust my life to him.

As a doctor myself, I knew the risks. I knew there was a possibility that I might not survive the operation as it was not, at that time, a common procedure. People still feared letting doctors open up their chests and fiddle with their hearts. But I told myself that if I was going to die, then that was it — I would leave it to Allah and the skill of the surgeon. It may sound dramatic now that so many people have successfully undergone heart surgery, but once I had accepted the possibility of death, I felt quite calm.

I rested for four days before the angiogram, which confirmed that I needed the operation. Dr Stertzer again offered the option of having the bypass done in California, although he also said that Dr Yahya was as competent as any heart surgeon in the US. When I was left alone with Hasmah, I asked her to call Dr Yahya and when he entered the room, I told him simply that I wanted him to do it. I had known his father well. Dr Awang had been a very good doctor and had been a Member of Parliament when I was also an MP from 1964 to 1969. At the time of my heart attack, Dr Awang was the Governor of Penang.

My admission into hospital precluded my attending the weekly Wednesday Cabinet meeting. The doctors warned that I could have no visitors, and Hasmah decided she would enforce the doctors' order herself. Many people came and insisted they had to see me but Hasmah was very firm, allowing only a few to peep at me as I lay sedated in bed. There was a by-election at that time and rumours were raging that I was critically ill. Some even said I had died. Hasmah never left the hospital and she stayed by my side the whole time. Dr Robaayah offered to give her a sedative that first night, but she was determined to stay awake to make sure no one came and bothered me.

On the eve of the operation, a phone call came at about 10pm from Lee Kuan Yew. He was very concerned and talked to Hasmah as I had already taken medication to get ready for surgery. Lee asked her to persuade me to postpone the operation because he had a medical team ready to fly to Kuala Lumpur, with the well-known cardiac surgeon Dr Victor Chang, a Singaporean living in Australia, to do the surgery. He said Dr Chang had a lot of experience, having performed more than a thousand such operations. When he asked who was going to be the surgeon, Hasmah named Dr Yahya, whom Lee had never heard of. But Hasmah said I had already made up my mind and the family agreed with me. She thanked him and promised to call as soon as the operation was over. She knew that once

I had made up my mind, I would not change it. Hasmah was also very confident that Dr Yahya could do the job. Apparently, Lee did not only appeal to Hasmah, but also contacted Tun Daim Zainuddin to ask him to intercede with her. Despite our many differences throughout the years, I appreciated Lee's concern.

Our three boys were away at the time and Marina was in Singapore. Ineza, her daughter, was sleeping in a cot in our room. In her haste to get me to hospital, Hasmah had almost left her locked in the room the night of my heart attack. She remembered just in time and shifted the cot to the children's room. Marina and Mokhzani, who was in Miri, flew in the very next day. Mukhriz was in Boston and Mirzan in Philadelphia, but both of them managed to return to Kuala Lumpur on the eve of the operation. Just before the surgery, they sent in Hasmah and then the kids one by one to kiss me. That was when Hasmah broke down for the first time.

The problem with being a doctor is that you know what they are going to do to you during surgery. In heart surgery they stop your heart and lungs and pass your blood through a heart-lung machine. I did not relish the idea, especially as the procedures were relatively new and the equipment was not as sophisticated as what is used now. Tun Hussein Onn had had a bypass and never really recovered afterwards. Another VIP who had undergone the procedure, Datuk Jaafar Hassan, the *Mentri Besar* of Perlis, died some time after. I asked Dr Yahya only one question — how would they open up my chest? He said they would use an electric saw. "Thank you very much," I said, "I do not need to know more."

As they lifted me onto a trolley and wheeled it into the operation theatre, I vaguely remember seeing the ceiling as I was rolled along the corridors and into the anteroom next to the theatre. I heard some soothing words from the anaesthetist as he went about his work. Then I was lifted onto the operating table and told to count backwards from 10. The next thing I knew, I was in the recovery room. In that respect, modern surgery is a miracle.

The operation took about six hours, though to me it seemed no more than two seconds. It was my family that had to sit and wait it out. The doctors took veins from both of my legs and constructed five bypasses. Dr Yahya, Dr

Rozali and their assistants did a good job and there were no complications. These days invasive surgery is less necessary and angioplasties give ever better results, while dieting and regular exercise can reduce the incidence of coronary atherosclerosis and infarction. Some say dieting can actually reverse the atherosclerosis of the arteries, which is what I am trying to do now.

When I woke up, all I could think about was the fact that I was still alive. I remember the discomfort though, as it hurt even when I tried to turn in my bed or coughed. There were tubes in my body, a drain in my abdomen, and an oxygen mask on my face. I was in the hospital for two weeks and took a much longer time than others to recover.

It was very isolated and surreal in the ICU. There were no windows and it was easy to lose track of time, and I found I could only keep track of the hours from the changing shifts of nurses. It was all quite depressing — I was 64 years old and it was the first time I had been admitted to a hospital, and for a major operation to boot. I had worked in many hospitals before, but had never been a patient in one. Being shy, I was also embarrassed by having to be cared for by the nurses.

My physiotherapist was a terror and would force me to cough to avoid any build-up of fluid in my lungs, which could lead to pneumonia or a lung infection. I may have resented her insistence then, but when I succumbed to a serious infection after my cardiac surgery of 2007 I could better appreciate her intentions and reasoning. In the meantime, I had to put off travelling and I avoided presiding over the Cabinet for a while.

During this time, one of the events which boosted my spirits was the Barisan Nasional's victory in the Ampang by-election the day after my operation. Stuck in the ICU, I heard a commotion and at first thought that we had lost. But when Ahmad Razali, Hasmah's brother, came in and gave me the thumbs-up sign, I realised the news was good. Sadly, however, Tun Ghafar's son, who was campaigning with him, died of a massive heart attack on the day of the election.

At the time of my stay, the operating theatre in the General Hospital was not very well equipped. Space was needed for the necessary equipment, including gas cylinders for the anaesthetics. The General Hospital's operating theatres were not really meant for highly complex heart surgery, and the surgeons and anaesthetists barely managed. I realised they were working under tremendous constraints and pressure, which was not fair to either the doctors or patients. But up until then, the Government had shown scant interest in their needs. After I had recovered, the doctors were not shy to point out the urgent need for better facilities.

They argued that instead of fully equipping the surgical theatres at general hospitals, it would be better to set up a special centre for heart diseases. I agreed and decided the Government should allocate adequate funds for this purpose, which was how the National Heart Institute or Institut Jantung Negara (IJN) was established.

Building and equipping such a facility was easy enough — it was staffing that posed a problem. Our specialists were leaving government hospitals in droves because of low pay; yet, we could not increase their salaries without other government employees demanding the same. This was simply unaffordable. We decided that while the specialist centre should be owned by the Government, it should also be run like an independent corporation. IJN was thus corporatised, which allowed it to draw up its own pay scheme, bonuses and the like. Terms of employment were still not as good as in the private sector, but good enough to permit committed specialists to stay and to greatly reduce the number of specialists leaving government service. Most of IJN's patients were government employees, and their treatment was paid for by the Government.

The whole experience of my heart attack was a tremendous strain on my family, perhaps more than on me since I had already resigned myself to the possibility of dying. To this day, Mokhzani gets worried around the time of his birthday, as many unfortunate events have uncannily taken place then, such as the first Gulf War, his breaking his ankle, and my operation. But none of the family, not even the children, tried to talk me into early retirement after I recovered. They knew that such a suggestion would only add to my stress and that I would make my own decision.

I have never felt much pressure when working but obviously the job of being Prime Minister entailed a constant undercurrent of stress. I always went about my work in my usual manner and tackled problems calmly, never getting unduly excited and rarely losing my temper. I would sometimes feel tired but always woke up the next day feeling refreshed and ready to go back to work. I enjoyed my job and the opportunity to do things which only a Prime Minister had the power to do. The challenges that I faced in 1986 and 1987 when Tengku Razaleigh Hamzah and Tun Musa Hitam tried to topple me must have been a great strain, as was Ops Lalang. But I had managed to handle them and did not feel any great undue pressure. At a deeper level, I suppose, my system must have reacted differently and experienced greater strain than I could recognise.

I was told to take three months off after my operation before making any decision about my future, but this was unnecessary as it never occurred to me to stop working. After leaving hospital, I was eager to go back to work, but my family and my doctors insisted that I take a vacation. So we went to Morocco and Spain. Even so, I resumed my old routine as soon as possible, going to my office, seeing my staff and Cabinet colleagues, meeting visitors and getting briefings on everything that was going on.

In fact, I was brimming with ideas about developing the country. I couldn't wait to see them take off and oversee their progress. I knew my disease might recur but that was something I had to accept, and so long as I remained Prime Minister my health held up well. I even felt strengthened by the challenges that I had to face and by my success in handling them. It was only after I retired that my cardiac difficulties returned.

I have not slowed down since my retirement and, aside from giving talks around the world and setting up an office at the Perdana Leadership Foundation in Putrajaya, I have also taken up horse-riding again. I made yearly trips to Argentina to ride in the Andes, sometimes for up to eight hours straight. But towards the end of 2006, after a strenuous trip to Saudi Arabia, Japan and New Zealand and several back-to-back engagements in Kuala Lumpur, I suffered a mild heart attack the evening after a Hari Raya open house held by my children.

I was at home on 6 November when I again felt that familiar tightness in my chest. Hasmah called Datuk Dr Nasir Muda, a cardiologist and my personal physician, and I was taken to IJN in the early hours of the morning. The doctors immediately put me on a drip and diagnosed a mild heart attack after conducting an ECG. I recovered fairly quickly and by the fourth day, I was sitting up in bed and ready to resume working. Hasmah always thinks it's a good sign when I ask for my writing tablet.

Despite my relatively quick recovery, it was clear that I needed to consider the possibility of another heart operation. In most cases patients remain reasonably healthy for 10 years after a bypass, but 18 years had already passed since I had had the procedure done. My doctors said I had to decide fairly quickly if I needed to undergo a second bypass, before my condition worsened and it became too dangerous to carry it out. I had to weigh my decision against the fact that I was already in my 80s and would likely find the post-operative recovery more difficult to deal with.

While I mulled over my decision, I started an exercise regimen that was designed to boost my blood circulation. I also went on the treadmill and cycled, sometimes up to 10 kilometres a day, which Hasmah thought was overdoing it. In fact, I was to find out later that she even asked for my horse to be trained not to gallop too fast.

579

Despite the exercise, by May of 2007 I noticed that my legs felt heavier and I could not catch my breath when I went up the stairs. That month we had a class of '47 reunion in Bukit Merah in Perak and spent several days with old friends from medical college, staying up late every night to talk. Hasmah and I flew to Langkawi immediately after the reunion for a brief holiday.

During our stay on the island, I suffered an acute attack of pulmonary oedema.[1] I was tired the day it happened and woke up from a nap feeling breathless. I used an inhaler but it had no effect. After that it all happened very quickly — as my lungs filled with fluid and I began to struggle to breathe, Dr Nasir called for an ambulance but quickly decided that it would take too long to wait for it to arrive. He assisted me to the car and we rushed to the hospital. I remember hearing him urging me to hang on even as I could feel myself slipping in and out of consciousness. We actually passed the ambulance on the way but Dr Nasir, knowing there was little time left

---

[1]     An acute pulmonary oedema is a potentially fatal condition where air sacs in the lungs fill up with fluid, preventing the absorption of oxygen.

to get me to the hospital, ordered our driver to keep going. Hasmah later said that she thought she would lose me that day. To make room for me and Dr Nasir in the car, she sat in the front seat and could only reach back to place her hand on my knee in an effort to comfort me.

At the hospital, they forced oxygen into my lungs and managed to stabilise me after half an hour. Dr Nasir contacted his colleagues at IJN and anaesthetist Dr Sharifah Suraya Syed Mohd Tahir flew in with all the equipment that the hospital in Langkawi did not have.

By this time it seemed as if most people on the island had heard about what had happened and they began to gather at the hospital. In order to get past the crowds the next day when we flew back to Kuala Lumpur, the hospital director had to use a decoy ambulance at the front of the hospital as we slipped out from the back. When we got to the airport, some of our children had just arrived on a commercial flight and had to turn back and board the same plane to Kuala Lumpur.

Getting me on the private plane to fly home proved to be a complicated task. The steps could not accommodate my stretcher so I had to be carried up, with one person supporting my head and shoulders and another holding up my feet. Not wanting to let my body sag, my physiotherapist Boey Ghod Chee insisted on crawling underneath me to support my back as we made our way up the stairs. I needed oxygen but it was dangerous to fly at high altitudes with oxygen tanks onboard so the plane flew at a low altitude all the way back to Kuala Lumpur.

The attack left me feeling weak and unwell and I began to seriously consider the doctors' advice to undergo a second bypass. Another operation, of course, would be far more risky because I was now 82 years old. Not going through with the procedure, on the other hand, meant that another attack was virtually inevitable. Eventually, even though I knew that undergoing a second bypass would give me no guarantees, I decided to take the risk. Again, my medical training proved to be less than useful, as I knew of the potential complications involved.

I did consider going overseas this time but, again, I worried that it would only undermine public confidence in our doctors. We brought in a consultant from the Mayo Clinic in the US, but the surgical team was ultimately led by Dr Yahya and Dr Rozali again.

I was admitted back into IJN on 2 September 2007 and had my second bypass two days later. Dr Yahya and Dr Rozali were not the only members of the original team that operated on me in 1988 to return. Virtually everyone else — including the operating theatre nurses — were involved as well. Some of them had already left IJN for private practice but they all came back for my operation.

For a while, during my post-operative recovery, I suffered from hallucinations and strange dreams that I was the son of a Sultan or that I was working as a horse trainer. Sometimes I thought I was elsewhere, in Jakarta, Thailand or China. I had to breathe with the help of a machine, which also stopped me from swallowing and speaking. Even after they had removed the tube from my trachea, I felt as if it was still there and had difficulty swallowing for a while. Because I could not speak, I tried writing, but found that I could not recall the right letters. My family gave me a keyboard so I could point to the letters I wanted but I was too uncoordinated to manage even that. At one point, when my frustration got the better of me, I wanted to pull out all the tubes from my body. Hasmah scolded me, saying that so many people had worked very hard to help me.

I developed an infection after staying in the ICU for two weeks. The doctors knew they had to go back in and were worried that I would not agree to another operation. But I decided to go ahead, hoping it would help me recover more quickly and end the nightmare of having to try and sleep with tubes in my neck, hand, back and chest.

I was wheeled back into the operating theatre on 22 September, but although the surgery went off without any problems, my recovery again proved complicated. Depression set in and I began to feel too tired to go on. To raise my spirits, several visitors were allowed to see me, including my horse-riding buddies, the Mufti of Perlis[2] Dr Mohd Asri Zainul Abidin, and my former personal physician Datuk Dr Zainal Hamid. Hasmah also tried to encourage me. She brought in one of her favourite pictures of me,

---

[2]   In Malaysia, 13 states including Perlis have appointed a Mufti, or Islamic scholar who advises the state government on matters of Islam.

pointed to it and gently said that she had brought this man to the hospital and fully intended to take him home.

Hasmah rarely left my side while I was in the hospital. During that time, she was home for only one night during the fasting month to spend time with our family, but otherwise slept at the hospital. All of this did take its toll on her —one day, out of sheer exhaustion, she literally toppled from her chair and woke up face-down on the floor. This caused a minor panic in the ICU but Hasmah insisted she was fine and was merely very tired.

In all I spent 49 days in IJN and was discharged on 20 October. I must admit that there were occasions when I felt perilously close to the end. In fact, I had gone into this knowing full well what the odds were and, on the day I was admitted, I had given Hasmah the combination number to the locked briefcase that held all my private papers. There was a time during my long stay at IJN, when it seemed that my condition would not improve, that Hasmah considered opening the briefcase. When she told Mirzan, however, he said the time had not come and it was best to leave it as it was.

Since these last two operations, I've been able to recover most of my old energy, but I tire easily and am still underweight. For once, I'm struggling to put on the pounds... this in a country where everyone is always determined to feed you to the gills.

As I write this, it has been more than three years since my second operation. The recovery had been much slower than the first time, but it has been progressive and I am now fully active.

I began riding again more than a year ago and have kept up a weekly programme. I also walk if the weather is fine, otherwise I use the treadmill. In the morning I exercise with weights. In February 2009 I went to Argentina and spent 10 days riding on the pampas, morning and evening.

I work at three separate offices daily from 8.30am to 6pm and often have to attend night functions. Most weekends I would be out and I would go abroad at least once every month to give talks.

Despite the two operations, I have generally enjoyed good health and people have repeatedly asked me about my stamina and how I manage to look younger than my age. I have brushed off these questions by jokingly replying that one should choose one's parents carefully.

But still the questions keep coming. Many believed and told others that I was getting injections in Switzerland. One lady came up to me in a supermarket and asked me if it was true I took some medicine costing RM5,000 a day. Many went to the pharmacy where I bought my vitamins and would buy whatever I bought.

Finally, I promised I would tell all in my memoirs. But what is there to tell? People feel disappointed if I begin to talk about healthcare or personal hygiene. They want a quick fix, but there isn't one. Certain things, however, can help us look younger than our age.

Keeping active is important at any age. But it is especially important after retirement. As far as possible I try to maintain my working routine. I get up early for my early morning prayers. After prayers, I shave, brush my teeth and have a very warm bath. Before breakfast I practise a few minutes of deep breathing and light exercise.

I have a light breakfast and then I begin the day with some writing. I feel lost if I do not write something in the early morning. I think it activates the brain and helps to retain its sharpness. I seldom do heavy exercise and certainly not in the morning on a working day. I do the treadmill infrequently, I don't walk as much as I would like to, and I don't play golf.

What I do like is horse-riding, which I learnt to do at the age of 60. I was invited by the late General Muhammad Zia-ul-Haq, the President of Pakistan, to review the annual parade on the country's national day. We went by car and then we got into a horse-drawn carriage flanked by Pathan horsemen in full military uniform. I was impressed by what I saw and I decided to buy two horses in Pakistan. President Zia got to know about my interest and decided to make me a gift of the two horses. And so I started to learn riding at the Selangor Polo and Riding Club.

Almost the first thing I learnt about riding was to sit up straight and erect in the saddle. This is very important. It prevents you from getting a backache. I think it helps me to stand erect and not slouch or stoop even when I am 80 years old. When people stoop they look old.

I developed a habit of walking as if I was marching. Most people at 80 would naturally slow down. They even shuffle and drag their feet. Younger people tend to help old people when getting up, when standing, walking and climbing stairs. Sometimes old people like to be helped. They enjoy the concern and attention of their children or grandchildren. If one allows oneself to be helped, it may develop into a habit. It is better to try to avoid the help and assistance for as long as possible. It gives the appearance of being young. And really it is good for muscle tone and balance.

I also always try to get sufficient sleep — six hours at night in a proper bed if possible. Then I would catnap for 15 minutes after lunch. For the catnap I would not lie down. I would sit in a comfortable chair with my head up. I do the same when travelling and when I have nothing to do. Napping with the head up is important. If you lie down, you will wake feeling groggy and be unable to work.

Besides being able to snatch short periods of sleep, my experience as a medical practitioner also helped me work long hours as Prime Minister. Having slept throughout a flight I would go straight to work. After all, when I visited foreign countries, I took no rest, starting work immediately upon arrival or the next day at most.

But most of all, if we want to look young, we must be happy. The happiness of being in love is very noticeable. It is difficult of course to be happy all the time. But if you count your blessings every morning, you will feel happy. There would be problems to tackle, misfortunes to be faced, but always there would be something to feel cheerful about. For me, to wake up alive is a great blessing, even in the past, and more so now.

As you can see I have no special formula for not looking my age. People who expect me to name the elixir of youth that sustains me will be disappointed. Truly there is no such thing.

# Chapter 44:
## New Challenges, New Solutions

I took some time to recover from my coronary bypass operation in 1989, travelling overseas to recuperate. Eventually, I regained my strength and was ready to face new political challenges.

By this time UMNO Baru, which had been registered after the court declared the original UMNO illegal in 1988, was succeeding in gaining support from most former UMNO members. The party's nationwide divisional structure had also been resuscitated.

In Sabah, however, the Sabah People's United Front, or Berjaya,[1] together with its Barisan Nasional partners, had lost ignominiously in the 1986 elections. Politics in Sabah had always been complicated. While the majority of Sabahans were Muslims and keen to ally themselves with the Federal Government, the Chinese-Kadazandusuns had never really felt well-disposed towards the Peninsula. This created a fractured political landscape, which was made more difficult by Sabah politicians frequently switching parties. This was so prevalent that it became a trademark of Sabah politics and continues to be a problem today.

The United Sabah National Organisation, or USNO, led by the state's first governor Tun Mustafa Harun, was allied with Tunku Abdul Rahman and UMNO. For a very long time Tun Mustafa was the single most powerful politician in Sabah. Once he was installed as Chief Minister in 1967, he ruled with a strong hand and was consistently able to deliver 16 seats to Barisan Nasional at every general election. Over time, however, Tun Mustafa showed less regard for the Federal Government, especially after the Tunku stepped down as Prime Minister. By then he had become extremely rich and did not hesitate to use his wealth. Once, during a visit to Kuala Lumpur, it was said that he sent back his plane all the way to Sabah to fetch his violin.

My relationship with Tun Mustafa was not good, especially after I criticised the Tunku in 1969. During a secret meeting, he demanded that I apologise to the Tunku, but I refused. Tun Mustafa and his party were eventually

---

1     Since it was formed in 1975, Berjaya has been a Barisan Nasional component party.

defeated in 1976 by Berjaya, the party Datuk Seri Harris Salleh had formed with the support of the Kadazandusuns, including Datuk Seri Joseph Pairin Kitingan. That victory put Harris in power and he became Sabah's next Chief Minister. He brought a lot of development to the state, including its island of Labuan, which, with his agreement, became Malaysia's second Federal Territory in 1984.

One of the reasons why Tun Mustafa lost the people's support was because he had become authoritarian. Harris made the same mistake and eventually his party was defeated by Pairin's Parti Bersatu Sabah (PBS)[2] or United Sabah Party in the 1985 elections.

I had been quite close to Harris but I was suspicious of Pairin because I did not have any clear indication as to his loyalty to the Barisan Nasional. Every time I visited Sabah when he was Chief Minister I felt as if I was in Opposition territory. To get him to commit to the Barisan Nasional I promised Sabah its own university should our coalition win there. I also took Pairin on my trip to South Korea and talked with him at length about Sabah and its future. As Chief Minister, he had registered his objection to Harris's consent to Labuan becoming a Federal Territory as he saw it as part of Sabah's domain which should be enhanced, not diminished. To emphasise his claim, he once held a state cabinet meeting on Pulau Layang Layang, an island in the South China Sea reclaimed by the Federal Government, to indicate that it too was a part of Sabah. He dwelt upon the 20 issues[3] which Sabah claimed had remained unsettled since it had joined Malaysia. I expected trouble from him so I had to consolidate elsewhere.

Beginning with Johor, I visited all the states to strengthen UMNO and Barisan Nasional. The failure of Tengku Razaleigh Hamzah to unseat me had meanwhile convinced the extremists and my detractors that I could not be easily overthrown. After Ops Lalang, racial issues were no longer played up as before by the Press and non-governmental organisations, even though most of the detainees had been released.

---

[2] Pairin broke away from Berjaya because of differences with Harris, and formed PBS in 1985.

[3] The 20-point Agreement, which included issues related to religion, language, the Constitution, immigration, citizenship, tariffs, the special position of indigenous races and education, was made on 16 September 1963.

A general election had to be held by 1990 and while I did not expect to do well, I still believed that the Barisan Nasional would get a two-thirds majority. In the midst of our preparations for the election, two former Prime Ministers passed away, Tun Hussein Onn in May and Tunku Abdul Rahman in December. Tun Hussein died in America while undergoing medical treatment, while the Tunku passed away at the Kuala Lumpur General Hospital. In accordance with their wishes, Tun Hussein was buried in the National Cemetery attached to the National Mosque, while the Tunku was interred in the Kedah Royal Mausoleum in Langgar, northeast of Alor Star.

Meanwhile, Pairin's younger brother Datuk Dr Jeffrey Kitingan began to agitate over the so-called 20 issues. A mercurial character, Jeffrey had a doctorate from Harvard University. He also harboured great political ambitions, but he was always backing the wrong people. He would jump from party to party without any qualms.

When he began to talk about the possible separation of Sabah from Malaysia, he was arrested and detained. After his release he supported the Barisan Nasional but was very disappointed when he was not made a Minister in the Sabah Government. Jeffrey currently supports Parti Keadilan Rakyat, the party which Datuk Seri Anwar Ibrahim created after his arrest.

When the 1990 elections were held, I went to Sabah to campaign, but the atmosphere there was not good despite my promise of a university for Sabah. On my return to Kuala Lumpur, as we were having a dinner at Angkasapuri (the national radio and television centre), the Minister of Information Tan Sri Mohamed Rahmat whispered into my ear that Pairin had pulled PBS out from Barisan Nasional. Tengku Razaleigh Hamzah was delighted when PBS aligned itself with the Opposition coalition. It was yet another example of the political switching that happened so often in Sabah.

I hastily called a meeting of the UMNO Supreme Council, which decided immediately to set up UMNO in Sabah. Until then, it had been our policy not to undermine the pro-Barisan Nasional indigenous parties in Sabah and Sarawak by starting UMNO there; now, to counter PBS's defection, we had to assert our presence in Sabah to maintain the Barisan Nasional's position.

It was no easy task, but Tun Ghafar Baba, the Deputy President of UMNO, spent a considerable amount of time in Sabah organising our party divisions in all the constituencies. The response was good, but not good enough to help the Barisan Nasional to win enough state seats to form the Government of Sabah.

Although by polling day UMNO had been set up in the state, it could not contest the election because Pairin's defection, and UMNO's response to it, had occurred after nomination day. All UMNO could do was to support USNO, Tun Mustafa's party. Berjaya, Harris's party, fielded 48 candidates but did not win a single seat. USNO managed to win only 14 of the 48 state assembly seats. PBS, on the other hand, had a huge victory. Of the parliamentary seats, PBS won 14 and Barisan Nasional only six. It was by far the worst performance ever by Barisan Nasional in Sabah.

But in the Peninsula, the Barisan Nasional decisively defeated the Opposition coalition headed by Tengku Razaleigh's Semangat 46. Pairin's hope of remaining a part of the Federal Government was shattered — he had backed the wrong horse. By deserting Barisan Nasional, Pairin lost whatever leverage he once had with the Federal Government to develop Sabah, in particular to secure a university for his state. Realising that PBS would no longer enjoy Federal Government cooperation, many of its members began to desert the party.

In the Peninsula, the Barisan Nasional once again lost Kelantan. Tun Hussein had won back the state in 1978 when PAS split into two factions and many had thought that this sounded the death-knell for PAS. I thought differently and I turned out to be right. By 1990 Berjasa, the PAS splinter group, had lost ground and could win only one seat. The Barisan Nasional lost all the seats it contested, while PAS and Semangat 46 together won 38 seats. Kelantan was now to be ruled by a loose coalition between PAS and Semangat 46 under Datuk Nik Aziz Nik Mat as *Menteri Besar*. Soon, however, cracks began to appear. Eventually, Semangat 46 was dissolved and its members as well as its leader Tengku Razaleigh rejoined UMNO. But resentment against Semangat 46 among UMNO members remained strong while many Semangat 46 members preferred to remain Opposition supporters.

Despite its losses in Sabah and Kelantan, the Barisan Nasional managed to maintain a two-thirds majority in Parliament. The strength of the Government had been restored, allowing us to concentrate on economic development and sustain the high growth rates from 1987 to 1997.

A new *Malaysia Boleh* (Malaysia Can Do It!) spirit seemed to take hold and coincide with this period of growth. The *Malaysian Book of Records* had also been started and people now tried to pull off unusual feats to get into it. This new competitive spirit, combined with the desire to show that Malaysians could do anything, generated much excitement in the country. Datuk Azhar Mansor sailed solo round the world; Datuk M. Magendren and Datuk N. Mohandas climbed Mount Everest; Datuk Abdul Malek Mydin swam across the English Channel; and Datin Paduka Sharifah Mazlina Syed Abdul Kadir trekked 1,100 kilometres across Antarctica to the South Pole. She later also mounted an expedition to the North Pole. People cheered these plucky Malaysians and saw their achievements as, if not world-beating, at least world-class.

Despite this new determination, however, the fact remained that we were not achieving our NEP targets. It was now more than 20 years since we had launched the NEP, and it looked like we were still not going to achieve the goal of 30 per cent Bumiputera ownership of corporate wealth. Except for those in the professions, most Malays and other Bumiputera Malaysians remained far behind the other races.

Since the implementation of the NEP, the economic disparities between the Malays and the Chinese have actually widened further in absolute terms. That is simply because the nation's wealth is now very much bigger and the 28 per cent difference in wealth between Malays and Chinese in 1970 was based on a smaller GDP. Today's GDP is many times bigger and 40 per cent of this enlarged GDP that is owned by the Chinese would be much more in absolute terms than the 30 per cent share of the GDP they held in 1971. However, the Malays continued to lag behind and the disparity had increased. Malay leaders do not want to point this out as it would anger Malays. The Chinese would not like to highlight this fact either, as it would result in the Malays demanding for more effective policies from the Government to correct the imbalance.

I needed to extend the NEP but with Tengku Razaleigh in the Opposition and his party making substantial gains, a wrong move might have precipitated a crisis. Most Malays were obviously unhappy over the failure to realise the 30 per cent corporate wealth target and they did not accept that they themselves were largely responsible for the shortfall. Instead, they blamed the Government for not doing enough for them; they blamed the Chinese; they blamed everybody but themselves and their own inability to achieve or even attempt to attain new levels of competence and confidence.

By 1990 we had achieved just 20 per cent Bumiputera control of national corporate wealth, but largely through the various Government-operated unit trusts. Although this holding grew in absolute size, the rapid growth of the country's economy meant that the wealth owned by Malays did not grow beyond 20 per cent. In fact, it shrank a little.

Increasing corporate wealth, or trying to do so, was one method we tried; providing educational opportunities was another. The huge number of Government scholarships dramatically increased the number of Bumiputera professionals. The number of Bumiputera doctors rose to about 40 per cent of the total, whereas before it had been only about five per cent. There was a similarly great increase in the number of Bumiputera engineers, architects, veterinarians, accountants, lawyers, hoteliers and in the other leading professions. Some became successful as developers, industrialists, fabricators and transport operators and a number of them, benefiting from the Government's privatisation policy, became substantial entrepreneurs capable of competing with the non-Malays.

One area where the Bumiputera failed almost completely was in retail business. They did not seem to like this sector because they could not get rich quickly. Those who want to succeed in business must accept the need for hard work, long hours, regular habits and disciplined time management. Rather than enjoy all one's profits today, one needs to accept delayed enjoyment and be prepared to invest some of the profits to grow the business in the hope of enjoying perhaps greater rewards at a later time. But again, the Malay attitude is not so much irrational as dominated by a short-term outlook. Short-term attractions seduce them away from the longer-term view. I believe that the roots of this outlook lie deep in Malay culture. Some Malays have become agents for Proton and operate petrol service stations, but apart from them, there are hardly any Malay retailers in urban areas. Our towns and cities, and certainly our commercial life, remain largely Chinese. The NEP failed to transform the basic character of Malaysian towns.

For my part I would have liked to stop the NEP and simply let the Bumiputera compete unaided, as standing on their own feet might have been exactly what they needed. But I feared that they would fail, and to allow them again to regress would be risky; to let the spectre of economic disparities once again rear its ugly head would be unforgivable. Most people remained very conscious of their race; if the situation that prevailed just before the 1969 riots was to recur, new racial clashes might easily be triggered.

Yet the non-Malays were watching the Government closely, and I felt sure that they would object violently if I extended the NEP. But if I did not, Tengku Razaleigh, PAS and the Malays might make an issue of it.

I finally decided to retain certain elements of the NEP and give it a more national and inclusive character by formulating a National Development Policy (NDP). Under the NDP, we would still favour the Malays in business. But if they did not respond or they were incapable of availing themselves of the opportunities created, then non-Malays would be eligible. The condition of 30 per cent Bumiputera participation was also made flexible. Even the unit trusts of PNB were to be made open, first to Malaysians of Thai origin and later those of Portuguese origin. Finally, the unit trusts were open to everyone. Under the NEP, non-Malays were sometimes able to benefit through sub-contracts, partnerships with successful Bumiputera, and in some instances by purchasing government contracts from Malays. Under the NDP, the non-Bumiputera could benefit more directly by taking up projects which no Malays made a bid for.

More scholarships were also given to non-Bumiputera students and many more places in institutions of higher learning were allocated to them. The NDP targets were less rigid as the Government wanted flexibility in its implementation. Many new ideas to increase Bumiputera participation were introduced. By now the privatisation programme could be freely used to increase big business opportunities for the Bumiputera, without excluding non-Malays.

In retail business, the Government encouraged franchising. All kinds of small businesses, such as small hotels, laundries, printing shops and fast-food restaurants were franchised. Non-Malays cooperated in the scheme, making their franchised outlets available to capable Malays. Training schemes were increased and more skilled Malay and Bumiputera workers were produced.

The NDP was not just the NEP by another name — we wanted to encourage meaningful cooperation between Malays and non-Malays and expected to see Malays put up the capital for their shares and then to work hard with their non-Malay partners. To some extent, this did happen. A number of Malay entrepreneurs and contractors emerged and some did very well, developing sufficient capacity to be independent. The Government was naturally inclined to give contracts to these capable companies. Again, the accusation was raised that it was favouring cronies, but favouring the incapable would have resulted in sure failure and financial problems. Convincing critics that the Government was not practising cronyism proved almost impossible.

Government companies owned by MARA and the state economic corporations were able to get many government projects and licences. Yet what they often ended up doing was depriving the Malay private sector of opportunities. Backed by government resources they would compete, often directly, against struggling Malay private companies. A case in point was the MARA bus company, which was supported by government capital and which plied the same routes as the Malay bus operators. They cared little if their buses were empty and they lost money, since their management and workers would lose nothing — they would keep their jobs and continue to draw the same pay. But the private bus companies could not afford to sustain losses. These government-owned companies were a bane to many Malay business people, but there was nothing they could do about it.

Since the establishment of the NDP, there have been a number of calls for the return of the NEP. As recently as 2005, the UMNO Youth wing demanded that it be reinstated to help the Malays.[4] However, this is unlikely to work because some of the key reasons why the NEP did not succeed fully the first time — the poor work ethic of the Malays and their unwillingness to learn how to do business properly — are still prevalent .

I spoke about this often enough within UMNO and to any Malay audience that I might address. I appealed; I prayed; I composed and recited poems; I implored; I even cried. But while people might say that they all agreed with my views, most of them continued to ignore my advice and went on doing all the wrong things. Certainly, a change in thinking was necessary, but by itself it was not enough. It had to be linked to a change in attitude and character. Functioning successfully in the modern economy and the modern world requires dedication, discipline, and consistent long-term and strategic thinking, which the Malays still needed to learn to acquire.

Malays enjoy being sleeping partners as it suits their temperament and pattern of living. In the past, *kampung* Malay farmers would let the Chinese village shopkeeper take all their harvest in return for goods and provisions from Chinese shops. The Malay farmer seldom knew, and had no way of knowing, whether what he received was equal in value to whatever his harvest would have yielded if sold for cash. He kept no account of the value of his harvest or of the goods he had already received, or would receive, in exchange. He may sometimes have borrowed money from the shopkeeper and not bothered to pay back, simply assuming that the harvest taken by the shopkeeper would cover everything. This was not the rational approach needed for the Malays to advance economically.

Even the big Malay owners of tin-mining land essentially did the same thing in the past. They gave concessions to Chinese tin miners and were happy to be paid whatever the latter chose to give. There is no evidence that they actually checked the amount of tin produced. If their Malay servants checked the number of sacks of tin ore, it is likely that the servants were also on the take. But the income that these owners of big tin-mining land received from the concessions they granted to Chinese tin-miners was far

---

[4] At the 2005 UMNO General Assembly, then Youth wing president Datuk Seri Hishamuddin Hussein called for the NEP to be revived to protect the interests of Malays. He was quoted as saying, "The NEP definition itself should be reapplied as part of the national development policy, so that the Malays will be empowered and not sidelined from now till the year 2020."

greater than they would have made had they mined the land themselves. Their mining methods were less efficient as they never bothered to learn, copy and adopt the Chinese mining methods to improve their own production. They were happy to see the Chinese do that and to be paid to sit idly by. The Chinese tin miners became very rich; the Malay landowners gradually became poor as the tin resources depleted. The Malays must have noticed this but they made no attempt to mine their own land.

In our own times, we see the same practice when licences, contracts and Approved Permits are sold to the Chinese. The few Malays who really entered the world of business became far richer than those who sold their contracts, licences and permits for easy short-term gain. Clearly those Malays also became very rich, though selling their permits, contracts and the like contributed virtually nothing to the NEP objectives or to the nation's economic growth. Nor would their wealth last long. We have seen Malays who were given forest concessions, for example, become millionaires overnight, but today they are paupers. Many Malays have become so used to a life of continual economic support, that when the flow stops they simply cannot continue on their own. Rather than learn about business and managing money, they spend their energies on cultivating contacts and gaining access to easy, short-term opportunities.

Outwardly, the Malays seem to be nationalistic, at times to the point of being racist. They can become very anti-Chinese and do not hesitate to be rude and unreasonable when criticising them. Their attitude recalls the behaviour of the Arabs in Palestine. When the Zionists first began their attempt to create their state of Israel in Palestine, the Jews owned only five per cent of the land. There was an equally small number of Jews in Palestine. Yet, while eloquently condemning the Zionist plan, the Palestinian Arabs willingly sold their land to the Jews. Nationalist or not, they could not resist the prices offered.

I am not suggesting that our Chinese Malaysians are like the Jews, only that the Malays have acted like the Palestinian Arabs. Strictly speaking, when Britain decided to leave Singapore, it should have reverted to becoming a part of Malaysia. But the Malays there had become a tiny and poor minority that owned practically no land, making Singapore's inclusion in Malaysia impossible. Had the Malays of Singapore and Johor ensured that large parts of Singapore still belonged to them, had they ensured that they remained the majority among the people of Singapore, then today Singapore would doubtless be a part of Malaysia. But for the Malays of Province Wellesley, Penang would be like Singapore.

Malays like to believe or claim that the Chinese have succeeded in business through cheating. Yet when a Malay wants to sign a contract (to build a house, for example), he will not give it to a Malay contractor. He would prefer a Chinese contractor. He obviously trusts the Chinese more than the Malays.

As a Malay myself, I am reluctant to denounce the bad work ethic of so many Malays. But this is what drags them down and prevents them from succeeding in business. I believe I see these things clearly, as many Malays do not. I have some definite ideas as to how these weaknesses can be overcome, partially and gradually if not completely and immediately. I believe I can best promote those ideas, as I have described, by meeting and talking with Malays brutally and frankly. I have also tried to set an example through my own work habits and attitude, but I don't think I made much impact. Now I don't have any more time or energy to continue doing so.

595

I continue to worry about the future of the Malays. If they do not learn how to face the challenges of the present and future as a people, what will happen to them is clear. They will again be pushed, as they were under colonial rule, to the margins where their survival as individuals or families, and as a people even, will become ever more precarious. Malay survival and continuity cannot be assumed, but must be continually pursued. I ask myself whether there will always be a place for the Malays in the world, even in their own country. I fear that those brave words of Malay defiance — *Takkan Melayu hilang di dunia* (we Malays shall never disappear from this world) — will one day come back to haunt us. Preventing this from happening has been the biggest challenge of my life and of my generation. It will also be that of the next Malay generation and its successors, as far into the future as we can imagine. I am sorry for those Malays who, after benefitting from affirmative action, demand that those who come after them should be denied the same benefits.

# Chapter 45:
# Vision 2020

As much as I was concerned about the progress of the Malays, I also wanted to make sure that Malaysia could move ahead as a whole. By the late 1980s we were experiencing an average growth rate of eight per cent a year, which was exceptionally good. Our policies appeared to be working and we were moving forward — but to where?

We decided that we needed an ultimate target, so Tan Sri Dr Noordin Sopiee of the Institute of Strategic and International Studies (ISIS) developed a conceptual blueprint that defined our path to social, economic and political development. As a doctor, I am attracted to the optometric measurement of vision: 2020 indicates 100 per cent vision in both eyes. That's what we eventually called our plan — Vision 2020 — as it implied a clear idea of where we wanted to go and what we wanted to be by the year 2020.

Vision 2020 was launched in 1991 and was a 30-year plan of what we needed to do in order to become a developed country. At that time, there were 19 countries that were considered to be fully developed, and they included the UK, Canada, Holland, Sweden and Japan. But did we want to follow the same path they had taken? Each of them had their strengths but they also had their weaknesses. There were many things about the developed countries that we did not like, such as their extreme materialism and their declining moral values. These were not features we wanted to imitate or reproduce. We wanted Malaysia to develop and become modern according to our own historic pattern, with our own distinctive ethical and moral values intact. We would chart our own journey and become a developed country in our own cultural mould. Over the years, I would repeatedly emphasise that we believed in establishing a fully caring and sharing society, one that would be ferociously dynamic but not rapacious. We wanted a society with a human face and a big human heart.

There was no criterion or single index for us to follow. Wealth as calculated from per capita income did not by itself indicate the level of a country's development. The oil-producing countries, for example, have high per capita incomes but few, if any, were considered developed. Most were categorised as developing countries, some even as countries of delayed or arrested development. Even so, a high per capita income is almost invariably a key attribute — necessary, but not sufficient in itself. We noted that most developed countries were also highly industrialised with high levels of education, particularly in science and mathematics. Their people's participation in public affairs and governance was extensive and their economies were based on free enterprise.

If Malaysia were to become a developed country it would have to display most of these typical features. Some would not be too difficult to achieve as we were already a democratic country with a strong private sector and a well-educated population. We believed that we had to increase the people's wealth so that their annual per capita income would be about USD16,000. To reach that goal, we would need to grow at seven per cent per annum over a projected 30-year period from 1991.

I presented the Vision 2020 paper at the first meeting of the Malaysian Business Council on 8 February 1991. Our development, I said, had to be more than just economic. We had to become a nation that was both politically sophisticated and socially and culturally advanced, but without losing our spiritual and moral values. The quality of life of Malaysians had to reflect and be commensurate with the level of development that we expected to achieve. Our people had to have reason to be proud of being Malaysians, proud of their country and its achievements. They had to stand tall in the eyes of the world, though among themselves they also had to always remain modest about their own social and economic status.

We needed to identify all possible obstacles from the outset and have some idea how we might tackle them. In doing all this, we also had to be conscious of our national affirmative action agenda spelt out in the NEP and its successor, the NDP. Altogether, I named nine challenges that we had to face. None were new but they now required focused attention if we were to progress towards our goal.

We needed to first establish a single, united Malaysian nation. Though born of different races, all Malaysians had to see themselves as nationals of one and the same country. Different though we were in our origins, ours was a common destiny. We might also differ politically but our loyalty and dedication to the nation had to be unshakeable. We were all, without reservation or limitation, part of a *Bangsa Malaysia* — a single Malaysian people, unified yet diverse.

The nation also had to be psychologically secure. We had to be proud of ourselves and our achievements, which meant that our society had to constantly pursue excellence and be satisfied with nothing less. But the quality that we sought had to be appropriate for us, not borrowed from others whose interests and outlook were not ours. We had to stop deferring to Westerners, especially our former colonial masters. We had achieved *Merdeka*, our Independence, in political terms and Malaysia had established its sovereignty. As individuals and as a society we had to achieve complete mental and psychological *merdeka* too. We had to stand up on our own terms and affirm our character and values. To be respected by others, we first had to respect ourselves.

In the meantime, our politics had to grow into something greater than it already was. Ours had to be a mature and truly community-oriented democracy based on the spirit and practice of consensus. That meant that individual Malaysians had to fully commit themselves to upholding a moral and ethical society that respected religious and spiritual values. We also had to break through the race barriers that had caused so much anguish and division in the past. If ours was to become a mature society, we had to accept that Malaysians of different creeds and colours had to be free to practise their religions, customs and cultures. Malaysians had to accept both those differences and also the common basis for their recognition and affirmation, which was the knowledge that we all belonged to something greater than our specific individual and inherited identities.

Progress in science and technology was also vital as we needed to stop being simply consumers of technology. We had to start innovating and developing on our own and not be just passive recipients or consumers as this would not enable us to make the major social changes we aspired to. We had to stand alongside other creative nations and be leaders in scientific discovery and technological innovation.

As a people and society we had to avoid the welfare-state mentality of the West. True, we needed to nurture a caring culture in our society but this

598

had to be based upon a strong and resilient family system. Encouraging a debilitating dependence upon the state would not create such a cohesive and self-reliant society. Neither would rampant and heedless individualism — the West had succumbed simultaneously to both these maladies at great cost. The strength of Asian society stemmed from its strong family foundation that held together and balanced individualism and collectivism. It provided a context for raising young people who were seriously goal-oriented, yet also ethically-minded and responsible.

We had seen the social damage that both capitalism and communism had done to the world. We wanted none of that. What we did want was a just and equitable society based on partnership in economic progress. Our advancement had to be socially integrative, not unbalanced and divisive, consistent with our national affirmative action agenda. We had to stop identifying particular races with certain jobs and we had to do away with race-based poverty.

Finally, we needed to develop a strong and diversified economy that would be fully competitive and dynamic, capable of withstanding and perhaps even prospering in difficult times. That meant encouraging the growth of a strong middle class, not just economically but in broad social terms. We needed to avoid becoming fixated on growth — especially on narrow economic growth and its key indicators — at the expense of the people, their human development and their capacity by their own efforts to meet their needs.

In the years following the launch of Vision 2020, the country's economy continued to grow at above seven per cent annually, which exceeded our Vision 2020 target. This did not last however. There was an attack on our currency in 1997 which led to economic recession. But we recovered quickly and growth was restored to between five and six per cent. Since we had exceeded our target in the early years, I was hopeful that we would average seven per cent growth overall and achieve our ambition to become a developed country by 2020.

Information technology was an area we had to focus on to fuel the country's development. We also needed to create innovative products that we could update regularly so as not to be left behind with dated technology. This required new knowledge, skills and researchers. Quite a few highly-qualified Malaysian scientists and engineers were working in research facilities overseas. We had to make a special effort to bring them back although they had become used to the lifestyles in the developed countries and were not keen to return. We could not offer them great incentives without causing resentment among their local counterparts and sometimes our bureaucrats made these people feel unwelcome. Despite the Government's stated wish to have these Malaysians come back to work for the country, bureaucratic obstacles tended to put them off and very few returned.

It was still government policy to favour the Bumiputera for scholarships to study specialised subjects, but there were not many who were qualified or keen to pursue scientific studies. On the other hand, quite a few non-Bumiputera students were more than qualified to study science and engineering. Our policy of favouring Bumiputera meant that these Chinese and Indian students found it difficult to get scholarships. This presented a dilemma: we had to uphold the NEP's objectives but could not afford to lose our best brains. I decided that we had to pursue the NEP judiciously.

I was all for affirmative action but when the Bumiputera were not keen to study and serve the country, I did not consider it fair to deny non-Bumiputera the scholarships they needed. We could attach conditions to their scholarships to ensure that they would return. More concerned about quotas and proportions between the different races, some government officers unfortunately failed to see, or ignored, our national needs for skilled manpower. Time and time again I had to intervene and recommend non-Bumiputera students for scholarships, but in many instances my recommendations were ignored and some flimsy excuse given for not awarding the scholarship. When we achieve developed country status, we would not want to see Malays and other Bumiputera not enjoying their due share of the nation's wealth and the good life, but that share will not simply fall into their laps — it is something they would have to work very hard for. I have always believed Malays and other Bumiputera are no less capable and intelligent than people of other communities, but intelligence alone does not suffice. Even the most intelligent must make the effort to acquire the needed capacities, no matter what the field.

When I visited Silicon Valley in the US I made a point of inspecting the research facilities there and discovered that many of the laboratories were manned by Asians — primarily Indians, Pakistanis and South Koreans. They had decided to work in America simply because there were no facilities in their own countries for them to apply their special knowledge and skills. They were also better paid and enjoyed a good quality of life. This observation became the basis for our Multimedia Super Corridor initiative, which I describe in Chapter 49.

When you go into an area involving new technologies you must be serious and committed and not expect immediate returns. If you become fixed upon the returns from investments in research, you would never invest as there are no guarantees that research will give a predictable return. Yet without research we would never discover anything new that might contribute to our wealth. You may strike gold from a line of research that can make all the funding seem like peanuts, but you can never know this in advance. It may seem to be a matter of luck, but success in technological innovation and application rarely is. It is built upon risks taken on the basis of informed intelligence, planning and thoughtful commitment. Still, you must be prepared to face that risk — not blindly or recklessly, but intelligently.

601

We have yet to acquire that mindset. When I introduced people to new ideas, their frequent response was to say that they could prove these ideas were unworkable. So long as that attitude prevails we will never progress. Granted, I got the Government to invest in some projects that failed, but that is the way things are in life. As it turned out, many of our industrial adventures did pay off because we were willing to take calculated risks.

Original research is an important marker of developed status, more important than per capita income. A number of Malaysian companies produced things that they could not sell in the country so they had to find markets abroad. We tend not to be receptive to our own new products. The Malaysian Agricultural Research Development Institute (MARDI), our leading research centre for agricultural and agribusiness-related science, for example, has produced important research results but they have not been taken up by our local companies. MARDI often had to go into product development, including commercial development, to convince investors to apply the results of its research. Because of this attitude, we lost out to Singapore, which is happy to grab our most promising students and scientific talent.

The success of Vision 2020 has always relied on our civil servants, who are the true custodians of the nation's policies. If they fail to understand our situation and objectives, the Government will be hamstringed. If they frustrate national policies and objectives, we will never transform this country and achieve developed nation status. By and large, the Malaysian Civil Service has delivered and we would not be where we are today had they not implemented most of the Government's policies. Yet there is always room for improvement, as long as the elected Government understands the problems which beset the country and the Civil Service knows its proper role and responsibilities.

One of the major difficulties in achieving Vision 2020 has always been getting people to understand the idea of *Bangsa Malaysia*. We are a multiracial country whose component races are mutually incompatible — they differ from one another in ethnicity, culture, language and religion and, most importantly, are divided in their economic and social achievements .

But *Bangsa Malaysia* is not a difficult concept to grasp. When I introduced it in 1991, I was confident that by 2020, we would have achieved a common identity. *Bangsa Malaysia* basically means that people should regard themselves, first and above all, as Malaysians. As citizens you must identify with your country and to that extent, you cannot be totally Chinese or wholly Indian and still be Malaysian. Even the Malays will have to lose some of their Malayness. In time, there will be one common identity in our country and it will be a Malaysian identity, but for a long time, there will still be a number of different ways of being Malaysian, including the Chinese, the Indian, the Iban, the Kadazan and others, and of course, the Malay way. The Malaysian identity will be inclusive enough to recognise and encompass all these differences. Our Malays, Chinese, Indians, Ibans, Kadazans and others may (and should still be entitled to) express their own historical identities in their own distinct ways, but not in a separatist form.

Ideally of course we should all forget the country of origin of our ancestors and be just Malaysian. But what is ideal is not always what is possible.

Achieving *Bangsa Malaysia* will require a focus on the education system. Our young Malaysians can get as good an education in Malay as in Chinese but when you insist that your child must be educated in Chinese, you are identifying yourself with another nation, China. The Chinese do not even want to come near a Malay in school. They even rejected the Vision School concept of a common campus jointly housing schools in all the three language streams. The Vision School idea was an attempt to bring Malaysians together when they were still in school, so that they would be equipped to deal with one another later on in their adult lives. The Chinese rejection of all attempts to bring together Malaysians of different races is very disappointing. In this country, much has always been made of racial issues. When religious matters were added to them, I feared we would have new and more complicated problems. By 2008, when the Bar Council held provocative forums on Malay dominance and the question of conversion to Islam in Malaysia, these fears started to materialise.[1]

People must remember that Malaysia is stable because the Malays have been willing to share what they have. In multiracial countries the indigenous people generally refuse to share their patrimony with people they consider newcomers. They will not give up their claim to primacy. If others want to claim citizenship they must become indistinguishable from the indigenous people. In Malaysia, the indigenous people not only agreed to share their country with others, but also adopted some characteristics of the people who came later.

We offered Vision 2020 as a blueprint and roadmap to become a country that has successfully and fully made the leap into economic, scientific and technological modernity; a country which, on that basis, might reach new levels of sophistication. But we intended to do this on our own cultural foundations and within our civilisation's framework — not by aping others and losing our soul.

---

[1]  In August 2008, the Bar Council pressed ahead with a forum to discuss conversions to Islam despite the Government's stand that it would only incite emotions among those with differing views. Demonstrators gathered outside the forum and the police advised organisers to shut it down for security reasons.

Ultimately, we realised, there could be no modern economy, society, industry or technology unless there were truly modern people at the heart and core of this new Malaysia. New buildings, systems and industries alone were not enough — the missing part was people. What was needed were Malaysians who, through education and science, could find their way forward while retaining their characteristically Asian values and human identities. At times I fear that while we have succeeded in producing modern industries and mastered new technologies, we have failed to fully advance ourselves — our psyches and mindsets and ways of thinking — as Malaysians.

If you look at our Kuala Lumpur International Airport or at our PETRONAS Twin Towers you will see great material symbols and manifestations of that brave new Malaysian modernity. They form the tangible and undeniable testimony of what we are capable of. I had hoped that in time we would be able to transform ourselves in similarly powerful and impressive ways, but recent events have suggested that this may now take longer than we had originally thought. Malaysia has always planned her development carefully but when these plans are abandoned, leaving us ill-prepared to meet new and unexpected challenges, then we jeopardise the dream that we had created for ourselves with the idea of Vision 2020.

# Chapter 46:
# Marketing Malaysia

Trading was nothing new to the Malay world and Malay culture. We lost our pre-eminent trading position only after the British deliberately destroyed Malacca in order to develop first Penang, from 1786, and then Singapore, from 1819. After a century and a half of British involvement and then "protection", we only had tin and rubber to export when we became independent in 1957. Our domestic market was small and our per capita income was not sufficient to support industrialisation. We were apparently doomed to remain a poor developing country unless our manufactured goods could penetrate the world market.

We decided upon a strategy of export-led growth so Tan Sri Rafidah Aziz, our Minister of International Trade and Industry, led numerous delegations to find markets for Malaysian products. At times I led the delegations myself. One continent with which we had minimal trade and knew little about was South America. I thought it was important to study these countries and their markets. So in 1991, I assembled a 120-member business delegation which flew on a chartered plane across the South Pacific to Santiago, Chile. Along the way, we stopped in Fiji, Tahiti and Easter Island. Tahiti is famous for its version of the hula dance, but we were not to be outdone. We brought Malaysian traditional dancers and they put on an impressive show. The troupe also performed well in all the cities of Latin America where we stopped, probably marking the first time that the Latin Americans had seen such dances.

The Latin American countries had not been doing well under their various military dictatorships. Argentina, with an area of 2.8 million square kilometres and 36 million people, had been the eighth richest country in the world before World War II. Its main product was high-quality beef, which it exported to the United States and Europe. But after Europe developed its own cattle industry it stopped importing beef from Argentina, while the United States would eventually claim that Argentinean cattle had foot and mouth disease. Lacking other exports, Argentina could not earn foreign exchange and its currency kept depreciating, even as new currencies were issued several times. While Argentina had a high per capita income, rapid inflation impoverished its people. It allowed its citizens and foreigners to make money in the country and keep it in the US, leaving the country without foreign exchange.

Brazil kept their market so tightly closed in those days that only locally-made TV sets could be used in the country. Inflation was so high that prices went up practically by the hour. Their supermarkets typically had 70 payment counters because the moment wage-earners received their weekly pay, they would rush to buy their supplies before the prices went up again. Chile was the most developed of the Latin American countries. They were already exporting wine to Malaysia before we went there, but investing posed many problems as their local authorities often disagreed with the central government.

Our relationship with Argentina was most interesting and began when our people went there to buy polo ponies for the royal polo teams. Later, after I encouraged horse-riding, more Argentinean ponies were imported. The importers made friends with well-connected Argentineans and came back to tell us about the country. They fuelled our curiosity about the great grasslands, the Pampas, and the Andean Mountains, which we had only read about in geography books. Argentineans are the greatest polo players in the world and they breed special ponies for the game. Our people talked about thousands of head of cattle and horses grazing on vast flat grasslands reaching to the horizons. I had taken up riding when I was 60 years old and many of my horses were from Argentina. After my first visit there I was easily persuaded by my riding instructor, Awang Kamaruddin, to go riding in Argentina. After my first riding trip on a farm belonging to a rich Argentinean businessman, I fell in love with the country. I persuaded my riding friends to buy a farm there and today, Malaysian businessman Tan Sri A.P. Arumugam owns farmland in the Pampas and a ski resort at the foot of the Andean mountains. For years now, I have spent my holidays in Argentina riding on the Pampas and in the mountains. Strangely, it was Malaysians who popularised horse-riding in the mountains and were responsible for improving the ski resort in the Las Leñas valley at the foot of the Andes.

Trade with Argentina also improved. Malaysians invested in one of the biggest leather tanneries there in a joint venture with Chileans, while one Malaysian trader sourced seamless steel pipes for the oil industry from

Argentina for distribution in the Far East. We also import Argentinean grain, and I persuaded Arumugam to bring 1,500 head of the country's cattle to Malaysia. Although they breed easily here, we lack sufficient grassland to have a good cattle-breeding industry. Since I retired, I have been trying to breed Argentinean polo ponies in Malaysia. I am happy to report that an Arab stallion, Al-Barik, given to me by Prince Sultan of Saudi Arabia, has since sired four foals by Argentinean mares. I have bought an Arab mare to try and breed pure Arabs by Al-Barik. So far I have not succeeded.

The Latin American business mindset is very different from ours. The only people who were aggressive were the Chileans. By contrast, Argentina did not export beef to Malaysia, nor can I remember ever receiving any trade delegation trying to push its products. Trying to improve trade with them was a tough job. It is still very much in their favour because we source a lot of grain from them, but we take a long-term view of developing bilateral trade. We thought we could develop markets here for their produce and we first tried to sell Proton cars there, but did not get the right agencies. Investing in growing cattle feed in Argentina would be a good idea as we currently import quite a lot from other countries.

Persuading Malaysians to go so far away — virtually to the opposite end of the earth — for trade was difficult. Fortunately, I was able to persuade Arumugam, a very determined man who showed that where there is a will there is always a way. Malaysians should not be content to seek only familiar and easy markets. In ancient times, Malaya was a trading nation, strategically located at the crossroads between East and West Asia and, by extension, between East Asia and Europe. Malaysia has once again become a great trading nation and our trade is twice the size of our GNP. But we must continue to nurture and expand it. To do so we need adventurous Malaysians: businesspeople who are genuine risk-takers, intelligent entrepreneurs who see opportunities, calculate risks, and prosper by achieving profitable results. The Government must encourage and lead the way but the real work must be done by Malaysian traders. The success that we have already registered proves the point. Today, Malaysian traders and contractors have an active presence all over the world and have even acquired foreign companies with well-known brand names. Latin America may have once seemed very far from us, but in a borderless world and a globalised economy, no place can be too remote to interest us and attract our businesspeople.

Latin America was not the only region I led delegations to. As Minister of International Trade and Industry, I had led many trade and investment missions but I believed I could open more doors for our businessmen as Prime Minister. Every year I led at least two business delegations to countries which Malaysians were not familiar with. I went to Eastern European countries and Russia, and later I went to the Central Asian countries after they gained independence. I led a huge delegation of 200 people to China as soon as it opened up to the world. Compared with Malaysia, it was poorly developed and our people quickly signed a large number of contracts to build and operate tolled roads and bridges. But the Chinese learnt very quickly and they could soon do everything on their own at a lower cost. Our people, however, are still welcome there and I am confident that the rapid growth of China will create business opportunities for Malaysians.

In Europe we traded mainly with the United Kingdom as we knew them best, but we very quickly expanded into other European countries, including those in Eastern Europe. We participated in their huge and well-organised trade fairs and Malaysian products eventually penetrated all the markets of Europe.

We were very welcome in African countries but the administration there was often problematic. In Ghana, for example, we bought into a telecommunications company, banks and broadcasting companies which had not been doing well. We turned them around, but when elections brought in a new government the new President accused the former administration of corruption and wanted to reject everything that his predecessor had made. This did not encourage foreigners to trade and invest there. We also built a power plant in Tanzania, but when it was completed we could not operate it. The United Nations had a hydroelectric power project and the Government decided that our tariffs, which they had already agreed to, were too high. We sold the power station in the end, but that is business. It involves taking risks and sometimes you lose money. The loss of hope, confidence and trust in such instances can be more painful than the loss of money. In business success is never guaranteed, but calculated risk-taking is the basis of the economic attitude and business culture that Malaysians, especially Malays, must learn.

In comparison, South Africa proved to have a more structured business environment. At one time, Malaysians were the biggest foreign investors with interests in telecommunications, oil distribution, hotels and more.

As for Japan, their companies manufacture goods like air conditioners in Malaysia for export back to Japan. We similarly manufacture components of various other products for the Japanese market. It was not a good way to industrialise but it was a way to get going. It also created jobs, improved skills and increased our receipts from exports.

I had read about how the Japanese had developed their country. Poor in natural resources, Japan had based its growth on importing raw materials, processing and adding value to them, and then re-exporting them. We decided to do much the same thing. People like to say Malaysia is a resource-rich country, but apart from tin and a climate suitable for some tropical plants, Malaysia is actually poor in natural resources. We followed what the Japanese did but much of the necessary manufacturing technology also had to be imported, which meant we could add less value to the final product. Still, this was better than exporting raw materials. Our trade increased by leaps and bounds as our manufacturing industry grew. Of our total exports worth USD100 billion, 82 per cent now consist of manufactured goods. Without them, our exports would amount to only USD18 billion and we would be a much poorer country. Our entire trade pattern changed and manufacturing industries superseded the production of rubber, palm oil and petroleum.

These days you see a lot of manufactured products with the words "Made in Malaysia" on them. When it comes to manufacturing, the Koreans have done well and have even developed their own innovative indigenous technology. In Malaysia, I had hoped the national car would have similarly helped develop our indigenous engineering capabilities. Then more exports would bear the "Made in Malaysia" label.

Japan remains a development model par excellence and every time I visit the country, there is something new to learn. If we could copy just some of their strategies and methods, I felt sure that Malaysia would be able to achieve accelerated growth and become a developed country much sooner. We even learnt from Japan's mistakes, as we studied the reasons behind their long recession so as to avoid the same situation in Malaysia.

Today we are losing out to China and Vietnam because of their cheaper labour. But our exports are still growing and they exceed our imports, which is quite an achievement for a country that is small and does not possess its own technology. When we went to the poorer countries, I always made a point of looking for things that we might import from them. People, I reasoned, were unlikely to welcome those who merely wanted to sell them things, especially when their trade balance was already adverse. Buying from poor countries was one way to help them prosper, and once they are prosperous, our sales to them would grow even more.

My critics often said that we moved too fast and I must admit that I was always in a hurry. I did not know how much time I had or how long I would be heading the Government, as there had already been several attempts to oust me. Besides, I might die suddenly. I had survived my first heart attack and I thought I might not survive the next. Fearing that, I had to do everything possible to develop the country and take it further towards the goal of Vision 2020 before I left office.

Others have remarked how tough it was to keep up with me during our overseas trade visits. I always had a very busy schedule every day, causing a few delegation members to drop out and miss some meetings. I did not care about sightseeing. I just wanted to meet the right government officials and business people to discuss bilateral relations and trade. I consider sitting down and doing nothing a waste of the time allocated to us in life. I have always hoped to lead by example, and in this too I believe I had some success. Malays emerged in increasing numbers during my time to master business. By learning to work diligently and study hard, more Malay professionals were produced during my time than ever before, and this without diminishing non-Malay aspirations and opportunities. Non-Malays also admit that they did well under my policies because I pushed them hard. On that basis, the development of the country proceeded at a fast pace.

The early 1990s were also a time of change for global trade. People talked about trade liberalisation at the General Agreement on Tariffs and Trade (GATT)[1] meetings but no agreement was achieved. The rich countries wanted access to the markets and resources of the poor countries, but they themselves were fiercely protective of their economies, particularly their agriculture. People ridiculed GATT saying the letters stood for General Agreement to Talk and Talk, where those with an unfair advantage and something to lose could delay unwelcome change with endless debate.

Trade negotiations are a strange part of international diplomacy. The objective seems not to be to make things happen but to ensure that nothing happens. GATT — and its successor since then, the World Trade Organization (WTO)[2] — have got nowhere mainly because of resistance from the rich countries. They talk glibly of change but want none that will affect their own interests. While they are happy to talk of the level-playing field that free market globalisation presumes and requires, they themselves will not accept the same logic when the issue is the application of fair, universal trade rules.

611

At these talks, the poorer countries were usually at a disadvantage as they could send only small delegations. Countries like the United States would send 200 delegates made up of experts in every field. Frequently, the poor countries would be unrepresented in the small working committee meetings, yet the powerful countries would insist that committee decisions be accepted by the general body. This meant that entire countries and populations would be bound by decisions in which they had no part in making. Just as the rich countries spoke readily of free trade principles when it suited them, they did the same with democracy. They were ever ready to impose their own notions of democracy upon the internal affairs of sovereign nations, which they must know were none of their business. But they would not accept the principle of democracy in the various

---

[1]  The General Agreement on Tariffs and Trade, created in 1947, was the result of the failure to establish the International Trade Organization, which was meant to regulate international trade as part of a global recovery plan after World War II.

[2]  Established in 1995, the World Trade Organization manages the liberalisation of international trade.

international bodies and trade organisations. The US itself was founded upon the call of "no taxation without representation", that all systems of levying taxes and tariffs imposed upon people without their consent or even participation were illegal. It was a pity that its leaders could not now recognise the force of this same principle in international trade in the global era.

In the early 1990s, when the Malaysian delegation returned yet again from another round of fruitless GATT negotiations, I decided that enough was enough. The Europeans had their European Community (not yet a Union at that time)[3] and the Americans had the North American Free Trade Agreement (NAFTA)[4] involving the United States, Canada and Mexico. I thought it was only right that East Asia should have its own grouping. So Malaysia proposed the formation of the East Asian Economic Group (EAEG). Such a body would enable Asia to be better represented when negotiating with Europe and America. Australia and New Zealand were excluded because they always favoured the European viewpoint, so the EAEG would be made up of Japan, South Korea and China in the northeast (we excluded Taiwan to avoid problems with China) and the ASEAN countries in Southeast Asia (Cambodia, Vietnam, Laos and Burma had not yet joined ASEAN so there were only six of us — Indonesia, Malaysia, the Philippines, Singapore, Thailand and Brunei). It would be a good grouping, we thought, combining the strength of the northeast with the dynamism of the emerging countries of the southeast. Before any negotiations at the international level, our group could meet first to develop a common stand. We did not have a free trade organisation or an EU-like grouping in mind, simply an East Asian forum on international trade issues.

But the US would not allow us to have even that, and they had great leverage with Japan and South Korea. The then US Secretary of State James Baker was particularly blatant in his approach. He told the Japanese that when he saw me during his 1991 visit to Kuala Lumpur, I was wearing a *sarung,* a loose cloth that is a part of our traditional Malay costume. It seems he thought that it was a backward thing to wear, and that it implied that

---

[3]  The European Community is a predecessor of the European Union. It is now one of the three pillars of the Union and oversees economic, social and environmental policies.

[4]  The North American Free Trade Agreement promotes trade among the three signatory countries and has been in effect since 1 January 1994.

Malaysia was still primitive. He did not realise that when we met it was late on a Friday morning and I would be heading to the National Mosque for Friday prayers. Cultural sensitivity was apparently not his strong suit. He also made the point to the Koreans that Malaysia did not fight for Korea during the Korean War. This was ridiculous — how could we have fought for the Koreans when we were a British colony at the time? He told the Japanese businessmen and government that the EAEG was not acceptable and they were not to have anything to do with the proposal. Japan and Korea listened to their powerful ally and withheld their involvement.

The Americans then influenced a few ASEAN countries to go against the EAEG, especially Indonesia and Singapore. The name was changed from EAEG to EAEC — with the "C" standing for "caucus", an informal grouping rather than a formal body. To me the difference did not greatly matter. The main thing was our intention to get together before the next WTO meeting or any other international economic negotiation. Our interests were not identical, of course; had they been the same, there would have been no need to develop a common negotiating position. Even so, there were enough shared interests and issues linking us all that we could work out, as we needed to do, a common stand at any international financial or trade meeting. There was no need to counter Baker's campaign as Asians had every right to hold their own discussions, but many were afraid of the Americans or felt that they were in some way indebted to the US. Still, it was an idea that merited Asian support. It remained in the minds of all Asians even though they could not yet do anything to promote it. Even after Baker retired from government, he went to Japan and summoned Japanese businessmen to remind them not to have anything to do with the EAEC. Indonesia and Singapore put up all kinds of obstacles to forming the group. The EAEC was held in abeyance until Kim Dae-jung became President of South Korea and proposed that the three northeast Asian countries have dialogues with ASEAN. These dialogues came to be known as ASEAN + 3, but effectively, it was the East Asian Economic Group.

I was still very insistent that Australia and New Zealand should have no place in this, and they, especially Australia, were very angry. I told them they were not Asians, but Europeans with the culture of the Europeans.

During the East Timor crisis,[5] Prime Minister John Howard even wanted to be America's Deputy Sheriff in Southeast Asia. Australia liked to be an appendage of the US and if that is what it wants to be, then so be it. It certainly is not East Asian or Asian. But Indonesia, Singapore and Japan wanted to include Australia and New Zealand. For as long as I was the Prime Minister, I remained opposed to the idea. Of course, after I stepped down, the other member countries brought them in and some even suggested that the US should be included. But there was already the Asia-Pacific Economic Cooperation (APEC)[6] forum, which included the US. The EAEG is purely Asian — it does not mention "Pacific".

The US, however, wants total control over the whole world. Nothing could be done anywhere without its dominating involvement. It fears China's influence in Asia and believes that China must somehow be contained. A grouping which includes China and Japan would be too powerful for the Americans to handle so the US does its best to keep Sino-Japanese enmity alive. But this strategy will eventually fail. US hegemony cannot be maintained forever. Whether or not the US or Japan or the rest of the world like it, China will become the world's biggest economic power and killing off the EAEG will not diminish China's potential. It is far better that China should always be associated with the non-belligerent countries of Asia.

We were quite happy with the ASEAN + 3 arrangement, but Asians must remain alert to the possible manipulation of the group by the US through Australia and New Zealand. Asians should not forget that the ouster of Indonesian President Sukarno[7] was the result of American machinations. When America became disenchanted with his successor Suharto, he too was ousted. Only those who pose no real or imaginary threat to the US can survive friendship with that country.

APEC was an Australian idea to counter the EAEC. East Asians refused to support it until Australia persuaded US President Bill Clinton to sponsor its formation. When he summoned East Asian leaders to Seattle,

614

---

[5] In 2006, East Timor, now Timor-Leste,was engulfed by a conflict that started as infighting among military factions. The violence eventually spread throughout the country and led to the resignation of Prime Minister Mari Alkatiri.

[6] APEC was established in 1989 to promote the economic growth of the Asia-Pacific region.

[7] Sukarno was formally deposed in 1968.

Washington, to initiate the formation of APEC, I refused to attend the meeting although many people asked me to go. I thought it improper for the Australians to use the President of the United States to force East Asian countries to promote an Australian initiative. The Japanese Ambassador to Malaysia, under instructions from his Government — which no doubt had been contacted by the US Government — was less than diplomatic in his language when he called at my office to ask me to attend.

I stood firm and refused. Paul Keating, then the Australian Prime Minister, was very upset. He saw the formation of APEC as a glorious Australian achievement. Awed by the power and wealth of the US, he could not imagine anybody refusing to do their bidding and he famously branded me a "recalcitrant".

I really did not mind because I did not set much store by what he thought. I preferred simply to ignore his indiscretion. But Malaysians and the Malaysian Press, thinking that I was being insulted, condemned Keating for his bad manners. After that I had to show my displeasure as well, because as a politician, I could not disassociate myself from strongly-held public opinion.

The next year when President Suharto hosted the APEC meeting, I went because I felt it was a decision made by the group, not just by President Suharto. As APEC is a Pacific organisation, I insisted that Peru and Chile should be included. I wanted to persuade other Pacific countries like Colombia and Ecuador to be members as well. Russia has since been included, a move I had pushed for, as has Taiwan although it was not able to attend the 2001 APEC meeting in Shanghai. If APEC calls itself "Pacific" then it should really be an inclusive Pacific entity, but the more inclusive it becomes of Pacific nations, the less an Asian grouping it is and the less plausible its claim to any legitimacy as one.

The "recalcitrant" episode was not the end of our adventures with APEC. When Malaysia hosted the APEC summit in 1998, President Clinton found some excuse not to attend and sent his Vice President Al Gore instead. In one of the most ill-mannered speeches ever delivered by a leader of a sophisticated, modern nation, Gore urged Malaysians to overthrow their government right in front of me. After finishing his speech he left the formal dinner that he had agreed to attend. There was an explosion of anger in Malaysia at this boorish behaviour of an official guest to his host. ISIS chairman Tan Sri Noordin Sopiee took out a full-page advertisement in the *New Straits Times* blasting Gore for his rudeness.

I chose to continue leading trade delegations to numerous countries. Our trade with the US and Europe made up more than 40 per cent of our total world trade and while I did not want to reduce its absolute volume, I wanted to lower its relative share in our overall trade. Among the countries which I thought would prove a big trading partner for Malaysia was China. I initially believed that China would not pose a threat to our ability to attract investment as it lacked the necessary legal and administrative framework as well as the required infrastructure. The Chinese were also still suspicious of the Europeans and the Japanese, and the Communist Party controlled all business enterprises while all Chinese companies were state-owned. But I was wrong. China, with its potentially huge domestic market, quickly made itself attractive to investors. Its per capita income may be far below that of Malaysia, but the GDP of 1.3 billion people must be very big. Taiwan was the first to invest in China to exploit the cheap labour there, and Japan, Europe, and the US followed. Before long China's industries grew, exports rapidly increased and they repeatedly achieved double-digit growth. China quickly became the factory of the world, producing for both foreign investors and their own entrepreneurs and exporting almost everything. Eventually, I believe its costs, like Japan's, will rise. But in China's case, because of its huge labour force, that will take a longer time. Come what may, the purchasing power of the Chinese people will grow and they will need many things from the rest of the world. Malaysia stands to benefit one way or another from its huge market.

I have great admiration for the Chinese leaders. They were smarter than the Russians. While the Russians tried to change both their political and economic systems at the same time, the Chinese retained their powerful centralised government while reforming only their economic system. They have managed to create a hybrid capitalist/socialist economy where the state owns and controls most of the big businesses but private entrepreneurs may still exploit opportunities and prosper. The superiority of the Chinese approach over that of the Russians is obvious. Despite the politics of central planning, the Chinese people of today are on average richer than the Russians in purchasing power terms. As earlier with the Japanese, the changes in China made themselves felt worldwide through their low-priced quality products and the country's huge purchases of raw materials and petroleum and vast numbers of Chinese outbound tourists. Malaysia is also seeing an increase in the number of Chinese tourists while our trade with China has grown. We still export electronics to China together with palm oil, gas and fabricated steel products, and we remain China's biggest trading partner among the Southeast Asian nations.

In East Asia however, North Korea is the odd man out. I went to North Korea when I was Deputy Prime Minister and it was one of the more memorable official visits I ever made. On our arrival on the first day, we were told that the Great Leader Kim Il-sung was concerned for our health. He sent a doctor to examine Hasmah and I. We consented at first but as the examinations got more thorough, we objected. In the end they acceded to our request that we should not be medically examined.

The second memorable thing was that at the official lunch, my wife was asked to make a speech in response to President Kim's toast to us. The Great Leader had earlier spoken in Korean and soon after that, the First Lady went to Hasmah and told her, "It's your turn." Hasmah said to me later that it was the most frightening moment of her life. In the silence that followed, she tried to catch my eye but I looked everywhere but at her. In the end, she got up from her chair and toasted with a glass of water saying, "Good wishes and good relationships" before sitting down abruptly. When we returned to Malaysia, Hasmah called the National Institute of Public Administraton (INTAN)[8] and told them to start teaching Ministers' wives how to toast their host or guest .

Internally, North Korea has not yet been able to transform itself sufficiently to take advantage of a changing world. North Korea had the same capacity as South Korea and, during the Japanese Occupation, it was North Korea that was industrialised. But today, South Korea is way ahead of the North, proving that when the leadership adopts the wrong strategy, the best of countries will fail. However, changes on the international stage in 2007 and 2008 have offered some hope that North Korea may gradually come in from the cold.

---

[8]  INTAN oversees training programmes for all government departments in Malaysia.

# Chapter 47:
# The Growth Of ASEAN

When he was Prime Minister, Tun Abdul Razak Hussein had decided that Malaysia would have relations with all countries, irrespective of differences in ideology or systems of government. My administration also believed in the idea of "prosper thy neighbour". This was not born out of altruism but was practical good sense — we realised that the best way to help ourselves was to help others. By doing so you don't simply generate gratitude and goodwill, you also create partners and friends.

It was on this basis that the Association of South East Asian Nations (ASEAN) was created in 1967 with Indonesia, the Philippines, Thailand, Singapore and Malaysia. During my term in office, Brunei joined the association in 1984, Vietnam in 1995, Laos and Myanmar in 1997 and Cambodia in 1999. When we had begun to think about expanding ASEAN in the early 1990s, there was a lingering fear of the Domino Theory,[1] a notion the Americans had invented to frighten us and get us to support their war against Vietnam. After America's humiliating defeat at Vietnamese hands, however, we did not fall to the communists as they had predicted we would. But old ideas die hard.

In the end there was little objection to Vietnam, Cambodia and Laos joining ASEAN, even though they had not renounced communism. Cambodia had seen the Khmer Rouge kill two million of its people and is today still recovering from this violent legacy. When I visited the country after Samdech Hun Sen established a government together with Prince Ranarridh, the capital city of Phnom Penh was still deserted. Most of the inhabitants had been killed and those who returned had problems reclaiming their houses. Laos, which was ruled by the Lao People's Revolutionary Party, was landlocked and very poor. Despite its history of prolonged struggle for power by various factions, Laos was able to resolve its problems and we welcomed its admission into ASEAN.

618

---

[1] According to the Domino Theory, if one country fell to communism then surrounding countries would soon follow suit.

Unified Vietnam continued to uphold communist ideology and practices. When I first visited Hanoi there were only bicycles on the road and the people were lean and muscular. Vietnam was eager to develop itself and invited foreign investments, and by joining ASEAN it was able to learn to expand its economy. Today Vietnam is the fastest-growing Southeast Asian nation, and even the Americans are investing there.

Malaysia, however, was especially keen to see Myanmar join the association because we believed that including the country in ASEAN might influence the thinking of its military government. We did not believe that enforced isolation from the dynamic Southeast Asian mainstream would change them. The US and Europe did not agree — whether in Myanmar or Iraq, they believed in applying pressure through sanctions to force people to rise against their governments. I have seen an actual revolt caused by sanctions happen only in South Africa; elsewhere, sanctions only hurt the people without affecting the ruling elite.

In 2001 we invited Senior General Than Shwe, the chairman of Myanmar's ruling State Peace and Development Council (SPDC), to Malaysia. We wanted to show him how democracy worked. I explained that he did not have to fear that it would deprive him of his power. In fact, it might even be a way for him to gain popular support if he formed a political party and the leaders visited rural areas and talked to the people. He followed my advice and later told me that the village people had indeed responded well and become much more open and approachable. But Than Shwe remained nervous about democracy. He tentatively appointed General Khin Nyunt as Prime Minister and the latter proved to be more relaxed and open to ideas about development and service to the people. Unfortunately, the senior generals were not happy with Khin Nyunt's accommodating ways. They charged him with corruption, branded him a traitor and placed him under house arrest. It was a very disappointing development.

Myanmar again seems to be isolating itself. I tried on several occasions to see Aung San Suu Kyi, the leader of the National League for Democracy who has spent years under house arrest, but the Myanmar Government refused permission. I wanted to touch base with her and had written to her, but although she had replied, we did not get very far. I thought that she herself needed to relax and be more flexible, for being too rigid and demanding would rub the leaders the wrong way. Tan Sri Razali Ismail, who was appointed by the United Nations to intercede with Myanmar, did not get very far either. The military leaders appeared unwilling to give up even a small part of their power. When an election saw Aung San Suu Kyi and her party winning, they modified the results. I believe they had seen how dictators who gave up power ended up being persecuted, so the SPDC's members were not willing to trust their fate to the people in democratic elections. In Bangladesh, South Korea and Indonesia, as soon as the autocratic leaders consented to democracy, they were charged with all kinds of misdeeds and thrown into jail. One was even sentenced to death. President Suharto was harassed and threatened, and only his ill health and the strength of his former party prevented him from being jailed.

Including these countries within ASEAN would bring greater stability to the region, and it also made good economic sense because it would enlarge the regional market. Together, we have about half a billion people in ASEAN. Even if our per capita income is small, it is still a considerable market. Intra-ASEAN trade was encouraged and it grew very fast. Malaysia's own trade with other ASEAN countries is very big and was already growing even before the preferential trading agreement, the ASEAN Free Trade Area or AFTA, was introduced. Now the pace of its growth is accelerating even more.

In managing ASEAN affairs and participating in ASEAN meetings, Malaysia and the Philippines had to come together. The Philippines' claim to Sabah had remained a stumbling block but both countries avoided open discussions about this claim. In 1995, Fidel Ramos brought the two countries closer together by visiting Malaysia soon after becoming President and ignoring his country's previous policy of avoiding direct bilateral contact. For my part, I readily approved his proposed visit to Malaysia. We now have diplomatic relations but the Sabah claim has always seemed incapable of being resolved.

The most lukewarm member of ASEAN was Singapore. I was familiar with Singapore's attitude towards cooperating with its neighbours from the time I was a Minister of Education and involved with the Southeast

Asia Ministers of Education Organisation (SEAMEO). It was thought that by exchanging information and experiences and by setting up educational facilities open to all member countries, we might avoid costly duplication. Malaysia was allocated the Mathematics and Science Centre while Singapore had the English Language Centre, both of which were intended for training teachers. Singapore made money from the fees charged since the English Language Centre was much in demand.

The Ministers met every year in a different member-country. I remember the meeting in the Philippines, held in the mountain resort of Baguio. That year Dr Sjarif Thajeb, the Minister of Education and Culture of Indonesia, was in the chair. A decision was made to increase subscription to the organisation and everyone agreed except Singapore. Bapak Sjarif adjourned the meeting because he wanted to talk personally to the Singapore delegates. Under the new agreement Singapore had to pay an additional USD10,000. Others had to pay more, yet they readily agreed. But Singapore threatened to leave the organisation, and Bapak Sjarif was only able to dissuade them from walking out with great difficulty. USD10,000 was a trifling sum for Singapore, which even then was the most prosperous Southeast Asian country, yet for that sum it was willing to dissociate itself from its neighbours.

But that is Singapore. It counts every cent that it has to pay for anything. It was always trying to reduce its commitments to any organisation, so its lukewarm support for ASEAN did not surprise me. Of course, when Malaysia proposed the East Asia Economic Group, Singapore was again its most unenthusiastic supporter.

Among the groupings of developing countries, ASEAN was the most successful. It had regular dialogues with the developed countries, which were often attended by heads of government. It was able to negotiate on trade and other matters with the major economies of the world. The countries of ASEAN proved themselves capable of growing into good trading nations and were favoured by foreign investors. Attracted by its success, countries outside Southeast Asia were interested in joining. Papua New Guinea and Timor-Leste were observers at ASEAN meetings, and at one time, Sri Lanka was keen to join.

ASEAN brought all 10 Southeast Asian countries together despite American and European pressure to keep Myanmar out. After it was admitted, attempts continued to be made to persuade ASEAN to expel Myanmar. After the World Trade Organization failed to make progress, an ASEAN Free Trade Area was proposed and accepted by the ASEAN countries. Trade among ASEAN countries would be promoted by reductions in import duty to five per cent. This meant that all the member countries had to lose tax revenue from import duties. Only Singapore would lose nothing. It was already a free port.

Because of its free port status, foreign goods were always cheaper in Singapore than in the Peninsula, and Malaysians flocked there to buy duty-free goods and smuggle them into Malaysia. Since Singapore did not tax imports, there was no tax that might be reduced or abolished so as to benefit any free-trade agreement partner. Entering into free-trade agreements with any country was therefore easy for Singapore. Singapore-made goods might enter the FTA-partner country with reduced tax or no tax, and in return, Singapore did not have to give anything that was not already available to others who exported their goods to the island-republic. Yet Singapore's FTA with the US was held up as a model to the other ASEAN countries. But should they follow suit they, unlike Singapore, would have to offer something substantial in return.

Some favoured the development of FTAs for trade among ASEAN countries. Our then Minister of International Trade and Industry, Tan Sri Rafidah Aziz, entered into negotiations with ASEAN members to lower or abolish taxes on goods entering one another's countries. The Cabinet was not consulted. In principle, an ASEAN FTA was basically a good idea, but labour costs were not all the same in the various ASEAN countries. Malaysia's labour costs were high, second only to Singapore, so our labour-intensive products would cost more than those from other ASEAN countries.

As I mentioned earlier, Rafidah also agreed that a 40 per cent local content would qualify a product for national status, as if it were entirely homemade, and on that basis it would enjoy a clear export advantage when it was sold to other ASEAN countries. The result was a rush from the developed, industrialised countries to the low labour cost ASEAN countries, where they set up production plants to produce goods for export to ASEAN neighbours. This was especially pronounced in the production of passenger vehicles, where the 40 per cent local content level was easily achieved. With its high labour costs, however, Malaysia was not a popular destination for the production of foreign cars and, worse still, we produced cars with 90 per cent local content and therefore incurred higher production costs. You see many cars made in Thailand and Indonesia on Malaysian roads, but very few Malaysian-made cars are sold in the other ASEAN countries.

Singapore has controlled the import of passenger cars by requiring buyers to bid for import certificates. These are very expensive and also act as a non-tariff barrier. So, while the ASEAN FTA gave Singapore's products free access into all the other ASEAN countries, Singapore not only made no corresponding tariff-cutting sacrifice but also effectively made imports of ASEAN-made cars subject to high tax. The cost of these licences is high because the Government limits the number of cars to be imported each year. As there is always a great demand from Singapore's prosperous society, the restricted supply of purchase certificates drove the prices ever higher. The burden that this may place on car buyers in Singapore is not my concern, but the scarcity of, and hence tight market for, purchase certificates effectively creates a high tariff barrier against the import of motor vehicles produced in ASEAN countries into Singapore. The restriction on imports is also a trade barrier. As far as cars are concerned, Singapore is anything but a free port.

The other Southeast Asian countries all appear to be adopting a similar development strategy. They have all begun to open their countries to foreign investments in industry, to pursue export-based economic growth and to develop their infrastructure. But their systems of government are hardly identical.

While the Vietnamese appear to want to retain their socialistic and authoritarian form of government, most of the others include some democratic practices in the choosing of their leaders. They all hold elections periodically, even if the same party is re-elected every time. Some may look askance at this, as many in the West do, including when they comment about

Malaysia, but so long as the elections are not rigged, one has to respect the right of the people to choose the same party at every election. Regrettably, while all the world's nations are urged to become democratic, the promoters of democracy are not that democratic themselves. If democratic elections produce governments friendly to the powerful democratic nations, that is fine with them. But if the outcome displeases them, these "selective" democrats feel entitled to effect regime changes in order to overturn the results of free and fair elections. I can accept their cynicism, but not the way it is disguised behind the mask of self-righteous principle.

Among the ASEAN countries, Myanmar seems to be the main candidate for regime change. Sanctions have been applied but force has not yet been used. Perhaps the great democratic nations of the world are pre-occupied with other problems, or perhaps Myanmar's oil reserves are too insignificant. Although regime change has not often been overtly enforced in the countries of Southeast Asia — few now remember what the US did in South Vietnam in 1962, or what they tried to do in Indonesia in the 1950s — covert pressure has often been applied quite effectively. Attacks upon the currencies of several ASEAN countries may not have been explicitly planned to effect regime change but at least in one case, it achieved that objective. During the Asian financial crisis, the rupiah's freefall led to the collapse of President Suharto's Government, but it was not just the leaders that were affected — the entire system of government was changed.

In contrast, the ASEAN countries believe in non-interference in the internal affairs of nations and, of course, in other member countries. It is a good policy as it shows respect for the sovereign independence of all member countries. It has also been the basis of European and worldwide international relations since the seventeenth century when, at the end of their terrible religious wars, they agreed that the world must be seen as a network of independent nation states that recognise one another's sovereignty.

Regrettably, that non-interference policy resulted in the systematic slaughter of two million Cambodians by their own government. Perhaps there is a case for interfering in the affairs of countries — but it cannot be by the sole fiat or unilateral action of a superpower. How such humanitarian intervention is to be justified, planned and managed needs to be thought out carefully. Perhaps ASEAN gave some indication of the way forward after cyclone Nargis devastated the Irrawaddy delta in May 2008. As usual the great powers wanted to come in and take over, not just the relief operation, but ultimately the whole socioeconomic and political development of the country. In the end the great powers, the European Community, and even the UN could find no way to deliver humanitarian assistance. It was only through ASEAN that agreements were made for the delivery of relief supplies and medical services.

Some in ASEAN were already prepared to jettison the policy of non-interference by calling for constructive engagement in Myanmar's case. After much thought, however, I concluded that doing so may have serious consequences. ASEAN cannot drop the policy of non-interference in the domestic affairs of its members as a matter of principle. ASEAN cannot assume the right to effect regime changes, as it would simply be wrong and too dangerous. But ASEAN must never again allow the kind of genocide that took place in Cambodia. There must be a formal provision in its charter which would allow ASEAN as a group to demand that the UN take action to stop genocide in any of its member countries. As a requirement for taking this course, ASEAN should have to produce acceptable evidence, but under no circumstance must ASEAN — or any other party — take the law into its own hands. ASEAN must not succumb to US pressure to take action against Myanmar.

ASEAN is a fantastic concept, one that can be the model for regional cooperation among neighbouring developing countries. Much more can be done and further benefits can be derived from close relationships among the countries of Southeast Asia. Perhaps ASEAN should revive the idea of jointly-owned industries situated within its various member-countries, while ministries could adopt and develop the SEAMEO model for educational cooperation. An equitable sharing of the benefits from such joint undertakings should not prove impossible.

Meanwhile, China and India will soon become powerful in every way, and individual ASEAN countries cannot expect to compete with these giants. But as a group, ASEAN can match much of their strength or at least find constructive ways of engaging with them. ASEAN can become the third Asian giant. But ASEAN must never allow itself to block, or be used by others to help block, either China or India. Southeast Asia has lived with China and India for 2,000 years and more, and neither country has ever tried to conquer this part of the world. It was the ethnic European countries which did, with consequences which all the peoples in the region are still trying to deal with.

The challenge of development that we all face is the challenge of reversing the economic and human impoverishment that colonial domination has brought on us. We fell under the domination of the English, French, Spanish, Portuguese and Dutch, and were made to underwrite and support their development, and in doing so to forgo our own. This is the origin of the so-called "backwardness" and stagnation that Europeans have for so long and so smugly characterised us with, and which we in ASEAN and beyond, must still overcome. The arrested development which we must contend with is not due to deficiency in our own cultures, our poor values or any lack of economic capacity. It is a backwardness that was imposed upon us after we were made to serve Europe's development at our expense.

626

The rise of China, India and the ASEAN nations is a key part of that historic response, that movement of developmental redress and repair. China and India turn to that task as vast countries that are each based upon an ancient civilisation; the ASEAN countries do so as a modern association or consortium of nation states that project themselves in matters of great regional and even global importance.

# Chapter 48:
# Law And Order:
# Police, Politicians And The Public

Sometime in 1993, the then Inspector-General of Police Tun Hanif Omar requested to see me. The police chiefs and their departmental heads periodically briefed me on current problems, but I was not prepared for the disturbing report that Tun Hanif had for me that day.

He revealed that the police had received certain information about Datuk Seri Anwar Ibrahim, who was the Minister of Finance at the time, and that they had followed up by placing him under surveillance. Tun Hanif informed me that it had become apparent that Anwar was engaging in homosexual activities. Tun Hanif presented no evidence at that meeting, only a verbal report of what his officers had observed. Although I had learnt by then that the IGP only came to me when he felt he had discovered something significant — and his information was usually proven correct — my first reaction to the news was scepticism.

Anwar had moved up UMNO's ranks very swiftly and he had made quite a few enemies along the way, so this seemed to me like someone's attempt to fix him. I could believe members of my Cabinet having affairs with someone of the opposite sex, but allegations of homosexuality involving someone as pious as Anwar frankly seemed far-fetched. He was such a religious person that I had trouble believing he was seeing other women, let alone men. That would have been a completely different person from the Anwar I knew. It was just too much for me to believe.

I think the IGP sensed this. Although I gave him no instructions to take any further action, I expected that the police would continue their surveillance and would return to make a report if they found anything more concrete. I was satisfied to leave it at that. When accusations of homosexuality were again thrown at Anwar five years later, I would remember my 1993 meeting with Tun Hanif. This time however, I was less surprised and was prepared to listen to any fresh evidence the police had uncovered.

Generally, I trusted Tun Hanif and never interfered with his work. I certainly would not protect a Minister from the law, but I always had to be sure that no one was victimised. I knew it was easy for politicians to be the subject of plots carefully designed to spike their future prospects. I had even experienced it myself. I knew how quickly a veiled attack could take effect and I did not like anyone to be subjected to that kind of political character assassination. In the next few years, however, it would no longer be possible to ignore these allegations.

I have been told that during my time as Prime Minister, the perception took hold among the public that the police could do as they pleased. There was a belief, for example, that the police could kill suspects with impunity, but that was not true. The police were not perfect but by and large, they followed the rules. When dealing with dangerous suspects, especially when it was believed that the suspects had guns, I don't think it was fair to expect the police to take unnecessary risks. Aiming at the legs may disable the suspect but often it was too easy to miss, so policemen were allowed to shoot at the body, which was an easier target. Of course, the suspect may be killed in the process — but I and many of my fellow citizens believed that that was a better outcome than for the policeman to be killed and the suspect to escape.

Giving power to an officer to kill is not something to be taken lightly but when they have to deal with violent people who may be armed, it is necessary to instil the well-founded fear of death if there is going to be any respect for those who enforce the law. In my time, the police were armed with handguns, but today many policemen in Malaysia have to carry a submachine gun. It is perhaps a sign of the deteriorating and ever more dangerous times we live in. Criminals today are better organised than ever and they take advantage of any weakness on the part of the law enforcers.

One of the reasons why we introduced mandatory death sentences for certain crimes was because people did not feel deterred by the prevailing laws. A life sentence actually meant 20 years, and with good behaviour, that period could be reduced to just 13 years. With that discount, a life sentence was no longer a deterrent. Judges seldom handed out a sentence of incarceration "for the term of the person's natural life" because they feared that criminals who knew they would die in prison would have no regard for or interest in good behaviour. Instead, they would not hesitate to kill a warder who might try to discipline them. However, many drug pushers and smugglers would not mind serving a finite jail sentence and collecting their ill-gotten gains upon their release. For them, only the death sentence would be a deterrent. But given a choice, judges would avoid passing the death sentence. As a result, the mandatory death sentence for drug trafficking was introduced when Tun Hussein Onn was Prime Minister, even though he himself was against this provision. Tun Hussein delayed approval of the amendment for quite some time.

I myself have very strong views against the death sentence, because taking the life of a person, even if he were a criminal, seems inhuman. The drug problem, however, had become very serious and drug pushers and smugglers were condemning young people to a terrible life and an early death. The pushers and dealers were worse than murderers. I had to overcome my own personal scruples and approve the mandatory death sentence. I can understand how the judges feel about imposing the death penalty — the first time I had to confirm a death sentence in a pardons board I could not sleep for several days. It is not pleasant to think of a man hanging at the end of a rope because of you. But we had a job to do.

By this time there were more than 100,000 drug addicts in Malaysia, mostly young people. Many had contracted HIV and drug users who injected themselves made up the majority of AIDS fatalities in the country. Most serious crimes, including rape and murder, were also drug-related. Drugs touched my own family — I had a nephew who was a drug addict. When he was young he was very sweet, but when he started using drugs he became a rogue, shifty and dishonest. The strain he caused his mother was terrible, especially after his father died. She was afraid to live in her own house because she did not know what her son might do to her. Somehow, after repeated treatments and relapses, he was able to give up drugs. I must admit that I had to get help from the police often. Unfortunately, after his rehabilitation he switched to riding motorcycles at a high speed, and one day he crashed and died. Other parents whose children never recovered from their addiction must have suffered even more than my sister did.

In Malaysia, most of the drug abusers are young Malays. I am no sociologist but I think the Malays have not been able to handle the great changes in their lives. Parental control is now weak and the schools have not been able to discipline and instil values in the children, especially after families have migrated to the towns and cities. Most Muslim religious teachers, as I have discussed in Chapter 36, concentrate principally and even obsessively on the performance of rituals, on the details of outward conformity and observance. They are less concerned with Islam as a way of life and on its incorporation into the inner life of the person and the core of his or her moral personality. They certainly place little emphasis on Islamic values that can strengthen the character of the Muslim individual. Since drug abuse is very much a Malay problem, and since Malays still have to do much to catch up with other Malaysians, I was very concerned.

Even so, the courts seemed not to like passing the death sentence. Even when it became mandatory — which meant that, without any exercise of personal discretion, the judge had only to decide the guilt or innocence of the accused since it was Parliament that had effectively passed the death sentence — the courts still managed to spare many criminals from the death penalty. They did so by the covert and often illicit exercise of personal discretion, such as by amending the charge or resorting to technicalities. Doing this may be humane and compassionate, but it was not wise from the standpoint of public policy. It was not the best exercise of judicial responsibility either.

In the meantime more youths became drug addicts and died miserable, untimely deaths. The drug abuse problem is still with us and, if anything, is getting worse. With it come more drug-related crimes, for when an addict feels the need for a fix he will do anything. Addicts have killed their mothers for not giving them the money they needed to buy more drugs. When an addict is high he will also commit crimes, including rape and murder. Drug abuse is a major social problem and governments must be prepared to go to extremes to eradicate it. When criminals are not deterred by the punishment they stand to receive, the work of the police becomes more difficult. When public criticism of the police is played up too vigorously, the police hesitate and become reluctant to exert their authority. This becomes dangerous as the public may find them unwilling to go to their aid.

A government's relationship with the police is very delicate. The Government needs police support but it must also ensure the police do not abuse their powers. In the final analysis, the police depend upon the

Government for their resources, support and authority, but the Government depends upon the police for society's well-being, protection and security. The Government, as I have explained in my account of Ops Lalang, not only has to coordinate a number of different functional departments but must also rely on their expertise and good judgment. It must trust a number of specialised professional agencies, such as the police, whose expertise and responsibility is the maintenance of public order.

The Constitution places the police under the authority and direction of the elected government but, it must be remembered, they are the men with the guns. Many countries have seen them seize power and set up authoritarian rule. They do this because the existing government may lack constitutional legitimacy or be headed by leaders who abuse their powers and who are corrupt. They may also intervene to rescue, as they put it, society and the nation from chaos and the politicians who they claim have created it. There is a clear lesson here: civilian governments that do not wish to see this happen must ensure that social order is maintained, that social breakdown and chaos are checked, in the first instance by the police. It must allow them reasonable means and conditions to do so and to discharge their duly-appointed tasks.

Once they get a taste of power, the pretexts for staging a coup are never too difficult to devise. At the slightest failure of the elected government, they may seize power, and it would take them a very long time before they return that power to the people with whom modern sovereignty — even in Malaysia, with its reverence for the historical *daulat* of the traditional Malay Rulers — resides. It serves the government to avoid misuse of power, either through excess or neglect. Above all, the Government must not use the men with the guns for purposes other than those provided for in the law. They must not be forced to do the dirty work of those in power — for example, to make threats against the opponents of the Government or to act against them illegally.

Any government that does this not only corrupts the police and army, but also places itself under a disabling obligation to the men with the guns. If they then misuse their powers, the Government cannot stop them. Over time, the abuses will escalate and, incapable of restraining them, the

Government itself must become incrementally complicit in their misdeeds. Such an unhappy country would soon degenerate into a police state, spelling an end to democracy and constitutional government.

For a developing country, Malaysia has one of the best professional police forces. This is evident from the frequency with which the UN invites the Malaysian Police to work in the world's many troubled places and also to train the police forces in many newly-independent countries. Our people should be proud of our police and the Government should be grateful for their loyal service. This gratitude should not be expressed merely in token form. The appreciation of the police by the people and the Government must be tangible. They should be fairly compensated for their work, and if they should fail or misbehave they should not be publicly scolded or unduly humiliated, especially by the Government. If there is a need to chastise them, their top officers should be called in and the criticism made directly to them. If criticism or rebuke needs to be passed on down the line, they will know how it can be best and most effectively done.

632

Most of our police are drawn from the Malay community, and Malays, it is important to remember, are especially sensitive. A public scolding would not only be regarded as humiliating but may worsen the situation. A Malay unduly challenged is a Malay provoked: that is their cultural psychology. An unmerited or poorly delivered reprimand may serve only to encourage an attitude of defiance. Such an attitude cannot be the basis of effective policing or fruitful cooperation among the police, the public and their political leaders.

# Chapter 49:
# The Multimedia Super Corridor

The British did not encourage industrialisation in their colonies so Malaya missed out on the Industrial Revolution. It was more convenient for our colonial masters that Malaya produced raw materials like tin and rubber to feed Britain's own industries. By the time the Information Age dawned many years later, we were, however, in full control of our destiny and did not want to be left behind in the new IT-based industries and businesses.

One of the greatest electronic advances of all time was the development of the transistor, which replaced vacuum tubes in radios and other wireless communication equipment. When Malaysia began its industrialisation it concentrated on electronics, so our workers became familiar with transistors. But we had no qualified electronic engineers specialising in transistors so tiny that they could be printed on a silicon wafer and function as well as ordinary transistors in all kinds of applications. In the early 1980s, Tengku Datuk Dr Mohd Azzman Shariffadeen Tengku Ibrahim, the Dean of the Faculty of Engineering at Universiti Malaya, and a Swedish professor began urging me to start local research in the area of microcircuits. Intrigued, I allocated RM5 million for them to set up their research unit. In a small government bungalow in the centre of town, Tengku Azzman set up a laboratory in 1984 to explore electronics and microcircuits. He named his organisation MIMOS — the Malaysian Institute of Microelectronic Systems. I visited the laboratory and was impressed by their ability to design microchips. We allocated more funds to MIMOS and I was frequently briefed on its progress, learning much about the new revolution based on the application of information technology. MIMOS went on to produce its own microchips and to establish Jaring, the first Internet service provider in the country.

633

When the computer was invented around the middle of the last century, there really was no idea that it would do anything other than speed up computing. But with transistors and then the microchip miniaturisation of switches, it became possible to put millions of switches on a square centimetre of silicon wafer. This massively increased "switch-on/switch-off" capacity, linked to binary logic, expanded the power of computers enormously, making them capable of receiving, storing and retrieving huge amounts of information of any kind. The information they carried also became more precise. With these enormously powerful computers and the information they could traffic and store, the Information Age was inaugurated. Scientific magazines and even general news magazines soon carried reports and published extended articles on the Information Superhighway and the advent of the Internet.

It was claimed that through these computer applications and advances in telecommunications, everyone would have access to unlimited information and data that might be applied to all human activities. It was as if a huge library would be placed in every office and home. Easy access to unlimited information would revolutionise the way we did things, and the Information Age would replace the Industrial Age. I found all these ideas mind-boggling but also exciting. Could the computer, which was getting smaller and smaller, carry the whole US Library of Congress? It did not seem possible, yet huge room-sized computers have evolved into desktops, then laptops, and then palmtops, capable of capturing and retrieving vast human cultural and technical information .

The person who helped me fully understand these rapidly unfolding developments was Kenichi Ohmae, a Japanese business consultant who was then working with the management consulting firm McKinsey & Co. He was a remarkable person who understood the new technology and the possible applications of computers. Through him, I began to see what information technology might do for Malaysia.

Ohmae suggested a unique approach — to create an identified area within which certain concessions and advantages would be made available to people working in the IT field. The designated area, roughly defined as a corridor extending from the PETRONAS Twin Towers in KL to the new Kuala Lumpur International Airport in Sepang, would constitute a Multimedia Super Corridor. An entirely new multimedia city to be called Cyberjaya would also be built within this corridor. Here, a range of industries using information and conducting research on information-based technology and its applications, together with various other businesses based on information technology and telecommunications, would be located.

Closely concentrated in this zone, they would be able to interact with one another and enhance Malaysia's IT capacities and industry generally. It would not be a Free Trade Industrial Zone but a Free-Flow Post-Industrial Zone. Foreigners involved in the industries there would have easy entry and exit from the country. The city would offer an attractive environment to both foreign and local researchers and the necessary infrastructure would be provided, with particular attention given to telecommunications.

The Multimedia Super Corridor or MSC was launched in Silicon Valley in California in 1996. We held a conference at Stanford University and invited the big names of the Information Age industries to attend. We set up an International Advisory Panel or IAP with IT luminaries such as Bill Gates of Microsoft, Lawrence Ellison of Oracle, Nobuyuki Idei of Sony, Scott McNealy of Sun Microsystems and Stan Shih of Acer. Members of the IAP guided the Government by offering their insight and expertise on appropriate policies, practices, legislation and standards for the MSC. At home, work began on building this city, which today faces the same lake as our new administrative capital Putrajaya. Cyberjaya was developed by three private sector companies: Country Heights, MK Holdings and Renong Bhd. For this undertaking they set up a jointly-owned company, Setia Haruman. Telekom Malaysia also became closely involved in the development, installing not only the needed telecommunications infrastructure but also locating its own Multimedia University in the new city.

635

It was a very exciting time, but getting things moving was not easy. Many investors came and I made time to see them all. Because I knew them well, I was able to persuade Nippon Telegraph and Telephone, Asia's biggest telecommunications company, to put up the first building in Cyberjaya. Big companies like Fujitsu, Ericsson and EADS either built their own premises or had the Multimedia Development Corporation (MDeC)[1] build to their specifications for them to lease. International banks also set up facilities to process their worldwide banking transactions electronically. For small start-up Malaysian companies, we built incubators, or small office and laboratory spaces equipped with basic needs for IT research. They developed all kinds of software for specific business applications and some of these products have found markets in other countries. Many

---

[1] The Multimedia Development Corporation is the Government agency that manages the MSC.

IT specialists said we were pioneers because we crafted a dedicated IT industry area, providing incentives to those who invested or worked there. Following the establishment of our MSC, many other countries began to use it as a model to create their own designated areas for IT research and industrial development.

Meanwhile, the IAP contributed greatly to the development of the Corridor. The CEOs and other senior officers of the large, well-known IT companies found the meetings useful as they otherwise did not often gather and talk about their business and the industry's longer-term outlook. At the IAP meetings, they could review technological and professional matters of common interest, and interact socially. The IAP's benefits spread all around as our advisers were able to share their ideas, listen to ours, and give opinions on what we proposed to do. They also told us about how they saw the future. An IBM executive predicted, for example, that the memory card developed for cameras might also be used to store entire books. Instead of carrying bulky books when travelling, one would only need memory cards and an electronic reader. The potential was enormous and growing quickly.

To protect the IT industry we formulated cyberlaws and cyber-security, neither of which was easy because our knowledge in these fast-evolving arenas was very limited. For example, we thought that we could somehow certify documents in the computer the way one does with hard copies. In the beginning, we also thought it was possible to protect signatures on the documents transmitted through computers. This has yet to be achieved. The world is still grappling with the problem of security for data stored and transmitted through the Internet. Hacking into what is stored and transmitted via computers is a growing problem, and viruses, worms, trojans and other sorts of malware have been developed to penetrate and destroy software and data. Previously unimagined, cybercrimes have arrived and the ordinary laws could not deal with them effectively.

We also ran into other problems. Our Government's desire to take a leading role in the IT revolution was unquestionable but it was often impeded by the actions of inflexible civil servants. Some bureaucrats were uncomfortable with the idea of foreigners moving in and out of the country at will and they could not get over the need to control this process. When I was still in office, some 270 Indian researchers destined for our industries were arrested and detained as they were thought to be illegal immigrants. Naturally, they were outraged and their Press prominently reported the incident. That huge blunder made it more difficult for us to attract foreigners to help promote IT industries in the MSC.

Another recurrent problem was the unwillingness of qualified, well-trained Malaysian researchers to return from the US and Britain. We had no choice but to look for foreign researchers who might be interested in doing their research in Cyberjaya. Using my contacts, I met a Libyan Arab-American who had a research laboratory near New York. I visited his laboratory where he demonstrated some of his inventions, one of which involved the production of electricity using aluminium foil and aluminium cans. Some of his inventions had been reported in American scientific journals and had been sold to major electronic companies in the US, so I persuaded him to visit Malaysia to see our facilities. When he agreed to carry out part of his research in Cyberjaya, we built a laboratory for him and financed the purchase of research equipment. The plan was for him to manage the facility and recruit researchers from Malaysia and abroad. He was also hoping to bring back some of the Malaysian scientists who were still working overseas. I did not expect the research laboratory we had set up to suddenly discover miraculous money-spinning products. As with all such things, time was needed and I was prepared to wait.

637

But others were impatient. Some civil servants and senior politicians in Malaysia expected money invested in research laboratories to give a guaranteed return within a specific time. Trouble soon developed between the minister in charge and the Arab-American researcher; after I stepped down as Prime Minister, the Government accused him of embezzling money. They raided the laboratory and seized all the documents, forcing all work to stop. His laboratory, which had cost almost RM300 million to set up and equip, was placed in the custodial care of an accounting firm which charged a tidy sum. It later transpired that there had actually been no embezzlement, but against good business sense, the Government decided that the money invested in the laboratory had been a loan to the Arab-American researcher. He was now accused of not paying back that loan. Later still he was told that, since he had only one share in the company, he had no locus standi to make any claim or to return and reopen his laboratory.

Another incident that damaged Cyberjaya involved a proposal to set up a computer animation business. I met the computer animator himself and studied his work and credentials. I supported his move from Singapore to Cyberjaya as I also wanted him to work with the Multimedia University to train computer animators. Even at that time the demand for people with these skills was very high. Unfortunately, for reasons I just cannot understand, the man was directed to go to Johor and he eventually decided to return to Singapore. We lost a golden opportunity in an area of IT which I noticed was growing rapidly and dominating the film industry.

Our chances of sustained growth may easily be blighted by such thoughtlessness, and while Cyberjaya is still growing, the pace is now very slow. I attended an IAP meeting the first year after I stepped down but what is happening in Cyberjaya now is unclear. I trust that the MSC, which has now been expanded to include the whole of the Klang Valley and many other parts of Malaysia, will yet contribute to Malaysia's progress in Information Technology.

When we privatised the Telecoms Department, I was cautious and reserved a large part of the company for the Government. Sure enough, after privatisation telecommunications usage grew rapidly and the enterprises became very profitable. Moreover, the Telecoms Department had several training facilities and with the expanded usage of telephones and related services, the demand for trained engineers increased. Very soon the training facilities were expanded and a university — which was subsequently named Multimedia University — was set up to specialise in telecommunications technology. The courses it offered included creative multimedia, electronics and engineering, and business administration. The university, where Hasmah today serves as Chancellor, has drawn a large number of foreign students and has also been able to partially meet our need for trained personnel to help us move into the Information Age.

In the meantime, new IT discoveries and applications were being developed almost daily. The capacity of the microchip is said to double every 18 months and as the transistor became ever smaller, more of them could be printed on microchip wafers. As their capacity increased the cost of the chips was also reduced and, together, this stimulated more new applications. Programming the chips enabled all kinds of functions to be added to them but we face some basic challenges here. The design of the chips requires certain skills which we need if we are to keep pace with IT development. New knowledge is being generated so quickly that we would be left far behind if we had to wait for research papers and publications to be translated into our national language. We lacked qualified people in these new disciplines who, fluent in both the national language and English, might carry out the translations. The few we did have could find far more important and rewarding employment: conducting research themselves, helping develop policy or pursuing entrepreneurial options rather than churning out translations. We risked being left behind in Information Technology just as we had been in the Industrial Age.

When the UMNO Supreme Council discussed this problem, the majority felt that we should use English to optimise the nation's access to this new knowledge. But we also feared the reaction of the language nationalists. Some of them would rather we remain ignorant than forsake our national language. If a nationalist says, "my country, right or wrong", then the credo of these critics was effectively "my language, right or wrong." In the end, we reached a compromise. We would teach Science and Mathematics in English but would still teach other subjects in Malay. Malaysians must be bilingual at least, fluent in Malay and English and, in the case of non-Malays, in their mother tongue as well. Our renewed emphasis on English was no betrayal of nationalism but a nationalist choice. We decided on this course precisely because we wanted our people to be as well-educated and technologically advanced as the peoples of the developed countries. Unfortunately, the language nationalists were not placated. They cursed me for betraying Malay nationalism's core belief, and the fact that a number of those who used hard words against me were my friends saddened me. Mostly they were people from the arts stream. They don't seem to think science is important. They know how I feel and have always felt about my own race and people — specifically our right to our own language, culture and heritage. How then could they accuse me of betraying my people when what I wanted to do was to make them more knowledgeable?

Still, I knew it was the right thing to do, so I was willing to be cursed and vilified for taking this step. I am told the Japanese managed to master modern science and mathematics without learning English, but I also know that the success of the Japanese in their industrial development and economic growth involved mastery of English by key personnel. A Nobel laureate in physics whom I met spoke English fluently. Today, China is also expanding the teaching of English in its schools and the country has apparently targeted having 200 million Chinese who will be fluent in English. I had always been impressed by the fluency of Chinese interpreters assigned to me. They studied English entirely in China, yet they seemed able to master it.

Like it or not, English has become an international language, the lingua franca of the entire world. It has certainly become the language of science and technology and of modern knowledge generally. We cannot afford narrow language nationalism. We must not allow a misplaced loyalty to the Malay language to make us an ignorant people — not if we want to become as developed and respected as the peoples of the developed countries. Whatever the opinion of the language nationalists, I believe I am more a nationalist than they are.

Unfortunately the Government of Datuk Seri Najib Razak decided to reverse the policy and to teach science and mathematics in Malay, Chinese and Tamil. Appeals by parents to be given the option to use English have been rejected out of hand. By the time I stepped down, the MSC had succeeded beyond our expectations, exceeding the targets originally set for it. I felt satisfied with our progress in the Information Age when I stepped down. My fear was that, after me, this emphasis might not be shared and sustained. Unfortunately, Tun Abdullah Ahmad Badawi's Government virtually reversed that IT policy, replacing it with one emphasising agricultural development. IT became a neglected, resented stepchild.

It is sad that our journey into the Information Age seems to have stagnated. We had a chance to participate in the new Information Age from the beginning, to start on an equal footing with other countries and with people eager to grasp the future and its new opportunities. We threw that chance away. Malaysia deserves and is capable of better.

# Chapter 50:
# PETRONAS Twin Towers

When I stayed in Kuala Lumpur during my university days, there was not a single tall building around. There were only a few "hotels" but they were mainly lodging houses for travellers. These were ordinary shophouses with flimsy partitions that divided the upstairs floor space into rooms. The tree-lined Jalan Ampang and Jalan Tun Razak were the domain of the rich Chinese *towkay*s, and there were so few motor vehicles on the road that I could cycle in safety all over the town.

Kuala Lumpur's first "skyscraper" was the nine-storey Federal Hotel, launched three days before *Merdeka*. It remained KL's tallest building until 1981, although by then it had been expanded to 21 storeys. In the next 40 years the city skyline[1] changed drastically and today, in the heart of Kuala Lumpur, we have the PETRONAS Twin Towers, which for a while were the tallest buildings in the world. They are still the tallest twin towers in the world.

The towers were built on a 100-acre piece of land bordering Jalan Ampang which belonged to the Selangor Turf Club (started by the British when Sir Frank Swettenham was High Commissioner). The site was then outside the town and so posed no problems for a long time. By the early 1980s, however, weekend traffic in Jalan Ampang clashed with the crowds and cars on race days at the club. The resulting congestion became intolerable even to the still-small number of motorists at the time, so the Government asked the club to move out. T. Ananda Krishnan,[2] who was a club member, bought the entire site, which by then was considered to be prime land. The Selangor Turf Club relocated to Sungai Besi by the North-South Expressway; unfortunately, on race days there are now traffic jams there too.

Ananda wanted to develop the site and recognised its commercial potential, especially since there was little chance that another piece of land of

641

---

[1]   Prominent on the Kuala Lumpur skyline in the 1970s were the 36-storey Crowne Mutiara Hotel (formerly the KL Hilton) built in 1972, the UMBC building and Menara Promet.

[2]   One of the wealthiest businessmen in Malaysia, T. Ananda Krishnan's interests are based around the world and include satellite television, telecommunications, farming, gaming, and even a cartoon studio in Hollywood.

comparable size would ever become available again in the centre of Kuala Lumpur. But he was also sensitive to Malay feelings and did not want the most expensive real estate project in Kuala Lumpur to be owned entirely by him. He was conscious that any initiative to develop the property should have some Malay participation. The only company with the financial resources to do it was PETRONAS, and it bought half of his share.

The Government, meanwhile, had decided that the centre of the city needed a park. We concluded that the former Selangor Turf Club was the most suitable site but the Government could not afford to buy it. It also did not seem fair to ask Ananda and PETRONAS to donate or sell the land they had acquired. Instead, it was decided that their plans would be approved for development if only one half of the site was used. The other half should be developed into a public park, and to this they agreed.

Since this was to be a very important part of the city, I involved myself quite closely in the planning. Originally, it did not cross our minds to build two towers, much less make them the tallest ones in the world. Ananda suggested we hold an international competition for the design of the development, and entries came in from Japan, the US and Britain. Most were for fairly low buildings, but the one we were especially drawn to featured two very tall towers, surrounded by lesser towers, a shopping complex and a garden. The design came from César Pelli, a US-based Argentinean architect who specialised in high-rise buildings. In his striking proposal, the twin towers were linked by a bridge at a very high level. Together, they would form a great arch that might suggest a gateway not just to Kuala Lumpur but to Malaysia's proud, modern future.

Like most skyscrapers seen in the US, his towers were initially based on a square design. We wanted them to have an identifiably Malaysian shape and to incorporate some Islamic features. There was precedent for our choice; built in the 1980s, the Dayabumi building[3] in Kuala Lumpur has Arabesque grilles which distinguish it stylistically. We also did not like the then-fashionable idea of glass towers, as they were neither beautiful nor suited to our climate. Pelli himself was not familiar with Islamic design,

---

[3]   The 39-storey Kompleks Dayabumi was the first Malaysian skyscraper to be designed in the modern Islamic style.

so I suggested that the building's base should have the shape of an eight-pointed star and that, as the building rose higher, it should taper off and become smaller. The Islamic motif here was evident — while the Muslim star usually has five points, the eight-pointed star is a common Islamic architectural pattern, notably in the design for Moroccan fountains and gardens. In my travels I had noticed that much of Moroccan architecture included this eight-pointed star. I had previously adopted this same motif in designs I had proposed for the fountain for my house and for two more at the National Mosque. I suggested that the proposed building should also stand and rise from a foundation consisting of two overlapping squares, placed at right angles to each other. Such a building would evoke and be a kindred structure to many of the great historic buildings of the classical Islamic world with their elegant architecture.

Pelli was quite taken with the idea and enthusiastically used it to redesign the whole building, creating something very beautiful in the process. He told us that having too many corners meant losing a lot of space, so he connected the star pattern with curved parts that softened the shape without losing the eight points. He then added what he called a "bustle" in front of the two towers, going up to 40 floors. Joined to the main towers, this device would provide more floor space yet would be serviced by the main tower lifts. Tall buildings need many lifts and the space they take up reduces the rentable floor area. The bustles would provide increased space without requiring additional lifts. To increase lift capacity without increasing the space required, double-decker lifts were planned. They were the first double-decker lifts in the world and they enabled us to reduce space requirements. Pelli decided to place the connecting bridge, which converts the towers into an elevated archway, between levels 41 and 42 of the 88-storey building. To stand on it is like floating in mid-air — there is nothing below, only empty space. Some people find crossing the bridge hair-raising; others, exhilarating.

The towers would be the tallest buildings in Malaysia, probably in all of Southeast Asia. They would become a Malaysian landmark, proof of what we had achieved, and a symbol of what we hoped to accomplish in the future. I casually mentioned to PETRONAS Chairman Tan Sri Azizan Zainul Abidin that since our buildings were only 10 stories shorter than the

643

Sears Tower in Chicago in the US, why not make them taller? Without my knowledge, he then instructed Pelli to add a few more floors and top the building with spires, which would be included in the towers' overall height. The spires increased the height of the Towers to 450 metres, making them the tallest buildings in the world at that time. There are not, in fact, all that many floors in the towers because two of the floors are for machinery, but the height of each floor is greater than in other famous buildings. Extra space was provided to install water pipes and electrical conduits under the floor and above the ceiling. I think Pelli was as elated as Azizan when they told me the buildings would be the tallest in the world.

We had the late Brazilian landscape artist Roberto Burle Marx plan the garden. The landscaping plans, which included a 1.3km jogging track, fountains, a children's pool, ornamental water features and a mosque, were both attractive and intelligent, and the park would enhance both the city's beauty and the value of the buildings. Today, the shopping centre, Suria KLCC, is very popular, especially with tourists. It continues to expand and remains a formidable competitor to the many other new shopping complexes that have risen all over town. Adjacent to Suria KLCC is the six-star Mandarin Oriental hotel, which overlooks the park. Overseas visitors cannot believe the comparatively low price of the rooms at this location with a view of the park.

PETRONAS set a precedent by awarding the building contract to two different companies from two different countries — Samsung Engineering & Construction from Korea and Hazama Corporation from Japan — to create competition and reduce costs. It would have cost three times as much to build the towers in the US or elsewhere, but we were able to keep costs down because we were not in an earthquake zone and had no volcanoes or strong winds to contend with. When there is an earthquake in Sumatra, we only experience minor tremors. Furthermore, Kuala Lumpur is built on firm ground, mostly limestone, unlike many Southeast Asian cities that have been built on swampy land where piling costs are prohibitive.

Even so, construction work was not completely free from problems; because of the towers' great height, we had to dig deep to lay the foundations and the engineers discovered that the site was astride an underground limestone cliff. This meant having to use piles of unequal length, which might provide uneven support. In the end, we had to shift the site slightly so that the foundations would stand on solid, levelled limestone.

Designing and constructing tall buildings is very complex, as many miles of water pipes and electrical wires need to be installed and hidden from sight. There are also tens of thousands of switches, innumerable toilets, air conduits and more. The Korean and Japanese contractors, however, did a marvellous job and managed to complete one floor every four days. Two Americans were engaged to oversee the work and they also did a great job, but in a documentary about the construction, CNN's Discovery Channel gave the impression that they had built the towers all by themselves. There was no mention of the Koreans, the Japanese and the thousands of other Asian engineers and workers who actually built the podium and towers and installed all the electrical and piping work. CNN later revised their documentary to acknowledge that many others were involved, including numerous Malaysians.

There were a few tense moments during the construction process. One was the discovery that one of the towers was tilting slightly, which I feared might jeopardise the whole project. The ever resourceful engineers, however, were able to correct it. They also had to manage the tricky problem of the skybridge, which they had initially thought could be installed quickly and without any difficulty. The bridge, a solid double-deck steel structure enclosed in glass, was fabricated completely in Korea. It had to be shipped to Malaysia and then lifted by crane and positioned between the two towers. Four slanting steel piers anchored it on the towers at level 41 and supported the middle part of the bridge. When the bridge was finally manoeuvred into place, it fitted snugly into the space prepared for it — truly a magnificent piece of engineering.

Apart from that, construction proceeded smoothly. The Japanese and Korean contractors were in a race to finish their half of the job but in the end it was the Koreans who finished one month earlier, even though they had started a month later. They did their fabrication on the site, while the Japanese had their fabrication yards in several places. The towers also had a "raft foundation", a technique that entailed putting in all the piles and then joining their heads with a great slab of cement. As the cement hardened it gave off tremendous heat, so ice had to be used to cool it. To ensure the slab would not harden at different times, the cement had to be poured in continuously over 24 hours. The building now stands on that huge block of cement, which joins all the heads of the piles together. They then had to build huge columns, each more than two metres in diameter at the base, to support the two towers. As the columns rose they had to taper, becoming ever smaller, and they also had to lean inwards slightly. How they made their calculations I do not know, but it was done with great precision. Not only the architects, who devised these innovative ideas, but also the engineers and workers who made them a reality, deserve to be congratulated.

I visited the site often, at least once every fortnight and sometimes even once a week. On weekends I usually drove myself out in a four-wheel drive vehicle and often dropped in to see the progress of the construction. Once, while construction work was still on, I went up in the lifts used by the workers. Because the tower tapered up, I had to change lifts three times, walking on steel walkways which did not look very safe. From the top I had a fantastic view of Kuala Lumpur and its surroundings.

The Malaysians who supervised the project were very good, as were the interior designers. Many Malay women engineers and architects were among the people who briefed me on the progress and on what they proposed to do inside: the décor, the rooms, everything. At times I was very disappointed when some of the Malays who had won the contracts were not there when I visited. Perhaps they thought that once they had the contract, they could hand it over to their subcontractors and overseers and not have to be there themselves. But if the job is yours, so is the responsibility of overseeing the work. I was also frustrated that there were so many foreign workers while Malaysian workers, especially Malays, just refused to do the work. They gave the excuse that the buildings were too high. Pakistanis, Bangladeshis and Indonesians were willing to work and were paid quite well. Malaysians should have also welcomed the opportunity to take part in building the tallest buildings in the world, especially in their own country.

One tower initially belonged to Ananda and the other to PETRONAS, but eventually Ananda sold his tower to PETRONAS. Renting out the vast space in the two towers took time, mainly because PETRONAS was choosy about its tenants. The company felt that as a prestige location, the towers could not be an address just for anyone. PETRONAS did not want to devalue the towers' prestige, so tenants had to be people and companies of some standing. Sometimes however, the managers may have been too selective and unduly fussy. Few Malays could afford to rent space in the shopping complex, but when a Malaysian producer of high-quality crocodile skin goods was to be evicted, I was annoyed. If we continued to look down on our own quality products, we would never develop high-profile, Malaysian-branded goods.

After the 11 September 2001 attacks in the US, we, like all proprietors and managers of tall buildings, had new concerns. We had not provoked anyone to warrant that kind of attack but anything, of course, was possible. The design of the Twin Towers and the use of steel in their construction made them very strong. I am told that in a strong wind or when there are tremors, the towers may sway, although I myself have never felt the buildings move. When there was an earthquake in Sumatra one night, all it did was to break some window panes in the towers.

As soon as the towers were completed, PETRONAS decided to provide me with an office on one of the top floors. It is the highest office in Malaysia, probably in Southeast Asia, and has its own lounge and boardroom. But I did not occupy it until I retired and needed an office in town. From my window, I enjoy a spectacular view of the whole of Kuala Lumpur and its surroundings, and on clear days I can even see Genting Highlands in the east and the coast to the west.

During the planning process, PETRONAS had also decided to include a Petrosains (petroleum science) Centre and a Philharmonic Hall, which would have a ceiling that could be lowered slightly to get the best acoustic effects. The Malaysian Philharmonic Orchestra is now very popular, with people coming from overseas to attend its performances. I did not realise at the time, however, that our orchestra would have so many European musicians. In time, I hope there will be more Malaysians in the orchestra, signalling a level of cultural advancement that I had always wanted for Malaysia.

Needless to say, many people complained about the money spent and asked why we needed the towers. In fact, they only cost about RM3 billion and would have cost three times as much in most other countries. People must remember that property appreciates in value over time, unlike cars and other engineering products that become outdated and depreciate in value. If we ever wanted to, we could sell the towers and make a handsome profit. Ultimately, I believe in moving money to make more money, and not letting it lie idle. PETRONAS in this case had the money. When it built the towers it stimulated the economy, with everyone from subcontractors to labourers and the *nasi lemak*-sellers[4] making money from the project. Ultimately, the Government would collect taxes from all these business activities.

Foreigners liked to point out that although we had built these towers, we still had a lot of squatter areas in the city. In a Hollywood film called *Entrapment,* starring Sean Connery and Catherine Zeta-Jones, they superimposed footage of a slum area in Malacca onto scenes of the towers, making it look as if they had been built while our people remained poor. When I was in New York I asked our TV people to film footage of a man in rags sleeping on a bench in the park as well as footage of the city's slums. But Malaysians still feel it is wrong to show anything unflattering about the *Orang Putih*. This inferiority complex is latent in the psyche of the Malays, perhaps even of Malaysians generally. When we built the towers, we were not unaware of poverty in Malaysia, but we could not wait until poverty was totally eradicated before we spent money on other things that would make a huge contribution to the country's economy. At the towers' opening ceremony, I said that when people are short, they need a soapbox in order to be seen and heard. We, I said, were little known and figuratively we were short, not players of tall stature in the international game. The towers were Malaysia's soapbox, but they have since also become the country's landmark, a part of our internationally-recognised and admired brand image. In any case, through Government efforts poverty in Malaysia has been reduced to less than five per cent.

648

---

4    Malaysians often eat *nasi lemak* — rice cooked in coconut milk, with side dishes of spicy sauce, anchovies, a boiled egg, and sliced cucumber — for breakfast.

Today PETRONAS has enough money to build 20 of these tower complexes and still have a lot to spare. The company is now regarded as a major international petroleum player and was once listed in *Fortune* magazine as the most profitable company in the world. Its profits in 2005 were bigger than our total collection from income and corporate tax. Therefore, if it could afford to build such towers, then why not? Other countries have shown greater extravagance, and often in far less productive forms that have impeded — not advanced — national economic development. It is hard to deny that the towers have been a major plus for Malaysia.

How could PETRONAS afford the towers when Malaysia is a relatively new and small producer of petroleum? Aside from small-scale onshore production in Miri, Sarawak, which Shell started during the colonial period, Malaysia's petroleum production and export only started in earnest in 1975. Unfamiliar with offshore production, we awarded the entire continental shelf east of the Peninsula to just one company. Fortunately, we were able to renegotiate the concession and regain most of it. Today most Malaysian oil is produced there and much of it belongs to us. Our highest total production is 700,000 barrels per day — we use some 400,000 barrels, leaving 300,000 for export. PETRONAS is 100 per cent Government-owned to ensure that oil revenues benefit all Malaysians.

At first we thought of operating as other national petroleum companies did — by simply collecting royalties from oil and gas production by foreign oil companies. Initially, no one thought we could involve ourselves in production or any of the upstream and downstream activities. Nobody believed we had or could acquire the necessary expertise and capability. The cost of exploring and producing oil was very high and seemed beyond our means, especially in the case of offshore production. But PETRONAS soon accumulated enough capital from our royalties, so the Government decided that it should invest in the oil business. We incorporated PETRONAS Carigali, an oil-prospecting company, while PETRONAS engineers and management staff studied the various upstream and downstream parts of the petroleum industry. They became involved in management, operations and marketing. Instead of sharing the production revenue under production-sharing agreements, PETRONAS began to take over the entire operation in their concession areas. There would be no more easy money for others from our resources. We had had quite enough of that under colonial rule.

When I became Prime Minister, I urged PETRONAS to reach out abroad. In Tun Hussein Onn's time there had been some talk of increasing trade overseas but the idea of actively going abroad only took off when I was Prime Minister. It was logical for PETRONAS to go abroad — our own reserves were small and, according to the experts, would be exhausted after 20 years. To secure future supplies, we needed to have concessions and produce oil in foreign countries. Unless we went abroad, all our acquired expertise would be wasted once our own reserves were finished.

In 1992, for its first overseas venture, the company opened PETRONAS Carigali Overseas Sdn Bhd in Vietnam. Although its war with the US had ended in 1975, Vietnam was still very distrustful of European companies. PETRONAS was welcomed by Vietnam. After that we looked elsewhere and went to many other countries to enter into all aspects of the oil business, from building pipelines to prospecting, from production to involvement in petrochemicals. Some welcomed us because they were rejected by the major American and European players. We made a point of training locals in every aspect of the oil business: from negotiating production-sharing agreements to training engineers and workers. We wanted the locals to operate, manage and control their own oil production, just as we did.

Sudan had earlier given contracts to US companies but then the US Government forbade American companies to work there, regarding it as a rogue country. The President of Sudan, who had attended Malaysia's Staff College when he was in the Sudanese army, knew our country. The Americans had said that Sudan's reserves were small, at just 10,000 barrels a day. But PETRONAS, working with the Sudanese Government and the Chinese, now produces about 350,000 barrels a day there. Other concessions were awarded to PETRONAS after that. The US Government would have liked to stop PETRONAS from operating in Sudan but a partnership with China's petroleum company protected PETRONAS. In other countries, PETRONAS teamed up with other major oil companies to avoid US Government harassment.

The company's successes in Sudan led to offers of oil exploration and production agreements from many countries that feared exploitation by the big Western oil majors. PETRONAS ventured into laying pipelines in Argentina and bought the South African oil company Engen, which refines and supplies oil to practically all the countries in southern Africa. In Egypt, PETRONAS built two LNG plants which produce liquid gas for export to Europe. We already had such a plant in Bintulu in Sarawak and had mastered the expertise so most of the managers at all these plants were Malaysians. PETRONAS retailed oil in many countries and has even bought some oil-retailing chains overseas. Highly-trained PETRONAS engineers are often enticed away by other petroleum companies, both national and multi-national. PETRONAS now operates in almost 40 countries and has one of the largest fleets of LNG tankers in the world.

PETRONAS went through a very stormy period in its early days. During my time it was decided that the company should have a non-executive Chairman and an executive President. Before the roles were split, Raja Tun Mohar Raja Badiozaman[5] had been both Chairman and CEO. Azizan, then Secretary-General of Home Affairs and my former Private Secretary at the Prime Minister's Department, was appointed President and Tan Sri Basir Ismail[6] Chairman. Later, Azizan became Chairman and Tan Sri Hassan Merican became President. The combination of Azizan and Hassan brought stability to the management and PETRONAS was at last able to move ahead and expand. Stable management is essential for overall company profitability but in the oil business, you can make very large profits simply from big increases in crude oil prices.

651

Profit margins in the industry are good and demand for petrol almost always exceeds current supply. Rumours of trouble in major producing countries are usually enough to push prices up further. When the price rose from USD30 to USD70 a barrel, the extra USD40 was pure profit. By the year 2008 we were forced to wonder whether the world had reached "peak oil" — a situation where demand continues to rise, where supply

---

5    Raja Tun Mohar Raja Badiozaman was also Chairman of Malaysian Airlines System from 1973 to 1991 and Special Economic Adviser to three Prime Ministers — Tun Abdul Razak Hussein, Tun Hussein Onn and me.

6    Among Tan Sri Basir Ismail's many posts were Malaysia Airports Holdings Bhd Executive Chairman, Kumpulan Fima Chairman, Sepang International Circuit Chairman and United Plantations Chairman.

and production must contract, and where oil prices must accordingly skyrocket. If so, the political economy of the oil industry would have reached a new stage worldwide. If that is ever the case, PETRONAS will be well positioned to adapt to the new situation and its demands, provided its own corporate leaders and the Malaysian Government act prudently. There is both a global economic and a domestic political dimension to the problem. In early 2008, the Malaysian Government delivered a huge shock when it suddenly withdrew much of its price subsidies to domestic consumers. It is a situation that requires very careful handling.

In Malaysia, the Government controls petrol pump prices but in England, there is a very high tax on oil because the roads are not tolled. There the cost of building and maintaining roads is funded from tax on oil, which is based on a percentage of the pump price. When the price of oil goes up, so does the tax, which the people have to pay. Even in the oil-rich Gulf States, the price of oil is higher than Malaysia. Yet Malaysians will create an uproar whenever the Government wants to raise oil prices. Many refuse to recognise or acknowledge the distortions caused by oil subsidies: cheap Malaysian oil can be smuggled out of the country, foreigners can come to our country to fill their tanks, and foreign-owned industries using oil for fuel and electricity also benefit — thus we end up subsidising foreigners, not only ourselves. Only when their petroleum products are for domestic consumption do Malaysians benefit. Yet some people here happily profiteered when the price of oil went up, raising the price of products by the same percentage as the increase in oil price even though oil may have constituted only 10 per cent of their costs. An oil price increase of 10 per cent would cause only a one per cent increase in their cost which does not justify a 10 per cent rise in price. The other nine per cent is claimed by greed, opportunism and a readiness for shady dealing.

PETRONAS pays the same petroleum tax as other petroleum companies, and since the Government owns the company, it also earns all its profits after tax. In 2005, PETRONAS made RM86 billion in profit and paid about RM30 billion as tax. The remaining RM56 billion belonged to the Government. If you compare this with the national income tax revenue at RM60 billion, PETRONAS profits are huge. It is the Government's cash cow. But in 2008, Tan Sri Hassan issued a warning — more than half the Government's funds now came from PETRONAS and its various subsidiaries. In relative, and in absolute terms, public expenditure in Malaysia was far more dependent on oil now than it had ever been on tin, rubber or electronics, or all three combined. This situation, he warned, could not continue indefinitely and the Government and Malaysian people were perhaps living in a fool's paradise.

Meanwhile, there are other demands on PETRONAS funds, but the company has to retain some of its profits to invest in new ventures. On average we still produce 650,000 barrels a day. I don't put much stock in the early predictions about supply running out after 20 years. When we first became involved in the petroleum industry we allocated practically all our reserves to PETRONAS, which also entered into production-sharing agreements with foreigners. They were reluctant to tie up with locals because they thought locals did not know how to do the job. That is not true anymore; and since we still prospect for oil in our waters I suggested we establish a second petroleum company, to be owned by the private sector. Such a company might get involved in certain small blocks at sea in which PETRONAS is not interested. So far, however, no Malaysian company has been given concessions locally, though some have been awarded concessions in other countries, such as Indonesia, and have been successful there.

The business side of PETRONAS was not its only important role. We also instructed the company to always be a good corporate citizen. In Sudan, for example, they built a hospital for their own staff and made it accessible to the locals, and they ran schools for local children. We generally treat local people as our friends, and are careful to employ them wherever we open an office. Many foreign students have been given scholarships to study at the prestigious PETRONAS Technological University.

PETRONAS is today one of the most successfully run national petroleum companies in the world. By going abroad to explore for and produce oil and to market its diverse products, PETRONAS has shown Malaysians that our companies and people can be successful outside of Malaysia. Because the company has successfully pioneered foreign business ventures, other Malaysians have been encouraged to follow suit. It is heartening and satisfying to see Malaysians doing business and providing professional expertise all over the world. It is yet another milestone in our progress towards becoming a developed country.

We have advanced, but not rapaciously in the way of many Western countries in colonial times. Even in these days, Western countries continue to impoverish their neighbours and other countries generally. We have progressed by winning friends and entering into mutually beneficial business partnerships. PETRONAS not only built our Twin Towers; it has made Malaysia a tower among developing nations.

# Chapter 51:
# Putrajaya

In the late 1980s and early 1990s Kuala Lumpur underwent a period of very rapid growth. Hundreds of construction cranes towered above the city skyline and, with the introduction of the national car stimulating car ownership, traffic jams became a daily occurrence all over the city. This was proof, but also an unwelcome and irritating aspect, of our astoundingly successful development.

Inching along the city's clogged streets took enormous amounts of time, energy and money, and made going to work a chore for civil servants, especially as the Government's offices were scattered all over Kuala Lumpur. Maintaining connections and making deliveries between different Government departments also became a challenge. Tan Sri Elyas Omar, then the Datuk Bandar or Mayor, suggested that the capital should be moved elsewhere as the city could no longer be home to the Government and its administrative apparatus. I saw his point — the need for some relief was obvious. But Kuala Lumpur had been our national capital since Independence. It is also where Parliament is located and where the Yang di-Pertuan Agong maintains his official residence. What we needed to build, I thought, was not a new capital but a new administrative centre.

I personally liked the coolness of our mountains and initially favoured building a new city at Bukit Tinggi or Janda Baik, both in the hills of Pahang. Delighted at the prospect, the Pahang state government readily consented. But the cost of compensation for the land there was prohibitive so we decided to look elsewhere. This proved to be a blessing because if we had gone ahead and sited the administration in either Bukit Tinggi or Janda Baik, it would have been much farther away from the new international airport than Kuala Lumpur. In the end, we decided to build it in Selangor and we chose an oil palm estate called Perang Besar as its site. It had been developed by a British company after World War I, hence its name "Perang Besar" or "Great War". It began as a rubber estate but after Independence, it was converted into an oil palm estate. About eight kilometres long and three kilometres wide, it occupied nearly 5,000 hectares of undulating land conveniently located halfway between Kuala Lumpur and the new international airport at Sepang. It met our needs and was sufficient for our purpose. The Government bought the entire estate for RM700 million and by 1993, development planning of Putrajaya (named after Tunku Abdul Rahman Putra), as the city was to be called, had started.

I had seen Washington DC and Canberra, and other purpose-built capital cities including Islamabad and New Delhi, and had noticed that many of them sat near expansive bodies of water. I like lakes so I asked the town planners to include one in the plan. Another feature which I wanted was a straight central boulevard for parades. France's President Jacques Chirac had once invited me to review with him the Bastille Day Parade in Paris and it had been a very impressive affair. The armed forces marched together with their armoured vehicles, guns and missiles down the Avenue des Champs-Elysées, the broad boulevard that stretches from the Arc de Triomphe to the Place de la Concorde. Kuala Lumpur lacked such a wide street for our Merdeka Day Parade, and the stretch of road in front of the Sultan Abdul Samad Building, which we usually used, was too short. I told the planners to provide a wide central boulevard with side lanes like the Champs-Elysées right through the centre of the city, and this they did.

We planned Putrajaya to be home to some 300,000 people, mostly civil servants. It was also planned as a garden city with seven parks, including a botanical garden. The boulevard, streets and roads would be lined with trees, bushes and flowering plants. As a symbol of the progress and sophistication of the nation, it was to be beautiful and full of colour. Its roads and streets were to be wide and well-planned, but there was a need for rapid mass transport. We were mindful of the transport gridlock in Kuala Lumpur, so right from the planning stage, a tunnel was provided under the central boulevard for a Malaysian-made monorail. Some RM600 million was spent on the tunnel, which ran parallel to another tunnel for water mains, electric cables, wastewater pipes and telephone lines. For some reason, however, Tun Abdullah Ahmad Badawi's Government decided not to build the monorail, which means the suspension bridge we built for it remains well and truly suspended. Perhaps one day soon, when government funds permit, the monorail will be built.

PETRONAS presented a Putrajaya development proposal in February 1995. It suggested the setting up of Putrajaya Holdings Sdn Bhd on a commercial basis as the owner and developer, while Kuala Lumpur City Centre Bhd would be the project consultant and manager. Perbadanan Putrajaya would be the local governing authority and would be independent of the state government. The entire piece of land would be transferred to Putrajaya Holdings Sdn Bhd, while its cost of RM700 million would constitute 30 per cent equity by the Ministry of Finance. The other equity holders were the Employees Provident Fund or EPF at 20 per cent, the National Trust Fund or Khazanah Nasional Berhad,[1] also at 20 per cent, and PETRONAS at 30 per cent. Except for a hotel and a few other buildings which would be built and owned by the Government, all other buildings would be built by Putrajaya Holdings Sdn Bhd and leased to the Government. After 30 years, the buildings would belong to the Government as the lease amounted to instalment payments.

When Putrajaya was being built, the late Sultan of Selangor, Al-Marhum Sultan Salahuddin Abdul Aziz Shah Al-Haj ibni Al-Marhum Sultan Hishamuddin Alam Shah Al-Haj, was the Yang di-Pertuan Agong. He was gratified that the nation's administrative city was being built in Selangor. During my weekly audience with him, I pointed out how this major development would contribute much towards the growth and development of his state. He showed keen interest in the progress of the development of Putrajaya.

I raised with him the problem of the city's administration. It had to be under the Federal Government and not the state government. Otherwise there would be difficulties as the policies between the two governments might differ.

I was very conscious of the sacrifice already made by Selangor in agreeing to transfer Kuala Lumpur to the Federal Government. It meant that Selangor had to accept excision of its land to create Kuala Lumpur as a Federal Territory. But by the 1990s, the rapid growth of Kuala Lumpur had spilled over into adjoining areas of Selangor, thus contributing to the growth and development of the state. I felt sure that the development of Putrajaya would have the same spillover effect on Selangor.

---

[1]  Khazanah Nasional Berhad is the Government's investment arm.

With some trepidation I suggested to the Sultan that it would be easier for Putrajaya to be developed if it were made a Federal Territory.

To my surprise, he readily consented. I believe many in the Selangor government, despite being of the same party as the Federal Government, were not happy. Be that as it may, all the legal procedures, including obtaining the approval of the state government, were meticulously followed before the transfer of Putrajaya to the Federal Government to become a Federal Territory was made. I believe it was to the benefit of everyone. It has certainly facilitated the management of the new administrative capital; it has stimulated the development of the adjoining areas of Selangor and beyond; and it has contributed to the national identity and pride of all Malaysians.

Witnessed by ambassadors from some 80 diplomatic delegations in Kuala Lumpur, I officiated at the groundbreaking ceremony on 19 September 1996. A monument in the form of an unfurled Malaysian flag on a low flagpole was constructed in steel to mark the site. Less than three years later, I moved into the new domed Prime Minister's Office. It was something

of a record and I know of no other capital city that was built in that space of time. I visited the construction site almost every week, at times wondering whether I would be its first occupant. I was already thinking of stepping down. Had I done so in 1998 as I had planned, I would never experience living in the new Prime Minister's residence or working in the Prime Minister's Office in Putrajaya. The impressive speed of construction was perhaps due to the fact that this was a greenfield site. There were no buried pipes or cables to avoid or re-site, no old roads to dig out, or existing buildings to demolish. Had we tried using a built-up area, re-siting services and the demolition of structures would have pushed up costs and delayed construction.

The lake I had asked the planners to include in the design was fed by a number of tiny rivulets which converged in the valley to become a constantly flowing stream. The planners thought it would take two years to fill the lake to the level of the spillway at the end of the valley, but in the end it only took two months. Nature proved to do a better job than we could in meeting our deadlines. There had been a small hillock in the middle of the estate but now the water filled up the surrounding lowland, turning it into an island. The boulevard and the ministry buildings flanking it were located on this island. The lake enhanced the city's beauty and though we had to build many bridges across it, pushing up the cost of development, we felt that it was worth it. Most of the bridges were very modern but one was of classic design. They are a great attraction to visitors, a source of pride to Malaysians, and a rendezvous point for people in the evening and on clear nights.

As for the boulevard, it is four kilometres long and I feel it adds grandeur to the heart of the administrative centre. The Prime Minister's Office sits at one end, and it was later decided that an International Convention Centre should be built at the other. We held the Merdeka Day Parade along this boulevard for the first time on 31 August 2003, and it was spectacular. It was also the last parade I attended as Prime Minister.

Predictably, Putrajaya was labelled a megaproject, first by my foreign detractors who, no less predictably, were echoed by local critics. Since I was no longer Prime Minister my detractors, including members of Tun Abdullah's Government, regularly had a field day condemning this "mega-waste-of-money project". It has been suggested that this was one of the projects which bankrupted the nation and caused all Government projects in the Eighth Malaysia Plan to be abandoned. It has also been said that even the Ninth Malaysia Plan could not be started because there was no money. Malay contractors who depended on government contracts to survive were told to blame the Government I led, and me in particular, for their dire straits.

Putrajaya is a big project, but most private-sector development projects in Malaysia are big. No one builds just one house or even a row of shophouses in Malaysia — private developers usually build whole towns complete with shopping areas and complexes, parks and gardens, kindergartens and schools, and even areas reserved for places of worship. Take Mont Kiara[2] for example. Only 10 years ago when I used to ride along the paths between the bushes which covered the area, there was not a single house to be seen. Today there are scores of high-rise flats, condominiums and offices,

---

[2]    Mont Kiara is a relatively new and wealthy suburb in the north of Kuala Lumpur.

a large area where shops and numerous restaurants line the streets, and roads which give access to elevated highways. Even outside Kuala Lumpur and Selangor, the housing developments in the other states are also big. Frequently they merge with other adjacent developments to form sizeable towns. Putrajaya had to be bigger than most private housing estates but it was not going to be built all at once. We envisaged completion in 2020.

A private-sector housing estate is just a housing estate but Putrajaya is much more — it is a part of the capital of Malaysia and is its administrative centre. No one, I hope, dares suggest that the administrative capital of perhaps the most developed of the developing countries should be the size of a private housing estate, or smaller. The new towns in the Klang Valley such as Sri Kembangan and Puchong are now bigger than Putrajaya and they will all continue to grow. So will Shah Alam, the new capital of Selangor. If Putrajaya were to be only the size of a housing estate, it would be overshadowed and rendered insignificant by the neighbouring new towns in the same area. As an administrative capital, it had to be of substantial size. We could not invite foreign visitors and overseas consultants to a dwarf-like urban complex. What would they think of us? Would we be seen as people of limited imagination? Our administrative capital has to be impressive and must truly reflect the country's development because it is to be our administrative capital not only for today but far into the future. It must be built to last, with ample space for growth, and its architecture should be admired by future generations. In its size, layout and architecture, Putrajaya had to be stylish and striking. And so it is — that has been the verdict of its many foreign visitors, including the leaders and officials of other countries who, having decided to build their own national administrative centres or new capitals, have openly said that they will use Putrajaya as their model.

But has the country been bankrupted by the building of Putrajaya? To the best of my knowledge, Malaysia's finances were healthy when I stepped down. Indeed, had the Government done as I advised, it would have cost us nothing to build Putrajaya. I had suggested that the many government properties in Kuala Lumpur, which would be vacated after the move to Putrajaya, should be sold to the public as these properties were located in some of the most commercially desirable and strategic parts of the city. The Perang Besar estate was sold to us by the acre; land in Kuala Lumpur is sold by the square foot, for as much as RM3,000 per unit. We bought some 10,000 acres (or 400 million square feet) but Government land in Kuala Lumpur also added up to millions of square feet. From the proceeds of their sale, the acquisition of land and the building of Putrajaya could doubtless have been easily financed — without any burden on the budget.

Had the civil servants taken my advice, Putrajaya could have been fully developed without the Government having to produce a single sen from its Consolidated Fund, where all Government revenue is collected. But, ever more sentimental than realistic, the civil servants were loath to part with the offices we had in Kuala Lumpur. They wanted to retain them and find some other use for them. They wanted to preserve the identity of Kuala Lumpur as the federal capital so they would not let it be owned entirely by the private sector. I can understand their feelings as I too have a feeling for our national past — but pride and sentiment cost money.

As a result of its development, the Perang Besar land has gained in value and price and if we cared to do so, we could sell off Putrajaya. A Government which pleads that it has no money could in fact make a pile. Alternatively, we could sell off the remaining undeveloped land in Putrajaya and recoup our original outlay. Land development companies are among the most profitable in Malaysia. Before I became a Minister, I had a housing development project in Alor Star, from which I made quite a lot of money despite my complete lack of experience in the business. As the developer of Putrajaya, the Government should also have been able to make a substantial profit, so financially, the Government has not lost any money from developing Putrajaya. The criticism that Putrajaya is a megaproject and waste of money is unwarranted; rather, it turned out to be a very good investment.

I have learned that assets which are not put to good use deteriorate and are eventually wasted. What enriches some people and some countries is their ability to develop and maximise the potential of their assets. When Kuala Lumpur was a sleepy hollow, few could become rich and even those who owned land in the city centre could not realise the full potential value of their properties. Undeveloped or developed, there were simply no takers. Businesses, including basic retail, did not do well in those days and there were certainly no elegant shops selling branded luxury goods. Tourists did not come, especially not the rich shoppers. Money did not flow in and Malaysians could not accumulate wealth as no one, local or foreign, was spending big.

But after the Government prodded the private sector by example — after it built the supporting infrastructure and invested in development — Kuala Lumpur began to grow. It eventually became a great city with all the amenities of a cosmopolitan urban centre. With that growth the assets that people owned — not just their land but also their intelligence, business acumen and skills — all became valuable. There was no longer any waste of assets, of idle and underutilised resources, in any form. In a country's development, what counts is the ability to amass, develop and exploit one's assets, as failure to do so means you remain poor. Even if there is gold in the ground, it will not enrich the landowner until he is able to extract and sell it.

In Putrajaya we have invested in and created increasingly more valuable assets. By themselves they will not yield returns unless and until we make good use of them. If you do not know how to make use of the assets and how to derive tangible benefits from them, they will only be a burden and a waste, yielding no returns from their ownership. That attitude, which encourages people to sit upon idle assets, is what has long held back the economic development of many rural Malays, to our people's and nation's great cost. It is not the kind of attitude that would yield a progressive and dynamic national development philosophy. Whether Putrajaya becomes a worthwhile project or a waste of money depends on the owners of the assets that Putrajaya and its facilities represent. If their owners do not know how to use those assets, how to exploit them productively, then they are likely to condemn them as a waste which in fact reflects their lack of enterprise. It is a verdict not on the assets but on those who so poorly understand their potential use. When governments lack entrepreneurial ideas, a country is not likely to grow and prosper. As one Malay proverb wisely puts it, *tak tahu menari, kata tanah tinggi rendah* (not knowing how to dance, you say the ground is uneven).

Putrajaya may be the manifestation of someone's ego and personal vision, but there can be no denying that it is more distinctly a response to Malaysia's urgent need for a new administrative capital. Without Putrajaya, the transportation problems of Kuala Lumpur would have long ago become unmanageable. In another 10 or 20 years, it would have totally defied any solution. Putrajaya helped to solve much of Kuala Lumpur's congestion problems while remedy was still possible.

We might have built just any dowdy town of simple standard buildings, just as we did immediately upon achieving Independence — it would certainly have cost much less. If Malaysians want to be proud of dowdiness, that is fine, but I sense that they want something better to be proud of; if so, then the striking architecture of Putrajaya is theirs to celebrate. It may have cost more to build but backward-looking sentiments and narrow pride, as I have indicated, also cost money. Government money is better spent on assets, like a new administrative capital that expresses and supports genuine national pride.

Putrajaya is a beautiful, functional city. When I visited the Versailles Palace outside Paris I heard the guide proudly extol its beauty. But when the Sun King Louis XIV built it, the people of Paris had no bread to eat. When we built Putrajaya, Malaysians had full stomachs. It was not built at the cost of neglecting their needs. It expressed the people's own pride, not their leader's vanity.

# Chapter 52:
# Currency Crumble

I was not familiar with the international monetary or financial system when it faltered and soon after threatened to implode on us in 1997. As a boy, I had experienced high inflation rates during the Japanese Occupation, when things were priced in thousands of dollars and people had to carry gunny sacks of the so-called "banana currency" to buy anything. There were no banks then and all transactions were carried out in cash.

Everything was in short supply during the Occupation and prices tended to go up very rapidly. The Japanese Military Administration overcame this problem by merely printing more currency notes in higher denominations, and even resorted to printing over new figures on the smaller denomination notes to meet the ever more inflated cost of paying their local employees and for their supplies. Somehow, we managed. In my family, I was better off than my brothers because I chose to sell bananas and other items at Pekan Rabu, the weekly Wednesday Market. I soon learned to raise my selling price in order to pay the expected higher cost of my supplies. My brothers held salaried jobs with the Government and its agencies, but their pay increases always lagged behind rising prices and came too late to meet increased costs. All of us were involved in the black market, and we sold old clothing, jewellery and some of our few possessions. When we could get Japanese cigarettes from the soldiers, we would sell them too.

By 1944, the war was not going well for the Japanese and I believed the British would return sooner or later. In anticipation, I paid a huge amount of Japanese banana money for 100 dollars of the old Straits Settlement and Malay States currency notes, as I was sure they would become legal tender again when the British returned. The way prices went down to pre-war levels as soon as the old currency came back into circulation again was quite miraculous. Government servants were given three months' pay to compensate them for not having been paid when the British left Malaya and in this way, the old currency was decisively returned into circulation. It flooded back into a battered economy that had been operating for some time without any effective, stable and credible currency. People then were not very sophisticated. They unquestioningly accepted the currency that the British Military Administration issued and got rid of the Japanese banana currency, which soon became worthless. That's the thing about paper currency — it's not worth anything in itself. It has value because, and only for as long as, people believe it does. That's how money works.

Unfortunately, the restoration of the Malayan economy and the reintroduction of the Malayan dollar to replace the Japanese currency has never been properly studied and documented. Perhaps we could learn something from that experience and about how to handle currencies and currency crises. I worked as a temporary clerk at the office of the Custodian of Enemy Property early in 1947 and was paid 80 dollars per month. Permanent clerks were paid 60 dollars per month, the same pay for clerks before the invasion. It was as if there had been zero inflation during the Japanese Occupation.

There was also very little inflation during the early years of the British Military Administration, the Malayan Union and then the Federation of Malaya. Supplies improved but unemployment was high, and the Colonial Government quickly introduced price controls. That kind of measure is often taken in wartime, but the Colonial Government found it a good way to reduce inflation. Even today Malaysia still controls the prices of essential goods, as we do not think this contravenes free market rules. The idea that demand and supply must always determine prices is not completely correct as traders can always cause artificial shortages or oversupply and so influence, even manipulate, prices. The market is not always a pure and impersonal mechanism that can be relied upon to deliver the uncontaminated truth about proper price levels. In fact, we were to learn 50 years later that free market principles permitted the unregulated freedom to manipulate prices, whether of basic domestic commodities or national currencies at the global level.

I learnt a few lessons about dealing with high inflation during my wartime forays into small business, and I learnt bookkeeping in school. But none of this equipped me with the knowledge to handle the currency crisis which hit Malaysia in 1997.

In May of that year I decided to take two months' leave, leaving Datuk Seri Anwar Ibrahim in charge as acting Prime Minister. I saw it as a good opportunity to observe how he performed as I was already thinking of stepping down in 1998. I wanted to be sure that when Anwar took over from me, he would be able to administer the country well.

While I was in Bledisloe in the Cotswolds in England, I received news about the Thai baht coming under attack by currency traders. Thai businessmen had apparently been borrowing a great deal of foreign currency at low interest rates compared with those of baht loans. Quick profits could be made from the differences between these interest rates — but only if the value of the baht remained stable. International currency traders, people who make a living from noting and exploiting such anomalies and vulnerabilities, thought the situation was suitable for their kind of trading. They spread the word that the baht was overvalued and that the Thai economy would prove unsustainable. The currency traders then sold large qualities of baht, causing it to depreciate against the US dollar, and throwing Thais who had borrowed US dollars into difficulties. They had

to find more baht to repay their foreign currency borrowings for if their trading profits were insufficient, they risked defaulting on their loans. If they defaulted, then the currency traders' allegation that the Thai economy was weak would appear vindicated. The traders then dumped more baht and the currency weakened further, causing more foreign currency loans to default. Yet the traders could appear to be simply responding as innocent bystanders to a crisis that they themselves had triggered.

A vicious cycle quickly developed: the more the baht depreciated, the more loan defaults increased and the more the Thai economy weakened. The Thai Government tried to buy baht with its US dollar reserves to sustain the baht's value, but the currency traders seemed to have limitless supplies of the currency to dump into the markets. Eventually, the Thai Government was landed with a lot of badly depreciated baht and greatly reduced foreign reserves. This started another round of selling as the baht weakened from a perceived lack of foreign currency reserve support. By the time I came home from leave in August 1997, things were looking very bad for Thailand. We decided to lend it some hard currency to strengthen its reserves but it was to no avail — the baht kept falling.

Malaysian finances were in good shape at the time, as neither the Government nor our business people had needed to borrow much foreign currency. Our interest rates had always been low and foreign currency borrowings would not have given us any advantage. Bank Negara's foreign currency reserves were also sufficient; at least we thought it was sufficient enough to support the ringgit if it came under attack. But that seemed hypothetical. We had not made ourselves vulnerable as the Thais had, through their foreign exchange borrowings and dealings with currency traders. What did we have to fear?

Then we began to hear talk about financial "contagion", and how our neighbour's troubles might soon infect us. It seemed that despite the soundness of our economy and finances, the ringgit might still come under attack. If the traders caused a loss of confidence in Malaysia as well, then the ringgit too would be devalued. I simply could not understand why this should be so, but the economists were certain it would happen.

They were right. Currency traders began selling the ringgit in huge amounts and it soon began depreciating. Before the attack began in mid-1997, the ringgit exchange rate was RM2.50 to the US dollar, but it would lose half its value by the end of the year. We did not know who was selling the ringgit nor did we know who they were selling it to. I was told about a man named George Soros who had attacked the British pound and the Italian lira — both England and Italy had a tough time fending off his attacks and their currencies were forcibly devalued. Not knowing who the currency traders were, I assumed that Soros was one of them. Whoever it was, I was furious. How could outsiders impoverish our country and our people? How could they knowingly and intentionally do such a thing? Even if that was not their main purpose, how could they choose to ruin us as a casual by-product of their own currency trading strategies? It made no sense to me, economically or morally.

Malaysians, particularly the business community, soon felt the effect of devaluation. Importers could not earn enough ringgit to buy the dollars needed to pay for the goods they had purchased from foreign suppliers, leaving them cash-strapped and unable to service their debts. Malaysians who were used to enjoying overseas travel suddenly found foreign trips too expensive. While our exports should have earned us more ringgit since sales were often denominated in US dollars, foreign buyers demanded to pay less. Malaysia's costs, they insisted, had gone down because the value of the ringgit had fallen. But imported raw materials and components were costing more, as were the capital goods. The fall in the ringgit did not make us more competitive, certainly not against our neighbours whose currencies were also devalued.

We felt helpless as the ringgit continued to sink and the economy moved further towards recession. Only recently we had been growing at eight per cent per annum for almost 10 consecutive years, but now we faced the prospect of negative growth. But I could say nothing about the currency traders — every time I made a public statement, the ringgit would immediately fall further.

On 17 June 1997, just before the attack on regional currencies began, IMF Managing Director Michel Camdessus praised the Governor of Bank Negara for a well-managed economy and financial regime at the Los Angeles World Affairs Council. "Malaysia is a good example of a country where the authorities are well aware of the challenges of managing the pressures that result from high growth and of maintaining a sound financial system amidst substantial capital flows and a booming property market," he said. Inflation, he had noted, was low and the ringgit had remained at RM2.5 to USD1 for a long time; it was truly a strong currency, reflecting the sound finances of the country. But now the same people were saying the economy was overheated and, as a result, the ringgit was reeling under the onslaught of the currency traders. I refused to believe that the depreciation of the ringgit was due to a weak economy or to any loss of market confidence in Malaysia.

I bought books on currency trading to better understand its mechanisms because I believed it was currency trading, not the basic condition of our economy itself or our currency which was affecting the ringgit. I had met Camdessus earlier and he seemed like a nice man. As Minister of Finance and Deputy Prime Minister, Anwar met the IMF head quite often. I asked Anwar to appeal to Camdessus to stop currency trading and argued that it was unnecessary and damaging to the economy of developing countries. I do not know whether Anwar stated my case to Camdessus, but no attempt was made to stop currency trading.

To me, trading in currencies as if they were commodities was absurd. Coffee, sugar, rubber and the like are real commodities and they have all kinds of substantive human uses. But currency is different. It has no value in itself, only in exchange as a way of procuring real commodities. It cannot be used in any other way and cannot be directly consumed. We are no longer in the Middle Ages, when the European economy did not have any credible currency and traders in the French markets used Southeast Asian pepper as their money and medium of exchange. Now we use pepper and spices to make our food tasty and we have money to buy the commodities we need.

I remember reading that once, when there was a glut in the coffee market and coffee prices were very low, the Brazilians dumped their coffee beans into the sea to create a shortage and raise the price. But can you dump or burn money in the same way to raise its value? In the case of currency, the situation is actually worse, for there is more money in circulation than there is issued by central banks and currency boards. It is no longer just real money that changes hands during transactions as there are also cheques, credit cards and electronic transfers. The total amount they represent must exceed the total value of currency notes issued and in circulation. Money has, in effect, become virtual.

Looking back now, I suppose I literally took to heart the economists' cliché that money is the lifeblood of the financial and economic system. As a doctor I understood that there is a finite amount of blood circulating in a person's body at any time (although you sometimes have to increase it with a transfusion). But I have learned not to take that medical idea or metaphor literally when it is applied to the economy. Money is different from debt, as there can be far more debt around than the money in circulation to support and denominate it. Economists think differently from doctors. For them, two plus two can sometimes be more than four.

After the US emerged from World War II as the dominant military and economic power, the world accepted the US dollar as the standard currency in international trade and as its reserve currency. The Bretton Woods

Agreement[1] had fixed the US dollar at 35 to one ounce of gold. All other countries then fixed their currencies against the US dollar, which in effect meant the value of gold. The post-war world economy recovered while this regime was in place, but when the US went off the gold standard in 1971, largely to pay for the accumulating costs of the Vietnam War, the world's currencies were destabilised. Market forces would now determine the rates and most currencies would "float" in relation to one another.

I felt that this destroyed the sovereignty of countries and left them at the mercy of the market and human greed. Greedy people will not take the welfare of others into account; they will certainly not be sensitive to the needs of developing countries. For profit, they will destroy whole countries and impoverish their people.

However, we had to accept the situation despite knowing that market mechanisms and forces could be manipulated. It did not take long for speculators to begin abusing the system. They had invented the short selling of commodities and shares; now, they invented the short selling of currencies.

670

They made fortunes by bankrupting countries, especially those in the developing world; these were quite literally financial killings. Enterprising people set up hedge funds and invited the rich to subscribe to them. The returns on investments would be far greater than through other channels, but the operations of these funds produced nothing that could be used in the market or for people.

The least that could have been done was to regulate them, but while their promoters kept insisting on transparency in every deal or transaction and in everyone else's plans — for how could serious investors possibly risk their money on anything that was shrouded in secrecy? — the operations of the funds themselves were allowed to remain mysterious. Who the traders were, where they got their money, how much they borrowed, to whom they sold and who bought the currencies that they sold: we did not know the answers to any of these questions. The funds could leverage their capital by as much as 20 times. With them, more than anywhere else in the economy,

---

[1]   Representatives from 44 countries met just before the end of World War II to discuss how to rebuild the global economy.

credit expansion outstripped the supply of money and ceased to have any coherent relation to it. The effect of their operations was devastating.

Camdessus was French and, I heard, a friend of President Chirac's. Since I knew Chirac well, I wrote to him about the depredations of the currency traders and asked him to intercede with Camdessus to stop the trading. Again, during the Commonwealth Heads of Government Meeting in Edinburgh, Scotland, in 1997, I met Tony Blair, who had only just become Prime Minister of Britain. I explained the effect of currency trading to him at length and asked him to take it up with the IMF, but my efforts came to nothing.

Malaysia had some prior experience in currency trading, in which we had become involved because we needed to ensure that our reserves would not be depleted because of the fluctuations in the currencies we kept. But we only dealt in the currencies of developed countries. We speculated as all in the market did, but we did not manipulate. It was a matter of taking calculated risks, and when one of our speculative ventures failed, we lost a lot of money. After that lesson, we got out of the business.

671

In September 1997, I was invited to speak at the annual meeting of the World Bank and the IMF in Hong Kong and took the opportunity to blast currency traders, accusing them of further impoverishing the world's poor countries. I mentioned Soros by name as one of the traders who had manipulated the currencies of Southeast Asian countries and undermined their development. The next day, Anwar spoke at the same meeting. I had left for Sabah and he rang me there. He sounded annoyed and informed me that my speech had caused the ringgit to depreciate further. He stopped short of telling me not to speak like that again, but I continued with my criticism of the IMF and the currency traders. At a later meeting in Santiago in Chile, I again condemned them and once again, the ringgit fell in value. That seemed proof to me that the currency traders were pushing the devaluation. It could not have been the market, as the reaction was instantaneous. This was not a general consensus from the market but a few key hidden players who were calling the shots. And for their own reasons — some people were deliberately trying to shut my mouth about currency traders.

At home Anwar started what became known as "the IMF solution without the IMF". But fundamentally, we were not in economic trouble. We had no need to borrow from the IMF to settle foreign debts because we had not borrowed much and few of our debts were due. Those that did fall due, we could still manage to pay. But regardless of whether we needed to borrow from the IMF, Anwar felt that Malaysia had to accept its advice. He believed that to maintain international confidence in our economic management, we should do as we were told and manage our economy the way they wanted. Anwar seemed to think that the IMF medicine was good for us and would help us recover from the international malaise, even if we had not yet fallen ill. So he raised interest rates and cut back on government spending. I warned Anwar that his actions might well deprive the Government of the revenue it needed to pay the salaries of our government servants. He also tried reducing the payment default period from six months to three months before declaring loans as non-performing. This landed the banks with a high percentage of non-performing loans, while making bankrupts of the borrowers. Business slowed down. The disease had arrived. The IMF medicine was not the cure but its cause. Still, Anwar pressed ahead.

672

The economy was now clearly heading towards a recession. Companies were going bankrupt and were defaulting on their bank loans, especially after Anwar's decision to reduce the default period and increase interest rates to 12 per cent. We decided to set up an operations agency along the lines of the National Operations Council which dealt with the aftermath of the race riots in 1969. We wanted to minimise political contentions so we brought in all the State Chief Ministers and *Menteri Besar*, including from PAS, into what we called the National Economic Action Council (NEAC).[2] Trade union and business leaders and think-tank heads were also included.

We were able to explain the problems faced by the country to them and heard their views on how to handle the situation. But because of its large size, the Council could not meet often. I decided to have a small advisory panel to follow developments and to suggest remedies. It had to be backed

---

[2]  The National Economic Action Council, or *Majlis Tindakan Ekonomi Negara* (MTEN), was created on 7 January 1998 to advise the Government on all issues related to the financial crisis.

by the Cabinet as a whole, though only a few Cabinet members would be in it. Fortunately, the Cabinet did not question the authority or the arrangements for setting up such a powerful body. Its members included Anwar; Datuk Mustapa Mohamed, a well-credentialed economist who now serves as Malaysia's Minister of International Trade and Industry; Tun Daim Zainuddin; the Chief Secretary Tan Sri Samsudin Osman; the Secretary-General to the Ministry of Finance Tan Sri Samsuddin Hitam; the Deputy Governor of Bank Negara Datuk Fong Weng Phak (for some reason the Governor never attended our meetings); Tan Sri Ali Abul Hassan Sulaiman who had headed the Economic Planning Unit; Oh Siew Nam, a man from the private sector who was familiar with banking and the financial markets; and ISIS chief Tan Sri Dr Noordin Sopiee.

This small committee met for at least three hours every morning in my office. We scrutinised all the statistics on the economy, commissioned studies of anything that we considered might influence the economic performance or prospects of the country, brought in experts to explain developments and give their views, listened to numerous briefings, and often decided on action that needed to be taken. Fortunately, we did not experience social unrest during this critical period. Malaysians could take a beating but a violent destructive response was not their way. We were also making final preparations for the Commonwealth Games to be held the following year, and we could not afford instability of any kind.

While managing the crisis, I continued to travel abroad to pursue both economic and diplomatic initiatives. I was in Buenos Aires in Argentina when I suddenly remembered Tan Sri Nor Mohamed Yakcop, who had headed the ill-fated Bank Negara currency trading operation. I had spotted him walking down a street in Kuala Lumpur before I had left for Buenos Aires. That image now came to mind and I decided that he might be able to explain currency trading and possibly suggest ways of countering it. Our loss-making venture into currency trading might yet yield Malaysia a valuable, even life-saving dividend as the currency traders now closed in on us. The matter was urgent and I could not wait to come home, so I asked my office to locate Nor Mohamed and fly him to Argentina. Soon after, in the hotel in Buenos Aires, we sat down together and he explained the intricacies of currency trading and why we had lost money. I asked him what lessons from that earlier experience could be applied to our present situation.

He suggested that we get some of our institutions with financial resources to set up a special fund to buy the ringgit. This we did, but again, we were no match for the funds the currency traders had at their disposal. They could leverage 20 times their capital and we would have exhausted our reserves trying to fight them this way. We were up against not one but several funds which were involved in currency trading so, inevitably, the exercise failed. Yet I found Nor Mohamed knowledgeable and decided to appoint him my financial adviser and a member of the NEAC.

We directed many questions to him in our efforts to grasp and to curb currency trading. I had to fully understand the banking and the financial systems and Nor Mohamed was able to explain it all. Not understanding these intricacies had made us institute measures which proved ineffective. At one stage I had thought of deliberately devaluing our ringgit and increasing salaries and wages to neutralise the effect of devaluation. When I took this idea to some of my colleagues and Ministers, they were adamant that it would not work. Yet I believed there had to be something the Government could legally do to stop the trade in our currency. I was still under the impression that actual money changed hands during all these transactions. I had not yet grasped the abstract and virtual nature of money, and how paper transactions in billions may flow across the world faster than you can pay for RM10 worth of vegetables at the local night market.

That was why when we were told that money was being taken out of the country, we thought people were actually taking cash out with them as they left. We asked the Customs officials at exit points to check travellers' bags but were mystified because no cash was being taken out of the country. Yet the amount of money in Malaysia was now considerably less than before, and we learnt that money had flowed to Singapore by the millions. That was why we asked the Singapore Government to deposit some of their ringgit in Malaysian banks. We were also puzzled as to how currency traders who operated outside Malaysia could have billions of ringgit to sell. Where, I wondered, did these international predators get their ringgit? They were short selling the ringgit and entering into contracts to deliver ringgit they appeared not to have. Still, they had to deliver some time.

I asked Nor Mohamed how such large amounts of our currency could leave Malaysia undetected and how the currency traders could physically handle billions of ringgit. We had no record of their acquiring the ringgit before they started trading it as a commodity and destabilising the exchange rate. Yet at some stage, I reasoned, they must have acquired their ringgit before selling it in the market.

Nor Mohamed explained to the NEAC that no cash was actually being moved. A million ringgit, even in RM100 bills, would be extremely bulky and would not be easy to transport. Certainly there was no way hundreds of millions or one billion ringgit could be moved around. The ringgit was legal tender only in Malaysia and it could not be used outside the country. Banks and money changers in other countries may accept the ringgit in exchange for local currency, but only in small amounts. In the end, they must repatriate the notes to Malaysia. Yet this was clearly not happening — if it were, endless streams of armoured vans would need to travel back and forth constantly between Singapore and Malaysia.

So what money was now being traded? No physical cash was involved, Nor Mohamed explained. Instead, the money was being held in Malaysian banks in cash, mostly in the accounts of the people to whom the money belonged. I asked Nor Mohamed what happened when the money was bought or sold. Small amounts may be deposited in the banks or taken out in cash, he said, but usually the money was simply credited to the recipient's account or debited from the accounts of the person making the payment. No cash transaction was involved at all as it was purely a paper transaction and only the figures in the bank books would change. When ringgit trades were made, no money ever left the country or entered it. The process might be slightly more complicated in the case of foreign currency accounts in foreign banks, but even then, the ringgit traded would never leave Malaysia.

I suddenly realised that this must be the way. We had asked Bank Negara to withdraw high denomination notes of RM1,000 to stop people from taking money out of the country. It turned out that the money was actually being held in Malaysian banks in the accounts of foreigners. Since the foreigners owned the money, we could not make use of it.

This was a revelation to me. I was not a banker and I had few dealings with banks. I always made payments by cheque without thinking about how the figures changed in my accounts. My own transactions were small and usually handled by my personal assistant. I was now appalled that I had been spending huge sums of government money without knowing anything about how banks operated. But from the moment I learnt that traded ringgit never left Malaysia physically, and that sales and purchases simply involved transfers of ownership of money from one account to the other in bank books, I began thinking about how the Government might use Bank Negara's control over Malaysia's banks to stop the currency trading.

I believed that many of my NEAC colleagues knew that the financial system generates far more credit than the money that is issued by the central banks, but they did not see how this knowledge might lend itself to instituting government control over currency trading. It may have been good to be ignorant about the financial system, as it allowed me to see with fresh eyes how to frustrate the currency traders.

I asked Nor Mohamed whether the Government could order the banks not to transfer ownership when currency traders bought and sold the ringgit. He said it was possible. I mulled things over and — with Tun Daim, Nor Mohamed and the bankers in the NEAC — began to discuss the possibility of blocking the currency traders' access to the ringgit. At the same time, we would have to put a stop to the buying and selling of Malaysian shares through the Central Limit Order Book or CLOB, the so-called "over-the-counter" stock exchange set up by Singapore to trade in Malaysian stocks after we separated our stock exchanges in 1989. The Singapore CLOB trading was causing our share prices to drop continuously. Our Composite Index (KLCI) was around 1,200 when the devaluation of the ringgit began. Not wanting to lose the money they had invested in Malaysia, foreign investors stampeded to the exit, selling off their shares and converting the ringgit they received into US dollars or other currencies. Their sales were causing our share prices to fall further, at one point to below 300. Market capitalisation of our stock exchange was now less than one quarter of what it had been before the crisis.

We found that the shares bought through CLOB were all registered in the names of trustee companies. It was completely legal, but when shares were sold within each trustee company, ownership did not change; it remained in the name of the holding trustee companies. There was therefore no need to inform the Malaysian Stock Exchange of the transaction. Still the continuous selling of these Malaysian shares caused their prices to drop. The KLSE could do nothing about CLOB and there was no need to register these transactions with the KLSE so long as they remained on paper with the same trustees.

We had to put a stop to this practice, and so decided that no sale would be recognised unless the real owners of the shares registered with the KLSE. Failing this, the transaction would not be valid and the shares would be legally considered as belonging to the seller. Once we imposed that condition, it was no longer possible for shares to be traded in CLOB without registering with the KLSE. No one would buy if the shares would not become legally theirs. Therefore, forcing the real owners to register their deals with the KLSE as a condition of having the acquisitions recognised was able to put a stop to the role of front-man trustees. Everyone had to register with the KLSE. CLOB had no more role in the trading of shares. It had to close.

677

Meanwhile, we made the decision to peg the ringgit to the US dollar, a move which was sure to be controversial. But we had to determine the exchange rate of the ringgit soon after instructing the banks not to transfer money in their accounts in any transaction. We also had to be sure we had enough foreign exchange (mainly US dollars) in the banks and at Bank Negara should traders need to pay for their imports. And of course we had to ensure that there was enough ringgit in the banks to exchange with foreign currencies at the rate we fixed.

Malaysia had always insisted that the proceeds of the sale of Malaysian products to foreigners must be brought back and deposited in Malaysian banks. Some developing countries, Argentina for example, allow such proceeds to be kept abroad. (In the case of some Middle Eastern states, a vast fund of so-called "petrodollars" was never repatriated but allowed to flow back and forth in search of profitable investments around the world.)

In our case, this would have resulted in a continuous drain of money out of the country. Without access to the foreign exchange it earned, the country would not be able to pay for imports or repay loans. Because of this practice of repatriating our foreign earnings, Malaysia always had enough foreign exchange for our importers wishing to buy goods or services from abroad. When the Government fixed the exchange rate, it had to be able to guarantee the availability of foreign currencies to pay for those essential imports at the fixed rate.

We might even have enriched ourselves by strengthening the ringgit to its former pre-crisis rate of RM2.5 to one US dollar, as the ringgit had by then recovered somewhat after falling to almost RM5 to the dollar and was now hovering at between RM3.8 and RM4 to one US dollar. But if the ringgit was too strong because we set the exchange rate too high, Malaysian products would not be able to compete internationally with similar products from Thailand, the Philippines and Indonesia. We had to decide on an exchange rate that would not impoverish us too much but would still make our products competitive. We decided on RM3.8 to one US dollar.

We kept this a secret, but we needed Bank Negara and the KLSE to implement our decision. The Government had to oversee implementation of its plans virtually minute by minute. When we began putting these measures in place, we could not be sure whether or not the controls would be effective, or whether our decision on the mandatory registering of CLOB share sales could be carried out or would prove sustainable. But when we made the decision in the NEAC, it is worth noting that Anwar was still the Deputy Prime Minister and Minister of Finance. He did not disagree with the plan to stop the currency traders and restrain the Singapore CLOB.

To play devil's advocate, Noordin of ISIS came up with over 30 reasons why we should not carry out these plans. I had to argue against and demolish every one of those objections. The other NEAC members displayed varying levels of enthusiasm, with some pointing out that this had never been done by anyone before. True, it was risky and there could be a total collapse of the ringgit. A black market might also emerge, selling the ringgit at below the price we fixed. The country's finances and economy might go into a tailspin and fly completely out of control — we could not be sure of anything. But the argument that nothing must ever be done for the first time is an argument that appeals to the timid and the orthodox, not to someone who was responsible for his country in times of unprecedented difficulty.

Some pointed out that in many developing countries, people refused to be paid in local currencies and instead insisted on payment in US dollars. The ringgit might also be rejected for payments and if so, it would not be worth the paper it was printed on. I was to later learn that some NEAC members told the *Menteri Besar* of several states to try and stop me, but they were not willing to confront me to argue about currency trading and the CLOB, about which they knew little. They understood even less the complexity of the measures we were planning to take and the risks these measures posed. Even if any of them had well-founded doubts, they were in no position to argue their cases.

That worked in my favour. I slept well on our decision, but that did not mean I was not worried that what we planned to do could bring disaster to the country. I was frightened at the prospect of going against conventional wisdom, of going against all the experts, including those at the IMF and the World Bank. Our strategy was undoubtedly "contrarian", as it was soon dubbed by its critics. It went against all conventional wisdom and if we crashed, no one would help us. I might even have had to make my exit in disgrace, something I truly feared.

But I hated the idea of losing control over the country the way the Government of Indonesia had lost to the IMF. I disliked that eloquent picture of Camdessus standing over President Suharto with his arms folded, watching with almost smirking satisfaction as the President signed away Indonesian's control over its economy, the basis of its national sovereignty for which it had fought so hard and bravely against the Dutch in the 1940s. I certainly did not want Malaysia placed in that same situation. We had tried to persuade Indonesia not to give in to the IMF. The Indonesian Minister of Finance, Marie Muhammad, was in close contact with Anwar, who said he had asked Marie to advise Suharto not to sign.

The President, I was told, could not sleep by then. Some 40 million Indonesians had lost their jobs. The rupiah had collapsed from 2,000 to 16,000 to the dollar and there were riots in the capital city of Jakarta. Shops were torched and people killed. The Indonesians put the blame for the crisis on the Chinese Indonesians. They did not see the Americans and their control of the IMF as responsible for the currency crisis. When the IMF took control of Indonesian finances, the measures they forced the country to take, such as stopping food and fuel subsidies, only made matters worse and there were more riots. Thailand and the Philippines, which had both also submitted to the IMF, fared no better. Only South Korea was able to make some tangible recovery.

I simply had no faith in the IMF solutions which Anwar had imposed on the country. Ministers began complaining that they had no money for their development projects. All their perks had been reduced and the austerity measures imposed on them were hurting. Anwar wanted a surplus budget but it was just not possible with the ringgit's lowered purchasing power, so he cut the budget by 25 per cent. If we had kept on doing that we would not have any money in the Treasury. Worse would follow, and we too would end up surrendering our economic sovereignty.

680

I was determined to go through with our solution. At the last minute, Anwar rang me to say that Tan Sri Ahmad Mohd Don, the Bank Negara Governor, and his deputy Fong had sent in their letters of resignation. I was shocked but I remained determined to go ahead. I asked the third most senior officer of Bank Negara to see me. At the time, Tan Sri Dr Zeti Akhtar Aziz was Assistant Governor responsible for economics, foreign and money market operations and exchange controls.[3] I knew her, but not well. There was no time to find a new Governor so I immediately appointed her as Acting Governor. She came to my residence and I explained the situation and what she had to do. Fortunately, she was very cooperative and able. She said she would contact the banks and stop all transfers of large sums of money involved in currency trading. She of course had to allow payments to be made for business transactions.

---

[3] Tan Sri Dr Zeti Akhtar Aziz is the only woman Central Bank Governor in Asia. She is also the daughter of Professor Ungku Abdul Aziz Ungku Abdul Hamid, the country's first Malay economist and former Dean of the Faculty of Economics at the University of Malaya, and is the grandniece of UMNO founder Datuk Onn Jaafar.

On 1 September 1998, Zeti formally announced the implementation of currency controls and the pegging of the ringgit to the US dollar. She told the Press: "We had to act on our own, considering the international community has failed to come up with any meaningful solution to the global financial turmoil. Ideally, the world should act in concert, instead of forcing countries to act individually."

Zeti, who went on to become Governor and win several international awards for her leadership of a central bank, joined the NEAC and gave it good feedback on the current situation in the market and the behaviour of the ringgit. We were on the lookout for a black market in ringgit to make its appearance. We monitored prices and tried to make sure that no one sought to profiteer. We ensured adequate supplies of all necessities. The daily NEAC meetings continued. The banks were required to deposit all the foreign exchange they received in Bank Negara, which meant we were never short of foreign money to sell to bona fide importers. The ringgit exchange rate against the US dollar was maintained strictly at RM3.80 to one US dollar, which proved good for importers as well as exporters.

Businesses were happy to accept the ringgit at RM3.80 whenever they changed their US dollars or other currencies. They were also comfortable with our assurances that we would maintain the exchange rate for as long as it took for the situation to stabilise. They could budget for the whole year and not have to hedge against fluctuations in the value of the ringgit, which reduced their cost of doing business. Requiring all owners of shares to register with the KLSE and stopping the sale of Malaysian shares held in trustee companies also stopped the plunge in the KLSE, and within a short period, the KLCI rose from below 300 to over 800. The number of non-performing loans declined after the period of default was returned to six months, and the economy began to show signs of recovery.

During the crisis we had introduced several measures to help mitigate the problem. When property sales became stagnant we arranged for home ownership campaigns that brought together developers, potential buyers, financiers, government officers and lawyers. At the first promotion exhibition, RM3 billion worth of property was sold. To get the construction industry going again we decided to build 40,000 flats to house urban squatters. Since retail sales were lagging, we found places for goods to be exhibited by retailers and we helped negotiate lower prices where necessary. We studied reports on electricity consumption, the movement of cargo and containers at the ports, incoming tourists and airline passengers, vehicles registered and many other things. We knew in detail how the economy was performing and often we found ways to stimulate it.

The NEAC gave particular attention to the operations of Pengurusan Danaharta Nasional Bhd (the National Assets Management Company), Danamodal Nasional Bhd (the National Bank Refinancing Company) and the Corporate Debt Restructuring Committee (CDRC) which had all been set up to address the problem of non-performing loans and bank recapitalisation.

We did not allow the shares acquired through CLOB to be sold immediately in the market, for this would cause all share prices to fall. The owners of the shares had to register first with the KLSE. Later we set up a special company to buy up these shares, oversee their repatriation and then manage their gradual sale into the market in order not to disturb share prices generally. At first, the owners of those CLOB-traded shares were unhappy. But as the KLSE recovered, share prices increased by 200 per cent by the time our special company bought up their shares. They were spared the great financial loss that they had feared, and waiting a while to cash in proved profitable for them. The company also made a profit in dealing with those shares and the Government recovered the money it had outlaid in its bold rescue exercise.

The world condemned our currency controls and many economists said that they were not in keeping with the open-market trading system. Experts predicted disaster for Malaysia and gleefully anticipated its return with a begging bowl. But we were not deterred. We believed we had found the right answer to the plundering of small countries by the rich currency traders. It may have been unconventional, but it worked. Let others uphold economic doctrine — we had a country and ourselves to save. In the end, we recovered faster than all the countries that, freely or under duress, accepted loans from the IMF and submitted to its one-size-fits-all solution. The currency traders ceased their operations. Even the IMF eventually admitted that our way had worked, though they would not recommend it to other countries.

Joseph Stiglitz, the Nobel Prize-winning economist, endorsed our view.[4] Even Soros later acknowledged that Malaysia had done the right thing in not submitting to the IMF.

Ours was a solution that worked for us, but not many other developing countries were in our situation. It could only work for us because, in addition to our political will and rich sources of practical policy expertise, we had ample foreign currency reserves at our disposal in Bank Negara to defend our economic sovereignty. We also had huge savings which, in turn, were due to our responsible economic management over the years. Our success in turning back the challenge of the currency predators and the IMF was not due solely to our decisive actions at the time. It drew upon and vindicated the Government's entire economic stewardship over the years, especially since the 1970s and 1980s.

The currency crisis, however, was not the only problem we were grappling with. Just one day after Zeti announced Malaysia's currency controls, my problems with Anwar came to a dramatic head.

683

---

[4]    Joseph Stiglitz's book *Globalisation and its Discontents* criticises the IMF's handling of the financial crisis.

# Chapter 53:
## Anwar's Challenge

Four years after IGP Tun Hanif first told me about allegations linking Anwar to homosexual activities, someone sent me the book 50 Dalil Kenapa Anwar Ibrahim Tidak Boleh Jadi Perdana Menteri (50 Reasons Why Anwar Ibrahim Cannot Become Prime Minister). It was written by Datuk Khalid Jafri, a former editor of the Malay-language daily Utusan Malaysia.[1] The book was clearly a sensationalist attempt to make money so I did not read it, but the rumours about Anwar refused to go away.

Then in 1997, I received a letter from a woman named Ummi Hafilda Ali. Its contents disturbed me as there were more specific and detailed allegations of sodomy against Anwar. I later learnt that Ummi was the sister of Anwar's political secretary Mohd Azmin Ali.[2] I must admit that even then, I thought the accusations were far-fetched. Had the contents been about Anwar having affairs with women, I would have been less incredulous, but how could such a seemingly pious person possibly be involved in homosexual activities? I found it very difficult to believe that anyone in such a high position, an adult and a decent Muslim at that, would do such a thing. Even though her allegations corroborated the IGP's report of four years ago, I did not take them seriously. About a month later, Ummi sent me another letter, this time saying that she withdrew her allegations. I wondered why she would now deny what she had said previously.

Meanwhile, the police had continued their observation of the Deputy Prime Minister's activities, as was their usual practice. Even if I had asked them to stop, I doubt they would have. This time they had evidence, including pictures and confessions of the people involved. When the new IGP, Tan Sri Abdul Rahim Noor and his investigating officer Tan Sri Musa Hassan presented the evidence to me, I realised that I could not ignore the information. I said I wanted to meet the witnesses and speak to them personally. That was tricky because it meant I was involving myself directly in the matter. I was already well on the way to getting the currency crisis

684

---

[1] On 18 August 2005, the High Court awarded RM4.5 million in damages to Anwar in his libel suit against Khalid, who died from complications arising from chronic diabetes just a few days after.

[2] Today Mohd Azmin Ali is Deputy President of Anwar's Parti Keadilan Rakyat (People's Justice Party) and Member of Parliament for Bukit Antarabangsa.

resolved and I wanted to concentrate on that as well as the approaching 1998 Commonwealth Games. The Games mattered a great deal to me, so I was annoyed that these distractions were also demanding my attention.

It was some time before I met the witnesses. I saw them individually, and in private, at my official residence at Sri Perdana in Kuala Lumpur. I assured them that our conversations were confidential and that I just wanted to hear their stories for myself. One of the witnesses was Azizan Abu Bakar, who was the driver for Anwar's wife Datin Seri Dr Wan Azizah Wan Ismail. The police said Anwar had sodomised Azizan many times. I asked Azizan about the allegations and he was naturally frightened because Anwar was the Deputy Prime Minister. During our meeting he was very nervous and a little incoherent. Azizan told me in detail where the first incident took place. He said he was afraid as Anwar was a powerful man and could cause him much trouble. He said that was why he had not resisted.

I know how difficult it is to remember the exact dates and times when things happen so I was not particular about these details, but the meeting was enough to convince me that he was speaking the truth. In court, exact dates and times are crucial and are sufficient to convict or acquit someone, but I doubt if even lawyers and judges can remember exactly what they did a year ago. Some people may keep a diary but no one records everything he does every day.

I also interviewed four girls who told me about how they were persuaded to see a very influential person by an Indian man they knew by the name of Nalla. He had taken each girl separately to a house in Kenny Hills, a rich suburb in Kuala Lumpur. There they met a person they recognised as the Deputy Prime Minister. They were asked to undress with the purpose of having sex. Two of them said they refused but the other two consented. They were willing to talk to the police and to me but were adamant that they should not appear in court to give evidence. The police briefed me in detail about the results of their investigations and their opinion of evidence they had gathered. They too were convinced that the witnesses who saw me were telling the truth.

Faced with all this information from the police and from my own interviews, I felt I had to do something. I simply could not have a person of such dubious character succeeding me as Prime Minister of Malaysia; in fact, I could not have him in the Government at all. His actions and hypocrisy in masquerading as a highly religious individual were unacceptable, and I found the despicable means he employed to ensnare people and then ensure their silence appalling.

I called all the UMNO Menteri Besar, Chief Ministers and state heads to Sri Perdana for a meeting and asked the police to make the witnesses I had interviewed available. I then briefed the party leaders about what I had learnt about Anwar and showed them pictures of the witnesses. I asked whether they wanted to question the witnesses themselves, but after a prolonged discussion they all said they were convinced and there was no need to interview them.

I then asked them what action I should take. If I hid the evidence and allowed Anwar to continue in office, his behaviour might be uncovered and used to blackmail him. He would always be vulnerable, and by extension, so would Malaysia. Even I would be compromised, for if it was discovered that I knew and yet failed to take necessary action then I would be accused of covering up. Either way, I could not let him remain in office — I had to come clean and remove him. Once people knew why I had taken such action, I was confident that they would approve. The gathered leaders unanimously endorsed my proposed plan and said that they would back me if there was any backlash.

Unlike the removal of a judge, sacking Anwar did not require following Constitutional procedure. As Prime Minister I had the power to remove him as Deputy Prime Minister and dismiss him from the Cabinet just as I had the power to appoint him. But even after he ceased to be a member of the Government, he would still be a member of UMNO and continue to be its Deputy President. That, too, was not a tenable situation, but his removal as Deputy President and member of the party could be effected only by a decision of the UMNO Supreme Council.

At that time I was seriously planning to step down, so I had to make a quick decision. On 2 September 1998, I issued a statement through the national Press agency Bernama that Deputy Prime Minister Datuk Seri

Anwar Ibrahim had been dismissed from the Government. By then many people had read Khalid Jafri's book, which had been distributed to all the delegates attending the most recent UMNO General Assembly and was selling briskly at neighbourhood night markets. Many had also heard about Ummi Hafilda's letter, but most people were either not aware or not convinced about what had actually happened. There was widespread belief that Anwar's dismissal was political, for it was no secret that he had been trying to undermine my credibility and support among UMNO party members. His supporters had accused me of cronyism and corruption, and at the 1998 UMNO Annual General Assembly, some of them had been openly critical of me and my leadership. People knew I was aware that Anwar was behind these attacks but I was not yet in a position to publicly denounce his wrongdoing. I could only signal, but not expose these matters in my closing address. What could be explained in detail to the Menteri Besar and UMNO leaders could not be revealed to the people at large, so most understandably assumed that his dismissal was prompted by my fear that Anwar would unseat me.

Even now it is difficult to explain convincingly that I was not afraid of this happening. Believing I was popular with the majority of UMNO members, I was confident that I would win any party contest against Anwar. I had won against Tengku Razaleigh Hamzah and Tun Musa Hitam before, both of whom were known and tried UMNO stalwarts, while Anwar was a rank outsider who had been against the party in the past. I had brought him in and helped him rise in the UMNO hierarchy until he became Deputy President and subsequently, Deputy Prime Minister. UMNO members, I was sure, would see the ungratefulness of this impatient protégé and newcomer. To party veterans he was an upstart who had bruised the dignity of many a stalwart as he elbowed his way up through the UMNO ranks.

He may have had strong supporters who were committed, even obliged and indebted to him for one reason or another, but I was convinced that I would be able to defeat him should he challenge me. The belief that I dismissed him because I was afraid he would oust me is without basis. I dismissed him for two reasons only: he was unsuitable to continue serving in the Government and he was unsuitable to succeed me as Prime Minister.

I now had to bring Anwar's case to the UMNO Supreme Council. Since the Menteri Besar and Chief Ministers who I had already taken into my confidence were all also members of the Supreme Council, I expected strong support from them. But Anwar was also a party member, indeed, its Deputy President. That meant he would be present at the Council meeting — in fact, he would be sitting at my side.

The meeting was convened a few days later at UMNO Headquarters in the Putra World Trade Centre to decide Anwar's fate. I began by explaining in as much detail as I could why I had to dismiss him from the Government. With the subject of my exposition sitting right beside me, the situation was tense and I felt very uncomfortable. But I had no choice — I could not send him out since, as a member, he was entitled to attend the meeting. After I finished, I said that the UMNO Deputy President could now answer the allegations against him and state why he should not be dismissed.

During his long explanation, Anwar never once referred to the question of homosexuality, focusing only on the affairs with women. He declared that he had done nothing unusual and insisted that everyone, including all the members of the Supreme Council, had done such things. He banged the table once or twice to show his anger. The Council members listened to him attentively and I did not try to interrupt or stop him.

When he finished, the first to speak was Datuk Paduka Ibrahim Ali. Ibrahim said he had known Anwar for a long time, since the 1970s when they had both been detained at the Kamunting Detention Centre.[3] He criticised Anwar for banging the table and said that he was inclined to believe what I said because he had read Khalid Jafri's book and had seen Ummi Hafilda's letter (copies of the letter were apparently being publicly circulated). Ibrahim said he believed Anwar should not only be dismissed as Deputy Prime Minister, but also as Deputy President of UMNO and even as an UMNO party member.

As was my custom, I allowed everyone to speak. The majority of them did, mostly against Anwar, though none as strongly as Ibrahim. They supported my earlier action in dismissing him as Deputy Prime Minister, and some now voiced support for the suggestion that Anwar also be removed from his

---

3    Kamunting is a maximum security detention centre located near Taiping, Perak.

UMNO position. A few went further to urge that his UMNO membership be revoked.

I was not ready to discuss the action to be taken. After everyone had spoken I asked Anwar to respond to the views expressed by the Council members. He refused — he just got up and left. I then asked the Council what was to be done. I reminded them that there had been two suggestions: dismissal as Deputy President and expulsion from the party. The majority favoured his expulsion, which of course meant Anwar would also cease to be the party's Deputy President.

It was almost midnight by the time the meeting ended, but I stayed back to sign some papers while the other members left. I was told Anwar's supporters had gathered on the ground floor but the police would ensure nothing violent would happen. When I later went downstairs, I found about 60 of his followers in an ugly mood. They threw plastic water bottles at me before I could get into my car. They shouted angrily, hurling words like zalim (unjust or unfair) and "dictator". Anwar had apparently brought this group of loyalists with him and had spoken to them after the meeting. Protected by my bodyguards and the police, I knew that these people could not hurt me and that the situation was under control.

689

Up until that night I had been used to people being polite to me wherever I went, but this was a different experience entirely. I was surprised to see Anwar's supporters there. Others had been sacked before him, including Datuk Harun Idris, Aziz Ishak and even myself, but nothing like this had ever happened. In my experience, this dramatic excess was vintage Anwar.

After his sacking, he continued to play to his admiring gallery. He went all over the country, telling people that his dismissal was part of a conspiracy to prevent him from becoming Prime Minister, that it had been a purely political machination. He made no mention of any involvement in immoral activities. PAS, which had condemned Anwar when he was in UMNO, now rallied to his cause. The PAS Member of Parliament Mohamad Sabu, who in his previous speeches had hinted at Anwar's homosexual activities, was now delighted and literally embraced him. PAS members organised and attended rallies, some as large as 30,000 people, where Anwar spoke.

Most members of the audience were from PAS or were supporters, but many UMNO members also attended.

I did not want to make a major issue of his national barnstorming campaign because the Commonwealth Games were by then in full swing and I could not go around the country to explain the situation. It was a delicate matter and not one that was easily explained to a large audience. I did, however, call in our UMNO grassroots leaders to give them the details. Most believed me but a few shouted incoherent words and left. It was difficult to convince people that Anwar was not the underdog, nor was he the paragon of virtue that he had made himself out to be. He had spent much time ingratiating himself with UMNO division leaders and branch members, because I had left it to him to maintain the leadership's connections and lines of communication with the party activists and rank and file. But he had used these visits to promote himself, especially among the kampung people. He was able to lead Muslims in public congregational prayers and to give persuasive sermons. Given this, it was difficult for people to believe that he could commit acts which were absolutely against the teachings of Islam. In their thinking, if he was good, then as his adversary, I must be bad. This kind of simplistic logic, craftily personified by a master orator, is not easily countered. As a result I appeared to be unjust in the eyes of many pious Muslims.

A few days after Anwar's dismissal from the Government, Lim Kit Siang, the Parliamentary Opposition Leader, issued a Press statement requesting that I as the Prime Minister owed the country and the international community an explanation for Anwar's dismissal. The President of Aliran,[4] P. Ramakrishnan, also said that the public had a right to know the reasons for Anwar's dismissal. Furthermore, 14 non-governmental organisations (NGOs) issued a joint Press statement calling on me to "account properly" for Anwar's dismissal.

With these growing calls for an explanation from various quarters, I held a Press conference at my office on 22 September. At this conference, a journalist asked me why I had dismissed Anwar as Deputy Prime Minister,

---

[4]  Aliran Kesedaran Negara (Aliran) is a civil society movement that began in Penang in 1977. It publishes a magazine, *Aliran Monthly*, that seeks to address important social issues in Malaysia.

Minister of Finance and Deputy President of UMNO. I explained that I had initially disbelieved the allegations of homosexuality made against Anwar when they first surfaced, but I was later convinced when I personally interviewed Anwar's partner. Anwar then launched a defamation suit against me claiming RM100 million in damages.

The High Court later struck out Anwar's defamation suit on the basis that I was protected by the defences of justification (truth) and qualified privilege. Justification or truth is a complete defence in a suit for defamation. The High Court said that as Prime Minister, I was under a legal, moral and social duty to inform the nation of the matters concerning Anwar and his fitness for the public offices he had previously occupied. It had become a matter of public interest. I was under a duty to explain to the nation the response of the Government and UMNO to the several attacks made by Anwar. All these were matters of general public interest, which the public had every reason and an interest to know about. The High Court said that I had acted bona fide (in good faith) and bore no malice when I spoke those words concerning Anwar. Therefore, I was protected by the defence of qualified privilege. The Court of Appeal dismissed Anwar's appeal and again said that I was sheltered by the defences of justification and qualified privilege. The Federal Court also dismissed Anwar's application for leave to appeal and upheld the High Court decision.[5]

691

Meanwhile, events in Indonesia seemed to encourage Anwar and his supporters. On 21 May 1998, President Suharto had been overthrown through massive and sustained street demonstrations. Taking a leaf from the Indonesian anti-Suharto campaign, Anwar began to talk about Reformasi (Reformation) and made me out to be corrupt and in favour of cronyism. On 20 September, the day before the Games closed, Anwar called a massive rally to be held at Dataran Merdeka in central Kuala Lumpur, at the historic site where we had proclaimed our national Independence in 1957. To him and his sympathisers the choice of location may have been symbolically shrewd; but to those who thought like me and felt as many UMNO members did, it was a travesty. His rally was timed to coincide

---

[5]    The judgments of the High Court, Court of Appeal and Federal Court are reported as Dato' Seri Anwar Ibrahim v Dato' Seri Dr Mahathir Mohamad [1999] 7 CLJ 32 HC; [2001] 1 CLJ 519 CA; [2001] 1 CLJ 663 FC.

with Queen Elizabeth II's visit to St Mary's Cathedral, adjacent to that historic site. This was an outrageous act of disrespect to a visiting head of state but Anwar did not care. We stationed police personnel in the area and made sure that Queen Elizabeth would not be in any danger.

He went as far as to urge his followers to burn down my house and the UMNO headquarters. One group actually did manage to break into the UMNO building and vandalise some rooms. Another group came within one kilometre of my house, but at that point the police arrived and managed to disperse them. The police, however, could not ignore Anwar's demonstrations any longer; Games or no Games. On the evening of 20 September, they arrested him at his house.

I knew there would be more problems but I hoped they would not unfold while the Games were still taking place. The many foreign journalists who were there to cover the event saw in Anwar's rebellion an opportunity to condemn Malaysia for arresting an Opposition leader. That is the kind of news they love. Local journalists who knew the background confined themselves largely to reporting on the progress and results of the Games, especially Malaysia's sterling performance. Their reporting on the demonstrations was factual. But when we gave a lunchtime reception to the Press at the Mint Hotel, which was the Press Centre during the Games, a woman journalist from Australia asked about Anwar. She was cynical about the accusation of immorality against him. I had forgotten that in most ethnic European societies, homosexuality and sodomy between consenting adults was normal. For them, Anwar had done nothing wrong.

At that time I was still overseeing the implementation of currency controls. Foreign journalists and observers said that the differences I had with Anwar over the handling of the currency crisis were also among the reasons why I dismissed him, but this was simply not true. Our differences were worth a good argument in the Cabinet, but they did not merit such drastic action. It was not necessary anyway, for as a member of the NEAC, Anwar agreed with my ideas on currency controls, at least outwardly. Some people also suggested that he was behind the resignations of the Governor and Deputy Governor of Bank Negara, but at that time I suspected nothing. The claim that I dismissed Anwar because of our differences in the handling of the currency crisis is flawed. Nor was he removed for political reasons, such as for his attempts to undermine party support for me — I could easily handle that as well without having to resort to dismissal.

When the IGP informed me that the police had decided to arrest Anwar for incitement to violence, I was apprehensive. I knew his sympathisers would not take the arrest quietly and, moreover, it would make a political martyr of him. I advised the IGP not to use violence or to handcuff Anwar when arresting him. Instead, the police did what they always do — they followed standard procedures and went to his house wearing hoods, broke the door down and handcuffed him. He was thrown into a police van and taken to police headquarters.

I expected him to be charged in court immediately but for several days, nothing happened. Then I was told he was being held under the Internal Security Act. I asked the police repeatedly why he had not yet been charged, but they only gave me vague answers. Finally, I learnt he had sustained a black eye during his detention and the police wanted it to heal before producing him in court in front of the cameras. The bruise, however, was taking a long time to fade away and as I was also anxious that he should not be detained under the ISA, I told the police that we simply could not wait any longer.

Anwar was charged on 29 September 1998, nine days after his arrest. It was his first appearance in public and the black eye was still clearly visible. As a doctor, I know how easy it is to get a black eye so I initially thought he had knocked his head. I never imagined that someone would assault him. It angered people when I suggested that his injury may have been self-inflicted, but I honestly did not think the police would beat him up, particularly after I had personally instructed the IGP to be careful.

As it turned out, it was IGP Rahim himself who was responsible for the black eye. He had allowed Anwar to provoke him and had lashed out, but in the process he handed over long-term political capital that Anwar and his supporters were able to use to great advantage. Rahim did me no favours politically — in fact, he did much harm to Malaysia's international standing. Anwar's supporters and the Opposition parties were glad to have tangible evidence of my "dictator-like" ways, and they displayed posters of

Anwar and his black eye all over the country. His supporters made it seem like I was personally responsible for this brutal treatment, even though I had tried to ensure that no such thing would happen.

Anwar was charged separately with corruption and sodomy but both charges were related to allegations that he had asked a senior police officer, Datuk Mohamad Said Awang, the Director of the Special Branch, to threaten Ummi Hafilda and cause her to withdraw her first letter to me. The corruption trial, which started on 2 November 1998, lasted more than five months. There was much excitement in the court during Mohamad Said's testimony when he related how Anwar had instructed him to "turn over" Ummi Hafilda and get her to withdraw and deny the contents of her letter to me. This constituted corruption and abuse of authority and the court found him guilty. Despite all of Anwar's legal efforts since then, all the appellate courts have upheld this conviction.

The sodomy trial began on 7 June 1999. Following its progress in the newspapers was depressing, as the prosecution bungled their case on several occasions. In one instance that particularly annoyed me, the defence claimed that sodomy had not taken place on a particular day as was charged. The Attorney-General Tan Sri Mohtar Abdullah did not say anything, as if agreeing that the crime had never occurred, and the newspapers then reported that there was no case of sodomy. But even if it had not taken place on a particular day, it did not mean that it had not happened at all. The problem with our prosecutors is that they are civil servants and they do not know the criminal mind. It was very frustrating to watch because they were not doing a good job and I could not do anything about it. They presented a lot of irrelevant evidence in court and the public became increasingly cynical, and began to be less convinced that there was a case. Even though the High Court eventually found Anwar guilty, he was able to score several points and leave many Malaysians convinced that he was the victim of a political conspiracy.

But how anyone could believe this, I really could not understand. To conspire against Anwar in this way I would have had to take the police, the Attorney-General and his prosecutors, their witnesses, the judge, the forensic laboratory experts and many others into my confidence. Surely someone in this small army of co-conspirators would have eventually leaked details of our plot to the public. Though some witnesses were hostile towards me, nobody came forward to say that I had forced him to tell lies to support me. One of these hostile witnesses was the former Director-General of the Anti-Corruption Agency (ACA), Datuk Shafee Yahya, who had earlier accused me of interfering with an ACA investigation into then-Director-General of the Economic Planning Unit, Tan Sri Ali Abul Hassan Sulaiman. In 1998 I had received a complaint that the ACA had been offensive during his investigation and so, knowing how Government officers could sometimes be overzealous in their duties, I asked Shafee to explain the situation. Our meeting did not go well and Shafee became angry, accusing me of interfering with his duties. Actually, the affair with the ACA had nothing to do with Anwar's case. But Shafee had his day in court and seemed to be happy to vilify me.

Though the Court of Appeal upheld the conviction by the High Court, the Federal Court, by a majority decision, quashed the conviction and freed Anwar of the sodomy charge. The Federal Court said that the evidence did not corroborate Azizan's story, i.e. that he was sodomised by Anwar and Sukma Darmawan Sasmitaat Madja (Anwar's adopted brother) at the specified time, date and place. Most Malaysians are ignorant of the contents of the judgment of the Federal Court, which acquitted Anwar on a technicality due to the error relating to the date of the incident. They are not aware that the majority of the Federal Court had held that in their judgment they found "… evidence to confirm that the appellants [Anwar and Sukma] were involved in homosexual activities and we are more inclined to believe that the alleged incident at Tivoli Villa did happen, …"[6] Although the conviction has been quashed on a technicality, the conclusive judicial findings of the Federal Court that Anwar and Sukma were involved in homosexual activities, remain intact.

695

Another alleged element of my "conspiracy" against Anwar involved my supposed interference with the judicial system. I have often been accused of emasculating the courts, humiliating the judges, and of being hostile to the legal profession. I have dealt with these matters elsewhere in these

---

[6]  The Federal Court Judgment is reported as *Dato' Seri Anwar Ibrahim v PP & Another Appeal* [2004] 3 CLJ 737 FC.

pages. Here I only need to say that Anwar was tried in court in a case that I thought was clear-cut. Malays are generally religious and conservative and, for them, sodomy is a sin. They will not condone such acts or show any sympathy for people who indulge in them. But Anwar's reputation for religious piety persuaded many people that it was simply absurd to accuse him of behaving as he did, even when the courts found that he had.

The local and foreign Press were also loath to let go of the image of me as a dictator. The foreign Press, especially, judged Anwar to be innocent and some Malaysians agreed with them. The Opposition parties and their newspapers never failed to put me in the worst light possible. I was made to feel as if I was the one who was on trial, and if one were to believe them, my whole life and work were devoted to destroying Anwar and his career.

Anwar again sued me for defamation based on the response I gave to a question posed by a journalist after I had delivered my opening address at the conference entitled "Human Rights and Globalisation", organised by SUHAKAM[7] on 9 September 2005. To a question relating to the Anwar issue, I explained that in our society, sodomy was not acceptable and that I could not have a person who was like that in my Cabinet, who might succeed me and become the Prime Minister. I also said: "Imagine having a gay Prime Minister, nobody would be safe".

However, the High Court struck out Anwar's defamation suit against me, again on the basis that I was protected by the defences of justification and qualified privilege. Anwar's subsequent appeal to the Court of Appeal was also struck out due to several defects in his Appeal Record filed by his lawyers.[8] On 24th November 2010, the Federal Court delivered its judgment dismissing Anwar's application for leave to appeal to the Federal Court.

At the time of Anwar's dismissal, members of the UMNO Supreme Council often complained about the Press and would invariably recommend that the critics be removed, especially if their criticisms were directed at me personally. Then, when senior editors were removed or transferred, I would be blamed by people outside the Supreme Council, who assumed that I was

---

[7] SUHAKAM is the Malaysian Human Rights Commission.

[8] The judgments of the High Court and the Court of Appeal are reported as *Dato' Seri Anwar Ibrahim v Tun Dr Mahathir Mohamad* [2007] 5 CLJ 118 HC; [2010] 1 CLJ 444 CA.

the one who had initiated or demanded their removal. I must admit that I never refuted these allegations, but I went along with the Supreme Council decisions because I did not want people who were so apparently concerned about me to feel that I was letting them down. I thought they were very sincere in their show of support. But once I stepped down from office, they became equally quick to turn against me in order to please their new boss. It was under the new boss' leadership, incidentally, that Tan Sri Abdullah Ahmad, the editor of the New Straits Times, was removed with no qualms. There were several other senior editors of the NST and Utusan Malaysia who were also removed. No one accused my successor of acting against the editors who did not support him.

Like it or not, I must accept that this is what Malaysians are like. When you are the top man people will try to read your mind and try to do what they believe you want. They get angry on your behalf, and you will disappoint them if you are not as angry as they are. As I related earlier, when former Australian Prime Minister Paul Keating called me recalcitrant I was not angry — he was just saying that I was refusing to fall in line with everybody else and that description generally applies quite well to me. I don't always do what others do. Most Malaysians like that side of me, as it has allowed our country to show that it is able and ready to stand up for itself. But people expected me to be offended by Keating's remark and they were insulted on my behalf. As I did not want to embarrass them, I played along.

The Anwar affair and the currency crisis destabilised Malaysia and it was my duty to restore the country's political and economic balance. By late 1998 the economy was already showing signs of restored health, but the political situation did not improve as much. Anwar's Reformasi movement and the setting up of his Justice Party, or Parti Keadilan, were accompanied by more street demonstrations and large public rallies.

Although I retired as Prime Minister some years ago, the allegations of Anwar's homosexual activities did not fade into oblivion. Eyebrows were raised again when fresh allegations of Anwar's homosexual activities surfaced. This time Anwar's 23-year-old aide, Mohd Saiful Bukhari Azlan, alleged that he was sodomised by Anwar on 26 June 2008 at a condominium in Kuala Lumpur. On 7 August that year, Anwar was charged in court for sodomising Saiful.

On 15 August Saiful swore on the Quran in front of mosque officials at the Federal Territory Mosque that he had been sodomised by Anwar. This was Saiful's way of proving that he was speaking the truth. Saiful then challenged Anwar to also swear on the Quran and deny sodomising him. On 16 August, I dared Anwar to swear on the Quran to prove that he was indeed innocent. I said that as a prominent figure on the Malaysian political scene, Anwar should act in accordance with public sentiment and take the oath on the Quran and give a sworn statement on the sodomy allegation made by Saiful. Anwar did not take the oath on the Quran to deny that he had sodomised Saiful. As the trial is ongoing, I will refrain from making any comment on it.

Anwar is an undeniably charismatic man and he knows how to get people to support him. All that I had done for Anwar in the past has been brushed aside. I was seen as having victimised him and throwing him into jail, as if there were no trial. Whenever my name is mentioned in a book or article, I am described as the Prime Minister who threw his deputy into jail. The fact that he was properly charged and tried in court is never mentioned.

698

I am a forgiving person by nature, and I rehabilitated the careers of many people who tried to undermine me politically. I even named one of them as my successor after Anwar was sacked as Deputy Prime Minister. But I find it difficult to forgive Anwar for demonising me in the eyes of the whole world.

Anwar should have been the Prime Minister of Malaysia today. But if he is not, it is because of his own actions. He left me no choice but to remove him and I did what I thought was best for the country. I may have made many mistakes, but removing Anwar was not one of them.

# Chapter 54:
# 1998: Great Games, Remarkable Gains

Today I think of 1998 as one of my most challenging years as Prime Minister. It was the year of the Asian financial crisis, the Commonwealth Games and Datuk Seri Anwar Ibrahim's dismissal. Ironically, it was also the year when I had planned to step down from office.

I had intended to go after the 16th Commonwealth Games, which was the biggest sporting event ever staged in Malaysia and the first Commonwealth Games to be hosted in Asia. I thought it would be the high point of my premiership and the perfect time to retire.

I had been keen to host the Games as they would raise Malaysia's profile and draw people to the country to see the progress we had made. I was fed up with people half believing that we lived on trees. Holding the Games would also be good for tourism, not just for the duration of the event but for long afterwards. The prestige that comes from holding international events is far-reaching, and the Commonwealth Games are second only to the Olympics in terms of the number of participating countries and athletes. Some of the competitors would even be Olympic champions.

699

The ability to organise such complex, large-scale, multifaceted events was also something we wanted to develop. I had set up a unit to stage international conferences shortly after becoming Prime Minister, but I noticed that our people were still not doing things properly. For example, they would fail to provide interpreters and protocol officers, and the routes to be taken by visitors were not correctly identified and mapped out.

We made our bid to host the Games in 1992 and it involved much effort. We were up against Adelaide and the Australian delegation went all out in their bid. They said Malaysia was only interested in boosting tourism, and they also claimed that athletes would find it very difficult to perform in our hot and humid climate. On our part, we simply invited those who were involved in organising the Games to see Malaysia and judge for themselves whether we were capable of hosting. This was where our policy of being friendly to developing countries proved to be useful, as they were now inclined to be fair to us. In the end, that made the difference. Small developing countries were not going to make us rich, but there would be occasions when we needed friends and supporters, and this was one of them. Malaysia was chosen by a majority of the 66 Commonwealth Games Federation members who cast their votes in a secret ballot on 21 July 1992 in Barcelona, Spain.

I took a great deal of interest in the preparations for the Games. We decided to build a new sports complex in Bukit Jalil outside the city centre. With huge numbers of vehicles already clogging the city streets, the old stadium in the middle of Kuala Lumpur was no longer suitable. We needed a new and bigger stadium, another for indoor events, an Olympic-sized pool and a games village for the participants. We identified a number of existing playing fields in and around Kuala Lumpur, which were suitable for various games, and which would be needed when several events had to be held simultaneously. We also built a shooting range in Langkawi. The organisers had wanted to hold the shooting competition in Kuala Lumpur, but I thought it would be good if the people of Langkawi were given a chance to attend at least a part of the Games. Besides, it was also an opportunity for participants to see what an attractive tourist destination the island is.

The new Games complex was designed and built entirely by Malaysians. It was important to me that venues were adequate not just for the impending Games, but perhaps for the Olympics as well. The day may come — maybe not in my lifetime — when we will host this most prestigious of sporting events. I don't like piecemeal extensions so by spending a little bit more at the initial stages, we might avoid the need for ugly and costly additions later. What we built served our purpose nicely. One of the features of the main stadium was the roof which was held up by cable tension, a considerable feat of engineering.

We held a series of dry runs to identify and correct any flaws in the facilities and arrangements. No matter how much you may have worked things out on paper, there is nothing like trying them out because you will always find things you thought would work that actually do not. We were also worried that we would not complete the work on time, so I went to the worksites often and asked for progress reports. I knew that if I didn't and, for example, supplies of a particular building material ran short, the project people would simply wait, pleading that they could not go on. Delay and inactivity do not bother some people. So sometimes you have to push.

The Games were held from 11 to 21 September and they were judged to be a great success. A record number of 70 countries and territories, and 3,638 athletes took part. A few team events such as rugby, hockey and cricket were included for the first time, drawing world-class sportsmen and women. For me, the highlight was that Malaysia did very well overall and we won 10 gold medals, our biggest Games haul ever.

My schedule was programmed so that I could attend most of the finals, with the most important one being the 100-metre dash. At the last minute, Olympic medallist Ato Boldon of Trinidad and Tobago had decided to take part in the Games, so everyone was looking forward to the race. Many of our guests told us that they thought this was among the best-organised Commonwealth Games ever, and everyone involved was pleased with the facilities and with how the events were programmed and coordinated. The spectators also seemed to have enjoyed themselves. When I rode in an open-top car around the track during the opening ceremony, the crowd's thunderous applause felt genuine and it really warmed the heart.

The Games were the one bright spot at a time when other matters in the country were not going well and I was fighting battles on many fronts. Besides the currency crisis, Anwar had begun going around the country campaigning against me. There was even the threat that he would lead a demonstration of his followers to the closing ceremony at the complex, so I was advised not to ride around in the convertible I had used at the opening. Security considerations cannot be ignored, but I was very disappointed.

There were also minor hitches disrupting the smooth flow of the Games. Queen Elizabeth II had flown in for the closing ceremony and things went without any problems until she was to make her speech. At the end she was supposed to say "I declare the Games closed", which was the cue for the fireworks to start. Unfortunately, the person who invited the Queen to the podium used the word "closed" before her and that set off the fireworks. She tried to speak above all the noise, but eventually gave up.

Still, the Games proved that we had the capacity to organise international events. After we had staged the Commonwealth Heads of Government Meeting (CHOGM) in Kuala Lumpur in 1989, Harare, the next host, was told it had a tough act to follow. Even if we had been asked to hold the Olympic Games, I felt confident we would now do a good job.

While we had proved ourselves to be efficient organisers, we continued to be poor at managing our facilities. We want beautiful buildings but we don't seem to know how to maintain them. At the old Seri Perdana for example, the Prime Minister's residence in Kuala Lumpur, a pool was built under the staircase for keeping Japanese koi fish. But it never saw a drop of water and it ended up being used as a storage area. In many places there are beautiful fountains and clocks which do not work. With our new impressive Games complex, we now sorely needed managers who could ensure events would continue to be held at the facilities long after the Games were over. They did not need to be just sporting events; concerts and other musical performances would also have been suitable. This did not happen often, although some schools do hold their sports carnivals there. We seem capable of building grand facilities but are less than talented at putting them to good use. Even the Putrajaya International Conference Centre[1] has been underutilised since its opening when the Organisation of the Islamic Conference summit was held there in 2003.

We tried as much as possible to encourage the managers to promote the use and maintenance of these facilities, but often they had no idea what to do. There is frequently no budget for it or, if there is, it is a trivial sum, insufficient even to keep the place clean. We have been developing our country for over 50 years and we have been able to transform it into quite a wealthy nation. But we have not developed an appreciation for what we have, nor do we have a strong sense of responsibility.

I think we did better with the Kuala Lumpur International Airport (KLIA) in Sepang, another of what critics call my "megaprojects". Originally we wanted to put in another runway at Subang International Airport but there was not enough land. To do so we would have had to acquire land

702

---

[1]    Located in the fifth precinct of the new administrative centre, construction of the Putrajaya International Conference Centre began in 2000 and was completed in 2003.

belonging to the Rubber Research Institute of Malaysia (RRIM), and cut down irreplaceable rubber trees planted long ago for research purposes.

History shows that we have never been very good at predicting the growth of air travel. Our first airport was located in Sungai Besi and as early as the Tunku's time, it became clear that it was too small for our needs and too near the city to be expanded. New aircraft were also making a great deal of noise. But the problem the Tunku faced was that people did not want the inconvenience of having the airport located too far away. They wanted it to remain near the city and even suggested relocating the nearby railway line underground so that the runway at Sungai Besi could be extended. The Tunku eventually moved the airport to Subang, where it encroached a little on land belonging to the RRIM. The Institute's expatriate British scientists protested and resigned over the cutting down of a few rubber trees.

The projection then was that Kuala Lumpur would handle a maximum of 400,000 passengers a year, which meant that an airport with one small terminal building and one runway would be sufficient. Subang International Airport also had the longest runway in Southeast Asia at the time, which made the Tunku very proud. The projection seemed valid since the cost of air travel was beyond what most people could afford at that time and so was not yet popular. But by the 1990s, passenger traffic had reached 10 million a year.

We now needed an additional runway to handle a greater number of flights. Besides requiring more land from the RRIM, building a new runway at Subang would involve relocating industries which had grown around the airfield. There were also housing estates which would be very costly to acquire, and, we had to ask ourselves, what would happen when traffic increased in the future and a third runway would be needed? Clearly, we needed a new airport with enough land for expansion, but it was difficult to find enough vacant land conveniently close to the city. People living close to the proposed airport site would also definitely object to its location. At Tokyo's Narita International Airport, for example, a second runway could not be built for years because local farmers refused to move out. Their protest against the airport even turned violent and high fences had to be erected and a large police contingent deployed to prevent vandalism.

To ensure enough room for future expansion, we had no choice but to find a location far from the city. We finally identified a parcel of land almost 50km south of Kuala Lumpur, and though this was quite a distance, it was the only piece of land available which had relatively few houses. We had to look ahead, beyond our own lifetimes, to think of expansion 100 years from now. We did not want the same demand for expansion to bedevil future governments. We could not anticipate what shape air travel would take that far into the future, but we knew that air travel would continue to grow. To cope with projected needs, we had to set aside enough land now, before people started building homes close by as airports naturally become growth centres. So we acquired 25,000 acres for the new airport, sufficient to build five runways, two terminal buildings, four satellite buildings and the ability to handle 125 million passengers a year.

I wanted KLIA to be built quickly but the tendering process for such a project could take as many as three years, with enough documents to fill three large rooms. Trying to make sure there would be no bias in the selection of consultants and contractors was important, although the process of doing this was, as I have discussed in an earlier chapter, tricky and unclear.

My desire to build the airport quickly may have resulted in cutting a few corners in the tender process, but when you build things on time or complete them ahead of schedule, you gain. You can save, for example, on the rental of another building leased for temporary use. I have always believed that if you are going to lose money anyway, it is better to get a building done well and early by someone capable than to rely upon someone who may be cheaper but who will do a slipshod job or may not even complete the project.

We appointed Public Works Department engineer Tan Sri Jamilus Hussein to oversee the construction of the entire airport, which began in 1994. A special unit was also set up under the chairmanship of a senior treasury official, Tan Sri Clifford Herbert, to manage the project and resolve any problems. It was gratifying to see our local team managing and coordinating construction work that at times involved an international force of 25,000 workers. The team was able to build roads, specialised and sophisticated buildings and other facilities simultaneously. Since the workers came from Pakistan, Bangladesh, Indonesia and other countries, naturally there were communication problems. Local and foreign contractors had to be managed and directed, and we had to provide accommodation and recreation for all of them. There were quarrels between the different nationalities from time to time, but these blew over. A temporary hotel also had to be built to accommodate the numerous experts and consultants who had to be close to the site for long periods.

Before building began, a few problems had to be solved. For example, the airport site was located on peat soil, which was too soft for the runways. Hundreds of lorries carried away the peat soil that had been dug up by dozens of mechanical hoes, and then carried in limestone and red earth to fill the void. Still, the airport took shape very quickly. Finally, the day came when a Boeing 747 made a trial landing on the first runway. It landed and took off perfectly to the cheers of visiting guests and officials.

Once the construction was completed, the biggest problem we faced was that the multifarious airport operations had to be moved from Subang to Sepang in a single night. Our people went to see how the Munich airport had carried out this transfer exercise. I was invited to take the first domestic flight out from KLIA to Langkawi at 7.20am on 30 June 1998, the morning after the big relocation exercise. The VIP bedroom where my wife and I slept was as cold as a freezer, but the flight went off without any problem. Once I got to Langkawi however, I was told that there had been chaos at the airport that morning as machines broke down and people got lost because of inadequate signage. The airport staff themselves were still not familiar with the facilities and were unable to help the passengers find their way. The local Press went to town with the failures, disregarding the dimension of the massive overnight transfer operation from Subang.

It was, frankly, an amazing feat, and things cannot be expected to work perfectly from the first hour of the first day. Modern airports are extremely complex in design and operation. Arriving passengers have to be separated from those who are departing. Their luggage, passports and health certificates have to be examined. They have to be moved along quickly to avoid congestion, and with the large commercial aircraft that are now flying the skies, the number of passengers involved is huge. When planes arrived at the main terminal building there was no problem, but the trouble started when passengers arrived at the satellite building. Their luggage had to be picked up, loaded onto trucks and brought to the conveyor belt in the main terminal building. These bags were exposed to pilferage, a problem that still has not been fully resolved.

Most other problems, however, were sorted out fairly quickly and KLIA has since become a showpiece for the country. It is repeatedly recognised as the best, intermediate-sized airport in the world. Foreigners, especially those who have read unfavourable comments about Malaysia, arrive at our airport and change their minds immediately. Seeing the huge, ultra-modern structure served by six-lane highways as well as the variegated development all the way to the city convinces them that this is not a typical Third World country mired in backwardness. The road to Sepang used to pass through a swamp but today, there are housing estates on either side. When you build infrastructure, I have always believed, you stimulate growth. The airport has been the catalyst for this multi-billion-dollar development.

The total cost of the airport was about RM9 billion. This compares well with the USD20 billion (RM72 billion) for Hong Kong's international airport, which opened a few days before KLIA and which took longer to resolve its teething problems. The investment by the Government was amply justified. I do not know how much we have earned from KLIA, but we now handle almost 23 million passengers annually and a great deal of cargo. I cannot imagine how things would have stood if we were still using Subang as our international airport. By the time we moved operations to KLIA, the Subang airport was handling some 14 million passengers a year. Despite having two terminals added to the complex, it was literally bursting at the seams.

KLIA is one of the best examples of Malaysia's project management and construction ability. After the airport was completed I told Jamilus — who was made a Tan Sri the night the Yang di-Pertuan Agong officially launched KLIA — to form a company to bid for other airport construction contracts elsewhere in Malaysia and abroad. That company now has the capacity to design and construct fully modern, well-equipped airports anywhere.

KLIA's first phase — with the main terminal building and one satellite building — was designed to handle 25 million passengers a year. The low-cost airline AirAsia[2] wanted to operate out of Subang, but that would have meant KLIA would lose out on aircraft movements and the number of passengers. The Government insisted that they stay in KLIA, but they did not want to use facilities such as the aerobridge, which would have increased their operation costs. They wanted a place where they could keep their costs low with minimum expenditure, so a low-cost terminal has now been built.[3] KLIA's main terminal building and satellite building lost several million passengers a year as a result. However, the low-cost airline has brought more than 10 million passengers a year.

Overall, KLIA has turned out to be the airport I had hoped it would be. Its infrastructure truly became world-class in April 2002 with the launch of the Express Rail Link (ERL), a RM2.4 billion medium-speed train service that connects it to the Kuala Lumpur Sentral transportation hub in the city. Passengers can check in at KL Sentral's City Air Terminal. With an ERL service, which runs at a top speed of 160km/hour, every 15 minutes, they can travel the 50km between KL and KLIA in just 28 minutes. Our ERL is very similar to the rail system that connects Heathrow Airport to Paddington Station in central London, but we were able to build our system to cover about double the distance, at a much lower cost. It usually costs about RM157 million/km to build such a train service — we did it for RM35 million/km. This reduction allows us to give world-class service at a third of world prices, and the ERL provides the cheapest fare-per-kilometre in the world for rapid rail transit. Since we had no knowledge or experience in this field, there was a lot of foreign input in constructing the ERL. The project was undertaken by Siemens of Germany and Express Rail Link Sdn Bhd, a stakeholder of which is YTL Bhd, one of the best-known construction companies in Malaysia. Together, they were able to complete the project ahead of schedule and within the budget. With the ERL, KLIA is now on par with other modern airports in the world, and it also remains competitive as a regional air transport hub.

---

[2]  AirAsia is Malaysia's first low-cost airline. Established by DRB-HICOM in 1993, it began operating in 1996. It was then acquired by Tune Air, a private company, in 2001.

[3]  The Low Cost Carrier Terminal or LCCT is located about 10km from KLIA and opened in March 2006.

Around the same time, we built our Formula One racing circuit, which was adjacent to KLIA. I had reasons for wanting Formula One racing in Malaysia — there was the tremendous exposure to be gained from television coverage of the championship, as well as the opportunity for Malaysian engineers to acquire racing car engine technology.

I remember telling the Press in 1996 that we had a definite agenda. We wanted Malaysia to become better known and this was one way of publicising the country. The exposure would be huge and the audience enormous, with over 6.1 million viewers from 201 countries. Based on my calculations, this translated into 26,400 hours of coverage with an average "live" viewing of 367 million people per race, backed by a trackside attendance of over 2.4 million people. In Japan, the charge for a three-minute advertisement on TV is RM1 million. We did not pay a single sen for the three days Sepang was on TV worldwide.

We endorsed the World Formula One Championship twice, well before the F1 came to Malaysia. PETRONAS also entered into a five-year contract with the Red Bull-Sauber team which, among others, allowed the team to carry the words "Malaysia and PETRONAS" on the sides, front and back of the cars.

In our bid to host a World Formula One motor racing championship event, we had to compete with China, South Korea and Indonesia, but my hopes were raised in 1994 when I received a letter from Bernie Ecclestone. As Vice President of the International Automobile Federation (FIA) and head of the Formula One Constructors Association — the latter holds the rights to the F1 — I was aware that Ecclestone was the man who could make or break a country's bid to host a leg of the F1. In his letter, he said: "To be included in the Formula One Grand Prix, countries must be in a position to support a world-class event. I have confidence that your country can do this."

I left the job of constructing the racing circuit to Malaysia Airports Berhad, in the capable hands of Tan Sri Basir Ismail, its Executive Chairman. We made sure that once it was completed, the RM300 million racing track would not affect the activities at KLIA. Up to 32 different races could be held at the track a year. It was no use building a circuit with just the Formula

One in mind, since it would only take place for three days annually. The circuit had to be for other events as well, such as the Formula Asia race and the weekly amateur races held at the Shah Alam racing circuit. Finally, after a record 14-month construction, the Sepang International Circuit was officially opened in early 1999.

While the Commonwealth Games displayed our organising capabilities, the Kuala Lumpur Airport at Sepang and the Express Rail Link took us several steps forward towards our target of becoming a developed country by 2020. Along that national journey, 1998 was a challenging year but in the end it proved to be a year of great Games and remarkable gains for us. Full of uncertainties at the time, in retrospect it stands out as a year of notable achievement.

# Chapter 55:
# Financial Crisis Fallout

The currency controls we imposed helped to staunch the bleeding caused by the financial crisis, but in the immediate aftermath, we still found ourselves facing the problem of having several high-profile companies teetering on the edge of bankruptcy. Among the big companies which faced the threat of collapse were recently-privatised corporations such as Malaysia Airlines, companies that managed the Light Rail Transit systems, the wastewater treatment company Indah Water Konsortium, and Renong, a conglomerate that had initially been set up to manage UMNO's assets.

We did not like companies to fail because they then became our problem in several ways. The Government collects no taxes from failed companies. Often it must also pick up the pieces, work out an alternative way for the delivery of essential services, deal with the human fallout of company failure, and, if the company is a recently-privatised one, suffer political consequences as well. When a company becomes bankrupt it tends to drag others down. Workers lose their jobs and subcontractors also incur losses. Loans may turn bad and the banks too are affected. When one company is bankrupted, it is difficult to appreciate the effect on the community and overall economy. If a large number of companies are bankrupted, the devastating results are soon felt by everyone and by the nation. If that can be avoided or if corrections can be made, there is no reason why even one functioning or remediable company should be allowed to go under.

A revived company can contribute towards the well-being of the owners and employees and will pay taxes to the Government. The idea that inefficient or struggling companies must immediately be closed down is the extreme rather than the reasonable version of capitalist thinking.

Among the measures we took to mitigate the impact of the crisis was the creation of three agencies to deal with banking and corporate liquidity. Pengurusan Danaharta Nasional Berhad (Danaharta) was set up in June 1998 to resolve the issue of non-performing loans. Danamodal Nasional Berhad (Danamodal) was created in August that year to recapitalise our banking system, while the Corporate Debt Restructuring Committee

(CDRC) focused on making sure that viable businesses continued to be financed. All three agencies successfully met their targets and recovered billions of ringgit in loans and debt restructuring.

Among the companies we had to salvage was Malaysia Airlines, which had been privatised and taken over by Tan Sri Tajuddin Ramli. He had borrowed RM1.8 billion to pay for his controlling shares but the financial crisis left the company severely in debt and haemorrhaging money. Since he had taken over the company, Malaysia Airlines had incurred debts of RM9.4 billion by the end of the year 2000.

The company had been doing well when it was sold to Tajuddin in 1994, and his acquisition of Malaysia Airlines had been seen as a coup. At that time Tajuddin was the owner of Celcom, a cellular telephone company that was doing very well. He had attempted to buy his 29 per cent stake in Malaysia Airlines through an exchange of shares between the company and Celcom, and had that happened, he would not have had to spend a sen. In the end, however, he had to borrow a lot of money to buy the shares. Had I known this, I would have put a stop to the acquisition.

By the end of 2000, when it was clear that Tajuddin could not service his debts, the Government decided to pay him RM1.79 billion for his controlling stake and re-acquire the company. Claiming that he had bought Malaysia Airlines out of national duty, Tajuddin demanded that he receive the price per share that he had paid when he bought them. But I knew that he had bought into the company because he felt it was a good investment — newspaper reports at the time had quoted him as saying that he was not the kind of person to invest RM1.8 billion unless he could get a good return. Our purchase of his stake received a lot of criticism because we paid him RM8 a share, at a time when the market value was RM3.62 per share. Tun Daim Zainuddin, who was the Minister of Finance at the time, negotiated the buyback. I was unhappy with the price but Tun Daim claimed it was the best he could do to salvage the national carrier.

The financial crisis also struck a heavy blow to Projek Usahasama Transit Ringan Automatik Sdn Bhd (Putra) and Sistem Transit Aliran Ringan Sdn Bhd (Star), companies which respectively managed the Putra and Star lines of the Light Rail Transit (LRT) system. At the time, the LRT was not being patronised by Malaysians as frequently as it needed to be as it takes time for any infrastructure facility to be accepted and used. Malaysians are a pampered lot and expect to be transported by vehicle to the very door of their workplaces or their homes. There was, admittedly, also a contradiction in public policy as we encouraged Malaysians to buy the national car. Incidentally, the number of cars per capita in Malaysia is the highest in Southeast Asia.

Not wanting the LRT to go under, the Government stepped in and paid about RM9 billion to take it over. Again, we were accused of bailing out politically-connected businessmen but the buyout has since proven to be a good investment. Today, everyone realises how important the light rail system is to Kuala Lumpur. Without it, the roads would be jammed with passenger cars and buses. The LRT lines now carry full loads of passengers and during peak hours it is standing-room only. Now, with oil prices rising and falling dramatically, the time for the full acceptance and development of public transport has arrived.

Another Malay businessman we had to help was Tan Sri Halim Saad, the Chairman of Renong Bhd who, like Tajuddin, was another one of Tun Daim's protégés. He had originally been brought in to kick-start the North-South Expressway project in 1987, which had slowed down and gone over budget. Although Renong had been associated with UMNO at one time, it had become a fully-private enterprise by the 1990s and was involved in a number of public projects. It built the National Sports Complex for the Commonwealth Games, for example, and its subsidiary UEM completed the North-South Expressway, which generated a great deal of income for the company and tax revenue for the Government.

Even before the financial crisis, however, Renong was already over-extended. When Datuk Seri Anwar Ibrahim was the Deputy Prime Minister and Finance Minister, Halim had gone to see him about a restructuring plan that involved about RM10 billion in government-backed bonds. Anwar had agreed to it in principle, although he later denied this and said he had rejected the idea. I found out about it only after Anwar had been removed and Halim came to tell me about the plan. When the financial crisis hit, Renong lost about 80 per cent of its value on the share market and its debts accounted for about five per cent of all debt in the entire banking system. CDRC got UEM to issue about RM8.5 billion in bonds and some of the money that was raised was used to pay off Renong's debts.

Through a series of very complicated manoeuvres, Halim attempted to maintain his position in Renong. He persuaded UEM to buy Renong shares at a very high price and promised he would buy them back later. But when the time came, he asked for a postponement as he did not have enough money and was trying to borrow more. In the end, we had to step in. I asked Khazanah Nasional Berhad to take over UEM because if Renong defaulted on its debts, it would have probably dragged several banks down with it. We simply could not allow that to happen.

My family was not spared the criticism that generally greeted these rescue packages. My son Mirzan's company, Konsortium Logistik Berhad (KLB), had made a profit of RM60.7 million in 1996, but it was so badly hit by the financial crisis that it had a debt of RM2.57 billion by 1997. Its interest payments alone amounted to RM90.6 million for that year. KLB had 40 vessels and three LNG carriers but most were still under financing. The company's management decided that the only way out was to divest its shipping business and assets. It was a buyers' market and the only company capable of putting up the money was MISC Berhad, a subsidiary of PETRONAS and one of the biggest international shipping lines in the country. For MISC, the acquisition was a strategic move that would allow it to become the country's leading shipowner and operator. With the acquisition of KLB's assets, MISC would have a fleet of 141 vessels. Two foreign companies evaluated KLB's shipping assets and fixed the price at USD367 million, inclusive of a 20-year charter and USD222 million without. PETRONAS elected to disregard the charter value and offered to pay USD220 million — less than the lowest estimated value. KLB had no choice but to accept, leaving it with an overall loss of RM457.8 million on its books.

Clearly, for MISC and PETRONAS, the acquisition of KLB's vessels was very profitable. There was no charity involved and the decision was based on good business sense. Anwar has repeatedly alleged that I asked PETRONAS to help Mirzan by buying KLB's assets for RM2 billion. I had nothing to do with the transaction and all these details can be verified through Government records. In any case, this was not a bailout. When a company in trouble is completely bought over, it is for the benefit of the buyer. This is what happens when foreign companies buy over banks and companies at fire-sale prices when they are in trouble. Bailouts happen when the owner is helped with funds in order to overcome his problems. PETRONAS not only bought KLB at a very low price, but when the shipping business recovered, PETRONAS sold some of the freighters at a handsome profit.

Another project that got into trouble was the Bakun hydroelectric power plant in Sarawak.[1] It was first proposed in 1982 at the beginning of my term as Prime Minister. Hydropower is usually best in snowy, temperate climates where water is drawn from melting snow. The snow melts throughout most of the the year so there is always water to drive the turbines. In the tropics, hydropower depends on rain and since it rains in Sarawak almost continuously throughout the year, it was possible to develop Bakun for electricity. True, the project would have had an impact on the environment, but there always is some sacrifice to be made for any development and certainly for a major project.

The initial idea was to carry the electricity across the seas over a distance of 600km, land the cable on the east coast of Johor, and then distribute the power throughout the Peninsula. In the process there would be voltage loss as you cannot boost the voltage at sea. When we first considered the idea, cable technology was not as advanced as it is now, but the manufacturers assured us they could do it. In the North Sea or the Baltic there were cables about 200km long, but nowhere was there a cable 600km long. We were not willing to take the risk that it might fail and since the cost of the cable was the same as that of a thermal power plant in the Peninsula, the idea of having it became less and less attractive.

Sabah and Sarawak did not consume much electricity. The total that might be generated from Bakun would be 2,400 megawatts, far in excess of the needs of the two states. We decided to maximise local use by creating power-intensive industries in Sarawak, which would also help in

---

[1]  Sarawak is the largest state in Malaysia and is located on the island of Borneo.

its industrialisation. The biggest user of electricity that we could think of was an aluminium smelter. It was initially very difficult to look for people interested in aluminium smelting, but as Chinese industrialisation picked up momentum, the demand for aluminium grew. At the same time, many countries decided that since their electricity costs were high, they should shut down their smelters and move them to where power generation was less costly. Malaysia is one of these places, as is the gas-rich Middle East. It took us a long time before we finally found a company, Dubai Aluminum (Dubal), that was willing to set up the smelter and buy the power.

We had started work on the dam before the financial crisis but once it hit, we decided to delay the construction of the main dam and power plant. After we recovered in 1998, we decided to go ahead once again, buying back control of the project from the Bakun Hydroelectric Corporation, the consortium led by Ekran Berhad that had been appointed to build the dam. We had to build the main dam with its spillway as well as the hydroelectric power plant. To ensure sufficient off-take of power from Bakun, we persuaded Dubal to invest in the power plant. With that they would have had to build an aluminium smelter to buy the electricity produced, which presented a win-win formula for them. If the electricity price was low, they would profit from the smelter; if it was high, then they would make money from the power plant. They agreed to build the smelter and take a 30 per cent share in the power plant. Since they were experienced aluminium smelters and had the technology and money to invest, we were quite happy with the arrangement. They paid RM90 million as a 10 per cent deposit on their 30 per cent share. Since the dam was to be built via tender, the price went down quite a bit. A Chinese company, which teamed up with Sime Darby, submitted the lowest bid and got the job.

Construction commenced but very soon after I stepped down, the Government decided they would not give the equity share in the power plant to Dubal after all. The deposit was returned and with this, the incentive for Dubal to invest in a smelter in Sarawak vanished. I was upset — it had taken us five years to get Arabs to come and invest, only to have the succeeding Prime Minister give back the money. Reneging on a contract is not a smart move. The reason our Government gave for the decision was that the Arab investor, Sheikh Rashid Saeed Al Maktoum, had no money. He is, in fact, the ruler of Dubai and he was developing his country and many others in the Arab world and Indian subcontinent. His three companies were capitalised in billions of dollars. To claim that he did not have money for the power plant is absurd. Dubai operates a very big aluminium smelter using natural gas as fuel for the electricity required. They understand the industry and the business so they did not decide to invest in Malaysia's hydroelectric project blindly or out of misplaced confidence. This was a genuine business opportunity for them.

I subsequently heard that our Government wanted this cheap electricity to benefit poor people in the country. Tun Abdullah Ahmad Badawi, before he stepped down as Prime Minister, said there were plans to bring the electricity by undersea cable to the Peninsula — an idea we had abandoned long ago for good reasons. By the time the electricity reaches here, it will no longer be cheap. The voltage loss over that great distance would be very high, even if cabling technology has improved. In the end the charges per unit would not be lower than a local power plant. So how would poor people benefit from Bakun's hydropower? The only ones who would benefit would be those who won the contract to lay the undersea cable. They would certainly not be the poor.

Attempts to rescue failing companies in Malaysia continued to be condemned, not least by local detractors. The Press and the public gleefully anticipated the fall of the newly rich, particularly those Malays who had benefited from the privatisation programme. While it is a general human characteristic to fawn upon the rich and famous and then revile them once they stumble, Malays seem to take a special delight in doing so when the fallen rich is one of their own. They labelled any attempt by the Government to help as a bailout and invariably assumed that those who were rescued had to be my cronies. The World Bank and the IMF actually urged that "inefficient" companies be allowed to go bankrupt as it would mean that only the hardiest and most efficient companies would survive the financial crisis. This may be good for the economy, but whether it would be good for our nation and its people was another matter. They did not take into account the extraordinary conditions caused by currency devaluation, nor did they care about the unemployment and other economic and social problems that would accompany these bankruptcies. You don't push a company over just because it is teetering on the edge.

As a result of taking the World Bank's and the IMF's advice, many companies in neighbouring countries literally closed shop, throwing millions of workers out of their jobs. They rioted, burnt down buildings and went on a rampage, raping and killing people. On top of that huge social cost, their economies deteriorated further. Banks and companies from the rich countries, however, were ever ready to come to the rescue. They would buy the financially-troubled companies and banks at fire-sale prices and turn them around. Then they would sell and make huge profits. After "bailing out" the country through loans to settle its foreign debts, the IMF claimed the right to manage the country's economy as it saw fit. All barriers to foreign takeovers had to be removed, which meant that these countries had to be open to foreign capital, forfeiting their economic independence and national sovereignty along the way.

Mindful of what had happened to some of our neighbours, we could not allow criticisms to prevent us from cushioning the effects of the currency crisis. Moreover, the Government was still committed to the objectives of the NEP — it had to be if the nation's social cohesion and long-term survival were to be assured.

Today, those rich countries have resorted to bailouts on an unbelievable scale, giving out trillions of dollars. They now know that if they don't bail out their banks and financial institutions, their whole economy would collapse. They no longer talk about our rescue plans now that they have to resort to the same strategies. However, they will find that their bailouts may not work for them as they did for us.

# Chapter 56:
## My Toughest Election

The 1999 General Election, the last in which I led the Barisan Nasional coalition, came only months after Datuk Seri Anwar Ibrahim was sacked as Deputy Prime Minister and expelled from UMNO. Especially with the black eye he got after the Inspector-General of Police hit him while in detention, we knew the Anwar issue would dominate the campaign and shape the election results. I could have delayed holding the election but I was not certain things would change in our favour. Anwar was a skilled politician and a persuasive demagogue — always convincing, he also knew how to endear himself to people.

By the time we decided to call for election, Anwar was behind bars but he had become a powerful symbol around which the Opposition rallied. Feelings ran high against me, even among UMNO members, and women who had loyally supported the party in the past suddenly turned against us and went on to vote for PAS.

718

Despite the hostility, I decided to go ahead with the election because we had just overcome the financial crisis and had the Chinese community on our side. Thanks to the measures that we had taken, Chinese businessmen who had been on the verge of bankruptcy suddenly recovered and pressure from their banks abated. Many were so grateful that they approached me at public functions to say that I had saved their lives. This convinced me that the Chinese would strongly support the Barisan Nasional, countering the anticipated loss of Malay votes.

The election was a tough one. Negative sentiment among the Malays was palpable with PAS trying to demonise me by calling me all kinds of names. This was hardly necessary — the notorious black eye sufficed to win them many votes and to cost UMNO dearly. Before his arrest Anwar had formed a new political party which he named the Justice Party, or Parti Keadilan. Unable to lead it himself because of his conviction,[1] he had his wife Datin Seri Dr Wan Azizah Wan Ismail step into his place to lead the party and

---

[1]   Under Malaysian election law, anyone who has served a jail sentence is barred from political office for five years from the date of his or her release.

run as a candidate in his parliamentary constituency of Permatang Pauh in Penang. Knowing how the Barisan Nasional always benefited from its inter-ethnic coalition, he had Parti Keadilan propose an election agreement with the other Opposition parties to form a coalition which he called Barisan Alternatif, or the Alternative Front. Tengku Razaleigh Hamzah had adopted the same tactic when he led Semangat 46 and tried to bring PAS and DAP into a pact with his party. Where Tengku Razaleigh failed, Anwar was to do better.

The success of any such coalition under our voting system lies in the willingness of its participating parties not to contest against each other. Instead, in every electoral district, they have to support the agreed coalition candidates no matter from what party they come. That was how the Barisan Nasional and before it, the Alliance, had been able to win repeatedly since Independence. The DAP could never accept PAS's Islamic state concept, which involved implementing the *hudud* Islamic laws as PAS understood them. For its part, PAS was equally unwilling to give up its quest for its version of an Islamic state, fearing that it might alienate rural Malay support. Ultimately, the Barisan Alternatif failed to function fully as a coalition and lost to the Barisan Nasional.

719

When I had been a vocal Member of Parliament in the 1960s, I had been labelled a Malay ultra by Lee Kuan Yew and the Chinese. I had even lost my seat in the 1969 General Election because the Chinese in my constituency turned against me. To find them supporting me so strongly in 1999 while many Malays were lukewarm at best towards me was strange, even ironic. So strong was our Chinese support that the Barisan Nasional did not just win, but again captured more than two-thirds of the parliamentary seats.

As always, I spent polling night monitoring the results at the UMNO headquarters on the 32nd floor of the Putra World Trade Centre. Most of the party's leaders were gathered there with me, watching the giant television screen that flashed the polling results as they came in. There were cheers whenever we won a seat, and an air of excitement when we had reached first a simple majority — when we knew for a fact that we would form the next Government — and then the two-thirds majority.

But we were not spared some painful losses. UMNO's share of the number of parliamentary seats dropped from 89 to 72. Besides failing to re-take Kelantan from PAS, the Barisan Nasional also lost control of Terengganu to them for the first time in 40 years. PAS increased its share of parliamentary seats to 27, up from the seven it had won in the 1995 General Election, and made significant inroads into Kedah and Perlis, and to a lesser extent, into Pahang and Malacca. Every member of the Cabinet won with a reduced majority and four Ministers lost their seats altogether. One of the most startling results involved then Education Minister Datuk Seri Najib Razak, who was only able to hang on to his seat with a 241-vote lead, down from the over 10,000-vote majority he had won in 1995. We had anticipated losing ground in this election and I estimated that the image of Anwar's black eye alone cost us some 300,000 votes.

The Barisan Nasional's defeat in Terengganu was a big disappointment, but it was not entirely due to Anwar. The state's *Menteri Besar* had stayed in office for far too long, longer than even my own premiership, but had insisted that he be given yet another term. Even loyal UMNO members could not bring themselves to support him and he lost. His defeat was not simply personal, however, as it also meant that Terengganu fell to PAS. Terengganu was and is the biggest producer of oil in Malaysia and five per cent of that revenue, worth almost RM1 billion a year, went to the state government. We knew that if the new PAS state government were to gain access to the money, they would likely use it to enhance their popularity and promote their cause. A way had to be found to deny them access to these funds. In September 2000, the Finance Ministry announced that the oil revenues, instead of going to the state government, would now be channelled directly into development projects to benefit the state's population. PAS took its case to court, but the issue was not resolved even when the Barisan Nasional recaptured Terengganu in the 2004 General Election.

In Kedah meanwhile, the *Menteri Besar* had managed to antagonise the Civil Service, religious teachers and even some UMNO divisions. He won his seat but the Barisan Nasional candidates, who were overwhelmingly UMNO members, barely managed to hold onto their two-thirds majority in the Kedah State Assembly. PAS was convinced it would capture Kedah at the next election.[2] After the election, I decided it was essential that a new *Menteri Besar* be appointed. After considering our options I settled on Datuk Seri Syed Razak Syed Zain Barakhbah, a member of the State Executive Council. On my recommendation, the Sultan gave him the authority to form a new Executive Council, the equivalent of a Cabinet at the state level.

I did not realise that Tan Sri Osman Aroff, a previous *Menteri Besar,* was also keen to be reappointed. When I told him of my choice he was very disappointed. Years later, after I had stepped down as Prime Minister, this man campaigned hard against me when I tried to get elected by my old UMNO division in Kubang Pasu to be one of its representatives to the UMNO General Assembly. He made it known that I had given him nothing. Considering that I had made him *Menteri Besar* three times before replacing him, this was not easy to understand. I wondered what else I should have given him to make him more grateful.

Since stepping down, I have learnt that very few politicians can sustain their loyalty to anyone. Once you lose your position and power, they ignore you and transfer their loyalty and support to whoever has taken your place. They will even condemn you if they think doing so will please their new leader. "Nobody knows you when you're down and out" the old song goes; the same wisdom holds true in Malay political life. While Malays like to talk about loyalty and claim to set great store by it, loyalty is not the dominant force in Malay politics, nor the main political motive or sentiment. In the Malay scheme of things, political loyalty is based not on the past, upon memory or gratitude, but on what the current leaders in power can offer. I was very sad to discover this.

721

The 1999 General Election results showed us that we needed to work harder to shore up Malay support for the Barisan Nasional. By that time, women made up almost half the members of UMNO, yet I noticed that the women's wing, Wanita UMNO, had lost its dynamism. It had not always been that way — in UMNO's early days, women played a big role in mobilising popular support. They were always very active during election

---

[2]    It failed to do so at the 2004 elections, but succeeded finally in 2008 amidst a wave of discontent directed at the administration of Tun Abdullah Ahmad Badawi.

campaigns and would fearlessly approach housewives to persuade them to support the party candidate and to vote. I always had great respect for Malay women. They were hardworking and responsible, often more so than men. In Kelantan, Malay women not only work in the padi fields but also make up most of the stallholders and traders in the town and city markets. In this way they provide the underlying network and the basic commercial infrastructure of the rural economy, while their menfolk sit about in coffee shops talking politics.

The women's political role was crucial, so I was alarmed by the decline in their interest in party work and believed that this might have contributed negatively to our election results. Many women, especially younger women, were obviously reluctant to join Wanita UMNO. Apparently they saw no prospects for themselves so long as older members dominated the wing and showed no inclination to vacate their positions, especially at the headquarters level. Some were also unhappy that their political ambitions and energies were diverted into a parallel party vehicle, and not through the men's mainstream divisional structure. For these capable and determined young women, new avenues for political participation, influence and achievements within UMNO had to be created.

One of the first hurdles was Tan Sri Rafidah Aziz, who had remained head of Wanita UMNO for years. She was challenged once and lost,[3] but at the next party election she won her position back. After that, she kept out all potential challengers and only those subservient to her could gain any position in the movement. This has since changed: in the 2009 UMNO elections, she was defeated by her deputy Dato' Sri Shahrizat Abdul Jalil.

But during my term in office, I felt strongly that we needed to gain the support of younger Malay women. They were a new generation, a different breed, the product of an independent country and of the New Economic Policy. They were generally better educated than their mothers and Wanita UMNO seniors. Many held professional qualifications and were successful in the professional world: as lawyers, architects, accountants, doctors and engineers. Some had risen to head government departments and ministries, while others had become executives, even chief executives

---

[3]    She was defeated by then Deputy Health Minister Datin Paduka Siti Zaharah Suleiman in 1996.

and financial officers in big companies, including foreign multinationals. A number were respected consultants and there were those among them who were well-known writers and journalists. Yet, while most of them could discuss current affairs, few displayed any interest in politics or in becoming involved in political life. I believed that their apparent apathy stemmed from a lack of opportunity, not of interest, confidence or capability.

By the 1990s we were also witnessing an unusual phenomenon. When I was at university, only one of the seven Malays who joined the College of Medicine in 1947 was female. But by the 1990s Malay female undergraduates at local universities had outnumbered the boys. Today they make up almost 70 per cent of the undergraduates in our local universities. This was a radical change that a political party like UMNO could not afford to ignore. It was clear that in future, women would play an increasingly important role in every sphere of professional and public life in Malaysia.

Malay women in Malaysia — whether middle-class career women or homemakers in the *kampung* — have always been more liberated than Muslim women in other countries. I realised that if there was to be an injection of wider thinking and deeper insight into UMNO politics, women had to be encouraged to provide it. To be able to do so, they would have to be able to join the party and make their contributions far more readily and easily than before.

But the senior women in Wanita UMNO feared the challenge that better-qualified younger Malay women would pose. They did not openly oppose their joining Wanita, but they were hardly encouraging. Unless something was done soon, UMNO would suffer a double loss: the ageing and thinning out of the current Wanita membership together with an inevitable, ensuing decline in their contribution to the party; and the disinclination of an entire rising generation of potential members. Forfeiting their energies and contributions was something neither the party nor Malaysia could afford to risk.

The suggestion was made in the Supreme Council to create a new wing that would cater to young women wanting to join the party. I gave it my full support. Immediately, Rafidah was up in arms and questioned the need for such a body. Wanita, she insisted, was already open to all women, old and young. When someone pointed out that the women in Wanita, especially the leaders, were quite old, she exploded with anger and resentment.

The male members of the Supreme Council were more positive, but I knew our party's men were no better than the women when it came to admitting highly-qualified applicants into branches. Branch chairmen often feared losing their positions and influence if qualified people were allowed to join either the UMNO Youth or as ordinary members in the branches. Not just existing divisional office-bearers but also many of their old-guard rival aspirants were reluctant to see capable new talent enter their divisions and local party branches. Many took the view that for party positions there was, in effect, a kind of queue or waiting list: that those who had waited their turn should get in first, and others should fall in behind them. Eager and capable, young members took a different view. But at least for young men there was the UMNO Youth; for young women, there was nothing. What was now proposed was hardly a radical innovation, simply the creation for Malay women of a counterpart or parallel section to the young men's wing.

724

This fear among the veteran party members was not really new. When I returned as a qualified doctor eager to play an active leadership role in Kedah UMNO, one leader told me that people like him had fought for Independence so that people like me could get a better education and achieve high positions in the Government. Now that I had those qualifications, I should not waste my time in politics but rather concentrate my efforts in public service. I had a great future there, on the permanent service side of government, he said. Over the years the older members' desire to hang on to party posts and eventually to become honourable Members of Parliament and the state assemblies grew ever stronger. For many of them, and especially those who did not have modern professional qualifications and prospects, election through UMNO to the state and federal legislative bodies represented a huge advance, not just in income and opportunity but in the social standing and public esteem that many Malays value so highly.

The increasing rewards open to those who hold party posts have made the contest for them even keener. Wanita UMNO's strong opposition to the formation of the new wing, Puteri UMNO, was not surprising. The Wanita stalwarts knew that at some stage Puteri candidates would have to be considered for election to the party's various councils and even to Parliament. For my part, I thought that qualified, young Malay women must be accommodated in UMNO. I was sure they would be able to contribute to the party's strength and to build acceptance and support for the party by young women generally. Exactly how they would play their part, I was not sure. We could think more about that once the new Puteri wing was formed.

By that time, we had co-opted a young woman lawyer named Datuk Sri Azalina Othman Said as a member of the Supreme Council. She was not active in Wanita but was well-known for her support of UMNO. On her own, she had defended the party and the Government's policies, especially its efforts to help Malay women. When the Supreme Council finally decided that Puteri UMNO should be formed, the lead role was given to her. Azalina proved very capable and soon every UMNO division in the country had a Puteri wing. Most of its leaders and many members were well-qualified professionals.[4]

Puteri adopted a striking pink for their outfits. It contrasted with the bright red of Wanita UMNO and suggested the youthfulness of the Puteri members. Under Azalina's leadership, Puteri became active in social work, and they even got me to read to orphans in kindergartens. They were soon making their presence felt everywhere but their political relevance was yet to be tested. During some by-elections they proved very diligent and campaigned hard. They did not just concentrate on women, they were active on many issues, and in all social circles. In fact, they were so effective that our opponents from PAS sought to discourage them with the most vulgar of dirty tactics.[5]

Puteri has unquestionably made UMNO relevant to the younger generation of Malays, in particular Malay women. It ignited a new enthusiasm for

---

[4]  Datuk Sri Azalina Othman Said, who was Tourism Minister, was dropped from the Cabinet line-up of Malaysia's sixth Prime Minister Datuk Seri Najib Razak.

[5]  At the Pendang parliamentary and Anak Bukit state by-elections in July 2002, Wanita and Puteri campaigners were called *jalang* (of loose morals) and *sundal* (prostitutes). In one instance a PAS supporter lifted his sarong and exposed himself to a Puteri campaigner.

politics in the rising Malay generation and made UMNO and its struggles known to those who had been the beneficiaries. Many who had gained a university education now realised how much they owed to UMNO and its policies. Beyond gratitude, they had become conscious that those same policies and benefits had to be extended to future generations. There was one clear way to do that: by becoming more involved in UMNO.

After the 1999 elections I again reconsidered my plans to retire. I decided I should first restore the strength of the party, re-establish the country's political and social stability, restart reasonable economic growth, and ensure that Government finances were in good shape. I did not want my successor to inherit a legacy of problems created during my tenure of office.

By now I had largely healed the rift in the party that had occurred in the wake of Anwar's dismissal. I had brought many, who had opposed me, back into UMNO. I had planned the succession process and decided upon my successor. UMNO was once again stable. Now, with the formation of Puteri UMNO, the party had been further strengthened and I was confident that Puteri would contribute greatly towards winning the next General Election after I stepped down.

# Chapter 57:
# 9/11 And The Muslim World

I was having dinner before going to the airport to take a flight to London when two aeroplanes crashed into the World Trade Centre buildings in New York on 11 September 2001. When my daughter-in-law Jane received a text message about what had happened, I first thought it was a minor accident. A small plane had once crashed into the Empire State building in New York. While there had been some damage to the building, it remained standing. But as more messages came in, we decided to turn on the TV to watch the news. To our horror, we saw the first tower building engulfed in smoke and flames. Then we saw the second plane crashing into the second tower. Like so many other people, we could hardly believe that what we were watching was really happening in faraway New York at that very moment. But it was real — we were watching a world-shattering event, an attack against the US which was to change everything that, until then, we had taken for granted.

I cancelled my London trip and we all stayed close to the TV, gripped by the disaster unfolding before our eyes. Suddenly, there was a gasp from the commentator. One tower fell straight down onto itself, then the other tower collapsed in the same way. I remember thinking how strange it was that the two towers collapsed vertically upon themselves in that way. When the dust clouds slowly cleared, there was nothing of the buildings left standing, just a total void — not even the steel girders remained. The TV commentators later explained that the construction of the 110-storey World Trade Centre towers was unique. They were supported the whole way by their outer walls so when the walls collapsed, all 110 floors came down with them. So apparently did the internal lift shafts, which must have been built from strong and very thick concrete to support the weight of the 110-story-tall shaft walls above. Clearly, there was something strange in all of this.

Soon people could talk only about terrorists and the need for the whole world to fight them and stop their violent onslaughts. President George W. Bush appeared on TV screens everywhere, obviously very angry. He blamed the destruction of the towers on Muslim terrorists and called for a "crusade" against them. I was startled and distressed. Having read much about the

Crusades, I thought that that reference was not altogether inappropriate. The Crusades had pitted the world of the European Christians against the world of Islam. To someone like Bush, fighting Muslims would really be another crusade, an echo and continuation of Europe's mediaeval struggle against the civilisation of Islam. Yet I, together with hundreds of millions of other Muslims, did not regard Christians as our enemies. We did not like the US and its unquestioning support of Israel, and I had often enough pointed out that the war in Palestine was not a religious war. It was a territorial issue — the result of seizing the land of the Palestinian Arabs, many of whom were Christians, and creating a Jewish state out of it. But Bush had clearly concluded that the attack against New York was a Muslim attack against Christians.

Bush later corrected himself and never used the word "crusade" again, but it was too late — using it once was sufficient to lay bare the underlying assumptions of his thinking. After that, he placed the blame squarely not on Islam itself but on Muslim terrorists, specifically on the Al-Qaeda led by Osama bin Laden. I did not question his assertion at the time, assuming that he knew things that I did not. The CIA is a formidable intelligence agency and I was sure its people would have pinpointed the culprits.

I am not so certain now. In June 2006, several Americans came to see me in my office in Putrajaya. What they told me and the DVD they produced cast doubt on what I had been told about the attacks against the World Trade Centre and the Pentagon. These people were not cranks. One of them was a janitor who had worked at the World Trade Centre for more than 10 years. William Rodrigues, a Hispanic US citizen, was there when the attacks took place. He held the master key to the rooms there and helped in the rescue of nearly 300 people in the towers. He was acclaimed by the US Government and the President as a national hero. Yet he joined a number of other Americans in demanding that a new investigation be carried out to determine who or what really destroyed the World Trade Centre. He did so because his statement to investigators had been excluded from the official report. He claimed he had heard explosions in the basement of the building, which could not have been due to the aircraft crashing into the towers high above. He believed explosives had been placed in the buildings, explosives which had detonated and were responsible for the collapse of the towers, or had at least contributed to their collapse.

I watched the three-hour video they brought with them, which featured a number of experts who gave their views regarding the collapse of the World Trade Centre and the damage suffered by the Pentagon building in Washington D.C. Accompanying the talk were video clips showing views, both of the towers and the Pentagon building at different times that morning during successive stages of the destruction of the buildings. Then I remembered thinking at the time of the attack that the way the towers collapsed had seemed strange. The video's principal narrator pointed out that it was most unusual for buildings to collapse straight down, except when they are deliberately demolished by the detonation of a succession of explosive charges. The video also showed a third building, building No 57, which, though it was not hit by the aircraft, also collapsed in the same way. I do not remember the media reporting about this building. This was the first time I heard about that third building also collapsing, though it had not been struck by any aircraft.

My visitors insisted that all three buildings were brought down, in calculated fashion, by demolition charges. As for the Pentagon building, the picture taken apparently soon after the plane had crashed into it showed no aircraft or aircraft wreckage at all. Surely they could not have removed the debris so quickly. Besides, the hole in the wall of the Pentagon building was too small for even the nose of the aircraft. Again, unlike other serious accidents, I have not seen the kind of extensive reports on the incident which the American Press loves to make.

On the basis of this and similar evidence, I now have doubts whether terrorists really crashed those planes or if the whole thing was an elaborately staged drama to convince the world that a serious terrorist attack had been made on the US, requiring an all-out war to be waged. Even within the US, there are groups who question the official account of the attack and the US Government's role in it, groups whose members include scientists, architects, engineers and scholars.

We now know that the excuse for invading Iraq was a blatant lie as there were no weapons of mass destruction. US intelligence agencies had told the President so, but he still went ahead to invade Iraq, to destroy the country and directly kill or cause the deaths of hundreds of thousands of people. A US President and his cohorts, who would lie about the presence of weapons of mass destruction to get the war that they wanted, would have no qualms about staging a terrorist attack involving the killing of 3,000 innocent people — if that was what it would take to get the world to back a war against Muslim terrorists, Afghanistan and Iraq.

We are living through terrible times. We are seeing an endless war in what is recognised as the cradle of world civilisation. The massive "shock and awe" attack has not been as the aggressors have claimed: to reduce strife and suffering, and the threat of a weapons of mass destruction war by Iraq. It was in fact just the opposite: the actions taken by the civilised West, by the same people who boast of having fought two great wars to end all wars, have only helped spread and promote the very terror which the West claims it wishes to uproot, and which it insists the whole world must join it to fight. Their arrogance and folly have brought greater oppression and the killing of the very people they claim they want to save. Whatever Saddam Hussein may have been guilty of, it was nothing compared to the death and destruction wrought by the self-appointed "saviours" of Iraq.

As a child I was terrified of the idea of fighting in a war and being killed in one. I could not believe that people would voluntarily become soldiers and accept that idea. Being killed violently and probably needlessly seemed inhuman to me. In school I had read books about the glory of war, the victories of the British in Europe and then in the rest of the world as they built their great Empire. But these books told only one side of the story. It was the same with movies, like the old Westerns in which brave cowboys shot down the Native Americans. The bodies of these "savages" were scattered across the wide prairies and I — knowing no better and with a child's easy enthusiasm — cheered the cowboys on, admiring their prowess with their six-shooters. I was always so happy that the beautiful heroines and all the pretty, fair-haired, white-skinned children were saved. My fear of war subsided somewhat and I came to think that it was glorious as only enemies were killed. I was on the side of the victors, which meant I would not be killed. It was a very reassuring thought. I too could become a soldier and go into battle against our enemies, and return a hero.

Then, in 1939, World War II broke out. At first it seemed to be confined to Europe with the Germans being the enemies, which meant they were the ones who would be killed and defeated. But, strangely, they seemed to be winning instead. On 7 December 1942, the war came to Malaya when the Japanese landed near Kota Baru and invaded the country from the north. To my horror, the British retreated. I saw them trudging in the mud and rain, totally unlike the proud Europeans I knew. All my fears of war and being killed returned.

I was overjoyed when the British and the Americans eventually won, but my fear and hatred of war did not go away. The killing that war entailed had become real to me. In earlier times it was mostly young men who were killed but today's wars are total wars. Everyone and anyone — combatants and non-combatants, soldiers and civilians — are killed. Taking Palestinian land to give to the Jews and thereby precipitating war was bad enough. Now the US and Britain are deliberately waging war against countries which cannot fight back.

As Prime Minister of Malaysia I was initially in agreement with President Bush that we should all fight against terrorism. But when Bush invaded Afghanistan, I decided Malaysia would not support it. Osama might well be there and he may have been responsible for the 9/11 attacks, but I was certain that invading Afghanistan would not end terror attacks but only increase their number, whether Bush and his allies won or lost. Of course, he could only imagine winning. He believed that the American will was unstoppable. Perhaps he did not know that Afghanistan had never been defeated by imperialist forces. I expected the Afghans to give the Americans a thrashing but Kabul fell and Hamid Karzai, a former employee of an American oil company, was installed by the US as the Prime Minister. The Americans were jubilant and it became evident that they were spoiling for another war and another easy victory.

To modify an old saying, "Those whom God wishes to destroy, they first make arrogant". The Americans had been hurt by 9/11. They did not want to appear weak and defenceless so like a cowboy posse they had to go after someone and teach them a lesson. If they could not strike at Osama, they would strike at Afghanistan and in that way send him and all his sympathisers and wavering Muslims a clear message: we are big, we are strong and we are angry, so don't mess around with us and don't resist us.

I was very worried by this turn of events. Malaysia would not be dragged in but that would not stop people from being killed. Iraq was openly named as the next target for American military action. It was weak enough for the Americans to bully and most importantly it had oil. After a short campaign a tame, compliant government would be installed and Iraq's oil would be available to the US. Even though Iraq was not hiding Osama and it could not be implicated in any way in the New York attacks, this posed no obstacle. Iraq was accused of having nuclear capability, of having chemical and other weapons of mass destruction. Possession of these WMDs provided sufficient excuse for the country to be invaded, its leader deposed, and its oil wealth made available to the world.

To me it was clear that what the Americans were planning to do in Iraq was similar to daylight robbery. A new concept was being introduced — that of a pre-emptive war to be waged on the mere suspicion that an enemy or a country might be planning to attack one's country. This made no sense in a world where every nation's Ministry of Defence had to draw up and keep updating contingency plans for all kinds of unlikely scenarios and improbable eventualities. War based on suspicion and pre-emption is a frightening concept. Anyone may have suspicions, but only a country with overwhelming military strength can initiate a pre-emptive war. A weak country, even one facing the real possibility of enemy invasion, would not have that option of striking first. Justifying a doctrine of pre-emptive war simply means authorising the most powerful to threaten and conduct war against whoever it pleases at any time. That is the blueprint for a world in which no country is safe, not even Malaysia.

I had met Bush several times at conferences and had made an official visit to see him in Washington DC. I had also written to him many times and he was gracious enough to reply personally. I thought I should write to him to warn him against invading Iraq, especially since I knew how strongly Muslims would feel about the invasion. They may not have liked Iraqi President Saddam Hussein but they would all feel very strongly against an American invasion of Iraq. I also knew something about terrorism and what drives the terrorists. Malaysia had dealt with its terrorists from 1948 to 1990. I had sat on the National Security Council since I first became a Minister in Tun Razak Hussein's time. I was very familiar with terrorist behaviour and I knew of the psychological war that we successfully waged against them. I believed I knew the mentality of the people who mount terror attacks. They may seem crazy and they may appear to have a death wish — but they are moved by very strong feelings. We can deal effectively with them only if we understand those feelings. We may not find them rational initially, but it is only after you begin to understand these emotions that you can begin to counter terror effectively. Malaysia did not rely entirely on the gun. The bigger battle that we fought was the one for the hearts and minds of the people, including the terrorists. In the end, we prevailed.

I was very sure that a US invasion of Iraq would not contribute to the fight against terrorism and would in fact cost the world infinitely more. So I wrote to Bush and Tony Blair, to Jacques Chirac and German Chancellor Gerhard Schröder. I appealed to them not to invade Iraq as doing so would only increase terror attacks and multiply the number of people willing to sacrifice their lives. But the president of the most powerful nation in the world was not about to listen to a leader of a small developing country. He did not reply to my letter. Instead, he announced his intention to invade Iraq. British Foreign Secretary Jack Straw told me Britain would try to persuade the Americans not to take that action but, as we now know, it was the British who were persuaded by the Americans to be belligerent.

People must realise that modern war is about killing people indiscriminately and on a massive scale. It is not about soldiers fighting soldiers on battlefields. Killing people is a crime in any society. Ordinarily, even in less advanced societies, killers are severely punished, often with death. Yet mass killings of people, combatants and non-combatants, authorised in their own brutal interests by the great state powers, is praised, honoured and rewarded. The Americans and the British people are as much against everyday murder as anyone else, yet they were willing to accept the massive "collateral" killings caused by war. What kind of people are these? Granted, their people had been killed by terrorists, but the people who would be affected by their agenda of retribution were not terrorists or even related to terrorists. Civilised people do not kill the families, the friends or the fellow citizens of murderers, and certainly not people not even remotely connected to the murderers. What kind of a society would we have if the family and friends of a murderer or murderers could be killed in vicarious retribution?

They only dared to form their "coalition of the willing" to invade Iraq because of their overwhelmingly superior strength. Yet they are really cowards because they pick on people who cannot match their military might. The US detention centres at Abu Ghraib and Guantanamo, which held terrorism suspects and subjected them to brutal torture, exposed the worst in them. The verdict of the world on their savage brutality and inhumanity is unanimous.

For the loss of some 3,000 combatants, 600,000 Iraqis, mainly innocent civilians, have been killed. God alone knows how many hundred thousands more have been wounded, disabled and traumatised for life; how many lives have been shattered and ruined. And all for what? It seems to me that the Iraq of today is worse off than the Iraq of Saddam Hussein. But the thirst for blood has not been satisfied. The Americans and the British still harbour the idea of extending the war to Syria, which is said to be harbouring terrorists, and Iran, which is supposedly developing a nuclear bomb.

A survey among the British people and other Europeans found that they regarded the United States as a greater threat to world peace than Iran or North Korea. No sensible person believes their country is in danger of being invaded by Iran or North Korea. Even the Japanese cannot seriously think that North Korea will attack Japan with one or two nuclear bombs. The North Koreans know that were they to use nuclear or even conventional weapons against Japan, the US would drop so many nuclear warheads on their country that their people would all be killed and North Korea would be made uninhabitable.

The only country that has used and can use nuclear weapons is the United States. It has probably more than 10,000 nuclear warheads and it has the means to deliver them anywhere in the world, to destroy any country. Their invasion of Iraq is proof that they can be foolish and irresponsible. Therein lies the danger. In fact, they have been using nuclear weapons in the form of depleted uranium. And they are developing so-called "safe" nuclear weapons so they can get around the world's objection to nuclear warfare. America's leaders have learnt nothing from their defeat in Vietnam. They still think that military might must prevail and win them their battles, gain them their objectives and cow the whole world. They should know that though battles may be won, the war could still be lost, especially in these modern times.

I am no expert in war, just as I am not an expert in finance or economics. Perhaps not being an expert is an advantage as you don't get trapped by conventional thinking and its ideas of what is proper and what is not, what is suitable and what is nonsensical. There are advantages to thinking outside the box. I may not have fought in one but I have gone through many wars in my lifetime: World War II, the Pacific War, the armed insurrection in Malaysia, the war in Palestine, the Vietnam War, the Gulf War, the war against Afghanistan by the USSR and then by the US, and then the post-9/11 war against Afghanistan and Iraq. I have also lived through the era of the many wars of independence waged by the colonies against the European imperialists. From all these, and from the unwillingness of evenly matched countries to take on each other, I have drawn certain conclusions.

735

Wars of conquest, I believe, are no longer possible. A conquered people will refuse to stay that way or allow their conquerors to remain their overlords for any worthwhile period. Their governments may surrender and be forced to submit to the victorious invaders but the people will not follow suit. Sooner rather than later, they will rise and fight to throw off the yoke of the overlord. In their struggle to liberate themselves, the people are prepared to sacrifice everything and will fight with whatever weapons they can lay their hands on. They will attack not just at home in their own countries but throughout the world. They will kill the citizens of the country which rules over them, even if in the process many more of their own people are killed. They may be killed themselves or captured and tortured, but others would be willing to take their places and carry on the fight.

Such people are labelled terrorists but they think of themselves as freedom fighters. They consider their own deeds glorious and their fellow citizens regard them as heroes and martyrs. Against them, all the powerful weapons and sophisticated technology of modern warfare are of no avail.

Even if the conquerors were to raze the whole country, they would not win. The survivors, exiled in other countries, would remember and their hatred would be so strong that, given half a chance, they would kill the enemy or the enemy's children and grandchildren. That hatred would be for eternity.

In other words, in today's world the most powerful nations, equipped with the most sophisticated weapons, cannot invade, conquer and prevail over even the weakest nation, at least not for very long. The Vietnam War provided a graphic illustration of this when one American field commander claimed that he had, with all his technological superiority, destroyed a certain village in order to save it from capture. In his mind he had prevented it from being held by the enemy. What he failed to recognise was that by doing so, he did not save the village. He lost it and his own country's moral credibility.

Modern wars are not going to be about fully equipped armies, navies and air forces facing each other, fighting set-piece battles on a grand scale. Modern wars will eventually become guerrilla wars in which ill-equipped people harass their adversary, snipe and kill, and mount "terror" attacks to undermine peace and stability. The more violent the conquest, the greater the violence employed by the conquered. Ultimately it is a war about credibility, a moral contest that the invaders must eventually lose; a war in which, if they persist, they must surrender whatever may be left of their international reputation and legitimacy. That was what happened in Vietnam. The might of America was defeated by pyjama-clad Vietnamese guerrillas armed mostly with handguns.

This is a truth upon which the rich and powerful countries and their leaders should reflect. To them I say: you are wasting your money developing ever more sophisticated killing machines. You may be attacked and killed anywhere in the world by explosives, handguns or even knives by the people you have oppressed and angered. So, reflect on the cost of your security.

You need armies of people to oversee visitors to your country, to check the cargo ships and the airplanes coming in and to stop the hijacking of civilian aircraft. But every time you have to ground planes or search for suspected terrorists, you deter businessmen, not terrorists, from visiting your country. You have to spend billions on research to develop devices to improve your security, only to find your enemies have discovered ways to get around your sophisticated devices and costly security measures. World trade and businesses have already been adversely affected by the terrorist attacks you have engendered and by the futile measures you have adopted to punish and counter them. Worst of all, there can be no end to all this. You cannot sign a treaty with "terrorists".

For the small, weak countries that the big powers wish to dominate, the cost of defending themselves is a minute fraction of the cost borne by their potential attackers. What they need most to do is to develop the necessary skills and capacity for a prolonged guerrilla war against the invaders. However great the human commitment involved, that will not cost them much in material terms. They may maintain relatively small conventional military forces at quite minimal cost. Knowing their own country, they would be able to hide their trained guerrillas and train non-military personnel in guerrilla warfare.

Vietnam defeated the US not by having the most powerful weapons or the biggest armed forces. It defeated America by digging hundreds of miles of underground tunnels at strategic locations, enabling their guerrilla force to appear and disappear at will.[1] There was no way the US forces could protect themselves. The Vietnamese had the most important resources: local knowledge and intelligence, together with political will born of necessity and elemental human pride. That is a formidable, in fact unstoppable, combination. At My Lai[2] the US became so rattled that its enraged forces decided to kill everyone. That only made the Vietnamese angrier, more determined, and more ready to kill or be killed. And it did much damage to the moral integrity of the US.

The US now admits that invading Iraq was a mistake, but the real mistake is its idea of military invincibility. It may have been true in the past but it is an anachronism today. War is no longer an option for the powerful, and

---

[1]   The Cu Chi underground tunnels allowed the Viet Cong to travel and communicate with each other undetected, and to store food and weapons caches. Sections of the tunnels also served as living quarters and hospitals.

[2]   On 16 March 1968, US soldiers attacked the village of My Lai in Vietnam, killing hundreds of unarmed citizens. The attack was reportedly carried out in retaliation after a squad of US soldiers sustained losses in a booby trap.

preparing for war does not guarantee peace. Yet ethnic Europeans love a good fight and a test of strength.

When the Cold War ended, the Europeans, led by the US, could not endure even a brief interlude of peace. They soon looked around for a new enemy. With his simplistic idea of "The Clash of Civilisations" — of an inescapable antagonism between Western (or ethnic European) civilisation and Islamic civilisation — Samuel Huntington[3] helped them find one.

During the Cold War the United States made full use of Muslim antipathy towards atheistic communism to gain their cooperation in expelling the USSR from Afghanistan. It was then that Al-Qaeda was promoted and equipped by the US. The US similarly encouraged Saddam to attack Iran, whose revolutionary regime regarded the US as Satan. But after the Soviets were expelled from Afghanistan and the Iraqi attack against Iran failed, the US turned against its former allies. Afghanistan was attacked and invaded because it played host to Osama. Iraq was then invaded, first because of its alleged possession of weapons of mass destruction and then because the US decided that its former ally, Saddam Hussein, was a dictator. Both reasons are spurious. The urge to make war is too strong, especially war against the weak.

The mistake of the US is to think of Al-Qaeda as an organisation which can be defeated militarily. But Al-Qaeda is a resistance movement, one that probably consists of many groups acting independently. Such groups have emerged in Malaysia and Indonesia — the Al-Maunah and the Gerakan Militan Malaysia in this country, and the Jemaah Islamiah in Indonesia. Their leaders and members may be identified and arrested but others will emerge to take their places.

Such people are not engaged in a war against the US because they are poor and uneducated. Their motivation is more precise and specific. Among Muslims worldwide there is a deep hatred and anger that Israel was created upon Palestinian Arab land. This anger has deepened since the Israelis occupied most of remaining Palestine after 1967, establishing numerous settlements, controlling the movement of people in and out of Palestine as

---

[3]   In 1993 political scientist Samuel Huntington published his book *The Clash of the Civilizations,* which outlined his ideas of the post-Cold War world order.

well as through it, and denying the existence of the Palestinian State and people. More recently, when the Palestinians held elections and Hamas defeated Fatah, the US and Israel refused to recognise Hamas as the elected Palestinian Authority. Taxes collected by Israel which were due to the Palestinian Authority were withheld from the elected Palestinian Authority to prevent the new administration set up by Hamas from functioning.

All this time Israel continued to attack the Palestinians using tanks, helicopter gunships and aircraft. Whole villages were bulldozed and houses demolished, killing all inside. Thousands upon thousands of Palestinians have been jailed by the Israelis. Yet when Hizbullah in South Lebanon arrested two Israeli soldiers, Beirut and other parts of Lebanon were bombed and many civilians were killed. The Israelis are allowed to commit aggression and atrocities against the Palestinians and the US supports them with arms and money. That means the Palestinians are effectively fighting against the armed might of the United States. Unsurprisingly, they always get nothing but bad Press coverage. They are portrayed as the cruel aggressors and Israel as the courageous defenders. Their desperate attempts to carry the war into Israel itself by sending suicide bombers have met with massive Israeli retaliation. Israel and the US have a simple strategy: to out-terrorise the terrorists. Inept Palestinian attacks are repaid by Israeli bulldozers, tanks and helicopter gunships that destroy whole villages and their inhabitants.

739

Recently, Israel attacked the Gaza Strip allegedly because Hamas had fired rockets into Israel. The Western Press ignored the fact that prior to the Hamas rockets, Israel had blockaded Gaza, preventing food, medical supplies and fuel from getting into the strip. The people of Gaza were starved to death, killed for lack of medicine and electrical power for their hospitals and for heating.

When the Israelis attacked Gaza with bombs and rockets, and then with tanks and guns, the Western media reported nothing of the horrors inflicted by the Israeli forces, of children and old people being killed. Instead, the whole Western world is regaled by a blockbuster movie showing the brutalities committed by the Germans in World War II. And so once again the so-called Holocaust is made the excuse for killing Palestinian people.

Britain in particular must be held responsible for the continuing war in West Asia between the Arabs and Israel. After the Ottoman Empire was defeated and dismembered in World War I, the League of Nations entrusted Britain with the administration of Palestine as a mandated territory. At that time the majority of the Palestinians were Arab Muslims. There were also some Arab Christians and only a handful of Jews because most of them lived in European countries. The Europeans had never welcomed the Jews. They were massacred periodically, the last and the worst time by the Nazis.

After World War II, the British were harassed by frequent Jewish terrorist attacks. Wanting to take the easy way out, the British agreed with the Zionist extremists to create a state of Israel in Palestine. So for the Jews, terrorism pays. The people of Palestine, however, were not consulted. After the United Nations partitioned the country, the Arabs were driven out from the Israeli sector and have had to live in refugee camps ever since. In the ensuing 60 years, Palestinians, other Arabs and Muslims worldwide have struggled to recover the land of the Palestinians.

740

But the Americans and British refuse to acknowledge that it was the creation of the state of Israel on Palestinian land that has destabilised the Middle East, pitting Arabs against Jews. With American and British help, more Palestinian land was occupied by Israel after 1967. Whenever the Palestinians fought back to recover their lost land, the British and Americans would help Israel to repulse the Arabs. There will be no solution to the conflict in the Middle East and no reduction of Muslim antagonism towards America and Britain until the Palestinian problem is resolved fairly. As long as that longstanding injustice is not redressed, attacks by Muslims will occur all over the world. The 2001 attack against the World Trade Centre may probably be one of them, albeit the most spectacular and dramatic. There have been several attacks in Britain and attempts have been made to shoot down Israeli aircraft in Africa. The American embassies in Kenya and Tanzania have also been bombed. The Indonesian resort island of Bali was attacked twice, causing deaths to Australians and Americans. In Malaysia, Al-Maunah's attempted armed uprising failed. But the Gerakan Militan Malaysia assassinated a State Assemblyman, robbed banks and exploded bombs in several places. Many of their activists have been arrested and detained. One or two have become explosives specialists for radical Muslim groups in Indonesia. Some of them remain at large. For the moment, Malaysia is free from such attacks, but the anger and bitterness of some of these young Malays have been made palpably worse by the American attacks against Afghanistan and Iraq.

One may label all these attacks as "terrorism", but that is not going to make stopping them any easier. In the eyes of many Muslims they are the work of righteous avengers responding to American assaults against Muslim countries. To a great number of Muslims, the real terrorists are the Americans and the British. Their bombings, shootings and rocket-launched grenade and missile attacks caused widespread terror among those helpless people. A study by Johns Hopkins University in the US verified that 650,000 Iraqis have been killed since the invasion by America. Iraq never had, and certainly does not now have, 650,000 soldiers, so the majority of those killed and the many thousands more wounded must be civilians. For the hundreds and thousands who were killed, wounded, maimed or mentally disturbed, the Americans are the terrorists.

This war between those who claim the legitimacy of state power and those who have been driven to take up arms on behalf of the weak, dispossessed and stateless Palestinians will not end in victory for anyone. But it can be ended if America and Britain put a stop to Israeli intransigence. Solve the Palestine issue and the world will see peace and enjoy better security. Faulting the religion of Islam will get us nowhere.

# Chapter 58:
## Education

I realised long ago that Malaysia needed to improve its education system so that our people would be equipped with the tools necessary to survive in the millennium. I was the only one among my siblings who went to university, which was a rare privilege before Independence. Education was undoubtedly the greatest gift my parents gave me and it was a gift that I always wanted everyone to have.

It was also an area that I was interested in from an early age. While at university I became involved with documenting the situation of Malay students and trying to find out why they were not doing well. I was among those who very early on suggested that the Government establish residential schools for Malay children from the *kampung*, as I knew they could not study at home where the home environment was not conducive and where there was no one to help them with their lessons. When I was a Member of Parliament I was appointed to the Council of the University of Malaya, then later, Chairman of the Malaysian Higher Education Council. I also took on the portfolio of Education Minister in 1974 and later, of course, that of Prime Minister, but despite all my efforts in these various capacities to improve our education system, many problems were to remain even at the time I stepped down from office.

There are more government residential schools in Malaysia than in any other developing country, and I pushed even harder for them when I became Minister of Education. Before that there was a small number of boarding schools, but most were designed to cater to the elite rather than the common people. In 1905 the Colonial Government had established the Malay College at Kuala Kangsar (MCKK) for the children of Malay royalty who were being groomed for senior posts in the Civil Service. MCKK was modelled after the so-called great public schools of England and became the Eton of the East.

When there was a need for better military leadership later, the colonial administration under High Commissioner Sir Gerald Templer established the Federation Military College[1] in 1952, based on similar institutions in England. There was also the Sultan Idris Training College,[2] established in 1922 to train Malay schoolteachers. The early young trainee teachers at this college were among the first nationalists — they set up the Kesatuan Melayu Muda or Young Malays Union, a clandestine nationalist movement whose fiercely anti-colonial members collaborated with the invading Japanese forces.

The push for a broad network of residential schools came only with the setting up of the MARA junior science colleges, or Maktab Rendah Sains MARA (MRSM),[3] starting in 1966. The brightest Malay students from all over the country — as well as a few non-Malays — were sent to these well-equipped residential schools. I was told much later that religious teachers tried to turn these MRSM schools into religious schools, where other subjects were subordinated to conventional spiritual instruction and the performance of religious rituals and more. I hope they will not succeed in subverting our objectives in setting up these schools. We need to know our religion well but not to the exclusion of other fields of knowledge.

743

We did not have a national school system at first, only different types of schools. The English schools established by the colonial administration and by the various Christian missions made up the bulk of the secondary schools in the country. The vernacular schools were divided along racial lines: there were Malay-language government primary schools; there were Chinese private schools which, at both primary and secondary levels, were much influenced by China's system of education; and there were a few small private Tamil primary schools. Pupils who attended these "mother-tongue" schools had no opportunity to mix with each other. Fortunately, some government English schools offered primary education and children of all races attended them. My own school, the Government English School, later renamed Sultan Abdul Hamid College, was of this kind and offered primary as well as secondary-level classes. My classmates were a

---

[1]  The Federation Military College is now known as the Royal Military College and is the foremost boarding school in Malaysia.

[2]  The Sultan Idris Training College was gradually upgraded through the years and became a university on 1 May 1997. It is now known as Universiti Pendidikan Sultan Idris.

[3]  The MARA junior science colleges were established to train secondary and pre-university Bumiputera students in science and technology in preparation for university.

diverse lot and as a result, I never had difficulty befriending or working with people of all races.

When Tun Abdul Razak Hussein held the education portfolio in 1955, he decided to streamline primary schools into a national system with Malay as the medium of instruction. This objective was embodied in the Razak Education Report,[4] but the Government was in no rush to implement it as the country was preoccupied with gaining Independence at the time. The British, who still wielded considerable power over the elected transitional government headed by Tunku Abdul Rahman, were also hardly eager to support it.

Shortly after Independence, there came an abrupt change in our education system. The then Minister of Agriculture and Cooperatives in the Tunku's Cabinet, Aziz Ishak, while acting as Minister of Education, ordered the conversion of all government primary schools to National Schools where the medium of instruction was Malay. The primary classes in the English schools were among those suddenly converted in this way. So too were the Chinese and Tamil government-aided primary schools. The Chinese community immediately protested, but the Cabinet could not easily reverse Aziz's decision since it was popular among Malay educationists and Malays generally. So the Cabinet decided to call the Chinese and Tamil primary schools "National-Type Schools" rather than National Schools. Their curriculum had to conform with that of National Schools, although the medium of instruction would be Chinese or Tamil.

744

The government secondary schools, meanwhile, retained English as their medium of instruction and Chinese and Indian children continued to attend these schools. New Malay-medium secondary schools were started but they did not attract non-Malay students. As a compromise, Chinese secondary schools were to be provided with government financial support if they followed the National School curriculum, but these schools were not popular with Chinese parents. They preferred to send their children to the English medium secondary schools, as did a lot of Malays and most Indians.

---

4   The Razak Report became the basis for the development of the National Education Policy.

After the 1969 General Election and the ensuing race riots in Kuala Lumpur, Tun Abdul Rahman Yaacob was appointed Minister of Education. Tun Razak asked me to help Tun Rahman, but after I had dinner with him I realised he did not want my advice. I was expelled from UMNO anyway a short time later and ceased to be the Minister's adviser. Out of the blue, Tun Rahman announced that all government secondary schools and government-aided schools would become National Secondary Schools, where the teaching would be in Malay. Schools in Sarawak and Sabah, however, were exempted. His decision made Tun Rahman very popular with the Malays, particularly Malay university students, but the move had a political rather than an academic agenda. He had become an UMNO Supreme Council member although, strictly speaking, as a Sarawakian he was not eligible to join the party. The most visible result of the conversion of the English-medium secondary schools to National Secondary Schools was the mass exodus of Chinese students to Chinese National-Type secondary schools, where the teaching was still in Chinese. The National Primary and Secondary Schools thus became almost exclusively Malay, and the only venue where young Malaysians of different races could mix was lost.

745

By the time I became Minister of Education, that pattern was set and it was too late to make any major changes. The only thing I could do was to make the Government National Secondary Schools as well-equipped and attractive as possible. The Government-aided Chinese schools did not get sufficient funds to expand or upgrade, and I hoped this policy might persuade increasing numbers of Chinese parents to send their children to the better-equipped schools in the National Secondary stream. But that was not to be — the Chinese community rose to the challenge and raised sufficient funds to support Chinese schools themselves. Some of their secondary schools were soon better in every way than the government schools.

After the 1969 riots, Malays generally became more intensely conscious of being Malay, the religious dimension of which was important. Levels of Islamic commitment and ritual observance increased, attendance at Friday prayers rose, and there was a constant demand for mosques to be built. There was also strong pressure to provide better religious instruction within the schools. The Colonial Government's English Secondary Schools had not included religious knowledge in their curriculum. The mission schools had taught Christian scripture, which even the Malay students had to study, but Islamic religious knowledge was not part of their curriculum. The Government now introduced Islam as a subject and since it would not be mandatory for non-Muslims, classes in moral education were provided for them instead. Although I was Minister of Education, the details of the Islamic syllabus were determined by Pusat Islam.[5]

I assumed that the religious curriculum would broadly cover all the teachings of Islam. If done properly, teaching the Islamic way of life (*ad-din*) would encourage students to become upright and diligent. Ritual instruction would not be neglected but would be just a part of Islamic instruction, enabling Muslim students to learn and perform all their religious rituals to gain merit for the afterlife. But other non-religious subjects would receive proper attention.

Unfortunately, the syllabus that was adopted neglected instruction in the Islamic way of life and its character-building values. Emphasis was instead placed largely on the proper performance of rituals. Islam was taught as a religion of ritual, of dos and don'ts, of formalistic requirements and prohibitions, not as a religion of far-reaching human and moral responsibility, not as a way of life. Worse, many of the Islamic religious teachers were supporters of PAS, who took the opportunity — and abused their position and public trust — to implant their political creed and outlook into the minds of their young students.

Although religious teachers were of junior status in most schools, they were powerful. Even the head teachers dared not discipline them for fear of being accused of failing to respect religion. When religious teachers required students to perform additional prayers and to recite religious texts for the whole night when the children should be doing their homework instead, head teachers were unable to override them. These religious teachers insisted that the children wear uniforms that they considered Islamic. Girls practically ceased to play games. In some schools the boys had to wear skull caps even when playing during recess.

---

[5] Pusat Islam administers all Islamic-related activities in the country.

Meanwhile, the Government decided that although the national language of Bahasa Malaysia should be the medium of instruction, English had to be a very important second language which everyone must learn and master. But many Malay students, encouraged by young activists and older-style nationalists, decided that knowing only Malay was sufficient for them. They didn't even need to learn it properly as it was their mother tongue. It was enough to know their own local dialects and they were not concerned about mastering modern written and spoken Malay. Very quickly, Malay students became less proficient in their own language and had little command of English to boot. But Chinese and Indian students studied both Malay and English assiduously, while also using their respective mother tongues. These worrying developments took hold largely after I had ceased to be the Education Minister. But there was an exception: the MARA Institute of Technology (ITM), which was developed from the Rural Industries Development Authority (RIDA) training schools, was allowed to use English in its classes. ITM developed into a very big institution — when it became a university it had more than 100,000 students, all of them Malays or other indigenous citizens. Thanks to their familiarity with English, many ITM graduates have been able to pursue postgraduate studies abroad and have done well in life.

I have defended and struggled on behalf of the Malay language as devotedly as any Malay nationalist, if not more so. As far back as the 1940s I was already fighting for the use of the Malay language. I wrote in the *Straits Times* that Malay was not just the language of five million people in Malaya but the language of 120 million people in Indonesia at that time. I dearly wanted Malay to be recognised as a major world language, but with age and experience I realised that a language would only spread if the people speaking that language were successful in life. Then others would want to learn their language too, to enter into their mental universe and cultural world and benefit from sharing in their wisdom.

At one time the Arabs who developed Islamic civilisation were regarded as incomparably knowledgeable, not only in religion but all other fields of knowledge. As a result most people in the Muslim world, extending from Spain to Central Asia, learnt and used Arabic. The Jewish philosopher

Maimonides (or Ibnu Maimun) wrote all his work in Arabic. The Europeans also learnt Arabic to gain access to the intellectual wealth of the great libraries in Cordoba and Baghdad, where the works of Greek philosophers, scientists and mathematicians, translated into Arabic, had been preserved for later ages and other peoples. Strangely, just when the Europeans were learning Arabic, the Muslims decided to pursue no other knowledge except religion and, as a result, Arabic ceased to be an important language of new and living knowledge. It was replaced by Latin and later by other European languages. Arabic became the language of ancient knowledge and wisdom, of an increasingly beleaguered religious tradition, and of an arrested and stagnating civilisation.

Similarly, the use of the English language spread because the English-speaking people were the most successful in colonisation and empire-building. One of those British colonies gained independence and became the most powerful nation in the world, capable of exerting its will and promoting its agenda on a global basis. The US is now responsible for the continued usage of English as the primary language of knowledge and

international relations. Canada, Australia, New Zealand, India and South Africa have also contributed to its world standing, as have the people of the Caribbean. The vast bulk of all scientific knowledge that has been produced and communicated worldwide is now in English. Even the once great national scientific traditions of the Germans, French, Dutch, Russians and Italians, among others, must now project themselves internationally in English, as do the newer scientific cultures of such dynamic countries as Japan and South Korea.

If Malay is to become an international language then the Malay-speaking people must be successful in every way, particularly in pioneering new knowledge. But as a realist I had to admit that Malays are not notably successful in life nor are they the authors of new knowledge. To do that, we will first have to learn from others. The Europeans had to learn Arabic in order to catch up with the Arabs of the days of the great Islamic civilisation. Now, in the same way, Malays must learn English. We can and should learn other languages too, but the inescapable reality is that English is now the lingua franca of knowledge and international commerce.

When looking into the problem of the rising number of unemployed graduates in the late 1990s, the UMNO Supreme Council discovered that part of the problem was that so many of them could not speak English. Some council members suggested that we return to teaching everything in English, but this proposal was rejected after much debate. Still, everyone felt something had to be done to make Malay graduates employable. Malay students had to take the learning of English in their schools more seriously, just as the non-Malay students seemed to do. But many council members felt that as long as English was not a compulsory subject, students would still get the required number of A's for admission into the local universities without doing well in English. We finally decided that some key examination subjects should be taught in English. As most areas of modern applied knowledge were in English, we felt that the best options would be Science and Mathematics.

There were other reasons for choosing Science and Mathematics to be taught in English. Most other subjects taught in schools are relatively static, i.e. they don't change much and little new knowledge is added with the passage of time. But science in particular changes and advances rapidly, so that old knowledge can be actually displaced by new knowledge added almost every day as research is carried out. Almost all this new knowledge is produced in the English language. It is quite impossible to have all of this translated into Malay. We just don't have people qualified in the different fields and fluent in both scientific English and Malay to do this. If there are, they would not want to spend a lifetime translating research papers and books. Failure to gain access to new scientific knowledge would mean we would be left behind. But if we study science in English, each scientist would be able to access the latest findings in his particular field by himself.

749

Conferences in the various scientific fields are held frequently, and participation in scientific discussion worldwide needs the mastery of scientific English. Even the use of Malay versions of English scientific terms will not work.

Furthermore, some Malaysians may want to go for further studies in foreign universities. In most instances teaching in these institutions would be in English. Without mastery of scientific English they will not be able to benefit from these studies. It is the same with mathematics. While mathematics does not change much in terms of content, the applications of mathematics have increased in many fields. It would not be possible to launch a satellite without mathematical calculations of force, trajectory and time. All this mathematical knowledge is available in English. There has yet to be advanced work on mathematical calculations in Malay. And we need many textbooks and papers on advanced mathematics.

For all these reasons I had strongly supported the teaching of Science and Mathematics in English. Malaysians must be as knowledgeable in science and mathematics as the people in developed countries if we wish to achieve Vision 2020.

The teaching of the two subjects was switched to English in 2003, just before I stepped down from office. When introducing anything new in schools, a recurrent problem is the need to begin in the lowest classes and to work gradually upwards as the students are promoted. Once a change is introduced in the lowest classes, it takes 11 years before pupils at all the school levels have been exposed to it, which meant it would take a long time before we could assess the success or otherwise of the change. There was another option: computer software could be designed so that the switch to English for Science and Mathematics could be done in all classes simultaneously. The teachers themselves need not be fluent in English. While teaching their own special subjects they could also improve their command of English together with their students. Whether the Ministry of Education actually took this course of action, I do not know, for they were still looking for retired teachers who used to teach in English. This may solve part of the problem but there are unlikely to be enough older teachers with the necessary experience available.

I have come in for a lot of condemnation by Malay language nationalists and there were many calling for Science and Mathematics to be taught in Malay again. Critics said that six years on, the policy had only opened up a gap between urban and rural students, and that Malay students were falling behind in the two subjects because their grasp of English was just not good enough. The Government resisted acceding to that political pressure for a time, but on 8 July 2009 Deputy Prime Minister Tan Sri Muhyiddin Yassin announced the Cabinet decision to revert to teaching the subjects in Bahasa Malaysia in 2012. I believe that this is a mistake. Education is not just about developing the language but also about acquiring all kinds of knowledge.

Apart from the employability of the graduates, there was also the problem of bringing schoolchildren of different races together. Ever since the English-language schools were converted to National Schools, most Chinese and Indian students ceased to mix with Malay students. Public universities draw students from all the communities, but on campus they do not integrate. The Islamic Studies faculties in Government universities have discouraged Malays from mixing with non-Muslims in the hostels, suggesting that contact or even close proximity with non-Muslims is polluting. The Chinese students also avoid staying in the same dormitories or hostels with the Malay students. This failure of local university students to mix bodes ill for the future of the country. If they create separate enclaves and parallel social spaces on campus, they will reproduce the same kind of racial separation in society at large after they graduate. Far from fostering the development of a cohesive multiracial society and encouraging a capacity in all students, especially Malays, for inter-ethnic interaction and sociability, our universities will instead ensure that the divisive educational streaming by race is carried forward from the primary and secondary levels and perpetuated through the universities to all areas of everyday public life. Malaysians cannot live within their racial compartments. In a multiracial society, it is important that they become familiar with one another while still young. If the schools cannot do this, then our universities should. If they don't, then it will never happen.

751

Earlier, I had suggested a new approach: multi-school campuses or educational precincts that would be known as Vision Schools. The idea was that we would build schools for the three main races within the same campus. In these compounds, students would attend classes in separate schools according to their language preference, but they would be brought together for certain school activities. School assemblies would be in a common assembly hall for all three schools. They would play games together but they would be divided into teams, not according to their schools or race. Each team would have a mix of students from all the schools. All non-academic activities would bring together the different students as participants while ignoring the divisions between their respective schools. Many school societies might also draw together students from all three schools.

Unfortunately, the Chinese educationists objected to this idea. Deferring to their views, many Chinese parents preferred to continue sending their children to their old dilapidated schools rather than let them attend the brand-new Vision Schools. It seemed the Chinese did not want their children to mix with Malay and Indian children. Perhaps they considered the Malay children too playful and inclined not to take their studies seriously. Perhaps they feared some contagion of bad attitudes, or perhaps it was something else — but I was upset by their attitude. Chinese schools were very willing to take in Malay and Indian children, using Chinese as the medium of instruction, and that made their refusal to support the Vision Schools concept even more hurtful. Many Malay parents, recognising that Chinese was the local language of business, were convinced that their children would do better if they knew Chinese. Quite a number also claimed that education in the Chinese schools was actually better, because their teachers were more dedicated and serious.

If these attitudes and practices were to become more widespread, national education in Malay would certainly fail. Yet at times I felt like agreeing with these Malay parents — Malay teachers were not putting their hearts and souls into their jobs and many seemed to be concerned only with their own careers and service conditions. They have always complained endlessly about inadequate pay. Even after pay scales were improved — and they were improved several times during my 22 years as Prime Minister — the same complaints continued to be voiced, as if nothing had been done.

Yet no developing country in the world has spent as much on education as Malaysia. All over the country, we have beautiful school buildings, and some secondary schools look like universities. Visitors from other developing countries have often remarked that Malaysian schools are luxurious and well-equipped. Now we also have Smart Schools, which are equipped with all kinds of modern teaching aids. The educational amenities provided by the Government cannot be faulted. Scholarships, too, are plentiful.

I was also always on the lookout for things that might make knowledge acquisition easier. One day a Malay educationist brought a man from China to my office, accompanied by several children aged five to 10. The man demonstrated how the children could solve arithmetical problems involving big numbers virtually in the blink of an eye. I was intrigued. I wrote down a number of about eight digits to be multiplied by an equally large number. The children rattled off the answer in a few seconds, without writing anything down. I was amazed. These, I thought, must be special children. The man said they were ordinary children trained to use special methods. He also showed me how calculation using the abacus could be as fast as, or faster than, an electronic calculator.

The Chinese man turned out to be a professor from China, and I asked him whether he could teach school children in Malaysia to do the same. He was willing to stay in Malaysia for as long as was necessary to teach Malaysian teachers his method. I was delighted and immediately requested the Ministry of Education to include in the curriculum both the use of the abacus and the Chinese professor's methods of mental arithmetic. It would surely help improve the mathematical skills of our children. But the idea of adding the abacus posed many bureaucratic problems. Government educationists wanted to compare the methods of the man I sent to them with those of another man with similar skills. Then they had to determine a pay scale for the man who, not unreasonably, wanted a special contract. The man was eventually hired after prolonged negotiations lasting for more than a year. I never received any report after that, but I remain convinced that by introducing the abacus, Malay children in particular would improve their mathematical skills.

But education should not only be about acquiring knowledge. It should also be concerned with character-building. It should cultivate the attitudes and attributes which make for good character and leadership, self-confidence, and the inquisitiveness that stimulates thinking and inventiveness. It must help develop a sound orientation towards the world based upon rationality and logical thinking. Intellectual and character development are not separate processes — they go together. A rational person is a decent and good person, and a good person will not act mindlessly or irrationally. A good person is also one who, as well as displaying good ethical values, can think clearly and rationally. Nothing is more dangerous than knowledge in the hands of a corrupt and untrustworthy individual.

Despite the inclusion of religious and moral education in the syllabus, character building and the implanting of good values do not get much attention in Malaysian schools and universities. Most things are learnt by rote and reproduced mechanically during examinations without understanding. Examiners rarely entertain and certainly do not encourage original thinking. One adjunct professor who lectured to a group of university students told me he was disappointed when not one of the students asked him a question. Either they did not understand him, he surmised, or else they had no capacity for analysis and critical thinking.

Many people do not even understand the need to be honest or to guard one's honour. In school, students are urged to be disciplined but are not told why, so they understand discipline simply as an imposition, not as mastery over base desires. It is not explained to them that their lives may one day depend on being disciplined, upon their ability to maintain control over themselves in the most trying of circumstances. Simply being told to be disciplined produces only resentment and resistance, and the end result is anything but the good character that is desired.

My parents instilled in me values which enabled me to face and overcome many challenges over the years. Most parents these days have little time to do that and neither, unfortunately, do schools and teachers. These values, though they may impose self-restraint since they require that we control and hold ourselves back in various ways, are also empowering as they encourage and enable us to do worthwhile and noble things which we would not otherwise be capable of. Some teachers are dedicated and inspiring — they do not simply talk about those values but personify them and, by doing so, persuasively communicate them to others, including their students. But most are just teaching to earn a living and they do not see moulding the character of their students as part of their jobs.

Religious teachers should be among those who have some notion of character development and should thus be committed to influencing the personal development of their students. Regrettably, this is not the case. The ideas they bring are hardly appropriate to these times. They encourage rote learning and dutiful conformity to the outward details of ritual practices, not the ability to understand, choose between and act upon moral choices and key values. Religious teachers should be involved in moral education and the implanting of strong and positive values, but they are not trained to do that. In fact, their understanding of the successful moulding of a mature and moral adult character can be very wrong. They hardly ever teach what made the Muslims successful during the golden era of Islamic civilisation. Their focus is on the mechanical performance of certain rituals and formalities to gain merit in the next world, not upon the individual's inner moral growth. In the end, they encourage the development of a subservient character with an inferiority complex and no self-confidence, a personality that cannot stand tall and be responsible and ethically aware. They encourage, in other words, the development of a personality type that will be obedient to religious dicta, as they themselves embody and understand it.

I believe that everybody is capable of great things, of acquiring knowledge and skills, and of succeeding in whatever they choose to do. God made us so that if we do anything repeatedly, we will improve our capacity and achieve success. That is how I learnt pathology in my third year at Medical College. I read the textbook repeatedly until I not only understood the text but could actually visualise the pages of the book. I could see in my mind's eye the actual text and illustrations when answering questions. It is not about deliberate memorising of the text. It is about becoming very familiar with the information — in the way we recognise faces, for example.

It is the same with practical work. I used to do wood-turning as a hobby. I produced very bad results at first, but by doing the work repeatedly I was able to master the technique and to produce reasonable pieces. For those who diligently master knowledge or skills, there is a bonus. The skills that a person acquires will somehow be passed on to their children and their children's children. I once watched a Balinese boy carving a piece of wood and was amazed at his skill. He was able to produce beautiful sculptured pieces almost effortlessly. I could not do that nor, I knew, could my children. Yet many Balinese people, young and old, can carve beautifully in wood or stone. It appears that they have inherited the skills from their forefathers and improved on them.

If the Malays were to set their hearts on acquiring business skills, for example, I am sure that within one or two generations they would match the Chinese in business. When I tell the Malays this, they are apparently not convinced. The Government provides them all kinds of support to help them acquire knowledge and skills. Unfortunately, they have developed a dependency on this support and demand that it be made permanent. What is the good of becoming an independent nation if internally as individuals and as a community we are always dependent on others?

I have found that it is not only positive attitudes that can be handed down from one generation to another; disabling ones can also be passed on. In one way or another, every child and every generation acquires attitudes and value orientations which become part of an individual and also of the group or race. Character expresses itself in action — in the actions of parents and teachers as they raise the next generation; and in a variety of specialised skills, techniques and attitudes that they hand down. This is how the Japanese became and remain Japanese, the English go on being English, and the thorough Germans continue to be thoroughly German. It is not the colour of the skin or the climate. It is the culture and the value system that they develop.

I have discussed the New Economic Policy at length in these pages and how it has contributed much towards overcoming the gross economic disparities and social disadvantages between the races in Malaysia. But affirmative action cannot go on forever. I had hoped that much of the disparity would disappear through education, which is why we endured criticism of discrimination in the award of scholarships. But it is now nearly 40 years since the NEP was first implemented and we still have not achieved our target of making the Malays own 30 per cent of the country's corporate wealth. The Government's provision of enhanced access to university education to Malays has seen a similar wasting of opportunities. To ask the non-Bumiputera to stand aside and wait while so many of the Bumiputera are happy to play around and not study is unfair.

To address this, the Government decided that admission into the country's universities should be based on merit. If not enough Malays were qualified, or if they had no desire to avail themselves of the opportunities, then qualified non-Malays would be admitted. The Malays raised a great hue and cry, yet the percentage of Malays in the next intake was actually higher than before merit was taken into account. I was mystified, until I discovered that the admission qualifications were not the same for the Malays and the non-Malays. Malay admissions were based on matriculation results while the non-Malays had to sit for the Higher School Certificate Examination. I had hoped to shock the Malays into waking up and taking their education seriously, but I failed. My action was frustrated by the desire of Malay officials to "help" Malay students. Malays will never learn to compete on a level playing field if their protectors keep tilting the ground in their favour.

In recent years, we have also had the problem of an imbalance in our university students, up to 70 per cent of whom are now female. It cannot be that so few boys are capable of qualifying for entry. Many say that they prefer to work and earn an income rather than spend several years in the universities earning nothing. Some say they prefer to be trained as technicians, but you do not see them working in these fields. Many are involved in activities which verge on the criminal. Almost all the *mat rempit* — the motorcycle daredevils — are Malays, as are most drug addicts.

Unless a way is found to draw Malay boys into university education, the qualified girls are not going to find husbands they can look up to and respect. Poorly-qualified husbands will earn less than their wives. Perhaps many Malay men like things that way, to be economically dependent upon and supported by their wives while they laze around in coffee shops or indulge in motorcycle stunts. Perhaps this kind of dependence and passivity suits them. If so, if they want to be sons of indulgent mothers, not responsible and socially-capable husbands to Malay wives and heads of strong Malay families, then they should not deny the rights of others. Their attitude makes me worry about the Malay future. Where, I wonder, have we gone wrong? We talk these days about lifetime education and there may well be a few late developers who can benefit from educational opportunities later in life, but they are surely far fewer in number than the legions of underperforming Malays.

As retirement approached, my time to deal with all these problems ran out. There was nothing that I could do anymore. Long before I became Prime Minister, the ideas that I had laid out in *The Malay Dilemma* had slowly crystallised in my mind since the time I had been a young medical student in Singapore in the early 1950s, and probably long before that. I was now nearing the end of 22 years of service as Prime Minister. Yet, for all of our achievements, some of the most basic problems of the Malay people that I had outlined in *The Malay Dilemma* still persisted. Some seemed no closer to being resolved than when I started.

All I can say is that I regret my failure to change the Malays, to mould the new Malay, to equip the Malay people with the knowledge and skills necessary for them to make a success of their lives and to take their rightful place in their country. If I seem to be concerned only with the Malays, it is because the other races, even the Indians, seem to be able to take care of themselves. I have met Indian students in the furthest corners of the world struggling to study medicine. Malays have been given reserved places in the universities at home but they cannot be bothered to qualify for these places. What more do they expect to be done for them?

# Chapter 59:
# Resignation

For 21 years I had done my job as best as I could, but I was becoming increasingly mindful of what my mother had always said when I was a young boy: never overstay your welcome. I chose to see my resignation as the end of one part of my life and the start of another, one that would be different and perhaps challenging as well. I could not imagine myself doing nothing. Apart from writing my memoirs, I wanted this to be a time for travelling and meeting people. I had hoped to contribute something different or extra during this quieter period of my life.

When I was finally sure that the time was right I kept it to myself. I did not tell anyone, not even Hasmah. Instead, I prepared letters to the King, the Chief Secretary to the Government and the UMNO Secretary-General in readiness for my public announcement. I wrote the letters by hand as I did not want anyone to see them. I had made up my mind to announce my resignation at the end of the 56th UMNO Annual General Assembly in 2002, when I was to give the closing speech. I chose that time and place because then the announcement would be a public statement that I would not be able to retract. I thought that if I told a few people, they would try to dissuade me. If I then reversed my position, my critics would say I had reneged. The foreign Press would also have a good laugh if they heard me say I would resign and then did not.

I planned my exit for months. Despite not telling anyone, a few friends told me not to resign. They had doubts about my successor. But I was determined to keep my promise to myself. It was nevertheless a strain — the feeling was indescribable. After 21 years as Prime Minister, the step was a huge one for me as at that time, I felt I was still reasonably popular. But while keeping my secret was a terrible burden, I felt I should not lessen it by burdening others . Hasmah had no inkling of my decision, but I knew I could count on her understanding and support at all times. The only thing I did was to ask my deputy Tun Abdullah Ahmad Badawi — almost a year before my announcement — whether he was ready to take over. He said he was. But still I did not indicate the actual time I would resign.

I announced my decision to step down as UMNO President and Prime Minister at 5.50 pm on 22 June 2002. It was towards the end of my speech to close the assembly. I anticipated some reaction but not the kind I received. All at once, people rushed up in a throng to the rostrum and asked me to withdraw my announcement. The then Wanita UMNO chief Tan Sri Rafidah Aziz and UMNO Youth chief Datuk Seri Hishammuddin Hussein were overcome with emotion. Rafidah, who later said she broke the heel of her shoe as she rushed up to me, kept asking me, "Why? Why? Why?" Datuk Paduka Ibrahim Ali, the perennial problem child of UMNO politics, also came up to the stage.

Hasmah, who was sitting in the gallery above, later told me how she experienced the surprising moment. When she heard my announcement she was just as stunned as everybody else. A camera crew from New Zealand zoomed in on her and caught her with her mouth agape. She sat there for a few minutes, trying to take it all in; then people around her nudged her to go down and get me to change my mind. Only then did she get up from her seat, although she remained fully aware of the fact that it was still an UMNO assembly and she could not interfere. She had known I would resign one day, but she had not known it would be at that time or in that way.

Before making the announcement I had feared that I might break down, but what happened was even worse. Despite having rehearsed my speech, when the moment came I found I could not say the few sentences coherently. I shed tears shamelessly. I was not able to handle this great turning point in my life as I had intended.

As UMNO leaders crowded around me on the rostrum, asking me to reconsider, I remember shaking my head and saying that I had made up my mind. Tun Abdullah went to the other rostrum on the stage and immediately asked UMNO Permanent Chairman Tun Sulaiman Ninam Shah to get the assembly to reject my decision.

Tun Sulaiman rose and tried to say something, to appeal for calm, but there was pandemonium in the hall. Delegates were chanting and singing party songs and shouting "No! No!" and "Don't resign!" A number of Supreme Council members then led me off the stage. We went to the presidential room next to the assembly hall where I was surrounded by more Supreme Council members and UMNO leaders, who kept pressing me to stay. All the Vice-Presidents were there and so were other party veterans including Tan Sri Aishah Ghani[1] and my sister-in-law Tan Sri Saleha Ali.[2] Even Tun Ghazali Shafie and Tengku Razaleigh Hamzah came in. It must have been a shock to everyone. They must all have wanted to know what was going on — or else they feared being left out in some way.

Soon after, Tun Abdullah, who was UMNO Deputy President, proposed that the Assembly reject my resignation. They agreed unanimously. Because I was in the room, I was not aware of what was happening outside. By now there were reporters everywhere and more and more people crowded into the room to see me. To spare me from the onslaught, I was smuggled out through a back door and driven back to the official residence in Putrajaya. All this overwhelming adulation and support may now appear excessively dramatic and probably insincere, but at the time I was touched by people's reactions and words.

The Opposition labelled my announcement a *sandiwara* — a play staged for sympathy votes ahead of a snap General Election. Others said it was all a cynical act to consolidate a mandate within the party for me to continue. None of this is true. Twenty-one years is a long time to be the Prime Minister of a country, and those who have not carried that burden cannot imagine what it feels like. I felt that I had overstayed and, anyway, had I not stepped down, my designated successor would think I would never do so. Now some people tell me my resignation was a mistake, but imagine what would have been said if I had not gone: "When is this old man going to stop?"; "Does he want to be Prime Minister forever?"; "Enough is enough."

That night, my children gathered at the residence to be with us. They were concerned about my health, specifically about a possible heart attack after the strain of the day. They and Hasmah all supported my decision to retire. Several UMNO leaders, including Tun Abdullah, came to convey the

---

[1]   Tan Sri Aishah Ghani was one of the most prominent women in UMNO politics, serving as a Member of Parliament from 1962 to 1986 and as Social Welfare Minister from 1973 to 1984.

[2]   Tan Sri Saleha Ali, Hasmah's sister, was an advocate for the rights of women and the disabled, a politician, and the first Malay woman to attend the London School of Economics.

feelings of the party representatives at the Annual General Assembly and I told them that I would give their request serious consideration. I decided that a transition period to allow for a smooth transfer of power would be best, so the following day, I confirmed that I would stay on for another year until after the NAM and OIC meetings in Kuala Lumpur in October of 2003.

Throughout my tenure, I tried hard to establish certain standards. Firstly, I did not encourage the adulation and excessive glorification that is often given to leaders. I was determined that there would be no personality cult. Even when I held the education portfolio, I stopped the practice of naming schools after the Minister. When I became Prime Minister I also refused to allow the naming of buildings and facilities after myself or any living person other than the Malay Rulers. I gave instructions that my official picture should not be displayed in government buildings, although this was widely ignored. To date, nothing has been named after me, except an orchid. I even rejected the idea of a memorial library.

I was and am still passionately against setting up political dynasties. While I was Prime Minister, my children were not given any role in the Government or in UMNO, and even if they had harboured interest in any political post, they would not have received my support. They may have been upset but I had to turn down several proposals to have them stand as candidates in elections. My position was this: if they were keen on politics, they would have to start at the grassroots level and work their own way up. I did not allow Mukhriz to take over my parliamentary constituency when the party proposed him upon my retirement. My dislike for nepotism extends to even distant members of my family. Although my brother-in-law was appointed *Menteri Besar* of Selangor by Tun Hussein Onn, I did not hesitate to remove him when accusations were made that he was corrupt.

Throughout my premiership, I worked hard to set a good example to people generally and to all UMNO leaders. I wanted to show that I could still get things done without being corrupt and that others should be able to do the same. Most people assume that those with the opportunity to be corrupt will be corrupt . Theirs is a very poor view of human nature. While they may be right about themselves, this does not make them right about others. Yet without any supporting evidence, and based solely on dubious inferences, such people have always assumed that I was corrupt while in office. It was not easy to convince them that I was not.

During my time as Prime Minister, I had adopted the slogan "leadership by example" and I tried to live by that slogan in every way. My stepping down voluntarily was part of that creed. Leaders should not cling to their position but should learn to recognise the signs of what their followers feel. If they felt it was time that their leaders should go, they should go. Although I now know that those who benefited from my decision will not always be grateful or even appreciative, I never regretted resigning voluntarily. I still think that leaders, no matter how popular they may be, should listen to their conscience and not wait until they are pushed out.

The first of several events which demanded my attention during the one year before retirement was the Non-Aligned Movement (NAM), which held its 13th summit on 24 February 2003. The Americans had not invaded Iraq yet, but I made a point of condemning their support of Israel. At that time Muslims were being condemned as terrorists and Prophet Muhammad (peace be upon him) was being called a terrorist leader by some born-again Christian preachers. This was clearly an attempt to make a reality of Samuel Huntington's clash of civilisations theory. I was incensed by the double standards shown by Americans and Europeans. When the Israelis committed terrifying acts such as the massacre at the Sabra and Shatila camps, they were not called terrorists. These blatant double standards infuriated Muslims. I told the NAM meeting that I condemned war as it "is about slaughtering people ... war must be outlawed".

A month later, on 20 March, Iraq was invaded. I had been against it and had written to Bush and Blair not to undertake this venture as it would worsen the situation. I am no clairvoyant. But seeing the desperation of the Palestinians and their suicide bombers, it was not difficult to foresee the acts of terror that would follow the attack on Iraq.

Apart from NAM and the OIC, I also had to attend the ASEAN Summit Meeting in Bali, the APEC Meeting in Bangkok and the ASEAN Federation of Engineering Organisations (AFEO) Meeting in Jogjakarta.

My last two official visits were to Timor Leste and Papua New Guinea. At home I had to preside over the 46th UMNO General Meeting, and present the 2004 Budget and the mid-term review of the Eighth Malaysia Plan.[3] I was pretty busy.

I had heard of lame duck presidents whose decisions and directives were not taken seriously in expectation of change when the new President took over. But I did not expect to be a lame duck Prime Minister. I fully expected my successor to at least implement the decisions that the Cabinet had agreed to. In the meantime, I carried on governing as there were infrastructure projects essential for the growth of the country that needed to be carried out. Among them were the transfer of water from Pahang to Selangor, the double-tracking and electrification of the railway from Johor Baru to Padang Besar, the bridge to replace the Causeway, and the high-tech incinerator for solid waste in Broga, Selangor.

In June 2003, UMNO was again scheduled to hold its assembly, the last such meeting I would preside over. I spent a lot of time writing my opening speech as I did not want it to be too emotional. It had to be about the nation, the people and the party — not about my personal farewell. I wanted to speak about what was likely to happen and the need for the party and its members to prepare for the future. Malaysia, I said, had changed greatly since achieving Independence 46 years earlier. The population had increased by 500 per cent from five million to 25 million. That the Barisan Nasional was still in power and still elected by the people to rule the country was remarkable. Most parties which fought for Independence had disappeared. The stability and the progress of the country had been made possible through the wisdom of the first Prime Minister, Tunku Abdul Rahman, who was responsible for setting up the coalition of parties which prevented Malaysian politics from becoming an unending conflict between different races. Despite their many failures, the Malays had made tremendous progress, displaying their ability to take over the administration of the country from the British and also rising to high positions in big multinational corporations.

---

[3] The key points of the Eighth Malaysia Plan were to: shift to a knowledge-based growth strategy; speed up the transformation of the agricultural, manufacturing and services sectors and; perpetuate the equitable distribution of national wealth to strengthen socioeconomic stability.

The whole world, I said, had changed. The principle of non-interference in the internal affairs of countries was now disregarded by the powerful ethnic European countries. We in Malaysia must therefore learn to know the Europeans well as they would continue to play a major role in our lives. The United Nations, I pointed out, would not be able to help us. I also warned against the kind of hedonism spread by the Europeans through their media and culture.

Internally we would face challenges, and the younger generation would find difficulty in race relations. Islam had not been taught properly. We had to also remember that we were not yet rich and should not behave as if we were. While we would like to see our people earn more, this would have to be based upon hard work and greater productivity. As for UMNO, its performance would largely depend on its members. Leadership struggles would only weaken it. Since its founding, there had been at least three groups that had broken away from the party: Dato' Onn Jaafar's Independence of Malaya Party (succeeded by his Party Negara), Tengku Razaleigh's Semangat 46 and Datuk Seri Anwar Ibrahim's Parti Keadilan. PAS, too, was formed by a group that had splintered from UMNO, but such splits were unproductive. The purpose of contests in the party should be about finding good leaders, not to carry on quarrels and further personal ambitions. Once a party election is over, the losers should close ranks with those who had won. This would be the conduct of those who really understood democracy. I again urged the party and its members to hold fast to the true teachings of Islam. Differing interpretations of Islam, I had always believed, made Muslims quarrelsome.

Finally, I reminded members that UMNO was not just any party, but the ruling party of Malaysia. This imposed a heavy responsibility on all its members and leaders, who had to be prepared to make sacrifices. Its struggles were for the wellbeing of all and not any one individual. Ultimately, everyone gains from the growth of the nation. People should remember that there would always be fewer positions in the party and government than the number of people aspiring to them. I thanked people for their support and prayed to Allah to save His people from evil influences, enabling them to achieve success and become models to all Muslims in the world.

I was calm throughout. Though many expected me to, this time I did not shed a single tear. Rereading my speech now, I feel I did not do justice to my predecessors. I mentioned Tunku Abdul Rahman's contribution only once, but, whatever my occasional, well-publicised differences with him, the Tunku had contributed so much that it made my own task easier. I also owed much to Tun Razak Hussein, who literally rescued me from the political wilderness and influenced Tun Hussein Onn into choosing me as his deputy. There were others too who had supported me who I should have mentioned, but the speech was already too long and I could not thank them all. I now regret my priorities in that speech. My main concern at the time was to impart my final advice to members, to UMNO and the people as a whole. Once I was no longer Prime Minister, I might not be able to do so as effectively. Those present gave me prolonged applause and a standing ovation. I was touched by this, and it made me feel that all the 22 years of toil and tears had been worthwhile. In the light of everything that has happened since then however, I wonder now what the applause and standing ovation were really worth .

766    On 21 June, the last day of the Assembly, I delivered my closing speech where I again said corruption was the bane of the Malays. This was because they loved to take *jalan yang mudah*, or the easy way out. Their Rajas in the past had lost their lands, even their sovereignty, because of their desire to get material things quickly and without great effort. Corruption, I warned, would destroy the Malays, cost them their independence and would enslave them.

For a while, I was amused by the new title that UMNO members bestowed upon me. They called me YDK for *Yang di Kasihi*, or The Beloved One, but I good-humouredly told them that while I appreciated it, the same love had to be shown to the incoming President and Prime Minister. Looking back I feared I did not do a good job in that last speech. By nightfall, when the General Assembly ended, I was exhausted. I flew to Langkawi intending to rest, but I could not resist checking out the new marina at Telaga Harbour and the work on the second phase of the Perdana Gallery, where all the official gifts I had received as Prime Minister were to be displayed for public viewing. The gifts were not given to me in my personal capacity so I did not consider them mine.

Perhaps I should have left the presentation of the 2004 Budget and the mid-term review of the Eighth Malaysia Plan to the incoming Prime Minister. But I presented it myself, believing — perhaps unwisely — that after I left office it would not see many changes. When I delivered my Budget speech on 12 September, I dealt at length with every aspect of development, as I wanted to warn the country of the challenges ahead.

After all my years in office, I realised that we could not always depend on foreign investments, a fact which I stated in my speech. We had to get our own people to save and invest, and for this there should be new incentives. The manufacturing sector would continue to be the primary contributor to the growth of the economy, which was expected to expand at 7.2 per cent in 2004. The day before I stepped down, I presented the mid-term review of the Eighth Malaysia Plan.

On 29 October, the Chief Secretary Tan Sri Samsudin Osman came to see me at the Ministry of Finance to tell me that the Agong had decided to confer on me the *Seri Maharaja Mangku Negara*, the highest award for a civilian, which carries the title "Tun". At first I said I would not accept it. Long ago, when I was first offered an award carrying the title "Dato'", I had given an excuse and turned it down. I had always felt that awards should not be automatically given to holders of posts. Rather, they should be given after you performed well in office, when a careful assessment could then be made of your contribution. If, after some time, you are still considered worthy, you may then be given the award.

767

I tried to apply this principle when I was in office, but the general feeling was that as soon as an officer was appointed to a certain post, he should be given the award and the title that was considered to be consistent with the dignity of that position. So, while we have kept some control over prices in the economy, we have suffered runaway status inflation in Malaysia. When I was still Prime Minister the award of a Tunship was offered to me several times, but I had turned down all those offers. However, when Samsudin urged me to accept the award, I changed my mind as I did not want to seem unappreciative and disrespectful of the Agong.

As the time approached for me to step down, I grew concerned about whether Tun Abdullah would choose Datuk Seri Najib Razak as Deputy

Prime Minister. I felt that I had been a little unfair to Najib — who had won the most number of votes for Vice-President — when I chose Tun Abdullah. So I wanted to be sure that Najib would take the number two spot, even though the appointment was the prerogative of the Prime Minister. In one of my impromptu speeches before I stepped down, I said openly that I hoped Tun Abdullah would choose Najib. The newspapers reported this prominently, reminding me that the choice of Deputy Prime Minister was Tun Abdullah's. When Najib was finally appointed as Deputy Prime Minister, I was relieved.

In the meantime, large advertisements began to appear in the local papers, thanking me and paying tribute to my 22 years as Prime Minister. This is an especially Malaysian practice. Full-page advertisements to thank and congratulate the Agong, Sultans, Prime Ministers and even Ministers on special occasions are common. State governments, companies and individuals all do this. UMNO state committees and divisions also place such full-page displays to congratulate and thank the President. Politically, the advertisements are all-too-often empty formality. While some people who placed such displays to thank me were doubtless sincere, I now realise they did not reflect real sentiment. Malays often like to *melepaskan batuk di tangga* (which translates literally as, "cough at the foot of the stairs"), to let you know that they are there and to get some credit for having been around. How reliable they are is not easily assessed. For myself, I saw the practice of placing such advertisements as an unnecessary waste of money. But the newspapers were unhappy when I suggested that the practice be stopped as it was a good source of income for them.

For the new Prime Minister, I had only goodwill. I chose him after UMNO had made him eligible by electing him as one of its Vice-Presidents. He was my choice because he was older and appeared to be free from corruption (he was popularly known as "Mr Clean"), even though I was not sure at first which of the three Vice-Presidents had won the most votes. Remembering that I myself had been the Vice-President with the smallest number of votes when Tun Hussein chose me as Deputy Prime Minister, I did not think that I should use votes as the only criterion. Tun Abdullah was 64 when he took office, which made him the oldest man to become Prime Minister in our history — I had been the oldest before that, at 56. I thought that Tun Abdullah's age would translate into experience and ability.

I did wonder: should anything go wrong with the country's progress, would I be able to refrain from interfering? But I had given a promise that I would not interfere once I stepped down so I did not dwell on the matter. I had made sure that the Government and the economy were in good shape. I had stayed on to make certain we recovered from the regional financial crisis, and to resolve the problem of Anwar. I also led the party in the 1999 General Election and won with the usual two-thirds majority, so I had nothing to worry about. I really could not foresee how drastically things would change just a few short years later.

# Chapter 60:
# The OIC Furore

In October 2003, just a few weeks before I stepped down from office, I gave a speech at the 10th summit of the Organisation of the Islamic Conference (OIC) that provoked the West, and the US in particular, into condemning me as anti-Semitic. We were playing host to the conference that year — I was the OIC Chairman and I wanted Malaysia to breathe life into the organisation. The summit was also the first formal meeting of Muslim leaders since the events of 11 September 2001, and my aim was to alert its members to the situation Muslims were now facing as the "war on terrorism" unfolded.

In my speech, I said that Muslims had to learn from the Jews, who had overcome centuries of oppression to become one of the most powerful peoples in the world. I quote: "They (the Jews) survived 2,000 years of pogroms not by hitting back, but by thinking. They invented and successfully promoted socialism, communism, human rights and democracy so that persecuting them would appear to be wrong, so they may enjoy equal rights with others. With these they have now gained control of the most powerful countries and they, this tiny community, have become a world power. We cannot fight them through brawn alone. We must use our brains also."

This is precisely what the Muslims in the US should do to counter the powerful Jewish lobby. When they strategise, Muslims can be a force to be reckoned with. It is said that the Jewish lobby is so mighty that when they vote, they can determine who will become the US President. During the 2004 US presidential election, I had written to the Muslims in the US not to vote for Bush. It was not because his opponent was any better. I just wanted the Muslims to show that they too could be a force in US elections. But the Muslims divided their votes between the two candidates and they failed to be relevant in US politics.

I used the Jews as role models for Muslim countries, who for too long have fought among themselves instead of seeking the unity that Islam enjoins upon them. Many of us Muslims are oppressed and humiliated by others but because of our disunity we have allowed this oppression and have often aided the enemies of Muslims to kill and wage war against other Muslims.

I tackled this question in my speech: "From being a single *ummah* we have allowed ourselves to be divided into numerous sects, *mazhabs¹* and *tarikats,²* each more concerned with claiming to represent true Islam rather than accepting that we all belong to the *ummah*, the Muslim community. We fail to notice that our detractors and enemies do not care whether we are true Muslims or not, whether we belong to one sect or another. To them we are all Muslims, followers of a religion and a Prophet who they declare promotes terrorism, and we are all their sworn enemies. They will attack and kill us, invade our lands, bring down our governments whether we are Sunni or Shiite or Wahabbi or whatever. And we aid and abet them by attacking and weakening each other, and sometimes by doing their bidding, acting as their proxies to attack fellow Muslims. We try to bring down our governments through violence, succeeding only in weakening and impoverishing our countries."

There was good reason for me to be harsh. Muslims make up 1.3 billion of the world's population and yet largely remain a backward community. There are some who would have us believe that only the afterlife matters, that it is Islamic to be poor, to suffer and to be oppressed in this world. These Muslims say all they have to do to be good Muslims is to wear certain garments and perform certain rituals and the joys of heaven will be theirs. They readily disregard whole sections of the Quran.

That October, I felt that the whole world was looking at us, at that meeting of the OIC. Over one billion Muslims were placing their hopes in us to lead and to guide them in restoring the honour of Islam and the Muslims. How can it be the Will of Allah that we stand by and do nothing about this, for doesn't it say in *Surah Ar-Ra'd*, verse 11, that "He will not change the fate of a community until the community has tried to change itself"? As host of the OIC Summit, it was crucial for me to remind Muslims not to let the *ummah* down. In doing so, I had to make comparisons with other,

---

¹   *Mazhab* is an Arabic term that refers to an Islamic school of thought.

²   *Tarikats* are Islamic religious orders devoted to a mystical search of divine truth.

more advanced communities and this was what the international audience picked up to demonise me.

Anyone who reads my OIC speech in its entirety will see that it is actually very balanced and fair. I may have been harsh with the Jews for the wrongs they have done, but I also praised them as role models. Despite their hardships, they acquired a wide range of skills and many became very rich and powerful financiers, politicians, scientists and businessmen. Similarly, I pointed out that many Muslims have done well the world over in terms of finance, politics and economics, but I condemned the Muslims for constantly fighting among themselves and for wilfully refusing to acquire the skills that would allow them to be competitive. I urged young Muslims to stop participating in suicide attacks and criticised those who believed that Islam was against science and progress. I wanted them to use their heads so that the Muslim community could recover its dignity and restore Islam's greatness.

To convince them, I made the following statement: "The Europeans killed six million Jews out of 12 million. But today the Jews rule this world by proxy. They get others to fight and die for them." The Jews claim they were almost exterminated by the Holocaust. They were nearly defeated both physically and spiritually and yet they came back even stronger. Once a nationless people, today they rule Israel with an iron hand and wield influence and authority in countries like the US.

This was an important comparison to make and both history and current affairs bear evidence to what I said. I was shocked when I visited Palestine in 2005 and saw that the whole country was occupied by Israel. There were roads there that Palestinians were not allowed to use and places in their own country they could not go to. It is patently clear why Arab anger is so terrible. It drives them to horrific acts, including turning their bodies into weapons by strapping on bombs. Terrible as this is, you cannot dismiss what they do as madness. They have been living in inhuman conditions for over 60 years, and they have to go to extremes to reclaim the land which belongs to them. I do not think they will ever succeed by doing what they have been doing and I find this recourse neither morally appropriate nor politically effective, but desperate people do desperate things. To state this is not to be an apologist for violence, it is to plead for human insight and understanding.

All this has added to the low self-esteem among Muslims, which I mentioned in the OIC speech: "There is still a feeling of hopelessness among the Muslim countries and their people. They feel that they can do nothing right. They believe that things can only get worse. The Muslims will forever be oppressed and dominated by the Europeans and the Jews. They will forever be poor, backward and weak."

I have always believed that creating Israel was a mistake. Even before the end of World War II, the Europeans had wanted to remove the Jews from their continent, considering places like South America and Uganda as potential homes for them. They did not want to surrender any of their own land but were happy to make available land that was not theirs. At that time, the number of Jews in Palestine was very small, so the Europeans decided to divide the country and apportion part of it to become the state of Israel. Naturally, the Arabs were furious. How would Americans have responded if half of Texas were taken away by a third party and given to the Mexicans? In the case of Palestine, the land was not only divided, but the long-resident Arabs were also expelled to make room for Israel, without any compensation. The few Arabs who have remained in Israel are treated worse than second-class citizens. If ever there was a racist country, it is Israel. Its citizenship is based on race, not on residence or loyalty.

773

Israel's strategy is to out-terrorise the Palestinians by officially committing worse acts of terrorism. As they do this, the world remains silent — out of guilt for the Holocaust. The West created the state of Israel and so they must justify their decision by supporting it come what may. Those who argue that Israel cannot simply be wished away should note that it occupies more land than was originally allocated by the United Nations in 1947. Israel must also accept the return of the Arabs they drove out — it is their land after all. But the Zionists are wary of letting the Arabs back in, fearing that if they return their numbers may grow quickly.

Given all these facts, it was not wrong of me to want to shake the Muslims out of their apathy and disunity. These were the reasons why, after more than 50 years of fighting in Palestine, the Muslims have not achieved any results. The situation has, in fact, gotten worse and I needed to remind members why the OIC was created. The principles of the Conference, according to its charter, are to sustain Islamic social and economic values and promote unity among member states. It also emphasises the importance of culture, science and technology. Malaysia has always taken its OIC role seriously since Tunku Abdul Rahman was appointed the Conference's first Secretary-General from its founding in May 1971 to 1973.

As the voice of the Muslim community, the OIC is very weak because its members can never agree on anything among themselves. The OIC works on the basis of consensus, but this can never be achieved. So it can never decide or act on anything. I thought that Malaysia might help find ways to make the group more effective. That, regrettably, did not happen. I quietly suggested abandoning the idea of consensus and suggested instead that a few member countries, a coalition of the like-minded, respond to developments without committing the whole OIC. You can get five countries to agree on something, but not 50, and certainly not 50 fractious Muslim countries. The principle of majority rule often works, but in the OIC getting even a majority is impossible. It is a gathering of minorities, many of them a minority of one. Some OIC leaders thought abandoning consensus was a good idea, but nobody has taken it up. Besides, it would require a consensus to give up consensus. This is the "infinite regress" of Muslim disunity.

Very few of the goals stated in the charter have been achieved and nowhere is the absence of unity so glaring than on the issue of Palestine. As far as I could see, Muslims had done little or nothing to help themselves and I did not shy away from asking tough questions in my speech: "But is it true that we should do and can do nothing for ourselves? Can we only lash back blindly in anger? Is there no other way than to ask our young people to blow themselves up and kill people and invite the massacre of more of our own people?" The constant bickering and endless infighting within the *ummah* only worsened their situation, and that is why I told them their prayers were not likely to be answered. This is a harsher judgment than the one I had passed on the Jews. Yet for this, I was never given due credit by the Jews and their apologists.

774

The condemnation of my speech was swift, with one Israeli official saying that my speech fuelled "further hatred and misunderstanding". A spokesman for the Israeli foreign ministry told CNN: "It comes as no surprise that in a summit like this, there is a search for the lowest common denominator among the members, which is Israeli bashing." A Bush administration official declared that my "hate-filled" remarks further cemented my legacy of "outrageous and misguided public statements". The then Australian Prime Minister John Howard called it offensive: "Let me make it clear — any invocation of rivalry between Jews and Muslims is very unhelpful," he said in a public address over radio. In Brussels, European Union leaders accused me of spreading falsehoods and sowing ethnic and religious divisions: "His unacceptable comments hinder all our efforts to further inter-ethnic and religious harmony and have no place in a decent world, " the EU leaders said in a statement.

Obviously, none of these people read the whole speech; if they did, they must have decided to pick only a few quotes and take them completely out of context. They had no idea that in May 1987, the Malaysian Government invited a group of Israeli schoolchildren to visit our country because we wanted to show them that Muslims here harboured no hatred towards them. Yitzhak Rabin was the Prime Minister of Israel then and he was less of a hawk than some of his predecessors, which made the visit possible. In 1997, despite objections from PAS, we allowed Israel's cricket team to play here in the second tier of the World Cricket Tournament. Again, the idea was to demonstrate to the world that Muslims, far from the stereotype, were not irrational.

775

But none of this stopped people from branding me anti-Jewish. It does not bother me much, however, because I know that if it were true, I would not have Jewish friends. I am not against Jews or Israelis, but I am against what the Zionists are doing to the Palestinians. Somehow though, it is impossible for me to say anything about this without being accused of being anti-Semitic. The world is strangely inconsistent this way. I cannot fathom why it is permissible to condemn all Muslims as terrorists but not to criticise some Jews for what they do. Even suggesting that the number of Jews killed in the Holocaust was less than six million can get you into serious trouble. In 2006, the British revisionist historian David Irving, was jailed in Austria for almost a year for questioning this figure when he was in the UK. I often wonder how the world would regard a Muslim country that jailed anyone who said that Muslims are terrorists or that the Prophet Muhammad's teachings are evil. This is the way things are: while some statements can be made with impunity, others can be stigmatised or even criminalised wherever they are uttered. It all depends on the power of those who uphold or reject such statements. All the talk about freedom of speech is just meaningless rhetoric.

As much as I have serious objections to what they have done, I also admire the Jews for their resilience. In the years immediately after World War II, they could not be admitted into Harvard University, either as students or staff. But these days many of the professors there are Jews. There was once a US Government restriction on financial institutions being run by Jews, and they overcame that too, by providing financial services that no one else could. Their numbers are small but their cultural and political influence is great, as they own most national and international media outlets. They also dominate the financial institutions and the policy-making think-tanks.

The Muslims, by contrast, give up easily and lack focus. However, the reports that came out after my speech conveniently ignored what I had said against them, even though I had been as tough in my criticism of them — for their ignorance and folly — as I had been of the Jews for their ruthless shrewdness. Several European leaders wanted to draft a resolution to denounce my statement as false and offensive. I can prove that everything I said was factually correct. I waited for them to do so as I already knew what I would say in reply. These were the same leaders who spoke so self-righteously about human rights and freedom of speech. People are free to read my speech any way they like, but the fact remains that I took pains to be fair. I am ready to criticise Muslims so it would be less than balanced if I did not also criticise the Jews. I was exercising my right of free speech.

The outrage generated by my OIC speech did not abate for some time. At the APEC Summit in Bangkok soon after, a number of media reports said that President George W. Bush had pulled me aside to rebuke me for what I said. What actually happened was quite different. In what seemed like an apologetic tone, he tried to explain to me the domestic politics involving Jews and Muslims in his country. I remember telling Hasmah that he sounded contrite for his harsh remarks about me. But Bush's spin doctors told the Press that he had verbally slapped me for my statement that the United States served as a proxy of the Jews.

The West is ever ready to turn a blind eye to the faults of the Jews, perhaps because Europeans carry so much guilt over their treatment of the Jews in their history and the Holocaust. They are right to feel guilty, because for ages they periodically massacred the Jews. But this does not justify ignoring Jewish depredations. Most people in the West may have forgotten the acts of terror committed by the Irgun[3] and Haganah militias[4] and the massacre of Palestinian Arabs in Deir Yassin[5] during the Jewish struggle against the British. Nobody dares point out that Israel's behaviour is not what the world would expect from victims of the Holocaust. To see them treat the Palestinians as they do makes it clear that they did not learn anything from the appalling persecution they suffered under the Nazi regime.

For this at least, the OIC must speak with a united voice. In my speech, I said that to survive the new world order, Muslims had to start thinking, as they were up against a people who think. "Whether we like it or not we have to change, not by changing our religion but by applying its teachings in the context of a world that is radically different from that of the first century of the *Hijrah*.[6] Islam is not wrong but the interpretations by our scholars, who are not prophets even though they may be very learned, can be wrong. We have a need to go back to the fundamental teachings of Islam to find out whether we are indeed believing in and practising the Islam that the Prophet preached. It cannot be that we are all practising the correct and true Islam when our beliefs are so different from one another."

777

---

[3] The Irgun Tsvai-Leumi was a militant Zionist group that carried out terrorist attacks in support of the Jewish state. The Irgun was later absorbed into the Israel Defense Forces.

[4] The Haganah was a Jewish paramilitary organisation that later formed the basis of the Israel Defense Forces.

[5] In March 1948, Irgun forces attacked the Palestinian village of Deir Yassin as part of a counter-offensive against the Arab Liberation Army's attempts to cut off supplies to Jerusalem. Over 100 villagers were killed.

[6] The Hijrah refers to the migration of Muslims that the Prophet Muhammad led in 622 CE from Mecca to Medina, where Islam first began to flourish.

I have stated repeatedly in my writings and speeches that I am against war and have always believed that there are different and peaceful ways of solving political conflicts, even between nations. I stand by my words at the 10th OIC Summit and once again quote from my speech to indicate my intentions: "We must not antagonise everyone. We must win their hearts and minds. We must win them to our side, not by begging for help from them but by the honourable way that we struggle to help ourselves. We must not strengthen the enemy by pushing everyone into their camps through irresponsible and unIslamic acts. Remember the considerateness of the Prophet to the enemies of Islam. We must do the same. It is winning the struggle that is important, not angry retaliation, not revenge."

I do not apologise for anything in my speech. I only apologise for the inevitable misunderstanding which may have hurt some people.

# Chapter 61:
## Problems With Singapore

One area of Malaysian foreign policy that has always been challenging has been our relationship with Singapore. I may be wrong, but I suspect that Lee Kuan Yew once nursed the thought of becoming Prime Minister of this country. At that time, Singapore was too small a stage for his great talent. If Singapore and its overwhelmingly Chinese population were to become a permanent part of democratic Malaysia, he stood a good chance of winning majority support and being elected Prime Minister. Events have shown that the Malays can be deeply divided against themselves so that their being in the majority poses no problem towards their being ruled by others.

But the Tunku frustrated Lee and his hopes when he confined the activities of the People's Action Party (PAP) to only Singapore, and virtually turned it into an Opposition party. In defiance, the PAP contested against MCA candidates in the 1964 General Election but it did poorly, winning only one seat. That put paid to Lee's hopes of displacing the MCA as UMNO's chief partner in the governing Alliance. The show of defiance convinced the Tunku that there could be no understanding with the PAP and he consequently expelled Singapore in 1965. Once Singapore became an independent country, the relationship between the two nations required considerable rethinking.

Enforced separation meant the end of Lee's dream. He cried when announcing it on television and never forgave the Tunku. He also remained unforgiving of Syed Jaafar Hassan Albar for the Sino-Malay clashes in Singapore that made separation necessary,[1] and of me who he labelled a Malay ultra. He did not attribute the expulsion to his own behaviour and obvious ambition, choosing instead to believe firmly that we were responsible for the Tunku's action. When he made the decision to part ways, the Tunku must have finally realised that with Singapore included

---

[1]   In 1964 a series of race riots between Chinese and Malays took place in Singapore. In the first incident in July, some 25,000 Malays gathered to mark the Prophet Muhammad's birthday, but the gathering turned violent and led to 36 deaths. Then in September, riots followed the death of a Malay trishaw-rider, who was widely believed to have been murdered by a group of Chinese.

in Malaysia, the Chinese would become the overall majority, capable of winning sufficient seats to form the Government.

I had clashed with Lee many times when we were Members of Parliament in the 1964 and 1965 parliamentary sessions. I did not like his endless preaching about what Malaysia should do or should be like. Bitter over the painful separation, he called Malays "the jungle Arabs", likening them to the desert Arabs of whom he seemed to have a low opinion. I doubt he would disparage the Arabs today as Singapore is now far more active than Malaysia in wooing investors from the Middle East, and being the model as well as their advisers for development.

Despite our past clashes, I was determined to have friendly relations with Singapore when I became Prime Minister. It should not have been difficult since many of our leaders had studied together in the same schools, colleges and universities. Yet, solving the serious problems we had with them over the years proved to be easier said than done.

The oldest of these problems had to do with water. In 1960 and 1961, before Singapore joined Malaysia, we signed an agreement whereby the Peninsula would supply 350 million gallons daily (mgd) of raw water at three sen per 1,000 gallons. Under the same agreement, Singapore would sell treated water to Johor, not exceeding 12 per cent of the raw water Singapore bought. The agreed price of the treated water was 50 sen per 1,000 gallons, although the cost of treating the water would probably have been in the region of RM1.20 per 1,000 gallons. This meant that the price Malaysia had to pay Singapore if it took the maximum 12 per cent would far exceed what Singapore would pay Malaysia for raw water. The amount paid for raw water daily by Singapore is RM10,500, while Malaysia pays RM21,000 a day for treated water. This means that Malaysia earns zero while Singapore gets RM10,500 per day after paying for raw water.

To add to this unreasonable equation, the prices could only be changed if both sides agreed to it. However, if Malaysia were to ask for an increase in the price of raw water, Singapore would surely respond by seeking a hike in the price of treated water. We were caught in a bind. The two agreements would expire in 2011 and 2061 respectively, but even before that, in 2001, Singapore wanted to negotiate a new water agreement for 100 years.

They wanted their 350 mgd of raw water at the same rate, under the same conditions as before and they also wanted it to come from the Johor River, as they said it was cleaner.

The only way out was for Malaysia to cease buying treated water from Singapore before seeking an increase in the price of raw water. A sum of RM700 million was accordingly allocated to Johor to build and operate a water treatment plant to supply the needs of the state. The plant was completed after I stepped down. I expected the Malaysian Government to seek a review of the price of raw water to Singapore without being worried about an increase in the price of treated water. At 30 cents per mgd, Johor could earn as much as RM105,000 per day or RM38,325,000 per year. Meanwhile, Singapore was making huge profits from selling the Malaysian water it treated both to Singaporeans and to ships. Released from any obligation to sell treated water at a subsidised price to Johor, Singapore could sell more water and earn larger profits. For our part, we did not want to deprive Singaporeans of water but we felt that the island state should pay a fairer price for the raw water.

Under the new 100-year agreement that Singapore tried to negotiate, they wanted an additional 400 mgd of raw water. Malaysia was willing to provide it but only at the right price. However, since I stepped down there has been no progress in the water agreement with Singapore and we are still being paid three sen per 1,000 gallons. Ironically, Johor sells raw water to Malacca at 30 sen per 1,000 gallons. Why should Malaysia have to subsidise the Singapore Government? And it really is the Government that we are subsidising, not the people of Singapore who are paying SGD17 (well over RM40) for 1,000 gallons of treated water. Malaysia is paying heavily to remain on good terms with Singapore but friends who have to be bought are not real friends.

The next problem was our railway station at Tanjong Pagar, in the southern part of the island. The railway line runs through its centre and since there are no level crossings, Singapore road traffic is not affected. From colonial times, Malayan customs and immigration officers have operated from this station, that is, inside Singapore. This arrangement facilitates travel and has never been a problem. We would like to maintain the line and station and to improve the service using modern electric trains.

But Singapore wants the land back. It is valuable, and presumably they have some new use for it in mind. Our agreement from the time of separation is that we could stay where we were so long as we ran trains into Singapore. But we agreed to renegotiate should Singapore want to develop the land. In November 1990, Tun Daim Zainuddin, then the Finance Minister, and Lee signed a document known as the Points of Agreements (POA). The POA involved moving the Tanjong Pagar Station to Bukit Timah, a point halfway between the Tanjong Pagar Station and the Causeway. For giving up the southern portion of the line and Tanjong Pagar station, Singapore would compensate us with land of equal value at Shenton Way, near the city centre, for Malaysia to develop.

For reasons that are unclear, Tun Daim told me that Singapore subsequently claimed that the POA had been altered because a Malayan Railways official had said that the terminus for our railway would be at Johor Baru. How any statement by a railway official could alter an agreement between governments, I do not know. Normally proper amendments would be made in writing and endorsed by both governments. The status of the POA is now murky, with Singapore demanding that we move our Customs, Immigration and Quarantine facilities (CIQ) to Woodlands, which is near the Singapore end of the Causeway. Meanwhile, Singapore began to claim that the land to compensate Malaysia for Tanjong Pagar and the railway line was not to be developed by us alone, but jointly.

Repeated meetings between Malaysian and Singaporean officials have failed to resolve the impasse. What will happen to the railway link may now be caught up in a larger complication between Malaysia and Singapore involving the new bridge which I had proposed. The Malaysian Government under Tun Abdullah Ahmad Badawi cancelled the project.

Another thorn in our bilateral relations was Pulau Batu Puteh, a rocky outcrop known on some maps as Pedra Branca ("white rock" in Portuguese). During the colonial period, the British built lighthouses on a number of islands along the peninsular coast. It did not mean that the British owned those islands or that Malay sovereignty over them was ceded or divided in any way. On Pulau Batu Puteh, in the sea lane approaching Singapore from the east side of the Peninsula, the British set up a navigation facility in 1851 which they named the Horsburgh Light. Since the Colonial Government was based in Singapore, all these lighthouses were administered from the same office there. After the formation of the Malayan Union and Singapore's separation from Malaysia, these coastal lighthouses continued to be administered from Singapore.

In our view, Pulau Batu Puteh had always belonged to Johor. We had allowed Singapore to continue operating the lighthouse after Independence as we did with the lighthouse on Pulau Pisang on the west side of the Peninsula, which also belongs to Johor. But Singapore claimed that Pulau Batu Puteh belonged to them. They built a small fortress on it and would not allow Malaysian fishermen, who had fished there for centuries and become accustomed to seeking shelter from storms on the island, to go near it. Once, when I approached the island on a Malaysian Police boat, Singapore immediately sent two of its navy boats to intercept us. Not wanting to create an incident, I asked the police boat skipper to leave the area.

Singapore finally agreed to refer the claim to the International Court of Justice (ICJ) for adjudication. On 23 May 2008 the Court delivered its long-delayed and much-awaited decision. By majority vote, it awarded Pulau Batu Puteh to Singapore. It did so on several grounds: first, that Malaysia could not produce the original letter stating the conditions under which the Sultan of Johor had agreed to the building of the Horsburgh Light in 1851. The letter was not in Johor's or the national archives, but may well be held in Singapore's collection of records of the colonial authority that operated from there, and perhaps also in the British national archives. Second, that Singapore had been operating the lighthouse for long unbroken periods without objection by Malaysia. And third, that in 1953, i.e. before Independence, the Sultanate of Johor, in a letter signed by the State Secretary had disavowed any claim to the island.

That the letter assuring the British authorities in Singapore of Johor's lack of desire to claim the island itself was signed by a temporary or acting State Secretary may well indicate that the desired consent was extracted conveniently during the time when the state was under British rule. But courts and lawyers, who understand their books of rules but are less attuned to how the world works and how the subtleties of Malay meaning are communicated, seem not to have appreciated this point. Despite giving Pulau Batu Puteh to Singapore, the Court declared that the adjacent Middle Rocks outcrop, which were further away from Malaysia, were Malaysian. It would seem that the island given to Singapore is lying in Malaysian waters.

The Court may have thought that by giving something to each of the disputing parties, it was being fair. This was the commonly expressed view in the days following the issuing of the Court's judgment: Malaysia and Singapore would soon agree to have their technical experts meet to work out all the complicated questions of delineating boundaries, and the practical details of managing all activities in the area subject to the ICJ's decision. The Malaysian Foreign Minister Datuk Seri Dr Rais Yatim thought and said so. Like it or not, he said, under the terms of the Court's judgment, all practical matters could now be amicably and cooperatively resolved.

It is nice to be so nice. But only those who trust others to be nice could have been surprised when Singapore unilaterally laid claim to all the territorial waters and the seabed resources of the entire surrounding area. This move pre-empted the work of the expert technical working groups which the Malaysian Foreign Minister was so looking forward to. It is hard to be a good, amicable and trusting neighbour to someone who is unable to concede that anyone else is entitled to anything. Losing this little island was unfortunate. The decision to go to the International Court of Justice was made while I was still Prime Minister, and we had opted for that route because we believed we had a stronger case than Singapore.

There was also the problem of Singapore's use of Malaysian airspace. We had allowed Singapore Air Force planes to use our airspace above southern Johor for training. But when they sent a helicopter north of the designated area to rescue a pilot who had crashed there without informing us first, we withdrew our permission. After that, whenever we tried to resolve problems with Singapore, they demanded that we concede our airspace to them first before they would agree to anything. Malaysia has never sought to train its air force over Singapore as surely such arrangements should be reciprocal.

But during my time, I did not ask for it as I preferred that training be done in our respective airspace.

At one stage, we had agreed that all our unresolved issues be settled together as a package. But because Singapore would never agree to a revision of the price of water, all other issues could not be resolved, making a package solution impossible. I wrote to the then Prime Minister Goh Chok Tong that since that approach would not result in a settlement, we should revert to dealing with each issue separately. He agreed, saying he would instruct his officers to deal with the water problem first.

A fourth bilateral issue had to do with Malaysians who worked in Singapore and had to contribute to its Central Provident Fund (CPF). Singapore had refused to allow Malaysians living in the Peninsula to withdraw their CPF money when they stopped working in the island state. Strangely, they did not put the same restrictions on Malaysians from Sabah and Sarawak. To me this was ridiculous. Sabah and Sarawak are both part of Malaysia, but Singapore seemed to regard us as separate states. I have related elsewhere the setting up by Singapore of an effective stock exchange to trade in Malaysian shares after the separation of the Singapore Stock Exchange from the Malaysian market. The Central Limit Order Book, as the Singaporean entity was called, was implicated in the attack against Malaysian shares during the currency crisis. We had to force it to close.

Very early on the Singapore Government did not like their people to fill up their petrol tanks in Johor Baru where the price of petrol was cheaper. Singapore had limited the number of cars registered on the island to encourage the use of the government-owned subway and other public transport. The sale of petrol was not a big business in Singapore and the taxes collected by the Government would have been quite small. Yet Singapore insisted that their cars crossing to Johor Baru must have at least half-full tanks. It was very petty, but it reflects on the mentality of the people who ruled Singapore.

The British had developed Singapore as the premier entrepot port in Southeast Asia. To meet the needs of the Malay states, the British built Port Swettenham in Selangor, now renamed Port Klang. To ensure that it would never grow to compete with Singapore, the charges for transporting goods by rail from the Malaysian hinterland to Port Swettenham were deliberately made higher than to Singapore. When Malaysia became independent we started to develop Port Klang, dredging the channel for the big ships and building new wharves for North Port and West Port.

We marketed Port Klang aggressively but failed to attract ocean liners to use it. A private company then decided to build the Port of Tanjung Pelepas next to Singapore. I asked the private developers to invite Singapore to participate in the Port of Tanjung Pelepas venture, but Singapore declined, probably believing that Tanjung Pelepas would never be able to compete with them. By 2002 however, the managers of Tanjung Pelepas were able to win two key clients from the Port Authority of Singapore: Evergreen Marine from Taiwan and Maersk Sealand, the world's leading container shipping firm.

Today ports in the Peninsula handle more than 10 million containers annually. Feeling the competition, Singapore started lowering their port charges and lending money to shipping lines. Malaysian port charges are lower simply because the cost of living in Malaysia is lower. Before the ports were built, the Malaysian Government imposed a levy of RM100 per truck going to Singapore to use their port. That levy I believe is no longer being charged. But whereas Tanjong Pelepas, Singapore's principal competitor, is privately owned, Singapore ports are Government-owned. The competition is hardly fair as the Singapore Government effectively subsidises its ports. Singapore cannot seem to accept that it is no longer the sole strategic location in Southeast Asia. Because of the huge trade generated by the countries of the region, it pays for shipments to be made directly from the countries concerned without having to be collected at entrepot ports, such as Singapore.

It made sense for Malaysia to export and import products via its own ports. Malaysia cannot languish forever as Singapore's hinterland. Port operations made Singapore a great trading centre and were a source of wealth for the country. Instead of seeing its wealth creamed off by Singapore, Malaysia is entitled to regain some of that wealth by building and operating its own ports for goods originating from and destined for the country. Yet Singapore seems to resent Malaysia's competition.

To encourage the two growing ports at the southern tip of the Peninsula, namely Pasir Gudang and Tanjong Pelepas, it was essential in my view to remove the obstructions placed by the Johor Causeway upon the movement of goods by sea between the two ports. Instead of a causeway, there should be a bridge sufficiently high for barges with containers to pass below. Besides, the traffic to and from the existing Causeway was causing terrible traffic jams in Johor Baru. That jam would only get worse as more cars are put on the road. So I proposed to the Singapore Government that we replace the Causeway with a bridge. Characteristically, Singapore did not say yes or no. Like the other problems with Singapore, this too would be allowed to remain on the agenda without any decision being taken. An agenda is literally a list of "things that must be done"; but with Singapore, a common agenda is often an itemisation of things that must be forever deferred, in this case at Malaysia's cost. I felt sure the bridge would never be built if we were to wait for Singapore to agree.

I spoke to Lee and urged him to persuade Goh. Lee wrote to say that Goh was nostalgic about the Causeway and that it could be removed only after he retired. Nostalgia can be an expensive sentiment. But it was not one that had stopped the massive redevelopment of downtown Singapore that Lee and Goh's Government's favoured. I raised the matter with Goh but could elicit no positive response. Yet the bridge was never part of the package when we tried to bundle together all our outstanding problems and resolve them simultaneously. In proceeding with the proposal for a new bridge, we did not need to be held up by those other problems. In any case, I had already told Goh that the package solution was proving unworkable. It was just another device for stalling, not carrying out, an agenda. If Singapore would not cooperate on the bridge, I had to find some other solution.

787

After discussions with interested parties in Malaysia, we decided that if Singapore refused to build the bridge together with us, then we would build a bridge on our side of the Tebrau Strait.[2] The deepwater line which formed the boundary between our two countries was almost exactly at the midpoint of the Causeway. By ending the southern end of our new bridge well on our side of the international boundary and the Causeway's midpoint, we

---

[2] The Tebrau Strait is also known as the Johor Strait, and separates Peninsular Malaysia from Singapore.

need not involve Singapore at all in the planning or construction of our bridge. Whether we wanted our own bridge to be flat and level, or curved with a high arch, was strictly our business.

A straight bridge on the Malaysian side only would be too short to be high enough for boats to pass below it. Its gradient had to be gentle enough for heavily-laden trucks to climb. So I suggested a curved bridge, one that would be long enough for the gradient to suit heavy motor vehicles but whose length, and gradual ascent and descent, would permit barge and boat traffic and other small ships to pass readily below the highpoint of its arch. An engineering study proved the concept entirely feasible. The bridge would have been about 1.5km long and would have carried an eight-lane highway about 25 metres above the straits. The train would not be able to climb a gradient that was suitable for motor traffic. The railway line had to be as near horizontal as possible. So we decided that a railway bridge should be built separately from the vehicular bridge. To allow ships to pass through, a part of the line would be able to swing open. Of course this section of the railway bridge would also be built on the Malaysian side of the straits and would join the old line on the Malaysian part of the Causeway.

There were other reasons for building the bridge. The water in the straits was stagnant and polluted. The bridge would allow the water to flow with the rise and fall of the tide. Yachts and other small boats would find the opening up of the straits very convenient. There would be a lot of commercial activity, especially the movement of tourists by boat between the eastern and western parts of both Johor and Singapore. I wrote to Goh to inform him that if he would not agree to the removal of the Singapore half of the Causeway, we would simply remove most of our half and replace it with a bridge that would land on our part of the Causeway. Traffic would then continue on to the Singapore part of the Causeway. Goh replied that he personally preferred a straight bridge; but if Malaysia wished to build its bridge on the Malaysian side, then he would accept it. Singapore did not indicate that it objected to the Malaysian curved bridge proposal, nor did Goh make any demands or impose any conditions. These were all made clear in the exchange of letters between us, which have been published by the Singapore Government.

With the bridge connected to an elevated highway, the obstruction to traffic flow in Johor Baru would be removed. Meanwhile the new CIQ was planned to be sited far enough inland for the road to have a sufficiently gentle gradient for trucks and buses. The contractor was directed to start work on the CIQ, the bridge and the railway bridge before I stepped down.

The Singapore Government was requested to relocate their water pipes which were in the way of the CIQ and the road. This they did, as required by the Singapore water-supply agreement. The water pipes on the Malaysian side might be buried in the seabed yet remain connected to the existing pipes on the Singapore side. The Singapore Government knew this. It had made no objection when Goh agreed in his letter to me to accept Malaysia's plan to build a bridge on its side. So when the construction of the CIQ building and railway station required relocation of Singapore's water pipes, Singapore did just that without any protest. The later claim that the Singapore Government had not foreseen the need to relocate the existing water pipes on the Causeway is not plausible. Certainly Goh did not make any reference to the pipes when he indicated in his letter that he accepted Malaysia's plan. The environmental impact study completed by the contractor had shown that there was no reason the bridge should not be built where we planned it to be. The Singapore Government made no special requests regarding the environmental impact. In the meantime, work had started on the CIQ, the elevated road and on the shifting of the railway station to the new site adjacent to the CIQ. The pipeline carrying water to Singapore that stood in the way of the CIQ had also been shifted.

789

The whole project was well under way and Singapore voiced no objection. They could not object as the bridge was to be entirely in Malaysian territory. Its southern end would land on a part of the Causeway that was also on the Malaysian side of the deepwater boundary. Singapore did not need to make any modification to its part of the existing Causeway. The railway line to be retained on the Malaysian part of the Causeway would not affect the alignment on the Singapore side at all. Only the Malaysian part, north of the international boundary with Singapore, would be connected to the new railway bridge. Everything, it appeared, would be carried out as planned.

Then in 2004, Prime Minister Tun Abdullah suddenly announced that work on the bridge would be stopped and new negotiations would be held with Singapore so as to build a straight bridge. Tun Abdullah's Government apparently did not like a crooked bridge. There may be other reasons which I do not know about. The new bridge was actually to be curved, not crooked, and this was hardly unusual. In the US, a famous bridge over a narrow straits between the mainland and an island is curved because the authorities wanted sufficient height for helicopters to fly under it. The highlight of the great new Trans-European highway is also a long curved bridge in France. Our new bridge, which had to be much longer than a straight bridge, would curve gradually and gracefully and would become an attraction for visitors. The bridge was designed to be both practical and picturesque. Who could sensibly object to that?

Our planned curved bridge would appear especially delightful at night, when it would be lit up. It would provide a clearance height of 25 metres, exactly the same as that of the Second Link at Tuas[3] which we had already built. It would serve its purpose just as well as a straight bridge so there was no reason to reverse the decision simply because of some sudden desire or belated liking for a straight bridge. Yet it was the Malaysian Government which made the decision to stop the construction and to renegotiate with Singapore. One year passed without results, then two, then more months passed. There had still been no indication that Singapore would agree to a straight bridge. So Malaysia continued to wait hopefully. But I know Singapore. I negotiated with them for more than 20 years but none of the outstanding issues between us were resolved. Singapore always delays, withholds agreement, and demands outrageous concessions in exchange for consenting to what is rightfully ours.

Then I heard that the Malaysian negotiators were offering to supply one billion cubic metres of sand to Singapore and to agree to Singapore Air Force planes to fly over southern Johor. I wondered whether it was the prospect of selling sand which made the Malaysian Government stop the bridge construction and to renegotiate the construction of a straight bridge. Meanwhile the Johor state government, which was directly involved in the

---

[3]   Launched in 1998, the bridge at the Second Link was built to mitigate the traffic congestion at the Johor-Singapore Causeway.

whole project, objected strongly to this retreat by the Federal Government. Loud protests were voiced against the new proposal. Deputy Prime Minister Datuk Seri Najib Razak, however, said that Malaysia would build the bridge on our side regardless of Singapore's stand. The Foreign Minister Tan Sri Syed Hamid Albar said Singapore had no right to object to the bridge that was being built in Malaysian territory. I thought we were about to go back to building the curved bridge to which the Singapore Prime Minister had already agreed. By then we had wasted two years, during which work on the CIQ had continued. Even if we had restarted building the curved bridge it would not have been completed by the time the CIQ was ready. We would be saddled with a white elephant which would have cost us almost RM1 billion to build.

I had stopped the sale of sand to Singapore when I was Prime Minister. Reclamation by Singapore around their islands in the Tebrau Strait was affecting the sea through which ships and our navy boats had to pass to reach Pasir Gudang port or the new naval base at the mouth of Johor River. To dredge one billion cubic metres of sand from the seabed around the Peninsula would cause erosion of the shoreline, destroy our fish breeding grounds, and so affect the livelihoods of our fishermen. A Government that is eager to dredge sand from the seas off our east and west coasts is one that does not care much for Malaysia's interest. Neither the Government nor businessmen who got the dredging concession would make much money from the sale, so who would the proposal really benefit?

Then came the bombshell. The then Prime Minister of Malaysia announced that the bridge would not be built at all. Malaysians, he said, did not want to sell sand to Singapore, nor did they want Singapore military aircraft to fly over and train in Johor airspace. He then added that Malaysians did not want the bridge anyway. Yet we had never once heard anything of the sort. The Sultan of Johor had actually given land in Johor Baru to enable people displaced by the new elevated highway to be moved. Clearly, he was not against any bridge, straight or curved.

The people involved in the negotiation with Singapore knew that the Malaysian Government of Tun Abdullah Badawi had offered to sell 50 million cubic metres of sand every year for 20 years, totalling one billion cubic metres. That would be sufficient to increase the size of Singapore to one and a half times its present size. In effect, Malaysia would be selling land to Singapore, providing the means for its expansion, even its encroachment upon us if they so chose. The great-grandfather of the present Sultan may have been swindled by the British into selling Singapore for 60,000 dollars. But by offering to sell one billion cubic metres of sand to Singapore, our Government was literally surrendering Malaysian soil.

Singapore might have some grounds for demanding concessions from Malaysia if we were to suddenly want to alter all our agreements and build a straight bridge. But it can demand no concession if we were to build our bridge on our side only. No conditions were imposed or agreed. Yet Tun Abdullah suggested that building a bridge, even one on our territory, would now require approval from Singapore. Apparently Malaysia does not exercise full sovereignty over its own territories and facilities. I wonder how this happened. I had asked for evidence of any agreement to that effect. I have been shown none.

This situation is manifestly absurd. Had Singapore actually made a claim against Malaysia's right to build its bridge? Will Malaysia have the self-respect to challenge this claim in a court of law, should it ever appear? We can draw only one conclusion from this whole sorry episode: the Malaysian Government simply did not want, or dare, to build the curved bridge. Perhaps a straight bridge would have made some people very rich as it would have required the sale of one billion cubic metres of sand to Singapore.

It angered me greatly that the Malaysian Government was so concerned about Singapore's interest and rights, and not our own. They went so far as to say the Causeway could not be touched by Malaysia as it belonged jointly to the two countries. Both sides, therefore, had to consent to any change in its structure and arrangements. To me this meant our Government had no guts. There is no agreement to say that the bridge is jointly owned. It showed its cowardice once again when, in September 2006, Lee remarked that the Malaysian Chinese were not well treated by their Government.[4]

---

[4]   On 15 September 2006, in a symposium in Singapore, Lee said "Our neighbours (Malaysia and Indonesia) both have problems with their Chinese. They are successful. They are hardworking and, therefore, they are systematically marginalised."

How did we respond? Najib merely said that Singapore was being "naughty". Belatedly, our Ministry of Foreign Affairs called the Singapore High Commissioner to convey its objection over Lee's remark. But it did so only after Indonesia summoned the Singapore Ambassador on the same issue. Not understanding diplomatic protocol, our Prime Minister then wrote to Lee to ask him for an explanation. Apart from making himself look foolish, this was wrong as it was Singapore that owed the apology, not Lee. Tun Abdullah should have written to the Prime Minister, the titular head of the Singapore Government. For the Malaysian Prime Minister to write to a mere minister was wrong, protocol-wise. Lee did not apologise for his remarks. He merely said he was sorry if they caused discomfort to Tun Abdullah.

Lee then dragged my name into it and said I had often said bad things about Singapore. Perhaps I have and I do. But during my term of office, he never asked me to apologise.

# Chapter 62:
## Legacy And New Dilemmas

Finally, it was time to let go. The night before my official retirement I slept very well, untroubled by thoughts about the next day.

At 3pm on 31 October 2003, I witnessed Tun Abdullah Ahmad Badawi's swearing-in ceremony as the new Prime Minister at Istana Negara. After that we went back to the Prime Minister's office where I officially handed over my duties to him. The next day all the newspapers showed pictures of me symbolically handing over a file to him. This had been staged for the media's benefit — the photographers wanted to show that the baton had been passed but in truth, there was nothing in the file.

Ordinarily, when I left my office to go home, I would go down the special lift to my car in the basement garage, but on that day hundreds of people had gathered to say goodbye to me at the front of the building. Slipping away would not have been proper, so I went down the steps to greet them. It was always heart-warming when people came out to show their support. If I had been unpopular, perhaps they would have thrown eggs at me or just ignored my departure. But as it was, many of the faces that surrounded me as I walked to my car looked very solemn and sad.

The same day, Hasmah and I were conferred the *Seri Setia Mahkota Malaysia* and *Seri Maharaja Mangku Negara* titles respectively, so we became Tuns together. I was amused when the Court Chamberlain addressed Hasmah as "Toh Puan", the title of the wife of a Tun, when calling upon her to come forward to receive her award. After receiving her own award from the Agong she was then addressed as "Tun" by the Court Chamberlain. She had been a "Toh Puan" for only a few minutes, but the brief interval between the conferment of the two awards was important and Hasmah's transitory status was not to be ignored while it lasted. Such is Malay meticulousness about status and their sense of precision in formal ceremonial etiquette.

Leaving the country's highest office after 22 years was a big step for me, but I was not concerned about how I might be treated. I have never seen myself as anything but an ordinary individual. During my time as Prime Minister I had tried to live my life as normally as I could — I went shopping, drove my car and where possible, I mixed freely with people. After retirement, I felt certain I could do the same.

In the months that followed, my schedule was as busy as ever. I continued to give talks within the country and at international conferences. I spoke on Islam, the importance of knowledge, good governance, globalisation, neo-imperialism, socio-political developments and the Malaysian economic model. People seemed keen to know my thoughts on these and other wide-ranging subjects. With my years of experience, during which we built a national car, modernised infrastructure, advanced our trading position and conquered the currency crisis, I was expected to have at least some solutions for the challenges involved in running a country.

Retirement also allowed me to devote full attention to the burning question of war. The Perdana Global Peace Organisation — of which I am founder and Chairman — was set up in 2005 to do just this. It is a tiny first step towards global peace. Together with internationally prominent peace advocates, I wanted the Organisation to be a serious and active presence in a sustained struggle against war. World War I and II were billed as wars to end all wars but after killing more than 70 million people, maiming millions more and razing innumerable towns and cities to the ground, we still continue to fight wars. While it may be easier to let things be, I strongly believe that it would be morally reprehensible for us to stand by and just watch people being killed while whole nations are being turned into battlefields and reduced to rubble.

795

In the past, people went to war for territorial gain, to build empires, promote ideologies, and in the pursuit of their dominance. If anyone stood in their way they would be hunted and killed and their lands occupied and new nations set up. Then, there were wars ostensibly to create egalitarian societies and for this, tens of millions were killed. Now, in the name of human rights and democracy, even more lives are being sacrificed. Through the Organisation, I try to promote the message that peace for us simply means the absence of war. We must never be deflected from the simple message.

I prepared most of my speeches at the Perdana Leadership Foundation (PLF) in Precinct 8, facing the Putrajaya lake. The Foundation was the result of an idea mooted by my former political secretary, Matthias Chang, and was set up to preserve the important papers and documents that went through the hands of the first four Prime Ministers. Headed by the late Tan Sri Azizan Zainul Abidin,[1] a special committee comprising members from the private sector — who were mostly my friends — funded its building. No Government money was channelled into PLF.

There was some talk at the time that I had received many gifts from the Government. It is true that the Government offered me a piece of land, but I said I would pay for it. This is where my fruit orchard stands today. I have never liked to take what is not mine, which is why I did not accept land offered by the Kedah State Government shortly after I became Prime Minister. It is the same with my cars — I own only two, a Kancil and a Proton Saga, which I paid for. The others were all registered with the Ministry of Finance and considered to be Government property. After retirement I returned them, including those given to me by Proton. A number of other cars that were given to me as gifts during my years in office are on display for public viewing at the Perdana Gallery in Langkawi. I never owned them. I regarded all of them as Government property when I received them as Prime Minister.

Just before the end of my tenure, I asked Tun Abdullah to appoint me as adviser to PETRONAS, Proton, Malaysia Airlines, the Langkawi Development Authority (LADA) and the Tioman Development Authority. Almost immediately upon retirement, I was appointed to PETRONAS, LADA and Tioman, but not to Proton and Malaysia Airlines. I had no right to demand anything of course, but I thought it was a reasonable request considering my personal involvement in all these entities. When I was Prime Minister, I had appointed Tun Hussein Onn as head of the Institute of Strategic and International Studies and adviser to PETRONAS.

My appointment as adviser to Proton came in April 2004. When I received the letter from Tan Sri Nor Mohamed Yakcop, who by now was the Second Finance Minister, I was delighted. Soon after, I went to Proton's main office for a briefing. At the briefing, I was shown various models which would

---

[1]    Tan Sri Azizan Zainul Abidin, Chairman of PETRONAS, passed away on 14 July 2004.

soon be launched. The employees were in good spirits and appeared ready to face challenges.

As I have written earlier, around this time I was informed that the Ministry of International Trade and Industry was issuing tens of thousands of approved permits (APs) to a handful of people. They went on to sell the permits, making millions from something they got free from the Government. The Proton CEO Tengku Tan Sri Mahaleel Tengku Ariff told me that unless the Government stopped giving out APs so freely and ensured that the importers did not under-declare their prices so as to pay less tax, Proton sales would suffer. Concerned, I wrote a letter to Tan Sri Rafidah Aziz, the Minister of International Trade and Industry, mentioning the malpractices which were taking place. However, I received no assurance that the problems would be attended to. I then turned to the Press to pursue this matter and several other problems affecting the automotive industry. At first they seemed keen to publish my views but shortly after, I found my comments and views blacked out by the media.

As adviser to Proton, I expected to play an active role and wanted to help turn the company into a leading brand for the country. Tengku Mahaleel did not train as an automotive engineer but he understood the business intimately. Under him Proton became a profitable company and I felt I could work with him closely.

When in office, I had urged Proton to work with Frazer Nash, a British research company owned by an Indian British citizen. To continue to be competitive, Proton needed to innovate by using multiplexing to replace the bulky wire harnesses. Frazer Nash could help with this and also in the development of a hybrid car using new technology. A hybrid car is the answer to the high price of oil. Frazer Nash had worked on this at my request and they had reached the point where they could get more than 100 miles to the gallon. Moreover, emissions would be almost completely eliminated. I had worked with the research company earlier on several harebrained ideas of mine and found that they had the capacity to develop workable solutions. By the time I became adviser, I noticed that Proton's share of the Malaysian market was rapidly dwindling. To keep Proton competitive, I was hoping to persuade Tengku Mahaleel to invest more in building the hybrid car.

Then the Government decided to appoint a new Chairman to the car company. I met Datuk Mohammed Azlan Hashim and he assured me that he was not there to get rid of Tengku Mahaleel. But he acted more like a Chief Executive Officer than a board Chairman and he removed Tengku Mahaleel from many of the posts he had held in the company's subsidiaries.

When Tengku Mahaleel reached the end of his contract, he was offered very unattractive terms to stay on. I think this was done deliberately. Naturally, he turned the offer down. Tengku Mahaleel was later replaced but the new management did not understand the business as well as he had and Proton's share of the market took a 50 per cent dip. Now it is even lower as foreign cars flood the market. At one point, I was told, the company only had RM500 million in its reserves, down from RM2.5 billion. Many senior executives and engineers began to leave Proton and there was talk that the company was going to be sold. I was very sad about this. Even though I was the Adviser, I refused to see Azlan — he seemed to believe that he was there to advise me, and not the other way round.

Proton's sale of Italian motorcycle company MV Agusta, which I discussed in an earlier chapter, was another distressing development. At the time of writing, the buyer's identity remains undisclosed. We tried to do a search for the company but discovered very little about it. All we knew was that the buyers were made up of two lawyers, and that the company was not even listed with the Italian registrar of companies.

Proton's position was not helped by the AP issue. Tengku Mahaleel had taken his concerns to the Chinese newspaper, the *Oriental Daily*, saying that the Government was not supporting Proton and was treating the national car company unfairly. When the board of Proton heard of this, they gave Tengku Mahaleel two days to explain his actions. As I also knew the truth, I defended him. I told the Press that of the 67,000 APs issued in 2004, only 12,600 were given to 82 companies while another 54,000 were issued to two companies. Tun Abdullah then stepped in and said that Rafidah should explain in writing the matters I had raised. Still, she refused.

In July 2005, the Opposition and a growing number of bloggers jumped into the fray, demanding an explanation. Under pressure, the Cabinet directed

Rafidah to give details as to why the bulk of the APs were issued to only a handful of companies. Instead, she merely dismissed the accusations and said that she was prepared for attacks at the UMNO General Assembly later that month. It was the Prime Minister's Office which finally released a complete list of individuals who received APs since 1970, including politicians, royalty and children of prominent Malaysians. What was glaring was that more than 60,000 APs were issued that year mostly to Datuk Seri Syed Azman Syed Ibrahim, Datuk Mohd Haniff Abdul Aziz and the late Tan Sri Nasimuddin S.M. Amin[2].

Rafidah got very emotional. She denied any wrongdoing and broke down during a Press conference which was widely covered. In some news reports she had been branded a villain who had been rude to me. This was made worse when she was booed at the UMNO General Assembly. Her only response was that she was "too hurt for words". I did not understand why she took it personally but she apparently did. In August, when she briefed the Cabinet on the AP issue, she was reportedly "combative", "confrontational", and "abrasive", especially to Cabinet colleagues who disagreed with her. In attempting to resolve the problem, the Prime Minister announced that he would chair a panel to review the AP system but, soon after, Rafidah declared that the system would be abolished altogether.

If there was much excitement in my role in Proton, there was almost none in my capacity as adviser to PETRONAS. Many believe that having a presence there means I exert continuous influence on the company when in fact, PETRONAS decisions are made by PETRONAS staff. The PETRONAS CEO reports to the Prime Minister. I only received occasional briefings and the statutory annual reports.

While I tried to settle into my new role, the Prime Minister decided to prove his legitimacy by holding a General Election in March 2004. I had let it be known that I would always be available to help with the campaign and I spoke at rallies in all states except Terengganu. UMNO wanted to

---

[2] Datuk Seri Syed Azman Syed Ibrahim is the Managing Director of Weststar Motorsport Sdn Bhd. He owns 80 per cent of the company, and the remaining 20 per cent is owned by his partner Datuk Mohd Haniff Abdul Aziz. Tan Sri Nasimuddin S.M. Amin was the founder, Chairman and Chief Executive Officer of the Naza Group, a leading automotive company in Malaysia.

recapture the state from PAS, but I was told I might cause the party to lose votes there. My name was associated with Tan Sri Eric Chia, whose Perwaja operations in the state had ended in a scandal and financial losses. Chia was accused of embezzling money from the company and I was blamed for appointing him. The court eventually concluded that he was not guilty. A sick man, he suffered terribly and died shortly after.

In any case, I was willing to contribute what I could. I had always remarked that many *Menteri Besar*, Ministers and Members of Parliament would disappear once they were no longer in office and would make no effort to help the party win. I believed that members who had received strong support from the party before should pay back by helping the party during elections. At the rallies, I emphasised that Tun Abdullah was a good man and supporting him was important for political continuity.

This was the first General Election in 40 years in which I was not a candidate. Tun Mohd Khalil Yaacob, the UMNO Secretary-General, had wanted my son Mukhriz to run in my old constituency of Kubang Pasu, but I refused. It looked too much like nepotism and I did not want to start a political dynasty. Mukhriz would have to do his own fighting, which he did when he won the Jerlun seat in Kedah in 2008, five years after I stepped down.

I expected a positive 2004 election result for the Barisan Nasional because the voters were energised and exhilarated. Datuk Seri Anwar Ibrahim's dismissal had become irrelevant while the Chinese community continued to enjoy the results of the fixed exchange rate that had helped many to escape bankruptcy. There was a new Government in power and people were expecting economic recovery and better growth to continue. They had had me for more than two decades and I imagine that there were those who were sick of my way of running the Government. Change always inspires optimism so the voters' support was very strong. Those who had voted against the Government in 1999 because of the Anwar issue came back and delivered a thumping victory to the Barisan Nasional in 2004.

There was much talk about how the triumph was attributed to the "Pak Lah factor" — he had a good image, was known as Mr Clean and was not belligerent like me. It was also a very cleverly-planned campaign and it was smart of Tun Abdullah not to respond personally to attacks from the Opposition, which was in direct contrast to how I would have reacted. Malaysians expected the new Government to be more dynamic and they foresaw a surge in national development. I was very happy about Barisan Nasional's outstanding performance because it validated my decision to appoint Tun Abdullah.

It did not take me long, however, to realise that he was not up to the job of being Prime Minister. This was a great disappointment to me because he had initially seemed to appreciate the rationale behind the many projects needed to keep the economy vibrant and moving. In my final week in office the most critical of these projects — the double-tracking and electrification of the railway from Johor Baru to Padang Besar — was on the verge of being approved. In my last meeting with Tun Abdullah, I explained the necessity for the project and he agreed to push it through when he took over. We had to have the double-tracking railway to transport the growing number of containers that were entering the country from Thailand. Trucks only carry one container at a time and since we handled 10 million a year, the roads would soon be choked by these semi-trailers. On the other hand, trains can carry up to 50 containers at a time and without level crossings, they would not cause traffic jams. I know for a fact that when I left there was enough money to build the railway.

I was in Japan two weeks after stepping down when word reached me that the Prime Minister had chosen to postpone the project. I had many misgivings and I would have said something then if not for my earlier promise not to interfere. I spoke to no one about it, but I was hurt and surprised that he had reneged on his word. It took place so soon after I left office that it was not possible for him to have forgotten his promise.

Other reversals quickly followed. The Arab investment in the Bakun hydroelectric project that I had worked for five years to secure was cancelled, and the deposit of over RM90 million for a 30 per cent share was returned to the investor. Then I began hearing accusations that I had spent all the Government's money on megaprojects which the country apparently did not need. I was even prepared to tolerate this. But when the project involving the bridge to Singapore was cancelled, I was flabbergasted. By allowing Singaporeans to dictate terms, the current administration had effectively undermined the sovereignty of our country. I had a choice: I could remain tight-lipped and maintain my image of a respected elder statesman or I could make myself heard again. I chose the latter — it was too much for me to see us submitting to Singapore.

When Tun Abdullah abruptly cancelled the bridge plan in April 2006, it meant that the Malaysian Government would have to shell out at least RM100 million to the contractor as compensation. It was later revealed by the Public Accounts Committee that the total cost of cancellation was RM740 million, more than half of what the bridge would have cost. Tun Abdullah's explanation was that he was abiding by the sentiments on the ground. If indeed that were the case, why did he take two years to cancel it?

It was at this point that I decided to speak out as I felt the Government should have gone ahead unilaterally with the bridge construction. My comment that we were a "half-past-six country with no guts" was picked up and reported across the world. Some foreign journalists said I was suffering from PPMS — Post-Prime Ministerial Syndrome — but the question is this: why were we scared of the Singaporeans? If we had proceeded with the plans we only needed to work on Malaysian land and in our territorial waters.

I was then informed that Malaysia had offered to sell sand to Singapore and allow the republic free use of airspace — all of which the Government denied. My statements were obviously causing discomfort to some. One by one, Cabinet Ministers and politicians came out to defend the Prime Minister. Over time, I found myself increasingly blacked out by the mainstream papers, especially with regard to my remarks about the involvement of Tun Abdullah's family members in his administration. The only response I received from Tun Abdullah was "an elegant silence", which was how Tun Musa Hitam described it. Much later I discovered that the elegant silence was due to his inability to explain himself.

My relations with party leaders, especially those who had been my colleagues in the UMNO Supreme Council and in Cabinet for so many years, also did not remain as cordial as I had hoped. In fact, as soon as I stepped aside, UMNO leaders and Cabinet Ministers began distancing themselves from me. I was made to feel not just like an outsider — it was as if I was some kind of enemy. This was not unlike the time when I was thrown into the political wilderness for going against the Tunku, except that this time I was alienated even more. Ministers who had originally been appointed by me and who were still in the Government, openly abused me.

In 2006, members of my UMNO division in Kubang Pasu urged me to make a bid to be one of the seven elected representatives of the division to the UMNO General Assembly later that year. As I wanted to bring my grievances to the delegates, I agreed — but I lost. Much later, I was told that the UMNO Supreme Council had been most agitated by my plans and actually decided at one of its meetings that action should be taken to stop me from being chosen. This was recorded in the minutes but when it was pointed out that it was illegal for the Council to decide such matters, all the minutes were withdrawn and new minutes issued without the original record.

803

At the urging of many senior UMNO stalwarts, who were worried that the rift between Tun Abdullah and me would weaken the party, the Prime Minister and I met in October 2006 for about two hours to discuss our differences. At first, I was satisfied that I had had the opportunity to speak to him about my concerns face-to-face, but in the end our meeting resolved nothing. I later told reporters that we were living in a police state because every time anyone invited me to talk, they would get a call from the police warning them or telling them to withdraw the invitation. The secretary of an UMNO branch in Johor, who insisted I address party members there, was later removed. Similar incidents took place in Terengganu. This was extra-legal — there was and is no law empowering the police to stop people from holding meetings unless there is a threat to national security.

My worries about UMNO were also escalating. As anyone who has read Malaysian history would know, UMNO is a democratic party and its leaders are elected from the branch to the division level and then on to the national level. If the members disagree with the leaders, they can express their disagreements anywhere, including the General Assembly. At party elections they may change their leaders if a majority wishes to do so. In the records of UMNO, only one President has had to withdraw while another chose to step down when he sensed that the majority was against him. To prevent frivolous challenges which can be costly and time-consuming, there are rules to reduce abuses of the democratic process. During the time I was President I was challenged once but I won. However, the challengers took the case to court, ending in UMNO being declared illegal.

Under Abdullah, the UMNO President had made himself into an institution. No challenges against him were allowed and his policies and actions could not be questioned. It seemed that the duty of every member and of every delegate to the General Assembly was to support the President and praise everything that he said. If any critical remarks were made about the President or his speech, then the person concerned would not only be hauled up and penalised, but also risked not being nominated to contest in future elections.

Sadly, UMNO members had become a collection of sycophants interested only in staying in the good books of the President in order to ensure personal gains. Actions and policies detrimental to the party no longer receive any attention. If a problematic issue was raised, then it would immediately be dropped if the Prime Minister instructed it. As a result, no one in UMNO questioned why the half-bridge could not be built in our territorial waters. No one asked why we had a billion-ringgit CIQ complex completely gone to waste. There were also no queries as to why the Government stopped negotiating other issues, including the water deals, with Singapore. In fact, other than a bunch of bloggers, no UMNO member or leader questioned why billion-ringgit Malaysian companies had been transferred to Singapore.

Tun Abdullah then announced a line-up of several big projects, including the Second Penang Bridge, a monorail for Penang, extensions for the Light Rail Transit system, and the monorail in Kuala Lumpur and economic development initiatives for key regions in the country, which would undoubtedly consume funds in the billions. However, until late 2008, it was not known whether any of these projects had taken off or made any difference to the country.

A number of projects which were halted — the double-tracking of the railway, a Pahang-Selangor water transfer project[3] and a new road to the causeway — have been partly reinstated. The double-tracking project, however, is only from Ipoh to Padang Besar and because of the delay, the cost of constructing just this short stretch would be around RM12 billion, when the original proposal which covered a rail line from Johor Baru to Padang Besar would cost only RM14 billion. The Bakun dam is also being attended to, although Tun Abdullah's Government reverted to a plan to lay down two 700-kilometre submarine cables to bring the power to the Peninsula, an idea which we had rejected in the late 1990s as it was technically difficult and too expensive to execute.

I was equally troubled by the impact of the National Automotive Policy, which Tun Abdullah announced in March 2006. When it was implemented, sales of motor vehicles began to plummet. Proton sustained huge losses and is now venturing into electric cars and other projects to remain profitable. With the policy, we now import more components and cars when we should be manufacturing and exporting them.

But nothing forced me into open criticism more than the shocking results of the 12th General Election in March 2008. I was in Kuala Lumpur the night the election results were announced. I was supposed to fly to Riyadh in Saudi Arabia the following day, and needed a good rest before taking the trip. After Hasmah called to tell me that Mukhriz had won the Jerlun parliamentary seat in Kedah, I was able to sleep peacefully. The next morning, however, I was stunned when I read the full results.[4] I had had some inkling that the Barisan Nasional would lose some seats but the extent of the coalition's humiliation was far greater than I expected.

---

3   This 11-year project, which includes building two dams in Pahang and a reservoir in Selangor, is designed to help meet a projected increase in demand for treated and piped water in Selangor and Kuala Lumpur.

4   The Barisan Nasional lost its traditional two-thirds majority, winning only 140 or 63.1 per cent of the 222 parliamentary seats. The Opposition also won control of five states — Penang, Selangor, Kedah, Perak and Kelantan — as well as the Federal Territory of Kuala Lumpur.

When I was told that my flight to Riyadh had been rescheduled, I immediately called for a Press conference, to state openly that Tun Abdullah must accept responsibility for the results and step down. It was only right, after such massive losses. I had anticipated Penang, Kedah and Kelantan falling to the Opposition but not Selangor and Perak as well. Losing Kedah was no surprise — we had nearly lost the state in 1999 because of Anwar and his black eye. In that election, however, Barisan Nasional had overwhelming Chinese support. This time, as surveys have shown, the Chinese and the Indians as well as the Malays all abandoned the ruling coalition.

I played no role in the 2008 elections as no one sought my assistance, so I only spent time in Mukhriz's constituency during the campaign period. There, I met a man who rather wistfully said that democracy in UMNO did not exist anymore. I mulled over his words and came to the conclusion that he was right.

Democracy should prevent a bad leader from staying in power, but this is no longer the case with UMNO. Even when it appeared that Abdullah was not getting support, he insisted that he was. He was truly in a state of denial. The *rakyat* had a leader who applied pressure upon them in order to perpetuate his rule. Just like the Malays of the past who submitted unquestioningly to their Rulers, UMNO leaders today have mistaken meek acquiescence for loyalty.

This, along with money politics and the misguided notion of their "superior" status as Malays, has contributed significantly to the party's weakness. And, as the law of nature dictates, when you are weak, you will also be subjected to pressure. The Sultans who insisted on having their say in the nomination of *Menteri Besar* in several states must have also noted that Tun Abdullah's hold was considerably diminished after the elections. In the past, when the Barisan Nasional had a commanding majority in the assembly, the Rulers merely endorsed the candidates named by the ruling party. This time, the Raja of Perlis, who simply did not want Datuk Seri Shahidan Kassim, withheld endorsing his re-nomination. Perlis today has a new *Menteri Besar*, Datuk Seri Dr Md Isa Sabu. A similar conflict arose in Terengganu, where for several weeks, the state was without a government.

This was because the Sultan — for some reason — did not want Datuk Seri Idris Jusoh re-appointed to the post. Tun Abdullah tried his best to retain Idris, but to no avail.

Although UMNO desperately needed a thorough post-mortem after the devastating losses of the 2008 General Election, all I saw was firefighting on a daily basis. There appeared to be no idea or identification of what needed changing and fixing and the party looked bereft of any strategy to pull itself together. For months Tun Abdullah received calls for his resignation, both from within and outside of UMNO. In some ways, I felt personally responsible for all of this as I had entertained great hopes that he would steer the country firmly in the direction set under Vision 2020 and chose him as my successor. To make amends, I joined the chorus of voices demanding for his resignation but he said he would not be dislodged until he had fulfilled his many "reform objectives" as Prime Minister. As a last-ditch measure, I quit UMNO in May of 2008. I had been a member for almost 60 years but I no longer recognised the party as the one I had served for most of my life.

The months after the election also saw the unravelling of the Barisan Nasional, with component parties hinting that they would leave or cross over to the Opposition. The ruling coalition was in the limelight for all the wrong reasons. Its response to the crisis was clearly underlined by desperation and this further weakened the Government's standing in the eyes of the people. It began to entertain extremist racialist demands which provoked protests from other races. The reasonable working relations between the component parties representing the different races became strained to the point of breaking.

There are those who insist that the problem went beyond Tun Abdullah. They claim the *rakyat* were moving away from race-based politics. Although voting patterns seem to support this argument, it is not true that ethnic parties are becoming irrelevant. If indeed people were leaning towards multiracial parties, Gerakan would have fared much better in the polls. Instead of interpreting the results as the end of ethnic-based politics, I am inclined to read them as nothing more than protest votes. I say this because Malaysia is still very deeply ethnocentric. Only when the Malays are confident that they can compete with the Chinese economically and the Chinese cease to emphasise their Chinese origins and their difference from others, will there be genuine multiracial politics.

Anwar is now exploiting the dissatisfaction on the ground, saying that he will introduce authentic, racially-integrated politics into the country. He has captured the imaginations of many with his apparently liberal and progressive talk. Upon close scrutiny, however, nothing he says reflects progressiveness. He was merely mouthing the racist sentiments of the extremists in every group to gain their support. He had always been supportive of the Israelis but when the Government appeared to be revising its anti-Israel policy he condemned the Government, to the annoyance of the Jews.

On 9 October 2008, Tun Abdullah announced that he would not defend his position at the UMNO General Assembly in March 2009, which paved the way for his Deputy, Datuk Seri Najib Tun Razak, to take over as UMNO President and Malaysia's sixth Prime Minister. Is this enough to save UMNO and the Barisan Nasional?

What is clear is that we need a strong leader to guide us out of this quagmire, and unless radical measures are taken, the Barisan Nasional will not survive the next General Election.

In my preface, I wrote that it was the wisdom of our founding fathers that led to the integrated and balanced system of government we had enjoyed under the Barisan Nasional. Despite the many shortcomings, we were able to resolve many of the multiracial and multi-religious problems in a democratic and non-violent manner. It was for this reason that I was willing to return to UMNO to help restore cohesion in the coalition. It broke my heart to see this country stumble under such ineffective management. However, recent political developments have shown that the divisions in Malaysian society run as deeply as ever.

As I come to the end of my memoirs, the world is still unable to recover from a global recession. Major US investment bank Lehman Brothers Holdings Inc filed for bankruptcy, and Merrill Lynch and the American

International Group had to be saved through billion-dollar bailouts. This triggered tumbles in stock markets around the world and governments in America and Europe took drastic measures to stop banks and financial institutions from collapsing. For a time, it looked more and more like a financial meltdown that only the toughest would survive. The Government under Najib unveiled two major economic stimulus packages, but it is still unclear if Malaysia is truly among the survivors. Still, Najib's administration is far better than Abdullah's

I am grateful to the people of Malaysia whose support had enabled me to lead this, my beloved country, for 22 years. I had tried my best although I cannot be a judge of my own work. It is up to the people of today and the future to pass judgment. As for me, I must admit that the greatest satisfaction that I get is from seeing physical evidence of the success of the plans and policies which were formulated while I was Prime Minister. I do not claim the results as my work alone. People from every stratum of society, the civil servants, colleagues in the Government, and members of my party have all contributed. I say prayers to Allah *swt* for His beneficence and for giving me parents who brought me up and instilled in me the values which made my career possible.

# Glossary

*Adat* The customs and traditions of Malay etiquette. It also refers to customary law, for example *adat perpatih,* which is the code of matrilineal law found in Negeri Sembilan.

**Agong** Formally styled "Duli Yang Maha Mulia Yang di-Pertuan Agong", the Agong, or Paramount Ruler, is elected for a five-year term by the Conference of Rulers of the states of Malaysia. The conference excludes Penang, Malacca, Sabah and Sarawak, which are ruled by Federally-appointed Governors rather than hereditary monarchs. Malaysia is one of the world's last elective monarchies.

**Approved Permits** An "approved permit" or AP refers to the system by which imports into Malaysia are controlled. The Ministry of International Trade and Industry issues individual APs for the import of a single unit of a given item, e.g. a car.

*Aya* In Hindi, originally a nursemaid or waiting-maid. Also spelt *aia* or *ayah.*

*Baju Melayu* Traditional Malay formal attire for men. The *baju Melayu* generally consists of a long-sleeved shirt with a stiff collar known as a *cekak musang* (fox's leash), trousers made from an identical fabric and colour, and a *kain samping* made from **songket**- or sarong-cloth and worn as a sarong. Regional variations exist.

**Barisan Nasional** Malay for the National Front coalition. The BN was formed in 1973 as the successor to the Alliance Party and has in this way formed the Federal Government in Malaya and Malaysia since 1957. There are 14 parties in the coalition today, which is led by the original Alliance partners UMNO, the MCA and the MIC.

**Barisan Alternatif** The so-called "alternative front" that opposition parties formed in 1998 against the **Barisan Nasional.** Its members were PAS, the DAP, **KeADILan** (later to become PKR), and Parti Rakyat

Malaysia. The coalition began to fall apart in 2001 when the DAP withdrew. The Barisan Alternatif has been superseded by the **Pakatan Rakyat.**

**Berjasa** The acronym for Barisan Jemaah Islamiyah Se-Malaysia (the Pan-Malaysian Islamic Front), founded in 1977 by a group of breakaway PAS members. The party did well in the 1978 General Election, winning 11 state seats in Kelantan, but faded away after that.

**Bendehara** The word was once the formal title of, and also meant, prime minister or commander-in-chief of the royal court. Today it is a royal title in a number of states: for example, the second son of the Sultan of Johor, and the Raja next in line to the heir apparent of Perak.

**Bumiputera** A term used to refer to Malays and other indigenous groups in Malaysia. It is formed from two ancient Sanskrit words meaning "Prince of the Soil".

*Ceramah* Political (or religious) speeches, often of the haranguing kind and an obligatory feature of election campaigns. The word once meant "garrulous" in Malay.

811

**DAP** The Democratic Action Party, formed in 1965. Originally a branch of the Singapore People's Action Party, the DAP came into being when its members chose to remain in Malaysia after Singapore left the Federation.

*Daulat* A Ruler's sovereign power, similar to the Divine Right of European monarchs.

**Datuk, Dato'** See **Malay Honours Encik** The Malay equivalent of "Mister".

**Federated Malay States** Formed in 1895 by the British for "administrative purposes", the FMS comprised Selangor, Perak, Negeri Sembilan and Pahang. Each was obliged to have a British Resident whose purpose was to "advise" the Sultan — but they effectively possessed full political and administrative power. The FMS was superseded by the Malayan Union in 1946. See also **Unfederated Malay States** and **Straits Settlements.**

**Gerakan** Parti Gerakan Rakyat Malaysia (Malaysian People's Movement Party), was founded in 1968 originally as an opposition party. It joined the **Barisan Nasional** in 1972.

*Haram* Arabic for "forbidden" and applies to anything or any matter legally forbidden by Islamic law.

*Hudud* The section of Islamic (or Shariah) law that applies to section of Islamic penal law dealing with fixed punishments.

*Imam* Prayer leader in the mosque, or, for Shi'ites, a Muslim leader.

**Japanese Occupation** The Japanese military occupation of Malaya and North Borneo (modern-day Sabah) and Sarawak began in 1941 with the invasion of Borneo and ended in 1945 when the last of the invasion force surrendered.

*Kampung* Malay for "village", though many of these are today modern towns and the names of these towns often reflect humbler origins.

**KeADILan** A political party formed by Datuk Seri Anwar Ibrahim after his arrest. See **Parti Keadilan Rakyat.**

*Kitab* A word of Arabic origin referring to religious commentaries in Islam.

**Malay Honours** Malaysia, as a elective monarchy with 14 individual heads of state, has a very complex system of honours. Sultans and Governors award the title Dato', Dato' Seri (and other variants including Datuk Seri Panglima and Dato' Amar), while the Agong awards the titles Datuk (*sic*), Tan Sri, and Tun.

For the purposes of this Memoir, all Dato' and their variants are spelt uniformly as Datuk with the exception of Dato' Onn Jaafar, whose name appears so often with that particular spelling that anything else would appear strange.

**MARA** Majlis Amanah Rakyat, or the Public Trust Council, formed in 1966 to help raise the status of **Bumiputera** especially in the areas of business and industry.

**MCA** The Malayan (later Malaysian) Chinese Association, a founding member of the Alliance Party and later the Barisan Nasional coalition. It was established in 1949.

**MCP** The Malayan Communist Party (also known as The Communist Party of Malaya or CPM) was founded in 1930. It was outlawed in 1948 and took up arms against the Colonial Government, provoking an emergency that lasted until 1989.

***Menteri Besar*** Literally "great minister", the Menteri Besar is the chief minister of a state ruled by a Sultan. In states ruled by a Governor the English term (or its Malay equivalent *Ketua Menteri*) is used.

***Merdeka*** Independence

**MIC** The Malayan (later Malaysian) Indian Congress was founded in 1946 and was one of the founding members of the Alliance Party.

813

***Orang puteh*** Literally "white people" or "white man". Another term frequently used for Europeans is "Mat Salleh", though the origins of this expression are obscure.

**Pakatan Rakyat** The "People's Alliance" of federal Opposition parties that came into existence after the General Election of 8 March 2008. The Pakatan comprises PAS, the DAP, PKR, and Parti Sosialis Malaysia.

**PAS** Parti Islam Se-Malaysia (the Pan-Malaysian Islamic Party). PAS was originally a faction within **UMNO** that eventually broke away to contest the 1955 General Election under its own banner.

**Parti Keadilan Rakyat** The "People's Justice Party". Originally known as **KeADILan,** PKR came into being after its merger with Parti Rakyat Malaysia in 2003. Datuk Seri Anwar Ibrahim has always been identified as the head of this party, although his wife Datin Seri Dr Wan Azizah Wan Ismail headed it during his term in prison. (She was also Malaysia's first woman Parliamentary Opposition leader.)

**PBS** Parti Bersatu Sabah (or the United Sabah Party) was founded in 1985 by Datuk Seri Joseph Pairin Kitingan. PBS formed the state government in the same year and joined the **Barisan Nasional** in 1986, but pulled out in 1990. It rejoined the coalition in 2002.

*Rakyat* The citizenry or, more commonly, the People. There are other words that mean similar things, such as *warganegara* (citizen) or *orang ramai* (the Public), but *rakyat* always carries with it the connotation of a duty owed to it by its leaders. It is hence a very popular term in political speeches.

*Sandiwara* The old word for a play, comedy, concert, or other form of live entertainment. The term is also popularly used to apply to shadow-puppetry (*wayang kulit*) and this, by extension, has turned it into a euphemism for the various kinds of machinations that go on in politics. When people speak of a *sandiwara* in Malaysia today, they are usually talking about a political drama with complex plots, hidden hands and the like.

814

**Sen** A basic unit of Malaysian currency worth one hundredth of the ringgit (formerly the Malaysian dollar). It is equivalent to the cent in other currencies.

*Songket* A luxurious, handwoven fabric intricately patterned with gold or silver threads.

*Songkok* A black oval cap made of cloth or velvet, worn by men (mostly Malay men, but also non-Malays in formal settings).

**Straits Settlements** Originally territories ruled by the British East India Company, the Straits Settlements of Penang, Malacca and Singapore (and Labuan in 1906) were British Crown Colonies until 1946. See also **Federated Malay States** and **Unfederated Malay States.**

**Syces** A word of Indian origin to mean a servant who looks after horses and drives carriages, etc. In Malaysia it was used to refer to a driver or chauffeur.

**Tanah Melayu** Literally and officially, "Malay States", in the forms of the **Federated** or **Unfederated Malay States.** More broadly, however, the term bears the connotation of "Malay homeland".

**Tan Sri** See **Malay Honors.**

**Towkay** Sir, master — a form of address of Chinese origin once intended as polite address to any Chinese employer or other Chinese above the working class. (Also spelt "*taukeh*").

**Tuan** Sir, master, lord — a title of respect for gentlemen once common Malaysia and Indonesia. However, due to its colonial implications (British colonial officers were invariably addressed as "*tuan*"), the term has fallen out of common use. It is still, however, the standard address for non-Malay men in official correspondence and is a courtesy title for *hajis* (i.e. those who have completed the Haj or pilgrimage to Mecca) and male descendants of the Prophet Muhammad who bear the title Syed.

**Tun** See **Malay Honours**

815

**Tunku, Tengku** Prince. The two variations are the titles of those descended from the royal lines of Malaysia's ruling houses and apply both to men and women.

**Ulama** Islamic religious scholars.

**Ummah** The worldwide community of Muslims.

**Unfederated Malay States** These were the states of Johor, Kelantan, Terengganu, Kedah and Perlis which would not accept British "protection" but instead tried to remain nominally independent. They were obliged, however, to have British "Advisors" who, like the Residents in the **Federated Malay States**, exercised full political and administrative control.

**UMNO** The United Malays National Organisation, founded in 1946 and the major partner of the Alliance Party and later the Barisan Nasional.

# INDEX

816

817

822

823

826

830

831

833